Comprehensive

Microsoft® Word 6.0 for Windows™

Comprehensive
Microsoft® Word 6.0 for Windows™

Cheryl L. Willis
University of Houston, University Park

Course Technology, Inc. One Main Street, Cambridge, MA 02142

An International Thomson Publishing Company

I(T)P

Albany • Bonn • Boston • Cincinnati • London • Madrid • Melbourne • Mexico City
New York • Paris • San Francisco • Singapore • Tokyo • Toronto • Washington

Comprehensive Microsoft Word 6.0 for Windows is published by Course Technology, Inc.

Managing Editor	Marjorie Hunt
Product Managers	Kathleen Finnegan, Barbara Clemens
Production Editor	Cynthia H. Anderson
Text Designer	Sally Steele
Cover Designer	John Gamache

© 1995 Course Technology, Inc.
A Division of International Thomson Publishing, Inc.

For more information contact:
Course Technology, Inc.
One Main Street
Cambridge, MA 02142

International Thomson Publishing Europe
Berkshire House 168-173
High Holborn
London WCIV 7AA
England

Thomas Nelson Australia
102 Dodds Street
South Melbourne, 3205
Victoria, Australia

Nelson Canada
1120 Birchmount Road
Scarborough, Ontario
Canada M1K 5G4

International Thomson Editores
Campos Eliseos 385, Piso 7
Col. Polanco
11560 Mexico D.F. Mexico

International Thomson Publishing GmbH
Königswinterer Strasse 418
53227 Bonn
Germany

International Thomson Publishing Asia
211 Henderson Road
#05-10 Henderson Building
Singapore 0315

International Thomson Publishing Japan
Hirakawacho Kyowa Building, 3F
2-2-1 Hirakawacho
Chiyoda-ku, Tokyo 102
Japan

Trademarks

Course Technology and the open book logo are registered trademarks of Course Technology, Inc.

I(T)P The ITP logo is a trademark under license.

Word 6.0 for Windows is a registered trademark of Microsoft Corporation and Windows is a trademark of Microsoft Corporation.

Some of the product names and company names used in this book have been used for identification purposes only and may be trademarks or registered trademarks of their respective manufacturers and sellers.

Disclaimer

Course Technology, Inc. reserves the right to revise this publication and make changes from time to time in its content without notice.

ISBN 1-56527-160-2 (text)

Printed in the United States of America

10 9 8 7 6 5 4 3 2 1

From the Publisher

At Course Technology, Inc., we believe that technology will transform the way that people teach and learn. We are very excited about bringing you, college professors and students, the most practical and affordable technology-related products available.

The Course Technology Development Process

Our development process is unparalleled in the higher education publishing industry. Every product we create goes through an exacting process of design, development, review, and testing.

Reviewers give us direction and insight that shape our manuscripts and bring them up to the latest standards. Every manuscript is quality tested. Students whose backgrounds match the intended audience work through every keystroke, carefully checking for clarity, and pointing out errors in logic and sequence. Together with our own technical reviewers, these testers help us ensure that everything that carries our name is error-free and easy to use.

Course Technology Products

We show both *how* and *why* technology is critical to solving problems in college and in whatever field you choose to teach or pursue. Our time-tested, step-by-step instructions provide unparalleled clarity. Examples and applications are chosen and crafted to motivate students.

The Course Technology Team

This book will suit your needs because it was delivered quickly, efficiently, and affordably. In every aspect of our business, we rely on a commitment to quality and the use of technology. Every employee contributes to this process. The names of all of our employees are listed below:

Tim Ashe, David Backer, Stephen M. Bayle, Josh Bernoff, Ann Marie Buconjic, Jody Buttafoco, Kerry Cannell, Jim Chrysikos, Barbara Clemens, Susan Collins, John M. Connolly, Kim Crowley, Myrna D'Addario, Lisa D'Alessandro, Howard S. Diamond, Kathryn Dinovo, Katie Donovan, Joseph B. Dougherty, MaryJane Dwyer, Chris Elkhill, Don Fabricant, Laura Ganson, Jeff Goding, Laurie Gomes, Eileen Gorham, Andrea Greitzer, Catherine Griffin, Tim Hale, Roslyn Hooley, Marjorie Hunt, Matt Kenslea, Susannah Lean, Suzanne Licht, Laurie Lindgren, Kim Mai, Elizabeth Martinez, Debbie Masi, Don Maynard, Dan Mayo, Kathleen McCann, Jay McNamara, Mac Mendelsohn, Kim Munsell, Amy Oliver, Michael Ormsby, Kristine Otto, Debbie Parlee, Kristin Patrick, Charlie Patsios, Jodi Paulus, Darren Perl, Kevin Phaneuf, George J. Pilla, Nicole Jones Pinard, Cathy Prindle, Nancy Ray, Christine Spillett, Susan Stroud, Michelle Tucker, David Upton, Mark Valentine, Karen Wadsworth, Anne Marie Walker, Renee Walkup, Donna Whiting, Janet Wilson, Lisa Yameen.

Preface

Course Technology, Inc. is proud to present this new book in its Windows Series. *Comprehensive Microsoft Word 6.0 for Windows* is designed for a full-term course on Word 6.0 for Windows. This book capitalizes on the energy and enthusiasm students have for Windows-based applications and clearly teaches students how to take full advantage of Word's power. It assumes no prerequisite knowledge of computers, the Windows environment, or Microsoft Word 6.0.

Organization and Coverage

Comprehensive Microsoft Word 6.0 for Windows contains ten tutorials that provide hands-on instruction. In these tutorials students learn word processing tasks by following a four-step "Productivity Strategy": create, edit, format, then preview and print. This strategy increases both efficiency and proficiency and is thoroughly reinforced throughout the text.

Moreover, the power of Word is unleashed by emphasizing the use of the Standard toolbar and Formatting toolbar. Using this book, students will be able to do more advanced tasks sooner than they would using other texts. By the end of the book, students will have learned all the important features of Microsoft Word 6.0, from basic document creation and formatting through merges, reports, customization, master documents, and integration.

Approach

Comprehensive Microsoft Word 6.0 for Windows distinguishes itself from other Windows textbooks because of its unique two-pronged approach. First, it motivates students by demonstrating why they need to learn the concepts and skills. This book teaches Word 6.0 for Windows using a task-driven rather than a feature-driven approach. By working through the tutorials—each motivated by a realistic case—students learn how to use Word 6.0 for Windows in situations they are likely to encounter in the workplace, rather than learn a list of features one-by-one, out of context. Second, the content, organization, and pedagogy of this book make full use of the Windows environment. The content that is presented, when it's presented, and how it's presented capitalize on the power of Word 6.0 for Windows to enable new users to perform complex word processing tasks earlier and more easily than was possible with non-Windows word processing packages.

Features

Comprehensive Microsoft Word 6.0 for Windows is an exceptional textbook also because it contains the following features:

■ **"Read This Before You Begin" Page** This page is consistent with Course Technology's unequaled commitment to helping instructors introduce technology into the classroom. Technical considerations and assumptions about hardware, software, and default settings are listed in one place to help instructors save time and eliminate unnecessary aggravation.

- **Tutorial Case** Each tutorial begins with a word processing problem that students could reasonably encounter in business. Thus, the process of solving the problem will be meaningful to students.
- **Step-by-Step Methodology** The unique Course Technology, Inc. methodology keeps students on track. They click or press keys always within the context of solving the problem posed in the Tutorial Case. The text constantly guides students, letting them know where they are in the process of solving the problem. The numerous screen shots include labels that direct students' attention to what they should look at on the screen.
- **Page Design** Each full-color page is designed to help students easily differentiate between what they are to do and what they are to read. The steps are easily identified by their color background and numbered bullets. Windows default colors are used in the screen shots so instructors can more easily assure that students' screens look like those in the book.
- **TROUBLE?** TROUBLE? paragraphs anticipate the mistakes that students are likely to make and help them recover from these mistakes. This feature facilitates independent learning and frees the instructor to focus on substantive conceptual issues rather than common procedural errors.
- **Reference Windows and Task Reference** Reference Windows provide short, generic summaries of frequently used procedures. The Task Reference appears at the end of the book and summarizes how to accomplish tasks using the toolbar buttons, the menus, and the keyboard. Both of these features are specially designed and written so students can use the book as a reference manual after completing the course.
- **Questions, Tutorial Assignments, and Case Problems** Each tutorial concludes with meaningful, conceptual Questions that test students' understanding of what they learned in the tutorial. The Questions are followed by Tutorial Assignments, which provide students with additional hands-on practice of the skills they learned in the tutorial. Finally, each tutorial ends with three complete Case Problems that have approximately the same scope as the Tutorial Case.
- **Exploration Exercises** Unlike DOS, the Windows environment allows students to learn by exploring and discovering what they can do. The Exploration Exercises are Questions, Tutorial Assignments, or Case Problems designated by an **E** that encourage students to explore the capabilities of the computing environment they are using and to extend their knowledge using Word's on-line Help facility and other reference materials.
- **References Section** This section provides simple listings of Microsoft Word commands, toolbar buttons, and field codes that students can refer to at any time.
- **Cases** Four cases help students incorporate all their knowledge of Microsoft Word in new, real-life settings. Each case integrates concepts and skills they have learned in more than one tutorial.

The CTI WinApps Setup Disk

The CTI WinApps Setup Disk bundled with the instructor's copy of this book contains an innovative Student Disk generating program designed to save instructors time. Once this software is installed on a network or standalone workstation, students can double-click the "Make Word 6.0 for Windows Student Disks" icon in the CTI WinApps group window. Double-clicking this icon transfers all the data files students need to complete the tutorials, Tutorial Assignments, and Case Problems to high-density disks in drive A or B. Tutorial 1 provides complete step-by-step instructions for making the Student Disks.

Adopters of this text are granted the right to install the CTI WinApps group window on any standalone computer or network used by students who have purchased this text.

For more information on the CTI WinApps Setup Disk, see the section in this book called "Read This Before You Begin."

The Supplements

■ **Instructor's Manual** The Instructor's Manual is written by the author and is quality assurance tested. It includes:
  • Answers and solutions to all the Questions, Tutorial Assignments, and Case Problems. Suggested solutions are also included for the Exploration Exercises.
  • Disks (3.5-inch or 5.25-inch) containing solutions to all the Questions, Tutorial Assignments, and Case Problems.
  • Tutorial Notes, which contain background information from the author about the Tutorial Case and the instructional progression of the tutorial.
  • Technical Notes, which include troubleshooting tips as well as information on how to customize the students' screens to closely emulate the screen shots in the book.
  • Transparency Masters of key concepts.
■ **Test Bank** The Test Bank contains approximately 50 questions per tutorial in true/false, multiple choice, and fill-in-the-blank formats, plus two essay questions. Each question has been quality assurance tested by students to achieve clarity and accuracy.
■ **Electronic Test Bank** The Electronic Test Bank allows instructors to edit individual test questions, select questions individually or at random, and print out scrambled versions of the same test to any supported printer.

Acknowledgments

I would like to thank the following individuals in the College of Technology at the University of Houston for their input and support: my undergraduate and graduate students, Maryann Pringle, Sharon Lund O'Neil, and Bernard McIntyre.

My appreciation goes to the Course Technology team assigned to this project—Barbara Clemens, Cynthia Anderson, Nancy Hannigan, Jane Pedicini, Andrea Star Greitzer, Jeff Goding, James Valente, Chris Greacen, Snehal Shah, Nancy Ray, Mark Vodnik, Dana Degenhardt, and Alexandra Nickerson—for their enthusiastic attention to detail. My undying gratitude goes finally to Kathy Finnegan for her invaluable suggestions, her wordsmithing abilities, and, perhaps more importantly, her gentle spirit in the face of tremendous pressure. Thank you all for your dedication to producing a quality textbook.

Thanks to my family, Lillian, Bill, and Denise, for their steadfast love and support. Thanks also to my colleague and friend, Marionette Beyah, who never got to see the finished product, but who was beside me in spirit with her words of encouragement and humor. God bless you!

Cheryl L. Willis

Brief Contents

Contents

TUTORIAL 5
Creating Reports

TUTORIAL 6
Desktop Publishing with Word

TUTORIAL 7
Customizing Word

TUTORIAL 8
Using the Master Document Feature to Manage Long Documents

TUTORIAL 9
Creating On-line Forms

TUTORIAL 10
Using Word With Other Microsoft Applications

Microsoft® Windows™ 3.1 Tutorials

1 **Essential Windows Skills**

2 **Effective File Management**

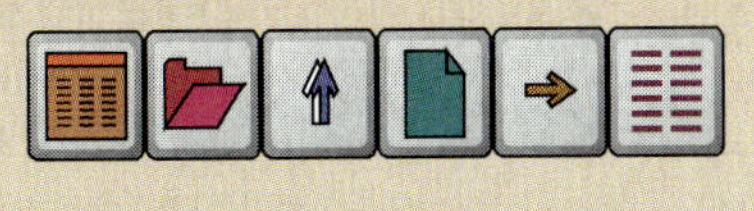

Read This Before You Begin

To the Student

To use this book, you must have a Student Disk. Your instructor will either provide you with a Student Disk or ask you to make your own by following the instructions in the section called "Preparing Your Student Disk" in Windows Tutorial 2. See your instructor or lab manager for further information.

Using Your Own Computer If you are going to work through this book using your own computer, you need:

- The Student Disk. ***You will not be able to complete the tutorials and exercises in this book using your own computer until you have the Student Disk.*** Ask your instructor or lab manager for details on how to get it.

- A computer system running Microsoft Windows 3.1 and DOS.

To the Instructor

Making the Student Disk To complete the tutorials in this book, your students must have a copy of the Student Disk. To relieve you of having to make multiple Student Disks from a single master copy, we provide you with the CTI WinApps Setup Disk, which contains an automatic Student Disk generating program. Once you install the Setup Disk on a network or standalone workstation, students can easily make their own Student Disks by double clicking on the "Make Win 3.1 Student Disk" icon in the CTI WinApps icon group. Double clicking this icon transfers all the data files students will need to complete the tutorials and Tutorial Assignments to a high-density disk in drive A or B. If some of your students will use their own computers to complete the tutorials and exercises in this book, they must first get the Student Disk. The section called "Preparing Your Student Disk" in Windows Tutorial 2 provides complete instructions on how to make the Student Disk.

If you have disk copying resources available, you might choose to use them for making quantities of the Student Disk. The "Make Win 3.1 Student Disk" provides an easy and fast way to make multiple Student Disks.

Installing the CTI WinApps Setup Disk: To install the CTI WinApps icon group from the Setup Disk, follow the instructions inside the disk envelope that was bundled with your book. By adopting this book, you are granted a license to install this software on any computer or computer network used by you or your students.

Readme File: A Readme.txt file located on the Setup Disk provides additional technical notes, troubleshooting advice, and tips for using the CTI WinApps software in your school's computer lab. You can view the Readme file using any word processor you choose.

System Requirements for installing the CTI WinApps Disk The minimum software and hardware requirements your computer system needs to install the CTI WinApps icon group are as follows:

- Microsoft Windows version 3.1 on a local hard drive or on a network drive
- A 286 (or higher) processor with a minimum of 2 MB RAM (4 MB RAM or more is strongly recommended).
- A mouse supported by Windows
- A printer that is supported by Windows 3.1
- A VGA 640 x 480 16-color display is recommended; an 800 x 600 or 1024 x 768 SVGA, VGA monochrome, or EGA display is also acceptable
- 1.5 MB of free hard disk space
- Student workstations with at least 1 high-density disk drive. If you need a 5.25 inch CTI WinApps Setup Disk, contact your CTI sales rep or call customer service at 1-800-648-7450. In Canada call Times Mirror Professional Publishing/Iwin Dorsey at 1-800-268-4178.
- If you wish to install the CTI WinApps Setup Disk on a network drive, your network must support Microsoft Windows.

Essential Windows Skills

Using the Program Manager, CTI WinApps, and Help

In this tutorial you will:

- Start your computer
- Launch and exit Windows
- Use the mouse and the keyboard
- Identify the components of the Windows desktop
- Launch and exit applications
- Organize your screen-based desktop
- Switch tasks in a multi-tasking environment.
- Use Windows menus
- Explore Windows toolbars

CASE

A New Computer, Anywhere, Inc.   You're a busy employee without a minute of spare time. But now, to top it all off, a computer technician appears at your office door, introduces himself as Steve Laslow, and begins unpacking your new computer!

You wonder out loud, "How long is it going to take me to learn this?"

Steve explains that your new computer uses Microsoft Windows 3.1 software and that the **interface**—the way you interact with the computer and give it instructions—is very easy to use. He describes the Windows software as a "gooey," a **graphical user interface (GUI)**, which uses pictures of familiar objects such as file folders and documents to represent a desktop on your screen.

Steve unpacks your new computer and begins to connect the components. He talks as he works, commenting on three things he really likes about Microsoft Windows. First, Windows applications have a standard interface, which means that once you learn how to use one Windows application, you are well on your way to understanding how to use others. Second, Windows lets you use more than one application at a time, a capability called **multitasking**, so you can easily switch between applications such as your word processor and your calendar. Third, Windows lets you do more than one task at a time, such as printing a document while you create a pie chart. All in all, Windows makes your computer an effective and easy-to-use productivity tool.

Using the Windows Tutorials Effectively

This tutorial will help you learn about Windows 3.1. Begin by reading the text that explains the concepts. Then when you come to numbered steps on a colored background, follow those steps as you work at your computer. Read each step carefully and completely *before* you try it.

Don't worry if parts of your screen display are different from the figures in the tutorials. The important parts of the screen display are labeled in each figure. Just be sure these parts are on your screen.

Don't worry about making mistakes—that's part of the learning process. **TROUBLE?** paragraphs identify common problems and explain how to get back on track. Do the steps in the **TROUBLE?** paragraph *only* if you are having the problem described.

Starting Your Computer and Launching Windows

The process of starting Windows is sometimes referred to as **launching**. If your computer system requires procedures different from those in the steps below, your instructor or technical support person will provide you with step-by-step instructions for turning on your monitor, starting or resetting your computer, logging into a network if you have one, and launching Windows.

To start your computer and launch Windows:

❶ Make sure your disk drives are empty.

❷ Find the power switch for your monitor and turn it on.

❸ Locate the power switch for your computer and turn it on. After a few seconds you should see C:\> or C> on the screen.

TROUBLE?   If your computer displays a "non-system disk" error message, a floppy disk was left in a disk drive at startup. To continue, remove the disk and press [Enter].

❹ Type **win** to launch Windows. See Figure 1-1.

Figure 1-1
Launching Windows

❺ Press the key labeled **[Enter]**. Soon the Windows 3.1 title screen appears. Next you might notice an hourglass on the screen. This symbol means your computer is busy with a task and you must wait until it has finished.

After a brief wait, the title screen is replaced by one similar to Figure 1-2. Don't worry if your screen is not exactly the same as Figure 1-2. You are ready to continue the Tutorial when you see the Program Manager title at the top of the screen. If you do not see this title, ask your technical support person for assistance.

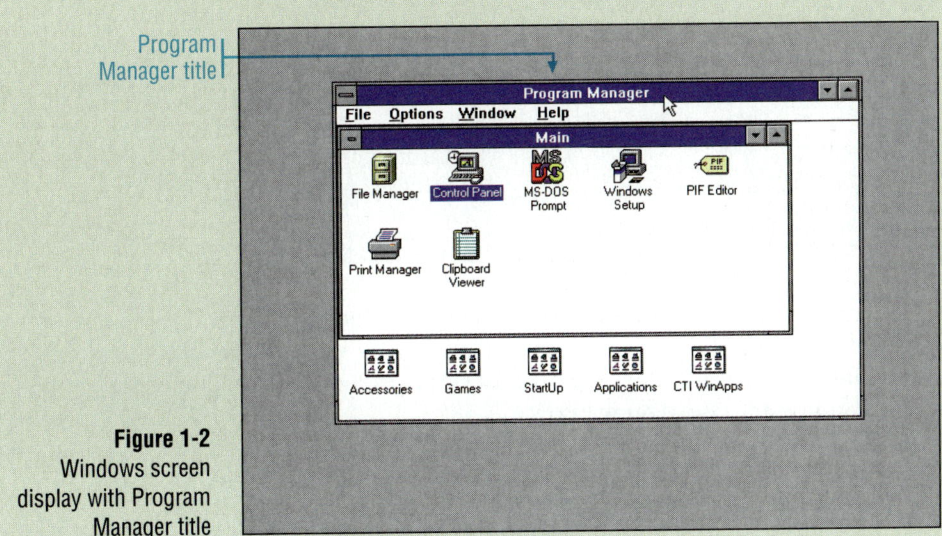

Figure 1-2
Windows screen display with Program Manager title

Basic Windows Controls and Concepts

Windows has a variety of **controls** that enable you to communicate with the computer. In this section you'll learn how to use the basic Windows controls.

The Windows Desktop

Look at your screen display and compare it to Figure 1-3 on the following page. Your screen may not be exactly the same as the illustration. You should, however, be able to locate components on your screen similar to those in Figure 1-3 on the following page.

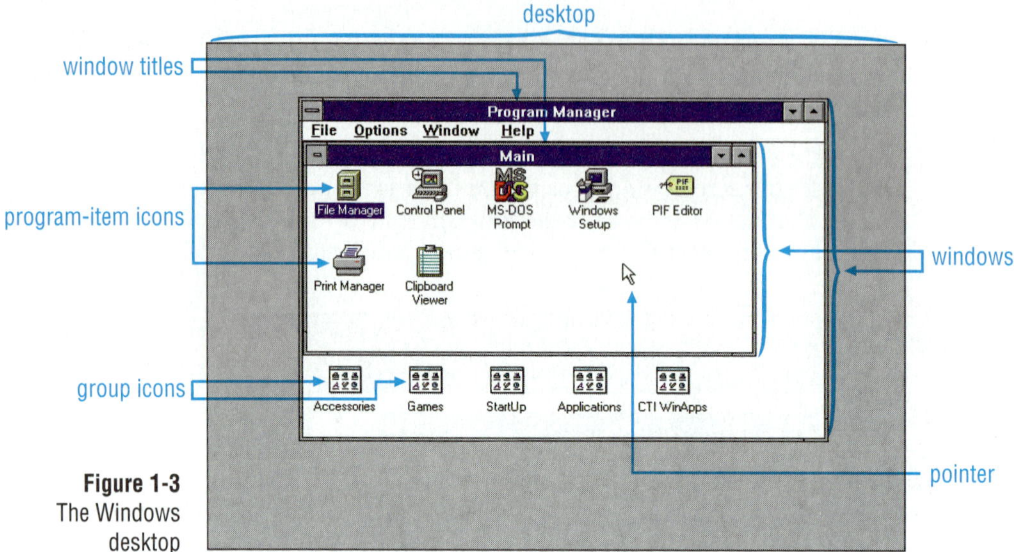

Figure 1-3
The Windows desktop

The screen represents a **desktop**, a workspace for projects and for the tools that are needed to manipulate those projects. Rectangular **windows** (with a lowercase *w*) define work areas on the desktop. The desktop in Figure 1-3 contains the Program Manager window and the Main window.

Icons are small pictures that represent real objects, such as disk drives, software, and documents. Each icon in the Main window represents an **application**, that is, a computer program. These icons are called **program-item icons**.

Each **group icon** at the bottom of the Program Manager window represents a collection of applications. For example, the CTI WinApps icon represents a collection of tutorial and practice applications, which you can use to learn more about Windows. A group icon expands into a group window that contains program-item icons.

The **pointer** helps you manipulate objects on the Windows desktop. The pointer can assume different shapes, depending on what is happening on the desktop. In Figure 1-3 the pointer is shaped like an arrow.

The Program Manager

When you launch Windows, the Program Manager application starts automatically and continues to run as long as you are working with Windows. Think of the Program Manager as a launching pad for other applications. The **Program Manager** displays icons for the applications on your system. To launch an application, you would select its icon.

Using the Mouse

The **mouse** is a pointing device that helps you interact with the screen-based objects in the Windows environment. As you move the mouse on a flat surface, the pointer on the screen moves in the direction corresponding to the movement of the mouse. You can also control the Windows environment from the keyboard; however, the mouse is much more efficient for most operations, so the tutorials in this book assume you are using one.

Find the arrow-shaped pointer on your screen. If you do not see the pointer, move your mouse until the pointer comes into view. You will begin most Windows-based operations by **pointing**.

To position the pointer:

❶ Position your right index finger over the left mouse button, as shown in Figure 1-4.

> **TROUBLE?**   If you want to use your mouse with your left hand, ask your technical support person to help you. Be sure you find out how to change back to the right-handed mouse setting, so you can reset the mouse each time you are finished in the lab.

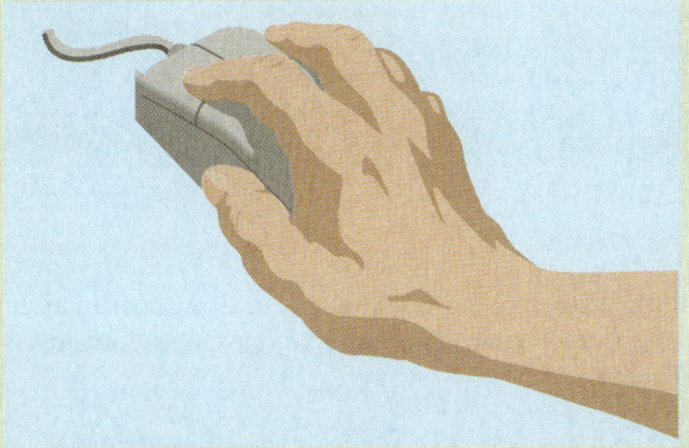

Figure 1-4
How to hold
the mouse

❷ Locate the arrow-shaped pointer on the screen.

❸ Move the mouse and watch the movement of the pointer.

❹ Next, move the mouse to each of the four corners of the screen.

> **TROUBLE?**   If your mouse runs out of room, lift it, move it into the middle of a clear area on your desk, and then place it back on the table. The pointer does not move when the mouse is not in contact with the tabletop.

❺ Continue experimenting with mouse pointing until you feel comfortable with your "eye-mouse coordination."

Pointing is usually followed by clicking, double-clicking, or dragging. **Clicking** means pressing a mouse button (usually the left button) and then quickly releasing it. Clicking is used to select an object on the desktop. Windows shows you which object is selected by highlighting it.

To click an icon:

❶ Locate the Print Manager icon in the Main window. If you cannot see the Print Manager icon, use any other icon for this activity.

❷ Position the pointer on the icon.

❸ Once the pointer is on the icon, *do not move the mouse*.

❹ Press the left mouse button and then quickly release it. Your icon should have a highlighted title like the one in Figure 1-5 on the following page.

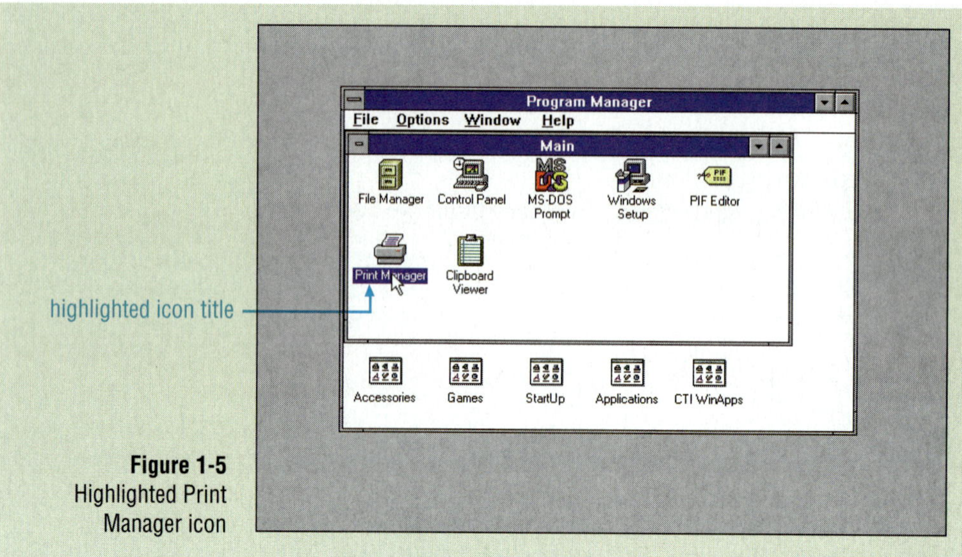

Figure 1-5
Highlighted Print
Manager icon

Double-clicking means clicking the mouse button twice in rapid succession. Double-clicking is a shortcut. For example, most Windows users double-click to launch and exit applications.

To double click:

❶ Position the pointer on the Program Manager Control-menu box, as shown in Figure 1-6.

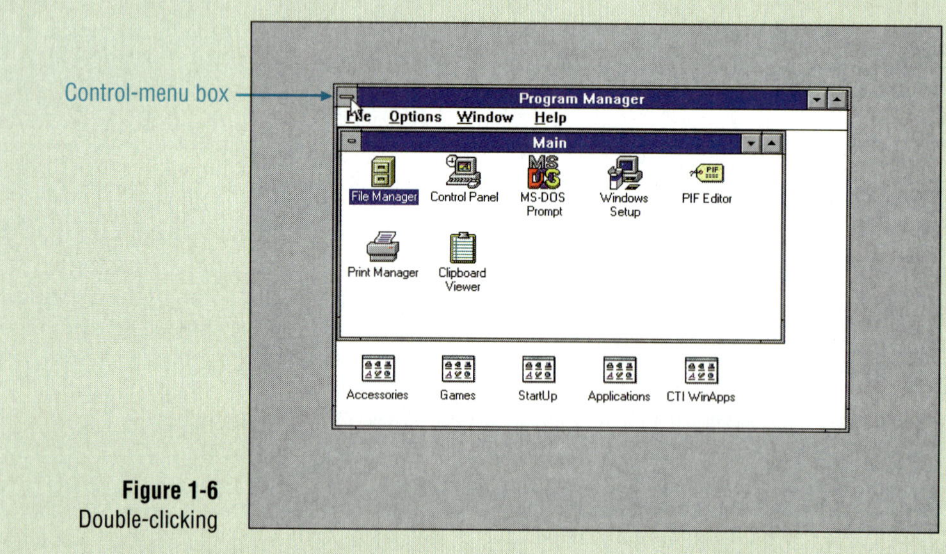

Figure 1-6
Double-clicking

❷ Click the mouse button twice in rapid succession. If your double-clicking is successful, an Exit Windows box appears on your screen.

❸ Now, single-click the **Cancel button**.

Dragging means moving an object to a new location on the desktop. To drag an object, you would position the pointer on the object, then hold the left mouse button down while you move the mouse. Let's drag one of the icons to a new location.

To drag an icon:

❶ Position the pointer on any icon on the screen, such as on the Clipboard Viewer icon. Figure 1-7 shows you where to put the pointer and what happens on your screen as you carry out the next step.

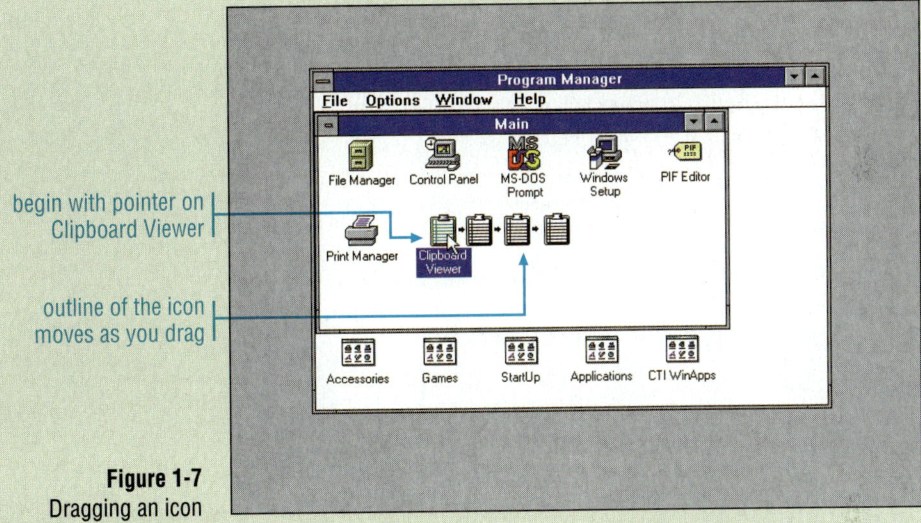

Figure 1-7
Dragging an icon

❷ Hold the left mouse button down while you move the mouse to the right. Notice that an outline of the icon moves as you move the mouse.

❸ Release the mouse button. Now the icon is in a new location.

TROUBLE? If the icon snaps back to its original position, don't worry. Your technical support person probably has instructed Windows to do this. If your icon automatically snapped back to its original position, skip Step 4.

❹ Drag the icon back to its original location.

Using the Keyboard

You use the keyboard to type documents, enter numbers, and activate some commands. You can use the on-screen CTI Keyboard Tutorial to learn the special features of your computer keyboard. To do this, you need to learn how to launch the Keyboard Tutorial and other applications.

Launching Applications

Earlier in this tutorial you launched Windows. Once you have launched Windows, you can launch other Windows applications such as Microsoft Works. When you launch an application, an application window opens. Later, when you have finished using the application, you close the window to exit.

Launching the CTI Keyboard Tutorial

To launch the CTI Keyboard Tutorial, you need to have the CTI WinApps software installed on your computer. If you are working in a computer lab, these applications should already be installed on your computer system. Look on your screen for a group icon or a window labeled "CTI WinApps."

If you don't have anything labeled "CTI WinApps" on your screen's desktop, ask your technical support person for help. If you are using your own computer, you will need to install the CTI WinApps applications yourself. See your technical support person or your instructor for a copy of the Setup Disk and the Installation Instructions that come with it.

To open the CTI Win Apps group window:

❶ Double-click the **CTI WinApps group icon**. Your screen displays a CTI WinApps group window similar to the one in Figure 1-8.

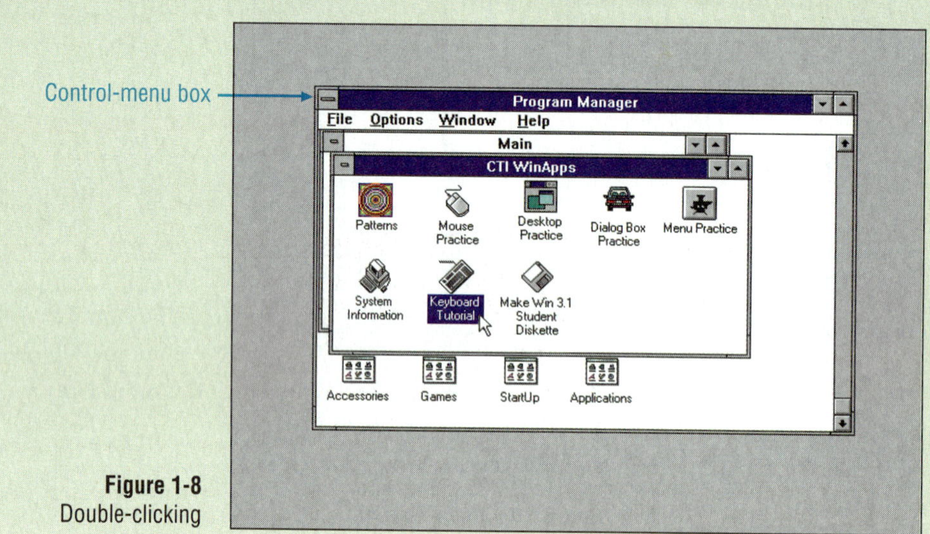

Figure 1-8
Double-clicking

The CTI WinApps group window contains an icon for each application provided with these tutorials. Right now we want to use the Keyboard Tutorial application.

To launch the Keyboard Tutorial:

❶ Double-click the **Keyboard Tutorial icon**. Within a few seconds, the tutorial begins.

❷ Read the opening screen, then click the **Continue button**. The CTI Keyboard Tutorial window appears. Follow the instructions on your screen to complete the tutorial. See Figure 1-9.

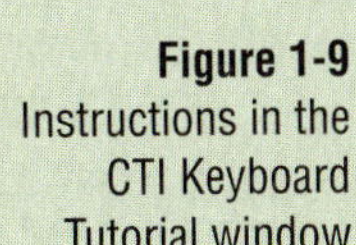

Figure 1-9
Instructions in the
CTI Keyboard
Tutorial window

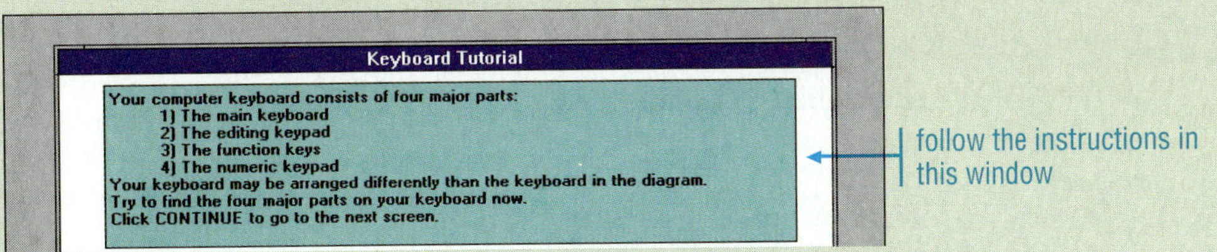

TROUBLE?   Click the Quit button at any time if you want to exit the Tutorial.

❸   When you have completed the Keyboard Tutorial, click the **Quit button**. This takes you back to the Program Manager and CTI WinApps group window.

TROUBLE?   *If you did not have trouble in Step 3, skip this entire paragraph!* If the Program Manager window is not open, look for its icon at the bottom of your screen. Double-click this icon to open the Program Manager window. To prevent this problem from happening again, click the word Options on the Program Manager menu bar, then click Minimize on Use.

Launching the CTI Mouse Practice

To discover how to use the mouse to manipulate Windows controls, you should launch the Mouse Practice.

To launch the Mouse Practice:

❶   Make sure the Program Manager and the CTI WinApps windows are open. It is not a problem if you have additional windows open.

TROUBLE?   If the Program Manager window is not open, look for its icon at the bottom of your screen. Double-click this icon to open the Program Manager window. To prevent this problem from happening again, click the word Options that appears near the top of the Program Manager window, then click Minimize.

❷   Double-click the **Mouse Practice icon**. The Mouse Practice window opens.

TROUBLE?   If you don't see the Mouse Practice icon, try clicking the scroll bar arrow button or see your technical support person.

❸   Click, drag, or double-click the objects on the screen to see what happens. Don't hesitate to experiment.

❹   When you have finished using the Mouse Practice, click the **Exit button** to go back to the Program Manager and continue the tutorial steps.

Organizing Application Windows on the Desktop

The Windows desktop provides you with capabilities similar to your desk; it lets you stack many different items on your screen-based desktop and activate the one you want to use.

There is a problem, though. Like your real desk, your screen-based desktop can become cluttered. That's why you need to learn how to organize the applications on your Windows desktop.

Launching the CTI Desktop Practice

The Desktop Practice application will help you learn the controls for organizing your screen-based desktop.

To Launch the Desktop Practice:

❶ Double-click the **Desktop Practice icon** to open the Desktop Practice window, shown in Figure 1-10. Your windows might be a different size or in a slightly different position. Don't worry. What's important is that you see a window with the title "Desktop Practice."

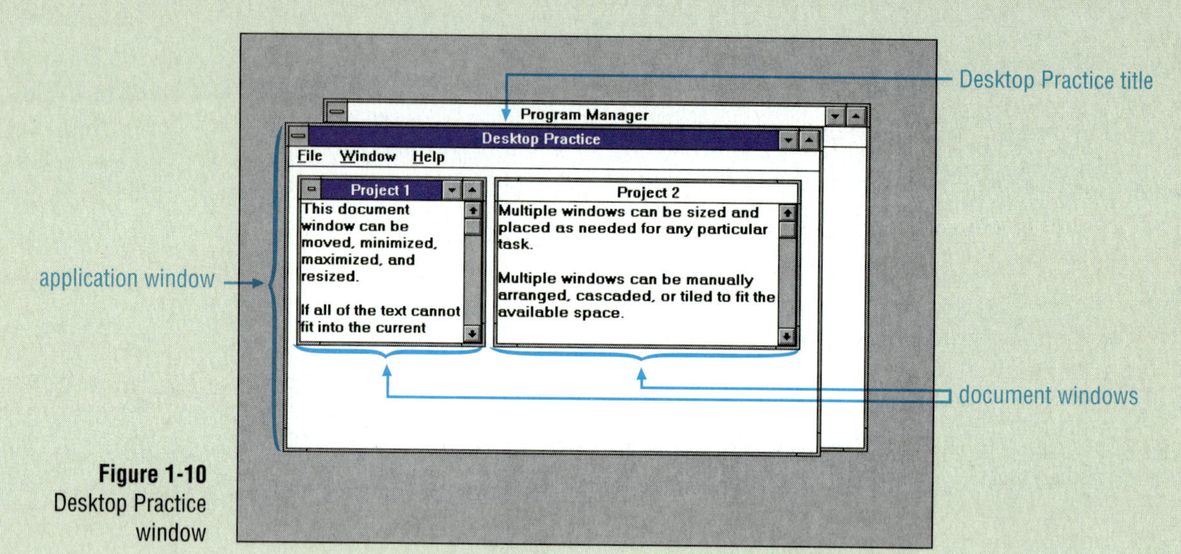

Figure 1-10
Desktop Practice window

Launching the Desktop Practice application opens three new windows on the desktop: Desktop Practice, Project 1, and Project 2. You might be able to see the edges of the Program Manager window "under" the Desktop Practice window. Essentially, you have stacked one project on top of another on your desktop.

The Desktop Practice window is an **application window**, a window that opens when you launch an application. The Project 1 and Project 2 windows are referred to as **document windows**, because they contain the documents, graphs, and lists you create using the application. Document windows are also referred to as **child windows**, because they belong to and are controlled by a "parent" application window.

The ability to have more than one document window open is one of many useful features of the Windows operating environment. Without this capability, you would have to print the documents that aren't being displayed so you could refer to them.

The Anatomy of a Window

Application windows and document windows are similar in many respects. Take a moment to study the Desktop Practice window on your screen and in Figure 1-11 on the following page to familiarize yourself with the terminology. Notice the location of each component but *don't* activate the controls.

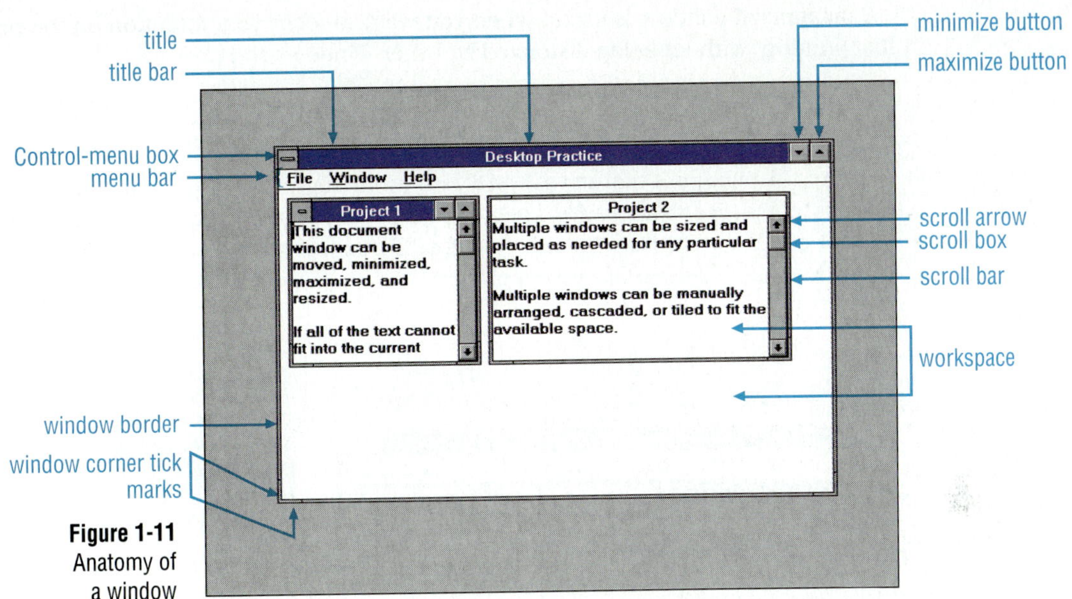

Figure 1-11
Anatomy of a window

At the top of each window is a **title bar**, which contains the window title. A darkened or highlighted title bar indicates that the application window is active. In Figure 1-11, the Desktop Practice application and the Project 1 document windows are active.

In the upper-right of the application window are two buttons used to change the size of a window. The **minimize button**—a square containing a triangle with the point down—is used to shrink the window. The **maximize button**, with the triangle pointing up, is used to enlarge the window so it fills the screen. When a window is maximized, a **restore button** with two triangles replaces the maximize button. Clicking the restore button reduces a maximized window to its previous size.

The **Control-menu box**, located in the upper-left of the Desktop Practice application window, is used to open the **Control menu**, which allows you to switch between application windows.

The **menu bar** is located just below the title bar on application windows. Notice that child windows do not contain menu bars.

The thin line running around the entire perimeter of the window is called the **window border**. The **window corners** are indicated by tick marks on the border.

The gray bar on the right side of each document window is a **scroll bar**, which you use to view window contents that don't initially fit in the window. Both application windows and document windows can contain scroll bars. Scroll bars can appear on the bottom of a window as well as on the side.

The space inside a window where you type text, design graphics, and so forth is called the **workspace**.

Maximizing and Minimizing Windows

The buttons on the right of the title bar are sometimes referred to as **resizing buttons**. You can use the resizing buttons to **minimize** the window so it shrinks down to an icon, **maximize** the window so it fills the screen, or **restore** the window to its previous size.

Because a minimized program is still running, you have quick access to the materials you're using for the project without taking up space on the desktop. You don't need to launch the program when you want to use it again because it continues to run.

A maximized window is useful when you want to focus your attention on the project in that window without being distracted by other windows and projects.

To maximize, restore, and minimize the Desktop Practice window:

❶ Locate the maximize button (the one with the triangle pointing up) for the Desktop Practice window. You might see a portion of the Program Manager window behind the Desktop Practice window. Be sure you have found the Desktop Practice maximize button. See Figure 1-12.

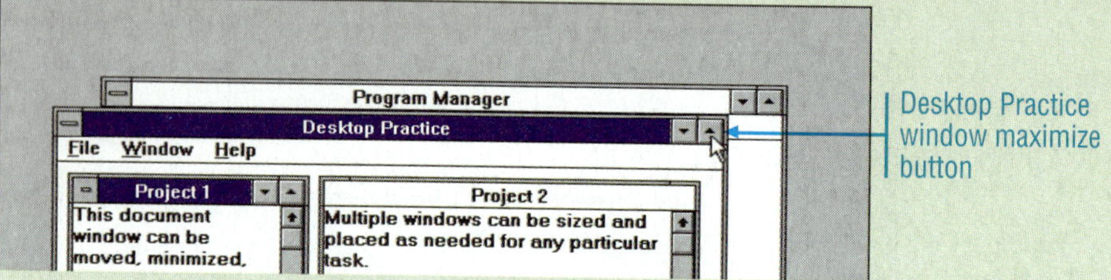

Figure 1-12
Maximizing a window

❷ Click the **maximize button** to expand the window to fill the screen. Notice that in place of the maximize button there is now a restore button that contains double triangles.

❸ Click the **restore button**. The Desktop Practice window returns to its original size.

❹ Next, click the **minimize button** (the one with the triangle pointing down) to shrink the window to an icon.

❺ Locate the minimized Desktop Practice icon at the bottom of your screen. See Figure 1-13.

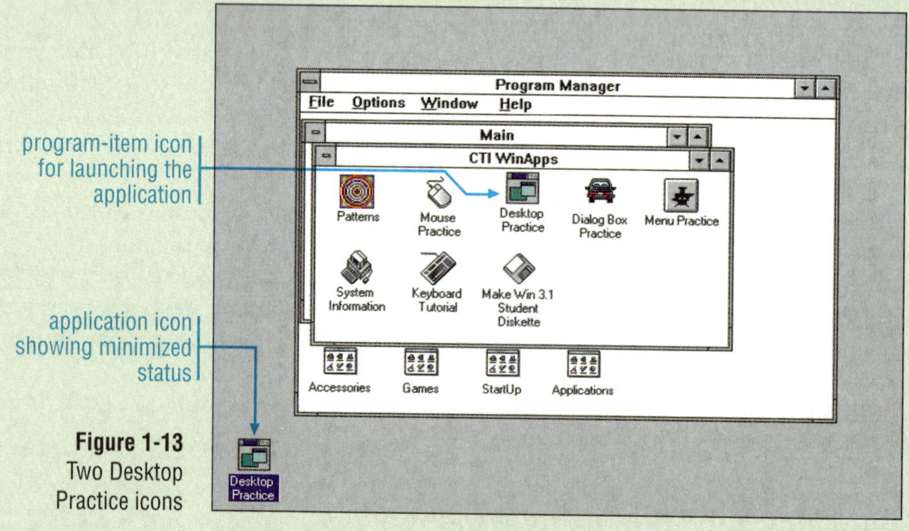

Figure 1-13
Two Desktop
Practice icons

TROUBLE?   If you cannot locate the Desktop Practice icon at the bottom of your screen, the Program Manager is probably maximized. To remedy this situation, click the restore button on the Program Manager Window.

When you *close* an application window, you exit the application and it stops running. But when you *minimize* an application, it is still running even though it has been shrunk to an icon. It is important to remember that minimizing a window is not the same as closing it.

The icon for a minimized application is called an **application icon**. As Figure 1-13 illustrates, your screen shows two icons for the Desktop Practice application. The icon at the bottom of your screen is the application icon and represents a program that is currently running even though it is minimized. The other Desktop Practice icon is inside the CTI WinApps window. If you were to double-click this icon, you would launch a second version of the Desktop Practice application. *Don't launch two versions of the same application.* You should restore the Desktop Practice window by double-clicking the minimized icon at the bottom of your screen. Let's do that now.

To restore the Desktop Practice window:

❶ Double-click the minimized **Desktop Practice icon** at the bottom of your screen. The Desktop Practice window opens.

Changing the Dimensions of a Window

Changing the dimensions of a window is useful when you want to arrange more than one project on your desktop. Suppose you want to work with the Desktop Practice application and at the same time view the contents of the Program Manager window. To do this, you will need to change the dimensions of both windows so they don't overlap each other.

To change the dimensions of the Desktop Practice window:

❶ Move the pointer slowly over the top border of the Desktop Practice window until the pointer changes shape to a double-ended arrow. See Figure 1-14.

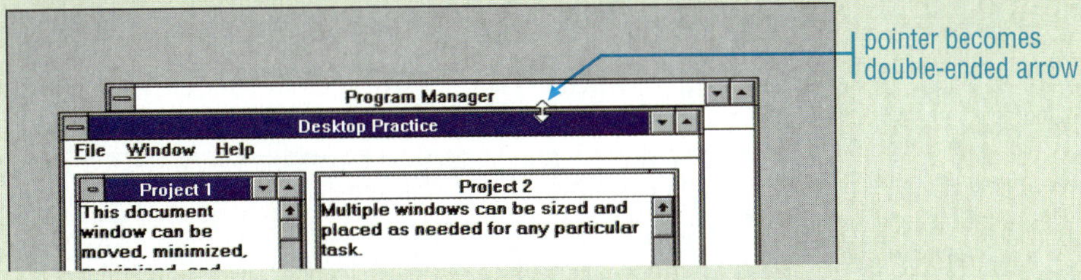

Figure 1-14
Preparing to change the window dimensions

❷ Press the left mouse button and hold it down while you drag the border to the top of the screen. Notice how an outline of the border follows your mouse movement.

❸ Release the mouse button. As a result the window adjusts to the new border.

❹ Drag the left border of the Desktop Practice window to the left edge of the screen.

❺ Move the pointer slowly over the lower-right corner of the Desktop Practice window until the pointer changes shape to a double-ended diagonal arrow. Figure 1-15 on the following page shows you how to do this step and the next one.

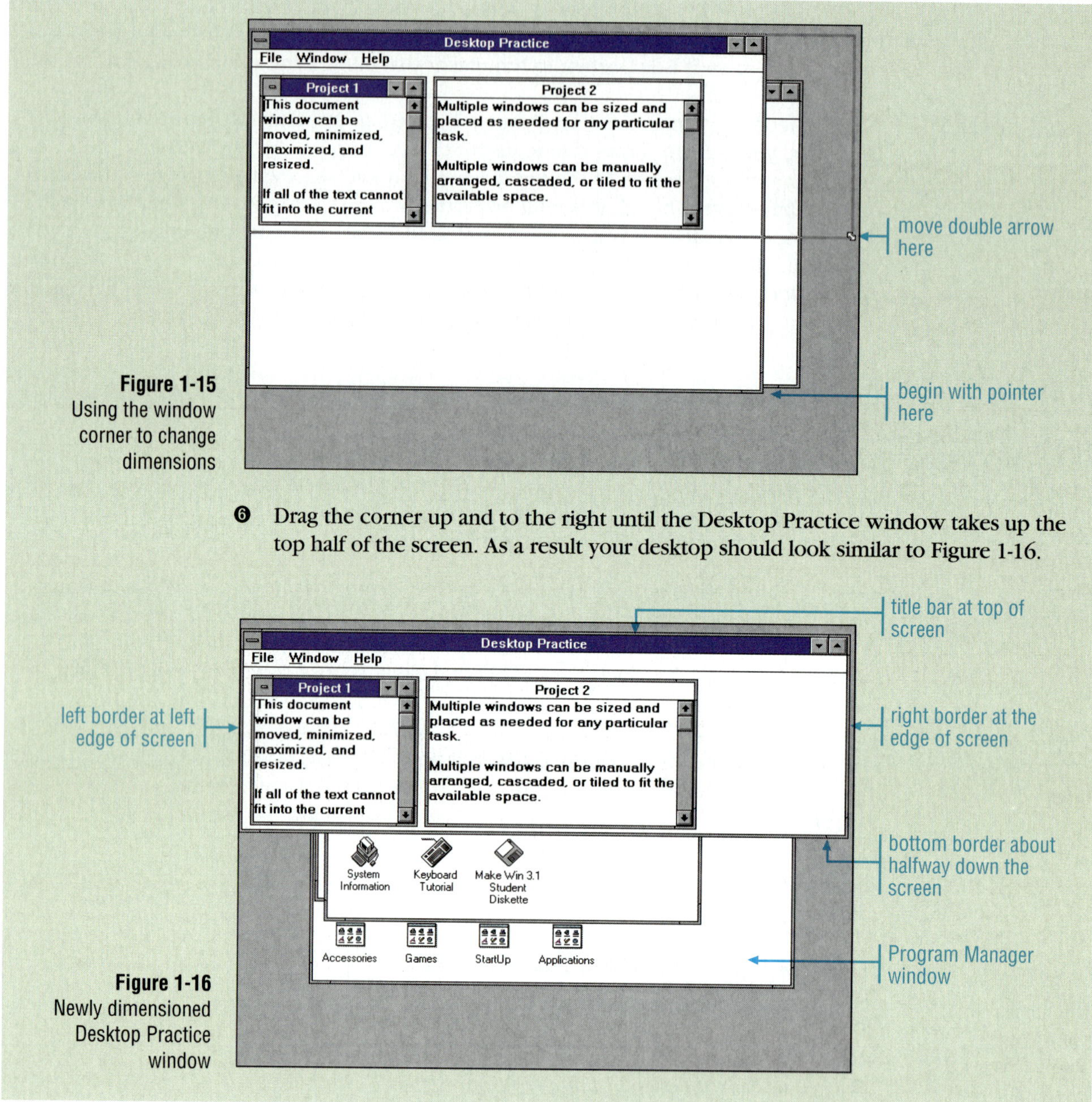

Figure 1-15
Using the window
corner to change
dimensions

Figure 1-16
Newly dimensioned
Desktop Practice
window

❻   Drag the corner up and to the right until the Desktop Practice window takes up the top half of the screen. As a result your desktop should look similar to Figure 1-16.

Switching Applications

In the preceding steps you arranged the application windows so they were both visible at the same time. A different approach to organizing windows is to maximize the windows and then switch between them using the **Task List**, which contains a list of all open applications.

Let's maximize the Desktop Practice window. Then, using the Task List, let's switch to the Program Manager window, which will be hidden behind it.

To maximize the Desktop Practice window and then switch to the Program Manager:

❶ Click the **maximize button** on the Desktop Practice title bar. As a result the maximized Desktop Practice window hides the Program Manager window.

❷ Click the **Control-menu box** on the left side of the Desktop Practice title bar. Figure 1-17 shows you the location of the Control-menu box and also the Control menu, which appears after you click.

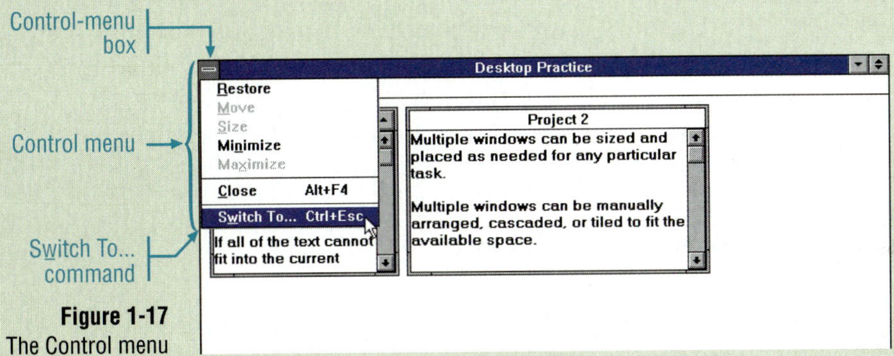

Figure 1-17
The Control menu

❸ Click **Switch To...** The Task List box appears, as shown in Figure 1-18.

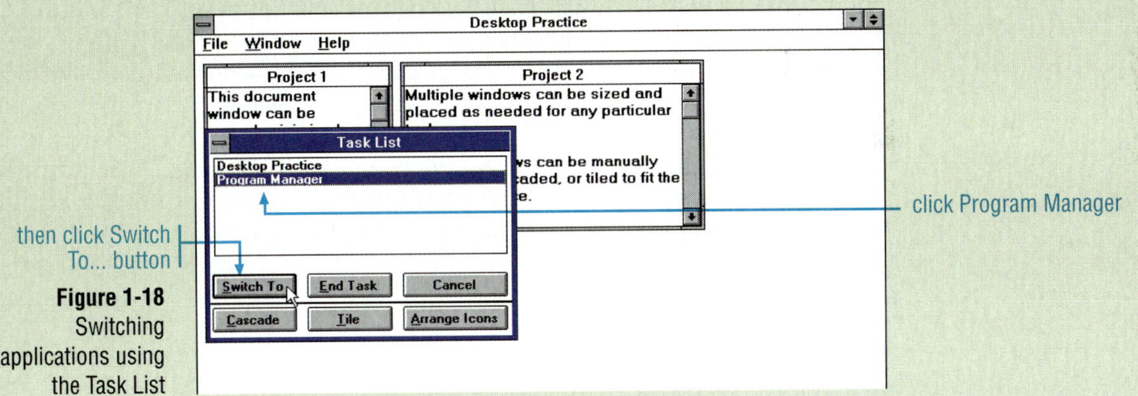

Figure 1-18
Switching applications using the Task List

❹ Click the **Program Manager option** from the list, then click the **Switch To button** to select the Program Manager. As a result the Program Manager reappears on the bottom half of your screen.

❺ If it is not already maximized, click the **maximize button** on the Program Manager window so both applications (Program Manager and Desktop Practice) are maximized.

The Program Manager window is active and "on top" of the Desktop Practice window. To view the Desktop Practice window, you will need to switch application windows again. You could switch tasks using the mouse, as we did in the last set of steps, or you can use the keyboard to quickly cycle through the tasks and activate the one you want. Let's use the keyboard method for switching windows this time, instead of using the Task List.

To switch to the Desktop Practice window using the keyboard:

❶ Hold down **[Alt]** and continue holding it down while you press **[Tab]**. Don't release the Alt key yet! On the screen you should see a small rectangle that says "Desktop Practice."

TROUBLE?   Don't worry if you accidentally let go of the Alt key too soon. Try again. Press [Alt][Tab] until the "Desktop Practice" rectangle reappears.

❷ Release the Alt key. Now the maximized Desktop Practice window is open.

When a window is maximized, it is easy to forget what's behind it. If you forget what's on the desktop, call up the Task List using the Control menu or use [Alt][Tab] to cycle through the tasks.

Organizing Document Windows

Think of document windows as subwindows within an application window. Because document windows do not have menu bars, the commands relating to these windows are selected from the menu bar of the application window. For example, you can use the Tile command in the Window menu to arrange windows so they are as large as possible without any overlap. The advantage of tiled windows is that one window won't cover up important information. The disadvantage of tiling is that the more windows you tile, the smaller each tile becomes and the more scrolling you will have to do.

You can use the Cascade command in the Window menu to arrange windows so they are all a standard size, they overlap each other, and all title bars are visible. Cascaded windows are often larger than tiled windows and at least one corner is always accessible so you can activate the window. Try experimenting with tiled and cascading windows. The desktop organizational skills you will learn will help you arrange the applications on your desktop so you can work effectively in the Windows multi-tasking environment.

Closing a Window

You close a window when you have finished working with a document or when you want to exit an application program. The steps you follow to close a document window are the same as those to close an application window. Let's close the Desktop Practice window.

To close the Desktop Practice application window:

❶ Click the **Control-menu box** on the Desktop Practice window.

❷ Click **Close** as shown in Figure 1-19 on the following page. The Desktop Practice window closes and you see the Program Manager window on the desktop.

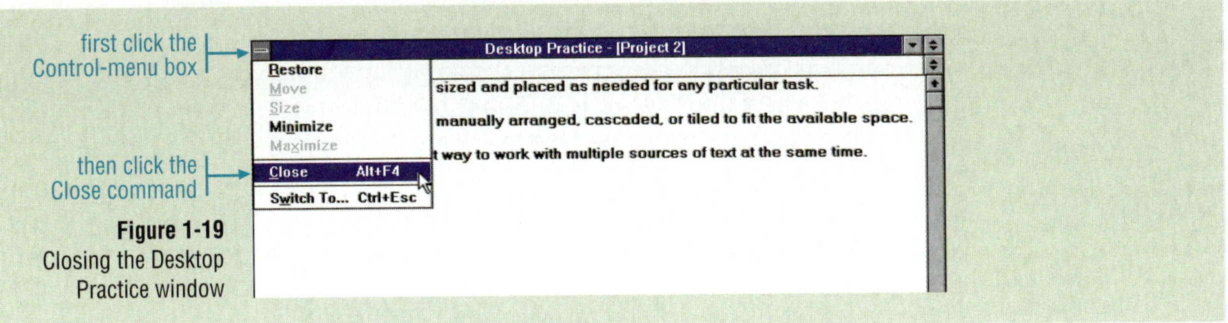

Figure 1-19
Closing the Desktop
Practice window

Using Windows to Specify Tasks

In Windows, you issue instructions called **commands** to tell the computer what you want it to do. Windows applications provide you with lists of commands called **menus**. Many applications also have a ribbon of icons called a **toolbar**, which provides you with command shortcuts. Let's launch the Menu Practice application to find out how menus and toolbars work.

To launch the Menu Practice application:

❶ If the CTI WinApps window is not open, double-click its group icon at the bottom of the Program Manager window.

❷ Double-click the **Menu Practice** icon to open the Menu Practice window. See Figure 1-20.

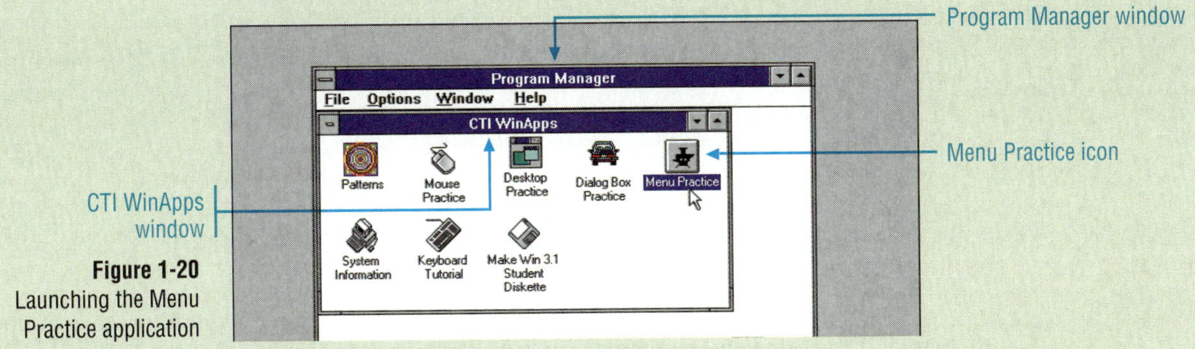

Figure 1-20
Launching the Menu
Practice application

❸ Click the **maximize button** (the one with the triangle point up) for the Menu Practice window. The maximized Menu Practice window is shown in Figure 1-21 on the following page.

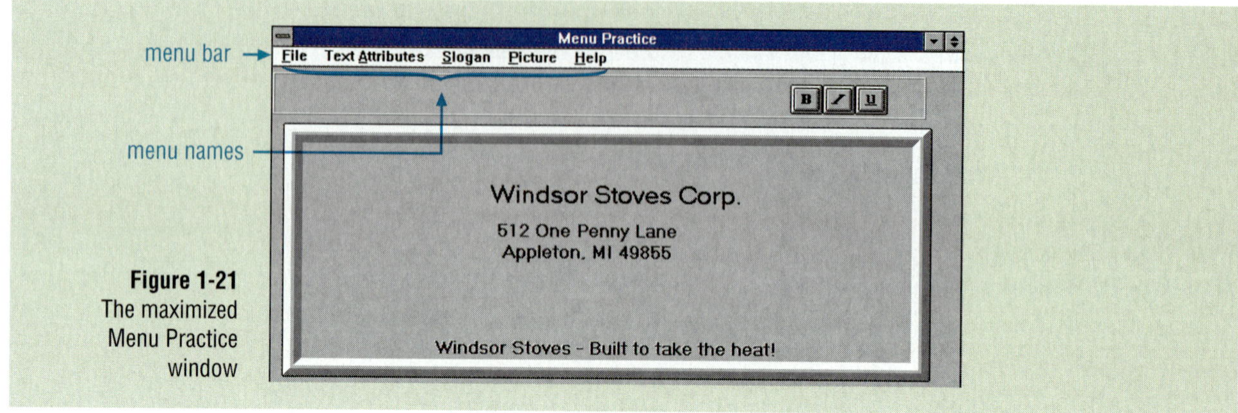

Figure 1-21
The maximized
Menu Practice
window

Opening and Closing Menus

Application windows, but not document windows, have menu bars such as the one shown in Figure 1-21. The menu bar contains menu names such as File, Text Attributes, Slogan, Picture, and Help. Let's practice opening and closing menus.

To open a menu:

❶ Click **File**. Figure 1-22 shows you where to click and the menu that appears.

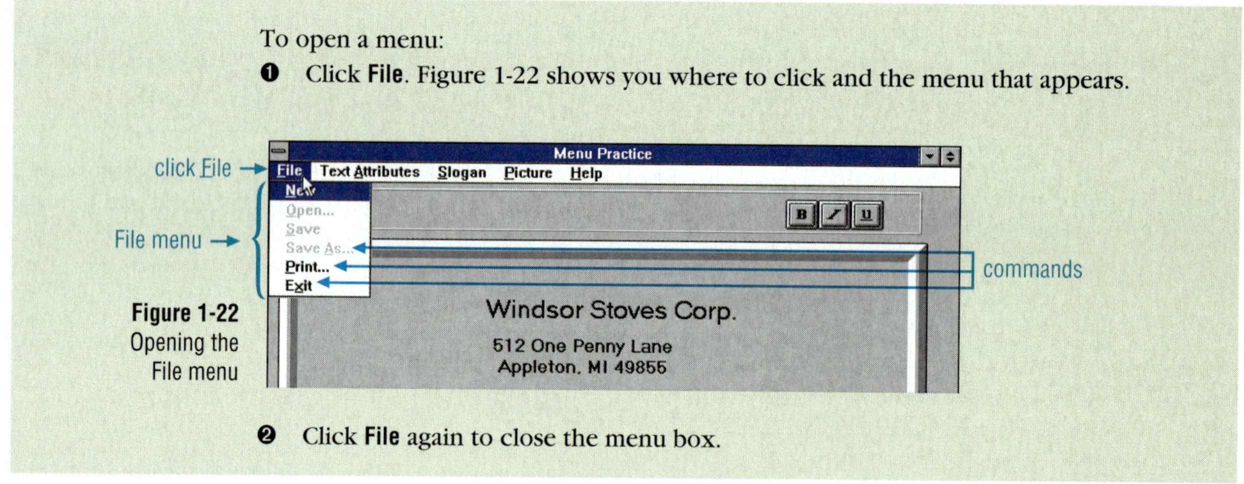

Figure 1-22
Opening the
File menu

❷ Click **File** again to close the menu box.

When you click a menu name, the full menu drops down to display a list of commands. The commands on a menu are sometimes referred to as **menu items**.

Menu Conventions

The commands displayed on the Windows menus often include one or more **menu conventions**, such as check marks, ellipses, shortcut keys, and underlined letters. These menu conventions provide you with additional information about each menu command.

A check mark in front of a menu command indicates that the command is in effect. Clicking a checked command will remove the check mark and deactivate the command. For example, the Windsor Stoves logo currently has no graphic because the Show Picture command is not active. Let's add a picture to the logo by activating the Show Picture command.

To add or remove a check mark from the Show Picture command:

❶ Click **Picture**. Notice that no check mark appears next to the Show Picture command.

❷ Click **Show Picture**. The Picture menu closes, and a picture of a stove appears.

❸ Click **Picture** to open the Picture menu again. Notice that a check mark appears next to the Show Picture command because you activated this command in Step 2.

❹ Click **Show Picture**. This time clicking Show Picture removes the check mark and removes the picture.

Another menu convention is the use of gray, rather than black, type for commands. Commands displayed in gray type are sometimes referred to as **grayed-out commands**. Gray type indicates that a command is not currently available. The command might become available later, when it can be applied to the task. For example, a command that positions a picture on the right or left side of the logo would not apply to a logo without a picture. Therefore, the command for positioning the picture would be grayed out until a picture was included with the logo. Let's explore how this works.

To explore grayed-out commands:

❶ Click **Picture**. Figure 1-23 shows the Picture menu with two grayed-out choices.

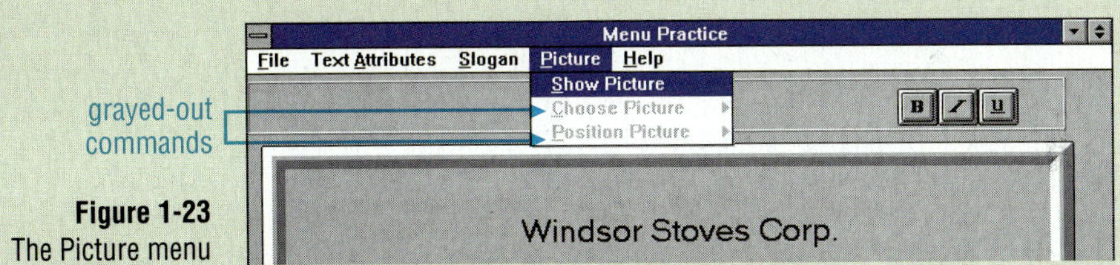

Figure 1-23
The Picture menu

grayed-out commands

❷ Click the grayed-out command **Position Picture**. Although the highlight moves to this command, nothing else happens because the command is not currently available. You cannot position the picture until a picture is displayed.

❸ Now click **Show Picture**. The Picture menu closes, and a picture is added to the logo.

❹ Click **Picture**. Now that you have opened the Picture menu again, notice that the Choose Picture and Position Picture commands are no longer grayed out.

A **submenu** provides an additional set of command choices. On your screen the Choose Picture and Position Picture commands each have triangles next to them. A triangle is a menu convention that indicates a menu has a submenu. Let's use the submenu of the Position Picture command to move the stove picture to the right of the company name.

To use the position Picture submenu:

❶ Click **Position Picture**. A submenu appears with options for left or right. In Figure 1-24 on the following page, the picture is to the left of the company name.

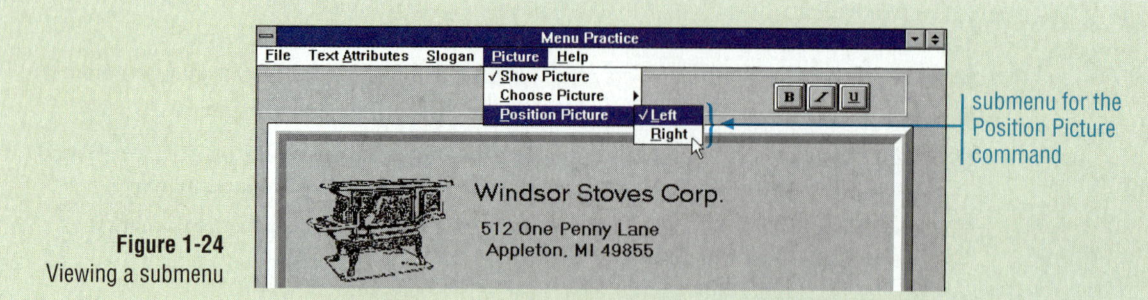

Figure 1-24
Viewing a submenu

❷   Click **Right**. Selecting this submenu command moves the picture to the right of the company name.

Some menu conventions allow you to use the menus without a mouse. It is useful to know how to use these conventions because, even if you have a mouse, in some situations it might be faster to use the keyboard.

One keyboard-related menu convention is the underlined letter in each menu name. If you wanted to open a menu using the keyboard, you would hold down the Alt key and then press the underlined letter. Let's open the Text Attributes menu using the keyboard.

To open the Text Attributes menu this way:
❶   Look at the menu name for the Text Attributes menu. Notice that the A is underlined.
❷   Press **[Alt][A]**. The Text Attributes menu opens.

TROUBLE?   Remember from the Keyboard Tutorial that the [Alt][A] notation means to hold down the Alt key and press A. Don't type the brackets and don't use the Shift key to capitalize the A.

You can also use the keyboard to highlight and activate commands. On your screen the Bold command is highlighted. You use the arrow keys on the keyboard to move the highlight. You activate highlighted commands by pressing [Enter]. Let's use the keyboard to activate the Underline command.

To choose the Underline command using the keyboard:
❶   Press **[↓]** two times to highlight the Underline command.
❷   Press **[Enter]** to activate the highlighted command and underline the company name. Now look at the **B**, **I**, and **U** buttons near the upper-right corner of the screen. The U button has been "pressed" or activated. This button is another control for underlining. You'll find out how to use these buttons later.

Previously you used the Alt key in combination with the underlined letter in the menu title to open a menu. You might have noticed that each menu command also has an underlined letter. Once a menu is open, you can activate a command by pressing the underlined letter—there is no need to press the Alt key.

To activate the Italic command using the underlined letter:

❶   Press **[Alt][A]**. This key combination opens the Text Attributes menu. Next, notice which letter is underlined in the Italic command.

❷   Press **[I]** to activate the Italic command. Now the company name is italicized as well as underlined.

Look at the menu in Figure 1-25. Notice the Ctrl+B to the right of the Bold command. This is the key combination, often called a **shortcut key**, that can be used to activate the Bold command even if the menu is not open. The Windows Ctrl+B notation means the same thing as [Ctrl][B] in these tutorials: hold down the Control key and, while holding it down, press the letter B. When you use shortcut keys, don't type the + sign and don't use the Shift key to capitalize. Let's use a shortcut key to boldface the company name.

Figure 1-25
The Text Attributes
menu

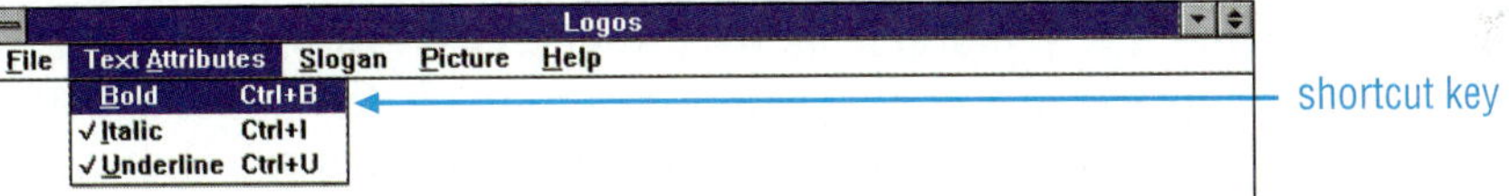

To Boldface the company name using a shortcut key:

❶   Press **[Ctrl][B]** and watch the company name appear in boldface type.

The **ellipsis (...)** menu convention means that when you select a command with three dots next to it, a dialog box will appear. A **dialog box** requests additional details about how you want the command carried out. We'll use the dialog box for the Choose Slogan command to change the company slogan.

To use the Choose Slogan dialog box:

❶   Click **Slogan**. Notice that the Choose Slogan command is followed by an ellipsis.

❷   Click **Choose Slogan...** and study the dialog box that appears. See Figure 1-26. Notice that this dialog box contains four sets of controls: the "Use Slogan" text box, the "Slogan in Bold Letters" check box, the "Slogan 3-D Effects" control buttons, and the OK and Cancel buttons. The "Use Slogan" text box displays the current slogan.

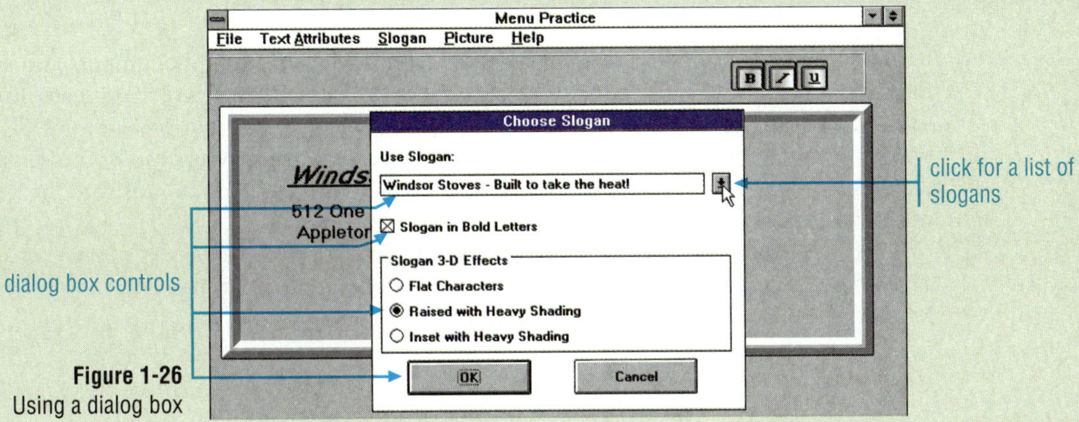

Figure 1-26
Using a dialog box

❸ Click the **down arrow button** on the right of the slogan box to display a list of alternative slogans.

❹ Click the slogan **Windsor Stoves - Built to last for generations!**

❺ Click the **OK button** and watch the new slogan replace the old.

You have used the Menu Practice application to learn how to use Windows menus, and you have learned the meaning of the Windows menu conventions. Next we'll look at dialog box controls.

Dialog Box Controls

Figure 1-27 shows a dialog box with a number of different controls that could be used to specify the requirements for a rental car. **Command buttons** initiate an immediate action. A **text box** is a space for you to type in a command detail. A **list box** displays a list of choices. A drop-down list box appears initially with only one choice; clicking the list box arrow displays additional choices. **Option buttons**, sometimes called radio buttons, allow you to select one option. **Check boxes** allow you to select one or more options. A **spin bar** changes a numeric setting.

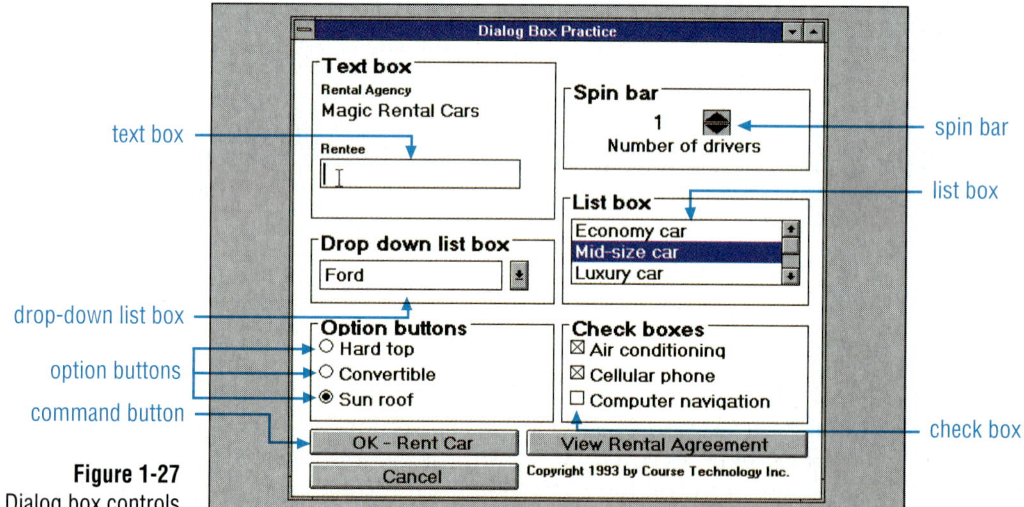

Figure 1-27
Dialog box controls

Windows uses standard dialog boxes for tasks such as printing documents and saving files. Most Windows applications use the standard dialog boxes, so if you learn how to use the Print dialog box for your word processing application, you will be well on your way to knowing how to print in any application. As you may have guessed, the rental car dialog box is not a standard Windows dialog box. It was designed to illustrate the variety of dialog box controls.

Let's see how the dialog box controls work. First, we will use a text box to type text. The Choose Slogan dialog box for the Menu Practice application has a text box that will let us change the slogan on the Windsor Stoves Corp. logo.

To activate the Use Slogan text box:

❶   Click **Slogan** to open the Slogan menu.

❷   Click **Choose Slogan...** and the Choose Slogan dialog box appears.

❸   Move the pointer to the text box and notice that it changes to an **I-bar** shape for text entry. See Figure 1-28.

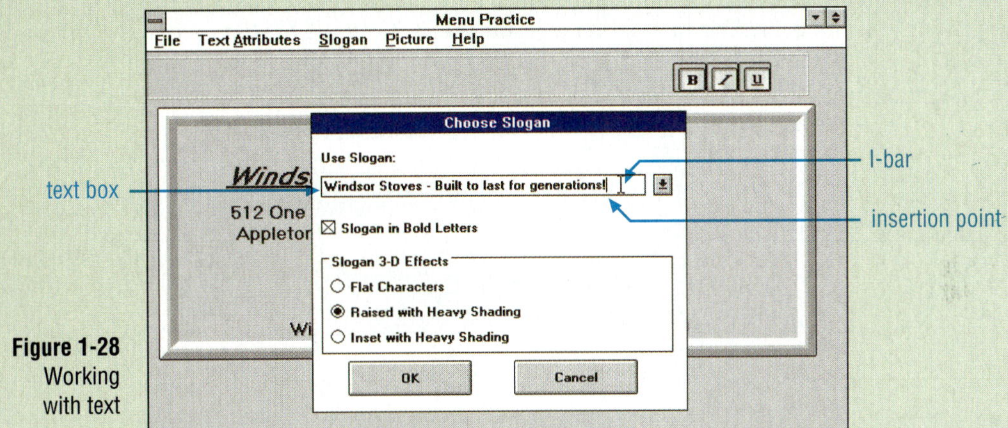

Figure 1-28
Working
with text

❹   Click the **left mouse button** to activate the text box. A blinking bar called an **Insertion point** indicates that you can type text into the box. Also notice that all the text is highlighted.

❺   Press **[Del]** to erase the highlighted text of the old slogan.

When you work with a dialog box, be sure to set all the components the way you want them *before* you press the Enter key or click the OK button. Why? Because the Enter key, like the OK button, tells Windows that you are finished with the entire dialog box. Now let's type a new slogan in the text box and change the slogan 3-D effect.

To type a new slogan in a text box:

❶   Type **Quality is our Trademark!** but don't press [Enter], because while this dialog box is open, you are also going to change the slogan 3-D effect.

   TROUBLE?   If you make a typing mistake, press [Backspace] to delete the error, then type the correction.

❷   Look at the Slogan 3-D Effects list. Notice that the current selection is Raised with Heavy Shading.

❸   Click **Inset with Heavy Shading**.

❹   Click the **OK button** and then verify that the slogan and the 3-D effect have changed.

   TROUBLE?   If you are working on a monochrome system without the ability to display shade of gray, you may not be able to see the 3-D effect.

Using the Toolbar

A **toolbar** is a collection of icons that provides command shortcuts for mouse users. The icons on the toolbar are sometimes referred to as buttons. Generally the options on the toolbar duplicate menu options, but they are more convenient because they can be activated by a single mouse click. The toolbar for the Menu Practice application shown in Figure 1-29 has three buttons that are shortcuts for the Bold, Italic, and Underline commands. In a previous exercise you underlined, boldfaced, and italicized the company name using the menus. As a result the B, U, and I buttons are activated. Let's see what they look like when we deactivate them.

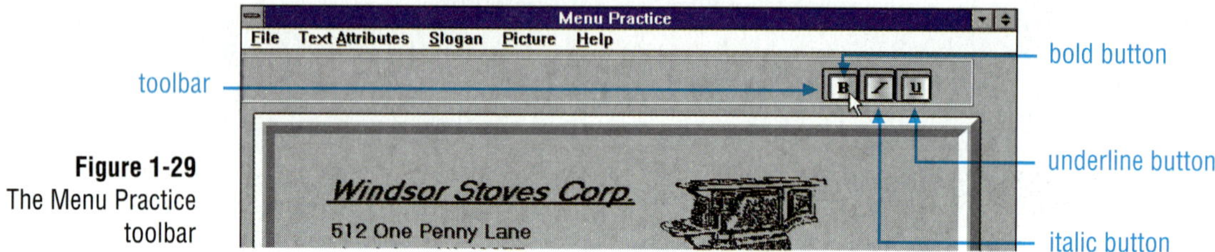

Figure 1-29
The Menu Practice toolbar

To change the type style using the toolbar:
❶   Click **B** to remove the boldface.
❷   Click **I** to turn off italics.
❸   Click **U** to turn off underlining.
❹   Click **B** to turn on boldface again.

You might want to spend a few minutes experimenting with the Menu Practice program to find the best logo design for Windsor Stoves Corp. When you are finished, close the Menu Practice window.

To close the Menu Practice window:
❶   Click the **Control-menu box**.
❷   Click **Close**. The Menu Practice program closes and returns you to Windows Program Manager.

You have now learned about Windows menus, dialog boxes and toolbars. In the next section, you will survey the Paintbrush application, experiment with tools, and access on-line help.

Using Paintbrush to Develop Your Windows Technique

After you have learned the basic Windows controls, you will find that most Windows *applications* contain similar controls. Let's launch the Paintbrush application and discover how to use it.

To launch the Paintbrush application:

❶ Be sure the Program Manager window is open. If it is not open, use the skills you have learned to open it.

❷ You should have an Accessories icon or an Accessories window on the desktop. If you have an Accessories group icon on the desktop, double-click it to open the Accessories group window.

   TROUBLE?   If you don't see the Accessories icon or window, click the Window menu on the Program Manager menu bar. Look for Accessories in the list. If you find Accessories in this list, click it. If you do not find Accessories, ask your technical support person for help.

❸ Double-click the **Paintbrush icon** to launch the Paintbrush application. Your screen will look similar to the one in Figure 1-30.

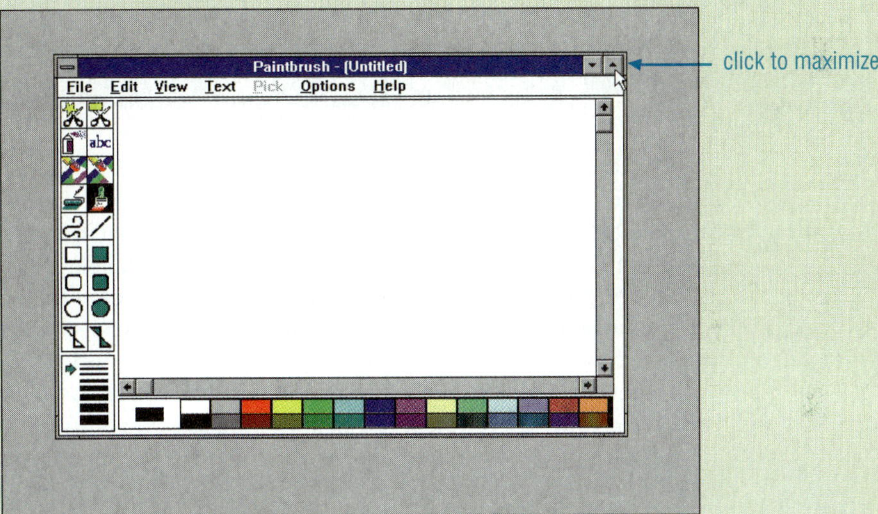

Figure 1-30
The Paintbrush
window

❹ Click the Paintbrush window **maximize button** so you will have a large drawing area.

Surveying the Paintbrush Application Window

Whether you are using a reference manual or experimenting on your own, your first step in learning a new application is to survey the window and familiarize yourself with its components.

Look at the Paintbrush window on your screen and make a list of the components you can identify. If you have not encountered a particular component before, try to guess what it might be.

Now refer to Figure 1-31 on the following page, which labels the Paintbrush window components.

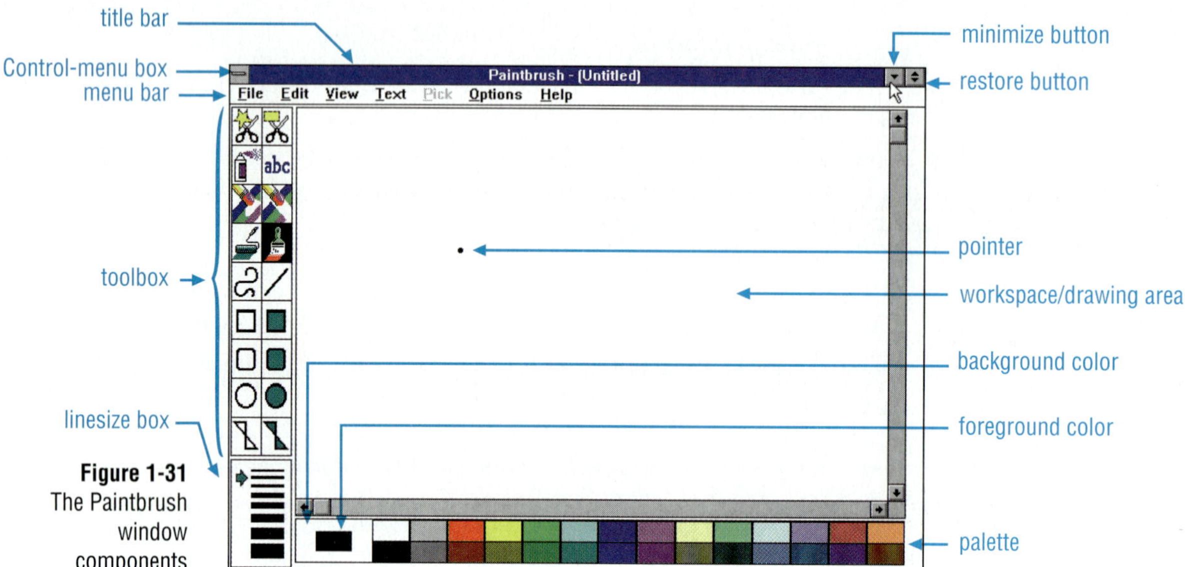

Figure 1-31
The Paintbrush window components

The darkened title bar shows that the Paintbrush window is activated. The resizing buttons are in the upper-right corner, as usual. Because there is a restore button and because the window takes up the entire screen, you know that the window is maximized. The Control-menu box is in the upper-left corner, and a menu bar lists seven menus.

On the left side of the window are a variety of icons. This looks similar to the toolbar you used when you created the logo, only it has more icons, which are arranged vertically. The Windows manual refers to this set of icons as the **toolbox**.

Under the toolbox is a box containing lines of various widths. This is the **linesize box**, which you use to select the width of the line you draw.

At the bottom of the screen is a color **palette**, which you use to select the foreground and background colors. The currently selected colors for the foreground and background are indicated in the box to the left of the palette.

The rectangular space in the middle of the window is the drawing area. When the pointer is in the drawing area, it will assume a variety of shapes, depending on the tool you are using.

Experimenting with Tools

The icons on toolbars might be some of the easiest Windows controls, but many people are a little mystified by the symbols used for some of the tools. Look at the icons in the Paintbrush toolbox and try to guess their use.

You can often make good guesses, when you know what the application does. For example, you probably guessed that the brush tool shown in Figure 1-32 is used for drawing a picture. However, you might not be able to guess how the brush and the roller tools differ.

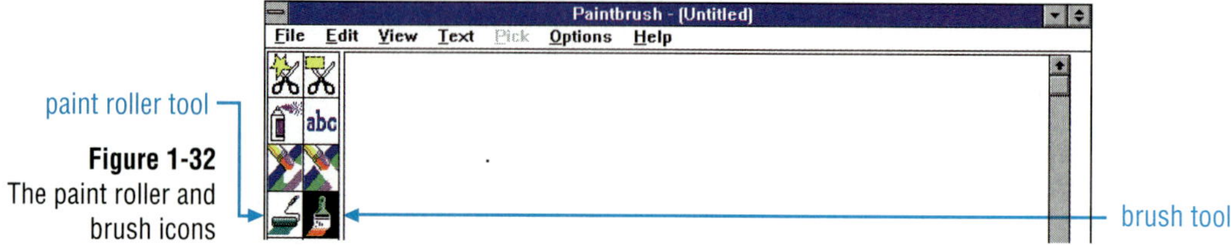

Figure 1-32
The paint roller and brush icons

If you can make some reasonable guess about how a tool works, it's not a bad idea to try it out. Can you write your name using the paintbrush tool? Let's try it.

To use the brush tool:

❶ Locate and click the **brush tool** in the toolbox. The brush tool becomes highlighted, indicating that it is now the selected tool.

❷ Move the pointer to the drawing area. Notice that it changes to a small dot.

❸ Move the pointer to the place where you want to begin writing your name.

When the left mouse button is down, the brush will paint. When you release the mouse button, you can move the pointer without painting.

❹ Use the mouse to control the brush as you write your name. Don't worry if it looks a little rough. Your "John Hancock" might look like the one in Figure 1-33.

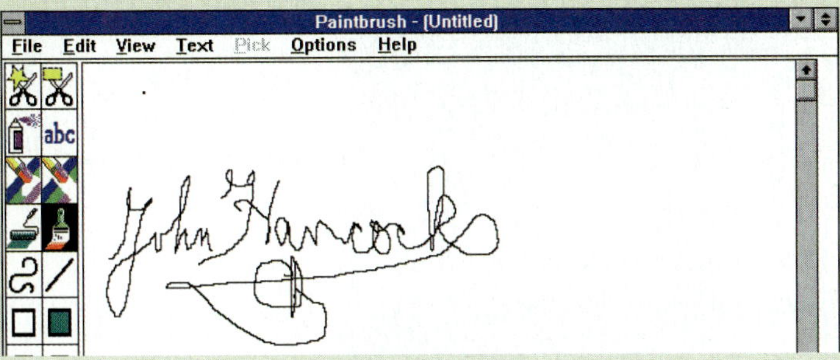

Figure 1-33
Your "John Hancock"

You will recall that we were curious about the difference between the brush and the paint roller. Let's experiment with the paint roller next.

To try the paint roller:

❶ Click the **paint roller** tool.

❷ Position the pointer in the upper-left corner of the drawing area and click. What happened?!

Did you get a strange result? Don't panic. This sort of thing happens when you experiment. Still, we probably should find out a little more about how to control the roller. To do this, we'll use the Paintbrush Help facility.

Using Help

Most Windows applications have an extensive on-line Help facility. A **Help facility** is an electronic reference manual that contains information about an application's menus, tools, and procedures. Some Help facilities also include **tutorials**, which you can use to learn the application.

There are a variety of ways to access Help, so people usually develop their own technique for finding information in it. We'll show you one way that seems to work for many Windows users. Later you can explore on your own and develop your own techniques.

When you use Help, a Help window opens. Usually the Help window overlays your application. If you want to view the problem spot and the Help information at the same time, it is a good idea to organize your desktop so the Help and application windows are side by side.

To access Help and organize the desktop:

❶   Click **Help**. A Help menu lists the Help commands.

❷   Click **Contents** to display a Paintbrush Help window similar to the one in Figure 1-34.

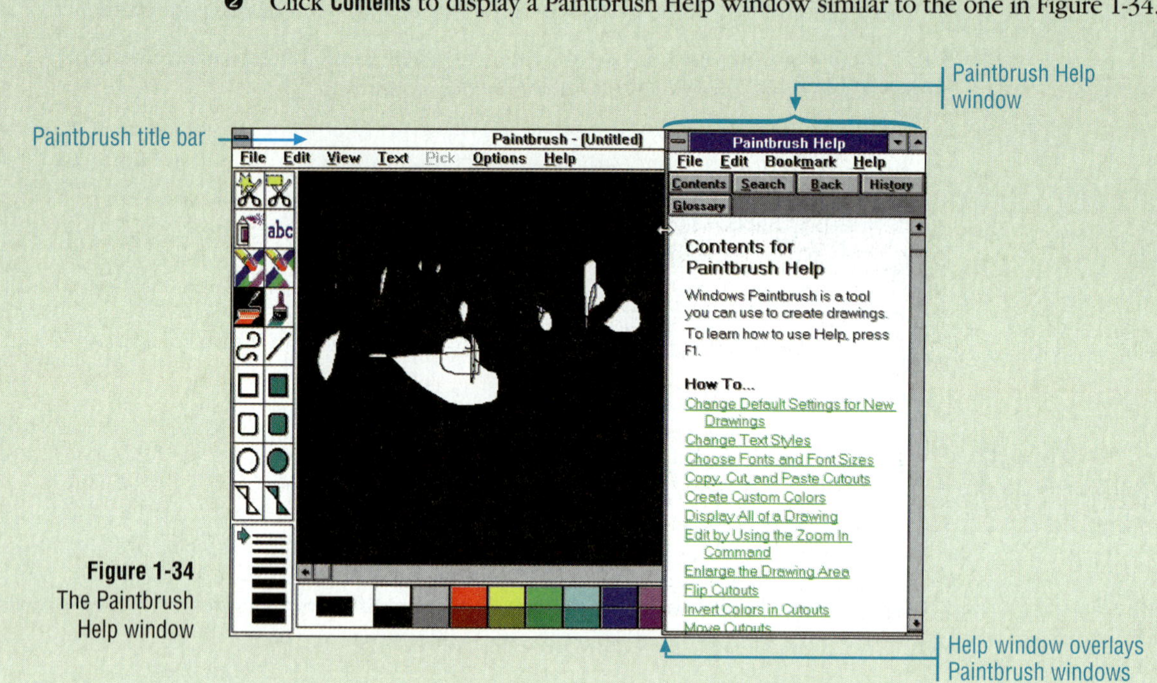

Figure 1-34
The Paintbrush Help window

❸   If the Paintbrush Help window is not the same size and shape as the one in Figure 1-34, drag the corners of the Help window until it looks like the one in the figure.

The Paintbrush application window is partially covered by the Help window. We need to fix that.

❹   Click the **Paintbrush title bar** to activate the Paintbrush window.

❺   Click the **restore button** to display the window borders and corners.

❻   Drag the corners of the Paintbrush application until your screen resembles the one in Figure 1-35 on the following page.

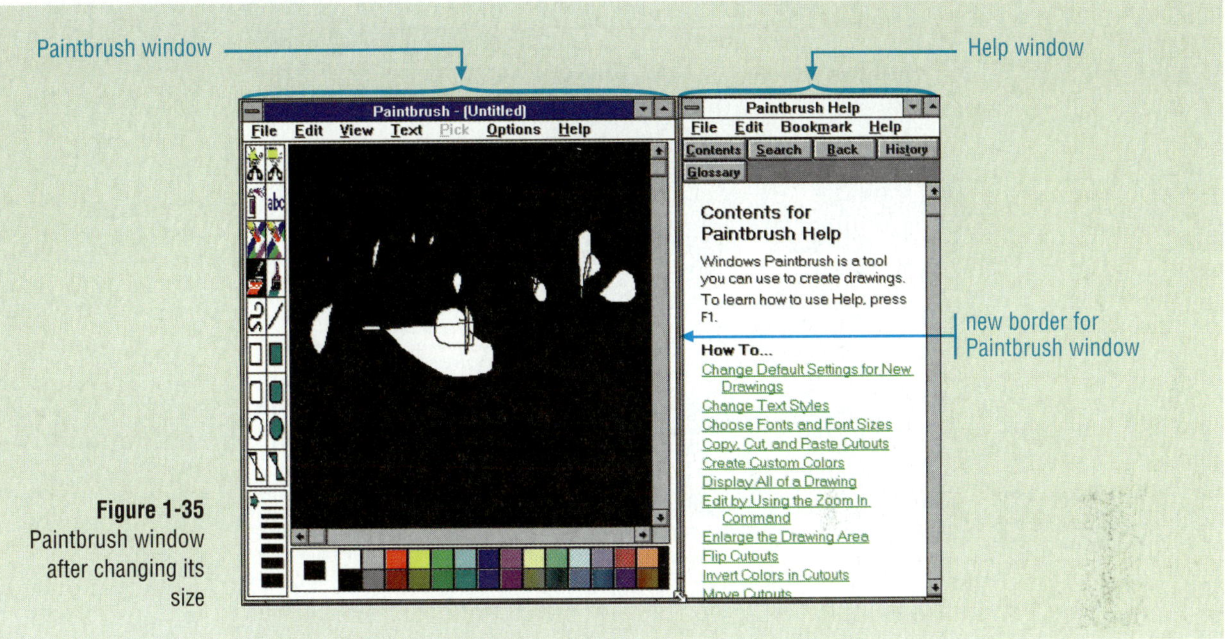

Figure 1-35
Paintbrush window
after changing its
size

Now that the windows are organized, let's find out about the roller tool. The Paintbrush Help window contains a Table of Contents, which is divided into three sections: How To, Tools, and Commands.

The **How To** section is a list of procedures that are explained in the Help facility. Use this section when you want to find out how to do something. The **Tools** section identifies the toolbar icons and explains how to use them. The **Commands** section provides an explanation of the commands that can be accessed from the menu bar.

To find information about the paint roller tool on the Help facility:

❶ Use the scroll box to scroll down the text in the Help window until you see the Tools section heading.

❷ Continue scrolling until the Paint Roller option comes into view.

❸ Position the pointer on the Paint Roller Option. Notice that the pointer changes to a pointing hand, indicating that Paint Roller is a clickable option.

❹ Click the **left mouse button**. The Help window now contains information about the paint roller, as shown in Figure 1-36 on the following page.

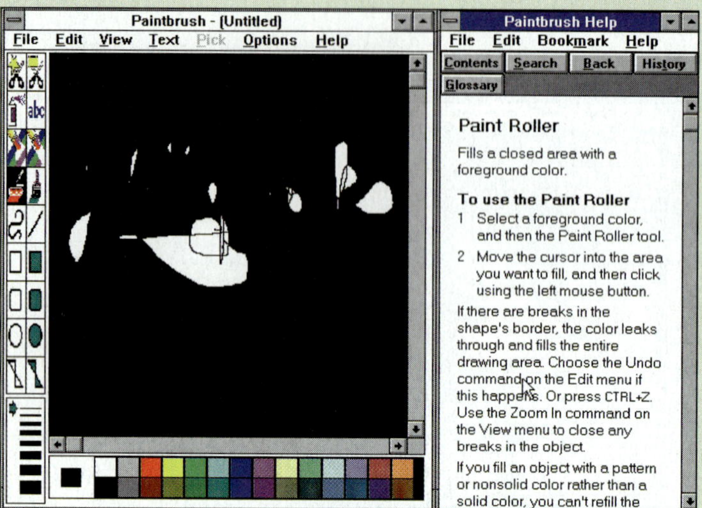

Figure 1-36
Paint Roller Help

❺   Read the information about the Paint Roller, using the scroll bar to view the entire text.

What did you learn about the paint roller? The first item you likely discovered is that the paint roller is used to fill an area. Well, it certainly did that in our experiment. It filled the entire drawing area with the foreground color, black. Next you might have noted that the first step in the procedure for using the paint roller is to select a foreground color. In our experiment, it would have been better if we selected some color other than black for the fill. Let's erase our old experiment so we can try again.

To start a new painting:

❶   Click **File** on the Paintbrush menu bar (not on the Help menu bar) to open the File menu.

❷   Click **New**, because you want to start a new drawing. A dialog box asks, "Do you want to save current changes?"

❸   Click the **No button** to clear the drawing area, because you don't want to save your first experiment.

Now you can paint your name and then use the roller to artistically fill areas. When you have finished experimenting, exit the Paintbrush application.

To exit Paintbrush:

❶   Click the **Control-menu box** and then click **Close**.

❷   In response to the prompt "Do you want to save current changes?" click the **No button**. The Paintbrush window closes, which also automatically closes the Help window.

You've covered a lot of ground. Next, it's time to learn how to exit Windows.

Exiting Windows

You might want to continue directly to the Questions and Tutorial Assignments. If so, stay in Windows until you have completed your work, then follow these instructions for exiting Windows.

To exit Windows:

❶ Click the **Control-menu box** in the upper-left of the Program Manager window.

❷ Click **Close**.

❸ When you see the message "This will end your Windows session," click the **OK button**.

■   ■   ■

Steve congratulates you on your Windows progress. You have learned the terminology associated with the desktop environment and the names of the controls and how to use them. You have developed an understanding about desktop organization and how to arrange the application and document windows so you will use them most effectively. You have also learned to use menus, dialog boxes, toolbars and Help.

Questions

1. GUI is an acronym for ____________________.
2. A group window contains which of the following?
    a. application icons
    b. document icons
    c. program-item icons
    d. group icons
3. What is one of the main purposes of the Program Manager?
    a. to organize your diskette
    b. to launch applications
    c. to create documents
    d. to provide the Help facility for applications
4. Which mouse function is used as a shortcut for more lengthy mouse or keyboard procedures?
    a. pointing
    b. clicking
    c. dragging
    d. double-clicking
5. To change the focus to an icon, you ______________ it.
    a. close
    b. select
    c. drag
    d. launch

6. What is another name for document windows?
   a. child windows
   b. parent windows
   c. application windows
   d. group windows
7. In Figure 1-37 each window component is numbered. Write the name of the component that corresponds to the number.

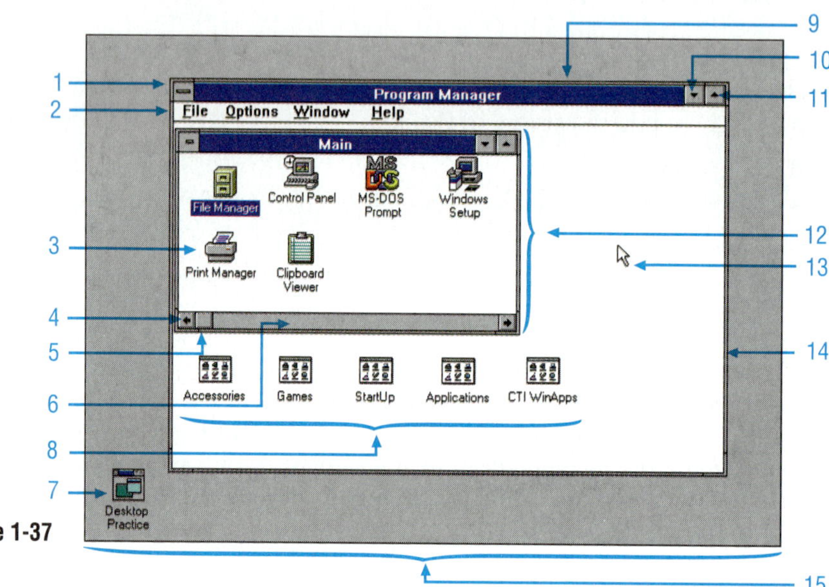

Figure 1-37

8. In Windows terminology you ________________ a window when you want to get it out of the way temporarily but leave the application running.
9. You ________________ a window when you no longer need to have the application running.
10. The ___________________ provides you with a way to switch between application windows.
    a. Task List
    b. program-item icon
    c. Window menu
    d. maximize button
11. How would you find out if you had more than one application running on your desktop?
12. ___________________ refers to the capability of a computer to run more than one application at the same time.
13. Which menu provides the means to switch from one document to another?
    a. the File menu
    b. the Help menu
    c. the Window menu
    d. the Control menu
14. Describe three menu conventions used in Windows menus.

E 15. The flashing vertical bar that marks the place your typing will appear is

___________________.

E 16. If you have access to a Windows reference manual such as the *Microsoft Windows User's Guide*, look for an explanation of the difference between group icons, program-item icons, and application icons. For your instructor's information, write down the name of the reference, the publisher, and the page(s) on which you found this information. If you were writing a textbook for first-time Windows users, how would you describe the difference between these icons?

 17. Copy the definition of "metaphor" from any standard dictionary. For your instructor's information, write down the dictionary name, the edition, and the page number. After considering the definition, explain why Windows is said to be a "desktop metaphor."

Tutorial Assignments

If you exited Windows at the end of the tutorial, launch Windows and do Assignments 1 through 15. Write your answers to the questions in Assignments 1, 2, 3, 4, 5, 9, 10, 11, 12, 13, and 15. Also fill out the table in Assignment 7.

1. Close all applications except the Program Manager and shrink all the group windows to icons. What are the names of the group icons on the desktop?
2. Open the Main window. How many program-item icons are in this window?
3. Open the Accessories window. How many program-item icons are in this window?
4. Open, close, and change the dimensions of the windows so your screen looks like Figure 1-38.
   a. How many applications are now on the desktop?
   b. How did you find out how many applications are on the desktop?

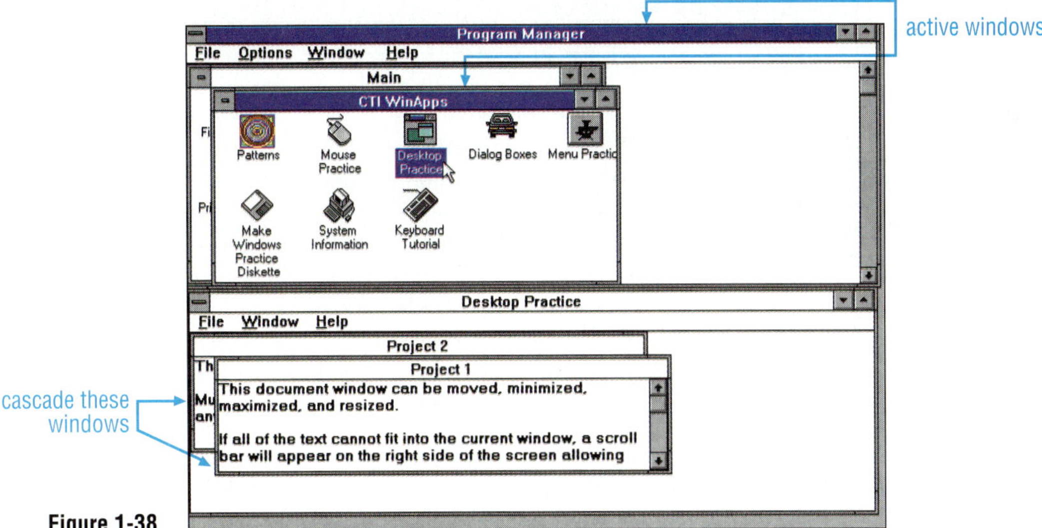

Figure 1-38

5. Open, close, and change the dimensions of the windows so your screen looks like Figure 1-39 on the following page. After you're done, close the Desktop Practice window using the fewest mouse clicks. How did you close the Desktop Practice window?

Open the CTI WinApps window and do Assignments 6 through 8.

Figure 1-39

6. Double-click the System Information icon.

7. Using the information displayed on your screen, fill out the following table:

CPU Type:	
Available Memory:	
Number of Diskette Drives:	
Capacity of Drive A:	
Capacity of Drive B:	
Horizontal Video Resolution:	
Vertical Video Resolution:	
Screen Colors or Shades:	
Network Type:	
DOS Version:	
Windows Version:	
Windows Mode:	
Windows Directory:	
Windows Free Resources:	
Available Drive Letters:	
Hard Drive Capacities:	

8. Click the Exit button to return to the Program Manager.

Launch the Mouse Practice application and do Assignments 9 through 14.

9. What happens when you drag the letter to the file cabinet?

10. What happens when you double-click the mouse icon located in the lower-left corner of the desktop?

11. What happens when you click an empty check box? What happens when you click a check box that contains an "X"?

12. Can you select both option buttons at the same time?

13. What happens when you click "Item Fourteen" from the list?

14. Exit the Mouse Practice.

Launch the Desktop Practice and do Assignments 15 through 17.

15. What is the last sentence of the document in the Project 2 window?

16. Close the Desktop Practice window.

17. Exit Windows.

Effective File Management

Using the File Manager

OBJECTIVES

In this tutorial you will:

- Open and close the File Manager
- Format and make your student disk containing practice files
- Change the current drive
- Identify the components of the File Manager window
- Create directories
- Change the current directory
- Move, rename, delete, and copy files
- Make a disk backup
- Learn how to protect your data from hardware failures

CASE

A Professional Approach to Computing at Narraganset Shipyard   Ruth Sanchez works at the Narraganset Shipyard, a major government defense contractor. On a recent business trip to Washington, DC, Ruth read a magazine article that convinced her she should do a better job of organizing the files on her computer system. The article pointed out that a professional approach to computing includes a plan for maintaining an organized set of disk-based files that can be easily accessed, updated, and secured.

Ruth learns that the Windows File Manager can help to organize her files. Ruth has not used the File Manager very much, so before she begins to make organizational changes to the valuable files on her hard disk, she decides to practice with some sample files on a disk in drive A.

In this Tutorial, you will follow the progress of Ruth's File Manager practice and learn how to use Windows to manage effectively the data stored in your computer.

Files and the File Manager

A **file** is a named collection of data organized for a specific purpose and stored on a floppy disk or a hard disk. The typical computer user has hundreds of files.

The Windows File Manager provides some handy tools for organizing files. Ruth's first step is to launch the File Manager. Let's do the same.

To launch the File Manager:

❶ Launch Windows.

❷ Compare your screen to Figure 2-1. Use the skills you learned in Tutorial 1 to organize your desktop so only the Program Manager window and the Main window are open.

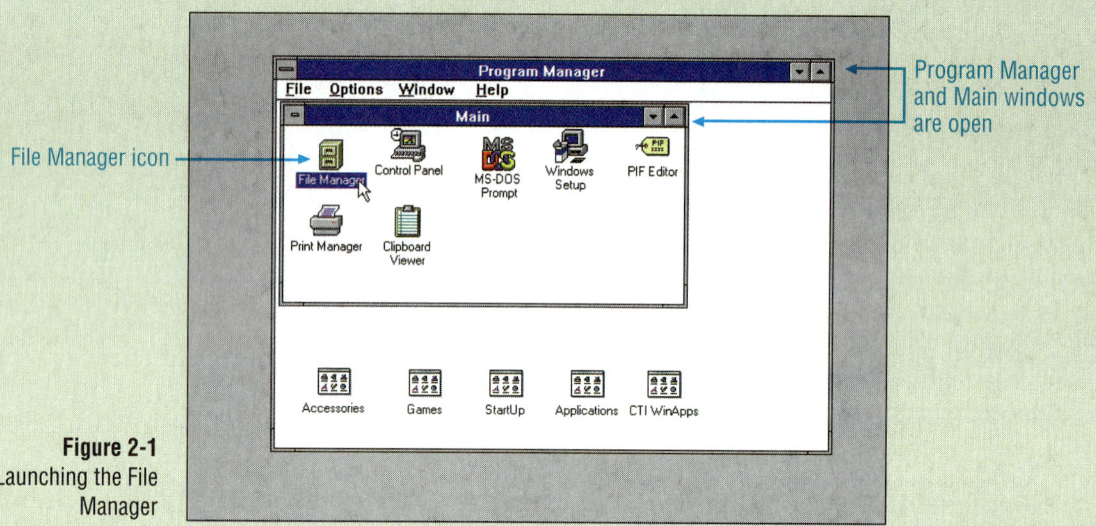

Figure 2-1
Launching the File
Manager

❸ Double-click the **File Manager icon** to launch the File Manager program and open the File Manager window.

❹ If the File Manager window is not maximized, click the **maximize button**.

❺ Click **Window**, then click **Tile**. You should now have one child window on the desktop. See Figure 2-2a on the following page. Don't worry if the title of your child window is not the same as the one in the figure.

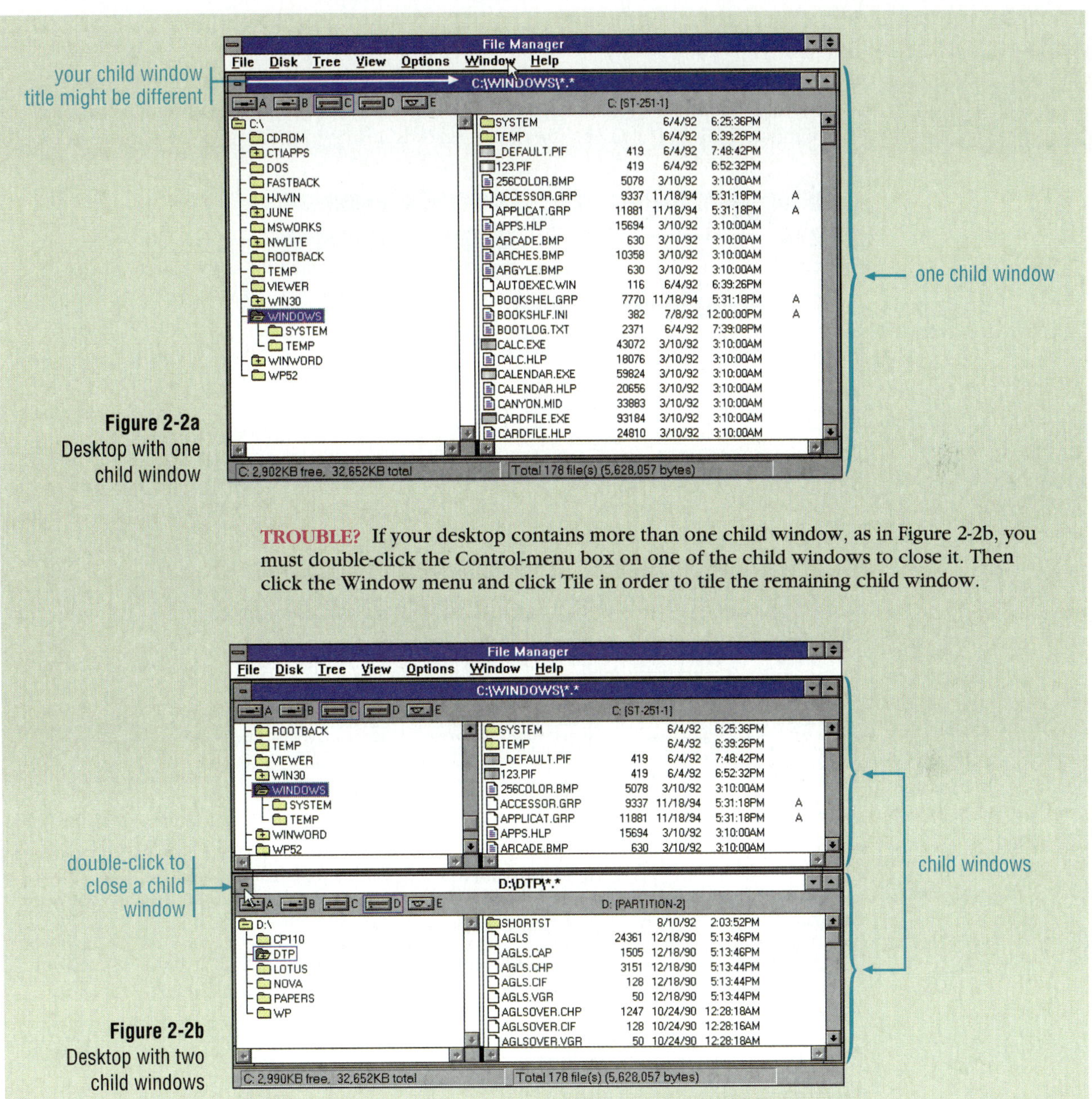

Figure 2-2a
Desktop with one
child window

Figure 2-2b
Desktop with two
child windows

TROUBLE? If your desktop contains more than one child window, as in Figure 2-2b, you must double-click the Control-menu box on one of the child windows to close it. Then click the Window menu and click Tile in order to tile the remaining child window.

Ruth decides to check her File Manager settings, which affect the way information is displayed. By adjusting your File Manager settings to match Ruth's, your computer will display screens and prompts similar to those in the Tutorial. *If you do not finish this tutorial in one session, remember to adjust the settings again when you begin your next session.*

To adjust your File Manager settings:

❶   Click **Tree**. Look at the command "Indicate Expandable Branches." See Figure 2-3. If no check mark appears next to this command, position the pointer on the command and click. If you see the check mark, go to Step 2.

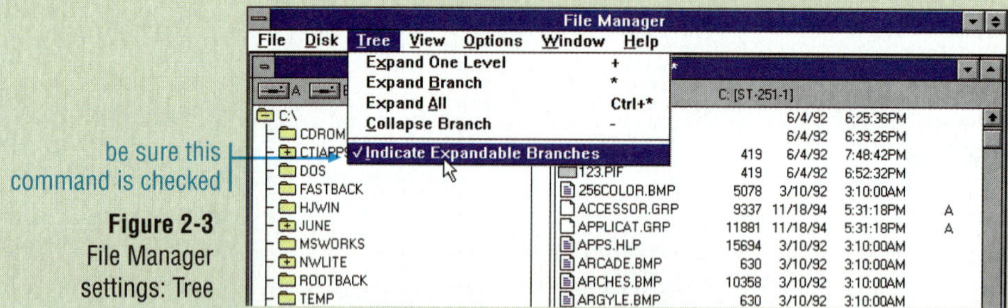

Figure 2-3
File Manager
settings: Tree

❷   Click **View**. Make any adjustments necessary so that the settings are the same as those in Figure 2-4.

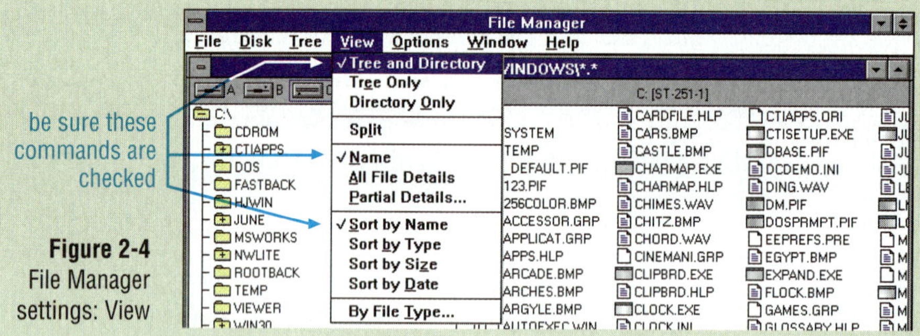

Figure 2-4
File Manager
settings: View

TROUBLE? When you click a command to change the check mark, the menu closes. To change another command in the menu or to confirm your changes, you need to click the View menu again.

❸   Click **Options** and then click **Confirmation…**. Referring to Figure 2-5, make any adjustments necessary so that all the check boxes contain an X, then click the **OK button**.

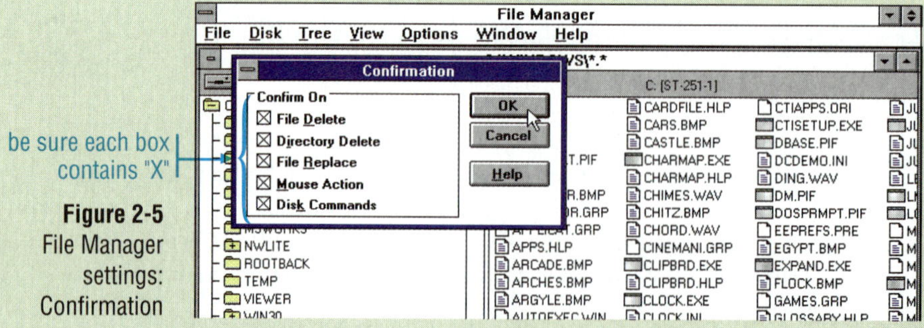

Figure 2-5
File Manager
settings:
Confirmation

❹   Click **Options** again and then click **Font**. Make any adjustments necessary so your font settings match those in Figure 2-6 on the following page. Click the **OK button** whether or not you changed anything in this dialog box.

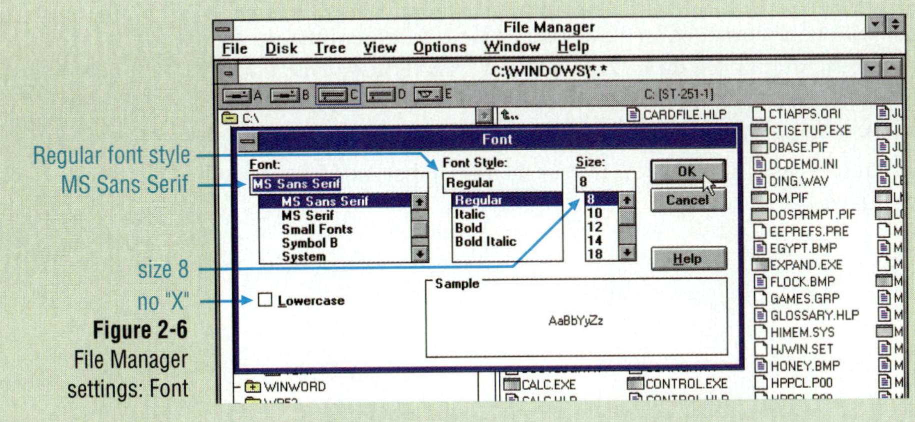

Figure 2-6
File Manager
settings: Font

❺   Click **Options** again. Make any adjustments necessary so that the settings are the same as those in Figure 2-7. If no adjustments are necessary, click **Options** again to close the menu.

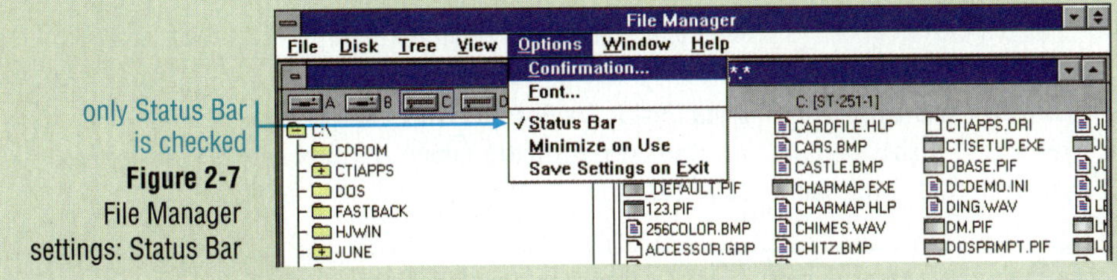

Figure 2-7
File Manager
settings: Status Bar

Formatting a Disk

Next, Ruth needs to format the disks she will use for her File Manager practice. Disks must be formatted before they can be used to store data. Formatting arranges the magnetic particles on the disks in preparation for storing data. You need to format a disk when:

- you purchase a new disk
- you want to recycle an old disk that you used on a non-IBM-compatible computer
- you want to erase all the old files from a disk

Pay attention when you are formatting disks. *The formatting process erases all the data on the disk*. If you format a disk that already contains data, you will lose all the data. Fortunately, Windows will not let you format the hard disk or network drives using the Format Disk command.

To complete the steps in this Tutorial you need two disks of the same size and density. You may use blank, unformatted disks or disks that contain data you no longer need. *The following steps assume that you will format the disks in drive A. If you want to use drive B for the formatting process, substitute drive B for drive A in Steps 3, 4, and 6.*

To format the first disk:

❶   Make sure your disk is *not* write-protected. On a 5.25-inch disk the write-protect notch should *not* be covered. On a 3.5-inch disk the hole on the left side of the disk should be *closed*.

❷   Write your name, course title, and course meeting time on an adhesive disk label. For the title of the disk, write Student Disk (Source Disk). Apply this label to one of the disks you are going to format. If you are using a 3.5-inch disk, do not stick the label on any of the metal parts.

❸   Put this disk into drive A. If your disk drive has a door or a latch, secure it. See Figure 2-8.

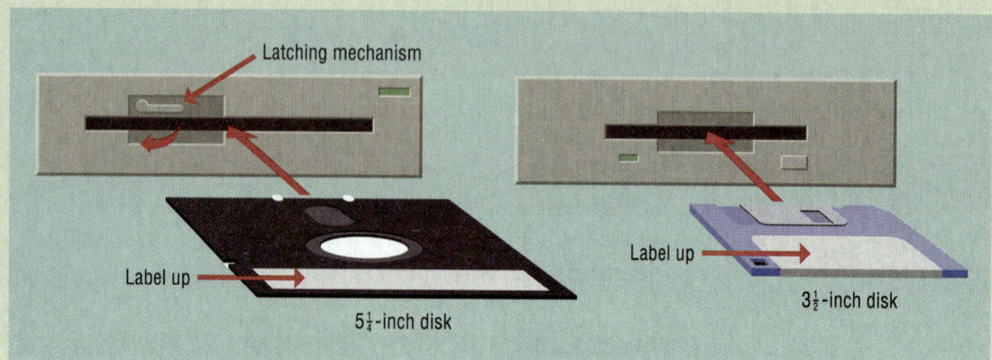

Figure 2-8
Inserting your disk

❹   Click **Disk** and then click **Format Disk....** A Format Disk dialog box appears. See Figure 2-9. If the Disk In box does not indicate Drive A, click the [↓] (down-arrow) button on this box, then click the Drive A option.

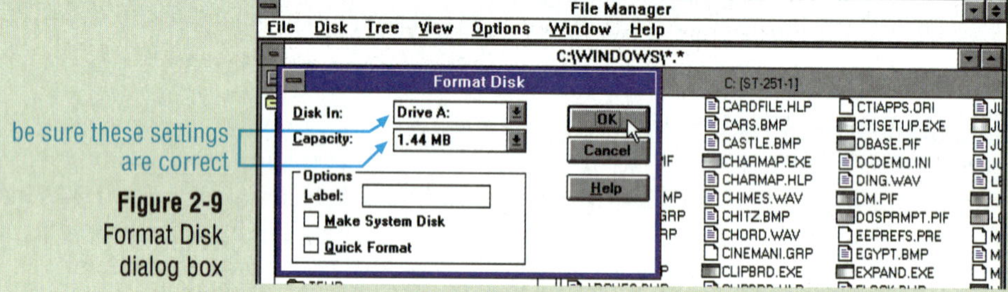

be sure these settings
are correct

Figure 2-9
Format Disk
dialog box

❺   Look at the number displayed in the Capacity box. If you are formatting a disk that cannot store the displayed amount of data, click the [↓] (down-arrow) button at the right side of the Capacity box and then click the correct capacity from the list of options provided.

TROUBLE? How can you determine the capacity of your disk? The chart in Figure 2-10 (on the next page) will help you. If you still are not sure after looking at the figure, ask your technical support person.

Diskette size	Diskette density	Diskette capacity
5¼-inch	DD	360K
5¼-inch	HD	1.2MB
3½-inch	DD	720K
3½-inch	HD	1.44MB

Figure 2-10
Disk capacities

❻ Click the **OK button**. The Confirm Format Disk dialog box appears with a warning. Read it. Look at the drive that is going to carry out the format operation (drive A). Be sure this is the correct drive. Double-check the disk that's in this drive to be sure it is the one you want to format.

❼ Click the **Yes button**. The Formatting Disk dialog box keeps you updated on the progress of the format.

❽ When the format is complete, the Format Complete dialog box reports the results of the format and asks if you'd like to format another disk. See Figure 2-11.

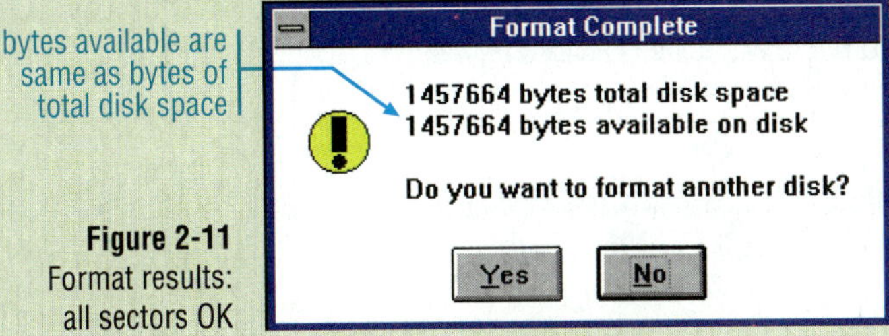

bytes available are same as bytes of total disk space

Figure 2-11
Format results: all sectors OK

Let's format your second floppy disk:

❶ Click the **Yes button** after you review the formatting results.

❷ Remove your Student disk from drive A.

❸ Write your name, course title, and course meeting time on the label for the second disk. For the title of this disk write Backup (Destination Disk). Apply this label to your second disk and place this disk in drive A.

❹ Be sure the **Disk In box** is set to drive A and the capacity is set to the capacity of your disk. (Remember to substitute B here if you are formatting your disk in drive B.)

❺ Click the **OK button** to accept the settings. When you see the Confirm Format Disk dialog box, check to be sure you have the correct disk in the correct drive.

❻ Click the **Yes button** to confirm that you want to format the disk. When the format is complete, review the format results.

❼ You do not want to format another disk, so click the **No button** when the computer asks if you wish to format another disk.

❽ *Remove the backup disk from drive A*. You will not need this backup disk until later.

Preparing Your Student Disk

Now that Ruth has formatted her disks, she is going to put some files on one of them to use for her file management exploration. To follow Ruth's progress, you must have copies of her files. A collection of files has been prepared for this purpose. You need to transfer them to one of your formatted disks.

To transfer files to your Student Disk:

❶ Place the disk you labeled Student Disk (Source Disk) in drive A.

The File Manager window is open, but you need to go to the Program Manager window to launch the application that will transfer the files.

❷   Hold down **[Alt]** and continue to press **[Tab]** until Program Manager appears in the box, then release both keys. Program Manager becomes the active window.

❸   If the CTI WinApps window is not open, double-click the **CTI WinApps group icon**. If the CTI WinApps window is open but is not the active window, click it. Your screen should look similar to Figure 2-12.

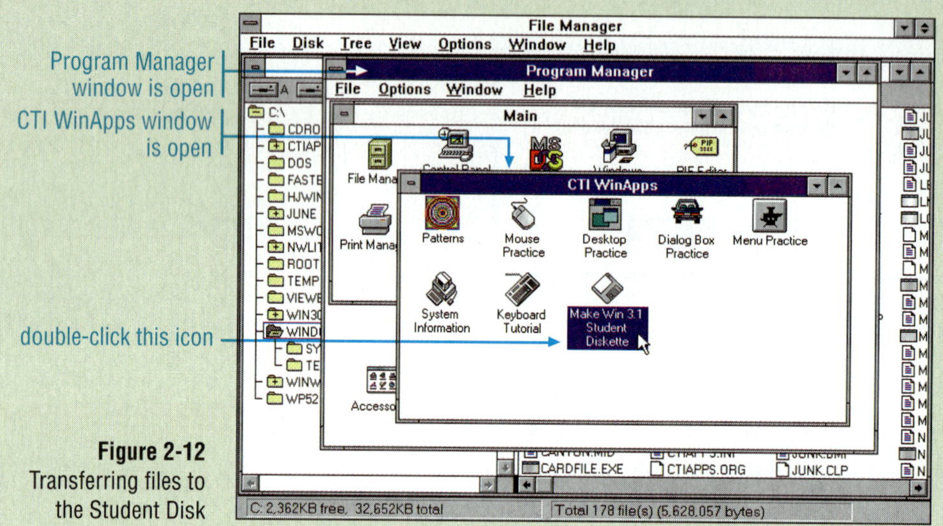

Program Manager window is open

CTI WinApps window is open

double-click this icon

Figure 2-12
Transferring files to the Student Disk

❹   Double-click the **Make Win 3.1 Student Disk icon**. A dialog box appears.

❺   Make sure the drive that is selected in the dialog box corresponds to the drive that contains your disk (drive A or drive B), then click the **OK button**. It will take 30 seconds or so to transfer the files to your disk.

❻   Click the **OK button** when you see the message "24 files copied successfully!"

❼   Double-click on the **CTI WinWorks Apps Control-menu box** to close the window.

Now the data files you need should be on your Student Disk. To continue the Tutorial, you must switch back to the File Manager.

To switch back to the File Manager:
❶   Hold down **[Alt]** and press **[Tab]** until a box with File Manager appears. Then release both keys.

Finding Out What's on Your Disks

Ruth learned from the article that the first step toward effective data management is to find out what's stored on her disks. To see what's on your Student Disk, you will need to be sure your computer is referencing the correct disk drive.

Changing the Current Drive

Each drive on your computer system is represented by a **drive icon** that tells you the drive letter and the drive type. Figure 2-13 shows the drive types represented by these icons.

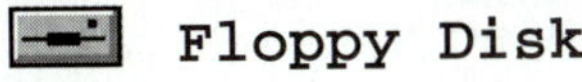

Figure 2-13
Drive icons

Near the top of the File Manager window, a **drive icon ribbon** indicates the drives on your computer system. See Figure 2-14. Your screen may be different because the drive icon ribbon on your screen reflects your particular hardware configuration.

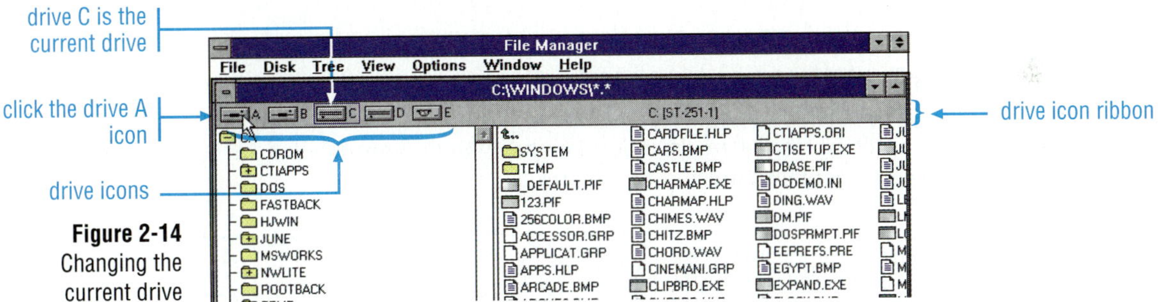

Figure 2-14
Changing the current drive

Your computer is connected to a number of storage drives or devices, but it can work with only one drive at a time. This drive is referred to as the **current drive** or **default drive**. You must change the current drive whenever you want to use files or programs that are stored on a different drive. The drive icon for the current drive is outlined with a rectangle. In Figure 2-14, the current drive is C.

To work with Ruth's files, you must be sure that the current drive is the one in which you have your Student Disk. *For this Tutorial we'll assume that your Student Disk is in drive A. If it is in drive B, substitute "drive B" for "drive A" in the rest of the steps for this Tutorial.*

Follow the next set of steps to change the current drive, if your current drive is not the one containing your Student Disk.

To change the current drive to A:

❶ Be sure your Student Disk is in drive A.

❷ Click the **drive A icon**. Drive A becomes the current drive. See Figure 2-15 on the following page.

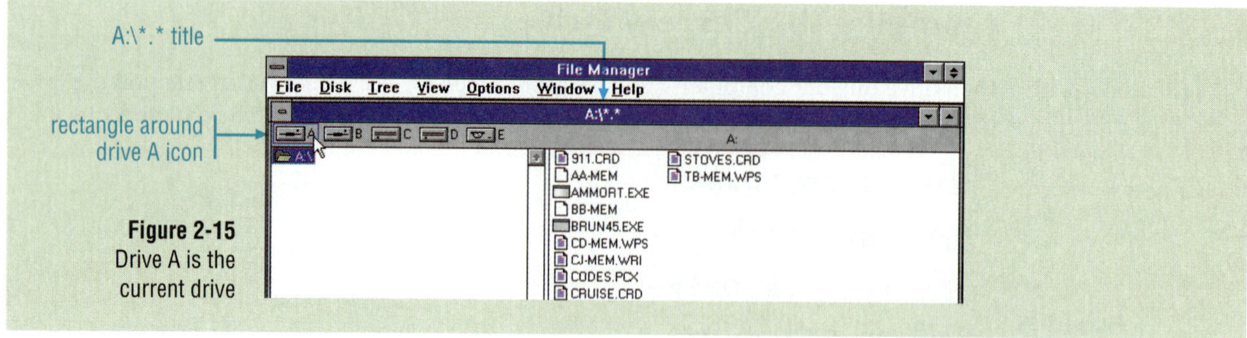

Figure 2-15
Drive A is the
current drive

After you make drive A the current drive, your screen should look similar to Figure 2-15. Don't worry if everything is not exactly the same as the figure. Just be sure you see the A:*.* window title and that there is a rectangle around the drive A icon (or the drive B icon if drive B contains your floppy disk).

The File Manager Window

The components of the File Manager window are labeled in Figure 2-16. Your screen should contain similar components.

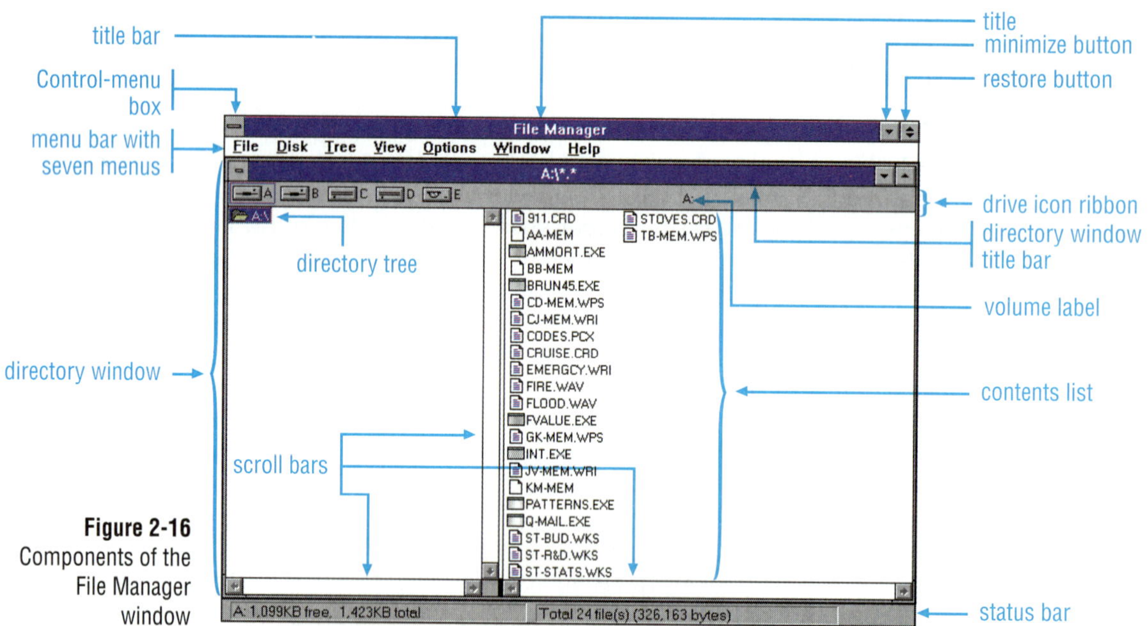

Figure 2-16
Components of the
File Manager
window

The top line of the File Manager window contains the Control-menu box, the title bar, the title, and the resizing buttons. The File Manager menu bar contains seven menus.

Inside the File Manager window is the **directory window**, which contains information about the current drive. The title bar for this window displays the current drive, in this case, A:*.*. This window has its own Control-menu box and resizing buttons.

Below the directory window title bar is the drive icon ribbon. On this line, the drive letter is followed by a volume label, if there is one. **A volume label** is a name you can assign to your disk during the format process to help you identify the contents of the disk. We did not assign a volume label, so the area after the A: is blank. Why is there a colon after the drive letter? Even though the colon is not displayed on the drive icons, when you type in a drive letter, you must always type a colon after it. The colon is a requirement of the DOS operating system that Windows uses behind the scenes to perform its file management tasks.

At the bottom of the screen, a status bar displays information about disk space. Remember that a byte is one character of data.

Notice that the directory window is split. The left half of the directory window displays the **directory tree**, which illustrates the organization of files on the current drive. The right half of the directory window displays the **contents list**, which lists the files on the current drive. Scroll bars on these windows let you view material that doesn't fit in the current window.

The Directory Tree

A list of files is called a **directory**. Because long lists of files are awkward to work with, directories can be subdivided into smaller lists called **subdirectories**. The organization of these directories and subdirectories is depicted in the directory tree.

Suppose you were using your computer for a small retail business. What information might you have on your disk, and how would it be organized? Figure 2-17 shows the directory tree for a hard disk (drive C) of a typical small business computer system.

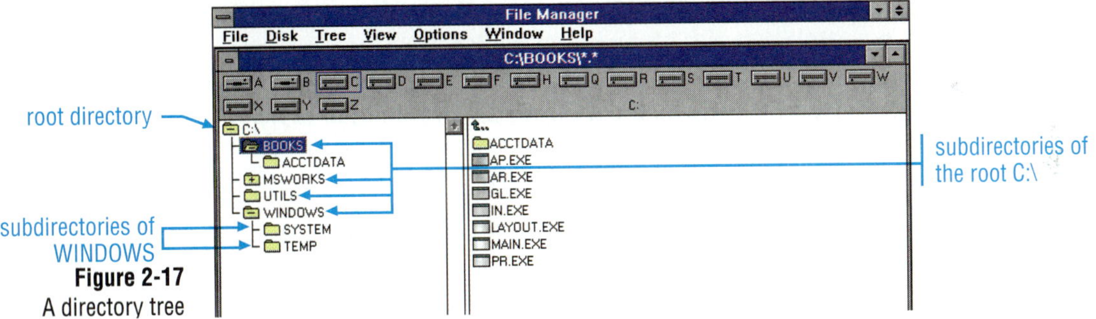

Figure 2-17
A directory tree

At the top of the directory tree is the **root directory**, called C:\ . The root directory is created when you format a disk and is indicated by a backslash after the drive letter and colon. Arranged under the root directory are the subdirectories BOOKS, MSWORKS, UTILS, and WINDOWS.

Directories other than the root directory can have subdirectories. In Figure 2-17 you can see that the BOOKS directory has a subdirectory called ACCTDATA. The WINDOWS directory contains two subdirectories, SYSTEM and TEMP. MSWORKS also has some subdirectories, but they are not listed. You'll find out how to expand the directory tree to display subdirectories later in the this tutorial.

Windows uses directory names to construct a path through the directory tree. For example, the path to ACCTDATA would be C:\BOOKS\ACCTDATA. To trace this path on Figure 2-17, begin at the root directory C:\, follow the line leading to the BOOKS directory, then follow the line leading to the ACCTDATA directory.

Each directory in the directory tree has a **file folder icon**, which can be either open or closed. An open file folder icon indicates the **active** or **current directory**. In Figure 2-17 the current directory is BOOKS. Only one directory can be current on a disk at a time.

Now look at the directory tree on your screen. The root directory of your Student Disk is called A:\. The file folder icon for this directory is open, indicating that this is the current directory. Are there any subdirectories on your disk?

The answer is no. A:\ has no subdirectories because its file folder icon does not contain a plus sign or a minus sign. A plus sign on a folder indicates that the directory can be expanded to show its subdirectories. A minus sign indicates that the subdirectories are currently being displayed. A file folder icon without a plus or a minus sign has no subdirectories.

Organizing Your Files

Ruth's disk, like your Student Disk, contains only one directory, and all her files are in that directory. As is typical of a poorly organized disk, files from different projects and programs are jumbled together. As Ruth's disk accumulates more files, she will have an increasingly difficult time finding the files she wants to use.

Ruth needs to organize her disk. First, she needs to make some new directories so she has a good basic structure for her files.

Creating Directories

When you create a directory, you indicate its location on the directory tree and specify the new directory name. The directory you create becomes a subdirectory of the current directory, which is designated by an open file folder. Directory names can be up to eight characters long.

Your Student Disk contains a collection of memos and spreadsheets that Ruth has created for a project code named "Stealth." Right now, all of these files are in the root directory. Ruth decides that to improve the organization of her disk, she should place her memos in one directory and the Stealth spreadsheets in another directory. To do this, she needs to make two new directories, MEMOS and STEALTH.

To make a new directory called MEMOS:

❶ Click the **file folder icon** representing the root directory of drive A. Figure 2-18 shows you where to click. This highlights the root directory A:\, making it the current directory.

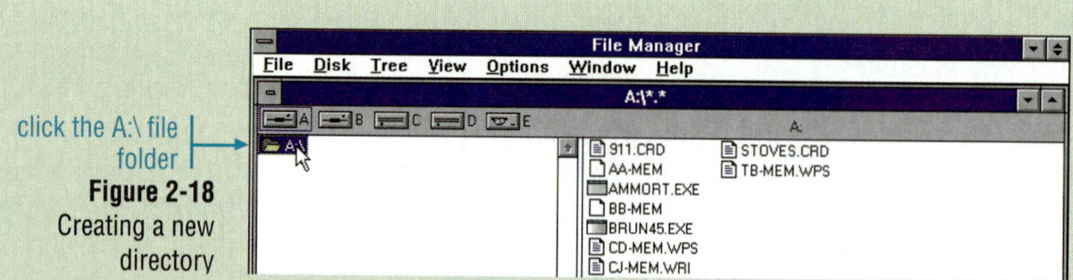

click the A:\ file folder

Figure 2-18
Creating a new directory

❷ Click **File**, then click **Create Directory…**. The Create Directory dialog box indicates that the current directory is A:\ and displays a text box for the name of the new directory.

❸ In the text box, type **MEMOS**, then click the **OK button**. It doesn't matter whether you type the directory name in uppercase or lowercase letters.

As a result, your screen should look like Figure 2-19. A new directory folder labeled MEMOS is now a subdirectory of A:\. The A:\ file folder now displays a minus sign to indicate that it has a subdirectory and that the subdirectory is displayed.

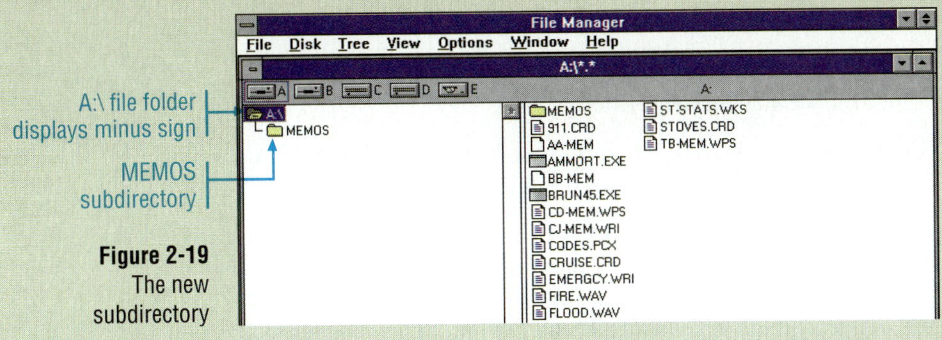

Figure 2-19
The new subdirectory

A:\ file folder displays minus sign

MEMOS subdirectory

TROUBLE? If you do not see the minus sign on the A:\ file folder, click Tree, then click Indicate Expandable branches.

Next Ruth will make a directory for the spreadsheets. She wants her directory tree to look like the one in Figure 2-20a, not the one in Figure 2-20b.

Figure 2-20a
SHEETS is a subdirectory of A:\

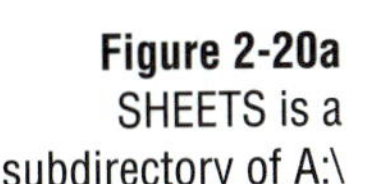

Figure 2-20b
SHEETS is a subdirectory of MEMOS

The spreadsheet directory should be a subdirectory of the root, *not* of MEMOS.

To make a directory for spreadsheets:

❶ Click the **directory folder icon for A:**

❷ Click **File**, then click **Create Directory….**

❸ In the text box type **SHEETS**, then click the **OK button**.

❹ Make sure that your newly updated directory tree resembles the one in Figure 2-20a. There should be two directories under A:\ — MEMOS and SHEETS.

TROUBLE? If your directory tree is structured like the one in Figure 2-20b, use your mouse to drag the SHEETS directory icon to the A:\ file folder icon.

Now Ruth's disk has a structure she can use to organize her files. It contains three directories: the root A:\, MEMOS, and SHEETS. Each directory can contain a list of files. Ruth is happy with this new structure, but she is not sure what the directories contain. She decides to look in one of the new directories to see what's there.

Changing Directories

When you change directories, you open a different directory folder. If the directory contains files, they will be displayed in the contents list.

First, Ruth wants to look in the MEMOS directory.

To change to the MEMOS directory:
- ❶   Click the **MEMOS directory file folder icon**.

Notice that the A:\ file folder icon is closed and the MEMOS file folder icon is open, indicating that the MEMOS directory is now current.

Look at the status line at the bottom of your screen. The left side of the status line shows you how much space is left on your disk. The right side of the status line tells you that no files are in the current directory, that is, in the MEMOS directory. This makes sense. You just created the directory, and haven't put anything in it.

- ❷   Click the **A:\ file folder icon** to change back to the root directory.

Expanding and Collapsing Directories

Notice on your screen that the A:\ file folder icon has a minus sign on it. As you know, the minus sign indicates that A:\ has one or more subdirectories and that those subdirectories are displayed. To look at a simplified directory tree, you would **collapse** the A:\ directory. You would **expand** a directory to redisplay its subdirectories. Ruth wants to practice expanding and collapsing directories.

To expand and then collapse a directory:
- ❶   Double-click the **A:\ file folder icon** to collapse the directory. As a result the MEMOS and SHEETS branches of the directory tree are removed and a plus sign appears on the A:\ file folder icon.
- ❷   Double-click the **A:\ file folder icon** again. This time the directory expands, displaying the MEMOS and SHEETS branches. Notice the minus sign on the A:\ file folder icon.

The Contents List

The **contents list** on the right side of the desktop contains the list of files and subdirectories for the current directory. On your screen the directory tree shows that A:\ is the current directory. The status bar shows that this directory contains 26 files and subdirectories. These files are listed in the contents list. Ruth recalls that she had to follow a set of rules when she created the names for these files. Let's find out more about these rules, since you will soon need to create names for your own files.

Filenames and Extensions

A **filename** is a unique set of letters and numbers that identifies a program, document file, directory, or miscellaneous data file. A filename may be followed by an **extension**, which is separated from the filename by a period.

The rules for creating valid filenames are as follows:

- The filename can contain a maximum of eight characters.
- The extension cannot contain more than three characters.
- Use a period only between the filename and the extension.
- Neither the filename nor extension can include any spaces.
- Do not use the following characters: / [ ] ; = " \ : | ,
- Do not use the following names: AUX, COM1, COM2, COM3, COM4, CON, LPT1, LPT2, LPT3, PRN, or NUL.

Ruth used the letters ST at the beginning of her spreadsheet filenames so she could remember that these files contain information on project Stealth. Ruth used the rest of each filename to describe more about the file contents. For example, ST-BUD is the budget for project Stealth, ST-R&D is the research and development cost worksheet for the project, and ST-STATS contains the descriptive statistics for the project. Ruth's memos, on the other hand, begin with the initials of the person who received the memo. She used MEM as part of the filename for all her memos. For example, the file CJMEM.WRI contains a memo to Charles Jackson.

The file extension usually indicates the category of information a file contains. We can divide files into two broad categories, program files and data files. **Program files** contain the programming code for applications and systems software. For example, the computer program that makes your computer run the WordPerfect word processor would be classified as a program file. Program files are sometimes referred to as **executable files** because the computer executes, or performs, the instructions contained in the files. A common filename extension for this type of file is .EXE. Other extensions for program files include .BAT, .SYS, .PIF, and .COM. In the contents list, program files are shown with a **program file icon**, like the one you see next to the file PATTERNS.EXE on your screen and in Figure 2-21.

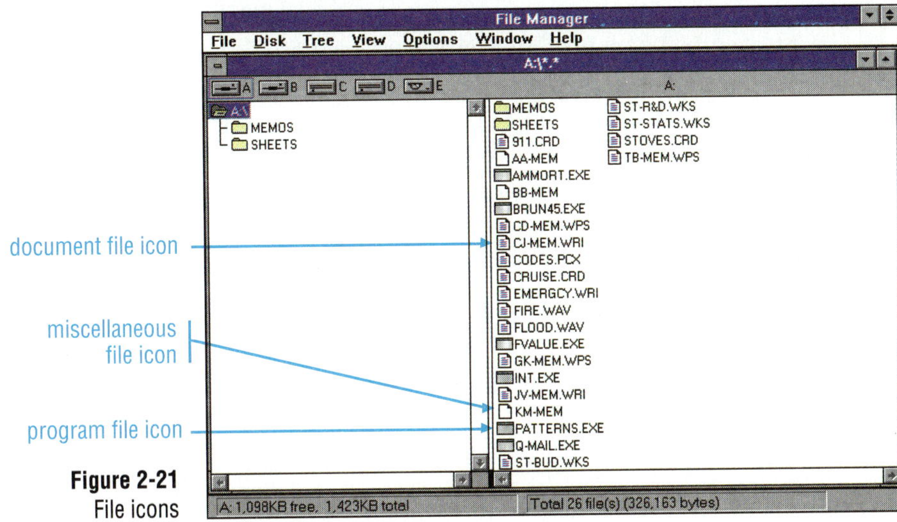

Figure 2-21
File icons

The second file category is data files. **Data files** contain the information with which you work: the memos, spreadsheets, reports, and graphs you create using applications such as word processors and spreadsheets. The filename extension for a data file usually indicates which application was used to create the file. For example, the file CD-MEM.WPS was created using the Microsoft Works word processor, which automatically puts the extension .WPS on any file you create with it. The use of .WPS as the standard extension for Works word processing documents creates an association between the application and the documents you create with it. Later, when you want to make modifications to your documents, Works can find them easily by looking for the .WPS extension.

Data files you create using a Windows application installed on your computer are shown in the contents list with a **document file icon** like the one you see next to CD-MEM.WPS on your screen. Data files you create using a non-Windows application or a Windows application that is not installed on your computer are shown in the contents list with a **miscellaneous file icon** like the one you see next to AA-MEM on your screen. AA-MEM was created using a non-Windows word processor.

Now that you have an idea of the contents for each of Ruth's files, you will be able to help her move them into the appropriate directory.

Moving Files

You can move files from one disk to another. You can also move files from one directory to another. When you move a file, the computer copies the file to its new location, then erases it from the original location. The File Manager lets you move files by dragging them on the screen or by using the File Manager menus.

Now that Ruth has created the MEMOS and SHEETS directories, the next step in organizing her disk is to put files in these directories. She begins by moving one of her memo files from the root directory A:\ to the MEMOS subdirectory. She decides to move JV-MEM.WRI first.

To move the file JV-MEM.WRI from A:\ to the MEMOS subdirectory:

❶ Position the pointer on the filename JV-MEM.WRI and click the mouse button to select it. On the left side of the status bar, the message "Selected 1 file(s) (1,408 bytes)" appears.

❷ Press the mouse button and hold it down while you drag the file icon to the MEMOS file folder in the directory tree.

❸ When the icon arrives at its target location, a box appears around the MEMOS file icon. Release the mouse button. Figure 2-22 on the following page illustrates this procedure.

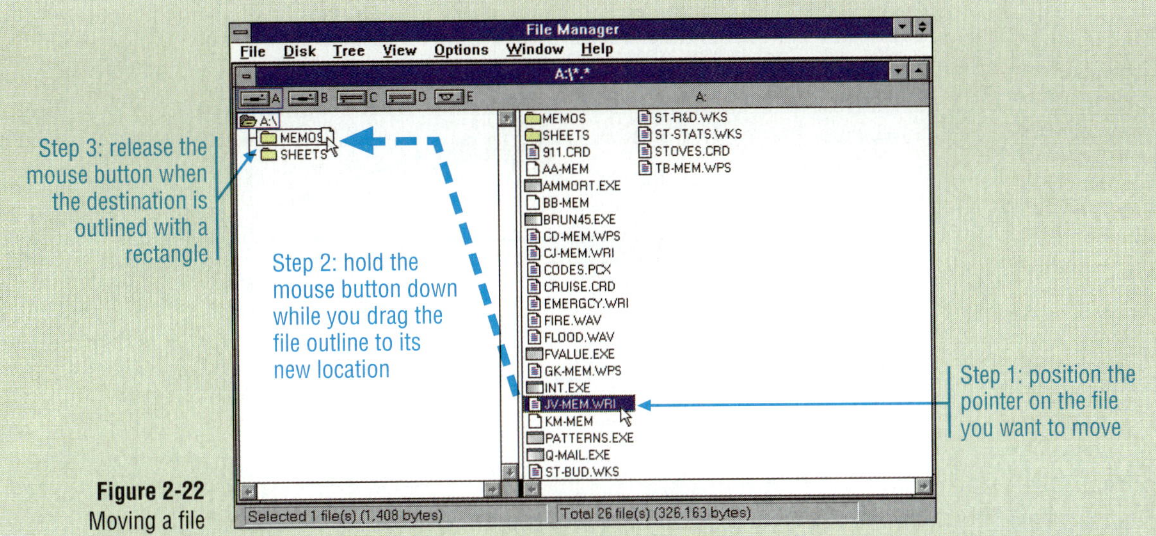

Figure 2-22
Moving a file

❹ Click the **Yes button** in response to the message "Are you sure you want to move the selected files or directories to A:\MEMOS?" A Moving... dialog box may flash briefly on your screen before the file is moved. Look at the contents list on the right side of the screen. The file JV-MEM.WRI is no longer there.

Ruth wants to confirm that the file was moved.

❺ Single click the **MEMOS file folder icon** in the directory tree on the left side of the screen. The file JV-MEM.WRI should be listed in the contents list on the right side of the screen.

> **TROUBLE?**   If JV-MEM.WRI is not in the MEMOS subdirectory, you might have moved it inadvertently to the SHEETS directory. You can check this by clicking the SHEETS directory folder. If the file is in SHEETS, drag it to the MEMOS directory folder.

❻ Click the **A:\file folder icon** to display the files in the root directory again.

Ruth sees that several memos are still in the root directory. She could move these memos one at a time to the MEMOS subdirectory, but she knows that it would be more efficient to move them as a group. To do this, she'll first select the files she wants to move. Then, she will drag them to the MEMOS directory.

To select a group of files:
❶ The directory A:\ should be selected on your screen and the files in this directory should be displayed in the right directory window. If this is not the case, click the directory icon for A:\.

❷ Click the filename **CD-MEM.WPS** to select it.

❸ Hold down [Ctrl] while you click the next filename you want to add to the group, **CJMEM.WRI**. Now two files should be selected. Ruth wants to select two more files.

❹ Hold down [Ctrl] while you click **GK-MEM.WPS**.

❺ Hold down [Ctrl] while you click **TB-MEM.WPS**. Release [Ctrl]. When you have finished selecting the files, your screen should look similar to Figure 2-23 on the following page. Notice the status bar message, "Selected 4 file(s) (4,590 bytes)."

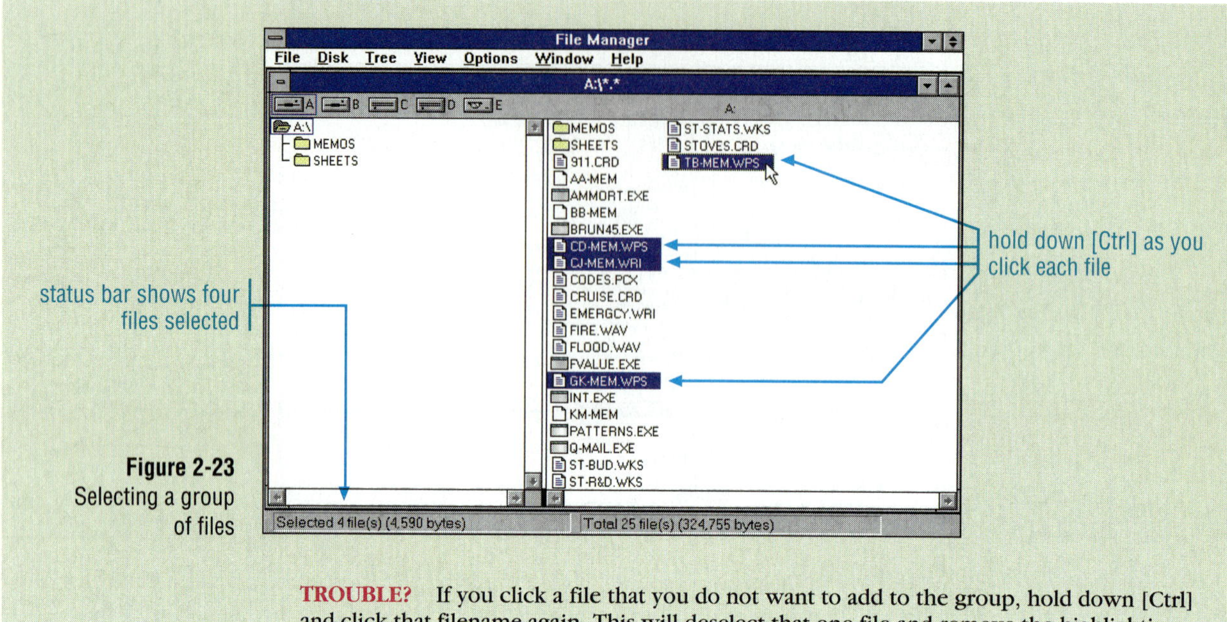

Figure 2-23
Selecting a group of files

TROUBLE?   If you click a file that you do not want to add to the group, hold down [Ctrl] and click that filename again. This will deselect that one file and remove the highlighting.

Now that Ruth has selected the files she wants to move, she can drag them to their new location.

To move a group of files:

❶   Position the pointer on any one of the highlighted filenames.

❷   Press the mouse button and drag the pointer, which now is attached to a multiple file icon, to the MEMOS directory icon. See Figure 2-24.

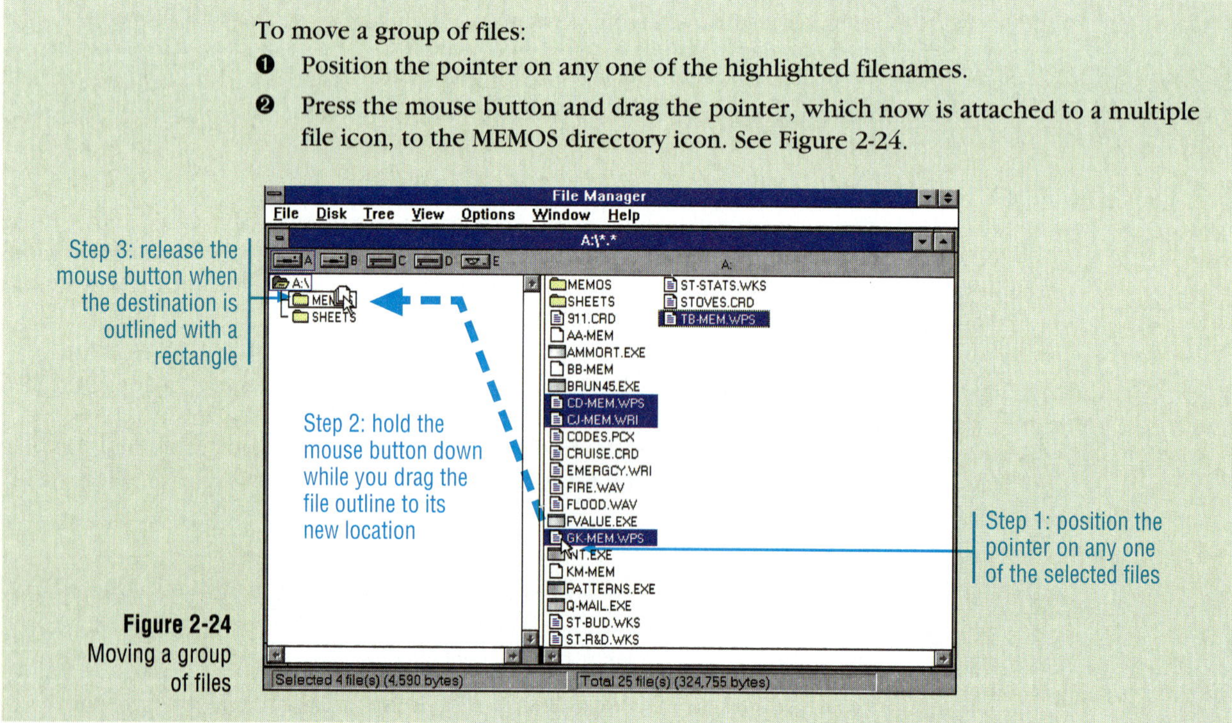

Figure 2-24
Moving a group of files

❸ When the you move the file icon onto the MEMOS directory, a box will outline the directory icon. Release the mouse button. The Confirm Mouse Operation dialog box appears.

❹ Click the **Yes button** to confirm that you want to move the files. After a brief period of activity on your disk drive, the contents list for the A:\ directory is updated and should no longer include the files you moved.

❺ Click the **MEMOS directory icon** to verify that the group of files arrived in the MEMOS directory.

❻ Click the **A:\ directory icon** to once again display the contents of the root directory.

Renaming Files

You may find it useful to change the name of a file to make it more descriptive of the file contents. Remember that Windows uses file extensions to associate document files with applications and to identify executable programs, so when you rename a file you should not change the extension.

Ruth looks down the list of files and notices ST-BUD.WKS, which contains the 1994 budget for project Stealth. Ruth knows that next week she will begin work on the 1995 budget. She decides that while she is organizing her files, she will change the name of ST-BUD.WKS to ST-BUD94.WKS. When she creates the budget for 1995, she will call it ST-BUD95.WKS so it will be easy to distinguish between the two budget files.

To change the name of ST-BUD.WKS to ST-BUD94.WKS:

❶ Click the filename **ST-BUD.WKS**.

❷ Click **File**, then click **Rename**. See Figure 2-25. The Rename dialog box shows you the current directory and the name of the file you are going to rename. Verify that the dialog box on your screen indicates that the current directory is A:\ and that the file you are going to rename is ST-BUD.WKS.

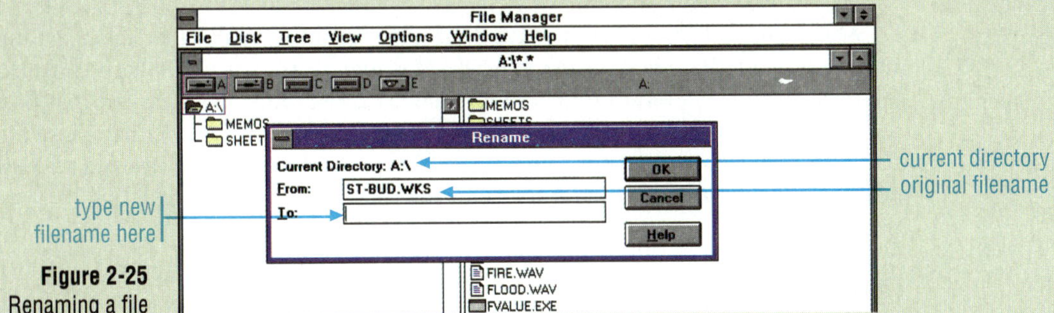

Figure 2-25
Renaming a file

TROUBLE? If the filename is not ST-BUD.WKS, click the Cancel button and go back to Step 1.

❸ In the To text box type **ST-BUD94.WKS** (using either uppercase or lowercase letters).

❹ Click the **OK button**.

❺ Check the file listing for ST-BUD94.WKS to verify that the rename procedure was successful.

Deleting Files

When you no longer need a file, it is good practice to delete it. Deleting a file frees up space on your disk and reduces the size of the directory listing you need to scroll through to find a file. A well-organized disk does not contain files you no longer need.

Ruth decides to delete the ST-STATS.WKS file. Although this file contains some statistics about the Stealth project, Ruth knows by looking at the file's date that those statistics are no longer current. She'll receive a new file from the Statistics department next week.

To delete the file ST-STATS.WKS:

❶   Click the filename **ST-STATS.WKS**.

❷   Click **File**, then click **Delete**. The Delete dialog box shows you that the file scheduled for deletion is in the A:\ directory and is called ST-STATS.WKS. See Figure 2-26.

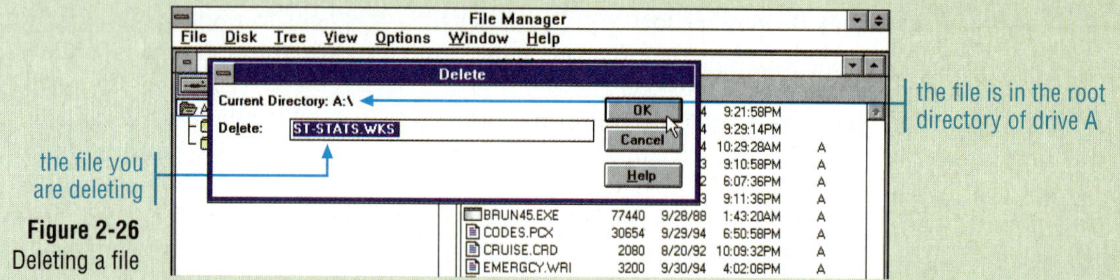

Figure 2-26
Deleting a file

TROUBLE?   If the filename ST-STATS.WKS is not displayed in the Delete dialog box, click the Cancel button and go back to Step 1.

❸   Click the **OK button**. The Confirm File Delete dialog box appears. This is your last chance to change your mind before the file is deleted.

❹   Click the **Yes button** to delete the file. Look at the contents list to verify that the file ST-STATS.WKS has been deleted.

After using a floppy disk in drive A to experiment with the File Manager, Ruth feels more confident that she can use the File Manager to organize her hard disk. However, she feels slightly uncomfortable about something else. Ruth just learned that one of her co-workers lost several days worth of work when his computer had a hardware failure.

Ruth resolves to find out more about the problems that can cause data loss so she can take appropriate steps to protect the data files on her computer.

Data Backup

Ruth's initial research on data loss reveals that there is no totally fail-safe method to protect data from hardware failures, human error, and natural disasters. She does discover, however, some ways to reduce the risk of losing data. Every article Ruth reads emphasizes the importance of regular backups.

A **backup** is a copy of one or more files, made in case the original files are destroyed or become unusable. Ruth learns that Windows provides a Copy command and a Copy Disk command that she can use for data backup. Ruth decides to find out how these commands work, so she refers to the *Microsoft Windows User's Guide* which came with the Microsoft Windows 3.1 software. She quickly discovers that the Copy and Copy Disk commands are in the Windows File Manager.

To prepare the File Manager for data backup:

❶ If you are returning from a break, launch Windows if it is not currently running. Be sure you see the Program Manager window.

❷ Relaunch the File Manager if necessary. Make sure your Student Disk is in drive A.

   TROUBLE?   If you want to use drive B instead of drive A, substitute "B" for "A" in any steps when drive A is specified.

❸ Click the File Manager **maximize button** if the File Manager is not already maximized.

❹ If necessary, click the **drive A icon** on the drive ribbon to make drive A the default drive.

❺ Click **View** and be sure that a check mark appears next to All File Details.

❻ Click **Window**, then click **Tile**. As a result, your desktop should look similar to Figure 2-27. Don't worry if your list of directories and files is different from the one shown in the figures.

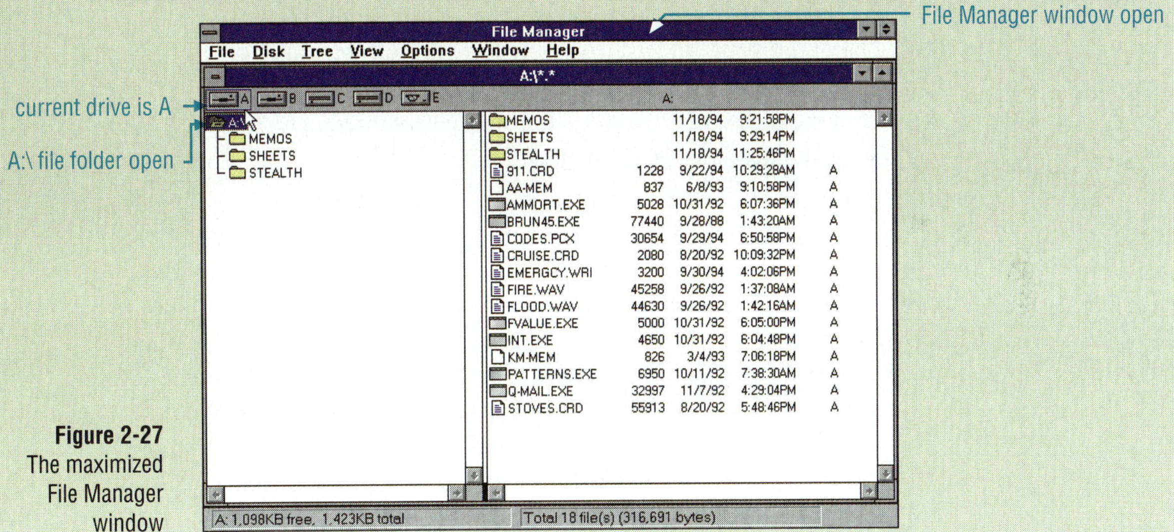

Figure 2-27
The maximized
File Manager
window

Now that Ruth has the File Manager window set-up, she decides to practice with the Copy command first.

The Copy Command

The Copy command duplicates a file in a new location. When the procedure has been completed, you have two files, your original and the copy. The additional copy of the file is useful for backup in case your original file develops a problem and becomes unusable.

The Copy command is different from the Move command, which you used earlier. The Move command deletes the file from its old location after moving it. When the move is completed, you have only one file.

If you understand the terminology associated with copying files, you will be able to achieve the results you want. The original location of a file is referred to as the **source**. The new location of the file is referred to as the **destination** or **target**.

You can copy one file or you can copy a group of files. In this Tutorial you will practice moving one file at a time. You can also copy files from one directory to another or from one disk to another. The disks you copy to and from do not need to be the same size. For backup purposes you would typically copy files from a hard disk to a disk.

Copying Files Using a Single Disk Drive

Ruth has been working on a spreadsheet called ST-BUD94.WKS for an entire week, and the data on this spreadsheet are critical for a presentation she is making tomorrow. The file is currently on a disk in drive A. Ruth will sleep much better tonight if she has an extra copy of this file. But Ruth has only one floppy disk drive. To make a copy of a file from one floppy disk to another, she must use her hard disk as a temporary storage location.

First, she will copy the file ST-BUD94.WKS to her hard disk. Then she will move the file to another floppy disk. Let's see how this procedure works.

To copy the file ST-BUD94.WKS from the source disk to the hard disk:

❶ Make sure your Student Disk is in drive A. Be sure you also have the backup disk you formatted earlier in the tutorial.

❷ Find the file ST-BUD94.WKS. It is in the root directory .

❸ Click the filename **ST-BUD94.WKS**.

❹ Click **File**, then click **Copy**.

TROUBLE? If you see a message that indicates you cannot copy a file to drive C, click the OK button. Your drive C has been write-protected, and you will not be able to copy ST-BUD94.WKS. Read through the copying procedure and resume doing the steps in the section entitled "Making a Disk Backup."

❺ Look at the ribbon of drive icons at the top of your screen. If you have an icon for drive C, type **C:** in the text box of the Copy dialog box. If you do not have an icon for drive C, ask your technical support person which drive you can use for a temporary destination in the file copy process, then type the drive letter.

❻ Confirm that the Copy dialog box settings are similar to those in Figure 2-28, then click the **OK button**. The file is copied to the root directory of drive C (or to the directory your technical support person told you to use).

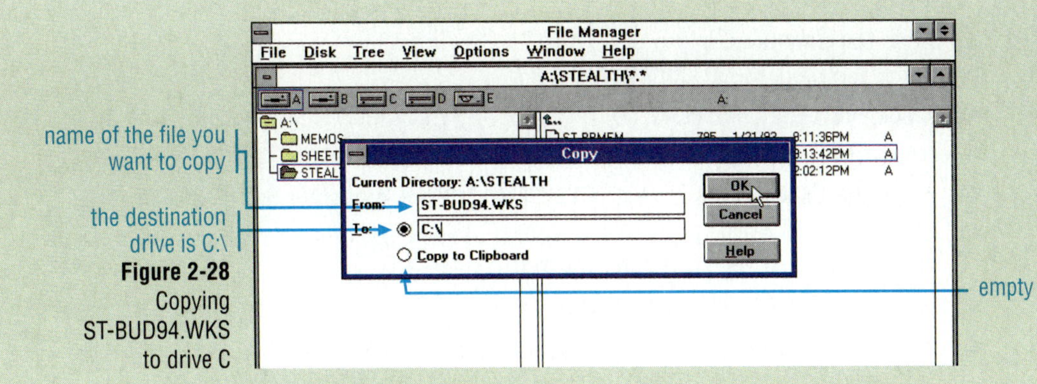

Figure 2-28
Copying
ST-BUD94.WKS
to drive C

TROUBLE?   If a dialog box appears and prompts you to verify that you want to replace the existing file, click the Yes button. This message appeared because another student left the ST-BUD94.WKS file on the hard disk.

After the file has been copied to the hard disk, Ruth needs to switch disks. She will take her original disk out of drive A and replace it with the disk that will receive the copy of the ST-BUD94.WKS file. After Ruth switches disks, she must tell the File Manager to **refresh** the directory tree and the contents list so they show the files and directories for the disk that is now in the drive.

To switch disks and refresh the contents list:

❶   Remove your Student Disk from drive A.

❷   Put your Backup Disk in drive A.

❸   Click the **drive A icon** on the drive ribbon to refresh the contents list. The directory tree will contain only the A:\ folder, because your backup disk does not have the directories you created for your original Student Disk.

Now let's look for the copy of ST-BUD94.WKS that is on drive C.

To locate the new copy of ST-BUD94.WKS:

❶   Click the **drive C icon** (or the drive your technical support person told you to use).

❷   Click the **C:\ file folder icon** (or the directory your technical support person told you to use).

❸   If necessary, use the scroll bar on the side of the content list to find the file ST-BUD94.WKS in the contents list.

Now you need to move the file from the hard disk to the backup disk in drive A. You must use Move instead of Copy so you don't leave the file on your hard disk.

To move the new file copy to drive A:

❶ Click the filename **ST-BUD94.WKS**.

❷ Click **File**, then click **Move**. (Don't use Copy this time.) A Move dialog box appears.

❸ Type **A:** in the text box.

❹ Click the **OK button**. As a result, ST-BUD94.WKS is moved to the disk in drive A.

❺ Click the **drive A icon** on the drive ribbon to view the contents list for the Backup disk. Verify that the file ST-BUD94.WKS is listed.

❻ Remove the Backup disk from drive A.

❼ Insert the **Student Disk** in drive A and click the **drive A icon** in the drive ribbon to refresh the contents listing.

Now you and Ruth have completed the entire procedure for copying a file from one disk to another on a single floppy disk system. In her research, Ruth also has discovered a Windows command for copying an entire disk. She wants to practice this command next.

Making a Disk Backup

The Windows Copy Disk command makes an exact duplicate of an entire disk. All the files and all the blank sectors of the disk are copied. If you have files on your destination disk, the Copy Disk command will erase them as it makes the copy so that the destination disk will be an exact duplicate of the original disk.

When you use the Copy Disk command, both disks must have the same storage capacity. For example, if your original disk is a 3.5-inch high-density disk, your destination disk also must be 3.5-inch high-density disk. For this reason, you cannot use the Copy Disk command to copy an entire hard disk to a floppy disk. If your computer does not have two disk drives that are the same size and capacity, the Copy Disk command will work with only one disk drive. When you back up the contents of one disk to another disk using only one disk drive, files are copied from the source disk into the random access memory (RAM) of the computer.

RAM is a temporary storage area on your computer's mother board which usually holds data and instructions for the operating system, application programs, and documents you are using. After the files are copied into RAM, you remove the source disk and replace it with the destination disk. The files in RAM are then copied onto the destination disk. If you don't have enough RAM available to hold the entire contents of the disk, only a portion of the source disk contents are copied during the first stage of the process, and the computer must repeat the process for the remaining contents of the disk.

Ruth wants to practice using the Copy Disk command to make a backup of a disk. She is going to make the copy using only one disk drive because she can use this procedure on both her computer at home, which has one disk drive, and her computer at work, which has two different-sized disk drives.

While Ruth makes a copy of her disk, let's make a backup of your Student Disk. After you learn the procedure, you'll be responsible for making regular backups of the work you do for this course. You should back up your disks at least once a week. If you are working on a particularly critical project, such as a term paper or a thesis, you might want to make backups more often.

To make a backup copy of your Student disk:

❶ Be sure your Student Disk is in drive A and that you have the disk you labeled Backup handy. If you want to be very safe, write-protect your source disk before continuing with this procedure. Remember, to write-protect a 5.25-inch disk, you place a tab over the write-protect notch. On a 3.5-inch disk you open the write-protect hole.

❷ Click **Disk**, then click **Copy Disk....** Confirm that the Copy Disk dialog box on your screen looks like the one in Figure 2-29. The dialog box should indicate that "Source In" is A: and "Destination In" is A:. If this is not the case, click the appropriate down-arrow button and select A: from the list. When the dialog box display is correct, click the **OK button**.

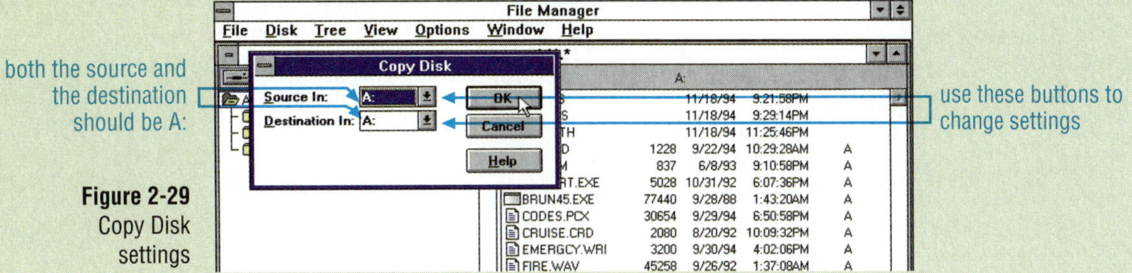

Figure 2-29
Copy Disk
settings

❸ The Confirm Copy Disk dialog box reminds you that this operation will erase all data from the destination disk. It asks, "Are you sure you want to continue?"

❹ Click the **Yes button**. The next dialog box instructs you to "Insert source disk." Your source disk is the Student Disk and it is already in drive A.

❺ Click the **OK button**.

After a flurry of activity, the computer begins to copy the data from drive A into RAM. The Copying Disk dialog box keeps you posted on its progress.

❻ Eventually another message appears, telling you to "Insert destination disk." Take your Student Disk out of drive A and replace it with the disk you labeled Backup.

❼ Click the **OK button**. The computer copies the files from RAM to the destination disk.

Depending on how much internal memory your computer has, you might be prompted to switch disks twice more. Carefully follow the dialog box prompts, remembering that the *source* disk is your Student Disk and the *destination* disk is your Backup disk.

❽ When the Copy Disk operation is complete, the Copying Disk dialog box closes. If you write-protected your Student Disk in Step 1, you should unprotect it now; otherwise you won't be able to save data to the disk later.

As a result of the Copy Disk command, your Backup disk should be an exact duplicate of your Student Disk.

Ruth has completed her exploration of file management. Now, Ruth decides to finish for the day. If you are not going to proceed directly to the Tutorial Assignments, you should exit the File Manager.

To exit the File Manager:

❶   Click the File Manager **Control-menu box**.

❷   Click **Close**.

❸   If you want to exit Windows, click the **Program Manager Control-menu box**, then click **Close**, and finally click the **OK button**.

Questions

1. Which one of the following is not a characteristic of a file?
   a. It has a name.
   b. It is a collection of data.
   c. It is the smallest unit of data.
   d. It is stored on a device such as a floppy disk or a hard disk.
2. What process arranges the magnetic particles on a disk in preparation for data storage?
3. In which one of the following situations would formatting your disk be the least desirable procedure?
   a. You have purchased a new disk.
   b. You have difficulty doing a spreadsheet assignment, and you want to start over again.
   c. You want to erase all the old files from a disk.
   d. You want to recycle an old disk that was used on a non-IBM-compatible computer.
4. If the label on your 3.5 inch diskette says HD, what is its capacity?
   a. 360K
   b. 720K
   c. 1.2MB
   d. 1.44MB
5. The disk drive that is indicated by a rectangle on the drive ribbon is called the _______________ drive or the _______________ drive.
6. Refer to the File Manager window in Figure 2-30 on the following page. What is the name of each numbered window component?

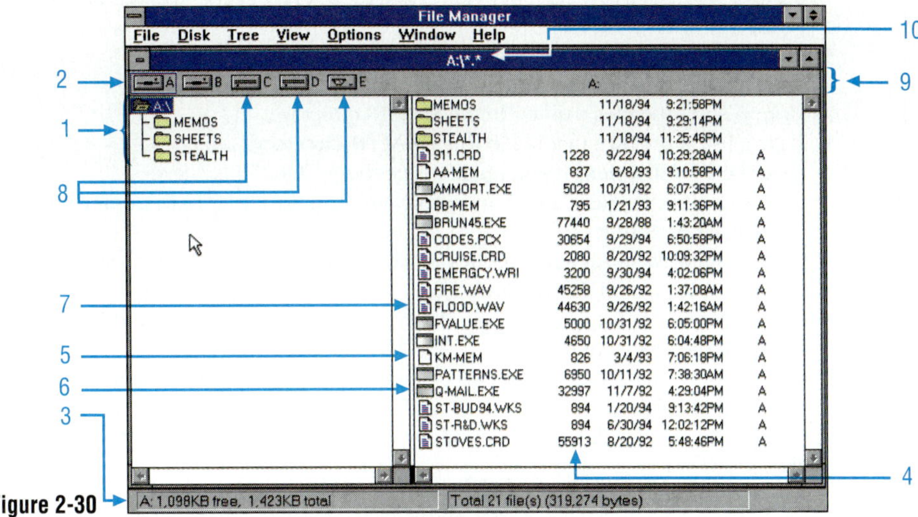

Figure 2-30

7. What is the directory that is automatically created when a disk is formatted?
8. What does a plus sign on a directory file folder icon indicate?
   a. The subdirectories are currently being displayed.
   b. The directory can be expanded.
   c. There are files in the directory.
   d. There are no subdirectories for this directory.
9. Indicate whether each of the following filenames is a valid or not valid Windows filename. If a filename is not valid, explain what is wrong.
   a. EOQ.WKS
   b. STATISTICS.WKS
   c. NUL.DOC
   d. VB-LET.DOC
   e. M
   f. M.M
   g. 92.BUD
   h. LET03/94
   i. CON.BMP
   d. Escape key

Tutorial Assignments

Launch Windows if necessary. Write your answers to Assignments 5, 6, 7, 8, 9, 11, 12, 13, and 14.

1. Move the two Microsoft Works spreadsheet files (.WKS extension) from the root directory to the SHEETS directory of your Student Disk.
2. You have a memo called BB-MEM that is about project Stealth. Now you need to change the filename to reflect the contents of the memo.
   a. Change the name to ST-BBMEM.
   b. Move ST-BBMEM into the MEMOS directory.
3. Create a directory called STEALTH under the root directory of your Student Disk. After you do this, your directory tree should look like Figure 2-30.
4. Now consolidate all the Stealth files.
   a. Move the file ST-BBMEM from the MEMOS directory to the STEALTH directory.

    b. Move the files ST-BUD94.WKS and ST-R&D.WKS from the SHEETS directory to the STEALTH directory.

5. After doing Assignment 4, draw a diagram of your directory tree.

6. Make a list of the files that you now have in the MEMOS directory.

7. Make a list of the files that are in the SHEETS directory.

8. Make a list of the files that are in the STEALTH directory.

9. Describe what happens if you double-click the A:\ file folder icon.

E 10. Click to open the View menu and make sure the All File Details command has a check mark next to it.

E 11. Use the View menu to sort the files by date. What is the oldest file on your disk? (Be sure to look at all directories!)

E 12. Use the View menu to sort the files by type. Using this view, name the last file in your root directory contents list.

E 13. Use the View menu to sort the files by size. What is the name of the largest file on your Student Disk?

E 14. Change the current drive to C:, or, if you are on a network, to one of the network drives.

    a. Draw a diagram of the directory tree for this disk.

    b. List the filename of any files with .SYS, .COM, or .BAT extensions in the root directory of this disk.

    c. Look at the file icons in the contents list of the root directory. How many of the files are program files? Document files? Miscellaneous data files?

    d. Review the file organization tips that were in the article Ruth read. Write a short paragraph evaluating the organizational structure of your hard disk or network drive.

Windows Tutorials Index

TASK	MOUSE	MENU	KEYBOARD
GENERAL / PROGRAM MANAGER			
Change dimensions of a window *WIN 15*	Drag border or corner	Click ▬, <u>S</u>ize	Alt spacebar , S
Click *WIN 7*	Press mouse button, then release it		
Close a window *WIN 18*	Double-click ▬	Click ▬, <u>C</u>lose	Alt spacebar , C or Alt F4
Double-click *WIN 8*	Click left mouse button twice		
Drag *WIN 9*	Hold left mouse button down while moving mouse		
Exit Windows *WIN 33*	Double-click Program Manager ▬, click OK	Click Program Manager ▬, <u>C</u>lose, OK	Alt spacebar , C , Enter , or Alt F4 , Enter
Help *WIN 30*		Click <u>H</u>elp	F1 or Alt H
Launch Windows *WIN 4*			Type win and press Enter
Maximize a window *WIN 14*	Click ▲	Click ▬, Ma<u>x</u>imize	Alt spacebar , X
Minimize a window *WIN 14*	Click ▼	Click ▬, Mi<u>n</u>imize	Alt spacebar , N
Open a group window *WIN 10*	Double-click group icon	Click icon, click <u>R</u>estore	Ctrl F6 to group icon, Enter
Restore a window *WIN 14*	Click ↕	Click ▬, <u>R</u>estore	Alt spacebar , R
Switch applications *WIN 16*		Click ▬, <u>S</u>witch To...	Alt Tab or Ctrl Esc
Switch documents *WIN 28*	Click the document	Click <u>W</u>indow, click name of document	Alt W , press number of document
FILE MANAGER			
Change current/default drive *WIN 45*	Click ▭ on drive icon ribbon	Click <u>D</u>isk, <u>S</u>elect Drive...	Alt D , S or Ctrl [drive letter]
Change current/default directory *WIN 50*	Click 🗀		Press arrow key to directory
Collapse a directory *WIN 50*	Double-click 🗀	Click <u>T</u>ree, <u>C</u>ollapse Branch	-
Copy a file *WIN 58*	Hold Ctrl down as you drag the file	Click the filename, click <u>F</u>ile, <u>C</u>opy	F8
Create a directory *WIN 48*		Click <u>F</u>ile, Cr<u>e</u>ate Directory	Alt F , E
Delete a file *WIN 56*		Click the filename, click <u>F</u>ile, <u>D</u>elete	Click the filename, press Del , Enter
Diskette copy/backup *WIN 61*		Click <u>D</u>isk, <u>C</u>opy Disk...	Alt D , C

TASK	MOUSE	MENU	KEYBOARD
FILE MANAGER *(continued)*			
Exit File Manager *WIN 62*	Double-click File Manager ▬	Click ▬, Close	Alt F4
Expand a directory *WIN 50*	Double-click 📁	Click Tree, Expand Branch	*
Format a diskette *WIN 41*		Click Disk, Format Disk...	Alt D , F
Launch File Manager *WIN 38*	Double-click File Manager	Press arrow key to File Manager, click File, Open	Press arrow key to File Manager Enter
Make Student Diskette *WIN 43*	Double-click Make Win 3.1 Student Diskette	Press arrow key to Make Win 3.1 Student Diskette, click File, Open	Press arrow key to Make Win 3.1 Student Diskette Enter
Move a file *WIN 52*	Drag file to new directory	Click File, Move	F7
Rename a file *WIN 55*		Click File, Rename	Alt F , N
Select multiple files *WIN 53*	Hold Ctrl down and click filenames	Click File, Select Files...	Alt F , S
APPLICATIONS			
Exit application *WIN 33*	Double-click application ▬	Click ▬, Close	Alt F4
Launch application *WIN 10*	Double-click application icon	Press arrow key to icon, click File, Open	Press arrow key to icon, Enter

Comprehensive Microsoft® Word 6.0 for Windows™ Tutorials

1 Creating, Editing, Formatting, and Printing a Document

2 Using Page, Paragraph, and Font Formatting Commands

3 Creating a Multiple-Page Document with Tables

4 Merging Documents

5 Creating Reports

6 Desktop Publishing with Word

7 Customizing Word

8 Using the Master Document Feature to Manage Long Documents

9 Creating On-line Forms

10 Using Word with Other Microsoft Applications

Additional Cases

Read This Before You Begin Microsoft Word 6.0

To the Student

To use this book, you must have Student Disks. Your instructor will either provide you with them or ask you to make your own by following the instructions in the section "Your Student Disks" in Tutorial 1. See your instructor or technical support person for further information. If you are going to work through this book using your own computer, you need a computer system running Microsoft Windows 3.1, Microsoft Word 6.0 for Windows, and Student Disks. *You will not be able to complete the tutorials and exercises in this book using your own computer until you have Student Disks.*

To the Instructor

Making Student Disks To complete the tutorials in this book, your students must have a copy of the Student Disks. To relieve you of having to make multiple Student Disks from master copies, we provide you with the CTI WinApps Setup Disk, which contains an automatic Student Disks generating program. Once you install the Setup Disk on a network or standalone workstation, students can easily make their own Student Disks by double-clicking the "Make Word 6.0 Student Disks" icon in the CTI WinApps icon group. Double-clicking this icon transfers all the data files students need to complete the tutorials, Tutorial Assignments, Case Problems, and Additional Cases to high-density disks in drive A or B. If some of your students will use their own computers to complete the tutorials and exercises in this book, they must first get the Student Disks. The section called "Your Student Disks" in Tutorial 1 provides complete instructions on how to make the Student Disks. The following table summarizes which tutorial files the Winapps program will place on each disk:

Tutorial(s)	Student Disk #
1-6	1
7 and 9	2
8	3
10 and Additional Cases	4

Your students will need a total of four blank disks when they run the Winapps Program.

Installing the CTI WinApps Setup Disk To install the CTI WinApps icon group from the Setup Disk, follow the instructions inside the disk envelope that was bundled with your book. By adopting this book, you are granted a license to install this software on any computer or computer network used by you or your students.

README File A README.TXT file located on the Setup Disk provides additional technical notes, troubleshooting advice, and tips for using the CTI WinApps software in your school's computer lab. You can view the README.TXT file using any word processor you choose.

System Requirements

The minimum software and hardware requirements for your computer system are as follows:

- Microsoft Windows version 3.1 or later on a local hard drive or a network drive.
- A 386 or higher processor with a minimum of 4 MB of RAM (6 MB or more is strongly recommended).
- A mouse supported by Windows 3.1.
- A printer supported by Windows 3.1.
- A VGA 640 x 480 16-color display is recommended; an 800 x 600 or 1024 x 768 SVGA, VGA monochrome, or EGA display is also acceptable.
- 20 MB of free hard disk space.
- Student workstations with at least 1 high-density disk drive. If you need a 5.25-inch CTI WinApps Setup Disk, contact your CTI sales rep or call customer service at 1-800-648-7450. In Canada call Times Mirror Professional Publishing/Irwin Dorsey at 1-800-268-4178.
- If you want to install the CTI WinApps Setup Disk on a network drive, your network must support Microsoft Windows.

Creating, Editing, Formatting, and Printing a Document

Requesting Information from a Supply Source

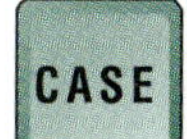

Sweet T's, Inc.   Denise Hill is assistant director of Research and Development for Sweet T's, Inc. Sweet T's owns and operates seven Sweet Tooth Cafe restaurants in Oklahoma and northern Texas. It has also sold franchises of the Sweet Tooth Cafe to individual licensees who operate another 13 restaurants throughout the southeastern United States. The Sweet Tooth Cafe is known for food that is moderately priced and served in a casual, family dining atmosphere.

Denise works with a staff of three food specialists responsible for creating new menu items for the restaurants. She also has responsibility for finding suppliers for any specialty ingredients required in any menu item. The current supplier of the brownie in Sweet T's famous Deep Fried Brownie is about to go out of business, so Denise must locate a new supply source. Denise calls Doug Stone, a salesperson for a wholesale food distributor, who tells her about Ram Food Purveyors in Dallas, Texas. She decides to write to Ram to inquire if it can produce a brownie that meets Sweet T's specifications.

The technician from Sweet T's Information Services office has just installed Word 6.0 for Windows on Denise's computer. She has learned Windows 3.1 and is anxious to get started learning Word 6.0 for Windows.

In this tutorial you will complete Denise's task. You will also learn an efficient strategy for producing a document, and how to use the features of Word to facilitate the document production process.

Using the Productivity Strategy

A **document** is any written item, such as a letter, memo, or report. Word 6.0 for Windows is a word processing program that allows you to create, edit, format, and print documents. Your ultimate goal in using this powerful tool, however, is to increase your ability to complete high-quality work in a minimal amount of time. To do so, you also need to use a plan for producing your documents efficiently. The plan you will use throughout this book is known as the productivity strategy.

The **productivity strategy** calls for you to approach the production of each document in four separate phases: creating, editing, formatting, and printing. Furthermore, to ensure that you produce the document efficiently, you complete each phase in sequence rather than switching among the four phases.

Using this strategy, first you will create your document. **Creating** a document involves much more than typing text; it begins with planning what you want to communicate to your intended audience. Once you have planned your document, you are ready to enter text. In general, you should not make editing or formatting decisions as you are entering text. In the Sweet T's example, Denise knows that the purpose of her letter is to inquire whether Ram Food Purveyors can supply the right type of brownie. She also knows that she must provide the supplier with the specifications for the brownie and a deadline for receiving the bid proposal.

Editing is the process of inserting, deleting, and moving text. To maintain a high degree of efficiency during this phase of the productivity strategy, you make only editing changes. For example, Denise will read through her document, then insert and delete text to make it clearer. Next, she will spell check her document for spelling errors. Finally, she will proofread her document thoroughly to make sure she has found all her errors.

Next you focus on formatting your document. **Formatting** involves changing your document's appearance to make it more readable and attractive. Use of white space and boldfaced or italicized text and headings are examples of formatting options you can use to make your document easier to read and more appealing to the reader. For her letter, Denise decides to use the standard business format, which includes a date, inside address, salutation, complimentary closing, and writer's name and title. She intends to emphasize several words in the body of her letter, as well as draw attention to the specifications for the brownie.

Printing is the final phase of the productivity strategy. You need a hard copy of your document to give to your reader. You should preview your document, however, before you spend time and resources printing it. Denise intends to use the Word Print Preview feature before printing her document to check its overall appearance. She will then print her letter and an envelope.

Of course, nothing prevents you from retracing your steps. To maximize your efficiency, though, you should concentrate on completing each phase of the productivity strategy in sequence.

In this tutorial you will create the letter and accompanying envelope shown in Figure 1-1. Just as in a real work situation, your document will go through various stages of development before it reaches the final result you see in Figure 1-1. This tutorial also takes you through each phase of the productivity strategy, so that you will learn to use Word 6.0 for Windows to produce professional-looking documents as efficiently as possible.

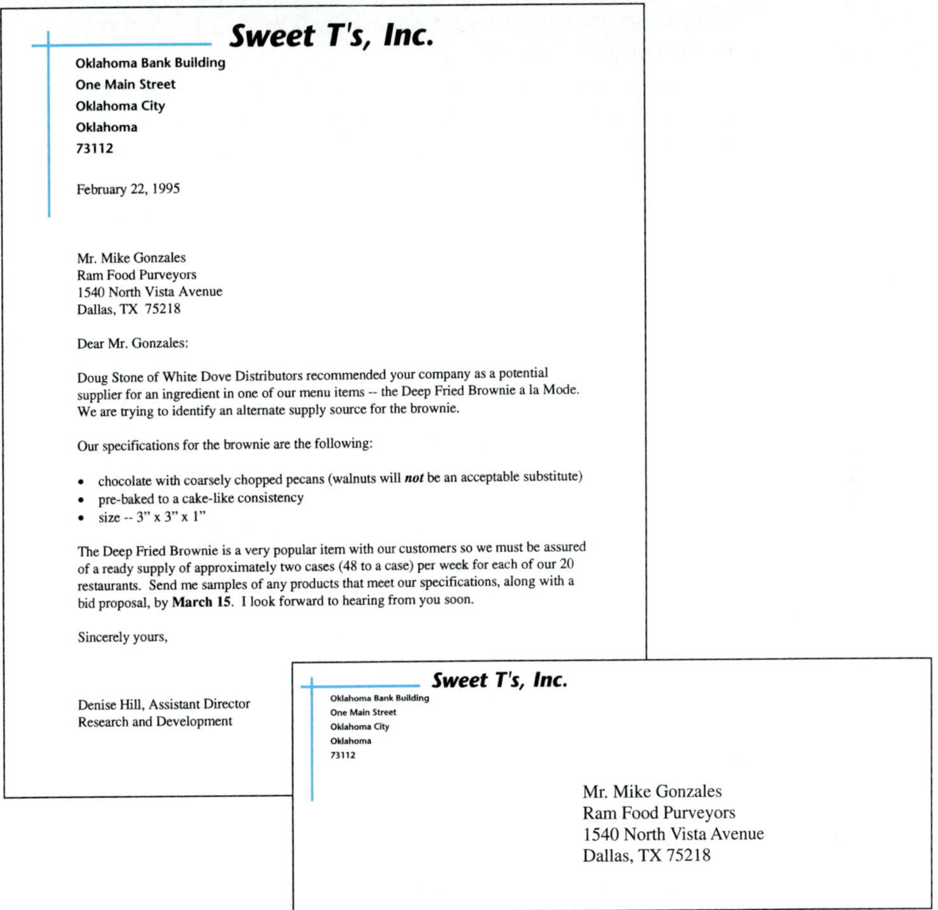

Figure 1-1
Completed letter
and envelope

Using the Tutorials Effectively

These tutorials will help you learn about Word 6.0 for Windows. These tutorials assume that you are familiar with the basics of Windows 3.1: how to control windows, how to choose menu commands, how to complete dialog boxes, and how to select directories, drives, and files. If you do not understand these concepts, please consult your instructor.

The tutorials are designed to be used in conjunction with your instructor's discussion of the concepts covered in the tutorials. Begin by reading the tutorial to be discussed by your instructor. After reading the tutorial and listening to your instructor's lecture, complete the numbered steps, which appear on a colored background, as you work at your computer. Read each step carefully and completely before you try it.

As you work, compare your screen with the figures in the tutorial to verify your results. It is relatively easy to change the appearance of Word's screen, so don't worry if parts of your screen are different from the figures. The important parts of the screen display are labeled in each figure. Just be sure these parts are on your screen. If you want to set up the basic Word screen used in this book, follow the procedures in the "Screen Check" section later in this tutorial.

Don't worry about making mistakes—that's part of the learning process. **TROUBLE?** paragraphs identify common problems and explain how to correct them or get back on track. Complete the suggestions in the **TROUBLE?** paragraphs *only* if you are having the specific problem described.

After you have completed a tutorial, you can do the Questions, Tutorial Assignments, and Case Problems found at the end of each tutorial. They are carefully structured so that you will review what you have learned and then apply your knowledge to new situations. When you are doing these exercises, refer to the Reference Window boxes. These boxes, which are found throughout the tutorials, provide short summaries of frequently used procedures. You can also use the Task Reference at the end of the book. It summarizes how to complete tasks using the mouse, the menus, and the keyboard.

Your Student Disks

To complete the tutorials and exercises in this book, you must have Student Disks. The Student Disks contains all the practice files you need for the tutorials, the Tutorial Assignments, the Case Problems, and Additional Cases. If your instructor or technical support person provides you with your Student Disks, you can skip this section and go to the next section entitled "Starting Word." If your instructor asks you to make your own Student Disks, you need to follow the steps in this section. To make your Student Disks, you need:

- Blank, formatted, high-density 3.5-inch or 5.25-inch disks. See the table on the "Read This Before You Begin" page for the number of disks you will need.
- A computer with Microsoft Windows 3.1, Word 6.0 for Windows, and the CTI WinApps icon group installed on it

  If you are using your own computer, the CTI WinApps icon group will not be installed on it. Before you proceed, you must go to your school's computer lab and find a computer with the CTI WinApps icon group installed on it. Once you have made your own Student Disks, you can use it to complete all the tutorials and exercises in this book on any computer you choose.

To make your Word Student Disks:

❶ Launch Windows and make sure the Program Manager window is open.

   TROUBLE? The exact steps you follow to launch Windows might vary depending on how your computer is set up. On many computer systems, type WIN at the DOS prompt then press [Enter] to launch Windows. If you don't know how to launch Windows, ask your instructor or technical support person.

❷ Place a formatted disk in drive A.

   TROUBLE? If your computer has more than one disk drive, drive A is usually on top. If your Student Disk does not fit into drive A, then place it in drive B and substitute "drive B" whenever you see "drive A" in the steps throughout this book.

❸ Look for an icon labeled "CTI WinApps" like the one in Figure 1-2 or a group window labeled "CTI WinApps" like the one in Figure 1-3.

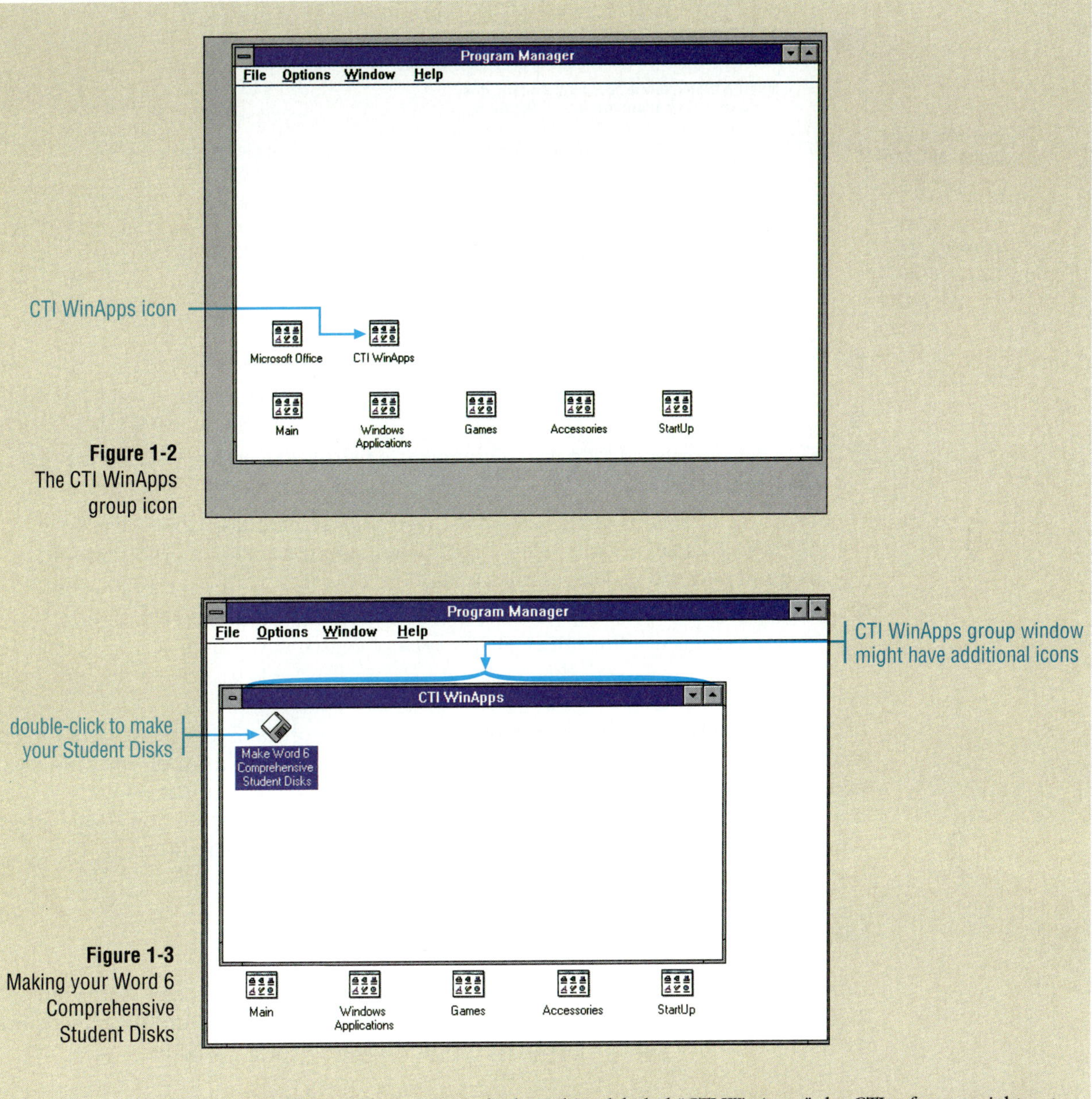

CTI WinApps icon

Figure 1-2
The CTI WinApps
group icon

CTI WinApps group window
might have additional icons

double-click to make
your Student Disks

Figure 1-3
Making your Word 6
Comprehensive
Student Disks

TROUBLE? If you cannot find anything labeled "CTI WinApps," the CTI software might not be installed on your computer. If you are in a computer lab, ask your instructor or technical support person for assistance. If you are using your own computer, you will not be able to make your Student Disks. To make it you need access to the CTI WinApps icon group, which is, most likely, installed on your school's lab computers. Ask your instructor or technical support person for further information on where to locate the CTI WinApps icon group. Once you create your Student Disks, you can use them to complete all the tutorials and exercises in this book on any computer you choose.

❹   If you see an icon labeled "CTI WinApps," double-click it to open the CTI WinApps group window. If the CTI WinApps group window is already open, go to Step 5.

❺   Double-click the icon labeled **Make Word 6 Comprehensive Student Disks**. The Make Word 6 Comprehensive Student Disks window opens. See Figure 1-4.

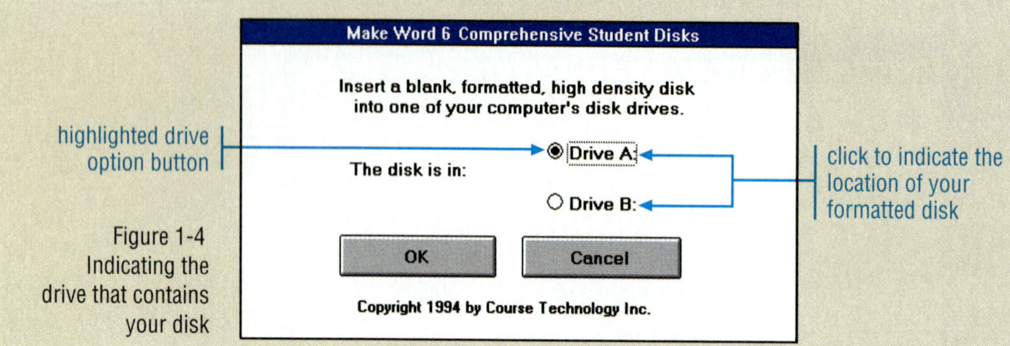

Figure 1-4
Indicating the
drive that contains
your disk

❻ Make sure the drive that contains your formatted disk corresponds to the drive option button that is highlighted in the dialog box on your screen.

❼ Click **OK**.

❽ When the copying of each disk is complete, a message appears indicating the number of files copied to your disk. Click **OK**.

Follow the directions on the screen to create your student disks. See the table in the "Read This Before You Begin" page to find out the number of disks you will need and how you should label each one.

❾ When you are finished copying disks, double-click the **Control menu box** of the CTI WinApps group window. The CTI WinApps group window closes.

Now the files you need to complete the Word tutorials and exercises are on your Student Disks. Throughout this book, you will be instructed to open files from your Student Disk. Be sure your disks are labelled with the correct tutorial number so you'll know which disk to use. Refer to the table on the "Read This Before You Begin" page if you are not sure which disk you should use. Your next step is to start Word.

Starting Word

You are now ready to create Denise's letter, so let's learn how to start Word. Although there are a variety of ways to start Word, this tutorial assumes that Word is launched from the Microsoft Office group window within the Program Manager window.

To start Word:

❶ Make sure Windows is launched and the Program Manager window is open. The Microsoft Office group icon should be visible in the Program Manager window.

TROUBLE? If you don't see the Microsoft Office group icon, ask your instructor or technical support person for help finding the icon. Perhaps Word has not been installed on the computer you are using.

❷ Double-click the **Microsoft Office group icon** in the Program Manager window. The Microsoft Office group window opens. See Figure 1-5.

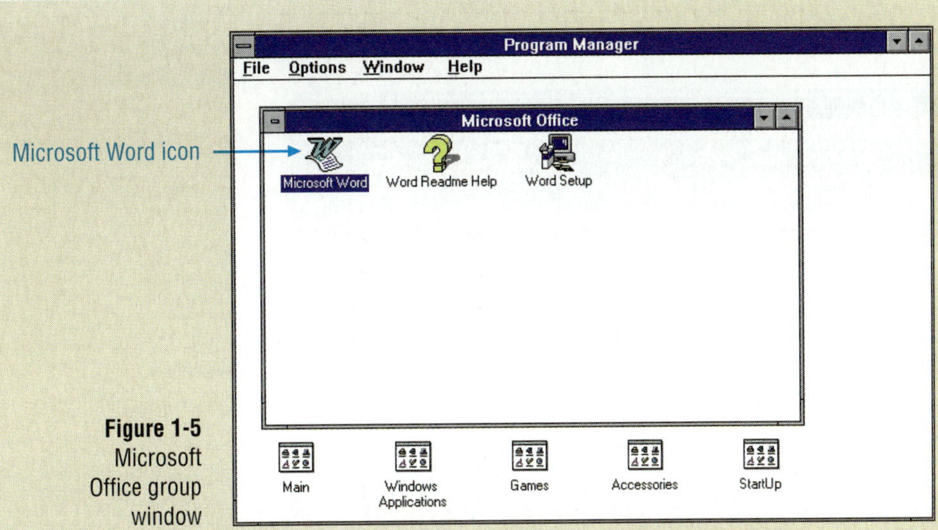

Microsoft Word icon →

Figure 1-5
Microsoft
Office group
window

TROUBLE? Don't worry if the Microsoft Office group window contains more program-item icons than shown in Figure 1-5.

❸ Double-click the **Microsoft Word icon** in the Microsoft Office group window.

Word displays a title screen briefly, then the Word screen appears. After starting Word, you might see a Word feature called "Tip of the Day" on your screen. The Tip of the Day provides useful information about different Word features and commands. If you do not see the Tip of the Day, your instructor or technical support person has deactivated this feature.

❹ If the Tip of the Day dialog box appears, read the tip, then click **OK** to close the dialog box. To deactivate this feature, click the **Show Tips at Startup check box** to clear it before clicking OK.

Elements of the Word Screen

Because you are familiar with the Windows screen, or interface, you can already identify several elements of the Word screen: the Word window Control menu box, the title bar, the Word window sizing buttons, the menu bar, the workspace, the mouse pointer, and the scroll bars. These appear as blue labels in Figure 1-6. In addition, you notice a few new elements: the document window Control menu box, the document window Restore button, the Standard toolbar, the Formatting toolbar, the ruler, the insertion point, the end mark, the document view buttons in the horizontal scroll bar, and the status bar. These appear as red labels in Figure 1-6.

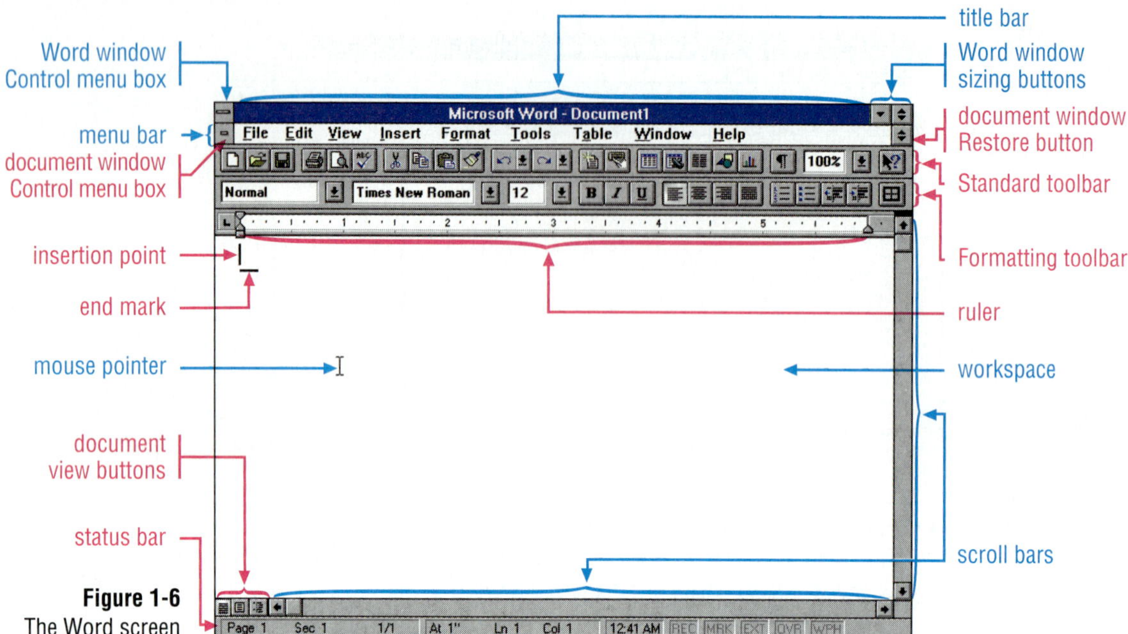

Figure 1-6
The Word screen

If your screen doesn't look like Figure 1-6, going through the next sections of this tutorial should resolve this. Just continue with the tutorial for now.

Figure 1-7 describes the function of each element of the Word screen. You need to become familiar with these elements to take full advantage of Word's features. You will learn to use all of them as you work through the tutorials.

Screen Element	Function
Word window Control menu box	Allows you to size, move, and close the Word window, as well as switch to other applications
Title bar	Identifies the current application (i.e., Word) and the name of the current document
Word window sizing buttons	The Minimize button reduces the Word application to an icon; the Restore button restores the Word window to its standard size
Document window Control menu box	Allows you to size, move, and close the document window
Menu bar	Contains all the Word commands
Document window Restore button	Restores the document window to its standard size
Standard toolbar	Contains buttons that represent some of Word's most often used commands
Formatting toolbar	Contains buttons that represent Word's most often used font and paragraph formatting features
Ruler	Allows you to adjust margins and indents quickly, set tabs, and adjust column widths
Document view buttons	Allow you to view a document in different ways
Scroll bars	Allow you to see different parts of the document
Status bar	Gives information about the location of the insertion point
Workspace	Area where text and graphics are entered
Insertion point	Flashing vertical line that marks the point where characters will be inserted or deleted
End mark	Identifies the end of a document
Mouse pointer	Changes shape depending on its location on the screen

Figure 1-7
Functions of the
Word screen
elements

If you want, you can take time now to browse through each of Word's menus.

Types of Word Windows

The Word screen is made up of two types of windows: an application window and a document window. Because both windows are maximized and share the same title bar and borders, they appear as one window. The application window, known as the **Word window**, opens automatically when you start Word. The **document window** opens within the Word window and will contain your document.

If you're not sure whether both the Word window and the document window are maximized, compare the shape of your screen's sizing buttons to the right of the title bar (the Word window sizing buttons) and to the right of the menu bar (the document window sizing button) with those in Figure 1-6. If the shapes are different on your screen, the next section gives you the information you need to solve this problem.

Screen Check

The appearance of the Word screen is easily changed. This ability to customize the appearance of the screen is an advantage in the business world, but it can pose problems in the academic world. Business people like Denise usually don't have to share a computer and so don't worry that another user will change the way the Word screen looks. To follow along with the tutorials as easily as possible, conduct a screen check each time you begin a new Word session. This section of the tutorial will help you cope with changes in the appearance of the Word screen from session to session.

Checking the Document View

The document view buttons in the horizontal scroll bar allow you to change the editing view you see on the screen (Figure 1-8). **Normal view** is the default view; you do most of your creating and editing of Word documents in normal view. You use **page layout view** to display your document as it will look when printed. **Outline view** allows you to create a topic outline of your document or to reorganize the sections of your document.

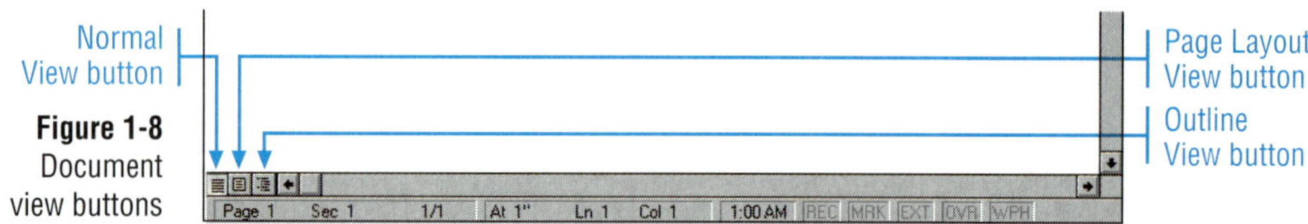

Figure 1-8
Document
view buttons

By default, Word displays the document view used by the last person opening Word, so you must know how to switch to normal view before you begin these tutorials. Let's practice that now.

To change document views:

❶ Position your pointer on the **Page Layout View button** 🔲 in the horizontal scroll bar.

You might notice a Word feature called a "ToolTip" as you move the pointer over the button. The ToolTip feature displays the button name and corresponding status bar message for any button on any toolbar when the pointer is positioned over a button (without clicking).

TROUBLE? If you do not see the ToolTip, the feature has been deactivated. Ask your instructor or technical support person how to activate this feature, if you want to see the ToolTips.

❷ Click 🔲. Notice that the Page Layout View button appears lighter to indicate that it is now activated. The document view changes—now a vertical ruler appears on the left side of the screen, and double-headed arrows appear at the bottom of the vertical scroll bar. See Figure 1-9.

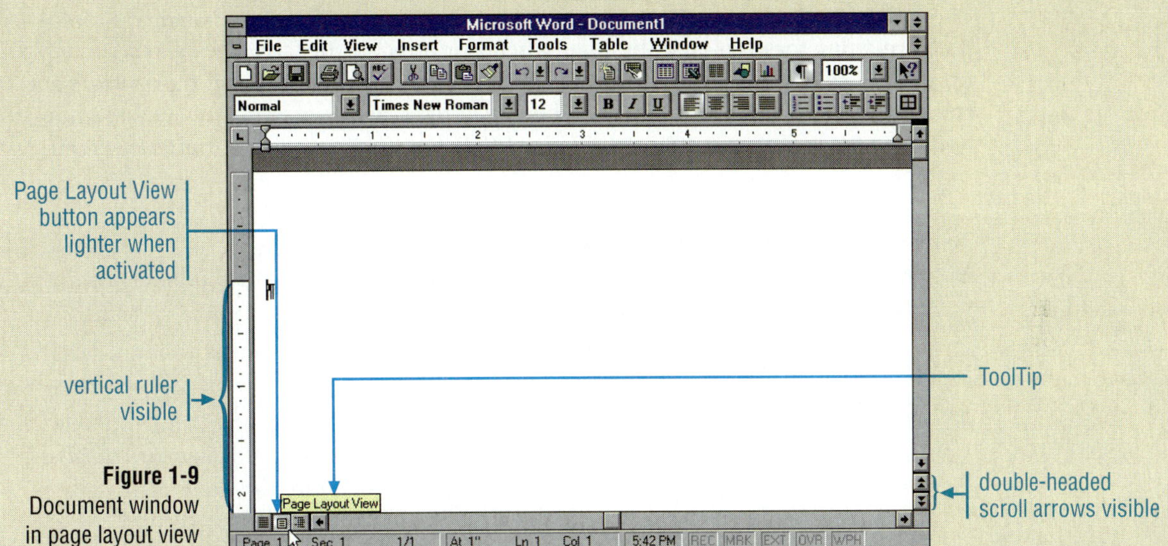

Page Layout View button appears lighter when activated

vertical ruler visible

ToolTip

double-headed scroll arrows visible

Figure 1-9
Document window in page layout view

❸ Click **View** on the menu bar. Notice that the Page Layout command has a bullet in front of it to indicate that it is activated.

❹ Click **Normal** on the View menu. The vertical ruler and double-headed arrows in the vertical scroll bar disappear. Also notice that the Normal View button in the horizontal scroll bar is lighter to indicate that it is once again activated.

Unless otherwise directed, use normal view when completing these tutorials. If the Normal View button is not selected, you can either click it or choose Normal from the View menu to reset the screen to normal view.

Sizing the Document Window

Unless you are instructed otherwise, the document window you are working in should be maximized. You can use either the document window Restore button or the document window Control menu box to change the size of the document window (see Figure 1-6). Whenever you start a new Word session to work on the tutorials in this book, make sure the document window is maximized.

Sizing the Word Window

The Word window should also be maximized unless otherwise stated. You can use the Word window sizing buttons or the Word window Control menu box to change the size of the Word window. Whenever you start a new session of Word, make sure the Word window is maximized (see Figure 1-6).

Viewing the Toolbars and the Ruler

The procedures in the tutorials instruct you to use the toolbars—the Standard toolbar and the Formatting toolbar—and the ruler whenever possible, because they allow you to speed up your work (Figure 1-6). Because the Word screen is easily changed, the toolbars and the ruler might not always be displayed when you start a Word session. You need to know how to display the toolbars and the ruler in case they have been removed from the screen.

To deactivate and activate the toolbars:

❶ Click **View**. The View menu opens. Notice that the Ruler command has a check mark in front of it to indicate that it is activated.

   TROUBLE? If the Ruler command doesn't have a check mark in front of it, click Ruler to display it on the screen, then repeat Step 1.

❷ Click **Toolbars...**. The Toolbars dialog box appears with Word's available toolbars listed. See Figure 1-10. Notice that the check boxes for both the Standard toolbar and the Formatting toolbar have been activated. Also, note the Show ToolTips check box. If this box is selected, the ToolTips feature has been activated.

Figure 1-10
Toolbars dialog box

❸ Click the **Standard check box** to clear it, then click **OK** or press **[Enter]**. The Standard toolbar disappears from the Word screen, but the Formatting toolbar is still visible.

You can also remove or display toolbars by using the shortcut Toolbar menu. To display the shortcut Toolbar menu, point to any visible toolbar, then click the *right* mouse button. Let's practice activating a toolbar with the shortcut Toolbar menu now.

To use the shortcut Toolbar menu:

❶ Point anywhere on the Formatting toolbar, then click the **right mouse button.** A menu appears containing all of Word's available toolbars, with a check mark in front of Formatting to indicate that the Formatting toolbar is displayed. See Figure 1-11.

TROUBLE? If you do not see the shortcut Toolbar menu, perhaps you did not click the *right* mouse button. Repeat Step 1.

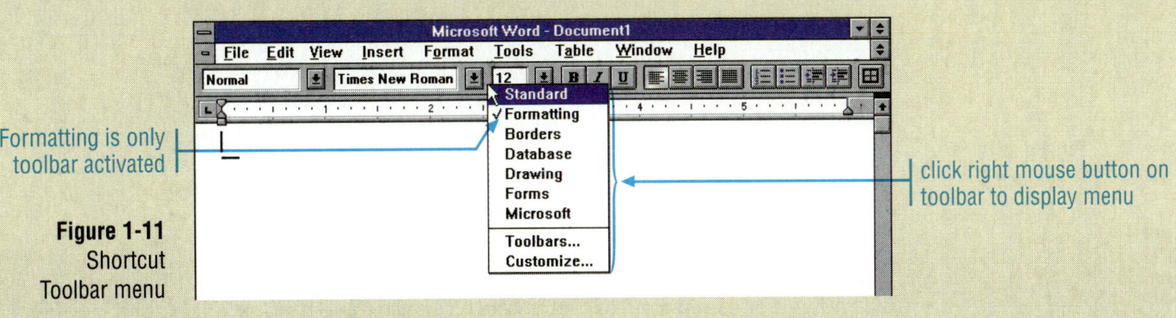

Figure 1-11
Shortcut
Toolbar menu

❷ Click **Standard** on the shortcut Toolbar menu. The Standard toolbar now reappears.

Now let's practice deactivating and activating the ruler using keyboard commands.

To deactivate and activate the ruler using keyboard commands:

❶ Press **[Alt][v]** to display the View menu.

❷ Press **[r]** to deactivate the Ruler command. The ruler disappears from the Word screen.

❸ Press **[Alt][v].** The View menu opens again. Notice that the Ruler command does not have a check mark in front of it. The ruler is deactivated.

❹ Press **[r].** The ruler appears once again.

As you complete these tutorials, the Standard and Formatting toolbars should be the only toolbars visible on your screen, unless otherwise instructed. The ruler should also be visible.

Displaying Nonprinting Characters

Word allows you to display paragraph marks, tabs, spaces, and all other nonprinting characters on your screen by activating the Show/Hide ¶ button on the Standard toolbar. To help you recognize the format of your document as you are working in it, and to avoid accidentally deleting one of these characters, work with the Show/Hide ¶ button activated.

To activate the Show/Hide ¶ button:

❶ Click the **Show/Hide ¶ button** ¶ on the Standard toolbar. A paragraph mark appears in the workspace of the document. The Show/Hide ¶ button now appears lighter to indicate that the button has been clicked—in other words, that the command is activated. See Figure 1-12.

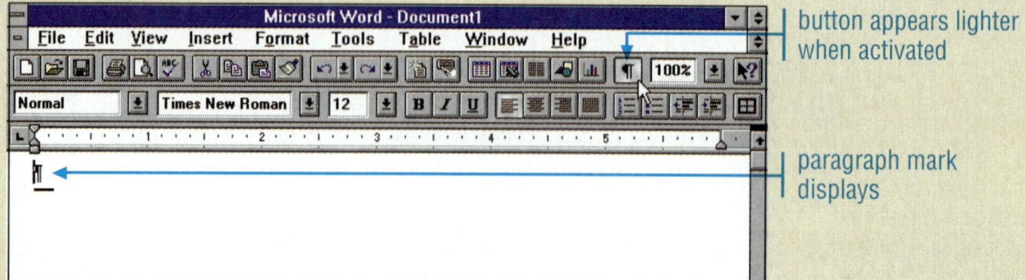

Figure 1-12
Show/Hide ¶
button activated

TROUBLE? If the paragraph mark in your workspace disappeared when you clicked ¶, the Show/Hide ¶ command had already been activated; by clicking the button, you *deactivated* the command. Click ¶ one more time to activate the command.

❷ Press **[Tab]**. A nonprinting character (→) appears to mark the location of the tab inserted into your document.

❸ Type **This is my first Word document.** A nonprinting character (•) appears to mark the location of the spaces inserted into your document. See Figure 1-13.

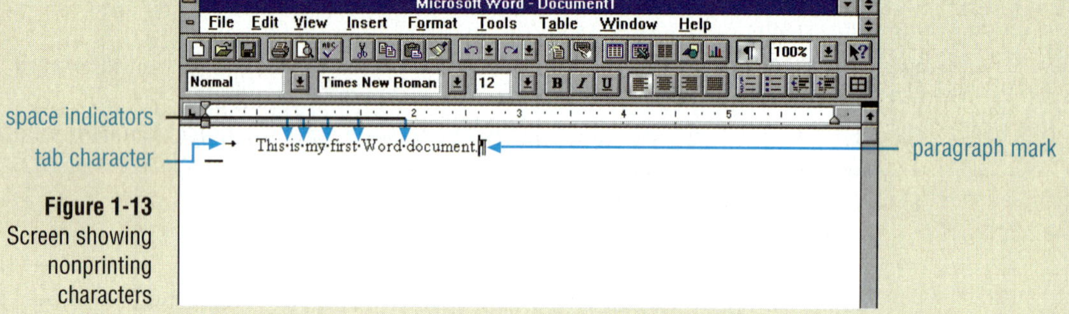

Figure 1-13
Screen showing
nonprinting
characters

❹ Click ¶ on the Standard toolbar. The nonprinting characters are no longer displayed in the workspace.

You can also activate the nonprinting characters through the Tools Options command.

❺ Click **Tools** then click **Options…**.

❻ Click the **View tab**, if necessary, then click the **All check box** in the Nonprinting Characters section.

❼ Click **OK** or press **[Enter]**. The nonprinting characters appear once again and the Show/Hide ¶ button is activated. Leave the Show/Hide ¶ button activated throughout these tutorials so you can see any special marks you insert.

Checking Font and Point Size Settings

Notice the term "Times New Roman" and the number "12" on the Formatting toolbar. These terms represent the shape (font) and size (point) of the letters used to create the documents shown in the figures throughout the tutorials. If the font or point size settings are different on your screen, ask your instructor or technical support person to adjust these settings for you. (By default, Word uses a 10-point font size in new documents; ask your instructor or technical support person to change the default setting to 12 if your screen shows 10 for the point size.)

In summary, each time you start a new Word session, conduct a screen check by asking yourself the following questions:

- Is the Word window in normal view?
- Is the document window maximized?
- Is the Word window maximized?
- Are only the Standard and Formatting toolbars and the ruler visible?
- Is the Show/Hide ¶ button activated?
- Is the font set to Times New Roman and the point size set to 12?

If you can't answer "yes" to all of these questions, adjust the Word screen appropriately.

Organizing Document Windows

Word makes it easy for you to open more than one document at a time—so easy, in fact, that you might not know it has happened. You need to know how to keep track of your open documents, as well as how to close them.

Opening a New Document

Currently you have one document window open; it is titled Document1. Within that document window, you create your document. You can have as many documents open at one time in Word as your computer's memory will allow. When you open a new document, it is displayed in a new document window. Word automatically assigns the new document a name—the word "Document" followed by a number. The Window menu contains a list of all open or minimized Word documents.

If the document name in your title bar has a different number, you have accidentally created a new document. Don't worry about it now; just continue with the tutorial.

Now let's practice opening two new documents.

To open a new document:

❶ Click the **New button** ☐ on the Standard toolbar. Notice the change in the title bar. It now reads "Document2." Document1 is still open but is not visible—it is open behind Document2.

❷ Type **This is my second Word document.**

❸ Click **File** then click **New...** The New dialog box appears. See Figure 1-14. The Template section contains a listing of Word's predefined document templates. You will learn about document templates later in this book.

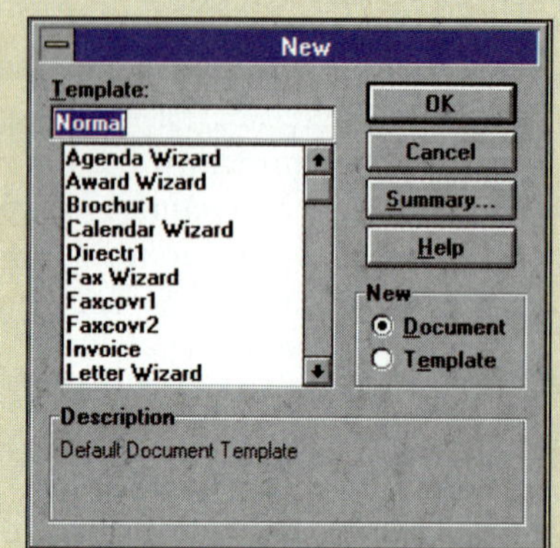

Figure 1-14
New dialog box

❹ Click **OK** or press **[Enter]** to open a new document. Notice the change in the title bar. Now it reads "Document3." Document1 and Document2 are still open but not visible.

❺ Type **This is my third Word document.**

Switching Between Open Documents

Although you can have many documents open at one time, you can work in only one document at a time. This document is called the **active document.** To work in another open document, you must first make it the active document.

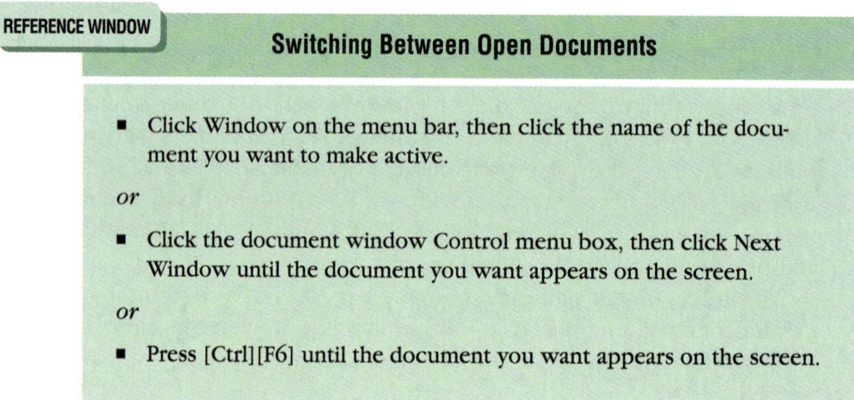

■ Click Window on the menu bar, then click the name of the document you want to make active.

or

■ Click the document window Control menu box, then click Next Window until the document you want appears on the screen.

or

■ Press [Ctrl][F6] until the document you want appears on the screen.

Let's practice switching between open documents.

To switch between the open documents:

❶ Click **Window** to display the Window menu. Three document names are listed at the bottom of the Window menu, and a check mark is in front of Document3, the active document. See Figure 1-15.

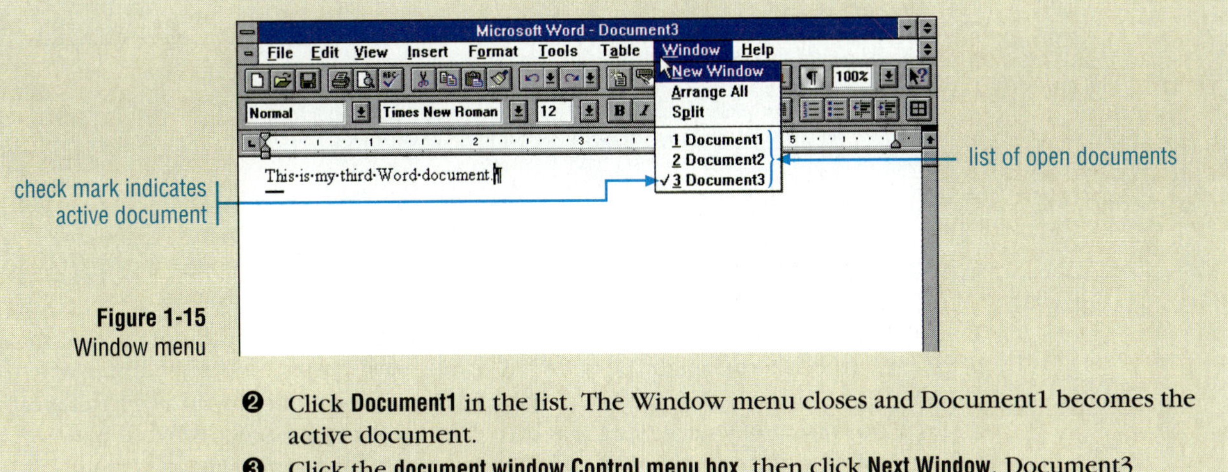

check mark indicates active document

list of open documents

Figure 1-15
Window menu

❷ Click **Document1** in the list. The Window menu closes and Document1 becomes the active document.

❸ Click the **document window Control menu box**, then click **Next Window**. Document3 becomes the active document.

❹ Press **[Ctrl][F6]**. Document2 becomes the active document.

If you ever lose sight of a document you have been working on, open the Window menu to see if your document is listed at the bottom of the menu, or try one of the other techniques to switch between open documents.

Closing a Document

Even though you can have several documents open at one time in Word, you should generally close your documents once you no longer need them. The more windows that are open, the more memory is used and the slower the performance of your computer. When you close a document, you remove that document from your computer's memory.

Let's practice closing a document without saving changes.

To close a document without saving changes:

❶ Switch to Document1.

❷ Click **File** then click **Close**. The message, "Do you want to save changes to Document1?" appears.

❸ Click **No** to indicate that you do not want to save any changes to the document. Document2 is now the active document.

❹ Click **Window** in the menu bar. Notice that Document1 is not listed.

❺ Close the Window menu by clicking outside the menu.

❻ Double-click the **document window Control menu box**. The message, "Do you want to save changes to Document2?" appears.

   TROUBLE? If you mistakenly double-click the Word window Control menu box, click Cancel to return to your document without closing Word. Then repeat Step 6.

❼ Click **No**. Document2 closes.

❽ Click **Window**. Notice that Document2 is not listed. Document3 is now the active document.

❾ Close the Window menu. Document3 is the only document remaining open at this point.

TROUBLE? If Document3 is not the only document remaining open at this point, use the previous set of steps to close all open documents except Document3 without saving changes.

Creating a Document

The initial phase of the productivity strategy, creating, requires you to do a great deal of planning. Although you might be tempted to just start typing, you must organize your thoughts first. Having a clear picture of what you need to say and how to say it will greatly improve the quality of your writing and help contribute to your success. Word is a powerful word processing program, but it cannot compensate for poorly planned writing.

Planning a Document

Denise decides that she will set the stage for her request in the opening paragraph of her letter, describe the specifications of the brownie in the second paragraph, and close with a request for a bid proposal in the last paragraph. With her writing plan for the body of the letter in mind, she also plans to enter the standard parts of a letter: the date, inside address, salutation, complimentary closing, and her name and title. During this phase of the productivity strategy, Denise is concerned only with typing the text of her letter as she has planned it, and not with editing or formatting the letter.

Entering Text

Each Word document is based on a **document template,** a set of predefined features. Unless you specify otherwise, new documents are assigned the features of the Normal template—8.5 x 11-inch print orientation, single spacing, 1.25-inch left and right margins, 1-inch top and bottom margins, tabs set at every 0.5 inch, and text aligned at the left margin only. These standard features of a document are called **default settings.**

The status bar, located at the bottom of the screen, is an extremely valuable feature when you are entering text because it keeps you informed of the location of the insertion point. Figure 1-16 describes the purpose of each element of the status bar.

This section of the status bar:	Indicates:
Page 1	Page number where the insertion point is located
Sec 1	Section number where the insertion point is located
1/1	Number of pages from the beginning of the document to the insertion point, followed by the total number of pages in the document
At 1"	Position of the insertion point as measured from the top edge of the page
Ln 1	Position of the insertion point as measured from the top margin of the page
Col 1	Position of the insertion point as measured from the left margin of the page
Time	Current time as determined by the computer's clock

Figure 1-16
Status bar elements

Denise doesn't want to change Word's default document settings, but she does want to start the date 2.5 inches from the top edge of the paper to allow room for the company letterhead. The "At" section of the status bar indicates that the insertion point is currently located 1 inch from the top edge of the paper. To insert a blank line in a document, press [Enter]. Each time you press [Enter], a paragraph mark is displayed (if the Show/Hide ¶ button is activated).

Denise must open a new document and then move the insertion point 2.5 inches from the top edge of the paper.

To insert blank lines:

❶ Click the **New button** ☐ on the Standard toolbar (or click **File**, click **New...**, then click **OK** or press [Enter]). A new document titled Document4 appears. Document 3 is still open, just not visible.

❷ Make sure the "At" section of the status bar displays 1".

TROUBLE? If the "At" section does not display 1", you have inadvertently inserted blank lines into your document. Press [Backspace] to remove the blank lines.

❸ Press [Enter] eight times. Notice the change in the status bar. The "At" section, which is the position from the top edge of the paper, is now 2.5"; the "Ln" section, the position from the top margin of the page, now reads "Ln 9."

TROUBLE? If the "Ln" section displays 9 but the "At" section does not display 2.5", ask your instructor or technical support person to change the default font to Times New Roman 12 point. If the default font or its size cannot be changed, continue with the tutorial, keeping in mind that your screen, and eventually your printed document, will look different from the figures shown in this tutorial.

Denise has moved the insertion point so that she has 2.5 inches of blank space at the top of her document, and now she is ready to type the date. In the following steps, you will make an intentional error by entering an incorrect date. This is so you can practice correcting errors in text as you type.

To type the date:

❶ Type **February 22, 1985**. Notice the change in the "Col" section of the status bar. The "Col" indicator in the status bar changes as you move the insertion point to the right. See Figure 1-17.

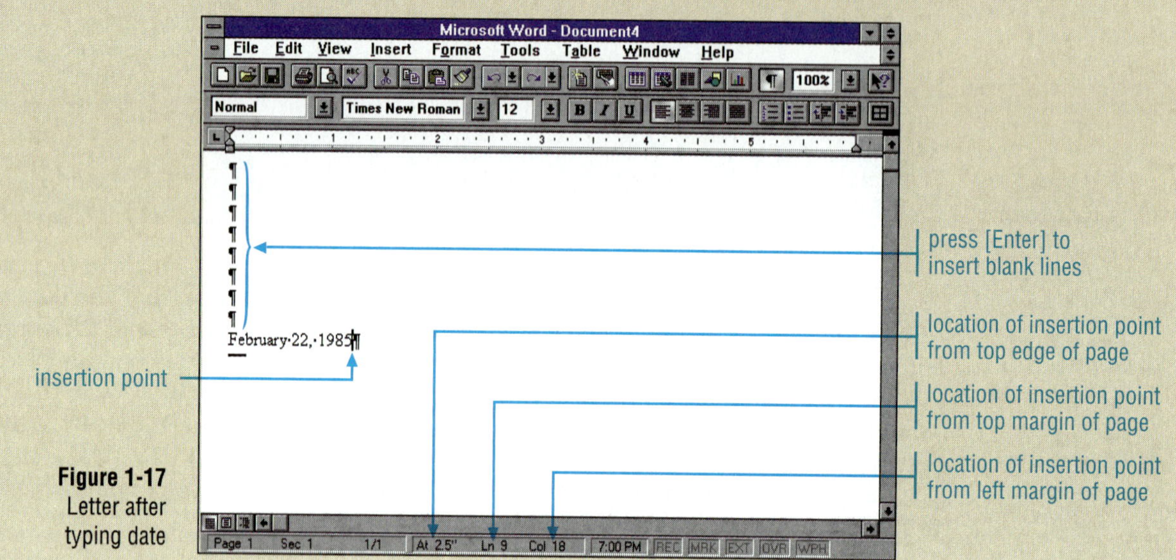

Figure 1-17
Letter after
typing date

Denise notices that she typed 1985 instead of 1995. Because she discovers this typing error shortly after making it, she can press [Backspace] up to and including the error and then type the correct text. Pressing [Backspace] deletes characters or spaces to the left of the insertion point. There are other ways to correct errors, but for now let's use this method to correct your typing errors.

To correct an error using [Backspace]:

❶ Make sure the insertion point is after the "5" in 1985.
❷ Press **[Backspace]** twice to delete the "5" and then the "8."
❸ Type **95**. The date is now correct.

Now Denise is ready to type the inside address. She needs to move the insertion point to the left margin and to insert three blank lines before the inside address.

To insert blank lines then type the inside address:

❶ Press **[Enter]** one time to move the insertion point to the left margin, then press **[Enter]** three more times to insert three blank lines after the date.

❷ Type **Mr. Mike Gonzales** (the first line of the inside address).

❸ Press **[Enter]**.

❹ Continue to enter the remaining three lines of the inside address, as shown in Figure 1-18. Press **[Enter]** at the end of each short line in the inside address to move the insertion point to the left margin of the next line. Make sure you press **[Enter]** at the end of the last line of the inside address as well.

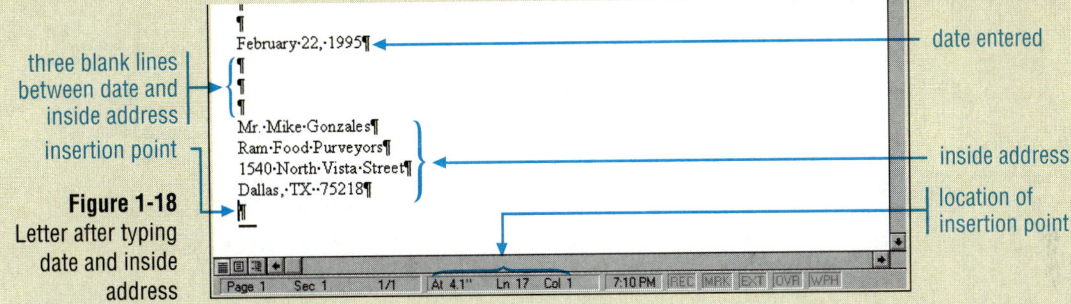

Figure 1-18
Letter after typing date and inside address

You have now typed the inside address of the letter. Next add a blank line after the inside address, then type the salutation.

❺ Press **[Enter]** to insert a blank line after the inside address.

❻ Type **Dear Mr. Gonzales:** then press **[Enter]** twice to leave a blank line between the salutation and beginning of the body of the letter.

Now you are ready to begin typing the body of the letter. As you type the letter, however, you do not have to press [Enter] at the end of the line as you did when you typed the date, inside address, and salutation. As you are entering text, if a word does not fit completely on the line, Word automatically moves it to the beginning of the next line for you. This feature is known as **word wrap**.

To type the body of the letter:

❶ Type the first paragraph of the body of the letter, as shown in Figure 1-19. Remember—do not press [Enter] at the end of each full line. Let Word do the work for you. Notice that some lines inserted at the top of the letter are now no longer in view.

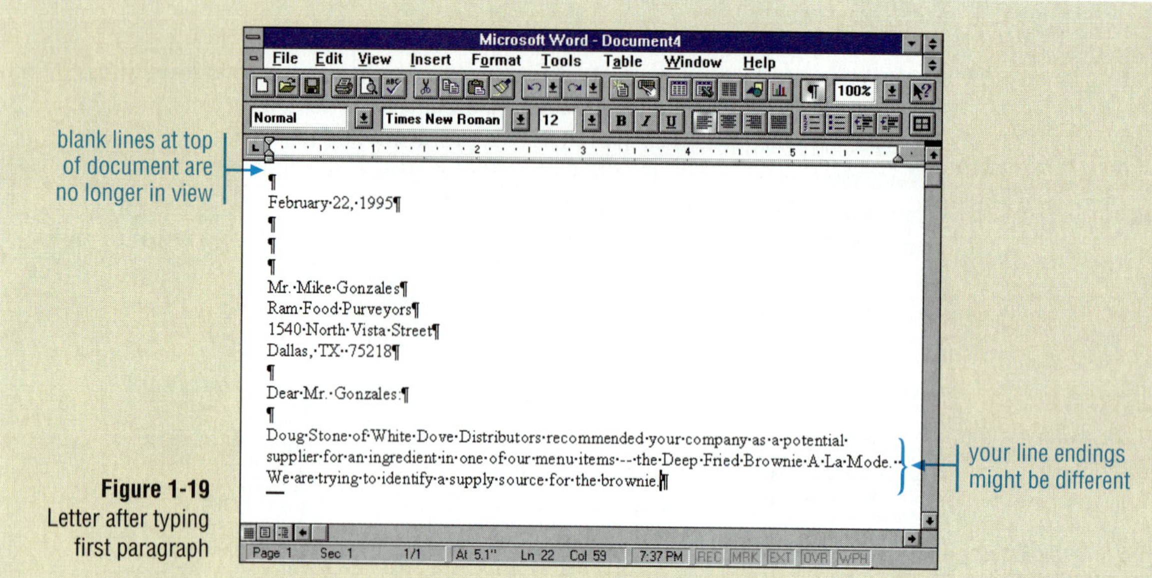

Figure 1-19
Letter after typing
first paragraph

TROUBLE? If your lines wrap differently from those shown in Figure 1-19, it could be because you have a printer selected that is different from the one used to prepare this tutorial. Don't worry; just continue with the tutorial.

❷   Press **[Enter]** to end the first paragraph, then press **[Enter]** again to insert a blank line between the first and second paragraphs.

❸   Finish typing the rest of the letter, as shown in Figure 1-20, *including the three deliberate typographical errors in the last paragraph*. Press **[Enter]** twice at the end of each paragraph to insert a blank line between paragraphs.

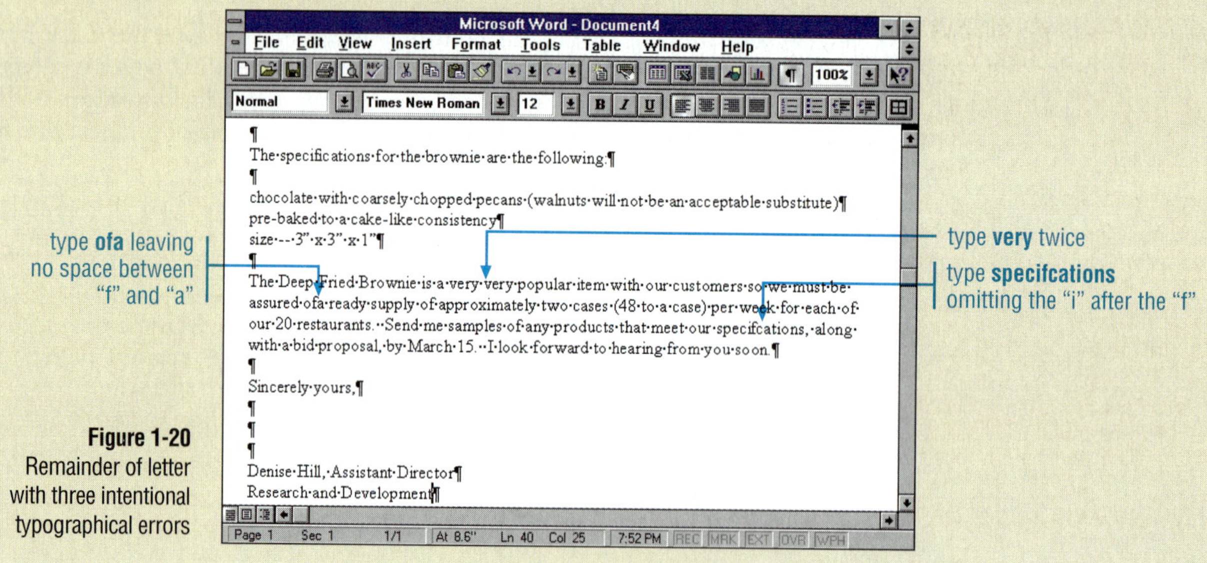

Figure 1-20
Remainder of letter
with three intentional
typographical errors

Denise has finished entering the text of her letter, and now she is ready to save her work.

Saving a Document

While you were creating Denise's document, it was not stored permanently to disk. A default feature of Word, AutoSave, automatically saves changes made to a document every specified number of minutes to a temporary file in case of a power failure. The changes are not saved to the permanent file, however, until you save the document. It is a good idea to save your work to disk at least every 15 minutes or when you finish something you wouldn't want to do again. When you save a document, it is preserved permanently on the disk in its own file with its own filename.

Naming Files

Word's filenames can be any legal filename; that is, they can contain from one to eight characters and no spaces. The extension "DOC" is added automatically to Word document files. Each filename must be unique, should be descriptive of the file's content, and should follow a naming scheme.

Before you save your work, you need to understand the file naming scheme used in this book, which was designed to help you and your instructor recognize the origin and content of documents. You will create many files, but some files have already been created for you and are stored on your Student Disk. As shown in Figure 1-21, you will be working with four categories of files. Those files provided for you on the Student Disk are for use in the Tutorial Cases, Tutorial Assignments, and Case Problems. The filenames of any files used in Tutorial Cases begin with C; Tutorial Assignments begin with T; and Case Problems begin with P. However, all files that you are instructed to save throughout these tutorials will have a filename that begins with S (for "saved").

File Category	Description
Tutorial Cases	The files you use to work through each tutorial
Tutorial Assignments	The files that contain the documents you need to complete the Tutorial Assignments at the end of each tutorial
Case Problems	The files that contain the documents you need to complete the Case Problems at the end of each tutorial
Saved Document	Any document that you save

Figure 1-21
Types of tutorial files

In the file naming convention used in these tutorials, the second character of the filename identifies the number of the tutorial to which the file relates. The last six characters of the filenames represent a description of the document's content—a word or an abbreviation that helps to identify the document. Thus, the filename S1RAM would represent a file you saved in Tutorial 1 that has something to do with Ram Food Purveyors.

Saving a Document for the First Time

The first time you save a document after it has been created, you must tell Word the filename that you want to give your document and where you want the document saved.

Let's save the work you have completed so far and name the document S1RAM.

To save the document for the first time:

❶   Make sure your Student Disk is in drive A.

❷   Click the **Save button** 🖫 on the Standard toolbar (or click **File** then click **Save** or **Save As...**). The Save As dialog box appears with the default filename doc4.doc highlighted in the File Name text box.

❸   In the File Name text box, type **s1ram**. *Do not press [Enter].* Because the default filename doc4.doc was highlighted, typing s1ram automatically replaces the selected text. Word automatically adds the extension "DOC" to the filename when you complete the dialog box. You can type the filename using uppercase or lower-case letters.

You want to save this document to your Student Disk, not the hard drive, so you must change the destination, or target drive, information.

❹   Click the **Drives list box down arrow**. A list of available target drives appears.

❺   Click the letter of the drive in which you put your Student Disk. This tutorial assumes that your Student Disk is in drive A. Notice that the Directories section of the dialog box also changes to reflect the change in the target drive. See Figure 1-22.

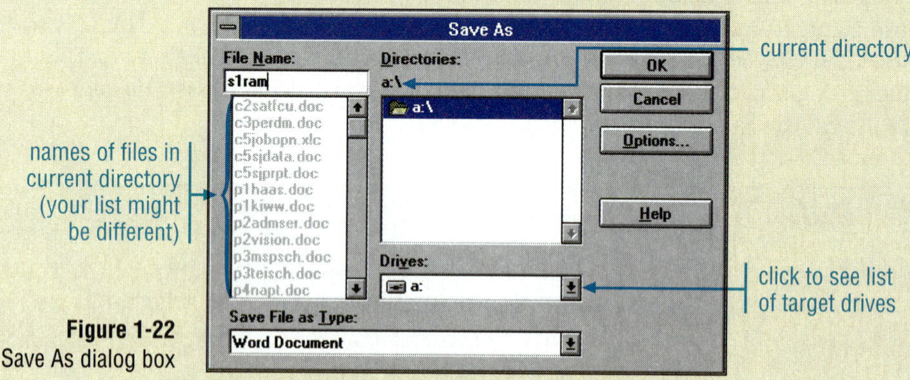

Figure 1-22
Save As dialog box

❻   Click **OK** or press **[Enter]** to save the document. Notice that the title bar has changed to reflect the new filename, S1RAM.DOC.

Now that Denise has created her letter and saved it, she decides to take a break before she begins editing her letter to Ram Food Purveyors. First, she needs to exit Word.

Exiting Word

You can exit Word by double-clicking the Word window Control menu box, or by choosing Exit from the File menu.

To exit Word:

❶ Double-click the **Word window Control menu box** (or click **File** then click **Exit**). Be sure not to double-click the document window Control menu box. The message, "Do you want to save changes to Document3?" appears because Document3 is still open.

❷ Click **No**. You do not need to save Document3.

❸ Double-click the **Microsoft Office group window Control menu box** to close it. You return to the Program Manager.

❹ At the Program Manager, either exit Windows or start another application.

If you want to take a break and resume the tutorial at a later time, you can do so now. When you want to resume the tutorial, start Word and place your Student Disk in the disk drive. Remember to complete the screen check procedure described earlier in this tutorial. Then continue with the tutorial.

Editing a Document

Editing a document involves changing its content by inserting, deleting, or moving text. The purpose of editing is to refine a document so that its meaning is clear and it is free of errors. The most efficient way to edit a document is first to make changes in content and then to check for spelling and typographical errors.

Opening an Existing Document

To resume work on the letter, you must first open the file that contains that document. You can either click the Open button on the Standard toolbar or choose the Open command from the File menu to display the Open dialog box, in which you specify the file you want to open.

You can also open a document that you have worked on recently from the File menu. The four most recently closed documents are listed at the bottom of the File menu. See Figure 1-23. (Your list might include other filenames.) Just click the name of the document on which you want to work, and it will open.

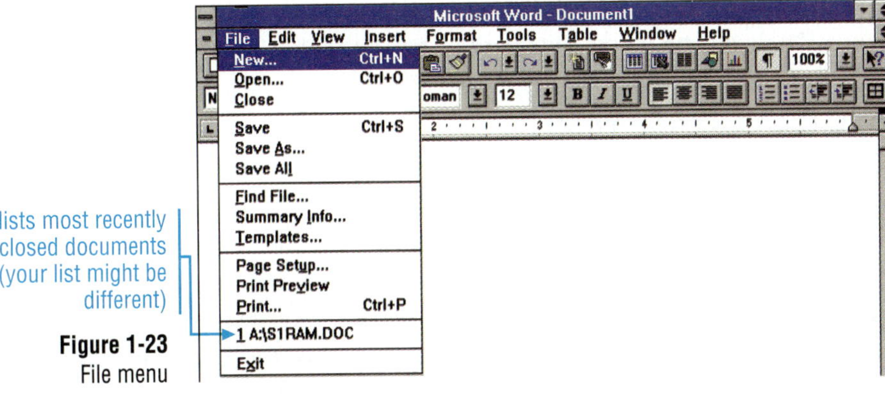

lists most recently closed documents (your list might be different)

Figure 1-23
File menu

Let's open the file S1RAM, which you saved on your Student Disk.

To open the S1RAM document:

❶ If necessary, start Word and conduct the screen check of your Word screen as described in the "Screen Check" section earlier in this tutorial.

❷ Click the **Open button** 📂 on the Standard toolbar (or click **File** then click **Open...**). Word displays the Open dialog box.

❸ Click the **Drives list box down arrow**. The list of available drives appears.

❹ Click the letter of the drive containing your Student Disk. Notice that the Directories section of the dialog box changes to reflect the selected drive. Scroll through the list of files until s1ram.doc appears.

❺ Click **s1ram.doc**. The name of the selected file now appears in the File Name text box. See Figure 1-24.

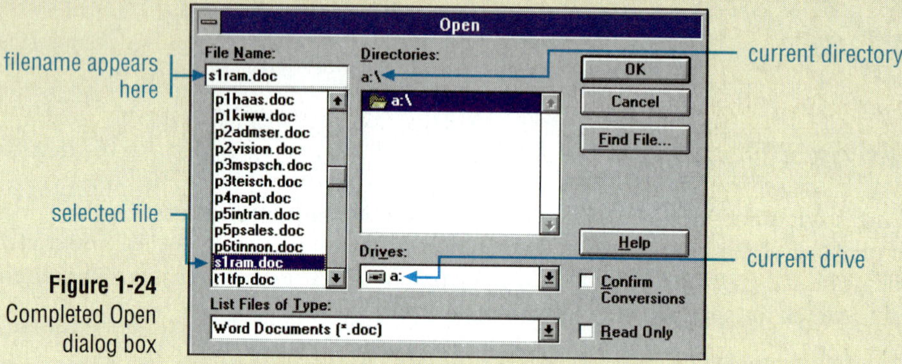

Figure 1-24
Completed Open dialog box

TROUBLE? If you can't find a file named S1RAM.DOC, make sure the Drives section indicates the location of your Student Disk. If the Drives section indicates the correct drive name, perhaps you accidentally saved the file to the hard drive. If you are working on the same computer as you were when you saved the document, check drive C. If you still cannot locate your file, check with your instructor or technical support person.

❻ Click **OK** or press **[Enter]**. The document S1RAM.DOC opens with the insertion point at the top of the document.

After reading through her letter, Denise decides to make a few changes to its content. Before she can make these changes, however, she must move the insertion point to the location in the document where the revisions will be made.

Moving the Insertion Point

The fastest way to move the insertion point to a new location in the window you are currently viewing is to move the mouse pointer to the new location, then click the mouse button. The mouse pointer takes the shape of an I-beam I when it is in the workspace of the Word window to aid you in the exact placement of the insertion point.

Keyboard Techniques

Skilled keyboarders might find it more efficient to move the insertion point with keyboard shortcuts rather than with the mouse, because they do not have to take their hands off the keyboard. The basic keyboard movement keys are the arrow keys: [→], [←], [↑], [↓]. To move the insertion point further with the keyboard, however, you need to use the keyboard movement techniques listed in Figure 1-25. To perform a movement that involves two keys, hold down the first key listed while pressing the second key listed. For instance, hold down [Ctrl] while pressing [End] to move the insertion point to the end of the document.

Figure 1-25
Keyboard movement techniques

To move the insertion point:	Press:
Left or right one character at a time	[←] or [→]
Up or down one line at a time	[↑] or [↓]
Left or right one word at a time	[Ctrl][←] or [Ctrl][→]
Down one paragraph at a time	[Ctrl][↑] or [Ctrl][↓]
To the previous screen	[PgUp]
To the next screen	[PgDn]
To the top of the screen	[Ctrl][PgUp]
To the bottom of the screen	[Ctrl][PgDn]
To the beginning of the previous page	[Alt][Ctrl][PgUp]
To the beginning of the next page	[Alt][Ctrl][PgDn]
To the beginning of the current line	[Home]
To the end of the current line	[End]
To the top of the document	[Ctrl][Home]
To the bottom of the document	[Ctrl][End]

Let's practice moving the insertion point using the keyboard. Look at the status bar to determine the location of the insertion point before you begin. Because you just opened the document, the insertion point should be at the top of the document.

To change the location of the insertion point using keyboard techniques:

❶ Press **[Ctrl][End]** to move to the end of the document. Notice that the status bar reflects the change in the location of the insertion point.

TROUBLE? If the insertion point didn't move to the end of the document, perhaps you released [Ctrl] before you pressed [End]. Try again; this time continue to hold down [Ctrl] while you press [End].

❷ Press **[Ctrl][Home]**. The insertion point moves to the top of the document.

❸ Press **[Ctrl][PgDn]**. Notice that you see the same text on the screen, but the insertion point moves to the last line on the screen.

❹ Press **[↓]** until the insertion point is in the first paragraph of the body of the letter.

❺   Press **[Ctrl][→]** once. Word moves the insertion point forward one word. Practice moving forward a word at a time a few more times.

❻   Press **[End]**. The insertion point moves to the end of the current line.

❼   Press **[Home]**. The insertion point moves to the beginning of the current line.

❽   Press **[Ctrl][↓]** once. The insertion point moves to the next paragraph. To Word, a paragraph is any string of characters that ends with a paragraph mark, including a paragraph mark on a line by itself.

❾   Press **[Ctrl][Home]**. The insertion point moves to the beginning of the document.

Mouse Techniques

Now let's practice moving the insertion point with the mouse by using the point-and-click method. The insertion point is at the top of the document, but Denise wants to move it in front of the word Street in the inside address.

To move the insertion point using the point-and-click method:

❶   Move the pointer so that the I-beam is in front of the "S" in Street. The insertion point is still at the top of the document. See Figure 1-26.

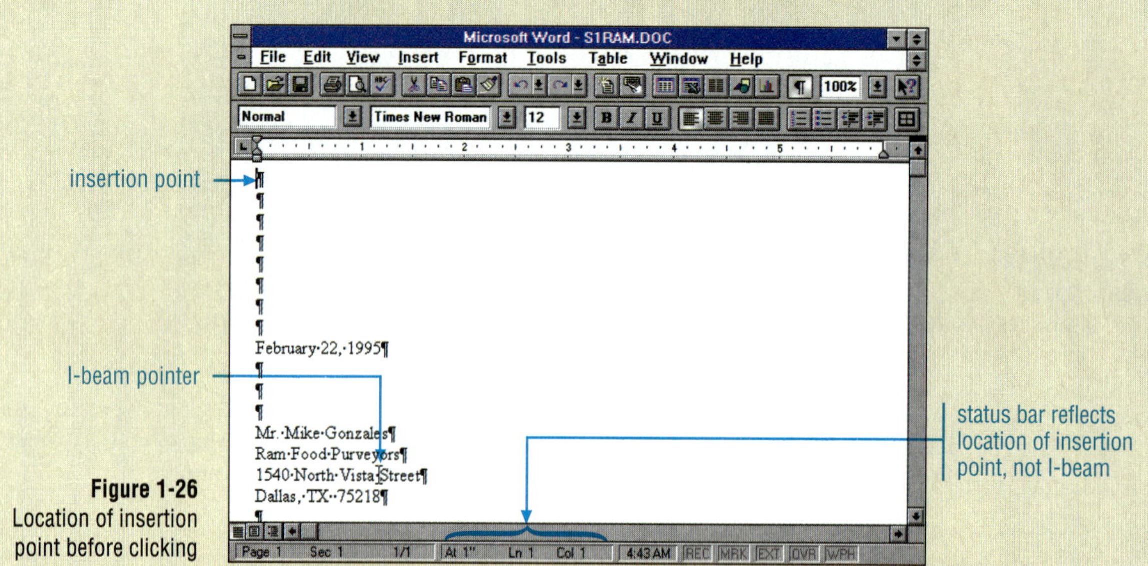

Figure 1-26
Location of insertion point before clicking

❷   Click the mouse button. Move the mouse pointer out of the way so that you can see the insertion point in its new location. Notice the change in the status bar.

The point-and-click method of moving the insertion point with the mouse is useful when the part of the document you need to move to is visible on the screen. If you can't see the place in your document to which you want to move, you must use the scroll bars first to move the new location into view, then click the I-beam at the point where the revision needs to be made.

Word's vertical and horizontal scroll bars contain the same elements as Windows' scroll bars—scroll arrows and a scroll box. Let's practice using the scroll bars. Take note of the status bar to determine the current location of the insertion point.

To scroll through a document:

❶ Click the **down arrow** at the bottom of the vertical scroll bar several times. Notice that the location of the insertion point does not change. You can use the down arrow and the up arrow on the vertical scroll bar to scroll through your document line by line.

❷ Click once below the scroll box in the vertical scroll bar. When you click below or above the scroll box, you scroll one window of text at a time.

❸ Drag the scroll box to the bottom of the vertical scroll bar to move quickly through the document. Although you can see the end of your document on the screen, you cannot see the insertion point.

❹ Move the I-beam anywhere in the last line of text you can see on the screen, then click. Now the location of the insertion point changes.

❺ Drag the scroll box in the horizontal scroll bar all the way to the right. You lose sight of your document. Drag the scroll box back to the left edge of the horizontal scroll bar. Your document comes back into view.

You can use the scroll bars to bring different parts of your document into view. However, until you click the mouse pointer, the insertion point does not move to a new location.

Inserting New Text

Now that Denise knows how to move within her document and change the location of the insertion point quickly, she can modify her document. She sees several changes she wants to make. First, she decides to insert the letter "n" and the word "alternate" before the word "supply" in the last sentence of the first paragraph.

To insert new text into previously created text, move the insertion point and type in the new text. Word's default typing preference mode is **Insert mode**; that is, as new characters are inserted into previously typed text, Word moves the existing text to the right and adjusts the line endings to accommodate the changes.

To insert the new text in the first paragraph:

❶ Place the insertion point in the first paragraph of the body of the letter, immediately after the "a" in "identify a..."

❷ Type **n** and press **[Spacebar]**, then type **alternate**. As you type the new text, the existing text moves to the right. See Figure 1-27.

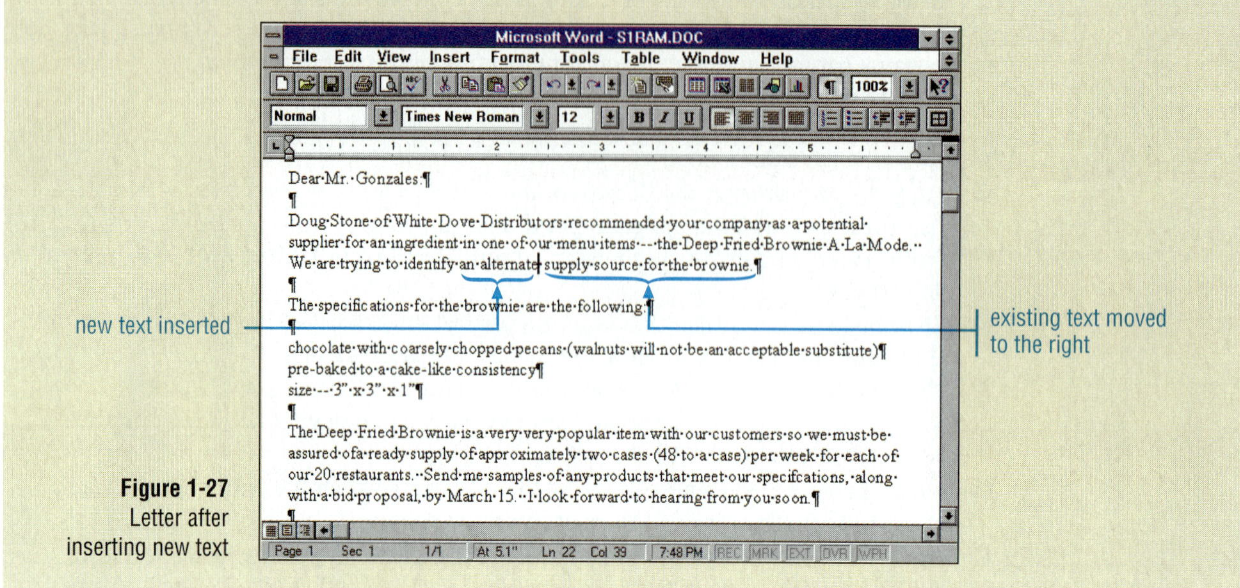

Figure 1-27
Letter after
inserting new text

new text inserted

existing text moved
to the right

Deleting Text

Thus far, you have been correcting your errors by backspacing over them. Backspacing deletes the character or space to the left of the insertion point. To delete a space or character to the *right* of the insertion point, you press [Del]. Denise notices that she capitalized the words "A La" in A La Mode, but they should be lowercase. Let's delete the capital A and capital L and replace them with lowercase letters.

To use [Del] to delete the text:

❶ Place the insertion point directly in front of the "A" in A La.

❷ Press **[Del]** three times to remove the "A," the space, and the "L." Notice that the text closes up after the characters are deleted.

❸ Type **a** then press **[Spacebar]** and type l. The correction is inserted, and the existing text moves to the right. See Figure 1-28.

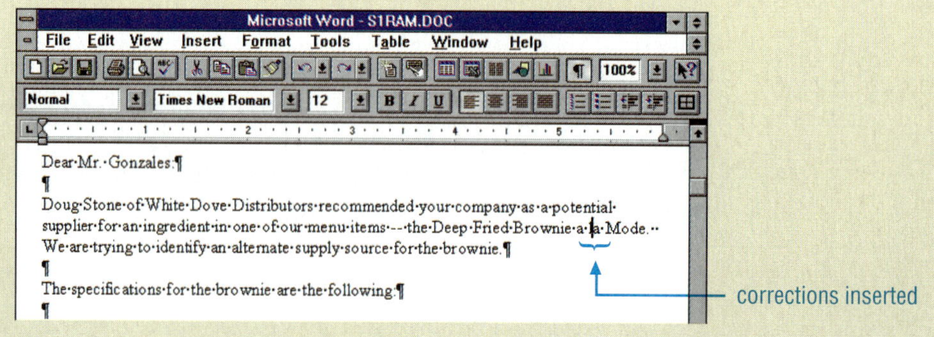

Figure 1-28
Letter after
corrections

corrections inserted

Deleting text one character at a time is inefficient if you have several characters to delete. Figure 1-29 describes other keyboard deletion techniques you can use.

To delete:	Press:
The character to the right of the insertion point	[Del]
The character to the left of the insertion point	[Backspace]
Text from the insertion point to the end of the word	[Ctrl][Del]
The word to the left of the insertion point	[Ctrl][Backspace]

Figure 1-29
Keyboard deletion
techniques

Denise wants to delete the word "The" in the sentence beginning "The specifications..." and change it to "Our."

To delete the word "The":
❶ Place the insertion point in front of "The" at the beginning of the second paragraph.
❷ Press **[Ctrl][Del]**. Notice that the word "The" and the space after it are deleted.

Using Undo

Sometimes Word makes it so easy to delete text that you might delete something unintentionally. In such a case, you could use another feature of Word, the Undo command. If you accidentally delete text, you can click the Undo button on the Standard toolbar or choose Undo from the Edit menu. The Standard toolbar also contains a Redo button, which redoes the previously undone action. The text you deleted reappears in its original location. The word or words that follow Undo on the Edit menu change to reflect the type of action that Word can undo at that point (for instance, "Undo Typing"). Note that some actions cannot be undone at any time. In that case, "Can't Undo" appears dimmed in the Edit menu to indicate that the command is not currently available for use.

Denise has just deleted the word "The" at the beginning of the second paragraph. Let's practice using the Undo feature to reinsert the deleted word.

To undo the text deletion:
❶ Click the **Undo button** on the Standard toolbar (or click **Edit** then click **Undo Delete Word**). The deleted word is recovered.

Now try reversing the undo action to delete the word "The" again.

❷ Click the **Redo button** on the Standard toolbar (or click **Edit** then click **Redo Delete Word**). Your previous undone action is reversed. "The" is deleted again.

Now you can insert the word "Our" in place of "The."

❸ Type **Our** then press **[Spacebar]**. The sentence is corrected. See Figure 1-30.

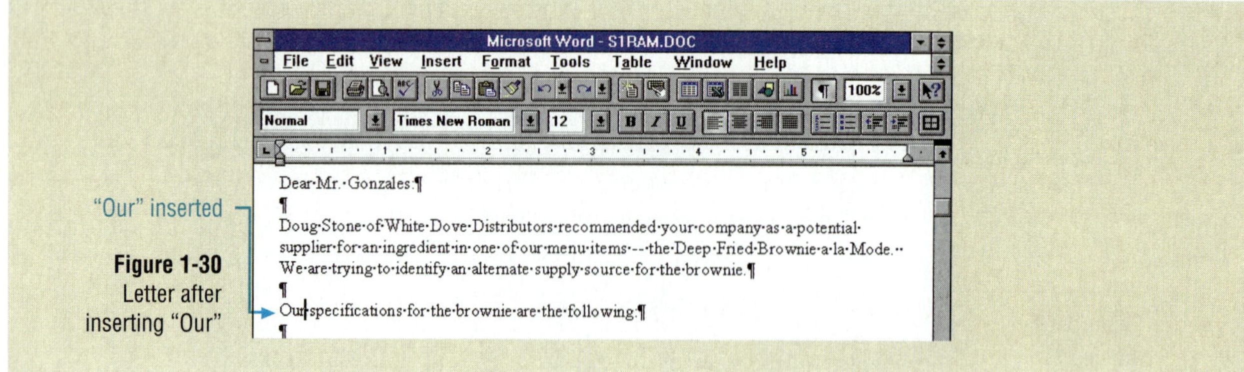

You can also undo more than just your last action. Clicking the down arrow next to the Undo button displays a list of all actions that can be reversed. You then select the action to be undone, and that action is undone as well as all subsequent actions. The Redo button has a similar list of all actions that can be redone.

Using Overtype Mode

As you learned earlier, Word's default typing preference is Insert mode. You can deactivate Insert mode by pressing [Ins] or by double-clicking the dimmed OVR indicator in the status bar. The Insert key acts as a **toggle switch;** in other words, you can activate and deactivate Insert mode by pressing the same key.

When you deactivate Insert mode, you overwrite existing text as you type new text. This mode of typing is called **Overtype mode.** When you activate Overtype mode, the abbreviation OVR changes from dimmed to bolded in the status bar.

Let's use Overtype mode to correct an error in Denise's letter. She notices that the address of Ram Food Purveyors is incorrect—it should be 1540 North Vista Avenue instead of Street. She wants to type Avenue over Street.

To type the word Avenue over the word Street:
❶ Place the insertion point in front of the "S" in Street in the inside address.
❷ Press [**Ins**]. In the status bar, OVR appears darker to remind you that you have changed to Overtype mode. See Figure 1-31.

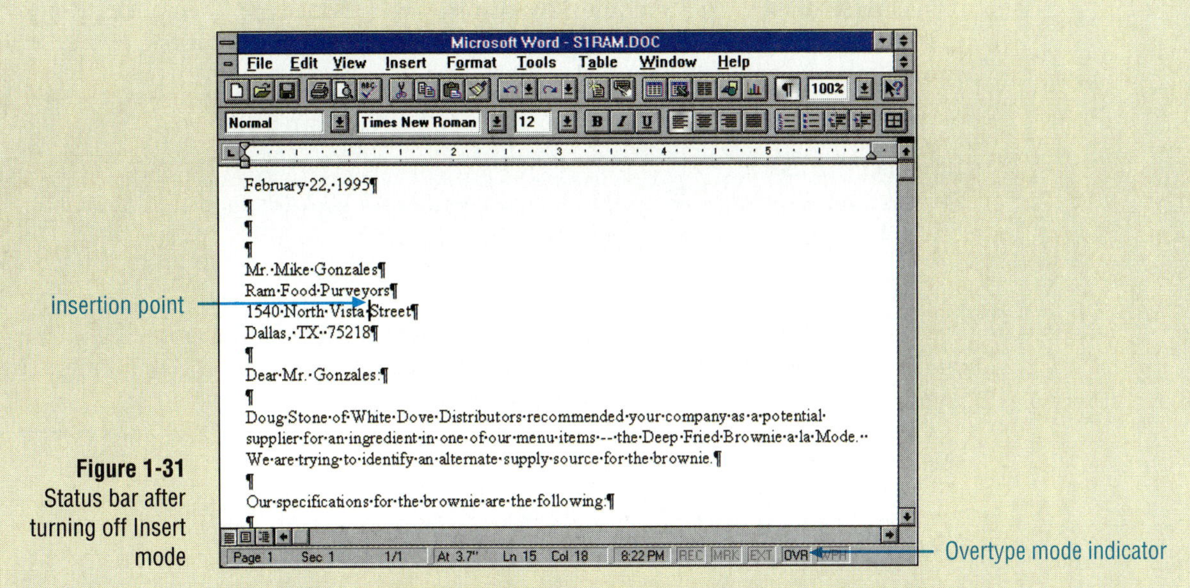

Figure 1-31
Status bar after turning off Insert mode

❸ Type **Avenue**. Word replaces, or overtypes, the existing text with the new text.

❹ Double-click **OVR** in the status bar. OVR appears dimmed once again in the status bar, and you are back in Insert mode. See Figure 1-32.

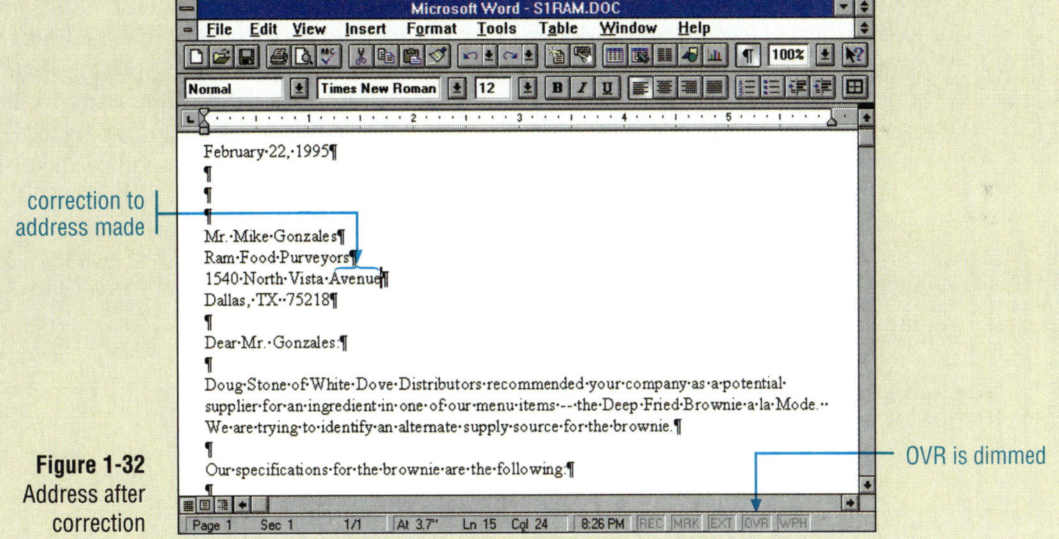

Figure 1-32
Address after correction

Updating a File

You have now made several changes to Denise's letter, but these changes are not automatically saved. You must instruct Word to update your file to reflect any changes made since you last saved your document. Once a Word document is saved and given a name, all you have to do to save again is click the Save button on the Standard toolbar or choose Save from the File menu. The Save As dialog box will not appear.

As mentioned earlier, the AutoSave feature saves changes to a temporary file just in case of a power failure. The changes are not saved to the permanent file, however, until you save the document in the usual manner.

To update the file:

❶ Click the **Save button** 🖫 on the Standard toolbar (or click **File** then click **Save**). Notice that the Save As dialog box does not appear.

If you wanted to save both the original file and the file with the most recent changes, you would choose the Save As command from the File menu, then give a different filename to the most recent version of your document.

Denise has finished revising the content of her document. Now she must correct any spelling and typographical errors.

Checking Spelling

After you have edited your document to get the wording right, you need to check it for misspelled words and typographical errors. Proofing a document for spelling and typographical errors can be tedious. Word's Spelling command considerably reduces the amount of time you spend on this part of the editing process.

Word contains a standard dictionary of approximately 130,000 words. As you spell check a document, Word compares each word in your document with the words in its dictionary. If one of your words doesn't match a word in its dictionary letter for letter, Word highlights the misspelled word in your document and opens the Spelling dialog box. Correctly spelled words would still be highlighted if Word did not find them in its dictionary. Examples of words that might not be in Word's standard dictionary include proper names, specialized vocabulary, foreign words, and acronyms. If you use a word consistently that Word doesn't recognize, you can add it to a custom dictionary. The Spelling command also points out instances of repeated or doubled words within your document.

A word of caution: don't rely solely on the Spelling command to catch all your errors. It does not catch grammatical and syntax errors. You should always proofread your documents to make the final decisions about their correctness.

REFERENCE WINDOW

Checking the Spelling of a Document

- Click the Spelling button on the Standard toolbar (or click Tools then click Spelling...).

- Change the spelling or ignore Word's suggestion for each flagged word.

- Click OK or press [Enter] when the spell check is finished.

Recall that you made some intentional typing mistakes in the last paragraph of Denise's letter. Let's use the Spelling command to locate and correct these errors. If you made other mistakes, Word will stop at additional places in your document.

To check the spelling of your document:

❶ Press **[Ctrl][Home]** to move the insertion point to the top of the document. Word checks your document from the location of the insertion point to the end of the document.

❷ Click the **Spelling button** on the Standard toolbar (or click **Tools** then click **Spelling…**). The Spelling dialog box appears. See Figure 1-33. The word "Gonzales" is not found in Word's dictionary, which is typical for most proper nouns. Notice that the word "Gonzales" is highlighted in the text and also appears in the Not in Dictionary text box of the dialog box. Word has no suggested correct spellings.

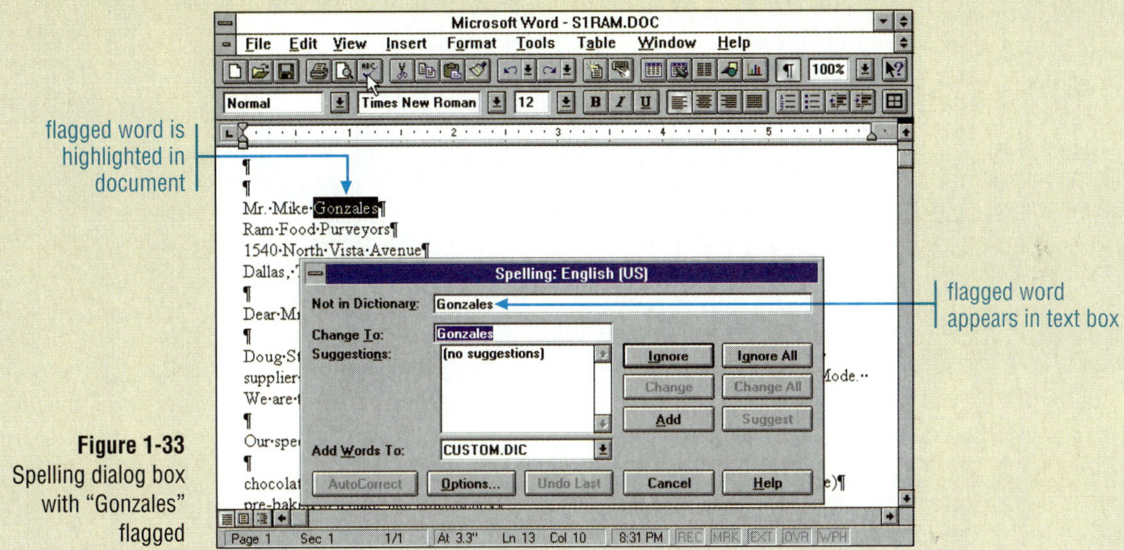

Figure 1-33
Spelling dialog box
with "Gonzales"
flagged

Denise knows that this is the correct spelling, so she wants to tell Word to ignore this word as well as all other instances of "Gonzales" in her letter.

❸ Click **Ignore All** in the Spelling dialog box. Word will not stop at the next instance of "Gonzales" in the salutation.

Word continues to check the spelling in the document and next flags the occurrence of a repeated word "very." The repeated word is highlighted in the document and flagged in the Spelling dialog box. Notice that the text box in the Spelling dialog box changes to Repeated Word instead of Not in Dictionary, and that the Change button is now a Delete button. See Figure 1-34.

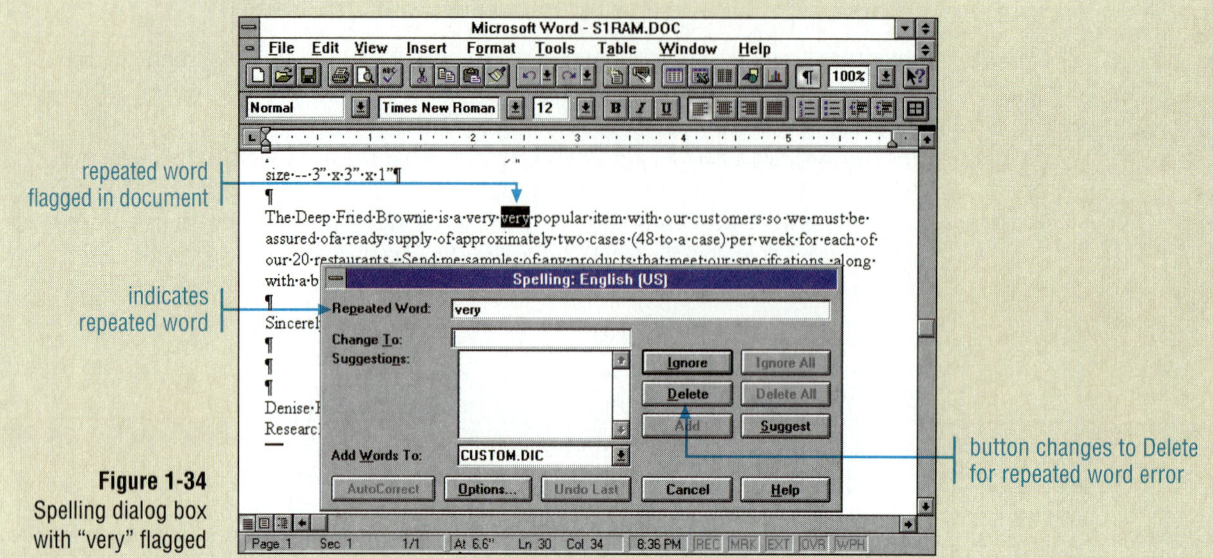

Figure 1-34
Spelling dialog box
with "very" flagged

Denise decides to delete the second occurrence of the word "very."

❹ Click **Delete** in the Spelling dialog box.

Word edits your document by deleting the second instance of "very," then stops at another typographical error, "ofa." As shown in Figure 1-35, Word's suggestions for correcting "ofa" are not appropriate, so you must edit this word manually.

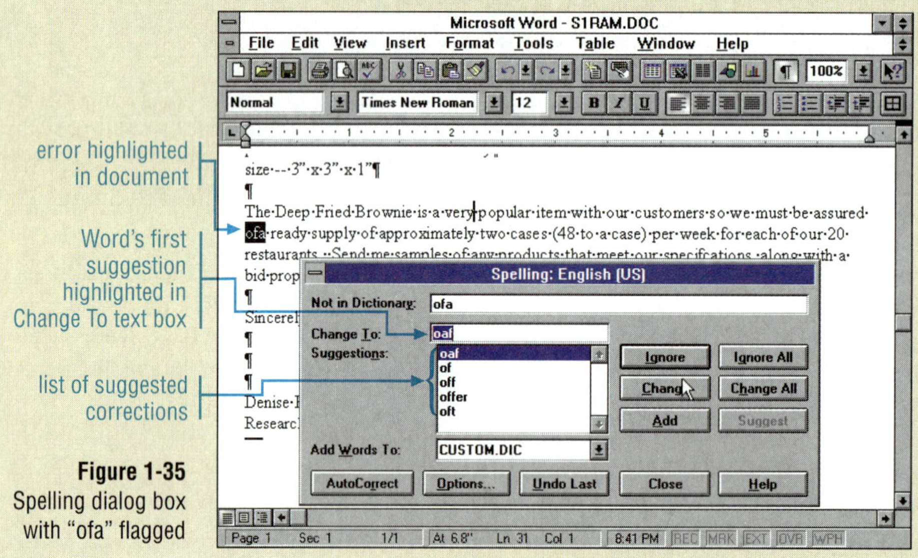

Figure 1-35
Spelling dialog box
with "ofa" flagged

❺ Click after the highlighted word "oaf" in the Change To text box to remove the highlighting.

❻ Press **[Backspace]** twice, then type **f** and press **[Spacebar]**, then type **a**. The Change To text box should now contain the correct text, "of a."

❼ Click **Change** in the Spelling dialog box to instruct Word to insert the correct text in the document.

Word moves to the next misspelled word, "specifcations." Notice that the Change To text box contains the correct spelling. If you accept the suggested spelling, Word edits your text for you by replacing the misspelled word in your document with the correct spelling.

❽ Click **Change** to accept Word's suggested spelling.

Word finds no more spelling errors (unless you made additional errors), and a message box appears. You're finished checking the document for spelling errors, so let's exit Spelling and save the corrections you've made.

To exit Spelling and save changes:
❶ Click **OK** or press **[Enter]**.
❷ Click the **Save button** 🖫 on the Standard toolbar (or click **File** then click **Save**) to save the changes you have made.

Denise proofreads her letter one last time, looking for any errors that the spell check would not catch. The content of her letter is correct and free from errors, and she has saved all of the changes she has made so far. Now she's ready to format her document.

If you want to take a break and resume the tutorial at a later time, you can do so now. Follow the procedure for exiting Word. When you want to resume the tutorial, start Word and place your Student Disk in the disk drive. Remember to complete the screen check procedure described earlier in this tutorial. Then open the file S1RAM.DOC and continue with the tutorial.

Formatting a Document

Formatting is the process of controlling how your printed document looks. The purpose of formatting is to improve the readability and attractiveness of your document so that the reader can concentrate on your message. To implement this phase of the productivity strategy efficiently, you should format your document only after you have created and edited the text.

Select, Then Do

When you want to format, you must first indicate to Word the portion of your document you want formatted. You give Word this information by selecting the text you want to change. To **select** text means to highlight it. You can select one character, the whole document, or any amount of text in between. Once you have selected the text you want to format, you then issue the commands to change the highlighted text. Simply stated, the process is "select, then do."

You can select text with either the mouse or the keyboard. Because the mouse is the most efficient way to select text, this book focuses on mouse techniques. The **selection bar** is the area located in the left margin of the document screen. It is one way you select a line or a paragraph of text. The I-beam pointer changes to ⌐Nwhenever it passes into the selection bar.

The mouse technique most frequently used to select small amounts of text is the click-and-drag technique: you click and hold the I-beam in front of the first character to be selected, then drag the pointer across all the text you want selected. The selected text is highlighted. Figure 1-36 summarizes the various techniques for selecting text.

To select:	Then:
A word	Double-click in the word
A sentence	Press [Ctrl] and click within the sentence
A line	Click in the selection bar next to the line
Multiple lines	Click and drag in the selection bar next to lines
A paragraph	Double-click in the selection bar next to the paragraph
Multiple paragraphs	Click and drag in the selection bar next to the paragraphs
Entire document	Triple-click in the selection bar or press [Ctrl] and click
Non-standard block of text	Click at beginning of block, then press [Shift] and click at end of block

Figure 1-36
Selection techniques

Selected text is extremely sensitive to change, so be careful. Word immediately carries out whatever command you issue after you have selected text. If you select text and then press [Enter], for instance, Word replaces your highlighted text with a paragraph mark. If you want your replaced text back, just click the Undo button on the Standard toolbar or select Undo from the Edit menu.

Once you become more familiar with Word and working with selected text, you will see that selecting and replacing text can be a very useful editing tool. For example, earlier you deleted the word "The" and typed the word "Our" to replace it. You could also select the word "The" then simply type "Our" to both delete the selected text and insert the new text in one step.

It is best to deselect text as soon as you can. To deselect highlighted text, you click anywhere off the selected text in the workspace or press any of the arrow keys.

Let's apply the principle of "select, then do" by practicing with the first sentence of Denise's letter.

To select the first sentence in the letter:
❶ Place the insertion point anywhere within the first sentence of the first paragraph of the body of the letter.

❷ Press and hold **[Ctrl]** and click within the first sentence. The entire first sentence plus the period and the spaces following are selected. The selected text appears highlighted. See Figure 1-37.

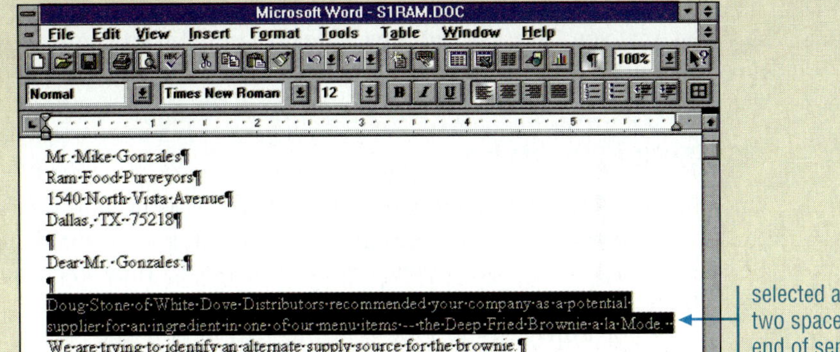

Figure 1-37
Letter with first sentence highlighted

selected area includes two spaces at the end of sentence

TROUBLE? If the entire first sentence is not selected, make sure the insertion point is visible within the first sentence, then press [Ctrl] while you click the left mouse button.

Now let's practice the "do" part of the principle: issuing a command to Word. Let's intentionally make an error, then undo it. If you type something rather than issue a formatting command after you select text, Word will replace your highlighted text with your typing. The principle here is "typing replaces selection." Let's try it.

❸ Press **[Enter]**. Your selection disappears and is replaced with a paragraph mark. See Figure 1-38.

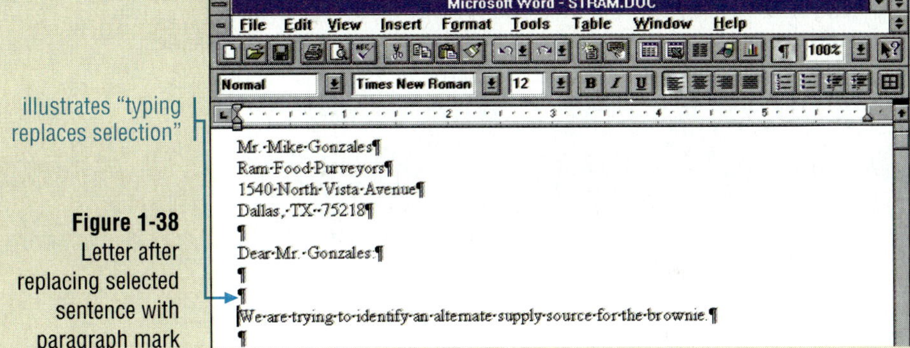

illustrates "typing replaces selection"

Figure 1-38
Letter after replacing selected sentence with paragraph mark

Don't worry that your sentence disappeared. Word carried out your command. You can recover your selected text by reversing the last command.

❹ Click the **Undo button** on the Standard toolbar (or click **Edit** then click **Undo Typing**). The text returns to its original location and is still highlighted.

To reduce the risk of error, it is always a good idea to deselect highlighted text as soon as possible after you are finished working with it.

To deselect the first sentence:

❶ Click in the workspace outside the selected area or press one of the arrow keys. The highlighting is removed from the first sentence.

Now that you have learned how to select text, you are ready to format Denise's document.

Applying Type Styles

One common formatting technique is to add emphasis to words by changing the style of the printed type. The three most popular type styles are **bold**, *italic*, and <u>underline</u>. Because these three type styles are used so often, they each have a button on the Formatting toolbar.

To add, or **apply**, these type styles to text, follow the "select, then do" principle. Select the text you want to change, then click the appropriate type style button on the Formatting toolbar. The type style is applied only to the selected text.

Denise wants to emphasize several words in her letter so that Mr. Gonzales will pay particular attention to them. She wants to italicize "not" in the first specification.

To italicize the word "not":

❶ Double-click **not** in the first specification ("walnuts will not be...") to select it. When you double-click a word, you select the word and the space after it.

Now let's issue the command to italicize the word you've selected.

❷ Click the **Italic button** *I* on the Formatting toolbar. Notice that the Italic button appears lighter to indicate that the italic type style is in effect, or activated, for the highlighted text. See Figure 1-39.

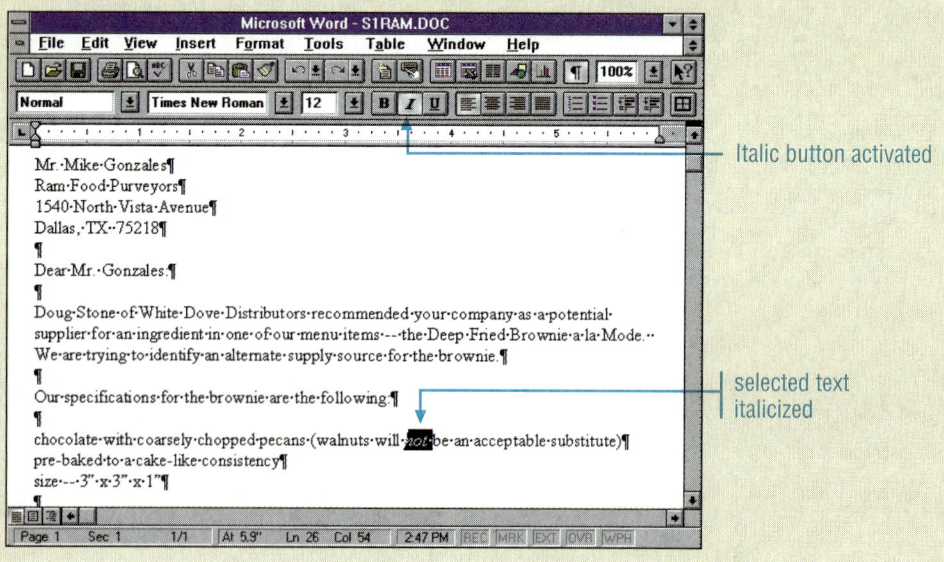

Figure 1-39
Letter with "not" italicized

You are essentially "pressing" the Italic button to activate that type style. By selecting the text first, though, you instruct Word to start and end the italic type style with the selected text.

❸ Click anywhere to deselect the highlighted text so that you can see the change in the type style of "not."

Next Denise wants to emphasize the date by which she needs the bid proposal from Mr. Gonzales. She decides to bold "March 15."

To bold the text "March 15":

❶ Click and hold the I-beam in front of the "M" in March, drag across and through March 15, then release the mouse button.

TROUBLE? If you have difficulty highlighting March 15, deselect the text by clicking in the workspace or pressing one of the arrow keys. Then start over. The insertion point serves as an anchor for whatever you want to select. As long as you do not release the mouse button, you can reduce or expand the amount of text you have highlighted. Once you have selected the text, you are ready to give a formatting command.

❷ Click the **Bold button** **B** on the Formatting toolbar. The Bold button appears lighter to indicate it has been applied to the selected text.

❸ Deselect the text to see the effect of the bold type style. See Figure 1-40.

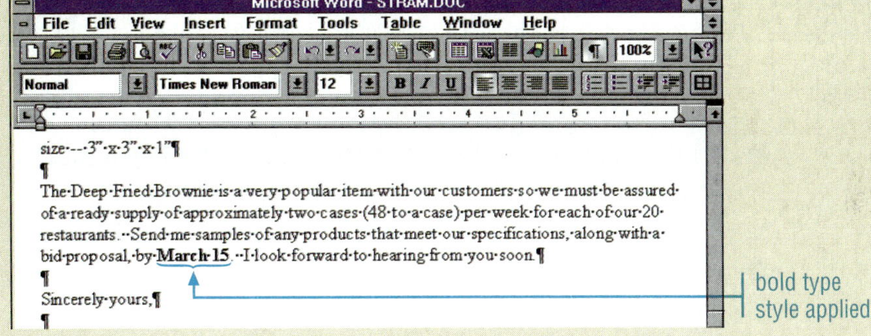

Figure 1-40
Letter with
"March 15" bolded

You can apply more than one type style to selected text. Denise wants the word "not," which she italicized in the first specification, to really stand out, so she decides to bold it, too. Let's do that now.

To apply more than one type style to the word "not":

❶ Double-click **not** in the first specification. Notice that the Italic button **I** becomes lighter because the word "not" has been italicized. The appearance of the button on the Formatting toolbar changes to reflect the format applied to the selected text.

❷ Click the **Bold button** **B** on the Formatting toolbar. Notice that the Bold button also becomes lighter. Both type styles have now been applied to the word.

❸ Deselect the text to see the effect of adding the bold type style to the italicized text.

❹ Click the **Save button** 🔲 on the Standard toolbar (or click **File** then click **Save**) to save the changes you have made so far.

Denise wants to emphasize "the Deep Fried Brownie a la Mode" in the first paragraph, so she decides to underline it. Although she could use the click-and-drag method to select the text, she decides to try a selection technique that gives her more control over what she wants to select.

Let's use the shift-click technique to highlight "the Deep Fried Brownie a la Mode" in the first paragraph before you underline it.

To underline the text:

❶ Place the insertion point in front of the "t" in the word "the" in the first sentence of the first paragraph.

❷ Move the I-beam after the "e" in Mode. Just move the I-beam to the end of the block—do not drag the mouse pointer over the text. See Figure 1-41.

Figure 1-41
Preparing to use
the shift-click
selection technique

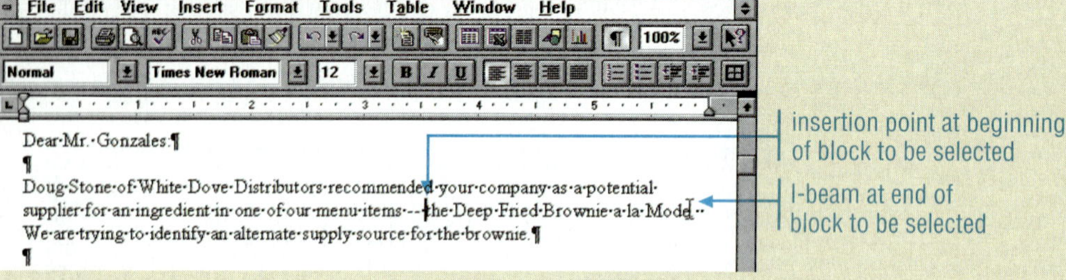

❸ With the I-beam after the "e" in Mode, press **[Shift]** then click. Just the block of text, "the Deep Fried Brownie a la Mode," is highlighted.

Now that you have selected the text, you are ready to underline it.

❹ Click the **Underline button** 🔲 on the Formatting toolbar to underline the selected text. The Underline button is activated. See Figure 1-42.

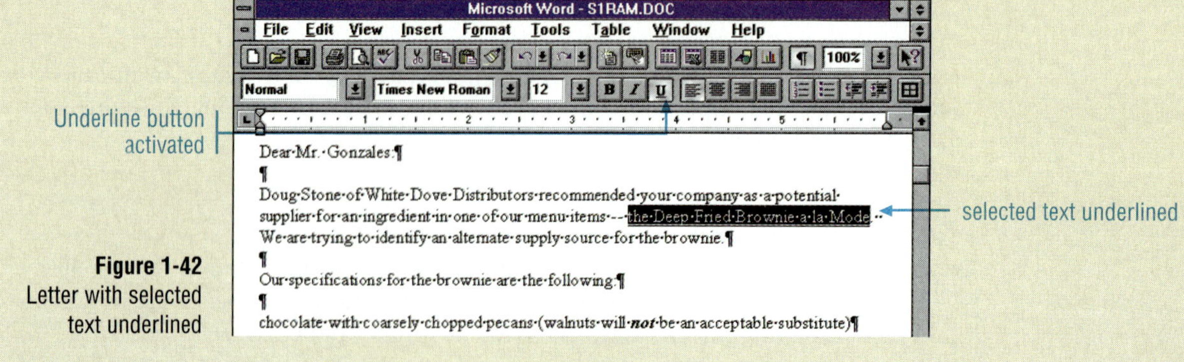

Figure 1-42
Letter with selected
text underlined

❺ Deselect the text to see the effect of the underlining.

Now you have seen how the shift-click technique gives you more control over the block of text you need to select.

Removing Type Styles

Denise changes her mind about the underlining and wants to remove it. She knows that to remove a type style format, such as bold, italic, or underline, all she has to do is select the formatted text she wants to change, then click the button of the type style she wants to remove. Let's try it.

To remove the underlining:
❶ Use the shift-click method again to select "the Deep Fried Brownie a la Mode." Notice that the Underline button ⊔ becomes lighter to indicate that it is activated for the selected text.
❷ Click ⊔ and notice that the button is deactivated.
❸ Deselect the text to see that the underlining is removed.

The type style buttons are toggle switches; you turn the type styles on and off with the same button.

Adding Bullets

Another way to format documents is to add special characters—often heavy dots—to call attention to a particular passage or list of items. These characters are called **bullets**. The Bullets button on the Formatting toolbar makes it easy for you to add or remove these special characters because it also acts like a toggle switch. To add a bullet to selected text, simply click the Bullets button; to remove a bullet from selected text, click the Bullets button again to deactivate the feature.

Denise decides to emphasize the three specifications for the brownie by placing a bullet in front of each of them. She could select each specification individually and then click the Bullets button, but the more efficient procedure would be to select all three specifications at once, then format the entire selection with the bullets. She decides to use the selection bar to highlight all three specifications.

To apply bullets to the list of specifications:
❶ Move the I-beam into the selection bar next to the first specification, "chocolate..." The pointer changes to ⇗ when you move it into the selection bar.
❷ Press and drag the pointer down until the last specification, "size ...," is highlighted.
❸ Click the **Bullets button** ⊞ on the Formatting toolbar. A special character, the rounded bullet, appears in front of each item. Notice that the button appears lighter to indicate that it is activated.
❹ Deselect the text to view the bullets. See Figure 1-43.

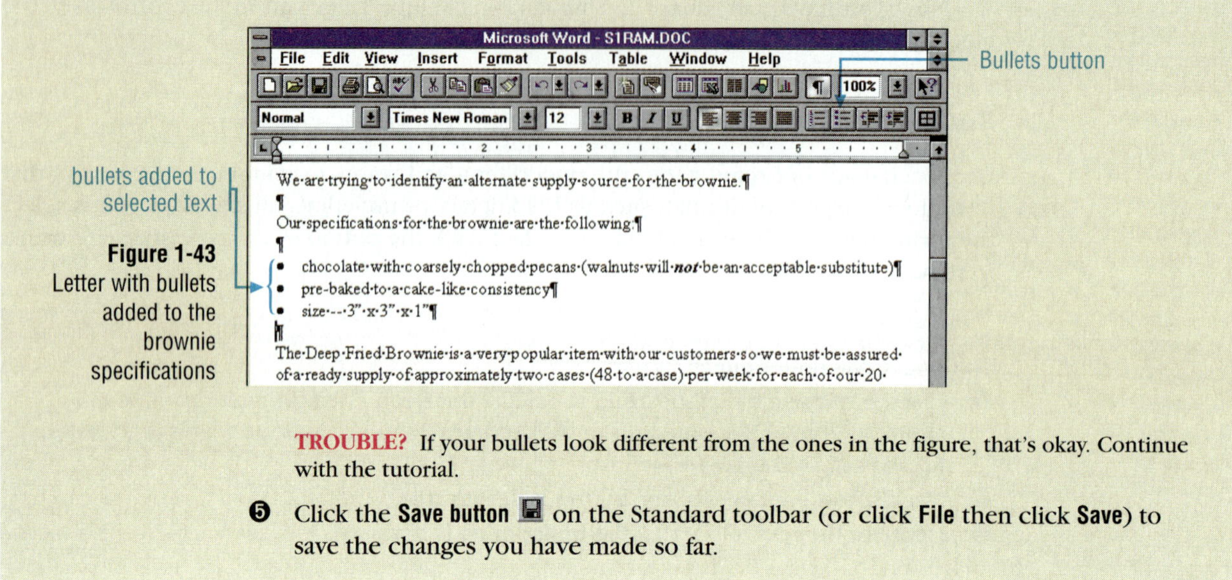

Figure 1-43
Letter with bullets
added to the
brownie
specifications

TROUBLE? If your bullets look different from the ones in the figure, that's okay. Continue with the tutorial.

❺ Click the **Save button** 🖫 on the Standard toolbar (or click **File** then click **Save**) to save the changes you have made so far.

Denise is now finished with three of the four phases of the productivity strategy. She began by entering the text, keeping in mind her plan for organizing her letter as she typed. Then she edited her letter by making changes in content and correcting any errors she found during proofreading, including spell checking her document. Next she used the various techniques for selecting text with the mouse to format her document so that it is more readable and attractive. Now she is ready to print her document.

Previewing and Printing a Document

During the first three phases of the production strategy, you typically use only Word's normal editing view. Now it is time to see a printed version of your document.

It is not necessary to actually print a hard copy of your document to see how it will look when printed. Rather, you can preview your printed document on screen. You can use the Print Preview button on the Standard toolbar to see a miniaturized view of your document as it would look printed. You can also choose Print Preview from the File menu. Then you can either edit the document while in print preview or return to your document to make adjustments. If the document needs no modifications, you can print it directly from the Preview window. Previewing your document before actually printing it saves time and resources.

To preview then print the document:
❶ Make sure your printer is on and contains paper.
❷ Click the **Print Preview button** 🔍 on the Standard toolbar (or click **File** then click **Print Preview**). The Preview window opens and displays a reduced version of your document. See Figure 1-44.

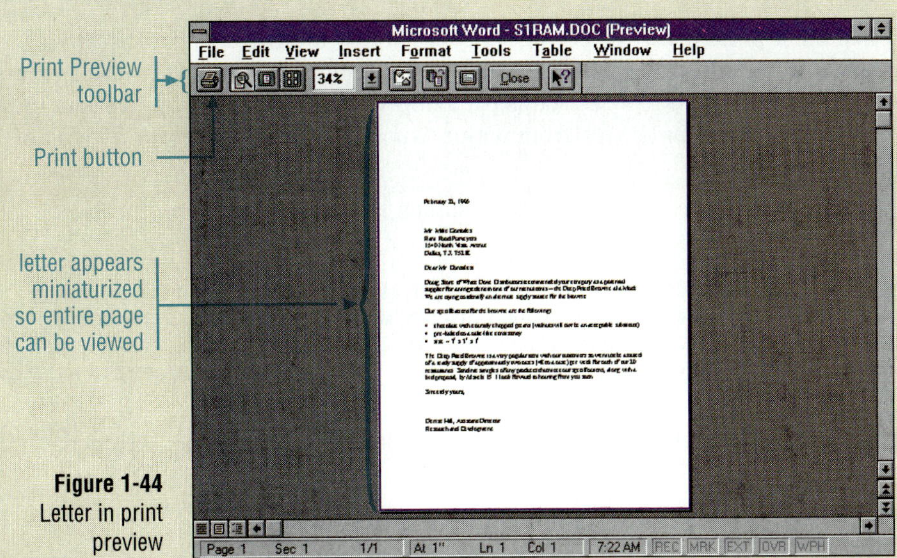

Figure 1-44
Letter in print
preview

The letter looks evenly balanced on the page, both vertically and horizontally, so Denise decides to print the letter. However, she wants to check the print settings first. To do so, she needs to choose the Print command from the File menu instead of clicking the Print button on the toolbar. The Print button sends the document directly to the printer; the Print command displays the Print dialog box in which you can modify the print settings. Both the Print button and the Print command are also available from the document window.

❸ Click **File** then click **Print...**. The Print dialog box appears. See Figure 1-45. Notice that the Print dialog box provides options for printing all the pages in your document, the current page only, or selected pages that you specify. You can also choose to print multiple copies of your document.

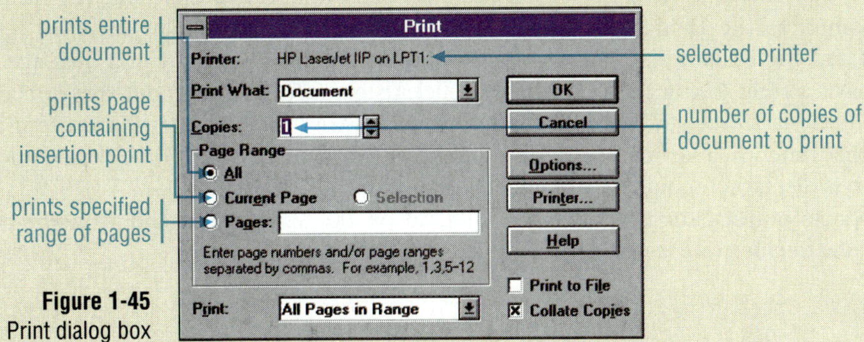

Figure 1-45
Print dialog box

Always check the Printer section of the dialog box to make sure that it shows the correct printer.

TROUBLE? If the correct printer is not selected, click Cancel in the Print dialog box. Click File, click Print..., then click Printer.... Select the correct printer from the list of available printers. If you change a document's printer after formatting a document, the way your document displays and prints might be different from the way you intended.

❹ Click **OK** or press **[Enter]**. A message appears briefly in the status bar letting you know that your document is being sent to the printer. A printer icon also appears briefly in the time slot of the status bar along with the number of pages sent to the printer. To cancel a print job from within Word, double-click the printer icon in the status bar.

Once your letter prints, it should look similar to Figure 1-1 without the Sweet T's letterhead.

TROUBLE? If your document hasn't printed yet, check the status of your document in Windows Program Manager by pressing [Alt][Tab] until the Print Manager title bar appears. Remove your document from the print queue before returning to your document, then send the document to print again. If it still doesn't print, check with your instructor or technical support person.

❺ Click the **Close button** on the Print Preview toolbar to return to the document.

Getting Help

Although the tutorials in this book will help you learn a great deal about Word's operations, you might want to explore a topic not taught yet or refresh your memory about a procedure already covered. In any case, you need to be able to find your own answers to word processing questions that might arise in the future.

Word's on-line Help system gives you quick access to information about Word's features, commands, and procedures. You can get help by using context-sensitive Help as you work, by looking up a topic in Word Help Contents, or by using the Help Search feature.

Using Context-Sensitive Help

Context-sensitive Help allows you to find out information about menu commands, buttons, toolbars, rulers, or other screen elements as you are working with them in your document. You click the Help button on the Standard toolbar or press [Shift][F1] to change the pointer to the Help pointer. Then you click the screen item you want to know about and the related Help topic appears automatically. Most dialog and message boxes also have a Help button, which you can click to get information about that specific feature's options. Once you have initiated context-sensitive Help, you can also use it to find out what function a key combination performs—just press the key combination and information is displayed about that command.

Denise noticed the Full Screen command on the View menu and wonders what it does. She decides to use context-sensitive Help to find out.

To use context-sensitive Help to learn about the Full Screen command:
❶ Click the **Help button** on the Standard toolbar. The mouse pointer changes to .
❷ Click **View** then click **Full Screen**. The Word Help window appears and displays the topic, "Full Screen command (View menu)."
❸ Read the information in the topic window, using the scroll bar to view the entire topic if necessary.

Denise is ready to exit Word Help.

❹   Double-click the **Word Help window Control menu box** (or click **File** then click **Exit** in the
Word Help window).

Using the Help Contents Window

If you want general information about Word's features, you should open the Word Help
Contents window, which serves as a table of contents for all topics in on-line Help. You
can even have Word demonstrate some of its features for you. To access the Help
Contents window, you press [F1] or choose Contents from the Help menu. From this window you can move to topics of interest by clicking the appropriate **hot topic,** a solid
underlined word or phrase.

Denise is interested in finding out more about Outline view. She decides to look it up
using the Help Contents window.

To use the Help Contents window to find information about Outline view:

❶   Press **[F1]** (or click **Help** then click **Contents**). The Word Help Contents window
appears in front of the document and becomes the active window. See Figure 1-46.

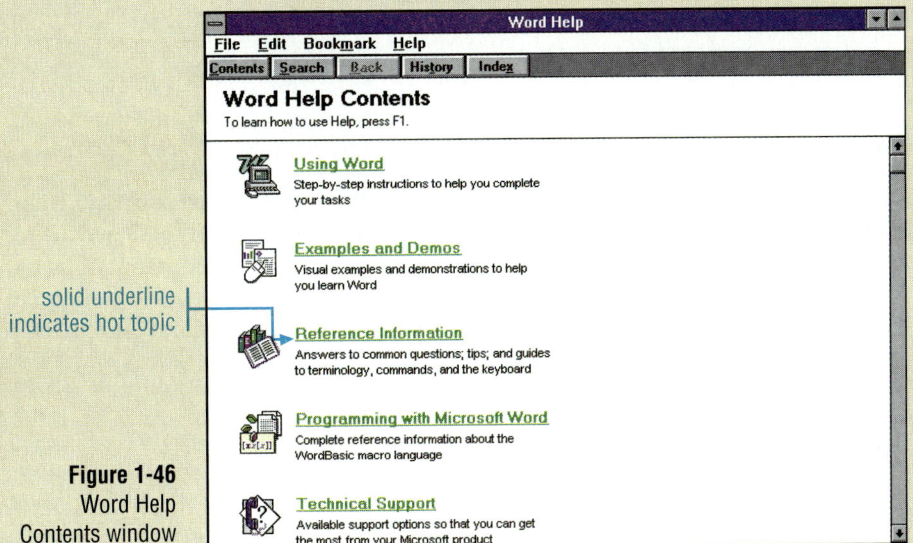

Figure 1-46
Word Help
Contents window

❷   Click the **Reference Information** hot topic, then click **Definitions** in the General
Reference Information section. Notice that the pointer changes to a hand when
placed over a topic. An alphabetical listing of terms opens. The dotted underlined
words are known as *hot words*. To see a definition of a hot word, simply click it.

Because you're looking for information on Outline view, you need to move to the topics that begin with the letter "O."

❸   Click the **O button** then click the **outline view** hot word. A definition of Outline view
appears in a separate window. See Figure 1-47.

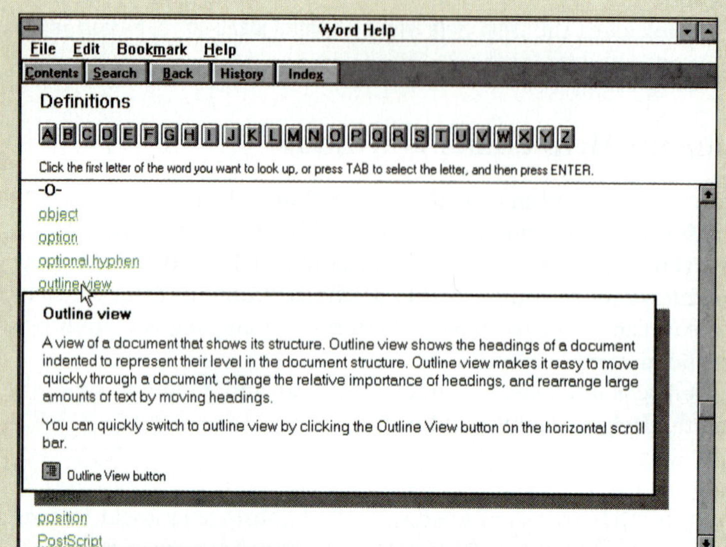

Figure 1-47
Definition of
outline view

❹   Read the information then press [**Esc**] to dismiss the definition window.

Denise now has a better understanding of outline view and is ready to exit Help.

❺   Close the Word Help Contents window.

Using Search

You can let Word do the leg work for you by using the Search feature of Word Help. You access the Search dialog box by double-clicking the Help button on the Standard toolbar or choosing the Search for Help on command from the Help menu.

Denise decides to use the Search feature to find information about printing envelopes, because she needs a printed envelope in which to send her completed letter to Ram Food Purveyors.

To search in Word Help for information on printing envelopes:
❶   Double-click the **Help button** ▶? on the Standard toolbar. The Search dialog box appears.
❷   Type **e** in the "search for" text box. The list of topics shown changes to those topics starting with "e."
❸   Type **nv** after the "e" in the "search for" text box. The list of topics shown changes to those starting with "env" and the topic "envelopes" is now highlighted.
❹   Click **Show Topics** or press [**Enter**]. Several related topics appear in the lower half of the window. See Figure 1-48.

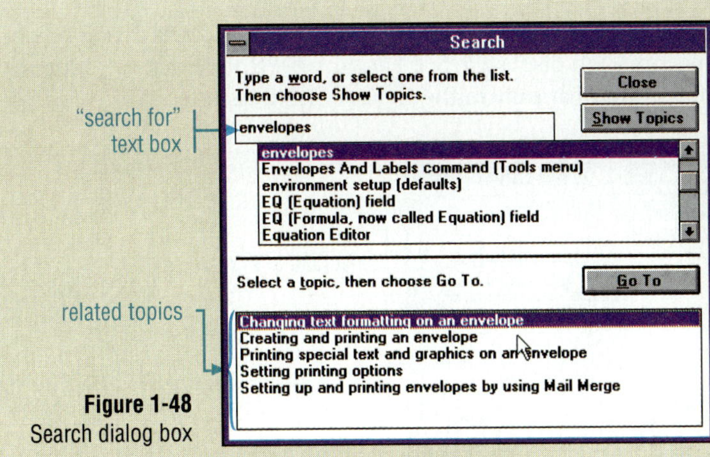

Figure 1-48
Search dialog box

❺ Click **Creating and printing an envelope**, then click **Go To** or press **[Enter]**. The How To window for Creating and Printing Envelopes appears.

❻ Maximize the How To window. How To windows have their own button bars, including an On Top button, which keeps the window visible so you can return to your document and still see the procedures for completing the task.

❼ Read the information about creating envelopes, double-click the **How To window Control menu box**, then double-click the **Help Contents window Control menu box** (or click **File** then click **Exit** in the Help Contents window) to close the window and return to the document.

Now that Denise has read the information about creating and printing envelopes, she decides to print the envelope for her letter to Mr. Gonzales.

Printing an Envelope

Envelopes have always been difficult to address on computers and, until recently, almost impossible to print on ordinary printers. It was generally easier just to type the address on an envelope using a typewriter rather than spend time figuring out how to do it on a computer. Word now makes it extremely easy to address the envelope, but you must still have a printer capable of printing envelopes. *Before you attempt this section of the tutorial, check with your instructor or technical support person to determine whether your printer can print envelopes.*

Denise inserts an envelope into the envelope feeder of her printer and is now ready to print her envelope.

To print an envelope:
❶ Insert an envelope into the envelope feeder on your printer. Check with your instructor or technical support person to make sure your printer can print envelopes before continuing. If your printer doesn't have an envelope feeder or you don't have an envelope, try printing the address on a regular sheet of paper.

❷   Click **Tools** then click **Envelopes and Labels…**. The Envelopes and Labels dialog box appears with the Envelopes tab displayed. See Figure 1-49. Notice that the address for Mr. Gonzales appears automatically in the Delivery Address box.

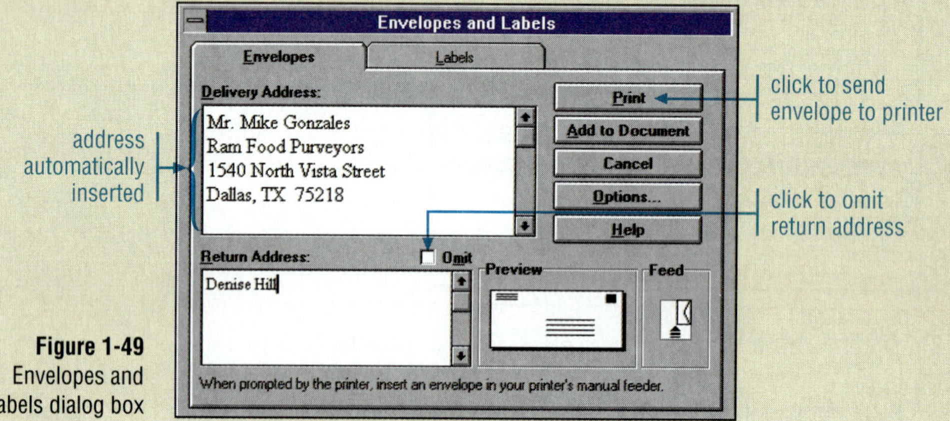

Figure 1-49
Envelopes and Labels dialog box

The information in your Return Address box will vary, depending on who installed Word on your computer. Generally in a business situation, the Omit check box would be selected because a company's return address is already printed on the envelope. However, you will enter your name and address in the Return Address box so that you can distinguish your printed envelope from those of other students.

❸   If the Omit check box is selected, click the box to clear it.

❹   Select any text that appears in the Return Address box, then type your name and address.

Ask your instructor or technical support person about your printer's ability to print envelopes before completing the next step. If your printer cannot print envelopes, click Cancel in the dialog box instead of completing the next step.

❺   Click **Print**. Because you have inserted your name and address in the Return Address box, Word wants to know if you want to change the default so that your name and address will automatically appear as the return address.

❻   Click **No**. A printing message appears briefly in the status bar.

❼   Save the changes you have made.

TROUBLE? If your envelope didn't print, your printer might not be able to print envelopes. Check with your instructor or technical support person to determine what to do next.

Your envelope should look like the envelope in Figure 1-1 except that your name and address will appear where the Sweet T's, Inc. preprinted address appears.

Now that Denise has printed both her letter and her envelope, she decides to close her document and exit Word.

To close the document and exit Word:

❶ Double-click the **document window Control menu box** (or click **File** then click **Close**). Notice the difference in the menu bar of the Word window—just the File and Help menus are available on the menu bar. Also, the status bar is blank. See Figure 1-50. When you have no other documents open, Word displays this window, known as the Nil menu screen.

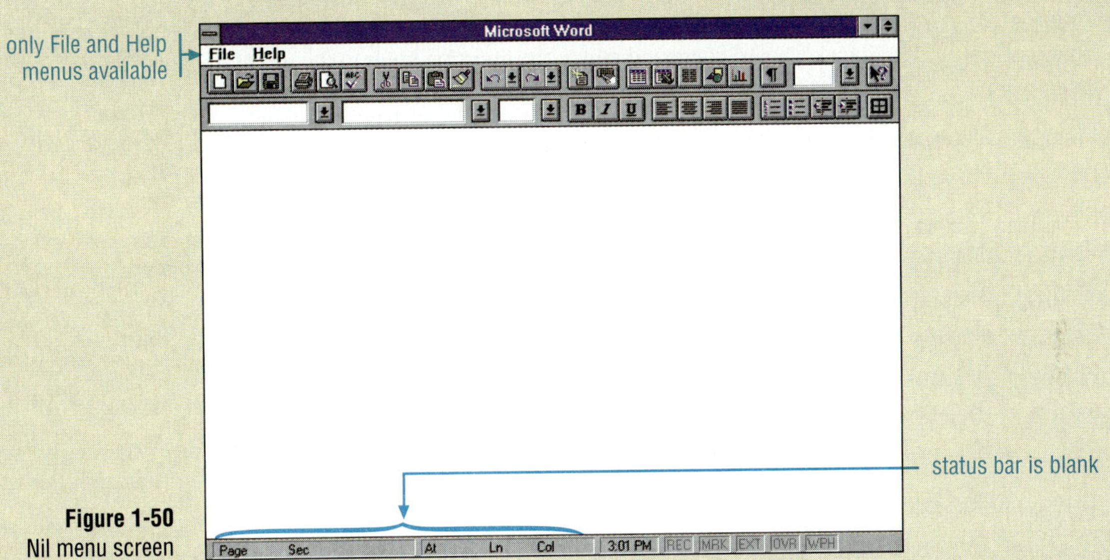

Figure 1-50
Nil menu screen

You could create a new document or open an existing document if you wanted to continue to work in Word, but in this case you will exit Word.

❷ Double-click the **Word window Control menu box** (or click **File** then click **Exit**). You return to the Program Manager. The Microsoft Office group window is still open.

TROUBLE? If you are asked to save changes to any documents other than S1RAM.DOC, click No.

❸ Double-click the **Microsoft Office group window Control menu box** to close this window.

❹ Exit Windows.

Denise has completed all phases of her productivity strategy—creating, editing, formatting, and printing—and is now is ready to mail her letter.

Questions

1. List and briefly describe the four phases of the productivity strategy.
2. Describe the differences between the Word window and the document window.
3. What are the six questions you should answer at the beginning of each new Word session to determine whether your Word screen is arranged properly?
4. How do you display the shortcut Toolbar menu?

5. What is the difference between an open document and an active document?
6. Describe two methods for switching between open documents.
7. What are default settings for a Word document?
8. In the status bar, what do the following indicate about the location of the insertion point?
   a. At 7.2"
   b. Ln 20
   c. Col 29
9. Which key do you press to insert a blank line in your document?
10. What is the difference between using [Backspace] and [Del] to correct errors?
11. Which keyboard command moves the insertion point to the top of the document?
12. Describe the difference between the insertion point and the I-beam.
13. What is the difference between Insert mode and Overtype mode?
14. What types of errors will the Spelling command discover?
15. Explain the principle of "select, then do." Give examples.
16. Where is the selection bar located?
17. What is the purpose of the print preview feature?
18. What is the difference between a dotted underscored word and a solid underscored word in a Word Help topic window?

Use Word Help to answer Questions 19 through 22:

E 19. How do you open a file in Word that was created by another application?

E 20. What is the purpose of the Summary Info dialog box?

E 21. How would you check the spelling of just one word in a document?

E 22. How do you modify the format of a bullet?

Tutorial Assignments

Start Word, if necessary, and make sure your Student Disk is in the disk drive. Conduct a screen check, then open T1TFP.DOC and complete the following:

1. Change the date to October 5, 1995.
2. Use the selection bar to select the inside address, then insert your name and address.
3. Change the salutation appropriately.
4. Move the insertion point into the last paragraph and change the date, March 15, to October 31. Bold and italicize the date.
5. Remove the applied type styles from "not" in the last brownie specification.
6. Spell check and proofread for additional errors.
7. Save the letter as S1TFP.DOC to your Student Disk.
8. Preview the letter.
9. Print the letter and an envelope, if your printer has the capability to print envelopes.
10. Save the changes, if necessary.

E 11. Apply bullets to the brownie specifications, but change the shape of the bullet to ⇒. Save the document as S1TFP2.DOC.

12. Print the document.

E 13. Use Word Help to look up how to remove bullets. Then print the Help Topic on "Adding or removing bullets or numbers in a list."

Case Problems

1. A Confirmation Letter to Haas Petroleum

Lillian May coordinates off-campus credit offerings for Western Hills Community College in Colorado Springs, Colorado. She has worked for several years with Fred Maxwell, Human Resources director at Haas Petroleum, to schedule academic classes for Haas employees at their site. She needs to write a letter confirming next semester's schedule. To save time, she uses the document she wrote last year, making a couple of changes.

　　Open P1HAAS.DOC from your Student Disk and complete the following:

1. Change the date to today's date.
2. Save the document as S1HAAS.DOC.
3. Insert the course description shown in Figure 1-51 one blank line below the course description for GOVT 2301.

Figure 1-51

> CSCI 1301. Introduction to Computer Information Systems. (3-0) Tuesday, 5-8 p.m.
>
> This course is designed to teach you computer concepts by providing a general knowledge of mainframes and microcomputers, their functions, and applications.

4. Delete the entire course description for PSYC 1301.
5. Edit the wording of the letter to make it appropriate for next semester.
6. Bold the course abbreviation and number for each course description.
7. Italicize each course name.
8. Remove the underlining from days and times in GOVT 2301 and ENGL 1302.
9. Spell check the document and proofread for all errors.
10. Save the changes.
11. Preview the letter.
12. Print the letter.
13. Print an envelope, if your printer supports printing envelopes. Include your name and address in the return address. Save the changes.
14. Close the document.

2. A Response to a High School Student

As program manager for KIWW, a radio station in your home town, you often receive requests from local high school students interested in radio and television. Marcus Vincente wrote to you asking for sources of information about radio or television for a research paper he has to write.

　　Open P1KIWW.DOC from your Student Disk and complete the following to respond to his request:

1. Insert seven blank lines at the top of the document.
2. Save the document as S1KIWW.DOC.
3. Type today's date then insert three blank lines after the date.
4. Insert the names of the three books shown in Figure 1-52 and insert a blank line after the sentence "Check with your school librarian for the following books."

Figure 1-52

> Handbook of American Popular Culture
> Les Brown's Encyclopedia of Television
> The Encyclopedia of Television Series, Pilots, and Specials, 1937-1973

5. Move to the end of the document, type your name, press [Enter], then type Program Manager.
6. Spell check the document and proofread for all errors.
7. Save your changes.
8. Format your document to improve its readability and appearance by italicizing the names of books and adding rounded bullets to the list of books.
9. Save your changes.
10. Preview then print your document.

E 11. Remove the bullets from the list of books, then print the letter again. Save the document as S1KIWW2.DOC.
12. Close the document.

3. Inquiring About a Sweet Tooth Cafe Franchise

You are interested in opening a Sweet Tooth Cafe franchise in your area. Write a letter to Jocelyn Titus, president of Sweet T's, requesting information about franchising and convincing her of the need for a Sweet Tooth Cafe in your town. Her address is Oklahoma Bank Building, One Main Street, Oklahoma City, OK 73112.

1. Plan your letter then type it.
2. Save the document as S1SWEET1.DOC.
3. Correct all errors, including spelling.
4. Save your changes.
5. Format your document to improve its readability and appearance.
6. Save your changes.
7. Preview then print your document.
8. Close the document.

Using Page, Paragraph, and Font Formatting Commands

Creating a Cover Memo and Agenda

OBJECTIVES

In this tutorial you will:
- Rename a file
- Move text within a document
- Change page formatting options such as document margins
- Change paragraph formatting options such as indentation, tabs, line spacing, alignment, borders, and rules
- Insert leader characters
- Number paragraphs
- Change font formatting options such as font type, point size, type style, and between-character spacing
- Insert special symbols
- Preview and print multiple pages

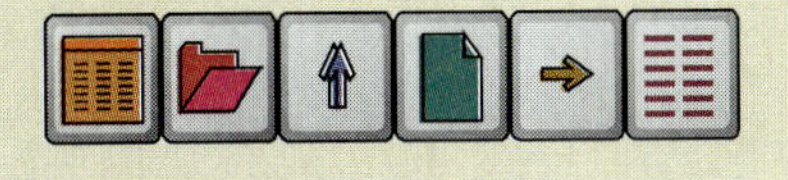

Seattle Area Teachers Federal Credit Union

CASE

Marcus Jenkins recently was hired by the Seattle Area Teachers Federal Credit Union as an administrative assistant to the president of the credit union, Michael Brown. The credit union provides financial services for its approximately 10,000 members, all of whom are employees or former employees of school districts within greater metropolitan Seattle.

Michael is responsible for the daily operations of the credit union and its staff. However, overall policy decisions are made by the Board of Directors, who are elected from the credit union's membership. Part of Marcus's new job is to develop the agenda for the monthly meetings of the board, along with a cover memo announcing the meeting and outlining the agenda for the board members. Because this is his first attempt at completing these documents, Marcus asks Michael to review them and make corrections. Michael suggests that Marcus submit his draft free of any formatting so that Michael can concentrate on the wording.

In this tutorial you will edit, format, and print the cover memo and agenda for Marcus. Marcus decides to use the productivity strategy to complete his assignment. He will first create a draft of the cover memo and agenda, then edit the document to include any additions or corrections Michael wants to make. Marcus will next format the cover memo and agenda and finally print his document.

Before creating the first draft of his cover memo and agenda, Marcus reviews the files from several previous meetings to see how his predecessor had created these documents. He notes that the content of the various cover memos and the order of the items on the agendas remain essentially the same from meeting to meeting. He also notices that occasionally more information is included in the memo than just the announcement of the meeting, and that the agenda items are sometimes rearranged. Marcus then creates a draft cover memo and agenda, which he submits to Michael, using basically the same wording as previous cover memos and the same order of agenda items, changing only the dates. As Michael requested, Marcus submits an unformatted document for his review.

Michael returns the draft of the cover memo and agenda with his edits. He attaches notes with additional information he wants inserted in the memo and some suggestions for reordering and formatting the agenda (shown in Figure 2-1). Marcus looks over his comments and is ready to begin editing the document.

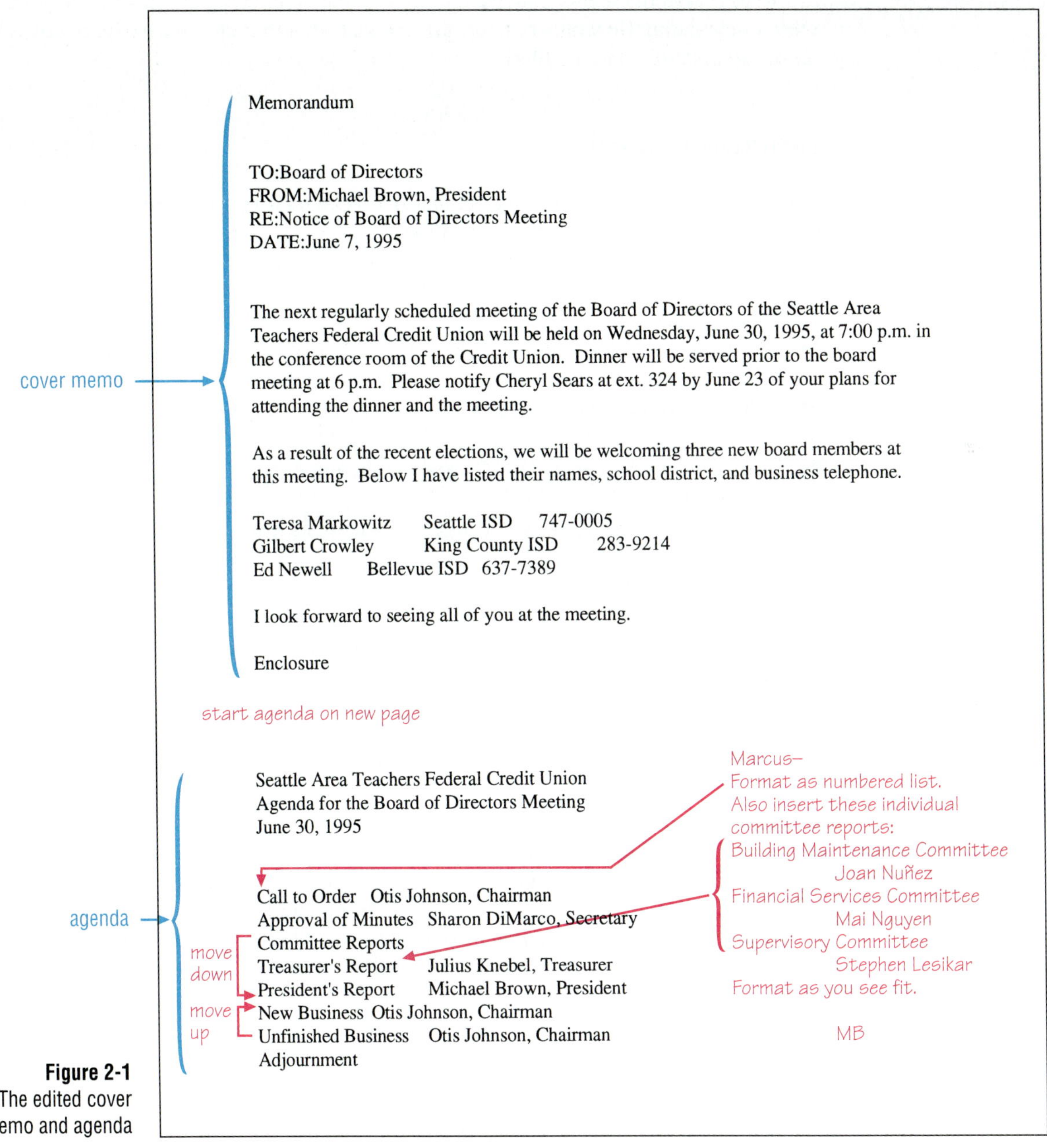

Figure 2-1
The edited cover
memo and agenda

Let's begin by opening Marcus's unformatted document.

To open the document containing the cover memo and agenda:
1. Start Word, if necessary, and conduct the screen check as described in Tutorial 1.
2. Insert your Student Disk in the disk drive, then open the file C2SATFCU.DOC from
   your Student Disk. If you do not remember how to open an existing file, refer to
   Tutorial 1. After C2SATFCU.DOC is open, scroll through the document to become
   familiar with it.

Before Marcus begins making changes to the document, he decides to save the file with a new name. He wants to keep the original version intact in case he needs it later. To do so, he must rename the file.

Renaming a File

You rename a file using the Save As dialog box, which you used in Tutorial 1 to name a document when saving it for the first time.

To rename the file:
❶ Click **File** then click **Save As…**. The Save As dialog box appears. The file's current name, "c2satfcu.doc," appears highlighted in the File Name text box.
❷ Type **s2satfcu** in the File Name text box. The new filename replaces the previous filename.
❸ Make sure the Drives list box displays the name of the drive containing your Student Disk.
❹ Click **OK** or press **[Enter]**. Word adds the extension "DOC" automatically to the filename.

Marcus saved the file he will work in as S2SATFCU.DOC, and he still has the original version of the file. Now he can begin editing the document.

Moving Text Within a Document

In the process of editing a document, you might want to rearrange the content by changing the location of an entire block of text. One of the advantages of word processing is that you can move text quickly and easily from its original location to another without retyping it. Word allows you to move text from one location in a Word document to another location in the *same document,* or to a *different Word document,* or to a *different application program,* such as a spreadsheet program. Furthermore, for each type of move you want to make, Word provides a variety of ways to make it.

The easiest method for moving text short distances within the same document involves the feature known as **drag-and-drop**, so named because you simply *drag* selected text to its new spot in your document and then *drop* it in place by releasing the mouse button.

Michael suggested a change in the order of the agenda items, and Marcus decides to use the drag-and-drop feature to relocate the Committee Reports agenda item after the President's Report agenda item and before the New Business agenda item.

To move the agenda items using drag-and-drop:
❶ Click in the selection bar next to Committee Reports to select that line (Ln 37), including the paragraph mark at the end of the line.

TROUBLE? If you don't remember how to use the selection bar or the other techniques for selecting text, refer to Tutorial 1.

❷ Move the mouse pointer over the selected text. Notice that the shape of the pointer changes to ⬉.

❸ Press and continue to hold down the mouse button. The drag-and-drop pointer appears. Use the dashed insertion point of the pointer to help guide you as you drag the selected text to its new location.

❹ Drag the selected text to its new location so that the dashed insertion point is in front of the "N" in New Business. See Figure 2-2.

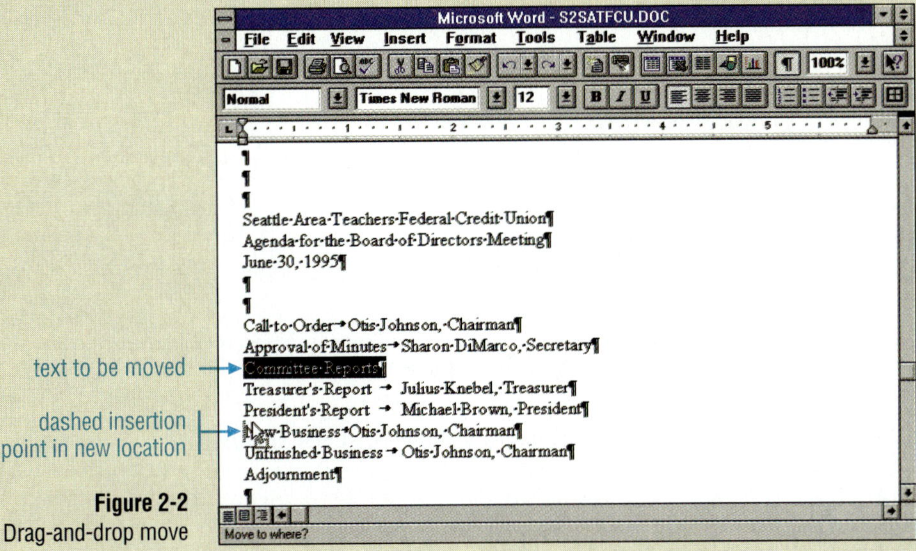

text to be moved

dashed insertion point in new location

Figure 2-2
Drag-and-drop move

❺ Release the mouse button. The selected text is moved to its new location and is still highlighted.

❻ Deselect the highlighted text.

TROUBLE? If the move did not work, click the Undo button ⬑ on the Standard toolbar (or click Edit then click Undo Move). Repeat the steps above, making sure that you do not release the mouse button until the dashed insertion point is in front of the "N" in New Business.

Moving Text with the Move Command ([F2])

The keyboard equivalent for the drag-and-drop feature is the Move command ([F2]). Marcus also needs to move the Unfinished Business agenda item before New Business, but this time he decides to use the Move command.

To move the agenda item using the Move command:

❶ Click in the selection bar next to Unfinished Business to select that line, including the paragraph mark.

❷ Press [F2]. Notice that the status bar displays the message "Move to where?"

❸ Place the insertion point in front of the "N" in New Business. Notice that the insertion point changes to a dashed vertical line.

❹ Press [Enter]. Unfinished Business is moved above New Business. See Figure 2-3.

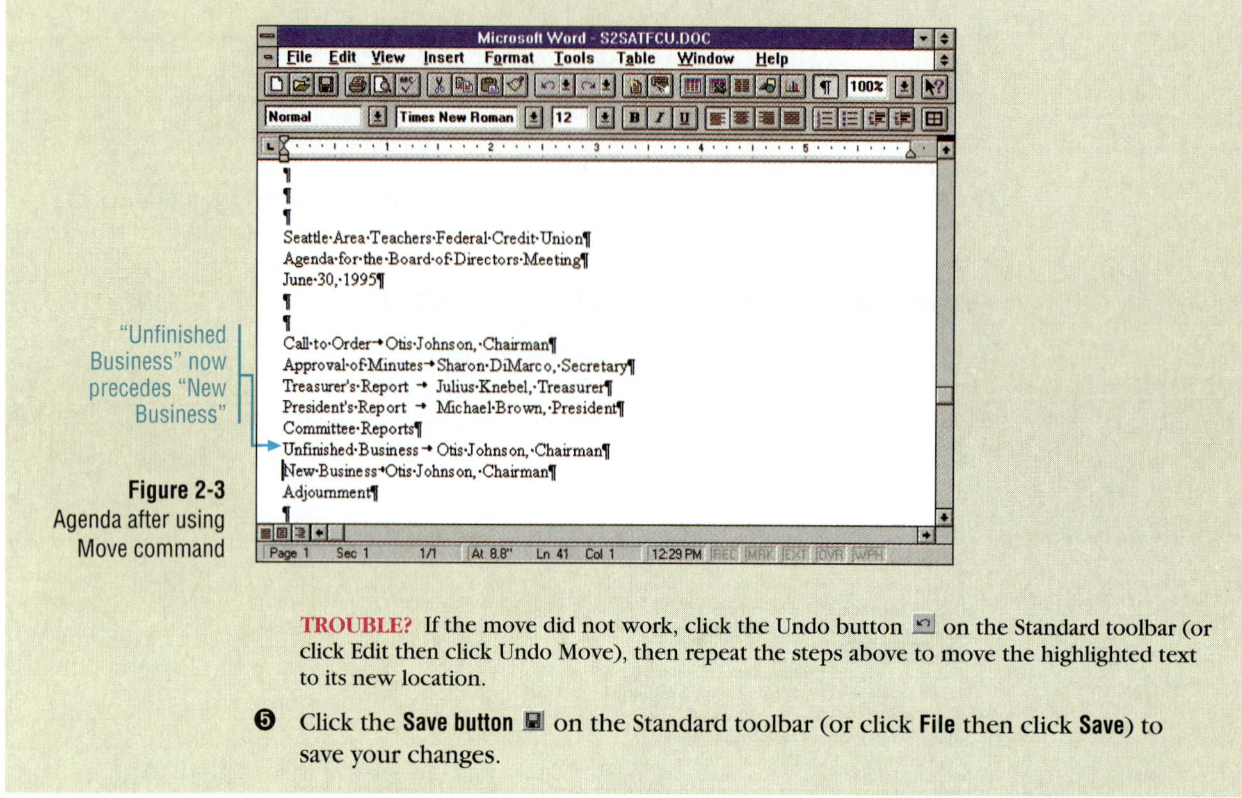

"Unfinished Business" now precedes "New Business"

Figure 2-3
Agenda after using Move command

TROUBLE? If the move did not work, click the Undo button 🔄 on the Standard toolbar (or click Edit then click Undo Move), then repeat the steps above to move the highlighted text to its new location.

❺ Click the **Save button** 💾 on the Standard toolbar (or click **File** then click **Save**) to save your changes.

Marcus is ready to move to the next phase of the productivity strategy: formatting the document.

Applying Direct Formatting Options

Word divides its formatting options into three groups: document-level or page setup commands, paragraph-level commands, and character-level or font commands. To work efficiently, start with decisions that affect the entire document (page setup decisions), then move to decisions about paragraph formatting options, and finally make decisions about font formatting options. By starting with those options that affect your entire document and moving to more specific formatting choices, you eliminate retracing your steps. You can apply individual formatting options directly to specific elements of your document by selecting the element and then choosing the appropriate formatting command, or you can apply several formatting options at once through the use of Word's styles. In this tutorial you will use direct formatting; in Tutorial 3 you will learn about using styles to apply formatting to a document.

Both the cover memo and the agenda require a great deal of formatting, so Marcus decides to begin by making the changes that affect the overall appearance of the document.

Page Setup Options

Word's page setup features govern the size of your document's text area—in other words, how many lines of text will fit on a page. Setting margins is a page formatting decision that affects the size of the available text area. Two other factors affecting your document's text area are paper size (8.5 x 11 or 8.5 x 14) and page orientation (tall or wide). The default page orientation is tall, or **portrait**, but you can change it to wide, or **landscape**. You can make changes to the margins, paper size, or page orientation by choosing Page Setup from the File menu.

Changing Margins

Word uses a default width of 1.25 inches for the left and right margins, and a default width of 1 inch for the top and bottom margins. Any changes to the margins affect the entire document, not just the current page. The area that remains after allowing for the margin settings is called the **available text area** (Figure 2-4).

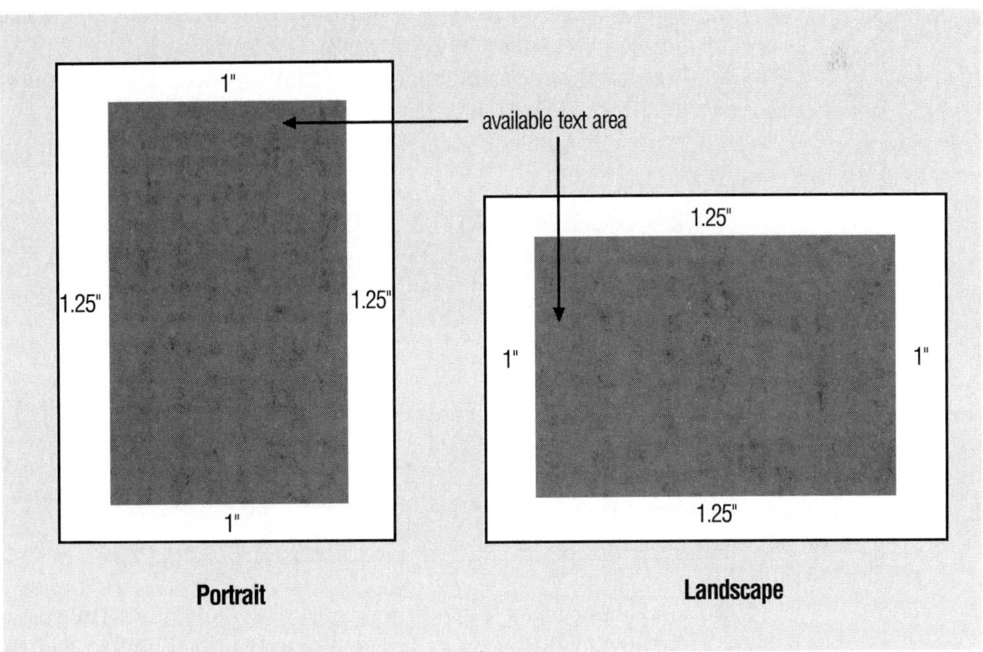

Figure 2-4
Available text area

　　The ruler, displayed below the Formatting toolbar on the Word screen, shows the length of the typing line, given the width of the current left and right margins. For instance, the default left and right margin settings of 1.25 inches provide a typing line of 6 inches (8.5 - 1.25 - 1.25 = 6). The numbers on the ruler scale indicate distances in inches from the left margin *not* from the left edge of the paper; therefore, the scale starts with 0. The tick marks on the ruler scale indicate increments of $\frac{1}{8}$ inch.

　　To create a more balanced frame of white space around the text, making the document more attractive to the reader, Marcus wants to increase the top margin to 1.5 inches and the left and right margins to 1.75 inches.

To change the top, left, and right margins:

❶ Press **[Ctrl][Home]** to move to the beginning of the document.

❷ Click **File** then click **Page Setup…**. The Page Setup dialog box appears. From this dialog box, you can also change paper size and orientation, and paper source. The Preview section allows you to preview any changes you make to the page setup.

TROUBLE? If you do not see the Page Setup dialog box with the Margins tab displayed, as shown in Figure 2-5, click the Margins tab at the top of the dialog box.

Marcus wants to increase the top margin to 1.5 inches.

❸ Click the **Top text box up arrow** until it reads 1.5". Notice that the Preview section changes as you change the value for the top margin.

Next, Marcus wants to change the left and right margin settings to 1.75 inches. This setting is not available in the list of settings, so he needs to type 1.75 in the Left and Right text boxes.

❹ Press **[Tab]** twice to highlight the Left text box.

❺ Type **1.75**. Note that you do not have to type the quotation mark to indicate inches; this is the assumed measurement.

❻ Press **[Tab]** once to highlight the Right text box. The Preview section now changes to reflect the new left margin setting.

❼ Type **1.75**. Figure 2-5 shows the completed Page Setup dialog box.

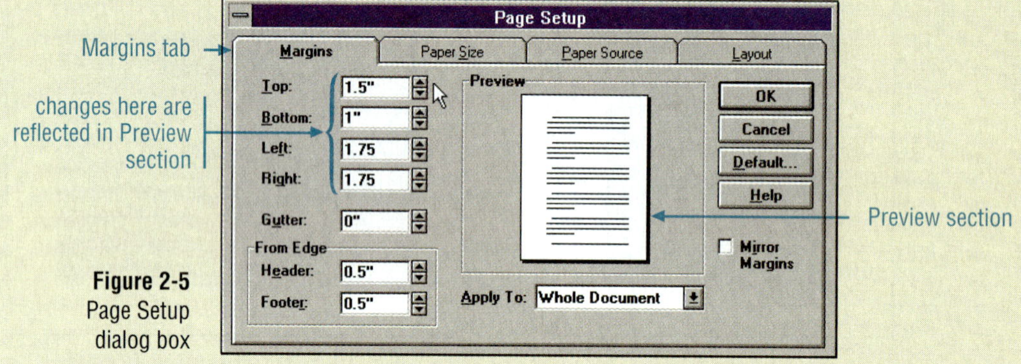

Margins tab →

changes here are reflected in Preview section

Preview section

Figure 2-5
Page Setup
dialog box

❽ Click **OK** or press **[Enter]** to return to your document. The ruler changes to reflect the new length of the typing line based on the new left and right margin settings (8.5 - 1.75 - 1.75 = 5). Also, notice the changes in the status bar, which now indicates that the first line begins 1.5 inches from the top of the page and that the document has two pages (as indicated by 1/2, meaning page 1 of 2). The increased top margin forced the text of the document onto a second page.

❾ Click the **Save button** 🖫 on the Standard toolbar (or click **File** then click **Save**) to save your changes.

Now that Marcus has made changes to the document's margins, he needs to adjust where the pages end within his document.

Soft Page Breaks

When you enter enough text to fill up a page, Word automatically starts a new page for you. To indicate the start of a new page, a row of dots appears across the page. This row of dots is called a **soft page break** because as you insert and delete text, the position of the soft page break can change. The status bar also changes to indicate the increase or decrease in the number of pages in the document.

Because his document has increased to two pages, Marcus must see where the second page starts. Michael wants the agenda to appear on a page by itself.

To view the soft page break in the document:

❶ Drag the vertical scroll box to the bottom of the scroll bar to move quickly to the end of your document. Notice the row of dots across the page. See Figure 2-6. This is Word's indication that you have filled one page of text and started another.

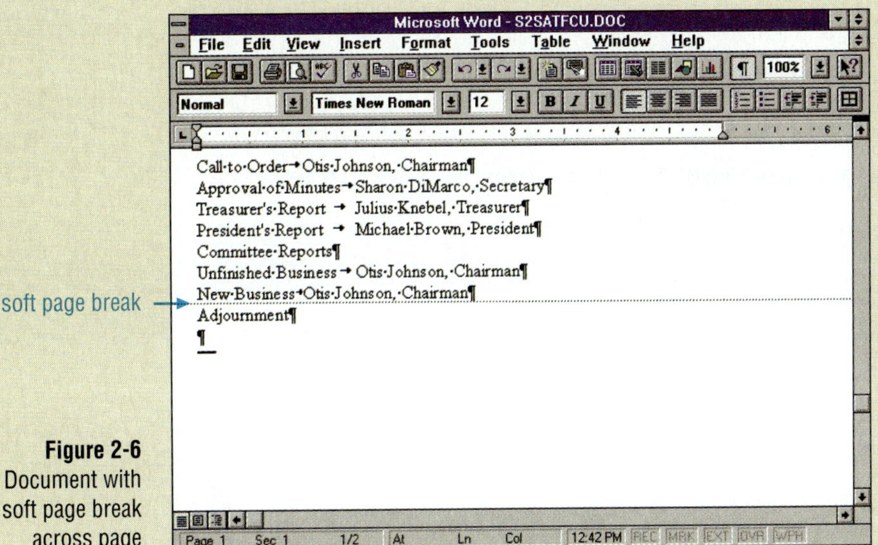

Figure 2-6
Document with soft page break across page

TROUBLE? Depending on the type of monitor or printer that you're using, the soft page break might occur in a different location. Just continue with the tutorial.

❷ Place the insertion point in the line of text directly *below* the soft page break. Notice the status bar. After the soft page break, the insertion point is located on page 2 of your document.

❸ Press [↑] to move the insertion point up one line of text, directly *above* the soft page break. The status bar now shows that the insertion point is on page 1.

Because the soft page break does not fall at the beginning of the agenda, Marcus must force the agenda to appear on a page by itself. He will do so by inserting a hard page break.

Inserting Hard Page Breaks

At times you might want to force a page to end at a particular spot in your document. To start a new page, you must insert a **hard page break**, also called a **manual page break**.

You can insert a hard page break by pressing [Ctrl][Enter] or by choosing Break from the Insert menu.

A hard page break is indicated by a row of dots across the page, like those used for a soft page break, but the words "Page Break" appear in the center of the row of dots. To delete a hard page break, select the page break then press [Del].

Let's insert a hard page break so that the agenda appears on a page by itself.

To insert the hard page break:

❶ Place the insertion point in front of the "S" in Seattle in the first line of the agenda heading (Ln 32).

> **TROUBLE?** If the first line of the agenda title in your document does not fall at the same point, perhaps you accidentally pressed [Enter] and inserted extra blank lines. Or, perhaps you have not changed the point size from 10 to 12. Ask your instructor or technical support person to do this for you. The line variation might also be due to the selection of a printer different from the one used in this book. Continue with the tutorial, keeping in mind this difference between your screen and the figures in this tutorial; use any line number indications as a point of reference.

❷ Press **[Ctrl][Enter]**. The status bar indicates that the insertion point is on page 2. See Figure 2-7.

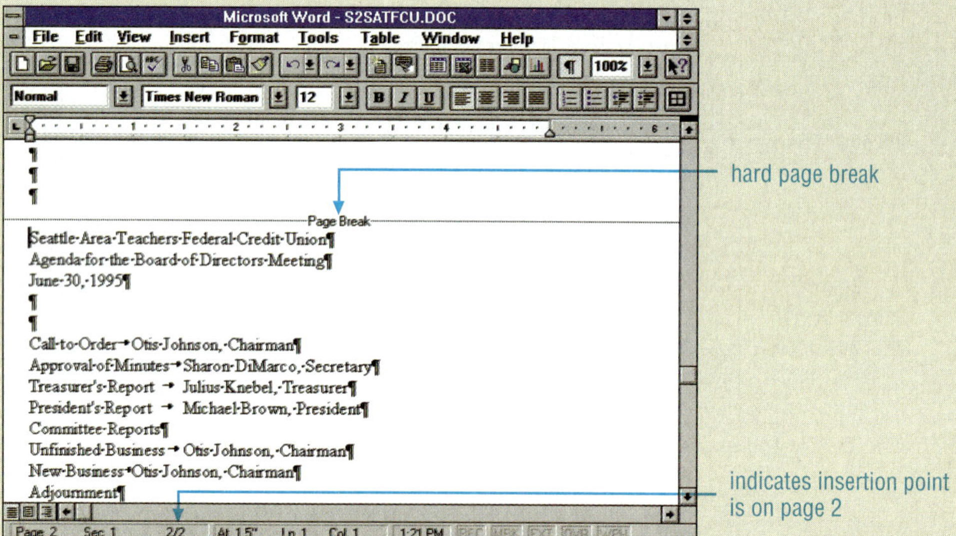

Figure 2-7
Screen after inserting hard page break

> **TROUBLE?** If you do not see a hard page break across your page, perhaps you did not hold down [Ctrl] while you pressed [Enter]. Click the Undo button ↺ on the Standard toolbar (or click Edit then click Undo Page Break), then repeat Step 2.

❸ Press [↑] to move the insertion point to the hard page break. Notice that the status bar changes to indicate that the insertion point is on page 1, Ln 32. Even though you have not filled page 1 completely with text, inserting a hard page break forced one page to end and another to begin.

❹ Click the **Save button** 🖫 on the Standard toolbar (or click **File** then click **Save**) to save your changes.

Marcus has completed making the document-level formatting decisions.

If you want to take a break and resume the tutorial at a later time, you can close the current document then exit Word by double-clicking the Control menu box in the upper-left corner of the screen. When you want to resume the tutorial, start Word, place your Student Disk in the disk drive, then complete the screen check procedure described in Tutorial 1. Open the file S2SATFCU.DOC then continue with the tutorial.

Now Marcus moves to the next group of formatting decisions: paragraph formatting options.

Paragraph Formatting

Paragraph formatting includes a wide variety of features such as paragraph indentations, tabs, numbered paragraphs, line spacing, paragraph alignment, paragraph borders, and rules. Some of the most often used paragraph formatting features are available on the Formatting toolbar; others are available only through the Paragraph command and the Borders and Shading command on the Format menu.

Remember that Word defines a paragraph as any amount of text that ends with a paragraph mark (¶). Word stores the paragraph formatting options that have been applied to a paragraph in the paragraph mark at the end of that paragraph. If you accidentally delete a paragraph mark, immediately click the Undo button or choose Undo from the Edit menu to restore the paragraph mark and any paragraph formatting changes that you might have made.

To make paragraph formatting changes, you first select the paragraph or paragraphs to be changed and then choose the paragraph formatting options you want to apply to the selection. To select a *single* paragraph, all you need to do is position the insertion point anywhere in that paragraph. Once you have selected a paragraph, you can make the necessary paragraph formatting changes. To make changes to *multiple* paragraphs, you can select the paragraphs and then apply paragraph formatting options. As you can see, the principle of "select, then do" pertains to formatting, too.

Marcus will begin formatting the paragraphs in his document by changing paragraph indentations.

Changing Paragraph Indentations

You might want to call attention to certain paragraphs within your document by indenting them from the left or right margin, or both, thus changing the length of your typing line. As you learned previously, changing margins is one way to change the length of the typing line; however, changing margins is a document-level option that affects the entire document, rather than just a paragraph. Word provides four ways to indent paragraph text from the margins without adjusting the entire document's margins—first-line indents, left indents, right indents, and hanging indents—as shown in Figure 2-8. The text in Figure 2-8 describes the different types of indents.

This is an example of a paragraph in which the first line is indented from the left margin. You can create this type of indent by moving only the *first-line indent marker* on the ruler.

This is an example of a paragraph in which all lines are indented from the left margin. You can create this type of indent by moving the *rectangle* below the left indent marker.

This is an example of a hanging indent, that is, a paragraph in which all lines except the first line are indented from the left margin. You can create this type of indent by moving only the *left indent marker* on the ruler.

This is an example of a paragraph in which all lines are indented from the right margin. You can create this type of indent by moving the *right indent marker* on the ruler.

Figure 2-8
Samples of
Word's indents

As usual, Word gives you a variety of ways to apply these features. You can create all these indents using the ruler or the Paragraph command on the Format menu. You can also use the Formatting toolbar to create left indents and hanging indents.

The ruler allows you to change paragraph indents quickly through the use of the indent markers (Figure 2-9). By default the indent markers are even with the left and right margins. The top triangle at the left end of the ruler, called the **first-line indent marker**, controls the amount of indentation from the left margin for the *first line* of a selected paragraph. The bottom triangle at the left end of the ruler, called the **left indent marker**, controls the amount of indentation from the left margin for *all* lines in the selected paragraph *except* the first line. The **rectangle** below the left indent marker controls the amount of indentation from the left margin for *all* lines in the selected paragraph, including the first line. The triangle at the right end of the ruler, called the **right indent marker**, controls the amount of indentation from the *right* margin for all lines in the selected paragraph. Any changes to the indentation level affect only the paragraph with the insertion point or any selected paragraphs. If you indent a paragraph and do not like the indentation you have chosen, you can click the Undo button and start again.

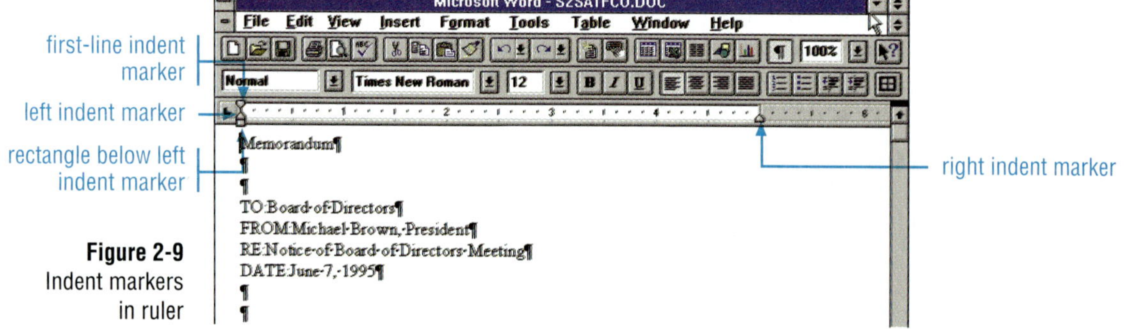

Figure 2-9
Indent markers
in ruler

You change the indent level for a paragraph by following the "select, then do" principle: select the appropriate paragraph or paragraphs to be changed and then drag the appropriate indent marker to a new position on the ruler.

Indenting a Paragraph

- Select the paragraph or paragraphs to be indented.

- Point to the indent marker you want to change and drag it to its new location on the ruler scale.

To indent:	*Do the following:*
Only the first line	Drag the first-line indent marker
All lines but the first line	Drag the left indent marker
All lines	Drag the rectangle under the left indent marker
All lines from the right margin	Drag the right indent marker

or

- Select the paragraph or paragraphs to be indented.

- Click Format then click Paragraph…. If necessary, click the Indents and Spacing tab in the Paragraph dialog box.

- From the Indentation section of the Paragraph dialog box, do one or more of the following:

  - In the Left text box, select or type the distance that you want to indent the paragraph from the left margin.

  - In the Right text box, select or type the distance that you want to indent the paragraph from the right margin.

  - In the Special section, select First Line, then select or type the negative or positive distance that you want to indent the first line of the paragraph from the *left indent*.

  - In the Special section, select Hanging, then select or type the negative or positive distance that you want to hang text after the first line.

- Click OK or press [Enter].

Marcus wants to try indenting the first line of each paragraph of the body of the memo by 0.5 inch, to see if this improves the appearance of the memo. He'll do so by changing the first-line indent marker. Because he's not sure if this is the format he wants, Marcus decides to indent just the first paragraph to see the results.

To indent the first line of the first paragraph:

❶ Place the insertion point anywhere in the first paragraph of the body of the memo, which begins "The next regularly…"

❷ Point to the first-line indent marker (top triangle), then click and drag it to the right 0.5 inch. The first line of the first paragraph is indented, but the remaining lines of the paragraph do not change. See Figure 2-10. Also notice that the other paragraphs in the memo were not affected by the change.

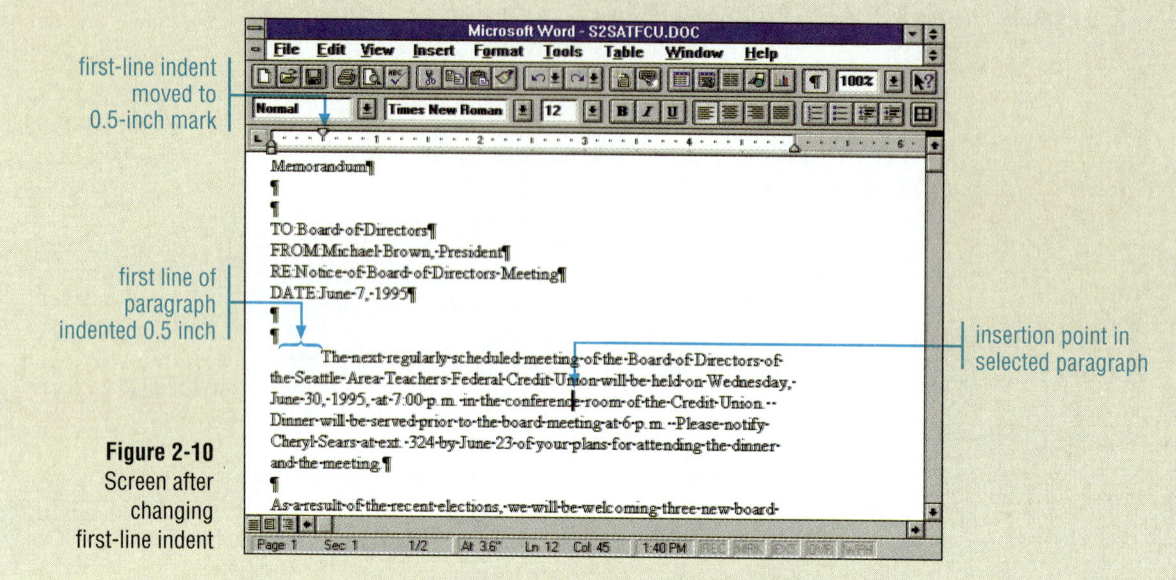

first-line indent moved to 0.5-inch mark

first line of paragraph indented 0.5 inch

insertion point in selected paragraph

Figure 2-10
Screen after changing first-line indent

Marcus doesn't like how this style looks, so he decides to undo it.

❸ Click the **Undo button** on the Standard toolbar (or click **Edit** then click **Undo Formatting**). The paragraph returns to its original format, with all lines even at the left margin.

Next Marcus decides to indent *all* lines of the paragraph 1 inch from the left margin. He could drag the rectangle to move both the first-line indent and the left indent to the 1-inch mark on the ruler, or he could use the Increase Indent button on the Formatting toolbar. Whenever you click the Increase Indent button, both the first-line and left indent markers move to the next tab stop to the right on the ruler. (You learn about tab stops in the next section.) You can just as easily "unindent" selected paragraphs by clicking the Decrease Indent button on the Formatting toolbar. Each time you click the Decrease Indent button, the first-line and left indent markers move to the previous tab stop to the left.

Marcus decides to use the Increase Indent button on the Formatting toolbar to indent all of the paragraphs of the body of the memo and the enclosure notation to the 1-inch mark on the ruler.

To indent the paragraphs using the Increase Indent button:

❶ Use the selection bar to select all the paragraphs in the body of the memo, from the first paragraph in the body of the memo ("The next regularly...") through Enclosure.

Next, let's make an intentional error and move the indentation too far to the right.

❷ Click the **Increase Indent button** on the Formatting toolbar three times. The selected paragraphs move to the right. Notice that the first-line and left indent markers have moved to the 1.5-inch mark on the ruler—half an inch too far to the right of where Marcus wants them.

❸ Click the **Decrease Indent button** 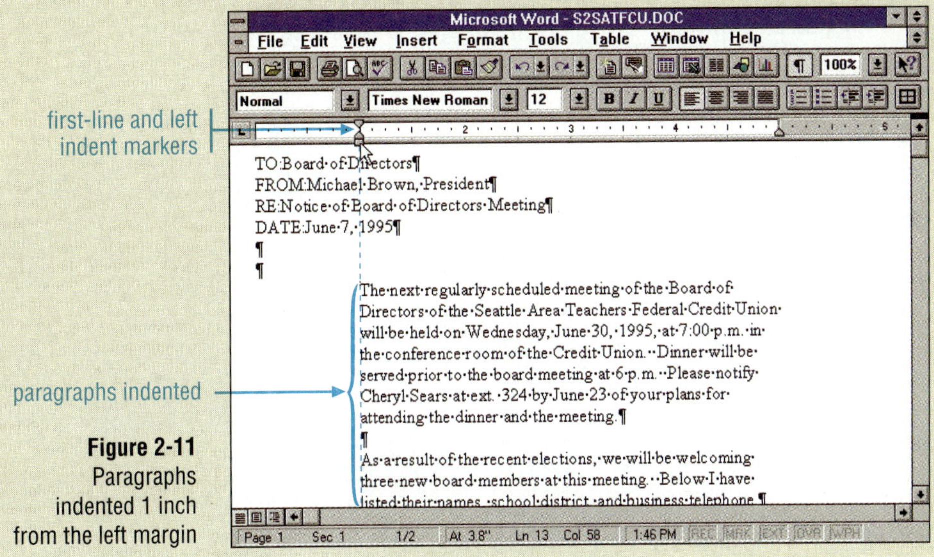 on the Formatting toolbar. All selected paragraphs move to the left 0.5 inch. Notice that the first-line and left indent markers have moved to the 1-inch mark on the ruler.

❹ Deselect the highlighted text and then scroll through the document. The body of the memo is indented to the 1-inch mark, but the rest of the document remains at the left margin. See Figure 2-11.

Figure 2-11
Paragraphs
indented 1 inch
from the left margin

❺ Save the changes you have made.

Next, to improve the appearance of the memo, Marcus wants to align the information vertically after the memo headings (TO:, FROM:, RE:, and DATE:) at the 1-inch mark on the ruler. This will match the indentation of the paragraphs in the body of the memo. To make this paragraph formatting change, Marcus will use Word's default tab settings.

Using Default Tabs

A **tab stop** is a predefined stopping point along your document's typing line. Each time you press [Tab], the insertion point moves to the next tab stop. If the Show/Hide ¶ option is activated, a tab character (→) appears on the screen at the point where you pressed [Tab]. Word's default tabs are set every 0.5 inch. To delete a tab character, you place the insertion to the left of the → then press [Del], or place the insertion point to the right of the → then press [Backspace].

Tabs are useful for aligning text or numerical data vertically in columns. Marcus will insert tabs to align the information after the memo headings.

To align the information after the memo headings by inserting tabs:

❶ Place the insertion point after the colon in the first memo heading (TO:).

❷ Press **[Tab]** twice. Notice that two tab characters appear and that the text aligns vertically under the 1-inch mark on the ruler. See Figure 2-12.

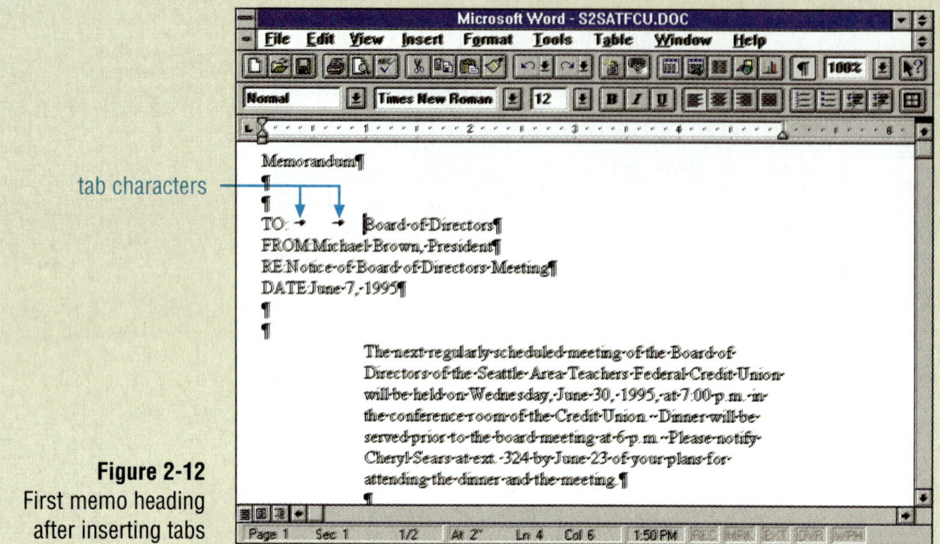

Figure 2-12
First memo heading after inserting tabs

> **TROUBLE?** If you don't see the tab characters on your screen, you need to activate the Show/Hide ¶ option by clicking the Show/Hide ¶ button ¶ on the Standard toolbar.

❸ Place the insertion point after the colon in the second memo heading (FROM:), then press **[Tab]** twice. The text aligns vertically at the 1.5-inch mark instead of at the 1-inch mark.

Marcus wants all the information to align at the 1-inch mark, so he must delete one of the tabs.

❹ Press **[Backspace]** once. The second tab character is deleted, and the text aligns vertically at the 1-inch mark.

❺ Place the insertion point after the colon in the third memo heading (RE:), then press **[Tab]** twice.

❻ Place the insertion point after the colon in the fourth memo heading (DATE:), then press **[Tab]** twice.

Because you inserted tabs between the headings and the information that follows them, the information aligns vertically.

Marcus now wants to format the information in the memo about the three new board members so that the three columns of information are more balanced on the page. To do so, he needs to set custom tab stops.

Setting Custom Tab Stops

Sometimes you might want to set tab stops at locations other than those of the default settings. In other words, you might want to customize the tab stops. Word allows you to set custom tabs using different alignment tab styles, namely, left, right, centered, or decimal (Figure 2-13). The default tab style, which you just used, is **left-aligned**, meaning that text at that tab stop is positioned even at the left and extends to the right from the tab stop. The **centered** tab aligns text evenly on either side of the tab stop, while the **right-aligned** tab creates text that is positioned even at the right and extends to the left from the tab stop. With **decimal-aligned** tabs, a number aligns at the decimal point, but text aligns to the right. You can use the tab alignment selector on the left side of the ruler or the Tabs command on the Format menu to set custom tabs.

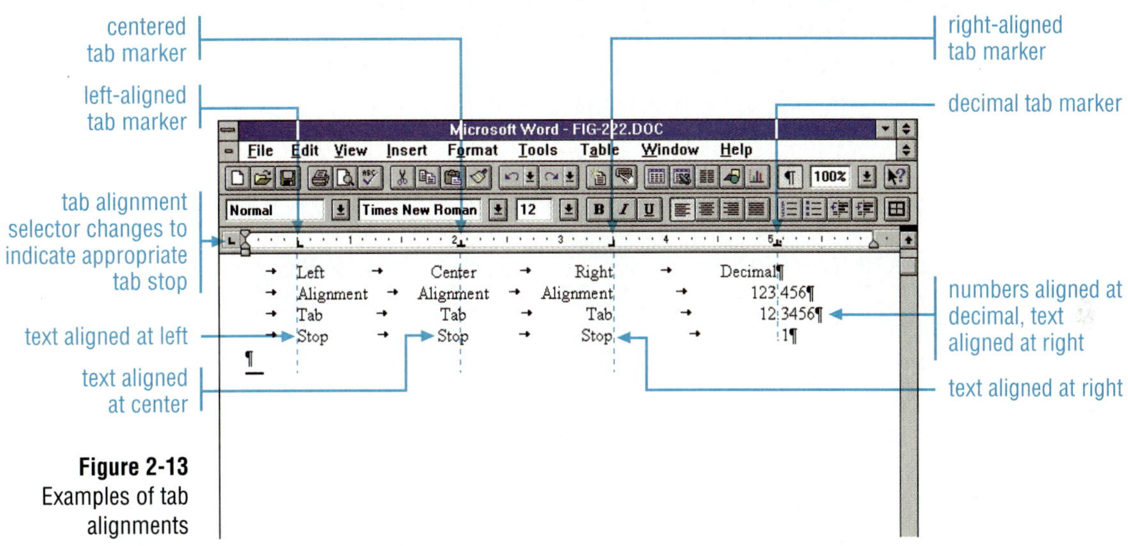

Figure 2-13
Examples of tab alignments

REFERENCE WINDOW

Setting Custom Tab Stops

- Select the paragraph or paragraphs for which you want to set custom tab stops.

- Click the tab alignment selector on the ruler until the appropriate icon for the tab alignment appears.

- Click at the point in the ruler where you want to set the custom tab stop.

or

- Click Format then click Tabs…. The Tabs dialog box appears.

- Type the position where you want to set the custom tab stop in the Tab Stop Position text box.

- Click the appropriate tab alignment option in the Alignment section.

- Click Set.

- Repeat the above steps for each additional tab stop to be set.

- Click OK or press [Enter].

Originally, Marcus entered the information about the board members by inserting a tab between each column of information, that is, between the board member's name and the school district, and between the school district and the telephone number. Now he wants to set a centered tab stop for the column containing the school districts, and a right-aligned tab stop for the column containing the telephone numbers.

To set the centered and right-aligned tab stops using the ruler:

❶   Select the three lines of information in the memo about the new board members ("Teresa Markowitz..." through "...637-7389").

❷   Click the **tab alignment selector** on the ruler until the **centered tab button** ⊥ appears.

❸   Move the tip of the mouse pointer below the 2.75-inch mark on the ruler, then click to set the centered tab at that point. A centered tab marker is inserted into the ruler. See Figure 2-14. Notice that the text *after* the first tab character in each of the selected lines shifts to the location of the centered tab stop.

centered tab marker at 2.75-inch mark

tab alignment selector changes to centered tab button

text centered at tab stop

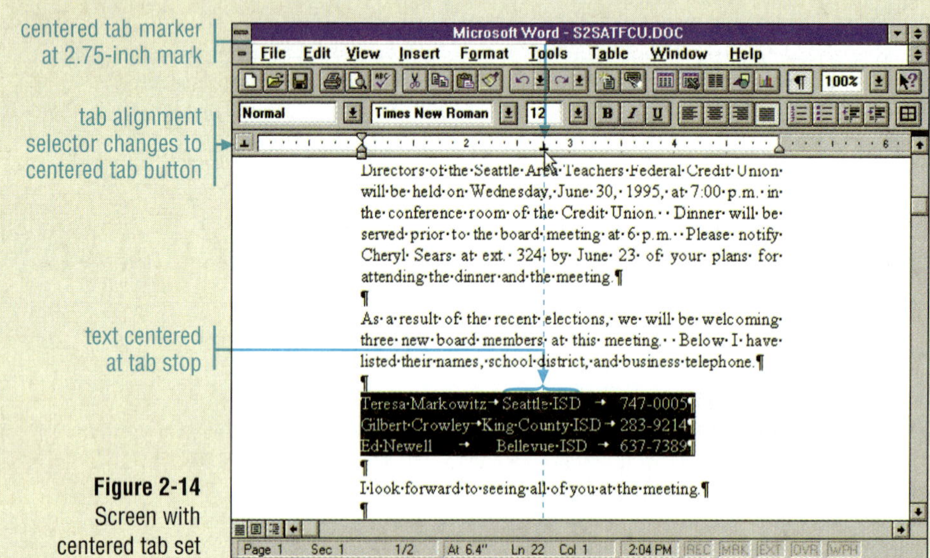

Figure 2-14
Screen with centered tab set

Now Marcus wants to set a right-aligned tab stop for the last column of information.

❹   Click the **tab alignment selector** on the ruler until the **right-aligned tab button** ⌐ appears.

Marcus decides to set the tab at the 4.75-inch mark on the ruler, but he wants to make sure he gets the tab exactly in place.

❺   Press and hold [Alt], move the mouse pointer to the 4.75-inch mark (approximately) on the ruler, then press and hold down the mouse button. As you do, the ruler indicates the exact distances from the left and right indents.

❻   When the ruler indicates that you are exactly 3.75" from the left indent, release [Alt] and the mouse button. A right-aligned tab marker is inserted into the ruler. The text after the second tab character in each of the selected lines moves to the new tab stop, and the default tabs between the centered tab marker and the right-aligned tab marker on the ruler are cleared. See Figure 2-15.

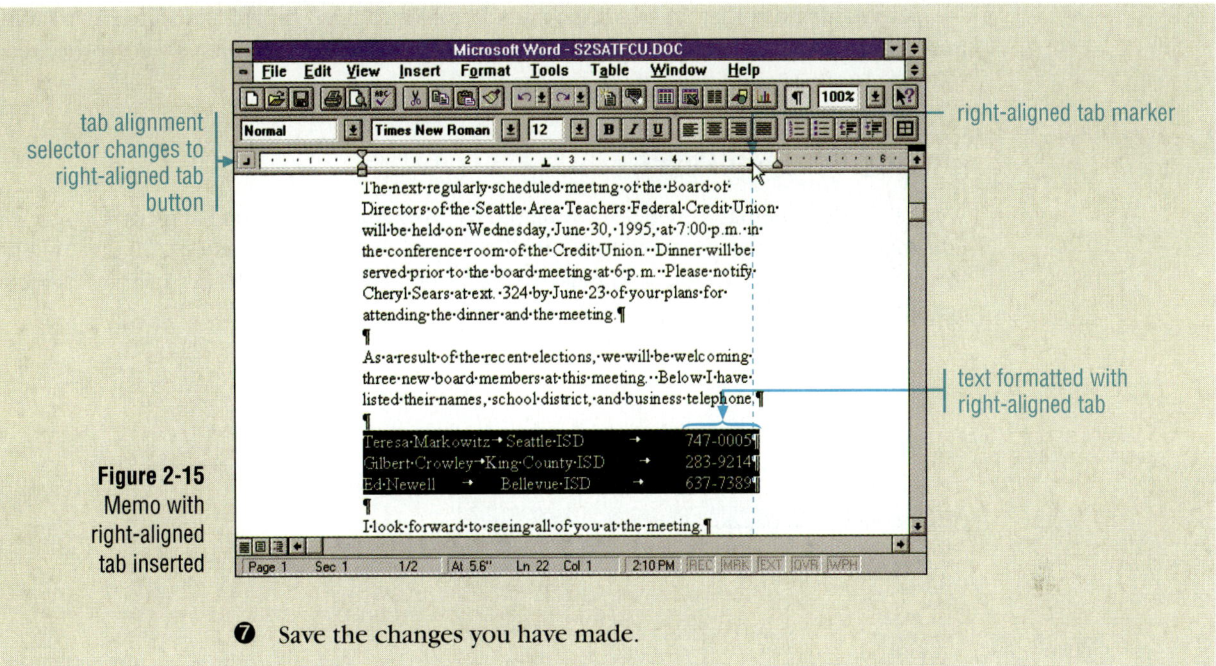

tab alignment selector changes to right-aligned tab button

right-aligned tab marker

text formatted with right-aligned tab

Figure 2-15
Memo with right-aligned tab inserted

❼   Save the changes you have made.

Marcus notices that the second column containing the names of the school districts is too close to the first column. He decides to move the second column to the right so that it looks evenly centered between the first and third columns.

Moving Tab Stops

You can adjust the location of a custom tab stop simply by dragging its marker to a new location on the ruler. Marcus will drag the right-aligned and centered tab markers to improve the format of the three columns.

To move the right-aligned and centered tab stops using the ruler:

❶   Select the information in the memo about the three new board members, if it is not already selected.

❷   Point to the right-aligned tab marker (at the 4.75-inch mark) in the ruler, then click and drag it to the 5-inch mark, on top of the right indent marker. The selected text adjusts to the new setting.

❸   Point to the centered tab marker (at the 2.75-inch mark) in the ruler, then click and drag it to the 3.25-inch mark. If necessary, continue to adjust the centered tab marker on the ruler until the items look evenly centered between the board members' names and their telephone numbers.

❹   Deselect the highlighted text.

❺   Save the changes you have made.

You can clear a custom tab stop just as easily as you can change its location. Simply point to the custom tab stop you want to remove, drag it down below the ruler, then release the mouse button.

Marcus decides that, to make the agenda easier to read, he will separate each agenda item from its presenter with a series of dots, called leader characters. To do so he needs to move to the second page of the document.

Moving Between Pages

Word's Go To command, which is available by pressing [F5] or choosing Go To from the Edit menu, allows you to move to a specified location in your document. Marcus will use the Go To command to move to page 2 so that he can insert the leader characters in the agenda items.

To move to page 2:

❶   Press **[F5]**. The Go To dialog box appears. See Figure 2-16.

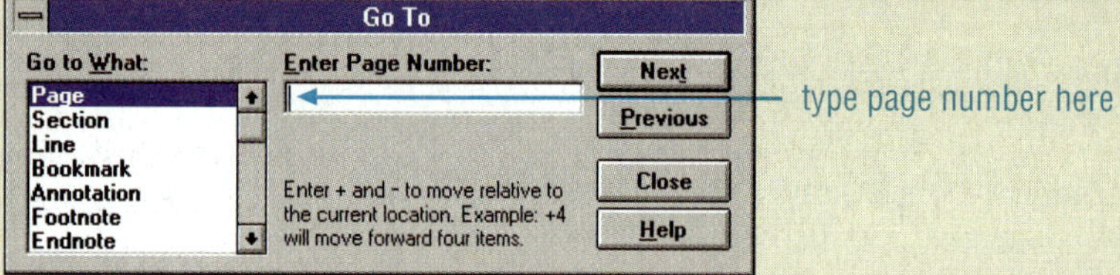

Figure 2-16
Go To dialog box

❷   In the Enter Page Number text box, type **2** then click **Go To** or press **[Enter]**. The insertion point moves to the top of page 2, and the Go To dialog box remains open on the screen.

❸   Click **Close** to close the Go To dialog box.

When formatting the rest of the document, you can use the Go To command to move between the two pages.

Now Marcus can insert the leader characters.

Inserting Leader Characters

Leader characters are repeated characters that help guide the reader's eye from one column of text formatted with tabs to another. Word provides you with three choices of leader characters: dots, dashed lines, or solid lines. The leader character you choose is inserted into the space preceding the designated tab stop.

Inserting Leader Characters

- Select the paragraph or paragraphs for which you want to set custom tab stops, or select the paragraph or paragraphs containing the existing tab stops.

- Click Format then click Tabs.... The Tabs dialog box appears.

- In the Tab Stop Position text box, type the position where you want to set the custom tab stop (if necessary).

- Select the appropriate type of tab alignment option from the Alignment section (if necessary).

- Select the appropriate type of leader character from the Leader section.

- Click Set then click OK or press [Enter].

Marcus originally entered the agenda items with a tab between the agenda item and the presenter's name. Now he will insert leader characters between the two columns. In addition, he will right-align the names of the presenters at the right indent (the 5-inch mark).

To insert leader characters in the agenda items:

❶ Select all the agenda items, beginning with Call to Order and ending with Adjournment.

❷ Click **Format** then click **Tabs...** The Tabs dialog box appears.

❸ Type **5** in the Tab Stop Position text box to set the location of the custom tab stop at the same position as the right indent.

❹ Click the **Right radio button** in the Alignment section to right-align text typed at this tab.

❺ Click the **2 radio button** (dot leaders) in the Leader section.

❻ Click **Set**. A tab is set at the position you have indicated in the Tab Stop Position text box with the options you have chosen in the Tabs dialog box. Dot leaders will be inserted in the blank space leading up to the right-aligned tab set at the 5-inch mark. See Figure 2-17.

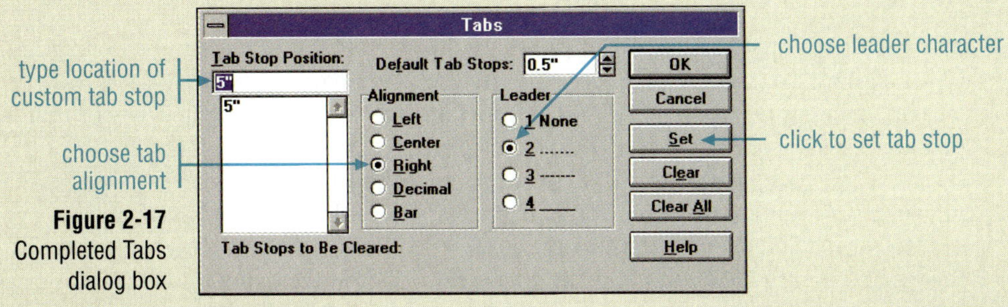

Figure 2-17
Completed Tabs dialog box

❼ Click **OK** or press **[Enter]**. A right-aligned tab marker appears in the ruler at the 5-inch mark (on top of the right indent). Dot leaders appear in the tab space leading up to the names of the presenters, and the names of the presenters are right-aligned at the 5-inch mark. All default tabs to the left of the right-aligned tab stop at the 5-inch mark are cleared (for the selected paragraphs).

❽ Deselect the highlighted text. See Figure 2-18.

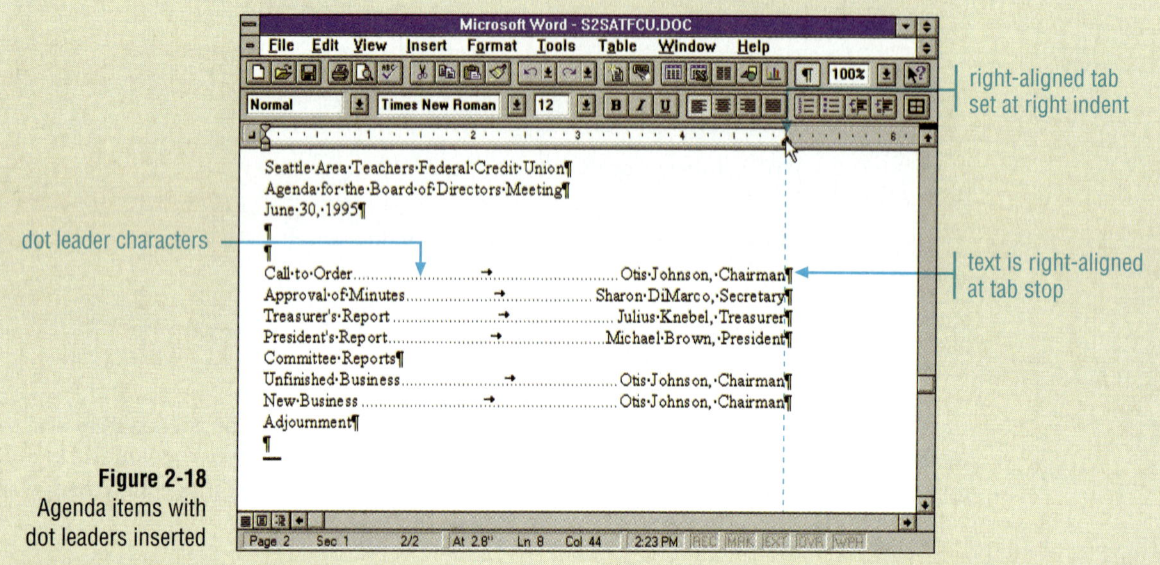

Figure 2-18
Agenda items with dot leaders inserted

Notice how the tab leaders guide the reader's eye from one column of text to the next.

❾ Save the changes you have made.

Marcus reviews the changes Michael requested (Figure 2-1) and notes that Michael wants to add three new agenda items (under Committee Reports), and he wants the list of agenda items to be numbered. However, the new items Marcus needs to insert under Committee Reports should not be numbered—only the main item (Committee Reports) should be numbered. To format the list in this way, Marcus will use Word's New Line command when entering the new agenda items.

Using the New Line Command

As you learned in Tutorial 1, Word treats any block of text that ends with a paragraph mark (¶), including a paragraph mark on a line by itself, as a paragraph. Because of the way Word formats paragraphs, treating a series of short lines as a single paragraph rather than several paragraphs is sometimes desirable. If you want to start a new *line*, but you do not want to start a new *paragraph*, use the **New Line command**, [Shift][Enter]. Word will insert a new line mark (↵) on the screen to indicate the use of the New Line command.

To format the agenda items in the numbered list as Michael requested, Marcus needs the line Committee Reports and the three new committee agenda items to be treated as *one paragraph* rather than as four short paragraphs. Therefore, when he types the new agenda items, Marcus must end all but the last item (Supervisory Committee) with a new line mark (↵).

To enter the new agenda items with new line marks:

❶ Place the insertion point after the "s" in the agenda item Committee Reports and before the paragraph mark.

❷ Press **[Shift][Enter]**. A new line mark (↵) is inserted after Committee Reports and Unfinished Business is forced to the next line.

> **TROUBLE?** If you inserted a paragraph mark instead of a new line mark, you did not hold down [Shift] while you pressed [Enter]. Press [Backspace] to delete the paragraph mark, then repeat Step 2.

Now let's enter the three new individual committee report items Michael wants inserted. You will separate the committee name from the presenter's name with a tab. When you do, the dot leaders will automatically be inserted because the Committee Reports paragraph mark stores the leader characters as part of its format.

❸ Type **Building Maintenance Committee** then press **[Tab]**. Pressing [Tab] inserts a tab character (→) and moves the insertion point to the next tab stop. The dot leaders are also inserted.

❹ Type **Joan Nunez** then press **[Shift][Enter]**.

❺ Type **Financial Services Committee** then press **[Tab]**.

❻ Type **Mai Nguyen** then press **[Shift][Enter]**.

❼ Type **Supervisory Committee** then press **[Tab]**.

❽ Type **Stephen Lesikar**. *Do not press [Enter]* because there is a paragraph mark already following Stephen Lesikar, signifying the end of the paragraph. The paragraph consists of the text "Committee Reports" through "Stephen Lesikar," even though the text appears on different lines. See Figure 2-19.

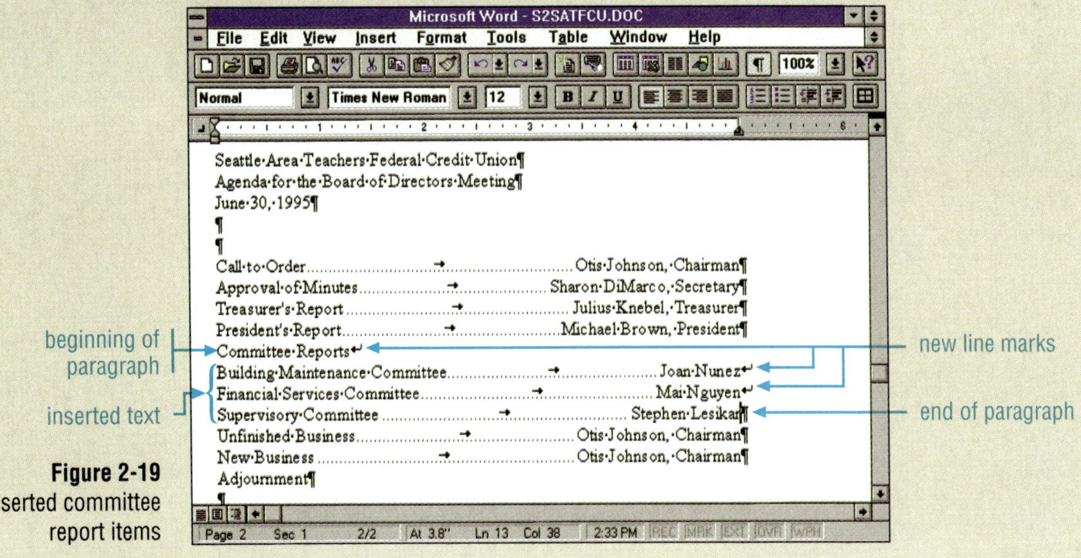

Figure 2-19
Inserted committee report items

Now Marcus can number the agenda items, as Michael requested, so that the order of presentation in the meeting is clear.

Numbering Paragraphs

Adding numbers to a group of paragraphs is another paragraph formatting option that might make your document easier to understand. To create a numbered list of paragraphs, you select the paragraphs you want to number and then click the Numbering button on the Formatting toolbar. Although you can use the Numbering button to apply or remove this option to selected paragraphs, you must choose Bullets and Numbering from the Format menu to reformat the numbers.

Marcus will use the Numbering button to number the agenda items.

To add numbers to the list of agenda items:

❶ Select all the agenda items, from Call to Order through Adjournment.

❷ Click the **Numbering button** on the Formatting toolbar. Each paragraph in the selected text is numbered consecutively.

❸ Click within the numbered list to deselect the highlighted text. Notice the indent markers in the ruler for the numbered paragraphs. See Figure 2-20.

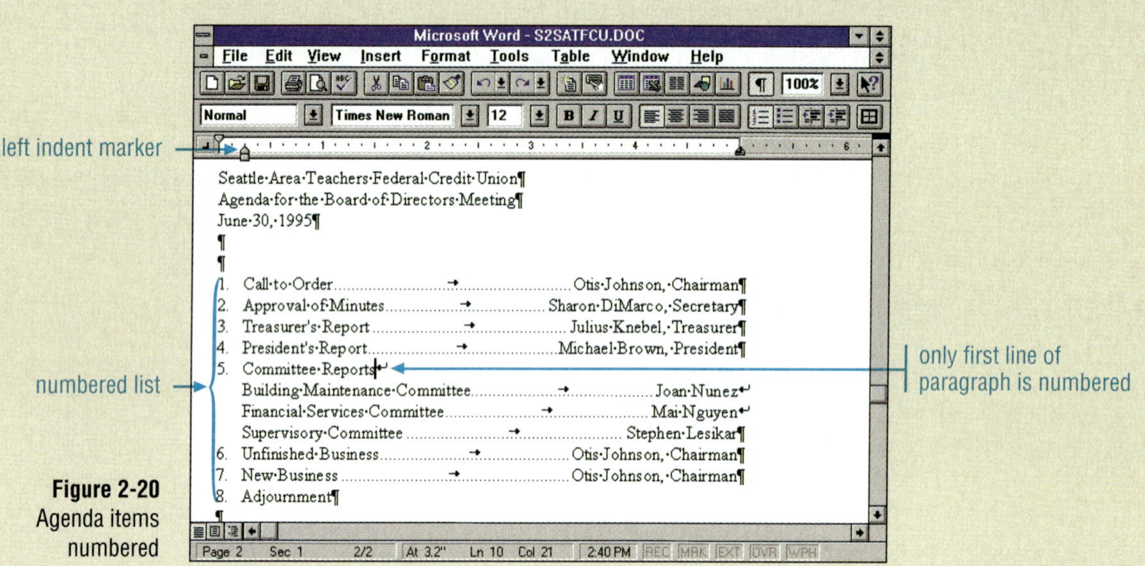

Figure 2-20
Agenda items numbered

Using the Numbering button formats the paragraphs as hanging indents, with the first-line indent marker at the left margin and the left indent marker at the 0.25-inch mark. For example, look at agenda item 5, Committee Reports. Notice that the individual committee report items were not numbered because Word did not consider them separate paragraphs, but they were indented because a hanging indent causes all lines of a paragraph except the first line to be indented.

Marcus wants the agenda items to start at the 0.5-inch mark instead of the 0.25-inch mark. Because of the change to the left indent, the agenda items moved to the point of the indent at the 0.25-inch mark instead of to the first default tab stop at the 0.5-inch mark. Marcus must adjust the amount of the hanging indent for the numbered agenda items.

To adjust the hanging indent for the numbered list:

❶   Select all the agenda items again.

❷   Click **Format** then click **Bullets and Numbering….** The Bullets and Numbering dialog box appears. Notice that the Numbered tab is selected.

Marcus needs to modify the numbering options.

❸   Click **Modify….** The Modify Numbered List dialog box appears.

❹   In the Number Position section, click the **Distance from Indent to Text up arrow** until it reads 0.5". See Figure 2-21. The Preview section changes to reflect the change in the value for the hanging indent.

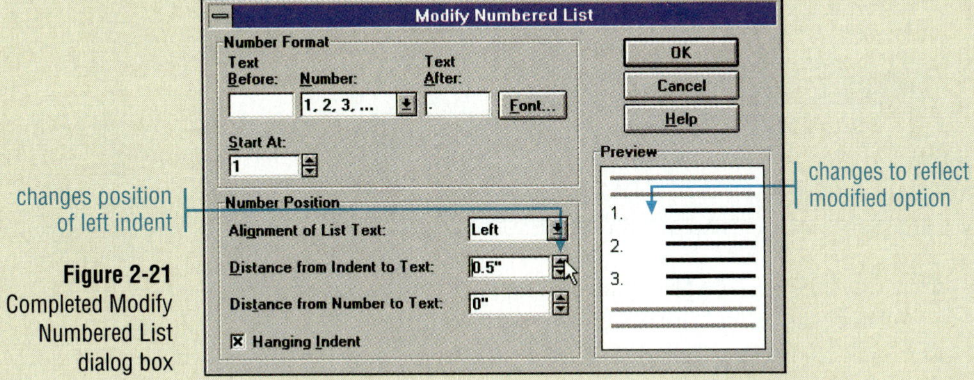

Figure 2-21
Completed Modify Numbered List dialog box

❺   Click **OK** or press **[Enter].** The amount of the left indent is changed, and the agenda items start at the 0.5-inch mark on the ruler.

❻   Deselect the highlighted text.

❼   Save the changes you have made.

Viewing the numbered list, Marcus decides that it would look better if he added more space between the lines of text in the list. This will help to distinguish the items from each other.

Adjusting Line Spacing

The default line spacing in Word documents is single spacing. Sometimes, however, you might want to use 1.5 spacing or double spacing. Because these options do not appear on the Formatting toolbar, the quickest way to apply line spacing options is through shortcut key combinations. The shortcut key combination for single spacing is [Ctrl][1]; for 1.5 spacing, [Ctrl][5]; and for double spacing, [Ctrl][2]. Other line spacing options are available when you choose Paragraph from the Format menu. Changes in line spacing affect only the selected paragraph or paragraphs.

Marcus wants to double space the agenda items to make them stand out more. He'll use the Paragraph command on the Format menu to do so.

To double space the agenda items using the Paragraph command:

❶ Select all the agenda items from Call to Order through Adjournment.

❷ Click **Format** then click **Paragraph...** to display the Paragraph dialog box.

❸ Click the **Line Spacing list box down arrow**. The list of line spacing options appears. See Figure 2-22.

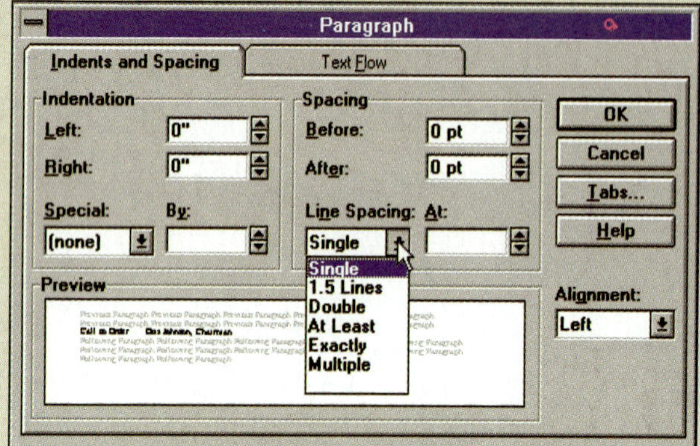

Figure 2-22
Line spacing
options on Indents
and Spacing tab

❹ Click **Double** in the list of line spacing options. Notice that the Preview section changes to reflect the new line spacing setting.

❺ Click **OK** or press [Enter]. The agenda items are now double-spaced.

❻ Deselect the highlighted text.

Marcus also decides to double space the memo headings on the first page, to make them stand out more. This time, he'll use the shortcut key combination.

To double space the memo headings using the shortcut key combination:

❶ Place the insertion point at the top of page 1.

❷ Select the four lines of the memo headings (TO:, FROM:, RE:, DATE:).

❸ Press [Ctrl][2]. Notice that only the selected area is affected by the paragraph format change to double spacing.

❹ Deselect the highlighted text.

❺ Save the changes you have made.

Next, Marcus wants to change how text aligns in some of the paragraphs in his document.

Aligning Paragraphs

Paragraph alignment involves specifying how you want the text within a paragraph to align horizontally in relation to its left and right *indents*. Remember, initially the left and right indents are located at the same point as the left and right *margins*. With **left alignment**, the paragraph text is set even with the left indent and ragged at the right; with **centered alignment**, the paragraph text is positioned evenly between the left and right indents; with **right alignment**, the lines of text within a paragraph are set even at the right indent and ragged at the left; and with **justified alignment**, the paragraph text at both the left and right indents is even. Left alignment is the default alignment setting.

Buttons for each of these alignment options appear on the Formatting toolbar. Alternatively, you can apply the different alignment options by using shortcut key combinations: [Ctrl][l] for left alignment, [Ctrl][e] for centered alignment, [Ctrl][r] for right alignment, or [Ctrl][j] for justified alignment. You can also choose the Paragraph command from the Format menu and then select the appropriate alignment option from the Paragraph dialog box.

Marcus wants to apply centered alignment to the memo title Memorandum and to the three-line agenda title, because titles are often centered on the page so that they stand out. He also wants to justify the text in the body of the memo, for a more formal appearance.

To apply centered alignment to the memo title:
❶ Place the insertion point anywhere within the paragraph, Memorandum. Remember that because of the way Word defines a paragraph, you merely position the insertion point anywhere within the paragraph to select it and Word will apply any paragraph formatting changes to the entire paragraph.
❷ Click the **Center button** ≡ on the Formatting toolbar. The text is centered between the left and right indents, and the Center button appears lighter to indicate that it is activated for the selected text. See Figure 2-23.

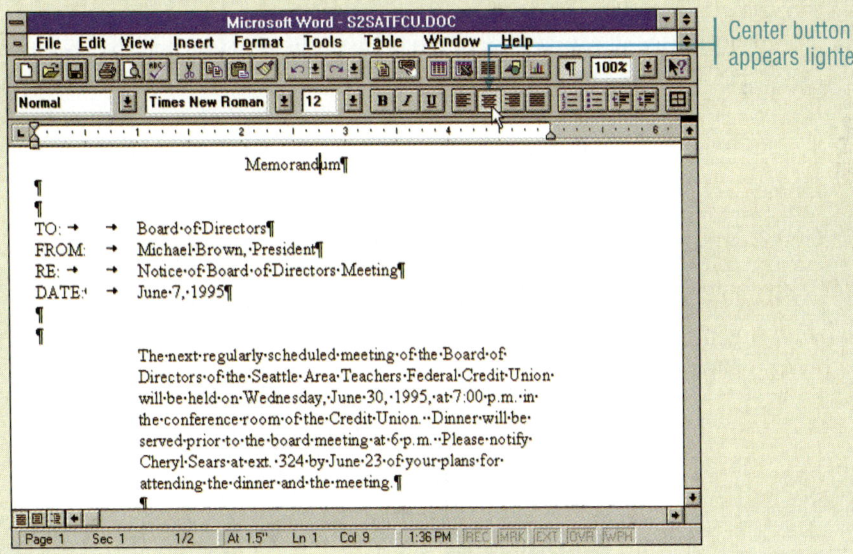

Figure 2-23
"Memorandum"
centered

Now Marcus needs to center the three lines of the agenda title. Because each line of the agenda title is a separate paragraph, he must first select all three paragraphs.

To apply centered alignment to the paragraphs of the agenda title:
❶ Move to page 2.
❷ Use the selection bar to select the three lines of the agenda title.

❸ Press **[Ctrl][e]**, the shortcut key combination for centered alignment. Notice that
the Center button on the Formatting toolbar appears lighter, and the three paragraphs that you selected are centered.

❹ Deselect the highlighted text. See Figure 2-24.

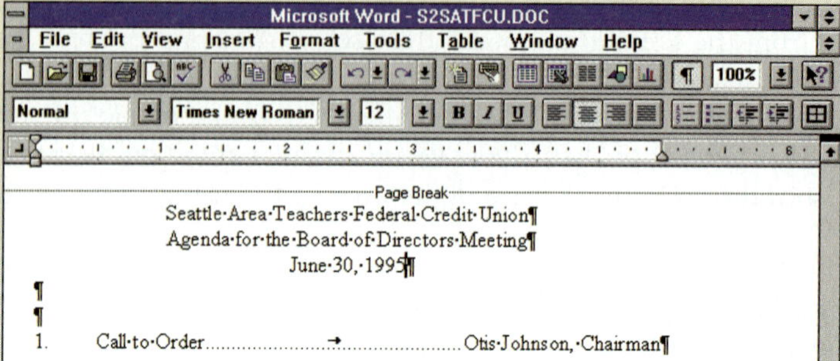

Figure 2-24
Agenda title
lines centered

Next Marcus decides to justify all paragraphs in the body of the memo to give the
memo a more formal appearance. He decides to use the shortcut editing and formatting
menu to do so.

To justify all paragraphs in the body of the memo using the shortcut menu:

❶ Move to page 1, then use the selection bar to select all the paragraphs in the body
of the memo from "The next regularly scheduled..." through "...at the meeting."

❷ Click the **right mouse button**. The shortcut editing and formatting menu appears. See
Figure 2-25.

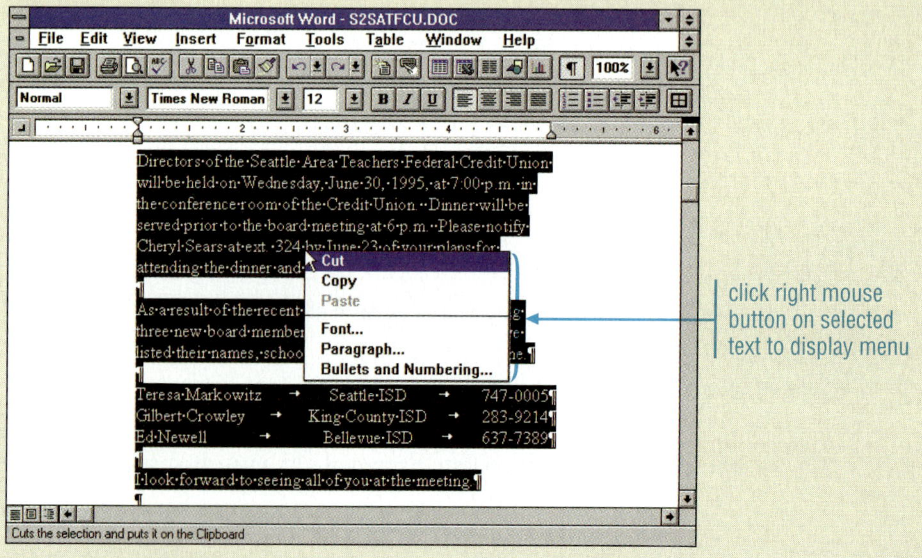

Figure 2-25
Shortcut editing and
formatting menu

❸ Click **Paragraph…**. The Paragraph dialog box appears.

❹ Click the **Indents and Spacing tab**, if necessary. Notice that the Alignment section on the right side of the dialog box currently shows "Left" as the alignment.

❺ Click the **Alignment list box down arrow**. The list of alignment options appears.

❻ Click **Justified**. The Preview section changes to reflect the new alignment option.

❼ Click **OK** or press **[Enter]**.

❽ Deselect the highlighted text.

❾ Scroll through the memo to see the effect of justifying the body of the memo. Notice that only those lines that take up a full line of typing are affected by justification.

❿ Save the changes you have made.

Marcus is pleased with how the agenda looks, but he wants to emphasize its three-line title by putting a border around it. He also wants to separate the memo headings from the memo text by inserting a rule from the left margin to the right margin.

Creating Paragraph Borders and Rules

Applying borders and rules to paragraphs is another paragraph formatting technique. A **border** is a box that you use to frame text or graphics. A **rule** is a horizontal or vertical line that you use to enhance the appearance of your document. You can add borders and rules using either the Borders and Shading command on the Format menu or the Borders toolbar.

Marcus decides to put a shadow border, also called a drop shadow, around the three-line title of the agenda. Remember that each line of the title is actually a paragraph.

To create a border around the agenda title lines:

❶ Move to page 2.

❷ Select the three lines of the agenda title from "Seattle Area..." through "...1995."

❸ Click **Format** then click **Borders and Shading...**. The Paragraph Borders and Shading dialog box appears.

❹ Click the **Borders tab**, if necessary. The Border section allows you to preview changes you make.

❺ Click the **Shadow icon** in the Presets section. Notice the change in the Border section.

Next Marcus needs to decide on the thickness of the line style. The choices are given in point sizes, with 1 point equal to $1/72$".

❻ In the Line section, under Style, click **¾ pt** (if it's not already selected). Figure 2-26 shows the completed Paragraph Borders and Shading dialog box.

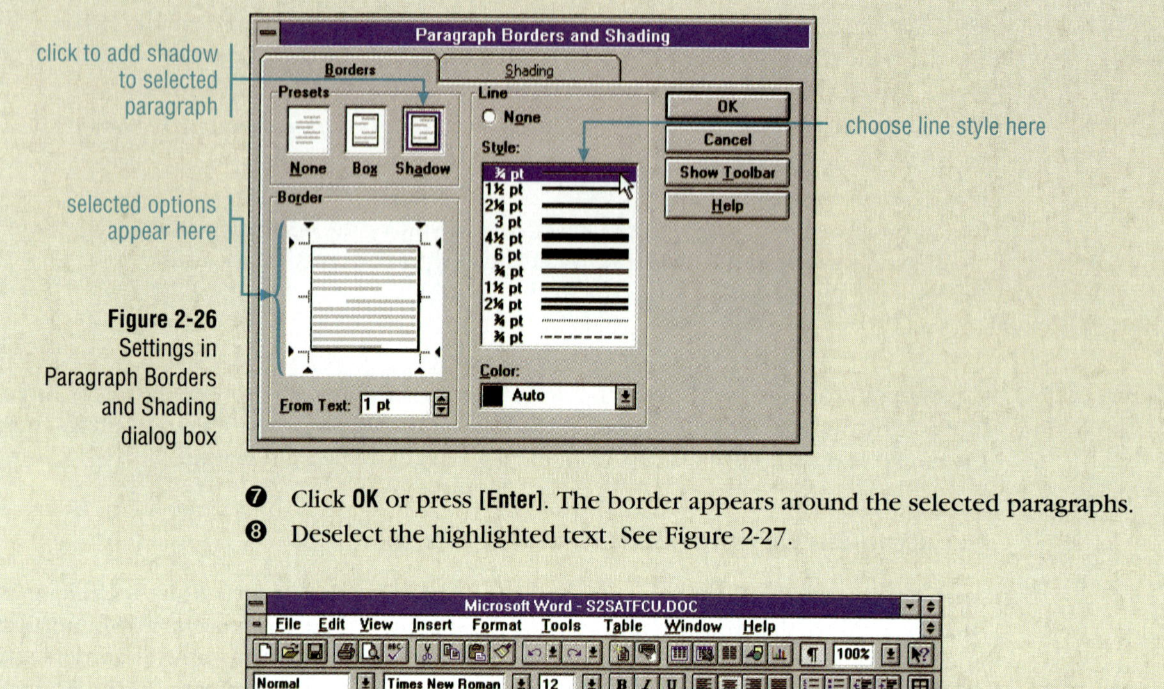

Figure 2-26
Settings in Paragraph Borders and Shading dialog box

❼   Click **OK** or press **[Enter]**. The border appears around the selected paragraphs.
❽   Deselect the highlighted text. See Figure 2-27.

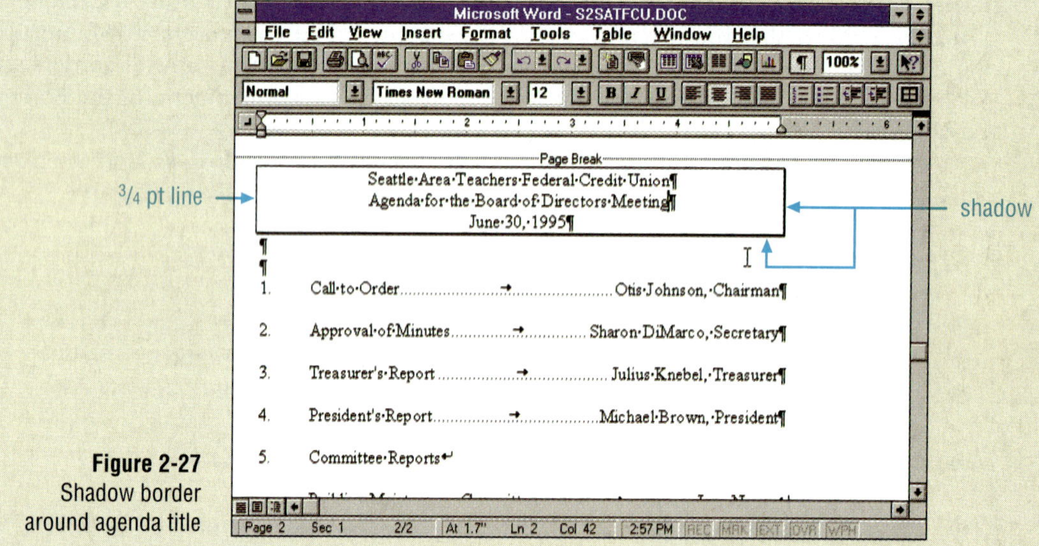

Figure 2-27
Shadow border around agenda title

Marcus follows basically the same procedure to add a rule between the date line in the memo headings and the body of the memo, except this time he'll use the Borders toolbar.

To insert a rule below the memo headings:
❶   Move to page 1.
❷   Place the insertion point in front of the first paragraph mark below the date of the memo. Even though this line has no text on it, Word considers it a paragraph.
❸   Click the **Borders button** 🔲 on the Formatting toolbar. The Borders toolbar appears. See Figure 2-28.

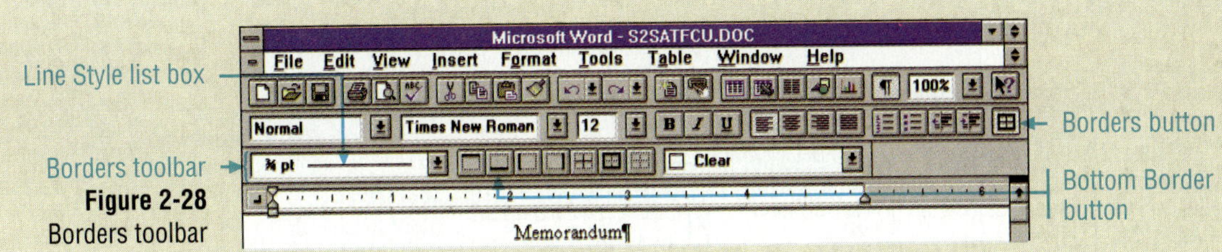

Marcus wants the rule to be heavier (thicker) than a typical underline, and he wants the rule to go along the bottom of the line space.

❹   Click the **Line Style list box down arrow** on the Borders toolbar, then click **1½ pt**.

❺   Click the **Bottom Border button** ⬜ on the Borders toolbar. The rule is inserted into the memorandum.

Marcus no longer needs the Borders toolbar.

❻   Click ⊞ on the Formatting toolbar. The Borders toolbar is dismissed.

❼   Save the changes you have made.

To remove a border or rule, select the paragraph or paragraphs to be changed. Choose Borders and Shading from the Format menu, then click the None radio button in the Line section of the Paragraph Borders and Shading dialog box. You can also click the No Border button on the Borders toolbar to remove a border or rule from a selected paragraph.

Marcus has now completed the paragraph formatting phase for his document.

If you want to take a break and resume the tutorial at a later time, you can close the current document then exit Word by double-clicking the Control menu box in the upper-left corner of the screen. When you want to resume the tutorial, start Word, place your Student Disk in the disk drive, then complete the screen check procedure described in Tutorial 1. Open the file S2SATFCU.DOC, press [Shift][F5], Word's Go Back command, to return to your last point in the document, then continue with the tutorial.

Next, Marcus begins the final stage of formatting: font-level formatting.

Font Formatting

A **font** is the general shape of the characters in your document. A **character** is any letter, number, punctuation mark, or symbol that you enter in your document. Font formatting involves choices about how the individual characters in your document appear on the screen and in print. These different choices are known as **character attributes**. Font formatting changes are made through the Formatting toolbar or the Font command on the Format menu. You can change the font type, the size of the characters, the style of the characters, the space between characters, the vertical position of characters, and even the color of the characters. In Tutorial 1 you learned how to change the type style of characters using the Bold, Italic, and Underline buttons on the Formatting toolbar. In this tutorial you will also use the Formatting toolbar and the Font command to make font-level formatting changes.

The available choices of fonts are listed in the Font list box. A partial listing of the available fonts is shown in Figure 2-29.

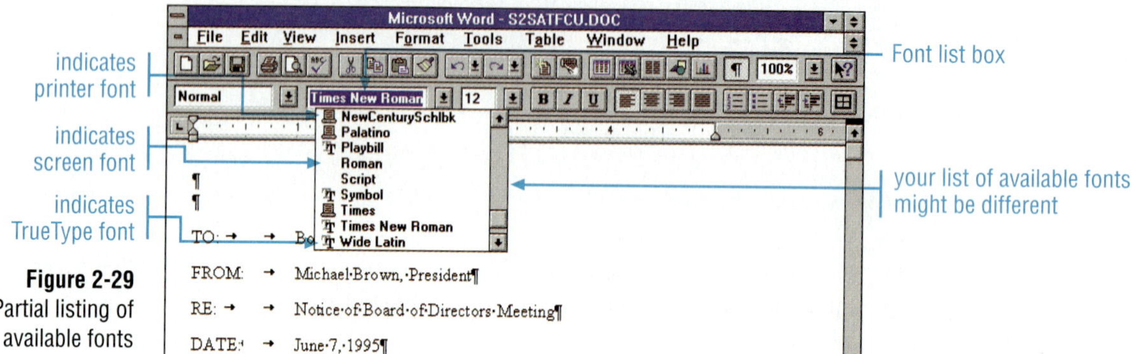

Figure 2-29
Partial listing of
available fonts

The fonts with a printer icon in front of them represent **printer fonts**—that is, fonts that are built into your selected printer. These printer fonts are limited, however, to just those sizes your printer is capable of producing. The fonts in the list with no icon beside them are **screen fonts** only; if you choose a screen font, the way your document appears on your screen might be different from the way it looks when it is printed. The fonts in the list with double "Ts" in front of them are TrueType fonts, a special type of font that is available only in Windows 3.1. **TrueType fonts** work with every printer, including dot matrix printers, and any size can be specified. Word provides you with several TrueType fonts. Figure 2-30 illustrates each TrueType font available in Word. Although all these different fonts are available to you, you should limit to two or three the number of different fonts you use in any one document.

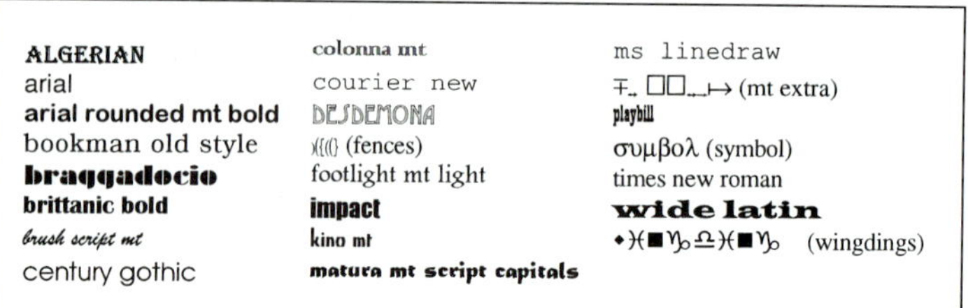

Figure 2-30
Example of
TrueType fonts
available in Word

The size of a font is measured in **points**; there are 72 points in an inch. The larger the point size of a font, the larger the font will be displayed and printed. The Font Size list box shows the sizes available for the font you have selected. Available point sizes vary depending on the font selected. The basic TrueType fonts are available, however, in sizes ranging from 4 points to 127 points. Figure 2-31 illustrates various font sizes.

This is Arial 12 point

This is Arial 24 point

This is Arial 36 point

Figure 2-31
Various font sizes

Another character attribute that you can change is type style. You have already used the bold, italic, and underline type styles, but Word provides other effects in the Font dialog box, such as strikethrough, all caps, small caps, and color (if you print on a color printer). The Character Spacing tab also provides you with the option to decrease or increase the space between characters and create superscript or subscript characters.

Marcus wants to change several character attributes of the memo title, Memorandum.

Changing Several Character Attributes at Once

Marcus wants to make the title Memorandum stand out from the rest of the memo text. He decides to change the font type of the memo title to the TrueType font Arial, make its size 14 point, make its font style bold and all caps, and expand the amount of space between each character. He decides to use the Font dialog box to change all these character attributes at once.

To change the character attributes at one time:

❶ Select the memo heading **Memorandum**. Because you are now changing font formats, you must select all the characters you want to change; you cannot simply click the insertion point in the paragraph.

❷ Click **Format** then click **Font...**. The Font dialog box appears.

The Font list box displays the available font types in alphabetical order.

❸ Scroll up the list of fonts, then click **Arial**. Notice that the Preview section changes to reflect the new font choice.

TROUBLE? If you cannot locate Arial at the top of your font list, then perhaps your system is using a previous version of Windows. Ask your instructor or technical support person which font to use instead of Arial.

❹ Click **Bold** in the Font Style list box. The Preview section changes to reflect the new type style choice.

❺ Click **14** in the Size list box. The Preview section changes to reflect the new point size.

❻ Click the **All Caps check box** in the Effects section. Figure 2-32 shows the completed settings on the Font tab of the Font dialog box.

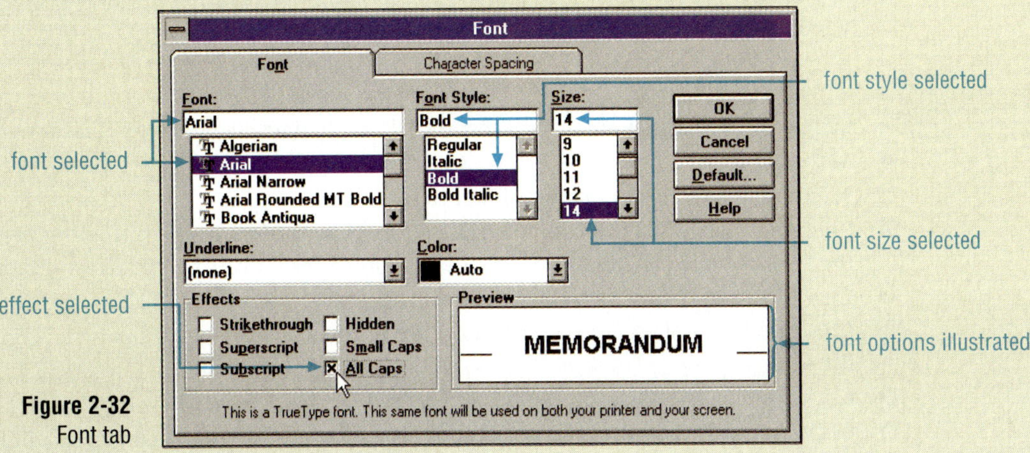

Figure 2-32
Font tab

Next, Marcus wants to increase the spacing between characters, so he needs to move to the Character Spacing tab of the Font dialog box.

❼   Click the **Character Spacing tab**, then click the **Spacing list box down arrow** to display the available spacing options.

❽   Click **Expanded**. An additional 1 point of space will be inserted between each character of the selected text. See Figure 2-33.

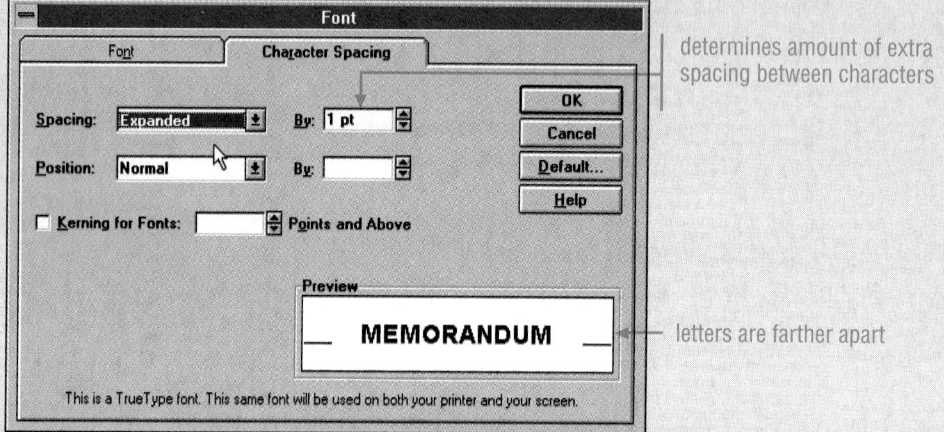

Figure 2-33
Character
Spacing tab

❾   Click **OK** or press **[Enter]**. All the character attribute changes you made are applied to the title Memorandum.

❿   Deselect the highlighted text, then save the changes you have made.

Next, Marcus wants to change the agenda's title to make it stand out more from the list of agenda items.

Changing Font and Point Size Using the Formatting Toolbar

Marcus decides to change the font and enlarge the type size of the agenda's title lines. He decides to change the font to Arial and the point size to 14 using the Formatting toolbar. He also wants to bold the title lines.

To change the font and point size of the agenda's title lines using the Formatting toolbar:

❶   Move to page 2.

❷   Select the three lines of the agenda title.

❸   Click the **Font list box down arrow** on the Formatting toolbar to open the font list. At the top of the list, Word keeps track of the fonts used most recently in a document.

❹   Click the **Arial**. The selected text changes to reflect the new font choice.

❺   Click the **Font Size list box down arrow** on the Formatting toolbar to open the Font Size list.

❻   Click **14**. The selected text changes to reflect the new point size choice.

❼   Click the **Bold button** B . The selected text changes to reflect the new type style choice.

❽ Deselect the highlighted text. See Figure 2-34.

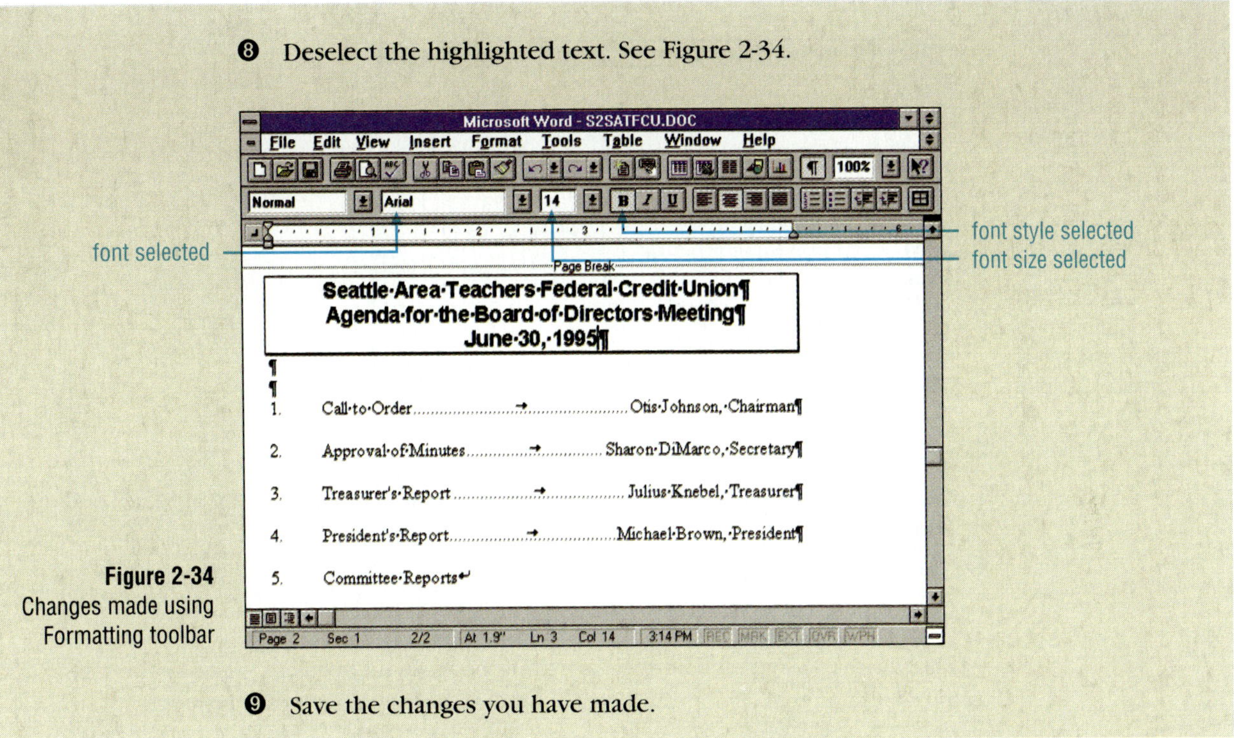

Figure 2-34
Changes made using
Formatting toolbar

❾ Save the changes you have made.

Marcus decides to insert the tilde (~) above the second "n" in Nuñez, the last name of one of the presenters on the agenda.

Inserting Special Symbols

Word provides an easy way to insert special symbols called **character sets** in your documents. The character sets available depend on the selected printer; you choose them using the Symbol command on the Insert menu. Each character set has a variety of available characters or symbols. Once you have selected a character, it is placed in your document at the insertion point. To delete an inserted symbol, you must first select it and then press [Del].

The (normal text) character set contains the symbol with the tilde above the letter "n," which is the symbol Marcus wants to insert in this document.

To insert the tilde above the "n" in Nunez:
❶ Move the insertion point to page 2, if necessary.
❷ Select the second "n" in Nunez, the last name of the presenter for the Building Maintenance Committee report. Only the "n" should be highlighted.
❸ Click **Insert** then click **Symbol…** The Symbol dialog box appears and the Symbols tab is selected.
❹ Click the **Font list box down arrow** to display the available character sets. Scroll up, then click **(normal text)** at the top of the list. The (normal text) character set is displayed.
❺ Click the **ñ symbol** to select it. (You will find it in the last row.) The symbol "ñ" now appears much bigger. See Figure 2-35.

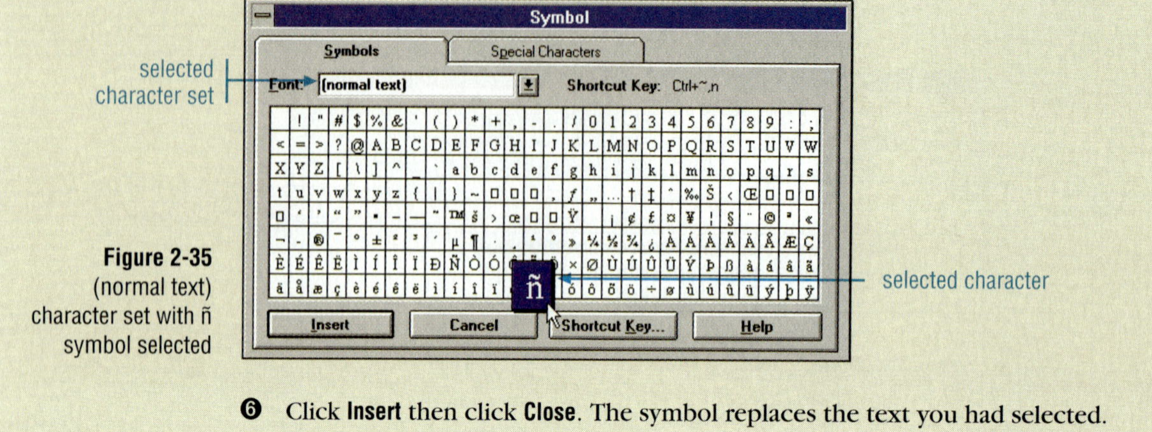

Figure 2-35
(normal text)
character set with ñ
symbol selected

❻ Click **Insert** then click **Close**. The symbol replaces the text you had selected.

   TROUBLE? If the letter didn't change, perhaps you did not select the "n" in Nunez prior to opening the (normal text) character set. Start again with Step 2.

❼ Save the changes you have made.

Marcus has completed all the formatting changes he needs to make to the memo and agenda. He is now ready to print his document—the final stage of the productivity strategy.

Previewing and Printing Multiple Pages

Now you are ready to print a copy of Marcus's memo and agenda. Before you do, you'll first spell check the document and correct any errors. Then, you'll view the document in print preview to see how it will look when printed. One of the options in print preview, Multiple Pages, allows you to view several pages of your document side by side.

To spell check the document:
❶ Press **[Ctrl][Home]** to move to the beginning of the document.
❷ Click the **Spelling button** on the Standard toolbar (or click **Tools** then click **Spelling…**). Follow the procedures described in Tutorial 1 for performing a spell check.
❸ Save your changes if necessary.

Now you can preview and print the document.

To preview both pages at the same time, then print the document:
❶ Click the **Print Preview button** on the Standard toolbar (or click **File** then click **Print Preview**).

   TROUBLE? If two pages are already displayed in print preview, skip to Step 4.

❷ Click the **Multiple Pages button** on the Print Preview toolbar.

❸ Drag the mouse pointer across two of the page icons to indicate that you want to view two pages side by side, then release the mouse button. Both pages of your document appear in the Preview window. See Figure 2-36.

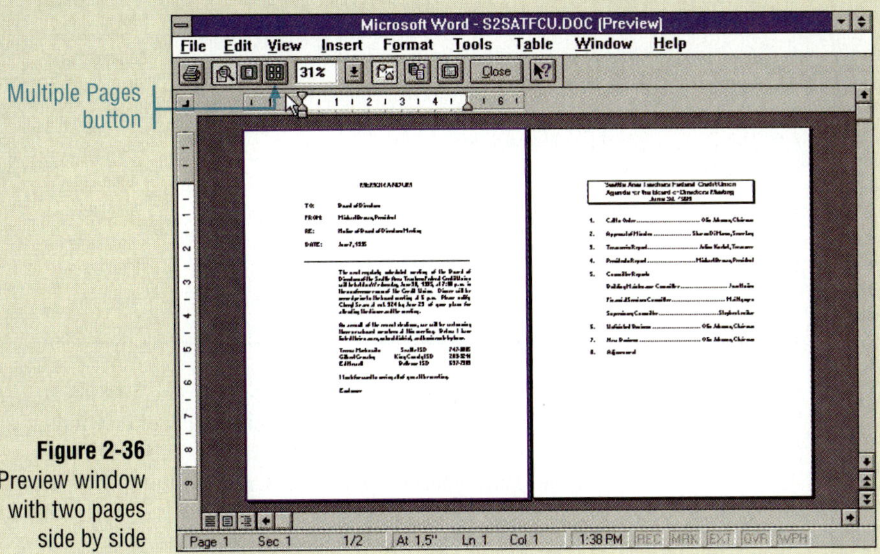

Figure 2-36
Preview window
with two pages
side by side

❹ Click the **Print button** on the Print Preview toolbar if you are satisfied with the appearance of your document. Otherwise, click **Close**, return to your document to make changes, then repeat Steps 1 through 4. Your final document should look like Figure 2-37.

❺ Click the **Close button** on the Print Preview toolbar to return to your document.

❻ Close the document and exit Word.

MEMORANDUM

TO: Board of Directors

FROM: Michael Brown, President

RE: Notice of Board of Directors Meeting

DATE: June 7, 1995

The next regularly scheduled meeting of the Board of Directors of the Seattle Area Teachers Federal Credit Union will be held on Wednesday, June 30, 1995, at 7:00 p.m. in the conference room of the Credit Union. Dinner will be served prior to the board meeting at 6 p.m. Please notify Cheryl Sears at ext. 324 by June 23 of your plans for attending the dinner and the meeting.

As a result of the recent elections, we will be welcoming three new board members at this meeting. Below I have listed their names, school district, and business telephone.

Teresa Markowitz	Seattle ISD	747-0005
Gilbert Crowley	King County ISD	283-9214
Ed Newell	Bellevue ISD	637-7389

I look forward to seeing all of you at the meeting.

Enclosure

Figure 2-37
Marcus's final document
(page 1 of 2)

**Seattle Area Teachers Federal Credit Union
Agenda for the Board of Directors Meeting
June 30, 1995**

1.   Call to Order .... Otis Johnson, Chairman

2.   Approval of Minutes............................ Sharon DiMarco, Secretary

3.   Treasurer's Report.................................... Julius Knebel, Treasurer

4.   President's Report....................................Michael Brown, President

5.   Committee Reports

       Building Maintenance Committee ....Joan Nuñez

       Financial Services Committee ....Mai Nguyen

       Supervisory Committee .... Stephen Lesikar

6.   Unfinished Business.................................... Otis Johnson, Chairman

7.   New Business... Otis Johnson, Chairman

8.   Adjournment

Figure 2-37
Marcus's final
document
(page 2 of 2)

Marcus is pleased with his final document. He gives it to Michael for distribution to the board members.

Questions

1. Explain the purpose of Word's drag-and-drop feature. What is another way to accomplish the same purpose?
2. Explain the uses of a new line mark.
3. What command do you choose to rename an existing file?
4. Explain the differences among page setup, paragraph formatting, and font formatting.
5. What would the length of your typing line be if you changed your left and right margins both to 1 inch?
6. Explain the difference between a soft page break and a hard page break.
7. What different methods can you use to move quickly between pages in a document?
8. What is the difference between portrait page orientation and landscape page orientation? What command do you choose to change page orientation?
9. What are Word's four types of indent formats? How do you create them using the indent markers on the ruler?
10. Describe the effect of the following paragraph alignment options:
    a. Left
    b. Centered
    c. Right
    d. Justified
11. What are the shortcut keyboard combinations for the following line spacing options?
    a. Single spacing
    b. 1.5 spacing
    c. Double spacing
12. Explain the difference between an indent and a tab.
13. What are the four types of tab alignments? How do you set tabs using the ruler?
14. What is the difference between paragraph alignment and tab alignment?
15. What are the three types of leader characters? How do you set leader characters?
16. What is the difference between a border and a rule? How do you create a border around a paragraph?
17. Describe the different types of character attributes.
18. If you wanted to print a word so that it appeared 1.5 inches high, what point size would you apply to the selected word?
19. What are the advantages of using TrueType fonts rather than printer fonts?
20. What is a character set?

Use Word Help to find the answers to the following questions:

E 21. What is the keyboard equivalent command to indent all lines of a paragraph to the next tab stop?

E 22. How do you remove the numbers from a numbered list of items?

E 23. How do you change the number format of a numbered list of items?

E 24. What is the keyboard equivalent command to remove all font formatting from selected text?

E 25. What is the procedure for inserting a vertical bar between tabbed columns of information?

Tutorial Assignments

Start Word, if necessary, and conduct a screen check. Open T2SATMIN.DOC from your Student Disk, then complete the following:

1. On the line after the Attendance section heading, type the names given below of the members in attendance. Press [Tab] once after the name in the first column, then type the name in the second column.

   Joan Nuñez   Michael Brown
   Gilbert Crowley   Sharon DiMarco
   Otis Johnson   Julius Knebel
   Stephen Lesikar   Teresa Markowitz
   Ed Newell   Mai Nguyen

2. Insert new line marks so that the Committee Reports section (from Committee Reports through the Supervisory Committee) is all one paragraph.
3. Move the President's report after the Treasurer's report.
4. Change the top margin to 1.5 inches and the side margins to 1 inch.
5. Center the three-line heading.
6. Indent the names of the members in attendance 1 inch from the left margin.
7. Insert a left-aligned tab so that the second column of the members in attendance starts at the 3.5-inch mark on the ruler.
8. Number the paragraphs of the body of the minutes.
9. Right-align the closing lines (Respectfully submitted through Board of Directors).
10. Change the three-line heading to 14 point, Century Gothic, bold.
11. Bold each of the section headings (Attendance, Treasurer's Report, etc.) and italicize the headings for each of the committee reports.
12. Save the document as S2SATMIN.DOC.
13. Spell check, preview, then print the document.

E 14. Number the paragraphs of the body of the minutes using roman numeral format.
15. Change the amount of the hanging indent for the numbered list to 0.5 inch.
16. Save the document as S2MIN2.DOC.
17. Preview then print the document.
18. Close the document.

Case Problems

1. The Cost of Administrative Services at Tyler Fasteners

Marjorie Rominofski is the administrative services manager for Tyler Fasteners, which manufactures a variety of fasteners for the construction industry. One of her responsibilities each month is to write a memo to the department heads in the plant. In this memo she informs the department heads about the cost of administrative services charged to each department's budget. You will format Marjorie's memo.

Open P2ADMSER.DOC from your Student Disk, then complete the following:

1. Insert the title Memorandum at the top of the document, then press [Enter] twice.
2. Align the information after the memo headings (TO:, FROM:, and so on) at the 1-inch mark.
3. Change the top margin to 2 inches and the left and right margins to 1.75 inches.
4. Double space the memo headings.
5. Move the sentence beginning "These amounts . . ." and the two spaces after it to the beginning of the last paragraph ("If you have . . .").
6. Center the title Memorandum.
7. Insert a 1½ point, double line border around Memorandum.

8. Indent the three expenditure lines (Photocopies, and so on) to the 1-inch mark.
9. Align the decimal for the amounts in the expenditure lines at the 4-inch mark.
10. Change Memorandum to 18-point Bookman Old Style, bold, and all caps.
11. Save the document as S2ADMSER.DOC.
12. Spell check, preview, then print the document.
13. Change the left and right margins to 1.25 inches and move the tab for the expenditures from the 4-inch mark to the 4.5-inch mark.

E 14. Remove the border from the title Memorandum.

E 15. Change the font to Arial for all the text except the title.
16. Save the document as S2TYLER.DOC.
17. Preview then print the document.
18. Dismiss the Borders toolbar, if necessary, and close the document.

2. Total Quality Management at English Engineering, Inc.

Janetta Coleman is the manager of the Human Resources Development Department for English Engineering, Inc., an aeronautical engineering systems firm in Huntsville, Alabama. As part of the team of contractors responsible for the life-support system on board the space shuttle, English is participating in the total quality management program mandated by the federal government of all space shuttle contractors. At a recent retreat, Janetta's staff developed its vision statement. Janetta created and edited a simple flyer that will serve as a reminder to her staff of their vision for the direction of the department. Now she needs to format and print it.

Open P2VISION.DOC from your Student Disk, then complete the following:
1. Scroll through the document. The flyer consists of three parts—the heading Vision on Ln 5, the vision statement on Ln 18 through 20, and the department identification on Ln 33 through 35.
2. Center the heading Vision and the vision statement.
3. Right-align and double space the department identification.
4. Place a $1\frac{1}{2}$ point double rule approximately 1 inch above and below the vision statement.
5. Add the following character attributes to Vision:
   a. Century Gothic font
   b. 36 point
   c. bold
   d. italic
   e. all caps
   f. expanded spacing
6. Add the following character attributes to the vision statement:
   a. Century Gothic font
   b. 24 point
   c. bold
   d. italic
7. Add the following character attributes to the department identification:
   a. Century Gothic font
   b. 18 point
   c. bold
8. Save the document as S2VISION.DOC.
9. Preview then print the document.

E 10. Insert the Wingdings character set symbol A (you will find it on the seventh row) at the beginning of the line, Human Resources Development Department.
11. Increase the amount of space between each character in the heading Vision to 3 point.
12. Save the document as S2HRD2.DOC.
13. Preview then print the document.
14. Dismiss the Borders toolbar then close the document.

3. Safety Measures at University General Hospital

Raul Fernandez is the director of the Environmental and Physical Safety Department of University General Hospital. He has decided to prepare a memo motivating employees to be aware of the potential safety hazards in their work environment and informing them whom to call for information or help.

Complete the following:

1. Create the document as shown in Figure 2-38. Type the memo headings, body of the memo, and telephone information without making any formatting decisions. When typing the memo headings (TO:, FROM:, and so on), insert one tab between the heading and the information that follows. When typing the personnel information, insert a tab between the title (for example, Director) and the name (Raul Fernandez).

Memorandum

TO: Hospital Staff
FROM: Raul Fernandez
RE: Safe and healthful work environments
DATE: September 2, 1995

Whether you work in a laboratory, hospital ward, or an office, it is important for you to be aware of the hazards and safety procedures for your work area. Attend safety meetings, learn about fire extinguishers, evacuation plans, personal protective equipment, and techniques for handling and storing potentially harmful materials.

The Environmental and Physical Safety Department maintains programs in chemical safety, radiation safety, biosafety, asbestos control, hazardous waste management, fire safety, hazard communication, and general safety. On the next page is a list of the individuals responsible for these programs. Please keep this sheet readily available, and contact the appropriate person whenever you have a question or concern about safety issues. Thank you!

Whom to Call

749-4271

Director   Raul Fernandez
Manager, Fire and Physical Safety   Bob Lane
Manager, Hazardous Materials   Janet Hunter
Manager, Radiation Safety   Le Chiu
Office Manager   Ann Schuler

Figure 2-38

2. Save the document as S2SAFETY.DOC.
3. Double space the memo headings and the personnel information.
4. Center the title Memorandum.
5. Justify the body of the memo.
6. Indent the body of the memo to the 1-inch mark.
7. Align the colons in the memo headings by inserting a right-aligned tab stop at the 0.75-inch mark, then inserting a tab in front of each heading.
8. Insert a hard page break before Whom to Call.
9. Insert a $^3/_4$ point single rule below Whom to Call.
10. Center the telephone number.
11. Indent the personnel information from both margins 1 inch.
12. Set a right-aligned, dot leader tab for the personnel information at the 5-inch mark.
13. Bold the title Memorandum.
14. Change the font for all the text on page 2 to Arial Rounded MT Bold.
15. Change the telephone number to 24 point.
16. Save the document.
17. Spell check, preview, then print the document.

E 18. Insert the Wingdings special character set symbol for the telephone above the telephone number.
19. Center the telephone.
20. Change the telephone special character to 36 point.
21. Save the document as S2UGH2.DOC.
22. Preview then print the document.
23. Dismiss the Borders toolbar and close the document.

Creating a Multiple-Page Document with Tables

Developing a Travel Expense Policy Report

O B J E C T I V E S

In this tutorial you will:

- Create a table
- Use AutoCorrect
- Use the Clipboard for cutting, copying, and pasting text
- Find and replace text
- Select cells, rows, columns, text, or an entire table
- Modify a table structure
- Sort information in a table
- Perform mathematical calculations in a table
- Insert a caption
- Insert headers and footers
- Use and apply styles
- Format a table automatically with borders, rules, and shading

Powell International Petroleum Services, Inc.   Barbara Svoboda is a recent business school graduate with a specialty in human resources management. For the last two years, she has been working for Powell International Petroleum Services, Inc. (PIPSI) at its corporate headquarters in Baton Rouge, Louisiana. PIPSI specializes in retrofitting older refineries and pipelines with the latest production technologies. Most recently, PIPSI has started numerous projects in the Commonwealth of Independent States; as a result, employee travel expenses have increased.

PIPSI's executive management has asked Barbara's manager, Nancy McDermott, to develop a new travel expense policy that will control domestic and foreign travel expenses. Nancy has almost finished the policy statement but has been called out of town. She gives Barbara the disk containing the report and tells her to finish the report, then edit and format it before submitting it to management.

Barbara decides to use the productivity strategy to complete her task. She will finish creating the travel expense policy, then edit the document for any changes or corrections she needs to make. Next, she will format the policy statement following the format used for other policy statements in the company's policy manual. Barbara will then print the completed travel expense policy.

To start Word and open the document that Nancy created:

❶   Start Word, if necessary, and conduct the screen check as described in Tutorial 1.

❷   Insert your Student Disk in the disk drive, then open the file C3PERDM.DOC from your Student Disk. After C3PERDM.DOC is open, scroll through the document to become familiar with it. Compare your document to Figure 3-1 on the following page. Notice that the document is two pages long and divided into four major sections—Standard Per Diem Allowance, Domestic Travel, Foreign Travel, and Exceptions. Eventually, the Domestic Travel and Foreign Travel sections will contain basically the same information arranged in the same order.

❸   Click **File** then click **Save As...** and save the document as S3PERDM.DOC to your Student Disk.

❹   Click **OK** or press **[Enter]**. The title bar changes to reflect the new document name.

Barbara begins by looking over the printed copy of the unfinished travel expense policy that Nancy left (Figure 3-1). She decides to begin her work in the document by adding the following: explanations for the components of the per diem allowance (Insert A), a table of information about the domestic travel per diem (Insert B), and a table of information about foreign travel per diem (Insert C). Depending on the printer selected, your document might break between pages one and two at a point different from that shown in Figure 3-1.

Barbara: Edit and format as you think best. Use policy manual
if you need a guideline. Thanks.　　-NM

Policy Governing Travel Expenses
Powell International Petroleum Services, Inc. (PIPSI) will pay for travel expenses only when the travel is directly related to company business. Transportation and accommodations must be consistent with the company's goals and conform to the per diem allowances and travel policies detailed below.
Standard Per Diem Allowance ← make this a section heading
Company employees will be authorized an equitable expense allowance when they are directed to perform company travel. Per diem allowances will be authorized and claims reimbursed in accordance with the provisions of the company's travel policies.

The company officers who are responsible for authorizing travel or for approving employee travel claims are required to authorize or approve only those per diem allowances that are justified by the circumstances of the travel. Such authorizations must be in accordance with the specific reimbursement rules and provisions of company policy.
Domestic Travel ← make this a section heading
make this a subsection heading → The maximum daily allowance is based on the actual cost of lodging plus an allowance for meals and incidental expenses -- the total not to exceed the applicable maximum per diem rate. The components of the per diem allowance are explained below:

Insert A
Add components and explanations here. Get text from policy manual.

Per Diem Allowance for Extended Domestic Work Assignments　　Insert B
On extended work assignments of more than 30 days but less than 120 days, the employee will be reimbursed 65 percent of the maximum per diem rate for that location.

Reimbursement will be based on a flat rate system. Employees are required to submit a copy of any leases for accommodations with the initial travel expense claim and for any future instances when another lease must be obtained. Receipts must also be submitted with each claim for furniture rental, utilities, and other expenses over $25.

Move after the domestic per diem table. Also put in Foreign Travel section; change "Domestic" to "Foreign."

Copy first sentence and edit for 120 days or more. Use 55 percent.

Table 1 illustrates maximum per diem allowances authorized for certain domestic travel locations. Contact the Assistant Comptroller for rates of destinations not listed.

Location	Maximum Lodging	MIE	Total Per Diem
College Station, Texas	$53.50	$26.75	
Alexandria, Louisiana	$53.50	$21.00	
Albuquerque, New Mexico	$69.00	$26.75	
Wheeling, West Virginia	$51.00	$26.75	
Midland, Texas	$59.50	$34.00	
Norfolk, Virginia	$65.00	$26.75	

I keyed this information with tabs between each column. Check with Al Simpson to see if we need all locations.

insert B here →
Foreign Travel ← make this a section heading
Subsistence reimbursement for foreign travel is based on lodging plus an amount established for meals and incidental expenses for the location. Actual expenses may be approved when per diem rates do not cover subsistence expenses. Reimbursements may be made for the actual expenses up to 150 percent of the location rate or $50 plus the location rate, whichever is greater. The components of the per diem allowance are explained below:

← insert A again here

Figure 3-1
Nancy's edited document
(page 1 of 2)

Table 2 illustrates maximum per diem allowances authorized for certain foreign travel locations. Contact the Assistant Comptroller for rates of destinations not listed.

← insert C here

← insert B here

Exceptions ← make this a section heading

Any exceptions to the standard per diem allowance must be in writing to the Assistant Comptroller's office.

Here's the information for the Foreign Travel Per Diem table. Check with Al to see if there are other locations.

Location	Maximum Lodging	MIE	Maximum Per Diem	
Usinsk, Komi	$23	$8	$31	
Baku, Azerbaijan	$35	$12	$47	
Lisitschansk, Ukraine	$40	$12	$52	Insert C

Figure 3-1
Nancy's edited document (page 2 of 2)

Creating a Table

Tables are an important means of communicating information in business documents, because they allow the reader to analyze complex data quickly. A **table** is simply information organized horizontally in rows and vertically in columns. The intersection of a row and column is called a **cell**.

In Tutorial 2 you learned to align text vertically by using tabs. That procedure works well for information in two or three columns, with each item in the table containing only one row of information. But if the information is more complex, or if you want a more professional-looking table, using tabs to create tables becomes awkward and tedious.

Word's table feature relieves the tedium of setting up data in columns and rows. It also enables you to lay out other types of information, such as text and graphics, side by side in a more readable format. The elements of a Word table are illustrated in Figure 3-2. Like text typed in a paragraph, text entered in a cell wraps automatically within that cell.

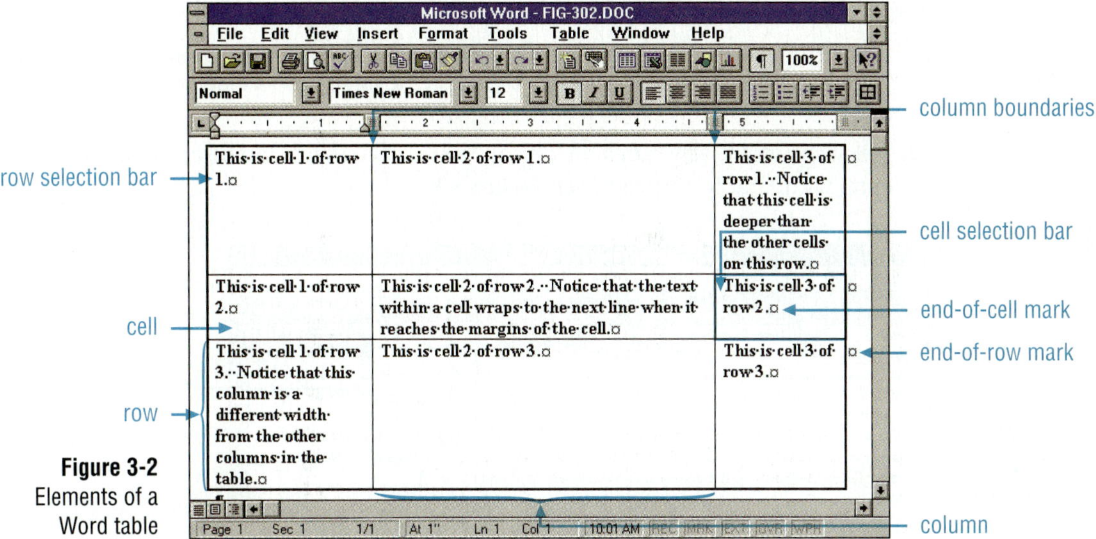

Figure 3-2
Elements of a
Word table

Word's table feature allows you to create a blank table, then insert information in it, or to convert existing text to a table. Whichever method you choose, Word makes it easy for you to create the **structure**—the number of rows and columns—of a table.

To see the outline of the table structure in your document, the Gridlines option on the Table menu must be activated, which it is by default. To check whether the Gridlines option is activated, open the Table menu and look for a checkmark in front of the Gridlines option. The gridlines that are used to display the blank table structure do not print, however. If you want a border around any part of a table, you must specifically format the table or individual cells with borders.

Creating a Table Using the Table Button

In addition to arranging data in rows and columns, Word's table feature allows you to create side-by-side text paragraphs, such as when you need to define words or include explanations of catalog items. One method to create a blank table structure is to use the Insert Table button on the Standard toolbar to specify the number of rows and columns you need in your table. Word then inserts a blank table structure with the specified number of rows and columns at the insertion point.

As she noted on page 1 of her draft, Nancy wants Barbara to insert explanations of the two components of the per diem allowance: "Maximum lodging expense allowance" and "Meals and incidental expense allowance." Barbara will use the table feature to create side-by-side text paragraphs, with the per diem component name on the left side and the explanation of the component on the right side. Barbara needs to create a table that has two rows and two columns. She decides to use the Insert Table button to specify the table structure.

To create a blank table structure using the Insert Table button:

❶ Scroll through the document until you see the Domestic Travel heading.

❷ Place the insertion point in front of the heading, Per Diem Allowance for Extended Domestic Work Assignments (Page 1, Ln 20).

TROUBLE? Your choice of printer might affect the location of the insertion point shown in your status bar. Use the line reference given in the tutorial as a guide, but continue to refer to the figures.

❸ Click the **Insert Table button** on the Standard toolbar. The Insert Table button grid, a miniature table, appears. See Figure 3-3.

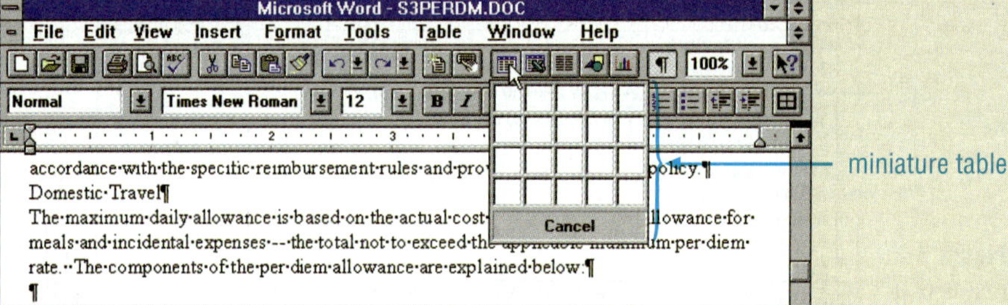

Figure 3-3
Insert Table button grid

❹ Place the pointer in the upper-left cell of the miniature table, then click and drag it across the grid so that two rows and two columns are highlighted. As you highlight cells, Word indicates the size of the table at the bottom of the grid (rows x columns).

❺ Release the mouse button. An empty 2 x 2 table grid structure appears in the document, and the insertion point is in cell 1 of row 1. See Figure 3-4.

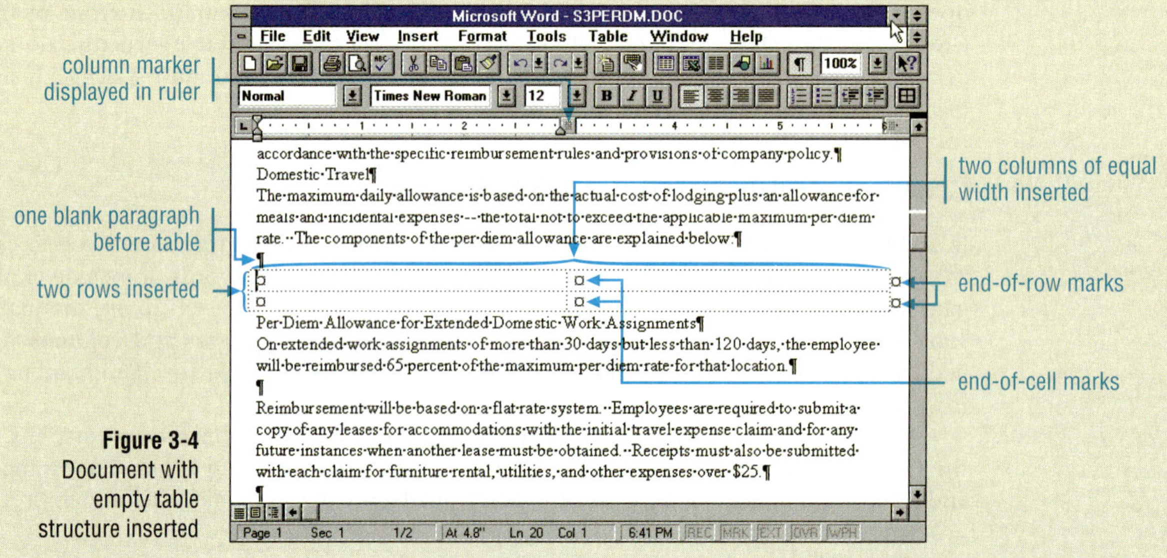

Figure 3-4
Document with empty table structure inserted

Notice that, by default, Word automatically creates two columns of equal width between the margins of the document. Each cell contains an end-of-cell mark, and each row contains an end-of-row mark. Also notice the change in the ruler: each column is indicated by column markers on the ruler, the indent markers for the active cell are displayed, and between column spacing has been inserted.

TROUBLE? If you are not satisfied with the table you created, immediately click the Undo button ⟲ on the Standard toolbar (or click Edit then click Undo Insert Table), then repeat Steps 2 through 5.

TROUBLE? If you do not see the end-of-cell and end-of-row marks, you need to click the Show/Hide ¶ button ¶ on the Standard toolbar.

❻ Click the **Save button** 🖫 on the Standard toolbar (or click **File** then click **Save**) to save your changes.

Now that Barbara has created the structure for her table, she is ready to enter text in it.

Entering Text in a Table and Using AutoCorrect

You enter text in tables just as you do in the rest of your document—simply start typing. If the text in a cell takes up more than one line, Word automatically wraps the text to the next line and increases the height of the cell. To move to a new cell, either click in that cell to move the insertion point or press [Tab]. Press [Shift][Tab] to move the insertion point to the previous cell. If a cell that you are moving to contains text or data, using [Tab] or [Shift][Tab] will highlight the contents of the cell. Figure 3-5 lists other keyboard techniques for moving within a table.

To move the insertion point:	Press:
One cell to the right or to the first cell in the next row	[Tab]
One cell to the left	[Shift][Tab]
The first cell in the current row	[Alt][Home]
The last cell in the current row	[Alt][End]
The top cell in the current column	[Alt][PgUp]
The bottom cell in the current column	[Alt][PgDn]

Figure 3-5
Keyboard techniques for moving within a table

When entering text in a table, you can correct errors just as you correct errors when typing text in the main document. In addition, the Spelling command will find spelling errors in the text of a table.

Word's AutoCorrect feature corrects some of the more common typing mistakes you might make when entering text anywhere in a document, including a table. For instance, if you mistakenly type *teh* for *the* or *adn* for *and*, AutoCorrect automatically corrects the error after you press the Spacebar. Figure 3-6 shows the AutoCorrect dialog box, which you display by choosing the AutoCorrect command from the Tools menu.

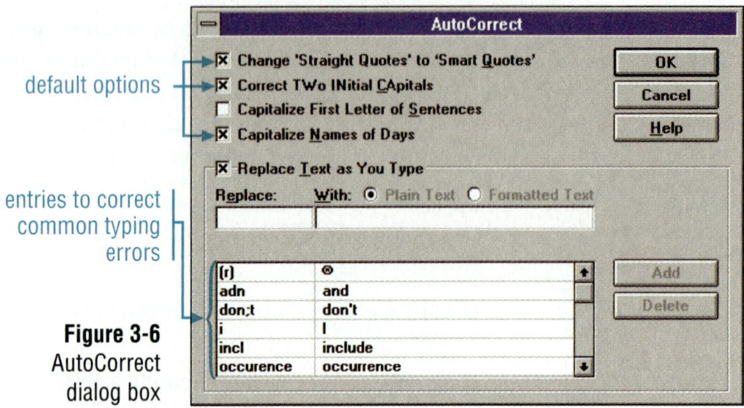

Figure 3-6
AutoCorrect
dialog box

Word provides AutoCorrect entries for many common typing errors, and you can also add your own entries for the typing errors you make most often. In addition, the dialog box provides default options that automatically change straight quotes to smart (curly) quotes; correct words typed with two initial capital letters; and capitalize the days of the week as you type.

Now that Barbara has created the table structure, she is ready to insert the components of the per diem allowance ("Maximum lodging expense allowance" and "Meals and incidental expense allowance") and their explanations in the table, as specified in Figure 3-1, Insert A. When she does, she'll make some intentional typing errors to see how AutoCorrect fixes them.

To enter the text in the table:

❶ Place the insertion point in the first cell in row 1, if it is not already there.

❷ Type **Maximum lodging expense allowance**. The end-of-cell mark moves to the right as you type within the cell.

❸ Press **[Tab]**. The insertion point moves to cell 2 in row 1.

   TROUBLE? If you accidentally press [Enter] instead of [Tab], you will create a new paragraph within a cell rather than move the insertion point to another cell. Simply delete the paragraph mark or click the Undo button ⟲ (or click Edit then click Undo Typing). Then press [Tab] to move to the next cell.

To see how AutoCorrect works, you'll make a typing error.

❹ Type **Teh** then press **[Spacebar]**. Notice how Word automatically corrects your typing mistake.

   TROUBLE? If the error is not corrected after you press [Spacebar], the AutoCorrect feature has been deactivated. Correct the error then type the remaining text for the explanation as shown in Figure 3-7, then skip to Step 7.

❺ Type **per diem rates authorized under this category**. When you reach the end of the first line in the cell, Word automatically wraps the insertion point to the next line, which increases the height of the cells across the entire row. By increasing the height of the cells, you can keep the explanation of the component next to the name of the per diem component.

The AutoCorrect feature also expands abbreviations you might substitute for text when typing. In the next step, you'll see how this works.

❻ Press **[Spacebar]**, type **incl** then press **[Spacebar]**. Notice how Word automatically expands the abbreviation "incl" to the complete word "include." Type the remaining explanation of the first term as shown in Figure 3-7.

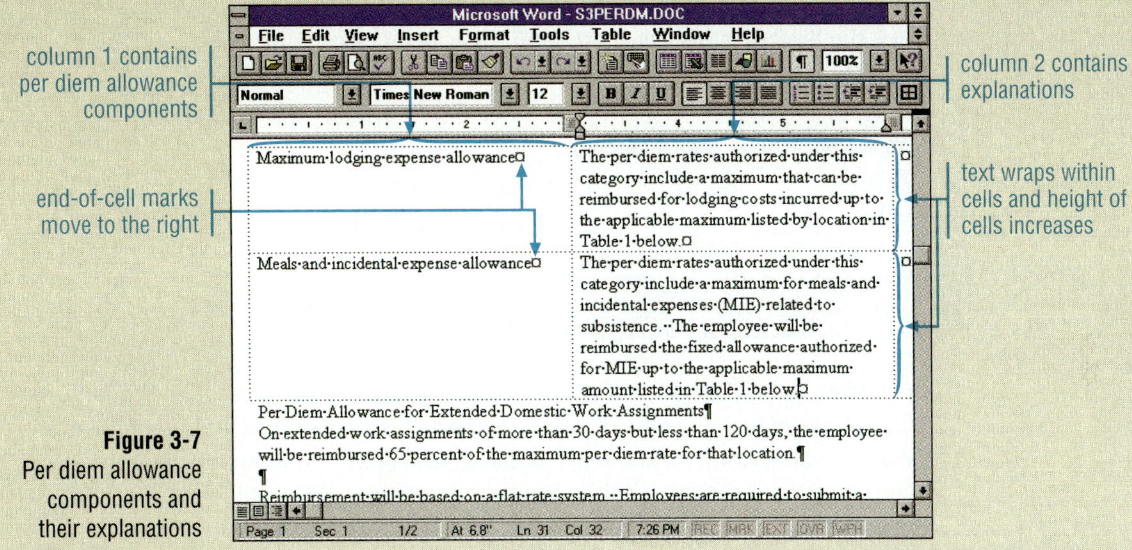

Figure 3-7
Per diem allowance components and their explanations

TROUBLE? Don't worry about correcting other errors now; you will edit the text later.

❼ Press **[Tab]**. The insertion point moves to cell 1 in row 2.

❽ Type **Meals and incidental expense allowance**, press **[Tab]**, then type its explanation as shown in Figure 3-7. This explanation also aligns next to its component name.

❾ Save the changes you have made.

Barbara next decides to create a table for the foreign travel per diem data that Nancy wants her to insert at the end of the Foreign Travel section (Figure 3-1, Insert C). Barbara thinks she needs a table structure that is four rows by four columns; she knows that if this is not the right size, she can easily change the table structure. She decides to use the Insert Table command to create this table.

Creating a Table Using the Insert Table Command

The Insert Table command on the Table menu displays the Insert Table dialog box. In this dialog box, you can specify additional features for your table that are not available with the Insert Table button, such as the exact width for each column or a predefined format for the table with the Table AutoFormat option. You can also have Word take you step by step through the creation of a table with the Table Wizard option.

Barbara will use the Insert Table command to create the table containing the foreign travel per diem data.

To insert the table using the Insert Table command:

❶ Scroll to the end of the document until you see the Exceptions heading, then place the insertion point in front of the "E" in Exceptions (Pg 2, Ln 17).

❷ Click **Table** then click **Insert Table...**. The Insert Table dialog box appears.

❸ Click the **Number of Columns up arrow** until it reaches 4.

❹ Click the **Number of Rows up arrow** until it reaches 4. See Figure 3-8. Barbara decides to create evenly spaced columns so she leaves the Column Width setting at Auto.

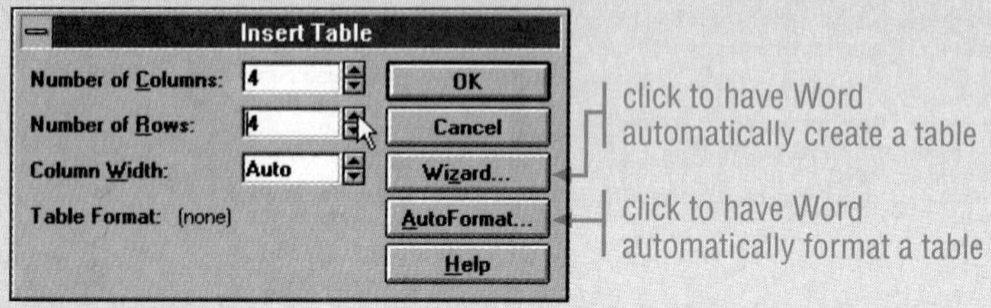

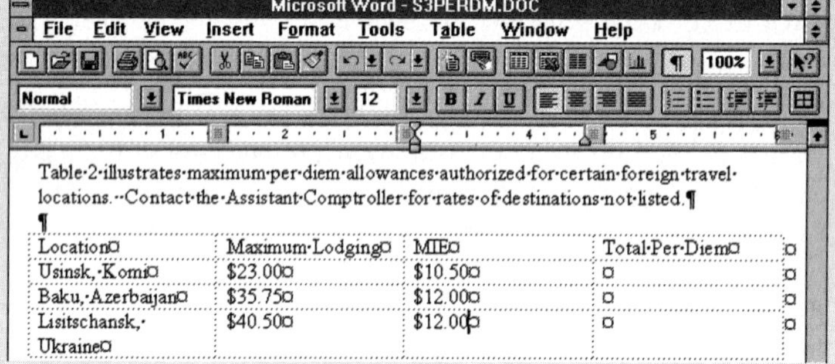

Figure 3-8
Insert Table
dialog box

❺ Click **OK** or press **[Enter]**. A blank 4 x 4 table appears on the screen, and the insertion point is placed in cell 1 of row 1. Notice that the columns are of equal width.

❻ Type the information for the table as shown in Figure 3-9. Remember to press [Tab] to move to the next cell; to move to a previous cell, press [Shift][Tab]. Leave the cells below the last column heading, Total Per Diem, blank for now.

Figure 3-9
Completed Foreign
Travel Per Diem table

❼ Save the changes you have made.

Word provides several ways to insert an empty table structure in a document. Moreover, Word can convert existing text to a table so that you can lay out the information more easily.

Converting Existing Text to a Table

You can convert existing text that is consistently separated by paragraph marks, tabs, or commas to a table. Word uses these three types of characters to separate the selected text into cells.

Converting Text to a Table

- Select the text to be converted to a table.

- Click the Insert Table button on the Standard toolbar (or click Table then click Convert Text to Table...). If the selected text contains a variety of possible separator characters, such as paragraph marks, tabs, or commas, then the Convert Text to Table dialog box appears.

- Choose the appropriate option to convert the text to a table according to either the paragraph marks, tabs, or commas in the text.

- Click OK or press [Enter].

Barbara needs to convert to a table the data about the domestic travel per diem rates that Nancy originally typed. This text will be easy to convert because Nancy separated each piece of data with a tab and put a paragraph mark at the end of each line.

To convert the text to a table:

❶ Scroll through the document until you see the data for the domestic per diem rates (Pg 1, Ln 45). Notice that each piece of information in a row is separated by a tab character and that each row ends with a paragraph mark.

❷ Use the selection bar to select the rows from "Location..." through "Norfolk, Virginia..."

❸ Click the **Insert Table button** 🖽 on the Standard toolbar (or click **Table** then click **Insert Table...**). Because the text was originally separated by tabs, Word creates a table with four columns of equal width, replacing the tabs with column boundaries. Eventually Barbara will calculate the total per diem amounts to complete the last column of the table.

❹ Deselect the table. Notice that the table splits across the page break between pages 1 and 2. See Figure 3-10. By default, Word inserts the page break *within* a row if the entire row won't fit at the bottom of the page. Word does not move the entire row to the next page.

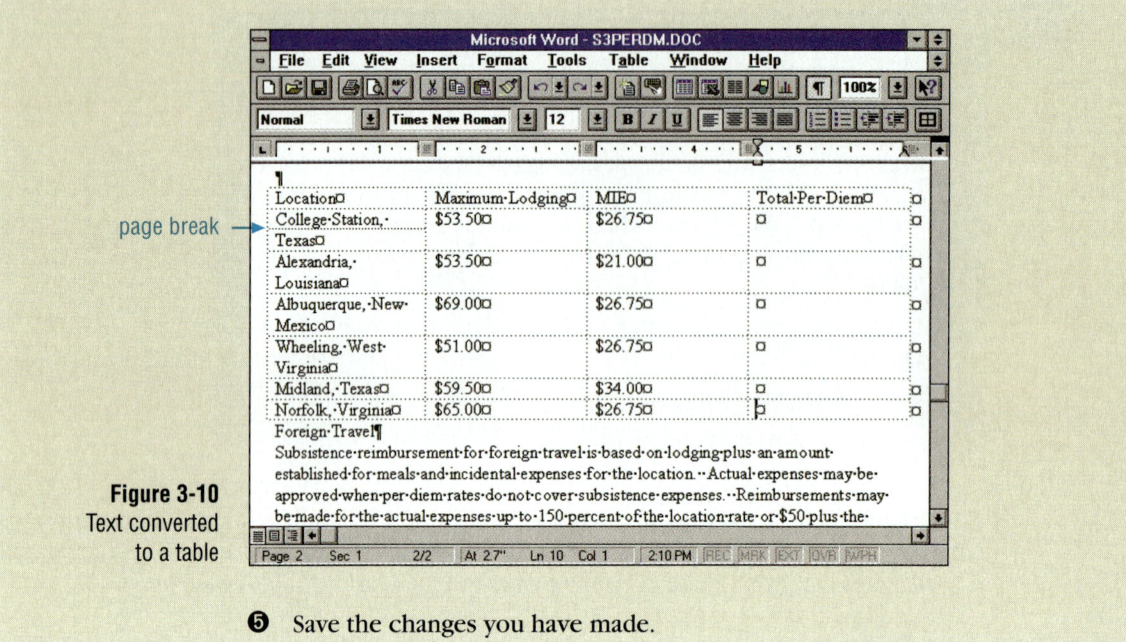

Figure 3-10
Text converted
to a table

❺ Save the changes you have made.

If you want to take a break and resume the tutorial at a later time, you can close the current document, then exit Word by double-clicking the Control menu box in the upper-left corner of the screen. When you want to resume the tutorial, start Word, place your Student Disk in the disk drive, then complete the screen check procedure described in Tutorial 1. Open the document S3PERDM.DOC, make sure the Gridlines option is activated on the Table menu, press [Shift][F5] to return to your last point in the document, then continue with the tutorial.

Barbara has several tasks to complete during the editing phase of the productivity strategy, some of which will be done more easily with the use of the Clipboard.

Using the Clipboard

The **Clipboard**, a standard feature in Windows applications, provides a temporary storage area for information that you need to copy or move from one location to another. To **copy** information means that the original text stays in its current location and a duplicate is created in a new location; to **move** information means that the original text is removed from its current location and placed in a new location. You would use the Clipboard when you need to copy or move information more than once or when you need to copy or move information between Word documents or between Word and other applications, such as spreadsheets. Clipboard operations using the Cut, Copy, and Paste commands from Word's Edit menu operate as they do in Windows. Word also provides Cut, Copy, and Paste buttons on the Standard toolbar.

Once you place information on the Clipboard by cutting or copying, you can paste the contents of the Clipboard as many times as you need. The contents of the Clipboard are overwritten, however, with any new text that you subsequently cut or copy.

Copying and Pasting Text

The Copy command is helpful when you need to use similarly worded text throughout a document. By using the Copy command, you eliminate possible keyboarding errors and you save time.

Barbara needs to add a second sentence to the end of the first paragraph after the heading, Per Diem Allowance for Extended Domestic Work Assignments, concerning work assignments of 120 days or more. The wording of the new sentence is similar to the first sentence with only a few corrections, so Barbara decides to copy the first sentence and paste it at the end of the paragraph; then she will edit the pasted sentence appropriately.

To copy and paste the sentence about per diem allowances:

❶ Place the insertion point in the first sentence of the first paragraph below the heading, Per Diem Allowance for Extended Domestic Work Assignments (Pg 1, Ln 34).

❷ Press **[Ctrl]** and click to select the entire sentence, including the period. Note that the ending paragraph mark is *not* selected. See Figure 3-11.

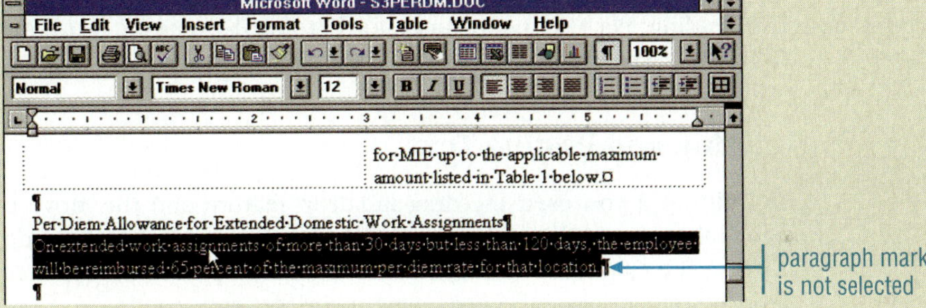

Figure 3-11
Selected sentence to be copied

❸ Click the **Copy button** on the Standard toolbar (or click **Edit** then click **Copy**). The selected text is copied to the Clipboard and remains highlighted.

TROUBLE? If the selected text disappeared, you chose Cut instead of Copy. Click the Undo button on the Standard toolbar (or click Edit then click Undo Cut). Then repeat Steps 2 and 3.

❹ Place the insertion point after the period at the end of the selected sentence. The text is deselected.

❺ Click the **Paste button** on the Standard toolbar (or click **Edit** then click **Paste**). The copied selection appears at the insertion point, with one space between the two sentences. Adding spaces to pasted text is part of Word's Smart Cut and Paste feature.

Barbara wants two spaces between sentences, and she needs to edit the pasted sentence.

❻ Place the insertion point between the two sentences, press **[Spacebar]**, then edit the pasted sentence to read "On extended work assignments of *120 days or more*, the employee will be reimbursed *55* percent of the maximum per diem rate for that location." See Figure 3-12. Do not type the quotation marks or use italics.

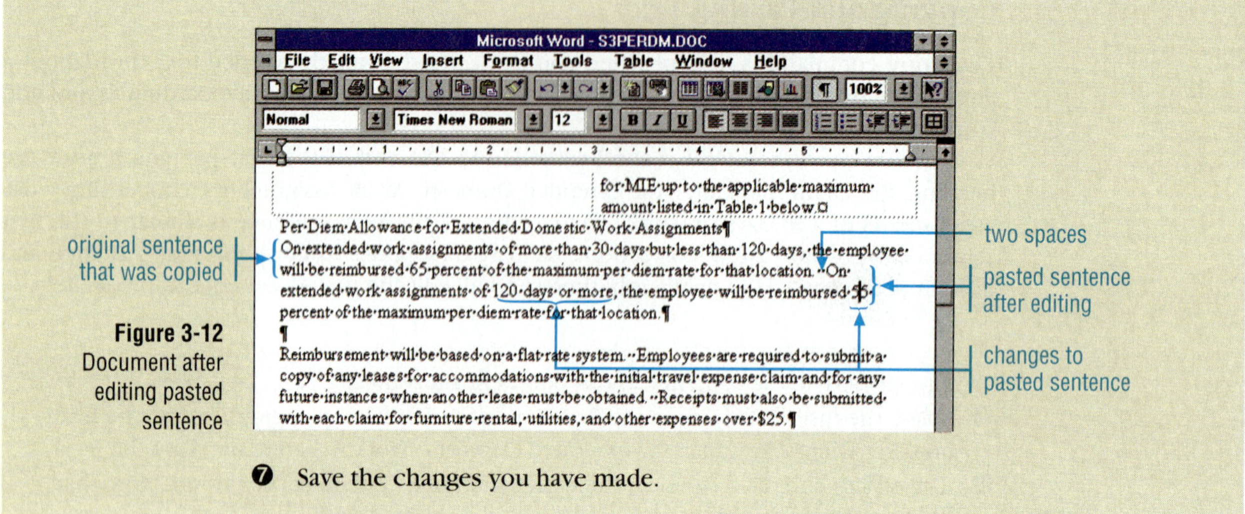

Figure 3-12
Document after editing pasted sentence

❼ Save the changes you have made.

Barbara checks Nancy's draft of the policy statement and sees that she needs to move the heading, Per Diem Allowance for Extended Domestic Work Assignments, and the two following paragraphs just before the Foreign Travel section.

Cutting and Pasting Text

In Tutorial 2 you used the drag-and-drop feature and the Move command to move text short distances within a document. These commands, however, do not place the selected text on the Clipboard. Using the Cut command places the selected text on the Clipboard so that you can paste the text as many times as you need.

Barbara will use the Cut and Paste buttons to move the heading about extended domestic work assignments and the two following paragraphs.

To cut and paste the heading and the two following paragraphs:
❶ Use the selection bar to select from the heading, Per Diem Allowance for Extended Domestic Work Assignments (Pg 1, Ln 33) through "...expenses over $25." Do not include the blank paragraph after the second paragraph. See Figure 3-13.

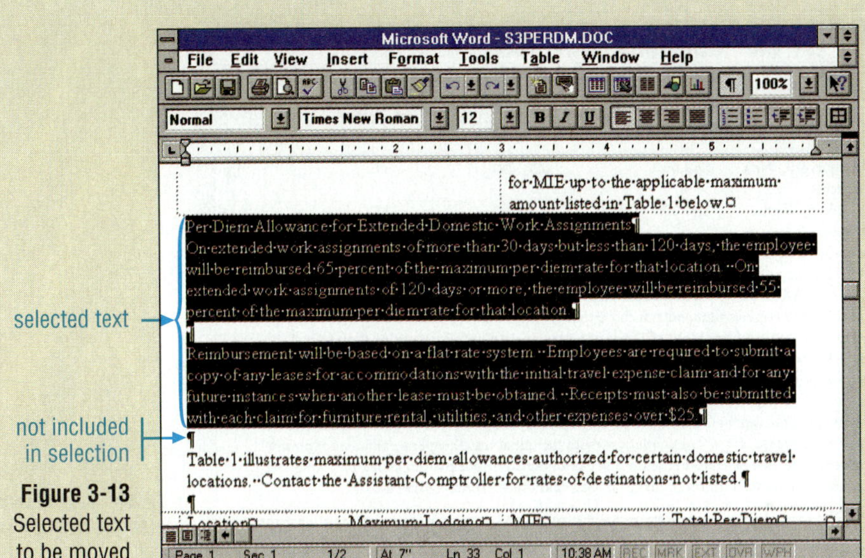

selected text

not included in selection

Figure 3-13
Selected text to be moved

❷   Click the **Cut button** on the Standard toolbar (or click **Edit** then click **Cut**). The selected text disappears. The Clipboard now contains the cut text instead of the previously copied text.

Barbara wants to move the text to the end of the Domestic Travel section.

❸   Place the insertion point directly before the "F" in the Foreign Travel heading (Pg 2, Ln 2).

❹   Click the **Paste button** on the Standard toolbar (or click **Edit** then click **Paste**). The cut text appears at the insertion point.

TROUBLE? If you moved the text to the wrong location, click the Undo button on the Standard toolbar (or click Edit then click Undo Paste). The pasted text is removed from the document, but it still remains on the Clipboard. Place the insertion point in the correct location, then paste again.

❺   Scroll through the document to see that the cut text has been pasted to the correct location. See Figure 3-14.

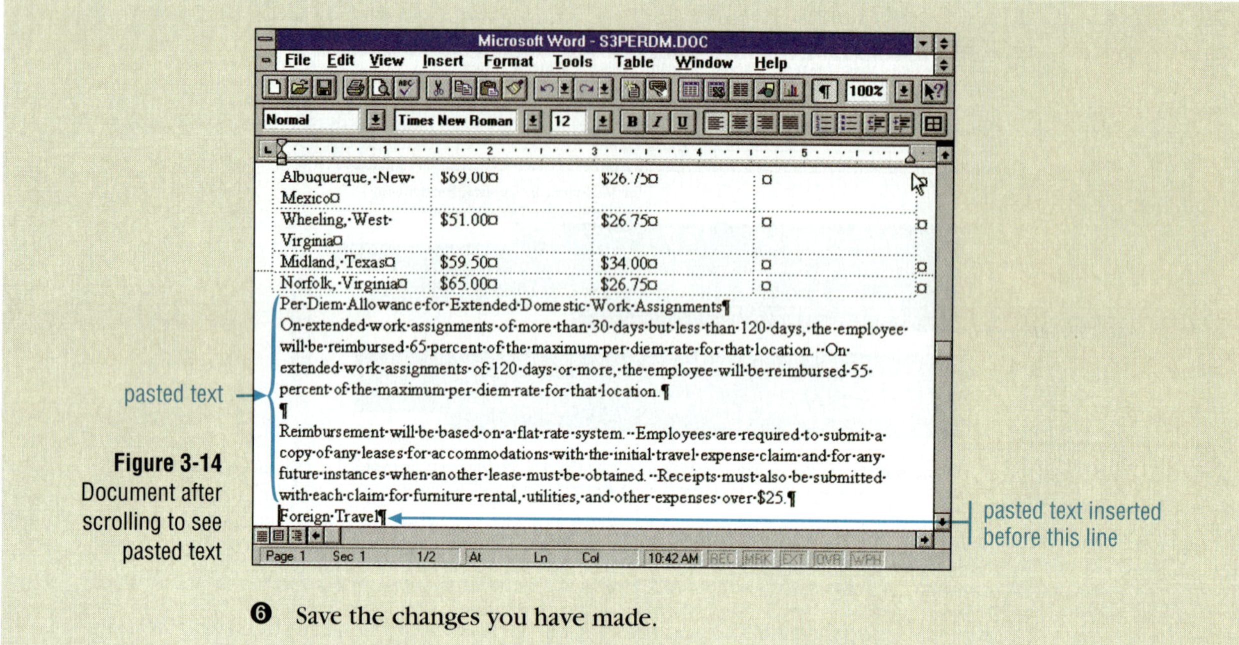

Figure 3-14
Document after scrolling to see pasted text

pasted text

pasted text inserted before this line

❻   Save the changes you have made.

Next, Barbara needs to put the same information at the end of the Foreign Travel section just before the Exceptions heading. Rather than retype it, she can paste that information again from the Clipboard, then edit the title appropriately.

To paste the heading and the two following paragraphs again:
❶   Place the insertion point in front of the "E" in the Exceptions heading at the end of the document (Pg 2, Ln 28).
❷   Click the **Paste button** 📋 on the Standard toolbar (or click **Edit** then click **Paste**). The previously pasted text is pasted again in the new location.
❸   Scroll through the document to verify that the text has been pasted at the proper location.
❹   Select the word **Domestic** in the second occurrence of the pasted text and change it to **Foreign**.
❺   Save the changes you have made.

Barbara now sees some editorial changes she wants to make to Nancy's draft. She wants to replace references to "the company" or "company" with the acronym of the company's name—PIPSI—to make the travel expense policy sound less formal.

Finding and Replacing Text

In editing long documents, you often need to change every occurrence of a word or string of characters within the document. Word makes this process easy with the Replace command on the Edit menu. This command allows you to find specified text or formatting, then replace it with different text or formatting. Word can also find and replace special characters such as tabs, paragraph marks, and hyphens within your document. Word starts the process from the current location of the insertion point.

With the Replace command, you specify the text, formatting, or special characters that you want Word to search for and the text, formatting, or special characters that you want to substitute for the search text. Word searches for all instances of the text you have specified, even if it is part of another word. For instance, if you search for the word "win," Word would stop at Window, window, winter, or swindle as well as win.

Barbara wants to replace the phrase "the company" with PIPSI, and she wants PIPSI bolded. She can do both tasks at the same time.

To specify the text and formatting options for the search and replace operation:

❶   Place the insertion point at the beginning of the document.

❷   Click **Edit** then click **Replace….** The Replace dialog box appears.

❸   Type **the company** in the Find What text box.

❹   Press **[Tab]** to place the insertion point in the Replace With text box.

❺   Type **pipsi** in the Replace With text box.

❻   Click **Format** in the Replace section, then click **Font….** The Replace Font dialog box appears.

❼   Click **Bold** in the Font Style list box, then click the **All Caps check box** in the Effects section.

❽   Click **OK** or press **[Enter]**. The completed Replace dialog box appears with the formatting options to be applied to the replacement text specified. See Figure 3-15.

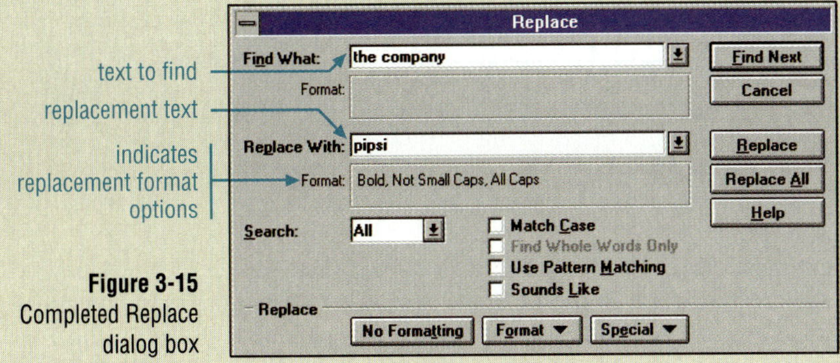

Figure 3-15
Completed Replace dialog box

Now that the Find What and Replace With options are specified, Barbara is ready to start the replace process. Because Barbara wants to check each instance of "the company" to determine whether she wants to replace it with **PIPSI**, she'll use the Replace button instead of the Replace All button.

To replace the specified text:

❶   In the Replace dialog box, click **Find Next** or press **[Enter]** to start the replace process. Word begins the search and stops at "… with *the company*'s goals…" Remember, Word searches for all matches of the characters specified, not just whole words, unless the Find Whole Words Only option is selected in the Replace dialog box. Barbara decides to replace this instance of the search text with **PIPSI**.

TROUBLE? If the Replace dialog box obscures the highlighted text, drag the dialog box out of the way.

❷ Click **Replace**. Word resumes the search and stops at "… provisions of *the company*'s travel…" Barbara decides to replace this instance also.

❸ Click **Replace** or press [**Enter**]. Word resumes the search and stops at "*The company* officers…" The Match Case option was not specified, so Word ignores differences in capitalization. Barbara wants this instance replaced also.

❹ Click **Replace** or press [**Enter**]. The following message appears: Word has finished searching the document.

❺ Click **OK** or press [**Enter**].

❻ Click **Close** in the Replace dialog box.

❼ Scroll through your document to verify that the replacements were done correctly. See Figure 3-16.

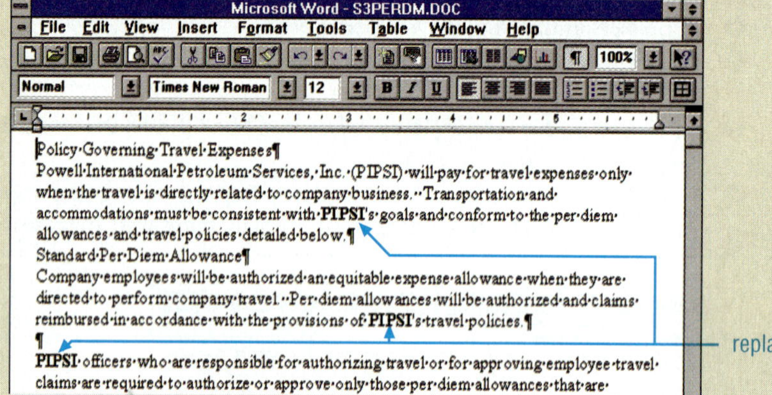

Figure 3-16
Document after replacing text

❽ Save the changes you have made.

Barbara next must edit the tables in the policy statement. She sees from Nancy's draft that the table she created in the Domestic Travel section, which contains the components of the per diem allowance and their explanations, must also be included in the Foreign Travel section. Also, some information she received from Al Simpson has shown her that she needs to add one location to the Foreign Travel Per Diem table and delete one location from the Domestic Travel Per Diem table. Barbara also decides that both the tables would be easier to read if the locations were arranged alphabetically. She also needs to calculate the total amounts in Tables 1 and 2, and finally, she wants to add captions to both tables.

Selecting Within a Table

To make all these editing changes in the tables, Barbara must select different parts of the table. You select text *within* cells just as you select text within a document. However, Word provides you with special techniques for selecting an *entire* cell, row, column, and the entire table. Once an area within a table is selected, you can follow the "select, then do" principle to modify it.

You are already familiar with using the selection bar to the left of your document to select text. Each element of a table—cell, row, column—also has its own selection bar. The selection bar for an individual cell is located at the left edge of the cell. The pointer changes to ⬈ when it moves into the cell selection bar, and it changes to ↓ when it moves into the column selection bar. Figure 3-17 describes different selection techniques for various elements of a table.

To:	Do this:	Or:	Or:
Select a cell	Click in the cell selection bar	Drag across the contents of a cell, including the end-of-cell mark	Press [Tab] to select the contents of the next cell
Select a row	Click in the row selection bar next to the row to be selected	Place the insertion point in the row to be selected, click Table, then click Select Row	Double-click in the cell selection bar of any cell in the row to be selected
Select a column	Click in the column selection bar above the column to be selected	Place the insertion point in the column to be selected, click Table, then click Select Column	
Select a table	Place the insertion point anywhere within the table to be selected, click Table, then click Select Table	Press [Alt][5] (on the numeric keypad) with Num Lock turned off	

Figure 3-17
Table selection techniques

Barbara needs to add the components of the standard per diem and their explanations to the Foreign Travel section. She decides to copy that information from the Domestic Travel section and paste it. First she needs to select the table before copying it.

To select the table:

❶ Place the insertion point anywhere within the table created for the explanations of the per diem allowance components in the Domestic Travel section (beginning on Pg 1, Ln 20).

❷ Click **Table** then click **Select Table**. The entire table is selected.

TROUBLE? If the Select Table command is dimmed, you did not have the insertion point within the table before you chose Select Table from the Table menu. Repeat Steps 1 and 2.

Now Barbara is ready to copy the selected table, then paste it after the first paragraph of the Foreign Travel section.

To copy and paste the selected table:

❶ Click the **Copy button** 📋 on the Standard toolbar (or click **Edit** then click **Copy**). The selected table is copied to the Clipboard.

❷ Deselect the table.

❸ Place the insertion point in the blank line between the first and second paragraphs in the Foreign Travel section (Pg 2, Ln 19), then press **[Enter]** once. This inserts a blank line above the table.

❹ Click the **Paste button** 📋 on the Standard toolbar (or click **Edit** then click **Paste**). The copied table is pasted in its new location.

❺ Scroll through the document to verify that the table has been pasted correctly.

Barbara notices that she must change the pasted text to read Table 2 instead of Table 1.

❻ Change the two instances of Table 1 to Table 2 in the pasted table. See Figure 3-18.

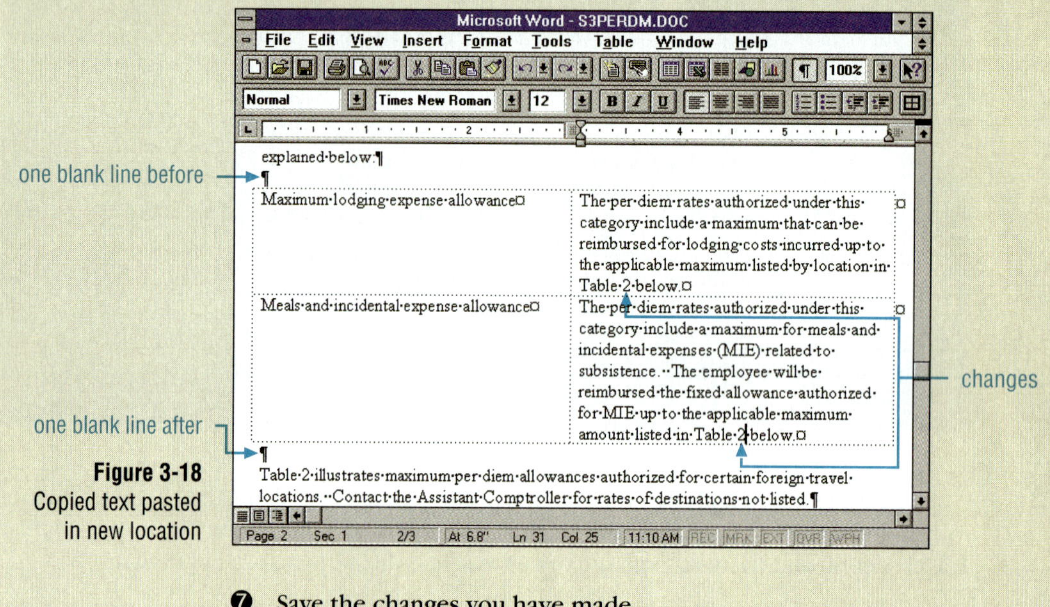

Figure 3-18
Copied text pasted in new location

❼ Save the changes you have made.

Next, based on the information from Al Simpson, Barbara needs to add the other location to Table 2.

Modifying a Table Structure

When you originally create the structure for a table, you often do not know how many rows or columns you will actually need. However, you can easily modify or change a table's structure after creating it. Figure 3-19 describes the various ways to insert or delete rows or columns in a table.

To:	Within a table:	At the end of a table:
Insert a row	Select the entire row below the one you want to add, click Table, then click Insert Rows	Place the insertion point in the last cell of the last row, then press [Tab]
Insert a column	Select the entire column to the left of the one you want to add, click Table, then click Insert Columns	Select the end-of-row markers, click Table, then click Insert Columns
Delete a row	Select the entire row or rows you want to delete, click Table, then click Delete Rows	
Delete a column	Select the entire column or columns you want to delete, click Table, then click Delete Columns	

Figure 3-19
Techniques for inserting and deleting rows and columns

Barbara decides to insert the new location at the bottom of Table 2. To do so she must insert a row.

To insert a blank row at the bottom of Table 2 and add the information about the new location:

❶ Place the insertion point in the last cell of the last row in Table 2 (Pg 2, Ln 40). This cell is currently empty.

❷ Press **[Tab]**. A blank row is added to the bottom of the table with the same characteristics as the row above it.

TROUBLE? If a blank row is not added to the bottom of the table, perhaps you did not have the insertion point in the last cell of the last row. Repeat Steps 1 and 2.

❸ Type **Radusny, Western Siberia** then press **[Tab]**; type **$23.00** then press **[Tab]**; type **$10.50**. See Figure 3-20.

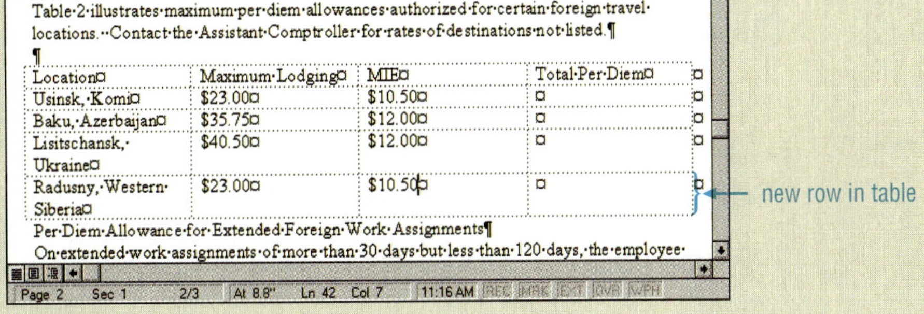

Table·2·illustrates·maximum·per·diem·allowances·authorized·for·certain·foreign·travel· locations.··Contact·the·Assistant·Comptroller·for·rates·of·destinations·not·listed.¶

Location¤	Maximum·Lodging¤	MIE¤	Total·Per·Diem¤	¤
Usinsk,·Komi¤	$23.00¤	$10.50¤	¤	¤
Baku,·Azerbaijan¤	$35.75¤	$12.00¤	¤	¤
Lisitschansk,· Ukraine¤	$40.50¤	$12.00¤	¤	¤
Radusny,·Western· Siberia¤	$23.00¤	$10.50¤	¤	¤

Per·Diem·Allowance·for·Extended·Foreign·Work·Assignments¶
On·extended·work·assignments·of·more·than·30·days·but·less·than·120·days,·the·employee·

Page 2   Sec 1   2/3   At 8.8"   Ln 42   Col 7   11:16 AM   REC   MRK   EXT   OVR   WPH

Figure 3-20
Table 2 after inserting row at bottom

❹ Save the changes you have made.

Barbara now needs to delete the row containing information about Wheeling, West Virginia, from Table 1 per instructions from Al Simpson.

With Word, you can delete either the *contents* of the cells in a selected row or the *entire row* from a table. To delete the contents of the cells in a selected row, just press the

Delete key. However, to delete the selected row entirely from the table structure, including the contents of the cells, you must choose the Delete Rows command from the Table menu.

According to Al Simpson, Barbara needs to remove the information about Wheeling, West Virginia, from Table 1 because PIPSI has completed work at the location and no longer sends employees there. Barbara decides to use the Shortcut Table menu, which contains the most often used commands for working with tables, to delete the row.

To delete the row for Wheeling, West Virginia, using the Shortcut Table menu:

❶ Place the insertion point in the Wheeling, West Virginia, row of Table 1 (Pg 1, Ln 44).

❷ Click **Table** then click **Select Row** (or double-click in the cell selection bar of any cell in the row).

To display the Shortcut Table menu, you simply place the insertion point within a table, then click the right mouse button.

❸ With the mouse pointer over the selected text, click the **right mouse button**. The Shortcut Table menu appears. See Figure 3-21.

Figure 3-21
Shortcut Table
menu

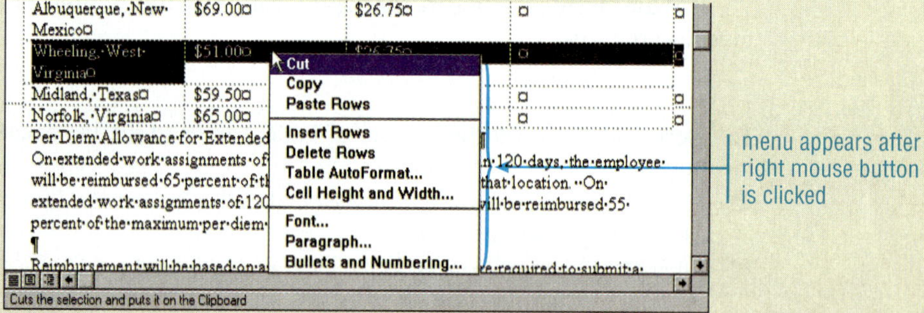

❹ Click **Delete Rows**. The selected row is deleted from the table structure.

❺ Save the changes you have made.

Barbara has finished changing the table structure of the tables in her document by inserting and deleting rows.

The next editing change Barbara needs to make is to arrange the travel locations alphabetically in Tables 1 and 2.

Sorting Rows in a Table

Word allows you to sort information in alphabetical, numerical, or date order quickly and easily. The most common use for sorting is to rearrange rows in a table, but you can use the sorting feature to sort any list of information. You can sort a table by up to three columns within a table. Word recognizes whether or not your table contains a header row, that is, whether the first row of the table contains column headings.

Barbara decides to arrange the locations in Table 1 in alphabetical order.

To sort the information in Table 1:

❶ Place the insertion point anywhere within Table 1, if necessary.

❷ Click **Table** then click **Sort…**. The entire table is selected, and the Sort dialog box appears. See Figure 3-22.

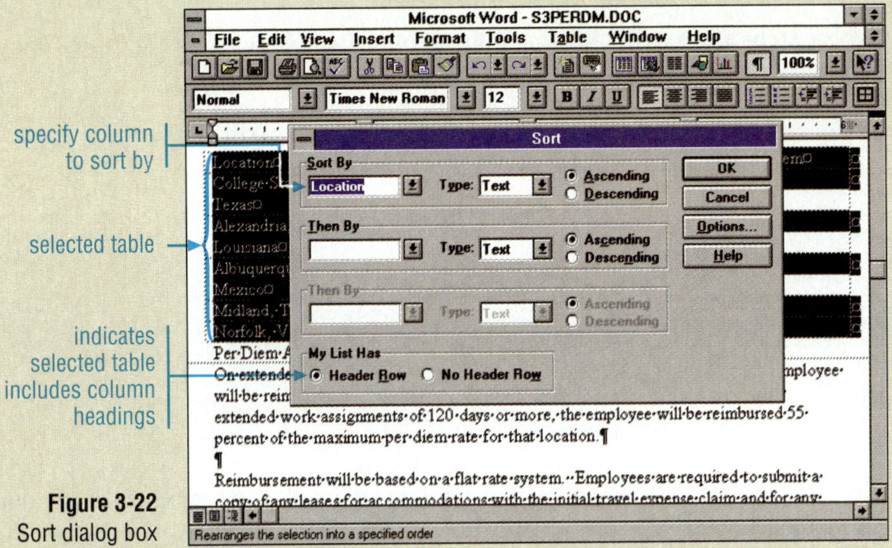

Figure 3-22
Sort dialog box

Barbara can sort by any column in the table, but she wants to sort by the Location column in *ascending* alphabetical order—that is, from A to Z—rather than in *descending* alphabetical order (from Z to A), so she doesn't need to change any of the settings in the dialog box. "Location" appears in the Sort By list box automatically because it is the first column heading in the table. Also, Word recognizes that the first row of the table contains the column headings; therefore, the Header Row option is selected in the My List Has section. This means that the contents of the first row will not be sorted. If you wanted to include the first row in the sort, you would click the No Header Row button.

❸ Click **OK** or press **[Enter]** then deselect the highlighted rows. Rows 2 through 6 of Table 1 are arranged alphabetically by the first word in the Location column. See Figure 3-23.

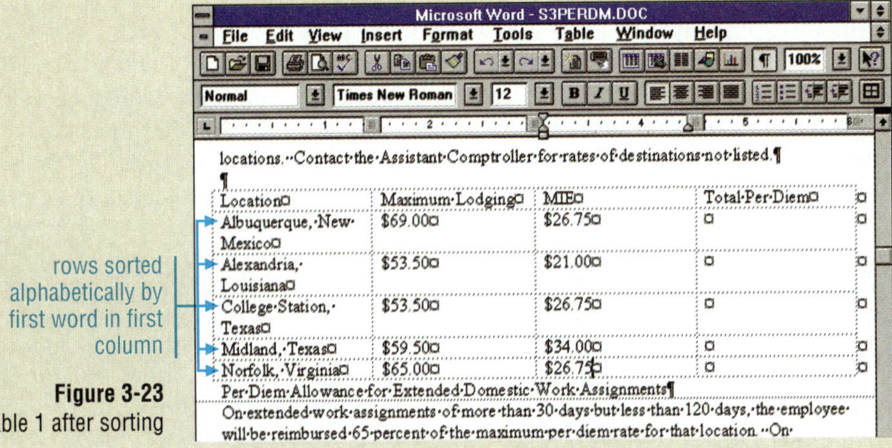

Figure 3-23
Table 1 after sorting

TROUBLE? If the sort was unsuccessful, immediately click the Undo button on the Standard toolbar (or click Edit then click Undo Sort). Then repeat Steps 1 through 3.

Now Barbara needs to sort the locations in Table 2.

4. Repeat Steps 1 through 3 to sort by location in Table 2. Deselect the table. See Figure 3-24.

rows sorted alphabetically by first word in first column

Location
Maximum Lodging
M&IE
Total Per Diem
Baku, Azerbaijan
$35.75
$12.00
Lisitschansk, Ukraine
$40.50
$12.00
Radusny, Western Siberia
$23.00
$10.50
Usinsk, Komi
$23.00
$10.50
Per Diem Allowance for Extended Foreign Work Assignments
On extended work assignments of more than 30 days but less than 120 days, the employee
Page 2 Sec 1 2/3 At 6.1" Ln 27 Col 39 11:39 AM REC MRK EXT OVR WPH

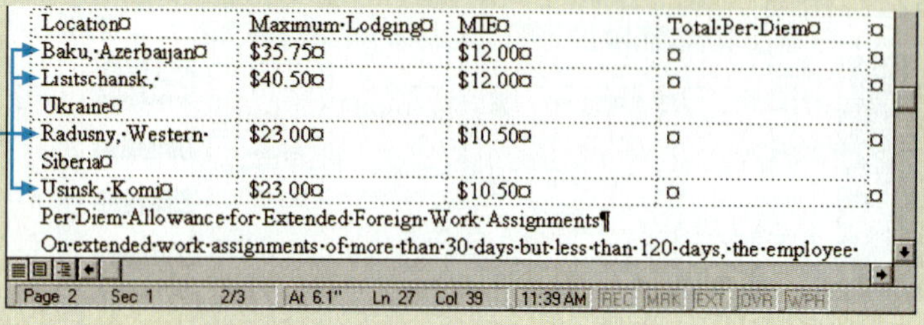

Figure 3-24 Table 2 after sorting

5. Save the changes you have made.

Next, Barbara needs to calculate the total per diem allowed for each of the domestic and foreign locations.

Performing Mathematical Calculations in Tables

A popular use of tables is to display data, perhaps showing the results of a mathematical calculation like a sum of numbers. Word's Table Formula command allows you to perform simple calculations, such as adding, subtracting, multiplying, dividing, and calculating percentages, averages, and minimum and maximum values. For involved calculations, you would use a spreadsheet application like Microsoft Excel, then link or embed the spreadsheet in your Word document.

Barbara needs to calculate the total per diem values for the domestic and foreign locations. Because these are simple calculations, she decides to use Word's Table Formula command.

To calculate the total per diem values in Table 1 and Table 2:

1. Place the insertion point in the last cell of the second row in Table 1(Pg 1, Ln 38).
2. Click **Table** then click **Formula...**. The Formula dialog box appears. Word analyzes the table, then displays a formula based on the data in the table, in this case one that will sum all numbers in the cells to the left of the insertion point. This is the correct formula. See Figure 3-25.

indicates that numbers to the left of the insertion point will be summed

Formula
Formula:
=SUM(LEFT)
OK
Cancel
Help
Number Format:
Paste Function:
Paste Bookmark:

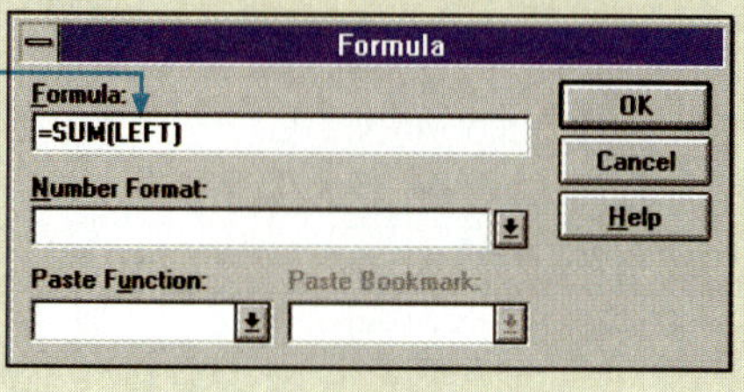

Figure 3-25 Formula dialog box

❸ Click **OK** or press **[Enter]**. The sum of the two numbers ($95.75) appears, properly formatted as currency.

Barbara needs to repeat this procedure for each total needed in this table, as well as those in Table 2. She decides to use Word's Repeat command [F4], which repeats the last change made to a document.

❹ Place the insertion point in the next empty cell below, then press **[F4]**. The sum for that set of numbers appears.

❺ Repeat Step 4 for each of the remaining rows in Table 1, scroll to Table 2 (Pg 2, Ln 36), then repeat Step 4 for each row in it also. Pressing [F4] will not repeat the scrolling; it will still repeat the last command, which sums the row of numbers.

❻ Save the changes you have made.

If a value used in a calculation subsequently changes, the new result will not be automatically updated. You must delete the current answer, then choose the Table Formula command again.

Next, Barbara wants to insert captions identifying the tables because the document refers to them as Table 1 and Table 2.

Inserting a Caption

A **caption** is a number or title that identifies tables or figures in a document. The Insert Caption command allows you to add automatically numbered captions easily to tables and figures.

Barbara decides to insert table captions containing both a number and a title so that employees reading the travel expense policy can better identify the tables' contents.

To insert captions for Table 1 and Table 2:

❶ Select all the rows in Table 1, click **Insert**, then click **Caption...**. The Caption dialog box appears with the text Table 1 inserted in the Caption text box. Word analyzes the selected text and inserts an appropriate label, in this instance Table. You can, however, change the caption label if you want.

❷ Type . (a period), press **[Spacebar]** twice, then type **Domestic Travel Per Diem**.

Barbara wants the captions to appear below the tables, so she needs to change the Position setting.

❸ If necessary, click the **Position list box down arrow**, then click **Below Selected Item**. See Figure 3-26.

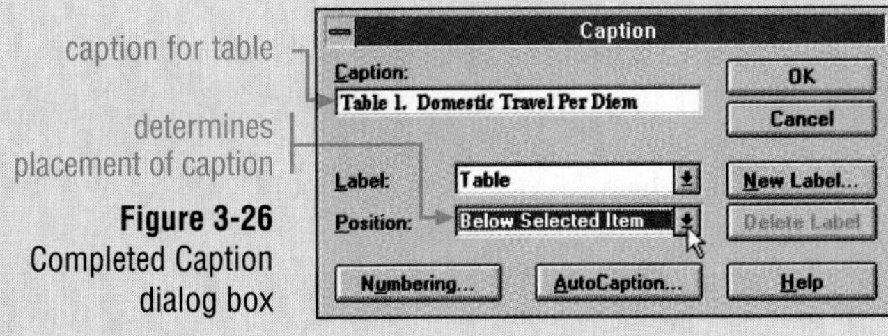

Figure 3-26
Completed Caption dialog box

❹ Click **OK** or press **[Enter]**. The specified caption is inserted below Table 1. See Figure 3-27. Notice that Word applied a predefined set of formats, also called a style, to the caption, which you can change if you want. You will learn more about styles later in this tutorial.

Location¤	Maximum·Lodging¤	MIE¤	Total·Per·Diem¤	¤
College·Station,·Texas¤	$53.50¤	$26.75¤	$80.25¤	¤
Alexandria,·Louisiana¤	$53.50¤	$21.00¤	$74.50¤	¤
Albuquerque,·New·Mexico¤	$69.00¤	$26.75¤	$95.75¤	¤
Midland,·Texas¤	$59.50¤	$34.00¤	$93.50¤	¤
Norfolk,·Virginia¤	$65.00¤	$26.75¤	$91.75¤	¤

Table·1.··Domestic·Travel·Per·Diem¶

Per·Diem·Allowance·for·Extended·Domestic·Work·Assignments¶
On·extended·work·assignments·of·more·than·30·days·but·less·than·120·days,·the·employee·

Page 1   Sec 1   1/2   At 7"   Ln 32   Col 88   1:40 PM   REC MRK EXT OVR WPH

Figure 3-27
Caption below
Table 1

caption

❺ Select all the rows in Table 2, then repeat Steps 1 through 4 to insert the following caption: **Table 2. Foreign Travel Per Diem**.

❻ Save the changes you have made.

If you delete a table with a numbered caption, Word will automatically renumber the captions for the remaining tables.

If you want to take a break and resume the tutorial at a later time, you can close the current document, then exit Word by double-clicking the Control menu box in the upper-left corner of the screen. When you want to resume the tutorial, start Word, place your Student Disk in the disk drive, then complete the screen check procedure described in Tutorial 1. Open the document S3PERDM.DOC, make sure the Gridlines option is activated on the Table menu, press [Shift][F5] to return to your last point in the document, then continue with the tutorial.

To follow the format used in the company policy manual, Barbara needs to insert page numbers at the top of her document on all pages but the first, and insert the title of the document and the revision date at the bottom of all pages.

Using Headers and Footers

As you learned in Tutorial 2, you should format a document starting with the page-level decisions, then proceed to the paragraph- and font-level decisions. One of Word's more popular page-level formatting features is the use of headers and footers.

A **header** is information that is repeated at the top of each page of a document. A **footer** is information that is repeated at the bottom of each page. In addition to including text in a header or footer, you can also insert page numbers, the date, and the time. You can format the contents of a header or footer just as you format text in the document, including inserting borders, rules, or graphics.

When you insert headers or footers in a document, Word changes to page layout view and the insertion point moves to the point in the document where the header will print. To speed the process of inserting headers or footers, Word provides you with a Header and Footer toolbar.

Inserting a Header

Barbara wants to insert the page number at the top right margin of all pages of her document except the first. It is a standard practice to omit the page number from the first page of a document.

To insert a header containing the page number:

❶ Press **[Ctrl][Home]** to move the insertion point to page 1, click **View**, then click **Header and Footer**. The Header and Footer toolbar appears, the insertion point is placed in the Header text area at the top of page 1 surrounded by a dashed line, the main text of the document becomes dimmed, and the screen changes to page layout view. See Figure 3-28.

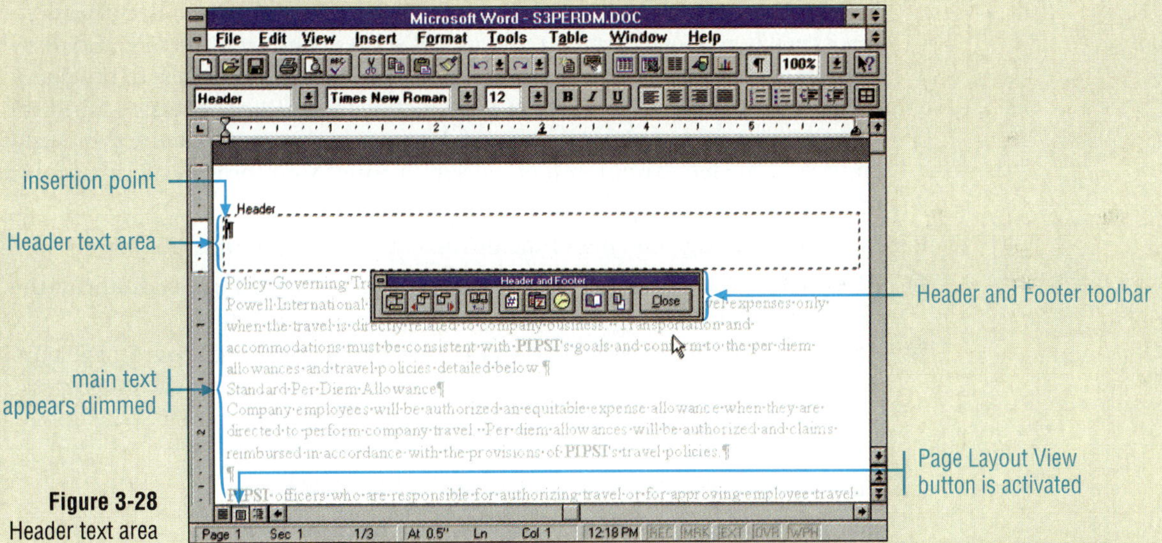

Figure 3-28
Header text area

TROUBLE? If the Header and Footer toolbar obscures the Header text area, drag the toolbar out of the way.

TROUBLE? Depending on the type of monitor you're using, the main text of the document might not appear on the screen; just continue with the tutorial.

Barbara does not want the header to appear on the first page.

❷ Click the **Page Setup button** on the Header and Footer toolbar (or click **File** then click **Page Setup…**). The Layout tab of the Page Setup dialog box appears.

❸ Click the **Different First Page check box** in the Headers and Footers section. See Figure 3-29.

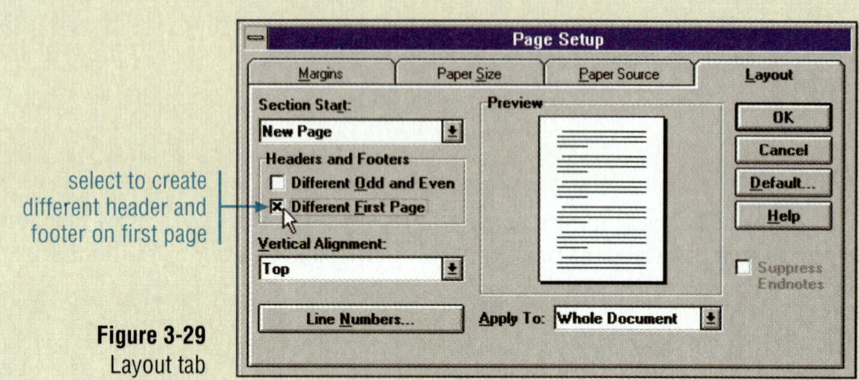

select to create different header and footer on first page

Figure 3-29
Layout tab

❹ Click **OK** or press **[Enter]**. You return to the document, but now the Header text area is labeled First Page Header. Any text typed here would print only on the first page.

Barbara does not want any text to appear in the header on the first page of the document so she can move to the Header text area on page 2.

❺ Click the **Show Next button** 🔲 on the Header and Footer toolbar. Notice that the insertion point moves to page 2. Now the Header text area is labeled "Header"; any text typed here would print on this and all subsequent pages. Notice also that the ruler in effect for the header is different from the ruler for the rest of the document: it contains a centered tab at the 3-inch mark and a right-aligned tab at the 6-inch mark, even with the right margin. Because header and footer text typically appears at the left margin, center, or right margin, Word provides formats for these text areas.

Barbara wants the page number of the document to appear at the right margin.

❻ Press **[Tab]** twice to move the insertion point to the right-aligned tab stop at the right margin of the Header text area.

❼ Click the **Page Numbers button** 🔲 on the Header and Footer toolbar. A page number appears at the right-aligned tab. Word also automatically places the correct page number on all subsequent pages of the document. See Figure 3-30.

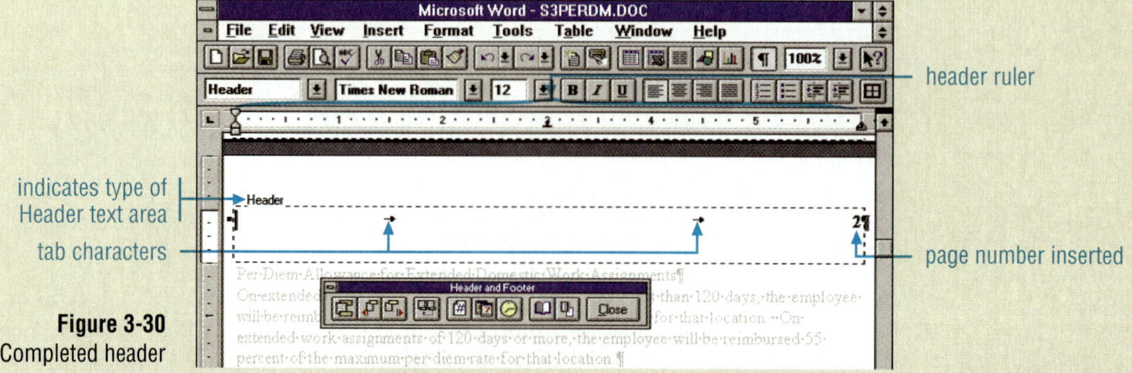

header ruler

indicates type of Header text area

tab characters

page number inserted

Figure 3-30
Completed header

❽ Click the **Close button** on the Header and Footer toolbar. You return to the document. Normal view does not display headers and footers; you need to switch to print preview (or page layout view) to see the header you just inserted.

❾ Click the **Print Preview button** 🔍 on the Standard toolbar (or click **File** then click **Print Preview**). Notice that the header does not appear on page 1 but that it does appear on pages 2 and 3.

> **TROUBLE?** If you cannot see all three pages at one time in print preview, click the Multiple Pages button 🔳 on the Print Preview toolbar, then drag across the grid to select three pages.

❿ Click the **Close button** on the Print Preview toolbar. You return to the document in normal view.

Next Barbara wants to add a footer containing the text, Policy Governing Travel Expenses, and the current date.

Inserting a Footer

Even though Barbara wants the same footer information to appear on all pages, including the first, she must insert it twice—in both the First Page Footer text area and the Footer text area—because the Different First Page check box is selected in the Page Setup dialog box. This setting affects both headers and footers. She also wants the footer text to appear in 10-point bold type.

To insert the footer:

❶ Click **View** then click **Header and Footer**. The insertion point appears in the First Page Header text area of the document.

Barbara needs to switch to the First Page Footer text area.

❷ Click the **Switch Between Header and Footer button** 🔲 on the Header and Footer toolbar. The insertion point is placed in the First Page Footer text area.

Barbara wants the text "Policy Governing Travel Expenses" to appear at the left margin of the footer and the date to appear at the right.

❸ Type **Policy Governing Travel Expenses** then press [Tab] twice.

❹ Click the **Date button** 📅 on the Header and Footer toolbar. The current date appears. The date will be updated automatically each time the document is printed.

> **TROUBLE?** If you chose the wrong button from the Header and Footer toolbar, you must select the incorrect text, then press [Del] before inserting the correct text.

Barbara wants to format the footer text in 10-point bold type.

❺ Click in the selection bar to select the entire footer, then use the Formatting toolbar to change the font format to 10 point and bold. Deselect the text. See Figure 3-31. Note that the date shown on your screen will be different from the one shown in the figure.

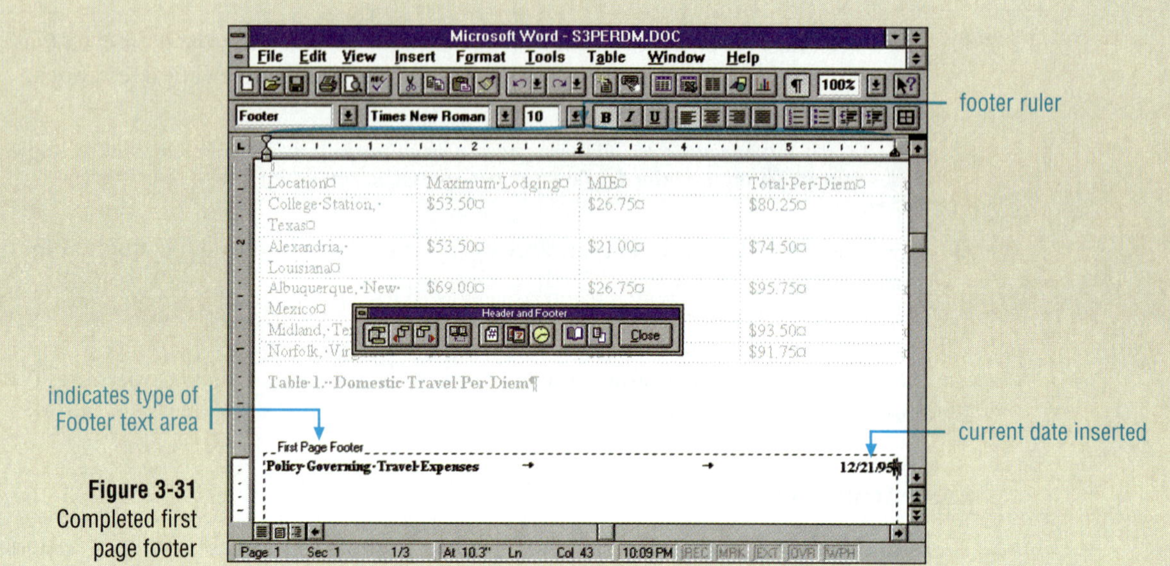

Figure 3-31
Completed first
page footer

Barbara decides to use the Copy and Paste buttons to copy the footer information from the First Page Footer text area to the Footer text area. Copying and pasting the footer eliminates the need to type and format the text again, and ensures that the same text appears in the footer on all pages.

6   Click in the selection bar to select the entire footer, then click the **Copy button** on the Standard toolbar (or click **Edit** then click **Copy**).

7   Click the **Show Next button** on the Header and Footer toolbar to move the insertion point to the Footer text area.

8   Click the **Paste button** on the Standard toolbar (or click **Edit** then click **Paste**) to paste the copied text in the Footer text area. You need to insert the footer on page 2 only, and it will appear on all remaining pages.

9   Click the **Close button** on the Header and Footer toolbar to return to your document.

Barbara wants to view the document in print preview to make sure she entered the footer information correctly.

To view the footer information in print preview:

1   Click the **Print Preview button** on the Standard toolbar (or click **File** then click **Print Preview**). Notice that the footer appears on all pages of the document.

   TROUBLE? If you cannot see all three pages at one time in print preview, click the Multiple Pages button on the Print Preview toolbar, then drag across the grid to select three pages.

2   Click the **Close button** on the Print Preview toolbar to return to the document in normal view.

3   Save the changes you have made.

Barbara wants the different parts of her document to be attractively formatted with a variety of paragraph and font formats. She doesn't, however, want to take the time to select each of the different parts and then directly apply formats one at a time. She decides to use Word's Style feature to speed up the formatting process.

Using Styles

In Tutorial 2 you used direct formatting to change the appearance of text within your document. Another method for changing the formatting of a document is to use Word's style feature. A **character style** is a collection of font formatting options that you save and reuse. A **paragraph style** is a collection of font and paragraph formatting options that you save and reuse. A paragraph style can include any and all of the following formatting options: tab settings, font, point size, type style, line spacing, borders, and indents. Rather than apply each formatting option individually, you apply a style that contains all the formatting options you want. A **style sheet** is a listing, which you can print, that describes the formatting characteristics of each style used in a document.

Each Word document comes with a set of standard paragraph styles: Normal (the default paragraph style for a Word document), Heading 1, Heading 2, and Heading 3. Word also contains a default character style called Default Paragraph Font. The current style is shown in the Style list box on the Formatting toolbar, and all styles available in a document are listed in the Style list, which you display by clicking the down arrow next to the Style list box. You can also use the Format Style command to view the paragraph and font attributes of each style in use. When certain other features, such as headers, footers, and captions, are used in a document, their styles are automatically added to the list.

You can define your own styles for use in documents, or you can use the predefined styles in Word's templates. A **document template** is a pattern, or model, on which a document is built. All documents based on a template take on the features defined for that template. In addition to its styles, a template's features can include boilerplate, or standard, text and specialized menu bars, toolbars, or keyboard shortcuts. These defined features help to automate the production of a document.

The NORMAL template is Word's default template, but Word contains many templates for other types of typical business communications. Figure 3-32 lists the names of the predefined templates available in Word. The file extension for a Word template is "DOT."

BROCHURE1	DIRECTR1	FAXCOVR1	FAXCOVR2
INVOICE	LETTER1	LETTER2	LETTER3
MANUAL1	MANUSCR1	MANUSCR3	MEMO1
MEMO2	MEMO3	NORMAL	PRESENT1
PRESREL1	PRESREL2	PRESREL3	PURCHORD
REPORT1	REPORT2	REPORT3	RESUME1
RESUME2A	RESUME4	THESIS1	WEEKTIME

Figure 3-32
Word's templates

To use the styles in one of the predefined templates, you can choose a template other than NORMAL when you first create a document, or you can *attach* a template to a document you've already created using the NORMAL template.

REFERENCE WINDOW

Attaching a Template to the Current Document

- Click File then click Templates…. The Templates and Add-ins dialog box appears.

- Click the Automatically Update Document Styles check box.

- Click Attach…. The Attach Template dialog box appears with all of Word's predefined templates listed.

- Click the template to be attached, then click OK or press [Enter] to close the Attach Template dialog box.

- Click OK or press [Enter] to close the Templates and Add-ins dialog box.

If you want to preview the predefined styles of a template before attaching it to the current document, you can use Word's Style Gallery feature. You can preview the styles of any template or document by using this feature.

Barbara's document contains several levels of headings, and she wants to differentiate among them with different paragraph styles. She decides to use the predefined styles of the MANUAL1 template. It has been a while since she used this template, so she decides to review its styles using Word's Style Gallery feature.

To use the Style Gallery to preview the MANUAL1 template styles:

❶ Click the **Style list box down arrow**. The list of styles assigned to the NORMAL template appears. The paragraph styles are bolded, and the character styles are shown in lighter type. Press **[Esc]** to close the list without selecting any styles.

❷ Click **Format** then click **Style Gallery**…. The Style Gallery dialog box appears with the current document displayed in the Preview section.

Barbara wants to review each style assigned to the MANUAL1 template.

❸ Click **Manual1** then click the **Style Samples radio button**. Each style defined for this template is displayed with the specific paragraph and font formatting characteristics applied to sample text. See Figure 3-33.

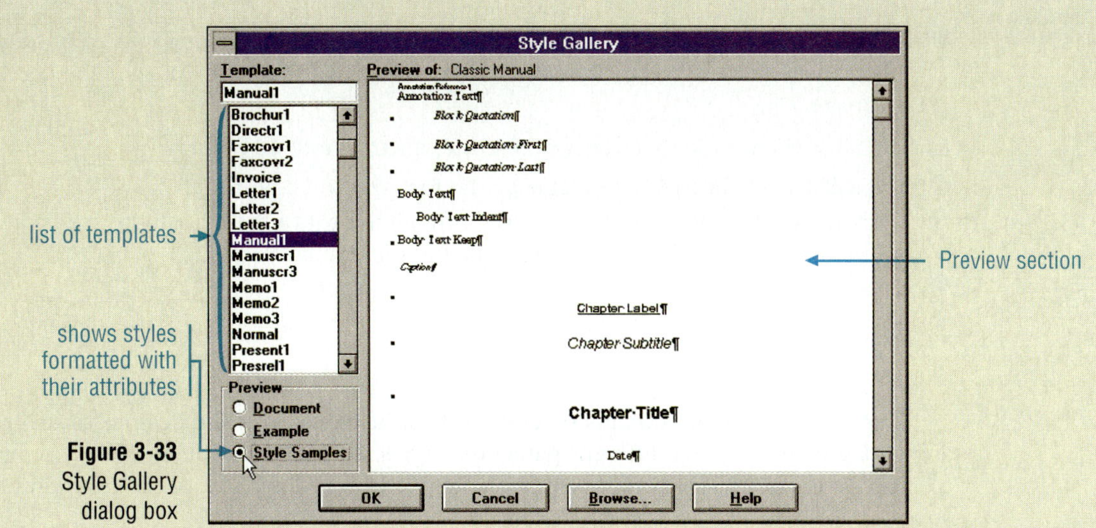

list of templates →

shows styles
formatted with
their attributes

← Preview section

Figure 3-33
Style Gallery
dialog box

❹   Use the scroll bar in the Preview section to view all the different styles defined for
the MANUAL1 template.

❺   Click **Cancel** to return to the document.

Barbara wants to attach the MANUAL1 template to her current document so she can
use the styles provided in the template. Note that any existing style in Barbara's document
having the same name as a style in the new template she attaches will be overwritten by
the new style.

To attach the MANUAL1 template to the document:

❶   Click **File** then click **Templates...**. The Templates and Add-ins dialog box appears
with "normal" in the Document Template text box.

❷   Click **Attach...**. The Attach Template dialog box appears. Only the template files are
listed in the File Name list box. See Figure 3-34.

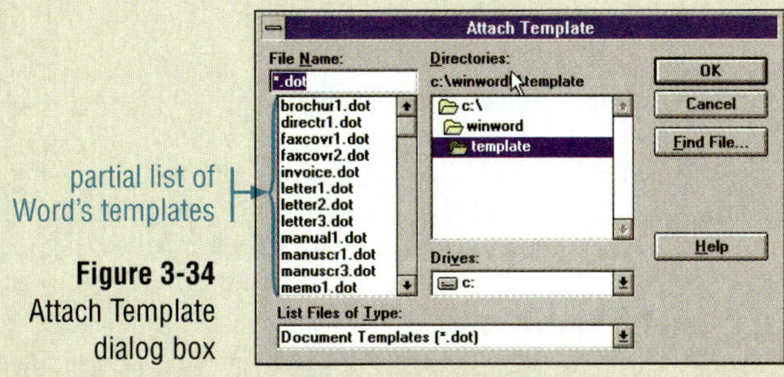

partial list of
Word's templates

Figure 3-34
Attach Template
dialog box

❸   Click **manual1.dot**, then click **OK** or press **[Enter]**. You return to the Templates and
Add-ins dialog box; the name and file location of the new template now appear in
the Document Template text box.

❹   Click the **Automatically Update Document Styles check box** to update your document
with the new styles.

❺ Click **OK** or press **[Enter]** to return to the document. Notice that the font size in your document has changed to 10 point, which is the default font size for the MANUAL1 template.

Barbara must change the font size for the entire document to 12 point.

❻ Click **Edit**, click **Select All**, then change the font size to 12 point.

❼ Click the **Style list box down arrow**. Scroll through the list to see that all the styles of the MANUAL1 template have been copied to the document.

❽ Press **[Esc]** to close the list without making any choices.

❾ Save the changes you have made.

Barbara's document contains several levels of headings, and she decides to differentiate among them by using different paragraph styles. She attached the MANUAL1 template to her document so she could use its predefined styles. Now she needs to apply those styles.

Applying Styles

Once you determine which styles you want to use—either Word's default styles or styles that you define—you must apply them to the text in your document to format it. The easiest way to apply a style to selected text is to use the Style list box.

Barbara is ready to apply paragraph styles to her document.

To apply paragraph styles to selected text using the Style list box:

❶ Click anywhere within the document title, **Policy Governing Travel Expenses**.

❷ Click the **Style list box down arrow** on the Formatting toolbar to open the Style list. Scroll through the list, then click **Title**. The combination of paragraph and font formatting attributes assigned to the Title style is applied to the selected paragraph. See Figure 3-35. Note that a small black box appears in the margin indicating that the text was formatted with one of Word's predefined styles. This box does not appear for text formatted with user-defined styles.

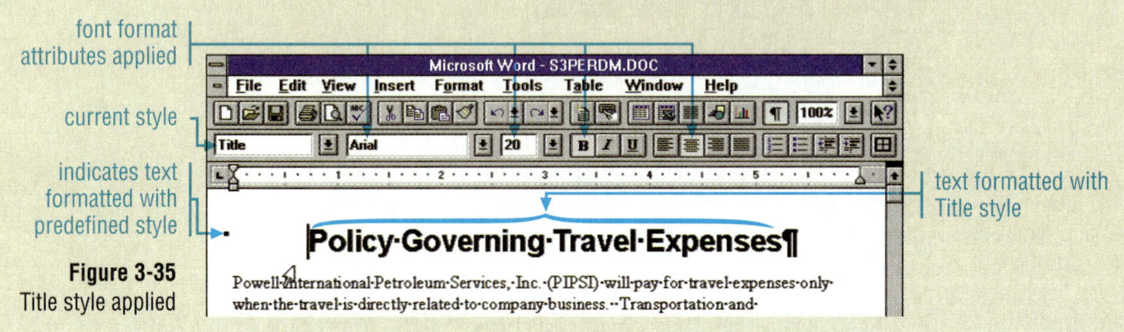

Figure 3-35
Title style applied

While she can see from the Formatting toolbar that the font format has changed, Barbara wants to review the exact attributes assigned to the Title style.

Using Reveal Formats

The Reveal Formats feature allows you to display information about the formatting that has been applied to paragraphs or characters either directly (as you learned in Tutorial 2) or through the use of styles. To use the Reveal Formats feature, click the Help button on the Standard toolbar, then click the Help pointer ▸? on the character or paragraph you want information about. Word displays an information box describing the formatting applied to the selected text. To dismiss the information box, press [Esc] or click the Help button.

To check the formats applied to the title:

❶ Click the **Help button** ▸? on the Standard toolbar, then click anywhere in the title, **Policy Governing Travel Expenses**. The Reveal Formats box appears. See Figure 3-36. The description indicates that the font used in the Title style has the following font formatting: Arial, 20 pt, bold; and the following paragraph formatting: a blank line equal to 18 pt inserted above the paragraph and a blank line equal to 8 pt inserted below the paragraph. Notice that no direct formatting has been applied to this text.

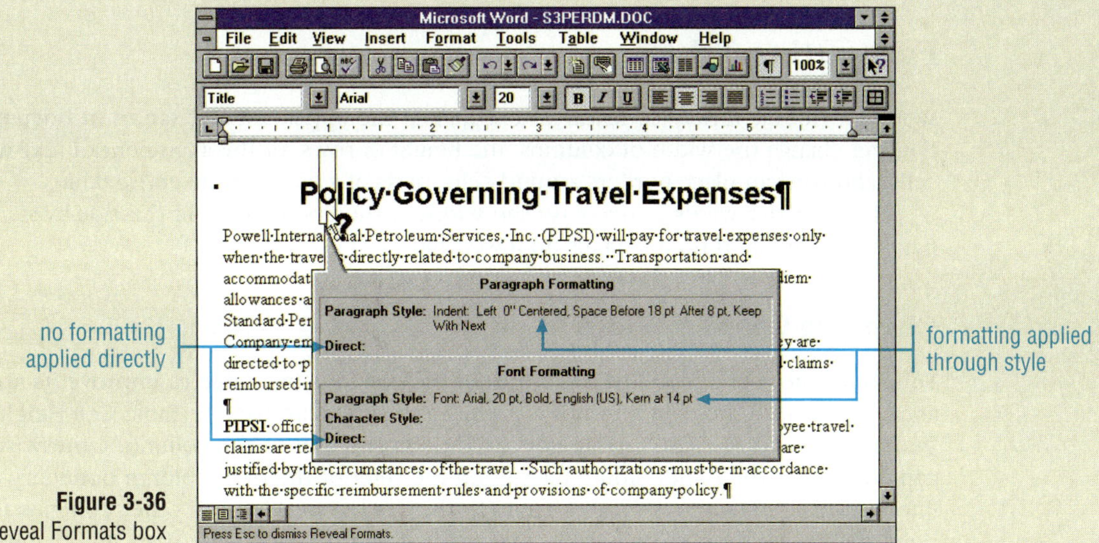

Figure 3-36
Reveal Formats box

❷ Press **[Esc]** or click ▸? to close the Reveal Formats box.

Barbara continues to apply styles to the rest of the document.

❸ Click anywhere within the **Standard Per Diem Allowance** heading (Pg 1, Ln 6) to select it.

❹ Click the **Style list box down arrow** on the Formatting toolbar, then click **Heading 1**. The formatting attributes for the Heading 1 style are applied to the selected text. Use the Reveal Formats feature to determine the attributes applied to the selected heading.

❺ Click anywhere in the **Domestic Travel** heading (Pg 1, Ln 15), click the **Style list box down arrow**, then click **Heading 1**. The formatting attributes of the Heading 1 style are applied to the selected paragraph.

❻ Click anywhere in the heading, **Per Diem Allowance for Extended Domestic Work Assignments** (Pg 2, Ln 8), click the **Style list box down arrow**, then click **Heading 2**. The Heading 2 style is applied to the selected text.

Barbara also notices that the Caption style has been applied to the table caption, which is now in italics and a smaller point size. Recall that when you attach a new template to a document, any style in the document having the same name as a style in the new template is overwritten by the new style. Use the Reveal Formats feature to determine the attributes applied to the selected heading.

❼ Repeat Steps 5 and 6 for those similar headings in the Foreign Travel section.

❽ Click anywhere in the **Exceptions** heading, click the **Style list box down arrow**, then click **Heading 1**.

❾ Save the changes you have made.

Barbara is now ready to format the tables in her document.

Formatting Tables

Word provides a variety of features to enhance the appearance of tables in documents. You can change the width of columns, the height of rows, or the alignment of text within cells; and you can place borders around cells, parts of a table, or the entire table.

First, Barbara wants to decrease the width of the first column in the side-by-side text paragraphs so that this table takes up fewer lines.

Changing Column Width

You sometimes need to adjust the width of the columns in a table to improve its appearance. If you need the column to be a precise measurement, use the Table Cell Height and Width command so that you can specify the exact width of the column. Otherwise you can drag either the right column marker on the ruler or the right column boundary (gridline) of the column you want to change to the desired position. All other columns to the right are resized proportionately, but the overall width of the table does not change. For more information about other options for adjusting the width of a column, see the *Microsoft Word User's Guide*.

Barbara wants to decrease the width of the first column in the side-by-side text paragraphs to 1.5 inches. She decides to do so by dragging the column boundary, using the ruler as a guide.

To change the width of the first column by dragging the column boundary:

❶ Place the insertion point anywhere in the table containing the side-by-side text paragraphs in the Domestic Travel section (beginning Pg 1, Ln 20). Make sure that you do not have any cells selected.

❷ Move the mouse pointer over the boundary between columns 1 and 2. The mouse pointer changes to ↔.

❸ Click and drag the pointer to the 1.5" mark on the ruler, then release the mouse button. Notice that as the first column decreases in width, the second column increases, but the overall width of the table does not change.

Barbara wants to make two other formatting changes to the table: she wants to increase the space between the two rows and bold the text in the first column.

To finish making formatting changes to the table:

❶ Place the insertion point in row 1 of the table, click the **right mouse button** to display the Table Shortcut menu, then click **Paragraph…**. The Paragraph dialog box appears.

❷ Increase the Spacing After box to **12 pt**, then click **OK** or press **[Enter]**.

❸ Select the first column of text, then click the **Bold button** **B** on the Formatting toolbar. Deselect the selected cells. See Figure 3-37.

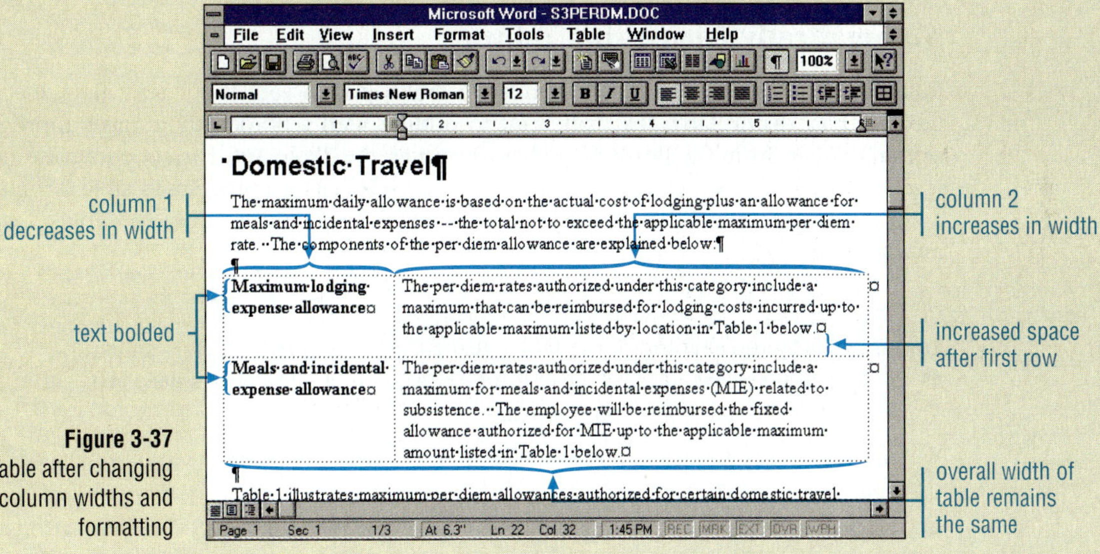

Figure 3-37
Table after changing column widths and formatting

❹ Save the changes you have made.

Next Barbara needs to make the same formatting changes to the same table in the Foreign Travel section of the document. This time she'll use the column marker instead of the column boundary to change the column width.

To format the table in the Foreign Travel section:

❶ Place the insertion point in the table containing side-by-side text paragraphs in the Foreign Travel section of the document (beginning Pg 2, Ln 21).

❷ Move the mouse pointer over the column marker in the ruler between columns 1 and 2. The mouse pointer changes to ↔.

❸ Click and drag the column marker to the 1.5" mark on the ruler, then release the mouse button.

❹ Place the insertion point in row 1 of the table, click the **right mouse button** to display the Table Shortcut menu, then click **Paragraph...**. The Paragraph dialog box appears.

❺ Increase the Spacing After box to **12 pt**, then click **OK** or press **[Enter]**.

❻ Select the first column of text, then click the **Bold button** **B** on the Formatting toolbar. Deselect the selected cells.

❼ Save the changes you have made.

Word also allows you to change the width of selected individual cells or groups of cells within a table. You would follow the same procedures to change their widths as you do for changing entire columns.

Next, Barbara decides to use the Table AutoFormat command on the Table menu to add borders and shading to Tables 1 and 2.

Automatically Formatting Tables

You can add borders, rules, and shading to tables just as you do for text: first select the table or part of the table that you want to outline with a border, then make appropriate option choices from the Borders toolbar. However, the Table AutoFormat command makes it much easier to create professionally formatted tables using a predefined table format.

Barbara will use Table AutoFormat to add borders and shading to Tables 1 and 2 automatically.

To add borders and shading to the tables using the Table AutoFormat command:

❶ Place the insertion point in Table 1, click **Table**, then click **Table AutoFormat...**. The Table AutoFormat dialog box appears.

Barbara is not sure which format she wants to use so she decides to explore her options.

❷ Click several different table format options in the Formats list to view the various formats available.

Barbara decides that the Classic 2 format is the one that suits her data the best.

❸ Click **Classic 2**. See Figure 3-38. Barbara wants Word to adjust the width of the column so that each column is only as wide as the longest item in the column, so she leaves the AutoFit option in the Formats to Apply section activated.

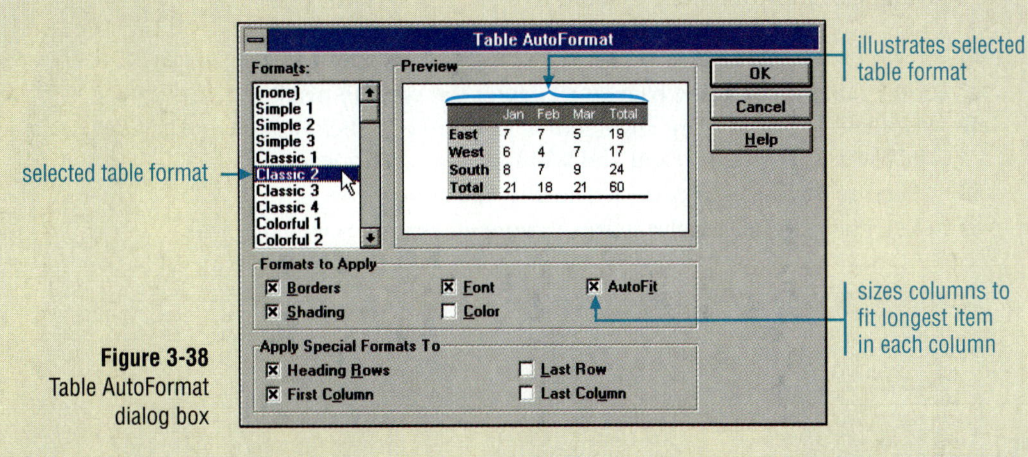

illustrates selected table format

selected table format

sizes columns to fit longest item in each column

Figure 3-38
Table AutoFormat dialog box

❹ Click **OK** or press **[Enter]**. The formatted table appears in the document. See Figure 3-39. Notice that the width of the columns has changed so that the columns are only as wide as the longest item in each column. Also notice that the table no longer extends across the entire line length.

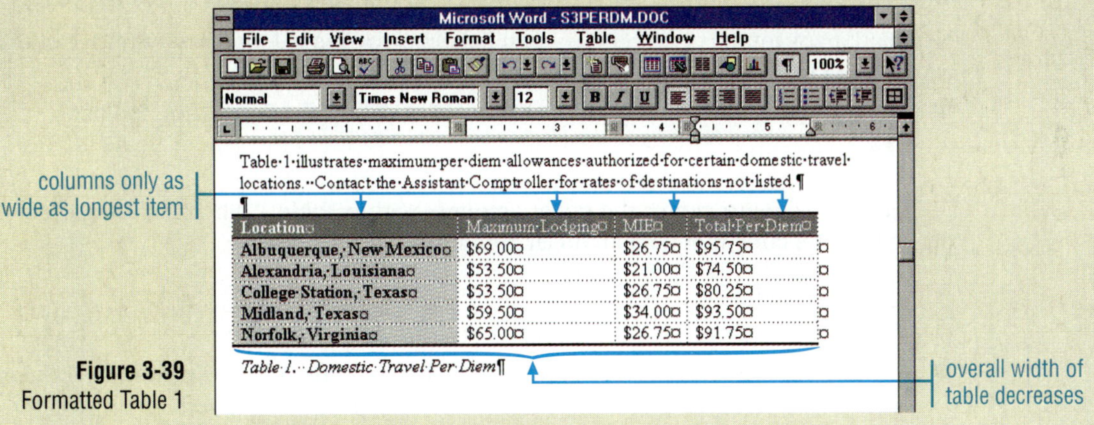

columns only as wide as longest item

overall width of table decreases

Figure 3-39
Formatted Table 1

❺ Repeat Steps 1 through 4 to format Table 2.
❻ Save the changes you have made.

Keep in mind that the gridlines you use to see the table structure on the screen are not the same as the borders that you apply using the Borders toolbar or the Table AutoFormat command; gridlines do not print.

Next Barbara decides to center the table across the page, center the dollar amounts within the cells, and center the caption below the table.

Centering a Table

If a table does not take up the entire width of a line, you might want to center it between the left and right margins. If you use the Center button on the Formatting toolbar to center a selected table, the *text* within the cells is centered between each cell boundary; the table is not centered across the page. To center a table, you must use the Table Cell Height and Width command.

Barbara begins by centering Table 1.

To center Table 1 across the page, then center the column headings:

❶ Place the insertion point anywhere within Table 1, click **Table**, then click **Cell Height and Width....** The Cell Height and Width dialog box appears.

❷ Click the **Row tab**, if necessary. The Row tab appears.

❸ Click the **Center radio button** in the Alignment section. See Figure 3-40.

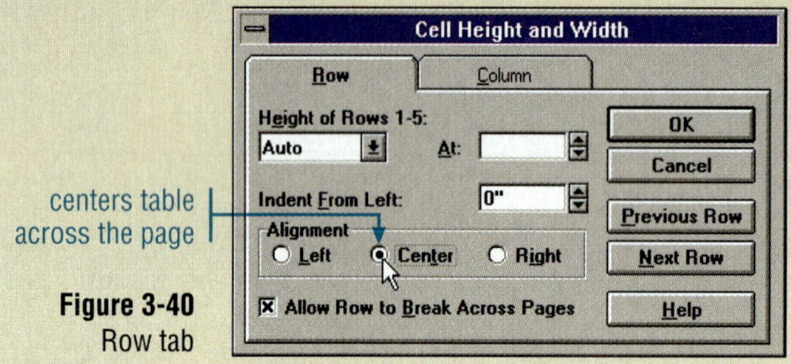

centers table across the page

Figure 3-40
Row tab

❹ Click **OK** or press **[Enter]**. Table 1 is adjusted so that it is centered across the page.

Next Barbara wants to center the column headings for Table 1. She must first select the row containing the column headings.

❺ Select the first row, then click the **Center button** on the Formatting toolbar.

Barbara wants to center the dollar amounts within Table 1. She must first select only the cells in the table that contain dollar amounts.

To center the text in the cells containing dollar amounts in Table 1:

❶ Click in the cell selection bar of the first dollar amount, $69.00 (Maximum Lodging amount for Albuquerque, New Mexico). The entire cell is selected.

❷ Press the mouse button, drag through $91.75 (Maximum Per Diem amount for Norfolk, Virginia), then release the mouse button.

TROUBLE? Just the dollar amounts within the table should be highlighted. If not, click the Undo button (or click Edit then click Undo), then start again.

❸ Click the **Center button** on the Formatting toolbar. Just the highlighted dollar amounts are centered. Deselect the text.

❹ Save the changes you have made.

Next Barbara wants the caption centered across the page below Table 1.

To center the caption for Table 1:

❶ Click anywhere within the caption for Table 1.

❷ Click the **Center button** on the Formatting toolbar. See Figure 3-41.

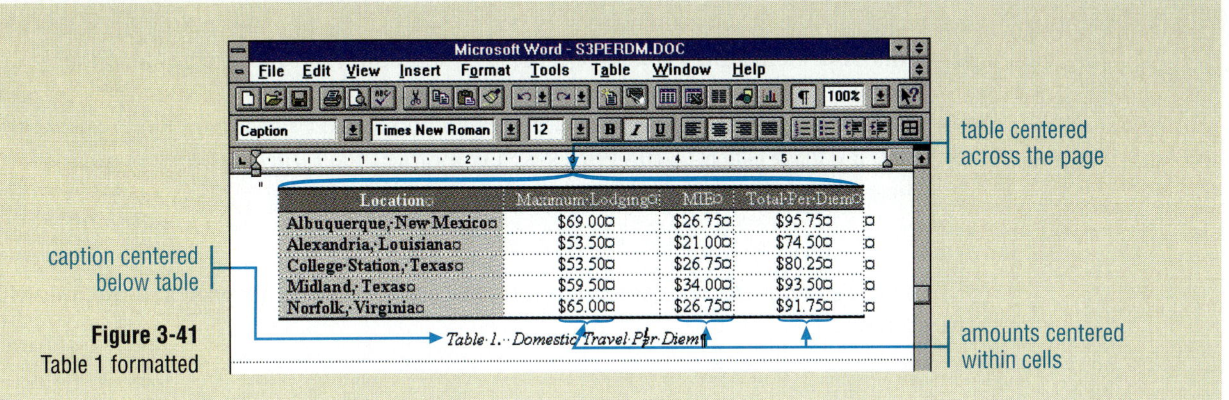

Figure 3-41
Table 1 formatted

caption centered below table

table centered across the page

amounts centered within cells

Barbara has applied formatting changes to Table 1. She now needs to make the same format changes to Table 2 (Pg 2, Ln 31). Use what you have learned in the preceding steps to help you make the changes to this table.

To apply format changes to Table 2:

❶ Center the table across the page, then center the column headings.

❷ Center the dollar amounts.

❸ Center the caption under Table 2. See Figure 3-42.

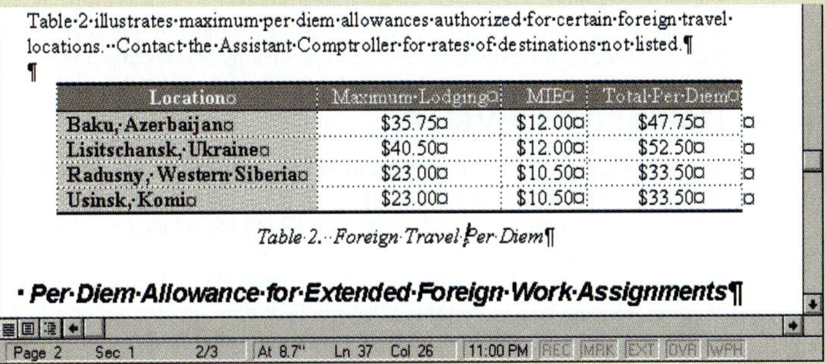

Figure 3-42
Table 2 formatted

❹ Save the changes you have made.

Barbara has finished formatting her document and now is ready to spell check, preview, then print it.

To spell check, preview, then print the document:

❶ Click the **Spelling button** 🔤 on the Standard toolbar (or click **Tools** then click **Spelling...**). Complete the spell check following the procedures you learned in Tutorial 1, then save your changes as necessary.

❷ Click the **Print Preview button** 🔍 on the Standard toolbar (or click **File** then click **Print Preview**).

❸ If necessary, click the **Multiple Pages button** 🖽 on the Print Preview toolbar, then select three pages to display all pages of the document.

❹ Click the **Print button** 🖨 on the Print Preview toolbar to print the document.

❺ Click the **Close button** on the Print Preview toolbar. You return to the document.

❻ Close the document then exit Word.

Barbara's completed document appears in Figure 3-43 on this page and the following two pages.

Policy Governing Travel Expenses

Powell International Petroleum Services, Inc. (PIPSI) will pay for travel expenses only when the travel is directly related to company business. Transportation and accommodations must be consistent with **PIPSI**'s goals and conform to the per diem allowances and travel policies detailed below.

Standard Per Diem Allowance

Company employees will be authorized an equitable expense allowance when they are directed to perform company travel. Per diem allowances will be authorized and claims reimbursed in accordance with the provisions of **PIPSI**'s travel policies.

PIPSI officers who are responsible for authorizing travel or for approving employee travel claims are required to authorize or approve only those per diem allowances that are justified by the circumstances of the travel. Such authorizations must be in accordance with the specific reimbursement rules and provisions of company policy.

Domestic Travel

The maximum daily allowance is based on the actual cost of lodging plus an allowance for meals and incidental expenses -- the total not to exceed the applicable maximum per diem rate. The components of the per diem allowance are explained below:

Maximum lodging expense allowance	The per diem rates authorized under this category include a maximum that can be reimbursed for lodging costs incurred up to the applicable maximum listed by location in Table 1 below.
Meals and incidental expense allowance	The per diem rates authorized under this category include a maximum for meals and incidental expenses (MIE) related to subsistence. The employee will be reimbursed the fixed allowance authorized for MIE up to the applicable maximum amount listed in Table 1 below.

Table 1 illustrates maximum per diem allowances authorized for certain domestic travel locations. Contact the Assistant Comptroller for rates of destinations not listed.

Location	Maximum Lodging	MIE	Total Per Diem
Albuquerque, New Mexico	$69.00	$26.75	$95.75
Alexandria, Louisiana	$53.50	$21.00	$74.50
College Station, Texas	$53.50	$26.75	$80.25
Midland, Texas	$59.50	$34.00	$93.50
Norfolk, Virginia	$65.00	$26.75	$91.75

Table 1. Domestic Travel Per Diem

Policy Governing Travel Expenses   **12/21/95**

Figure 3-43
Completed document
(page 1 of 3)

2

Per Diem Allowance for Extended Domestic Work Assignments

On extended work assignments of more than 30 days but less than 120 days, the employee will be reimbursed 65 percent of the maximum per diem rate for that location. On extended work assignments of 120 days or more, the employee will be reimbursed 55 percent of the maximum per diem rate for that location.

Reimbursement will be based on a flat rate system. Employees are required to submit a copy of any leases for accommodations with the initial travel expense claim and for any future instances when another lease must be obtained. Receipts must also be submitted with each claim for furniture rental, utilities, and other expenses over $25.

Foreign Travel

Subsistence reimbursement for foreign travel is based on lodging plus an amount established for meals and incidental expenses for the location. Actual expenses may be approved when per diem rates do not cover subsistence expenses. Reimbursements may be made for the actual expenses up to 150 percent of the location rate or $50 plus the location rate, whichever is greater. The components of the per diem allowance are explained below:

Maximum lodging expense allowance
The per diem rates authorized under this category include a maximum that can be reimbursed for lodging costs incurred up to the applicable maximum listed by location in Table 2 below.

Meals and incidental expense allowance
The per diem rates authorized under this category include a maximum for meals and incidental expenses (MIE) related to subsistence. The employee will be reimbursed the fixed allowance authorized for MIE up to the applicable maximum amount listed in Table 2 below.

Table 2 illustrates maximum per diem allowances authorized for certain foreign travel locations. Contact the Assistant Comptroller for rates of destinations not listed.

Location	Maximum Lodging	MIE	Total Per Diem
Baku, Azerbaijan	$35.75	$12.00	$47.75
Lisitschansk, Ukraine	$40.50	$12.00	$52.50
Radusny, Western Siberia	$23.00	$10.50	$33.50
Usinsk, Komi	$23.00	$10.50	$33.50

Table 2. Foreign Travel Per Diem

Per Diem Allowance for Extended Foreign Work Assignments

On extended work assignments of more than 30 days but less than 120 days, the employee will be reimbursed 65 percent of the maximum per diem rate for that location. On

Figure 3-43
Completed document
(page 2 of 3)

3

extended work assignments of 120 days or more, the employee will be reimbursed 55 percent of the maximum per diem rate for that location.

Reimbursement will be based on a flat rate system. Employees are required to submit a copy of any leases for accommodations with the initial travel expense claim and for any future instances when another lease must be obtained. Receipts must also be submitted with each claim for furniture rental, utilities, and other expenses over $25.

Exceptions

Any exceptions to the standard per diem allowance must be submitted in writing to the Assistant Comptroller's office.

Policy Governing Travel Expenses   12/21/95

Figure 3-43
Completed document
(page 3 of 3)

Barbara faxes Nancy a copy of the finished travel expense policy. Nancy is pleased with the document's appearance and gives Barbara her approval to submit it to management.

Questions

1. Describe three methods for creating tables.
2. Describe the elements of a table.
3. Explain the purpose of the AutoCorrect feature.
4. Explain the difference between the Cut and Paste procedure and the Copy and Paste procedure.
5. Explain the purpose of the Replace command on the Edit menu.
6. Explain the process for inserting a row:
   a. Between existing rows of a table
   b. At the bottom of a table
7. Explain the procedure for inserting a column:
   a. Between existing columns of a table
   b. At the end of a table
8. Explain the procedure for sorting information within a table.
9. What is the function key that repeats the last change to a document?
10. Explain the procedure for adding a caption to a table.
11. Explain the difference between a header and a footer.
12. Briefly define each of the following terms:
    a. template
    b. paragraph style
    c. character style
    d. style sheet
13. Describe the procedure for attaching a template other than the NORMAL template to the current document.
14. Describe the procedure for using the Style Gallery to preview a template's styles.
15. Describe the different methods for changing column widths.
16. Describe the procedure for using the Table AutoFormat command to apply formatting to a table.

Use Word Help to answer Questions 17 through 23.

E 17. What is a Table Wizard?

E 18. How do you copy and paste or cut and paste from one Word document to another Word document?

E 19. How do you print the style sheet for a document?

E 20. What is the purpose of the Find command on the Edit menu?

E 21. What is the procedure to merge cells within a table?

E 22. How do you change the numbering format used in a caption?

E 23. How do you print a range of pages within a document?

Tutorial Assignments

Start Word, if necessary, and conduct a screen check. Open the file T3PIPSI1.DOC from your Student Disk, then complete the following:

1. Save the document as S3PIPSI1.DOC.
2. Move the entire Domestic Travel section after the Foreign Travel section.
3. Change all occurrences of "company" to PIPSI (not bolded).

4. Change the header so that:
    a. The page number is centered rather than at the right margin.
    b. It is Arial 12 point bold.
    c. It does not print on the first page.
5. Apply the Heading 1 style to the heading Standard Per Diem Allowance.
6. Apply the Heading 2 style to the headings Domestic Travel and Foreign Travel.
7. Apply the Heading 3 style to the Per Diem Allowance for Extended Work Assignments headings in both sections.
8. Replace all instances of three consecutive paragraph marks with one paragraph mark.
9. Save your changes.
10. Preview, print, then close the document.

Open the file T3PIPSI2.DOC from your Student Disk, then complete the following:

11. Save the document as S3PIPSI2.DOC.
12. Decrease the width of the column containing the component names (Maximum lodging expense allowance and Meals and incidental expense allowance) to 1.25 inches without decreasing the overall width of the table.
13. Bold and center the component names, then change the font to Arial.
14. Insert a 12 point blank line after row 1 of the side-by-side text table, which explains the per diem components.
15. Insert a row at the top of the Foreign Travel Per Diem table to contain column headings: Location (in cell 1), Maximum Lodging (in cell 2), MIE (in cell 3), and Total Per Diem (in cell 4).
16. Insert the two rows of information shown in Figure 3-44 at the bottom of the Foreign Travel Per Diem table without changing the overall width of the table.

Figure 3-44

Volgograd, Russia	$40.25	$12.50
Tbilisi, Georgia	$35.75	$12.50

17. Calculate the total per diem amounts in the Foreign Travel Per Diem table.
18. Add a caption above the Foreign Travel Per Diem table that reads: Table 1. Foreign Travel Per Diem. Center the caption across the page.
19. Sort the rows in the table in descending order based on the total per diem amounts in the last column, then alphabetically by the Location column.
20. Insert a footer to appear on all pages with your name at the left margin, the current date at the right margin, and a 1½ point single rule across the top of the line space.
21. Use the Style Gallery to view the styles in the MANUSCR1 template, then attach the template to the document.
22. Apply the Part Title style to the heading Policy Governing Travel Expenses.
23. Apply the Heading 1 style to the headings Standard Per Diem Allowance and Exceptions.
24. Apply the Heading 2 style to the heading Foreign Travel.
25. Apply the Heading 3 style to the heading Per Diem Allowance for Extended Foreign Work Assignments.
26. Apply the Body Text style to all the text paragraphs in the document, but not to the tables.
27. Format the Foreign Travel Per Diem table using the predefined Columns 5 table format. Deselect the shading option in the Formats section, and select the Last Column option in the Special Formats to Apply section.
28. Save your changes.
29. Preview then print the document.
30. Insert a tab at the beginning of each text paragraph. (*Hint:* Each paragraph is preceded by one paragraph mark. Tab characters and paragraph marks are special characters.)

31. Save the document as S3PIPSI3.DOC.
32. Preview then print the document.
33. Close all documents.

Case Problems

1. Hiring Practices at Teisch Manufacturing, Inc.

Jerome Ellis is the assistant director of Personnel Services for Teisch Manufacturing, Inc., of St. Louis, Missouri. His manager, Felicia Santana, has asked him to write a memo covering the company's hiring practices during the past year. Jerome is to report on how many males and females were hired so that Felicia can determine whether Teisch has complied with Equal Employment Opportunity Commission (EEOC) guidelines.

Open the file P3TEISCH.DOC then complete the following:

1. Save the document as S3TEISCH.DOC.
2. Insert a memo heading at the top of the document, including the title Memorandum and heading information: TO: Executive Committee; FROM: Jerome Ellis; RE: New Hire Mix; DATE: February 26, 1995.
3. Insert a hard page break at the end of the document.
4. Create a table on page 2 for the data shown in Figure 3-45.

Figure 3-45

Position	Female	Male	Total
Equipment Operator	17	10	
Plant Supervisor	1	4	
Administrative Assistant	2	4	
Salesperson	11	10	
Total			

5. Add a caption below the table that reads: Table 1. Gender Mix Among 1994 New Hires.
6. Save your changes.
7. Replace all instances of "the corporation" in the body of the memo with "Teisch."
8. Insert a first-page footer that includes the page number centered. Insert a header for subsequent pages that includes the text "Executive Committee" at the left margin, the page number at the center, and the memo date at the right margin. Add bolding to Executive Committee.
9. Apply the Document Label paragraph style to the title Memorandum.
10. Apply the Message Header First paragraph style to the memo heading TO:; apply the Message Header paragraph style to the memo headings FROM: and RE:; apply the Message Header Last paragraph style to the memo heading DATE; apply the Message Header Label character style to just the memo headings.
11. Apply the Body Text style to the body of the memo.
12. Format the table using the Columns 3 predefined table format. Select the Last Row option in the Apply Special Formats section.
13. Center the table across the page, and center the caption below the table.
14. Center the numbers of new hires within the cells.
15. Save your changes.
16. Preview then print the document.
17. Delete the caption below the table.
18. Insert one row at the top of the table.
19. Merge the cells in the inserted row.
20. Type "Gender Mix for 1994 New Hires" in the cell.

21. Apply the Heading 2 style to the cell, then center the text across the cell.
22. Save the document as S3MIX.DOC.

E 23. Preview then print just page 2 of the document.

24. Close the document.

2. AMICI Training Schedule

Cecilia Vance is the coordinator of staff development programs for AMICI Exploration and Production's headquarters in Houston. She asked Murry Kyle, the manager of the Information Support Services division, to provide her with a schedule of dates in June and July when the staff of the Help Desk Department could offer several training classes requested by the Headquarters' employees. Cecilia received the file today from Murry and wants to send out a flyer for distribution to all personnel.

Open P3MSPSCH.DOC then complete the following:

1. Save the document as S3MSPSCH.DOC.
2. Select all of the lines of text in the file, then convert them to a table.
3. Insert a row at the top of the table.
4. Type the following column headings in the cells of the new row: Course Name, Dates, Prerequisite.
5. Sort the table alphabetically by course name. Specify that the table contains a header row.
6. Insert the following three-line title above the table: Microsoft Products, Training Schedule, Summer Session.
7. Type the text shown in Figure 3-46 below the table.

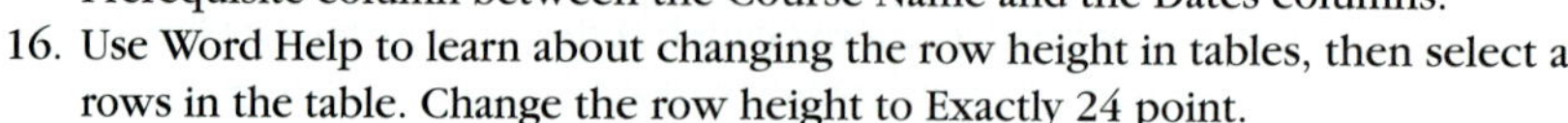

Figure 3-46

8. Change the top margin to 2.0".
9. Format the three-line title with the following attributes:
   a. Center alignment
   b. Matura MT Script Capitals (If this font is not available, choose another script font.)
   c. 24 point
10. Insert a 12 point blank line below the last line in the title and above the last paragraph ("Class size is …").
11. Format the table using the Grid 8 predefined table format.
12. Center the table across the page and the column headings within their cells.
13. Save the document.
14. Preview then print the document.

E 15. Use Word Help to learn about moving columns in a table, then move the Prerequisite column between the Course Name and the Dates columns.

E 16. Use Word Help to learn about changing the row height in tables, then select all rows in the table. Change the row height to Exactly 24 point.

17. Save the document as S3MOVCOL.DOC.
18. Preview, print, then close the document.

3. Creating Your Own Résumé

Complete the following:

1. Create a new document.
2. Type your name, address, and telephone number on separate lines.
3. Press [Enter] twice.
4. Create a five-row by two-column table. (Note: If your résumé extends beyond one page, you will need to adjust the table structure and formatting accordingly.)

5. Decrease the width of column 1 to 1.5 inches, but do not change the overall size of the table.
6. Type the following section headings in the cells in the first column: Career Objective (in row 1), Education (in row 2), Employment (in row 3), Extracurricular Activities and Honors (in row 4), and References (in row 5).
7. In cell 2 of row 1 (next to Career Objective), type your career objective. Use the Paragraph command to insert a 12 point blank line at the bottom of the cell.
8. In cell 2 of row 2 (next to Education), list your college, its location, degree earned or expected to be earned, major, and date of graduation. Press [Enter] twice then list all the courses you have completed in your major. Use the Paragraph command to insert a 12 point blank line after the last line in the cell.
9. In cell 2 of row 3 (next to Employment), list the position title, company, location, and dates of employment for each position you have held. Start with your most recent position. On the next line, give a brief description of your duties. Skip a line between each job. Use the Paragraph command to insert a blank line after the last entry in the cell.
10. In cell 2 of row 4 (next to Extracurricular Activities and Honors), list any organizations you participate in and any awards you have received. Use the Paragraph command to insert a blank line after the last entry in the cell.
11. In cell 2 of row 5 (next to References), type "Available upon request."
12. Center your name, address, and telephone number. Change the font to 14 point Arial, then bold your name, address, and telephone number.
13. Change the section headings in column 1 of the table to bold and all capitals.
14. Insert bullets in front of each course in your major.
15. Bold each title of the positions you have held.
16. Spell check the document.
17. Save the document as S3RESUME.DOC.
18. Preview, print, then close the document.

Merging Documents

Writing a Confirmation Form Letter

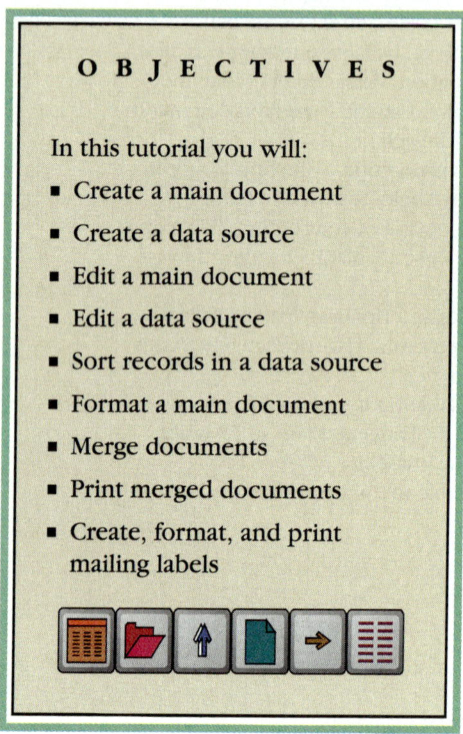

CASE — **Mecklenburg County Roads and Bridges Department** Paul Krueger is the administrative assistant to Greg Sterling, superintendent of the Roads and Bridges Department for Mecklenburg County in North Carolina. The department is responsible for building and maintaining all roads and bridges within the county that are not within any city's corporate limits.

Because of declining state revenues, the state of North Carolina established a volunteer cleanup program, called the Adopt-a-Highway program, for state highways through the State Department of Highways and Public Transportation. In conjunction with the state's program, Greg recently established the Adopt-a-County-Mile program, whereby civic and nonprofit organizations within Mecklenburg County could assist the local government with county road cleanup.

After a recent local television report on the Adopt-a-County-Mile program, several organizations contacted the Roads and Bridges Department to volunteer their services for the project. Now Greg wants Paul to write a confirmation letter that explains the details of the program to the contact person for each of these organizations (Figure 4-1).

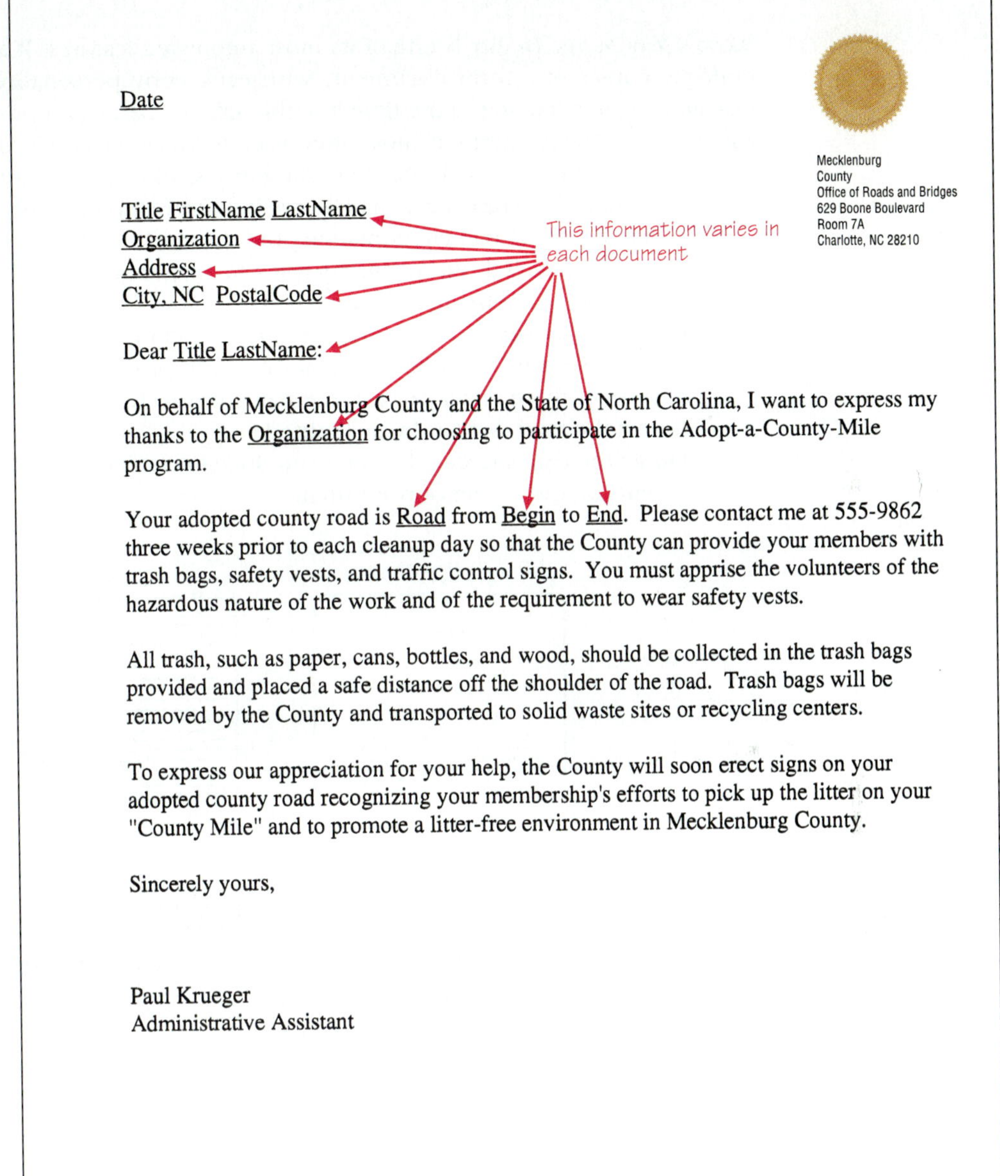

Figure 4-1
Paul's confirmation form letter

Paul's task requires him to send the same basic letter to several different people. He needs to determine the best productivity strategy to complete this task. The letters should be personalized for each volunteering organization, but Paul doesn't have the time to create each letter individually or to edit an existing letter several times.

Word provides a time-saving procedure to help Paul solve his problem. The Mail Merge command on the Tools menu allows him to combine a main document—a file containing text that stays the same for every printed copy—with a data source—a file containing information that varies for every printed copy—to produce customized documents. Paul will follow the productivity strategy by creating the main document and the data source, then editing and formatting them. Finally, he will merge the two documents before printing.

The Merge Process

Word's Mail Merge facility is one of its most automated features. It allows you to produce multiple copies of a form document, with each copy personalized according to your instructions, in a fraction of the time it would take to create and print each copy individually. The Mail Merge feature is most often used to create customized form letters, but you can also use it to create labels, catalogs, directories, and legal documents.

As illustrated in Figure 4-2, a mail merge is a three-step process:

1. Create a main document containing the standard text that does not vary from letter to letter, as well as merge instructions to Word about where to insert the variable information from the data source.
2. Create a data source containing the information that varies from letter to letter. In Paul's case, this variable information is the organization's name, the name and address of the contact person, the name of the adopted county road, and the portion of the road that has been adopted.
3. Merge the data source with the main document. Then either view the merged documents on the screen or print them.

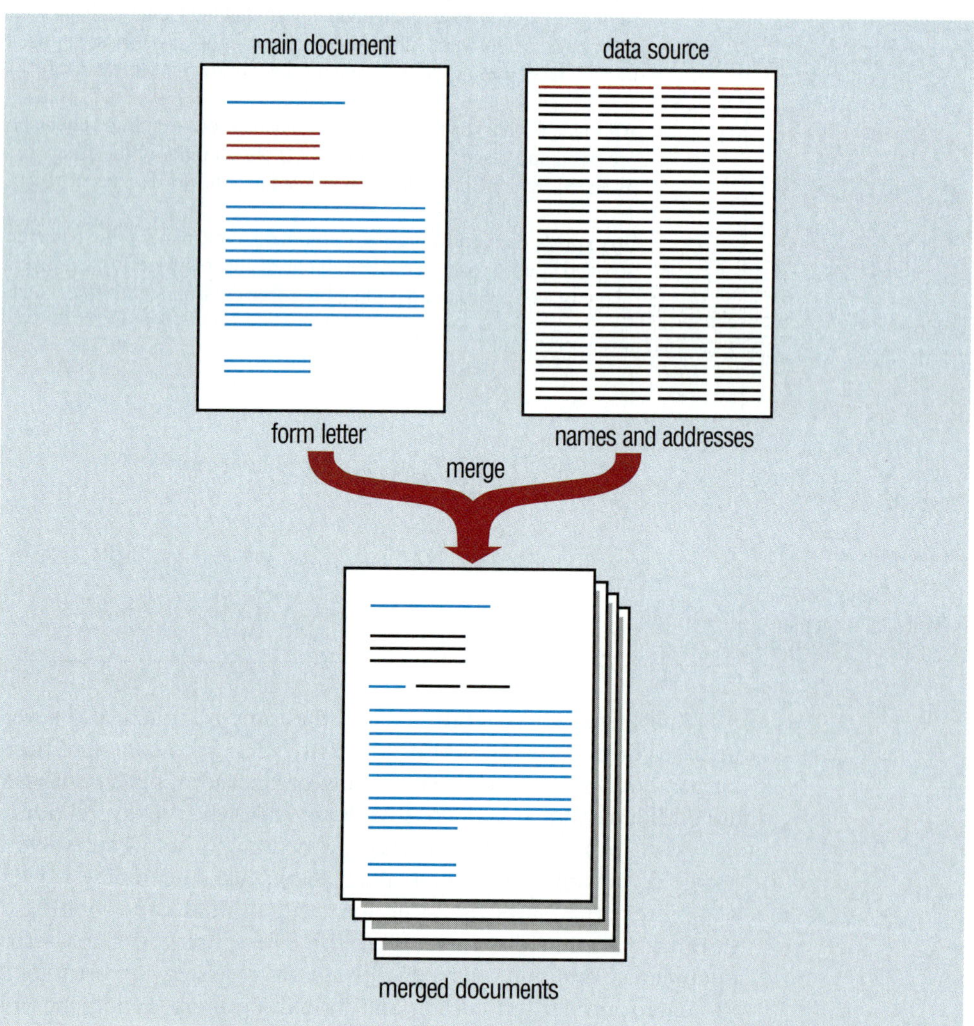

Figure 4-2
Merge process

Word gives you a variety of ways to complete the steps in the merge process. In this tutorial, you will use the most automated way to complete the merge process for situations in which you create both the main document and the data source from scratch. This tutorial will explain when and how the procedures would be different if you had previously created either the main document or the data source.

Creating a Main Document

The **main document** contains the text that stays the same in all the merged documents, as well as the instructions that tell Word where to place the information from the data source. In this first step of the merge process, you must indicate which document you intend to use as the main document. You can either create a new document or use an existing document as the main document.

Paul will create a new document—the form letter—as his main document.

To start Word and set up the main document:

❶ Start Word then conduct the screen check as described in Tutorial 1.

❷ Insert your Student Disk in the disk drive, then save the new blank document as S4ACMAIN.DOC. This will be Paul's form letter document.

If you had already created a main document, you would open it instead. The important point to remember about Word's Mail Merge feature is to make sure that the main document is the active document when you begin the merge process; that is, when you choose the Mail Merge command from the Tools menu.

❸ Click **Tools** then click **Mail Merge....** The Mail Merge Helper dialog box appears. See Figure 4-3. It indicates the step-by-step procedure you follow to create merged documents.

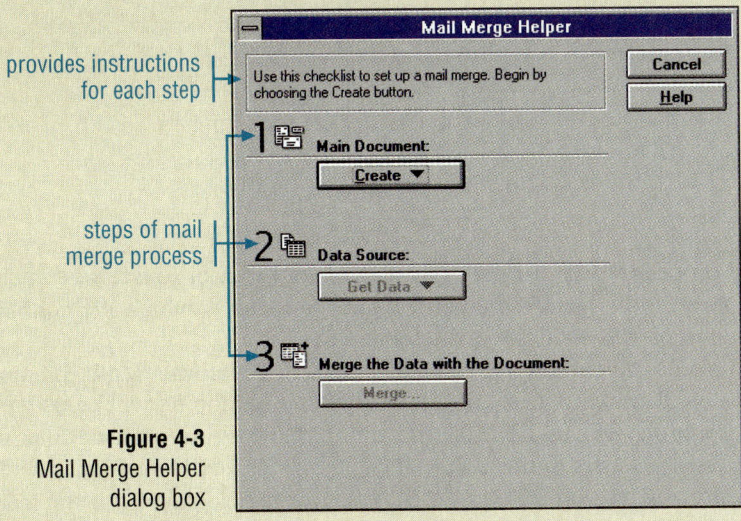

Figure 4-3
Mail Merge Helper
dialog box

❹ Click **Create** in the Main Document section. The list of main document types appears.

❺ Click **Form Letters…**. A message box appears with choices for which document to use as the main document. You'll use the document in the active window as the main document.

❻ Click **Active Window**. You return to the Mail Merge Helper dialog box. Notice that the type of merge and the name of the main document are specified in the Main Document section. You have now established the active document— S4ACMAIN.DOC—as the main document.

Paul will type the text of the letter and add the merge instructions to the main document after he creates the data source, which is the next step in the Mail Merge process.

Creating a Data Source

The **data source** is a document that contains all the variable information used to personalize the main document. As shown in Figure 4-4, the data source is basically a Word table made up of three components: data records, data fields, and a header row. Each row, except the first, is a **data record** that contains all the information necessary to customize one merged document. Each column is a **data field** that contains a single type of information; for instance, the last name of the contact person for each volunteering organization.

The **header row**, the first row of the data source, contains the **data field names**, or descriptions, of the different types of information in each of the columns. Each data field name in the header row must be unique, can contain up to 40 characters (including numbers, letters, and underscores), cannot contain spaces, and must start with a letter.

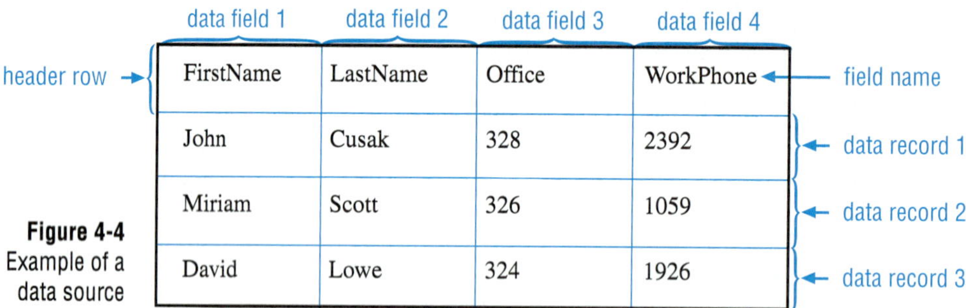

Figure 4-4
Example of a
data source

In the mail merge process when you specify the name of the data source document, you *attach* that document to the main document. Word then knows which file contains the variable information to be placed in the main document.

Paul has not created a document that contains the data source information so he must do that now. He begins by identifying the types of variable information he will be using in his letter. He lists descriptions of this information; then, following the conventions for naming data fields, he assigns names to the different categories of variable information for use in the header row of the data source. Figure 4-5 lists the data field names for the information Paul will use in his letter. Notice the field name "City_NC." Because all the organizations are located within North Carolina, Paul includes "NC" in the field name. Otherwise, he would have had a separate field for "State."

Category of Information	Data Field Name
Name of volunteer organization	Organization
Title of contact person	Title
First name of contact person	FirstName
Last name of contact person	LastName
Street address of contact person	Address
City location of contact person	City_NC
Zip code for location of contact person	PostalCode
Name of adopted county road	Road
Beginning point of county mile	Begin
Ending point of county mile	End

Figure 4-5
Data field names for
Paul's data source

First, Paul begins by attaching the data source to the main document.

Attaching the Data Source

Word must know which document contains the variable information that is to be inserted into the main document during the merge process. You can either open an existing document that was set up as a data source, or you can create a new data source document. Paul needs to create a new data source document.

To attach the data source to the main document:
❶ Click **Get Data** in the Data Source section of the Mail Merge Helper dialog box. The Data Source menu appears.

Paul has not created the data source information yet. He will start by creating the header row of the data source.

Creating the Header Row

Paul has established the data fields for each of the categories of variable information, and he is ready to create the header row for his data source.

To create the data field names for the header row in the data source:
❶ Click **Create Data Source…**. The Create Data Source dialog box appears. See Figure 4-6. The Field Names in Header Row list box provides commonly used data field names for a header row in a data source.

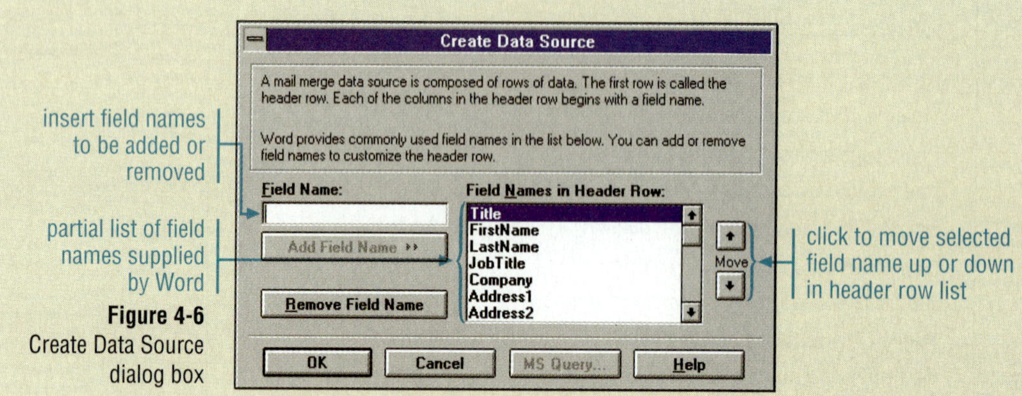

Figure 4-6
Create Data Source
dialog box

Paul wants to see if he can use any of the data field names that Word has supplied.

❷   Scroll through the list of data field names.

Paul can use some of the field names—Title, FirstName, LastName, Address1 (for Address), and PostalCode—but he will need to add other field names for Organization, City_NC, Road, Begin, and End.

❸   Type **Organization** in the Field Name text box, then click **Add Field Name** or press **[Enter]**. "Organization" is added to the end of the Field Names in Header Row list.

❹   Repeat Step 3 to add the following four data field names to the list: **City_NC**, **Road**, **Begin**, **End**.

Next Paul needs to remove the unnecessary field names.

❺   Scroll to the top of the field name list, click **JobTitle**, then click **Remove Field Name**.

❻   Repeat Step 5 for each of the following unnecessary field names: **Company**, **Address2**, **City**, **State**, **Country**, **HomePhone**, **WorkPhone**.

To make it quicker to add the specific information he has received for each data record, Paul needs to rearrange the order of the data field names.

❼   Click **Organization** then click the **Move up arrow button** until Organization is moved to the top of the field name list, directly above Title.

   TROUBLE? The field names in the list scroll continuously. Make sure you move Organization immediately above Title.

❽   Click **City_NC** then click the **Move up arrow button** until City_NC is between Address1 and PostalCode.

❾   Click **OK**. The Save Data Source dialog box appears.

❿   Type **s4acmdat** in the File Name text box. Make sure the drive for your Student Disk is selected, then click **OK** or press **[Enter]**. The data source document, S4ACMDAT.DOC, is now attached to the main document, S4ACMAIN.DOC.

A message box appears with choices for either entering the variable information into the data source or editing the main document. Paul wants to complete the data source by inserting the variable information for each organization. To do so he'll use the data form.

Using the Data Form

You can either enter the data directly in the data source, just as you would enter information in a table, or you can use the on-line data form that Word provides to make the process easier.

Paul decides to use the data form to enter the information about the volunteering organizations in the data source.

To enter information in the data source using the data form:

❶   In the message box, click **Edit Data Source** or press **[Enter].** The Data Form dialog box appears with the data field names for the header row listed next to blank text boxes, which you complete with the necessary variable information. See Figure 4-7.

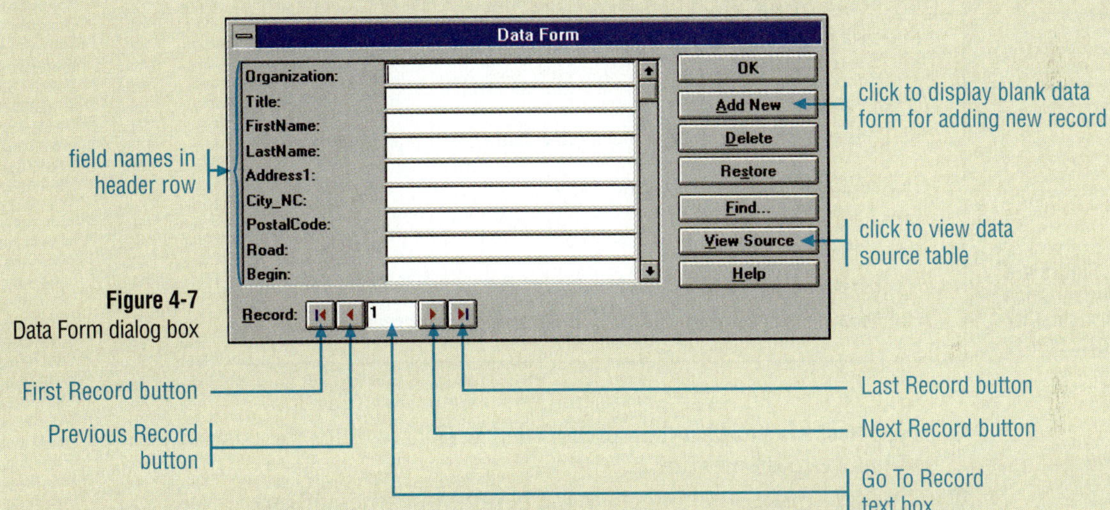

Figure 4-7
Data Form dialog box

To move to the next blank text box, press [Tab] or [Enter]; to move to the previous text box, press [Shift][Tab]. Do not enter any trailing spaces at the end of a text box—you will add the necessary spacing around the merge instructions in the main document rather than in the data records.

Figure 4-8 lists the information Paul has gathered about each organization that has volunteered for the Adopt-a-County-Mile program. To help him complete the data form, he has marked off the different pieces of data that he must enter for each field.

/Noon Kiwanis Club/
/Ms./Leola/Williams/
/1887 Goldston Lane/
/Charlotte, NC/ 28078/
/Grier Road/from/W. T. Harris Blvd./to/John Russell Road/

/Mint Museum Employees/
/Mr./John/Diaz/
/13523 Primwood Street/
/Pineville, NC /28134/
/Lebanon Road/from/Margaret Wallace Road/to/Lawyers Road/

/Charlotte Association of Retired Persons/
/Mr./Brian/Anderson/
/10038 Wrentree Drive/
/Charlotte, NC / 28211/
/W. T. Harris Blvd./from/Mallard Creek Blvd./to/Research Drive/

/Huntersville Chamber of Commerce/
/Mrs./Oma/Cristini/
/Rt. 4, Box 51/
/Huntersville, NC /28210/
/Huntersville Road/from/Alexandria Road/to/Hambright Road/

Figure 4-8
Organization
information for
Paul's data source

❷ Type **Noon Kiwanis Club** then press **[Enter]** or **[Tab]** to enter the data for the first field and move to the next field.

❸ Type **Ms.** (make sure to include the period) then press **[Enter]** or **[Tab]**.

❹ Type **Leola** then press **[Enter]** or **[Tab]**.

❺ Type **Williams** then press **[Enter]** or **[Tab]**.

❻ Type **1887 Goldston Lane** then press **[Enter]** or **[Tab]**.

❼ Type **Charlotte, NC** then press **[Enter]** or **[Tab]**.

❽ Type **28078** then press **[Enter]** or **[Tab]**.

❾ Type **Grier Road** then press **[Enter]** or **[Tab]**.

❿ Type **W. T. Harris Blvd.**, press **[Enter]** or **[Tab]**, then type **John Russell Road** to complete the form. See Figure 4-9.

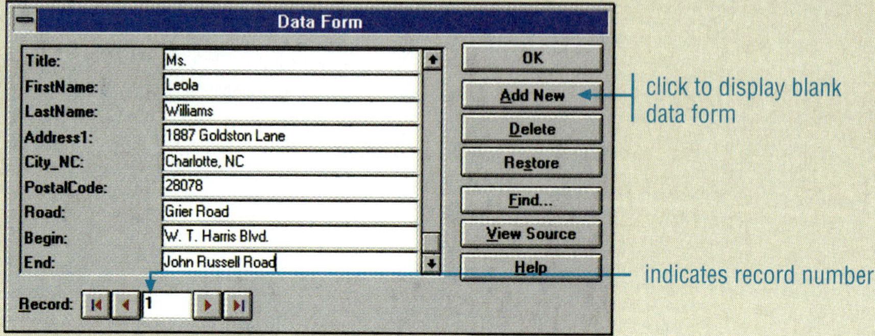

Figure 4-9
First data record in
Paul's data source

Paul has entered all the information for the first record in the data source. Now he is ready to enter the information for the remaining three records shown in Figure 4-8.

To enter the remaining information in the data source:

❶ Click **Add New** to display a blank data form. Notice that the text box at the bottom of the data form now shows record 2.

❷ Enter the information for the second and third data records shown in Figure 4-8.

❸ Enter the information for the fourth data record shown in Figure 4-8, but *do not click Add New* when you are finished. Clicking Add New would add a blank record as the fifth record.

   TROUBLE? If you accidentally insert a blank fifth record, click Delete.

Paul wants to proofread each data record to make sure he typed the information correctly. He wants to move to the beginning of the data source using the data record access buttons at the bottom of the dialog box.

To move to records within the data source:

❶ Click the **First Record button** at the bottom of the form. The data record number changes to 1, and the information for the first data record you entered is displayed in the form.

❷ Proofread the data, making corrections if necessary, then click the **Next Record button** at the bottom of the form. The data record number changes to 2, and the information for the second data record is displayed in the form.

❸ Repeat Step 2 until you have viewed all four records, making corrections where necessary.

Now that Paul has proofread the records using the data form, he needs to save the data source document. He cannot save the document while the data form is displayed; he must first view the data source.

To save the data source:

❶ Click **View Source**. The inserted data in the form of a table is displayed. Note that the Database toolbar also appears. This is the toolbar you use for working with the data source.

Paul wants to be able to see the full width of the data source table on the screen.

❷ Click the **Zoom Control list box down arrow** on the Standard toolbar, then click **Page Width**. The entire table is displayed across the screen. Notice that the contents wrap within the cells. You do not need to worry about the appearance of the text in the table because you will not print the table. See Figure 4-10.

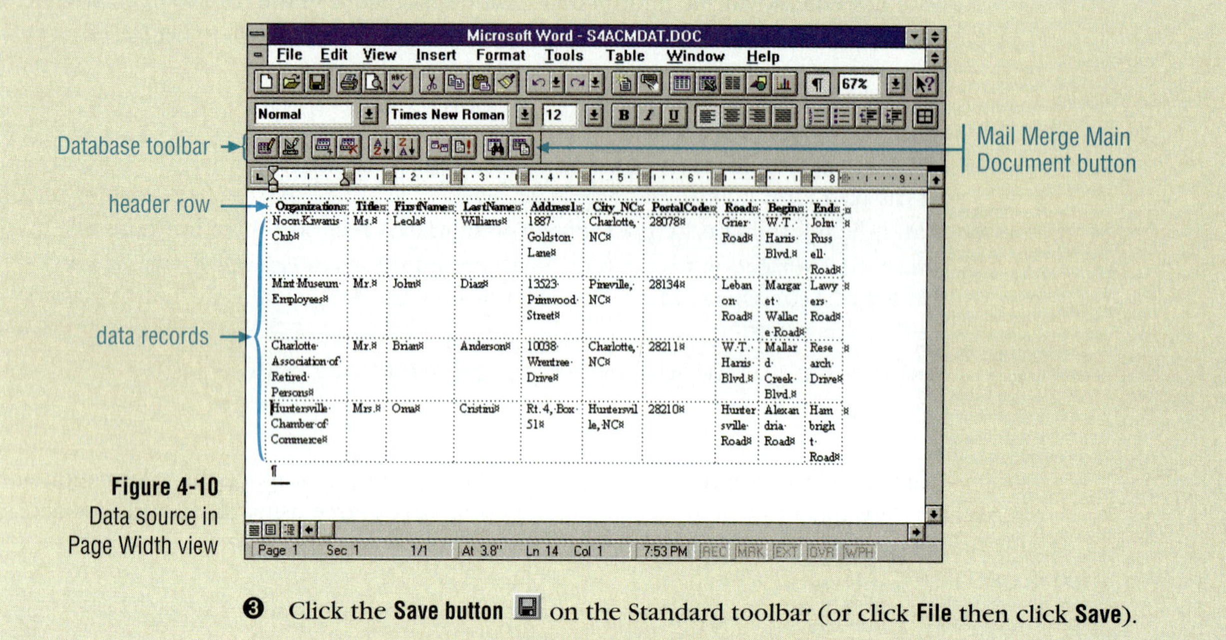

Figure 4-10
Data source in
Page Width view

Database toolbar

header row

data records

Mail Merge Main
Document button

❸ Click the **Save button** 🖫 on the Standard toolbar (or click **File** then click **Save**).

Although Paul's data source eventually will contain many more volunteering organizations, it contains enough records now to demonstrate Word's Mail Merge feature. He is ready to type the text of his confirmation form letter and insert merge instructions in the main document.

Editing a Main Document

You created the main document earlier, but you did not enter any text or merge instructions yet. You are now ready to edit the main document.

Paul knows he needs to begin his letter with a date, but he also knows that if he types the current date he will have to modify the main document each time he sends this letter to a new volunteering organization. He decides to insert a **date field code** that will automatically insert the current date each time the document is printed.

To insert the date field code:
❶ Click the **Mail Merge Main Document button** 📄 on the Database toolbar. You return to the blank main document—S4ACMAIN.DOC. Notice that the main document contains the Mail Merge toolbar, which appears between the Formatting toolbar and the ruler. See Figure 4-11.

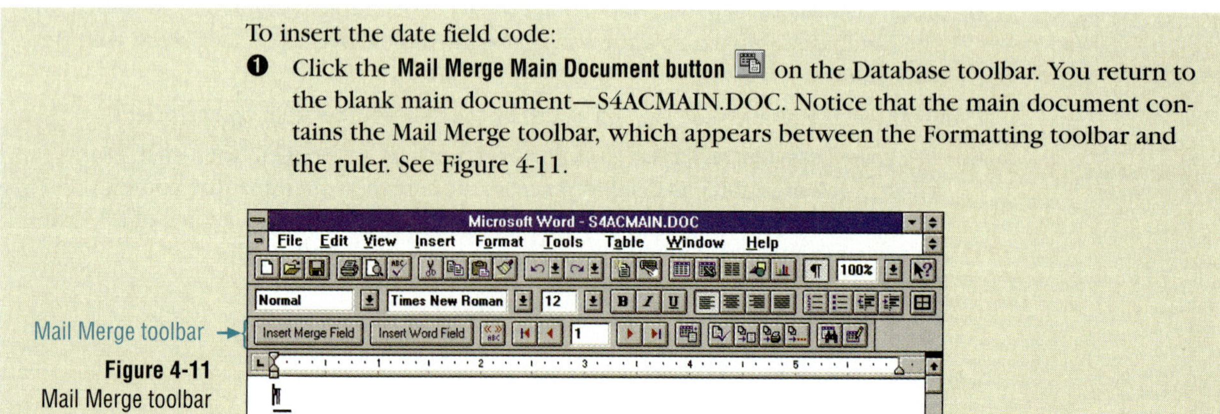

Mail Merge toolbar

Figure 4-11
Mail Merge toolbar

❷ Click **Insert** on the menu bar, then click **Date and Time...**. The Date and Time dialog box appears.

❸ Click the fourth date format from the top of the list of available formats (Month xx, 19xx). See Figure 4-12.

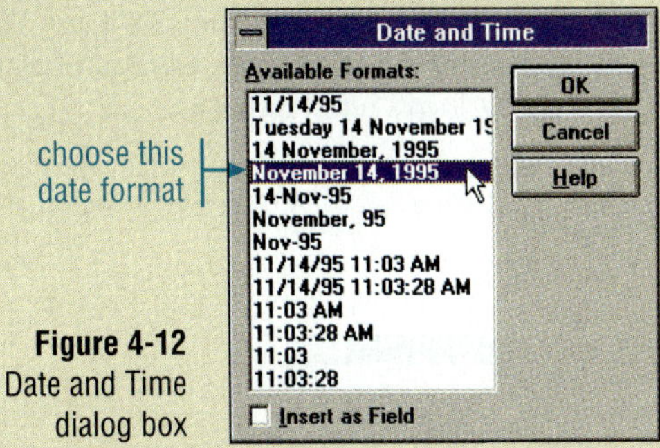

Figure 4-12
Date and Time
dialog box

❹ Click **OK** or press **[Enter]**. The current date appears in the document. In the future, whenever Paul prints the merged document letters for new volunteering organizations, the current date will appear.

TROUBLE? If you see text surrounded by curly brackets {} instead of the date, click Tools, click Options..., then deselect the Field Codes option in the Show section on the View tab.

Inserting Merge Field Codes

The main document contains the text that stays the same in all the merged documents, as well as the instructions that tell Word where to place the information from the data file. These instructions in the main document are called **merge field codes.**

Paul has entered the date and now is ready to enter the merge field codes for the inside address. Recall from Figure 4-1 that the variable information for the inside address includes the title, first name, last name, organization name, and address of the contact person for each organization. As you enter these merge field codes, be sure to insert the proper spacing and punctuation around the codes so that the personalized documents will print correctly.

To insert the merge field codes:

❶ Press **[Enter]** four times to leave three blank lines between the date and the first line of the inside address.

❷ Click the **Insert Merge Field button** on the Mail Merge toolbar. A list appears containing all the field names that you previously created for the header row in the attached data source.

❸ Click **Title** in the data fields list. The data field name, Title, appears in the main document, surrounded by chevrons (« »). The chevrons distinguish merge field codes from the rest of the text in the main document.

❹ Press **[Spacebar]** to insert a space after the Title merge field code, click the **Insert Merge Field button**, then click **FirstName** in the list. The FirstName merge field code appears.

❺ Press **[Spacebar]** to insert a space after the FirstName merge field code, click the **Insert Merge Field button**, then click **LastName** in the list. The LastName merge field code appears.

❻ Press **[Enter]** to move the insertion point to the next line, click the **Insert Merge Field button**, then click **Organization** in the list. The Organization merge field code appears.

❼ Press **[Enter]** to move the insertion point to the next line. Continue inserting the appropriate merge field codes to complete the inside address and the salutation (Dear «Title» «LastName»:) until your document looks like Figure 4-13.

TROUBLE? If you make a mistake inserting merge field codes, you must select the entire field code, including the chevrons, then press [Del]. You can then continue to insert the correct merge field code.

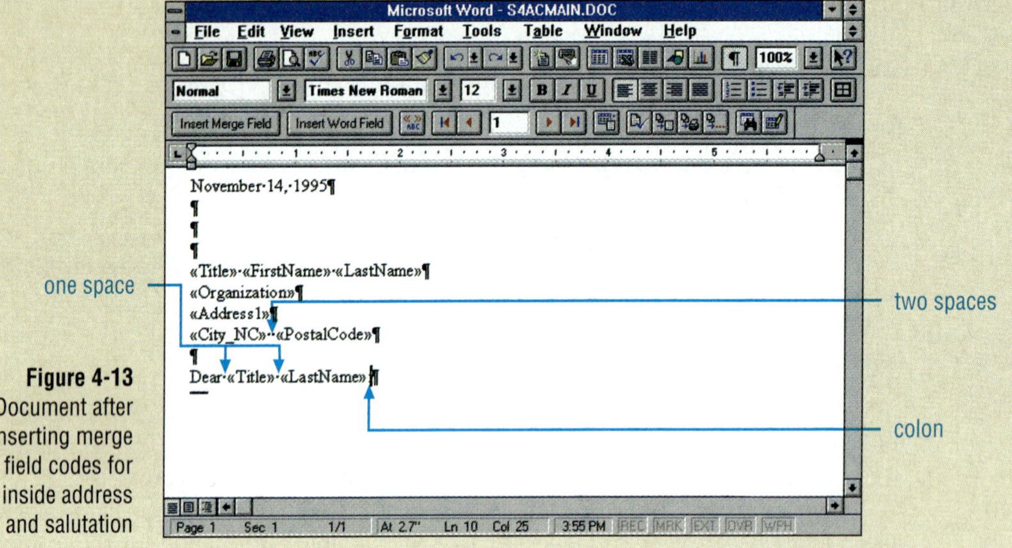

Figure 4-13
Document after inserting merge field codes for inside address and salutation

Now Paul can continue typing the body of the letter and the remaining merge fields.

To finish entering the main document:

❶ Press **[Enter]** twice after the salutation to insert a blank line between the salutation and the body of the letter.

Paul wants to further personalize the letter by including the name of the organization, the adopted county road, and the beginning and ending points on the road.

❷ Continue typing the body of the letter, including the appropriate merge field codes, as illustrated in Figure 4-14.

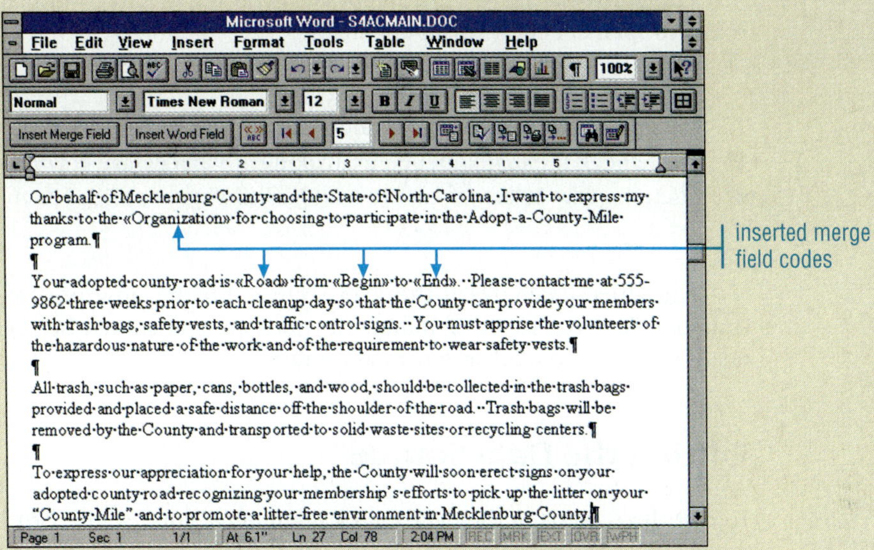

Figure 4-14
Document with
merge field codes
inserted in body
of letter

You are now ready to type the closing lines.

❸ Press **[Enter]** twice, type **Sincerely yours**, press **[Enter]** four times, type **Paul Krueger**, press **[Enter]**, then type **Administrative Assistant**. Your completed document should look like Figure 4-15. You will need to scroll up and down to see the entire document.

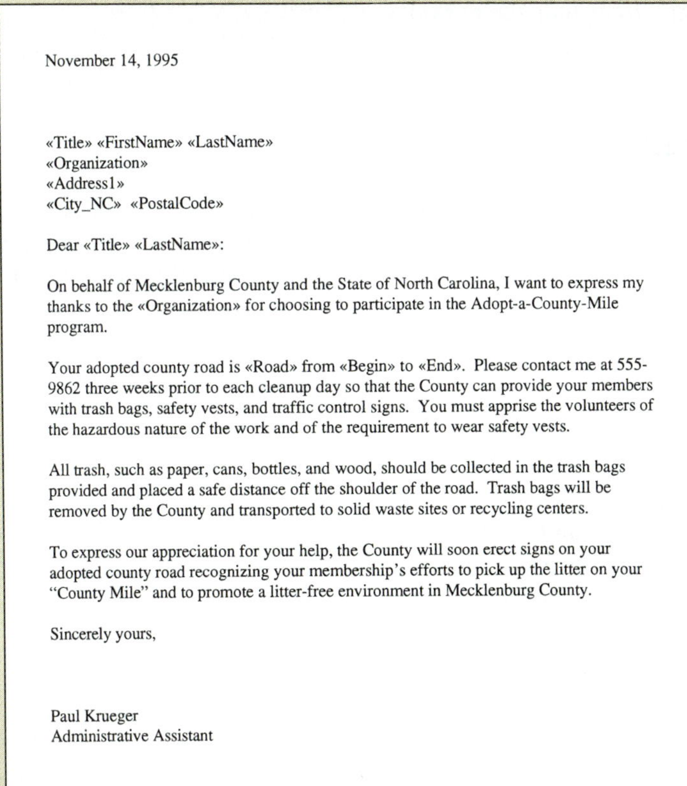

November 14, 1995

«Title» «FirstName» «LastName»
«Organization»
«Address1»
«City_NC» «PostalCode»

Dear «Title» «LastName»:

On behalf of Mecklenburg County and the State of North Carolina, I want to express my thanks to the «Organization» for choosing to participate in the Adopt-a-County-Mile program.

Your adopted county road is «Road» from «Begin» to «End». Please contact me at 555-9862 three weeks prior to each cleanup day so that the County can provide your members with trash bags, safety vests, and traffic control signs. You must apprise the volunteers of the hazardous nature of the work and of the requirement to wear safety vests.

All trash, such as paper, cans, bottles, and wood, should be collected in the trash bags provided and placed a safe distance off the shoulder of the road. Trash bags will be removed by the County and transported to solid waste sites or recycling centers.

To express our appreciation for your help, the County will soon erect signs on your adopted county road recognizing your membership's efforts to pick up the litter on your "County Mile" and to promote a litter-free environment in Mecklenburg County.

Sincerely yours,

Paul Krueger
Administrative Assistant

Figure 4-15
Completed main
document

Paul is satisfied with the content and wording of the confirmation letter, and now he wants to spell check the main document.

To spell check and save the main document:
❶ Spell check the main document, making any necessary corrections.
❷ Click the **Save button** 🖫 on the Standard toolbar (or click **File** then click **Save**).

Paul already proofread the data source, but he now notices that the title for the Huntersville Chamber of Commerce contact person should be "Dr." instead of "Mrs." He needs to correct the error in the data source.

Editing the Data Source

To edit the records in the data source document, you use the Edit Data Source button on the Mail Merge toolbar. Paul needs to make one correction to a record in his data source.

To edit the data source:
❶ Click the **Edit Data Source button** 🗐 on the Mail Merge toolbar, then click **View Source**.
❷ Use the cell selection bar to select the contents of cell 2 of row 5, then type **Dr.** (be sure to include the period).
❸ Save your changes.

Sorting Records

In his job Paul is accustomed to mailing large numbers of letters and brochures. Whenever he does this, he needs to bundle together letters going to the same postal code, as required by the U.S. Post Office, to speed processing. He saves himself time by printing the letters in postal code order. To print the letters in postal code order, he must first organize the data source in postal code order by sorting it. He decides to do this by using the Database toolbar.

To sort the data source records by postal code:
❶ Place the insertion point anywhere in the PostalCode column.
❷ Click the **Sort Ascending button** 🔼 on the Database toolbar. The records are sorted from the lowest to the highest postal code, and the column is selected. Deselect the column. See Figure 4-16.

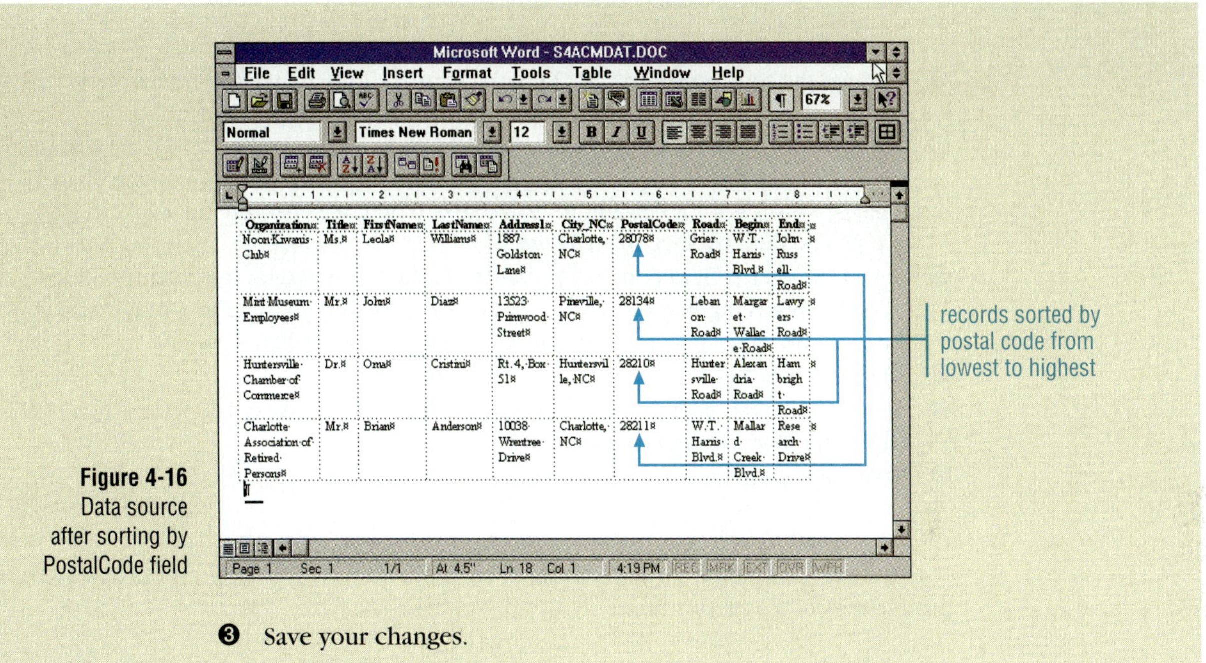

Figure 4-16
Data source after sorting by PostalCode field

❸   Save your changes.

Paul is now finished editing both the main document and the data source. He needs to make a few slight formatting changes to the main document before he is ready to merge the two documents.

Formatting a Main Document

Paul has some minor formatting changes to make to the main document. He does not plan to print the data source by itself, so he doesn't need to format it.

Paul must switch to the main document to make his formatting changes. Let's do that now.

To switch to the main document:
❶   Click the **Mail Merge Main Document button** 🖼 on the Database toolbar to return to the main document. The main document becomes the active document. The data source is still open but not visible.

Paul wants to change the top margin of the main document to 1.5 inches. He also wants to bold the volunteering organization's name in the first paragraph, as well as the words "three weeks prior" in the second paragraph. To apply format options such as bolding to a merge field code, you must select the entire field code, including the surrounding chevrons.

To format the main document:

❶ Change the top margin to 1.5". Refer to Tutorial 2 if you need to review how to change margins.

❷ Place the insertion point in the merge field code «Organization» in the first paragraph of the body of the letter. Notice that the entire field code becomes shaded. This is Word's way of helping to distinguish field codes from regular text in a document. The field code is *not selected*.

❸ Select the merge field code **«Organization»** in the first paragraph; the entire field code becomes highlighted with a darker shade of gray than before. Make sure you include the chevrons on either side of "Organization" when selecting.

❹ Click the **Bold button** [B] on the Formatting toolbar.

❺ Select **three weeks prior** in the second paragraph of the body of the letter, then click [B] on the Formatting toolbar. Deselect the text.

❻ Save your changes.

Paul has completed formatting his document and now moves to the final stage of the productivity strategy: printing.

Merging Documents

Paul has created his main document and has attached the completed data source to it. He has also made all the necessary editing and formatting changes. Now he is ready to merge the two documents to produce the customized letters. Paul has only four letters to print now, but he doesn't want to waste time and resources printing letters that contain mistakes. He decides to view the document as it will appear when merged.

To view the merged document as it will appear when printed:

❶ Click the **View Merged Data button** [«»] on the Mail Merge toolbar. Word inserts the information for the first data record into the text of the main document. The beginning of the first letter (to Leola Williams) appears in the document window.

❷ Scroll through the letter to see that you have inserted the merge field codes and the spacing around them correctly. If you see errors, it is best to correct them here in the main document, then save the changes; do not merge the letters then correct each individual merged document.

Paul is satisfied that the merge will work properly and is ready to merge and print the documents.

❸ Click [«»] again to return to the usual display of the main document.

❹ Click the **Merge to Printer button** [□] on the Mail Merge toolbar.

❺ Click **OK** or press **[Enter]** in the Print dialog box. During the merge process, Word inserts the appropriate variable information for each data record in the data source document wherever a merge field code appears in the main document. All four merged documents print. The complete merged document to Leola Williams appears in Figure 4-17.

❻ Save your changes.

November 14, 1995

Ms. Leola Williams
Noon Kiwanis Club
1887 Goldston Lane
Charlotte, NC 28078

Dear Ms. Williams:

On behalf of Mecklenburg County and the State of North Carolina, I want to express my thanks to the **Noon Kiwanis Club** for choosing to participate in the Adopt-a-County-Mile program.

Your adopted county road is Grier Road from W. T. Harris Blvd. to John Russell Road. Please contact me at 555-9862 **three weeks prior** to each cleanup day so that the County can provide your members with trash bags, safety vests, and traffic control signs. You must apprise the volunteers of the hazardous nature of the work and of the requirement to wear safety vests.

All trash, such as paper, cans, bottles, and wood, should be collected in the trash bags provided and placed a safe distance off the shoulder of the road. Trash bags will be removed by the County and transported to solid waste sites or recycling centers.

To express our appreciation for your help, the County will soon erect signs on your adopted county road recognizing your membership's efforts to pick up the litter on your "County Mile" and to promote a litter-free environment in Mecklenburg County.

Sincerely yours,

Paul Krueger
Administrative Assistant

Figure 4-17
Merged document
to Leola Williams

If you want to take a break and resume the tutorial at a later time, you can close both the main document and the data source document, then exit Word by double-clicking the Control menu box in the upper-left corner of the screen. When you want to resume the tutorial, start Word, place your Student Disk in the disk drive, then complete the screen check procedure described in Tutorial 1. Open the main document, S4ACMAIN.DOC, then continue with the tutorial.

As Paul looks over the last merged document, he receives a telephone call from Molly Suen of the Student Political Action Committee at the University of North Carolina, Charlotte campus. Her organization wants to adopt a county mile, too. Paul takes down the information he needs so he can get her letter in the mail along with the others.

Selecting a Data Record to Merge

Paul needs to add the information for the Student Political Action Committee to the data source. Because he has already printed the merged documents for the other data records in the data source, he needs to merge only the variable information for the new organization with the main document.

First, Paul needs to add the information for the new volunteer organization to the data source. This time he'll enter the new record directly in the data source.

To add the new record to the data source:

❶ Click the **Edit Data Source button** 📝 on the Mail Merge toolbar of the main document to switch to the data source form.

❷ Click **View Source** to switch to the data source table. Now you can enter the new record, then save this change to the data source.

❸ Click the **Add New Record button** 📇 on the Database toolbar. A blank row is added to the bottom of the table.

Paul can now add the data for the new organization just as he would enter information into any table.

❹ Type **Student Political Action Committee** in cell 1 of the new row.

❺ Using Figure 4-18, continue typing the remaining information for the new volunteer organization into the data source table.

/Student Political Action Committee/
/Ms./Molly/Suen/
/2911 Lakeview Drive/
/Charlotte, NC/28211/
/Rocky River Road West/from/University City Blvd./to/Old Concord Road/

Figure 4-18
Information for
new data record

❻ Proofread the new data record carefully, correcting errors if necessary.

❼ Save your changes.

Now that Paul has entered the information for the new organization, he is ready to print that record. He can specify that Word merge only the new record and the main document, then print just that letter.

To find the new record:

❶ Click the **Mail Merge Main Document button** 📇 on the Database toolbar to switch to the main document. Notice that the Go To Record text box on the Mail Merge toolbar indicates data record 1.

Paul wants to print just the letter to Molly Suen, but first he must move to that data record.

❷ Click the **Find Record button** 🔍 on the Mail Merge toolbar. The Find in Field dialog box appears. See Figure 4-19.

Figure 4-19
Find in Field
dialog box

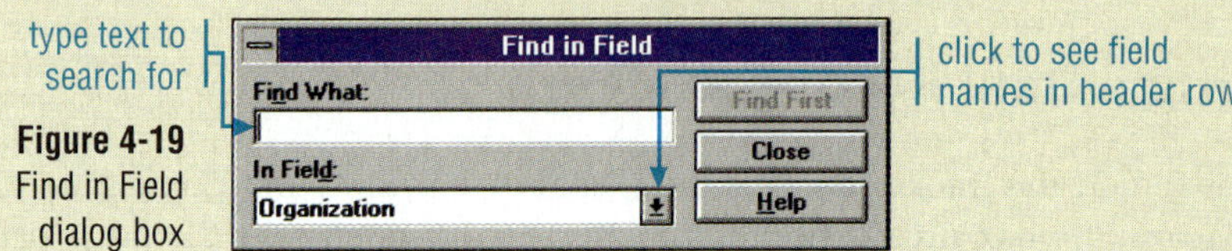

❸ Type **Suen** in the Find What text box.
❹ Click the **In Field list box down arrow**, then click **LastName**.
❺ Click **Find First** or press **[Enter]**. Now the Go To Record text box indicates record number 5.
❻ Click **Close** to close the Find in Field dialog box.

Paul wants to print just the merged document to Molly Suen, data record 5.

To print the merged document to Molly Suen:
❶ Click the **Mail Merge button** on the Mail Merge toolbar. The Merge dialog box appears. See Figure 4-20.

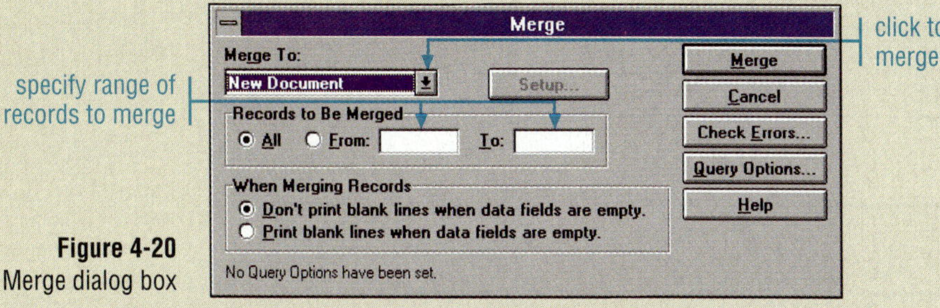

Figure 4-20
Merge dialog box

❷ Click the **Merge To list box down arrow**, then click **Printer**.

Now Paul must specify the number of the data record that he wants to print, in this case, 5.

❸ Click the **From radio button** in the Records to Be Merged section, type **5**, press **[Tab]**, then type **5** in the To text box.
❹ Click **Merge**. The Print dialog box appears.
❺ Click **OK** or press **[Enter]**. The merged document to Molly Suen prints.
❻ Save both S4ACMAIN.DOC and S4ACMDAT.DOC, then close both documents.

Paul has completed the personalized letters to those organizations that volunteered to participate in the Adopt-a-County-Mile program. He can now use the merging process to help him quickly create a mailing label for each merged document.

Creating Mailing Labels

Paul uses transparent address labels for the laser printer that are each 1 inch x 2⁵/₆ inches. They come on sheets that look like Figure 4-21. Word uses the product numbers of a popular manufacturer of labels, Avery, to specify the various formats for labels it can produce. You must know the product number or the Avery equivalent of the specific label type you will be using. The Avery product number for the labels that Paul uses is 5660.

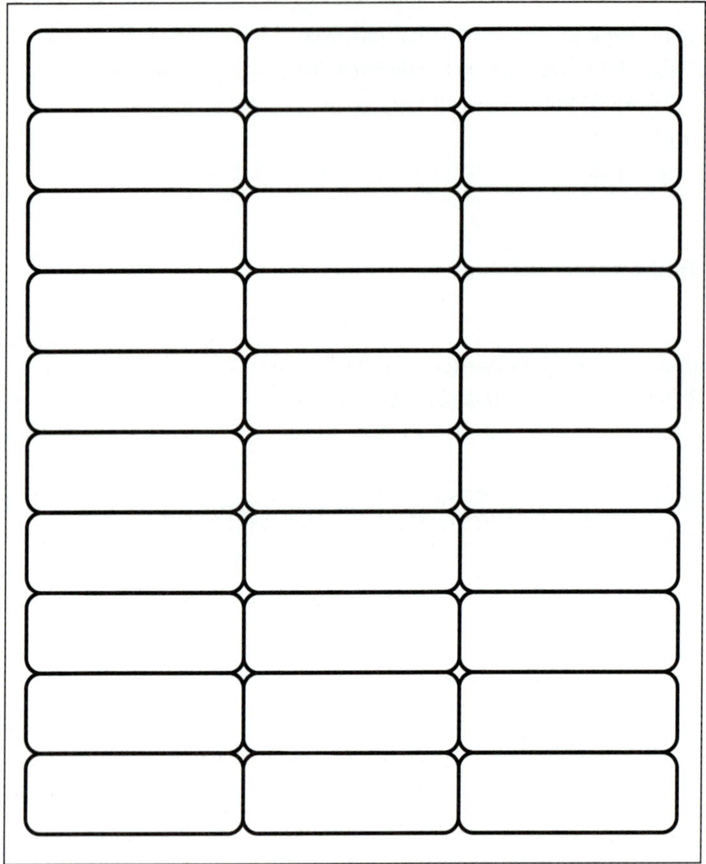

Figure 4-21
Layout of sheet of
mailing labels

Paul already has a data source that contains the names and addresses of the contacts for each of the volunteering organizations (S4ACMDAT.DOC), but he needs to create the main document that will contain the merge field codes arranged as they would appear on a mailing label. Then he can merge the mailing label main document with the data source document.

To create the mailing label main document:
1. Click the **New button** ▢ on the Standard toolbar. A new blank document appears.
2. Click **Tools** then click **Mail Merge...**. The Mail Merge Helper dialog box appears.
3. Click **Create** in the Main Document section, then click **Mailing Labels...**. A message box appears.
4. Click **Active Window** in the message box. You return to the Mail Merge Helper dialog box.

Paul will use the addressee information in the data source document he just created—S4ACMDAT.DOC.

5. Click **Get Data** in the Data Source section, then click **Open Data Source...**.
6. Select S4ACMDAT.DOC from your Student Disk. A message box appears for setting up the main document.
7. Click **Set Up Main Document**. The Label Options dialog box appears.

❽   Make sure the Laser radio button is selected in the Printer Information section, then click **5660 - Address** in the Product Number list box. See Figure 4-22.

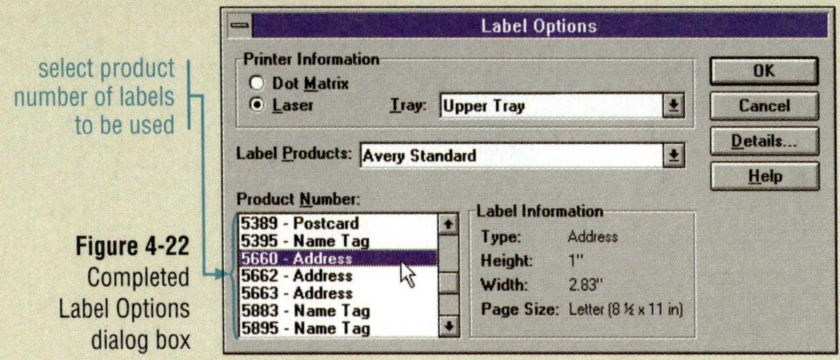

select product
number of labels
to be used

Figure 4-22
Completed
Label Options
dialog box

TROUBLE? If you are using a dot matrix printer, your document will not print exactly as shown.

❾   Click **OK** or press **[Enter]**. The Create Labels dialog box appears.

Now Paul must build the contents of the mailing label. He wants the mailing label to look like the inside address of the letter. Paul creates the label by selecting the merge fields he wants to appear on the label from the Insert Merge Field list, then inserting any necessary spacing, just as he did when he inserted the inside address into the confirmation form letter.

Now let's place merge field codes into the mailing label document.

To insert merge field codes into the mailing label document:

❶   Click **Insert Merge Field**, click **Title** in the list, then press **[Spacebar]**. The selected merge field appears in the Sample Label box.

TROUBLE? If you make a mistake after you add an item, you can edit the text directly in the Sample Label box.

The first name of the contact person is the next item to be added to the mailing label.

❷   Click **Insert Merge Field**, click **FirstName**, then press **[Spacebar]**.

Next you need to enter the last name of the contact person, then return the insertion point to the beginning of the next line.

❸   Click **Insert Merge Field**, click **LastName**, then press **[Enter]**. The LastName field code is added to the mailing label, and the insertion point moves to the beginning of the next line.

Now that you have entered the first line of the label, you can enter the remaining three lines.

❹   Set up the remaining lines of the mailing label address as shown in Figure 4-23. Remember to press [Enter] at the end of each line to return the insertion point to the beginning of the next line.

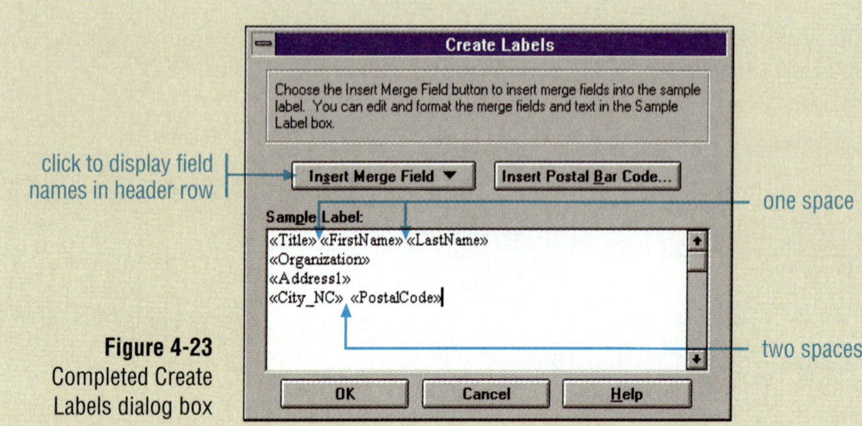

Figure 4-23
Completed Create Labels dialog box

❺   Click **OK** when you are finished building the address for the label. You return to the Mail Merge Helper dialog box.

Before Paul merges the label main document with the data source, he wants to make sure that the main document is set up properly.

❻   Click **Edit** in the Main Document section of the Mail Merge Helper dialog box. The name of the current label main document appears.

❼   Click **Mailing Label: Document2**. Notice that the label main document is a table, with each cell being the equivalent of one label on a sheet of mailing labels. The label you built is copied to each cell of the label main document you created.

TROUBLE? The document name of your mailing label main document might be different; click the name of your label main document, then continue with the tutorial.

Paul can't see the entire last column of the mailing label main document on the screen.

❽   Click the **Zoom Control list box down arrow**, then click **Page Width**.

Paul decides to save the label main document so he doesn't have to create it each time he has a mailing to send out.

❾   Click the **Save button** 🖫 on the Standard toolbar (or click **File** then click **Save As...**). Save the label document to your Student Disk as S4ACMLAB.DOC.

Paul sees that he needs to format the label main document so that the necessary information will fit on the label.

Formatting Labels

You can format the mailing label main document the same way you format other Word documents. Paul decides to change the font of the label main document to Arial to make the labels more readable and to reduce the size of the font to 10 point so that the text will fit better on the label. Let's do that now.

To change the format of the mailing label main document:

❶ Place the insertion point anywhere inside the table, click **Table**, then click **Select Table**. The entire table is selected.

❷ Click the **Font list box down arrow** on the Formatting toolbar, then click **Arial**.

❸ Click the **Font Size list box down arrow** on the Formatting toolbar, then click **10**. The font and the font size for the label document have been changed. Deselect the mailing label main document.

❹ Save your changes.

Paul wants to see what the formatted labels will look like after they are merged.

❺ Click the **View Merged Data button** on the Mail Merge toolbar.

Paul is satisfied that the text will fit properly on the labels.

❻ Click again to return to the usual view of the label main document.

Printing Labels

Now that Paul has formatted the label main document, he inserts a sheet of labels in the printer and prints the merged documents. You will simply print the labels on a sheet of paper.

To print the mailing labels:

❶ Click the **Merge to Printer button** on the Mail Merge toolbar. The Print dialog box appears.

❷ Click **OK** or press **[Enter]**. Word merges the label main document with the data source and sends the resulting merged document directly to the printer. See Figure 4-24.

❸ Save the changes you have made to S4ACMLAB.DOC.

❹ Close the label main document then exit Word.

Figure 4-24
Printed mailing label
merged document

Ms. Leola Williams Noon Kiwanis Club 1887 Goldston Lane Charlotte, NC 28078	Mr. John Diaz Mint Museum Employees 13523 Primwood Street Pineville, NC 28134	Dr. Oma Cristini Huntersville Chamber of Commerce Rt. 4, Box 51 Huntersville, NC 28210
Mr. Brian Anderson Charlotte Association of Retired Persons 10038 Wrentree Drive Charlotte, NC 28211	Ms. Molly Suen Student Political Action Committee 2911 Lakeview Drive Charlotte, NC 28211	

Paul now has the confirmation letters and the accompanying labels. He attaches the labels to the envelopes, inserts the letters in the envelopes, and mails them.

Questions

1. Describe the merge process.
2. Define each of the following terms:
   a. main document
   b. data source
   c. header row
   d. data record
   e. data field
   f. field name
   g. merge field code
   h. date field code
3. How do you establish the document you need to use as the main document?
4. Which of the following names are legal field names:
   a. ProductInventoryNumber
   b. 1995_Sales
   c. Employee_ID
5. What are two methods for entering data into a data source?
6. Describe the purpose of the Page Width option provided by the Zoom Control feature.
7. When formatting a merge field code in a main document, what must you remember to do?
8. Describe the process you would follow to merge then print one specific data record only.
9. Describe the process for creating and printing mailing labels if you have a data source already created.

Use Word Help to answer Questions 10 through 12:

E 10. How do you add a field to an existing data source?

E 11. What is the purpose of the Query button in the Mail Merge Helper dialog box?

E 12. How do you return a main document to a regular Word document?

Tutorial Assignments

Start Word, if necessary, then conduct a screen check. Complete the following:

1. Open a new document then create a form letter main document. Save it as S4ACMAGR.DOC.
2. Attach T4MECDAT.DOC from your Student Disk as the data source.
3. Scroll through the data records. Notice the two new data fields—Date_1 and Date_2.
4. Save the data source as S4MECDAT.DOC.
5. Switch to the main document.
6. Create the main document shown in Figure 4-25, inserting merge field codes as indicated.

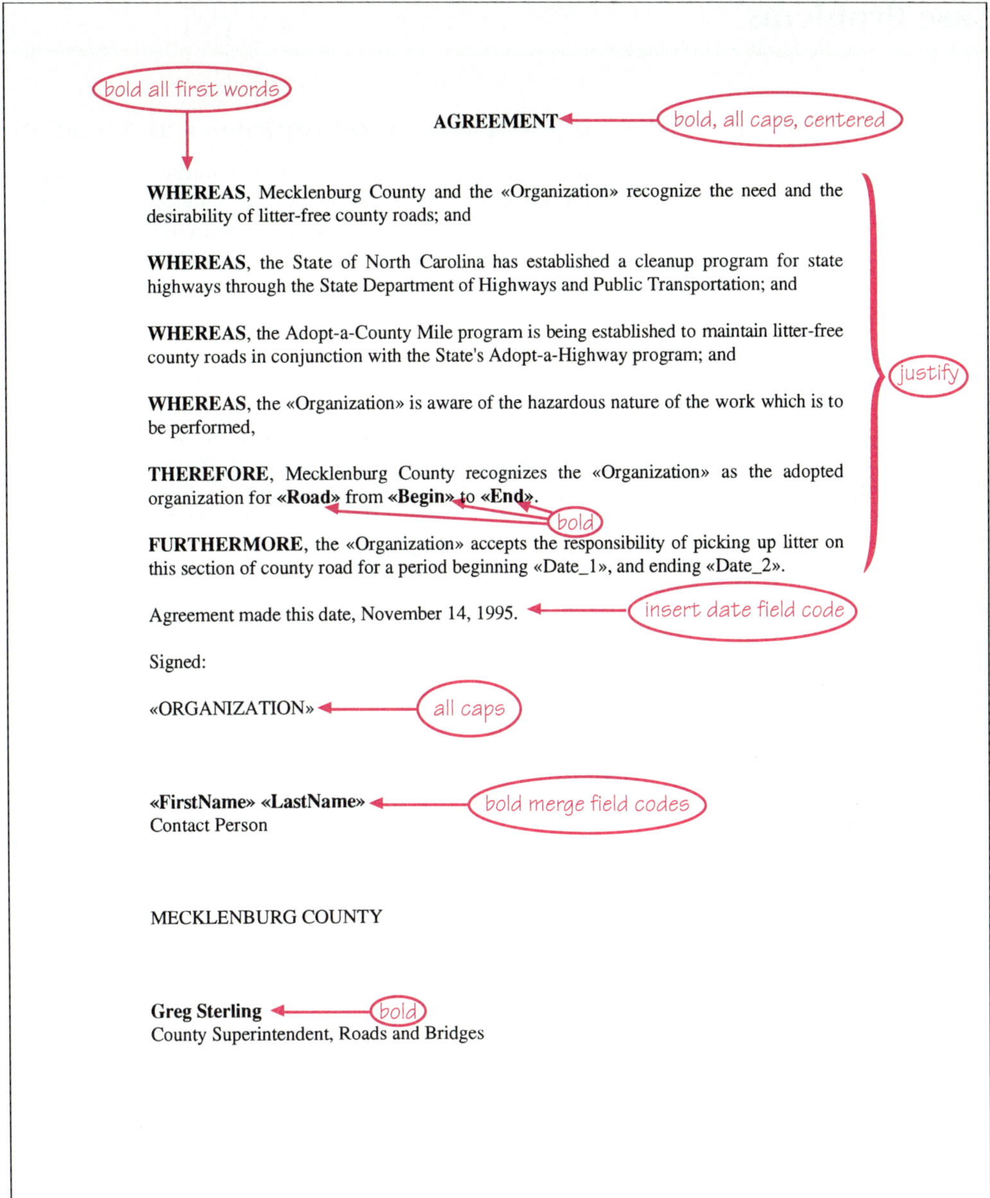

Figure 4-25

7. Spell check the document.
8. Format the document as indicated in Figure 4-25.
9. Save the changes to the main document.
10. View the document as it will appear when merged, and check for any mistakes.
11. Merge and print records 3 and 4.
12. Close all documents.

Case Problems

1. Writing a Form Memo to Employees at Associated Credit Services

Tommy Hiebert is the assistant director of the Telecommunications Department for Associated Credit Services of Boston, Massachusetts. One of his responsibilities is to publish the company employee directory. Because of the recent installation of a new telephone system, he wants to update the directory. He decides to send a memo asking employees to confirm the accuracy of their information before he publishes the final version of the directory.

Complete the following:

1. Open a new document then create a form letter main document. Save the document as S4DRMAIN.DOC
2. Create a data source, S4DIRDAT.DOC, with the following field names in the header row: FirstName, Middle, LastName, Department, Phone, Office.
3. Insert the information shown in Figure 4-26 into a data source.

Linda F. McCown	Accounting	3-9035	409
Charles A. Abbate	Online Services	3-9276	312
Richard L. Swartz	Online Services	3-9279	310
Ronnie D. Gajeske	Accounting	3-9052	411
Leroy L. Keese	Support Services	3-9167	493
Joel Y. Aldape	Telecommunications	3-9641	385
Hillary Abramson	Accounting	3-9038	407
Leah T. Abbate	Online Services	3-9274	308

Figure 4-26

4. Sort the data records by office number in descending order.
5. Switch to the main document.
6. Create a standard memo heading:
    a. After TO: insert the merge field codes FirstName, Middle, LastName, and Department with appropriate spacing between each code.
    b. After FROM: insert Tommy Hiebert.
    c. After RE: insert Directory Listing.
    d. After DATE: insert the date field code, using the date format you prefer.
7. Type the message shown in Figure 4-27, substituting the appropriate merge field codes for the blank lines.

We are in the process of updating the employee directory to reflect the latest telephone number changes. According to our records, your current telephone number is ____________ and your office number is ____________. Is this information correct? Please respond immediately.

Figure 4-27

8. Spell check the memo.
9. Change the top margin to 2 inches and the side margins to 1.5 inches.
10. Bold the memo headings and the phone and office merge field codes in the message.
11. Save the changes to the main document.
12. View the document as it will appear when merged, and check for any mistakes.
13. Merge and print documents for records 5 and 6 only.
14. Close all documents.

2. Creating Mailing Labels for the NAPT Newsletter

Marilyn Taff is chair of the Communications Committee for the National Association of Performance Technologists (NAPT). She has just completed the quarterly issue of the NAPT newsletter and is ready to mail it to the members, but she still needs to prepare mailing labels. Marilyn purchased a box of Avery number 5160 address labels for a laser printer. She already has a disk copy of the membership data source.

Open a new document then complete the following:

1. Create a mailing label main document, making appropriate choices for Laser 5160 address labels.
2. Use the data source P4NAPT.DOC from your Student Disk.
3. Add your name and appropriate information to the data source.
4. Build the layout of the mailing label as shown in Figure 4-28.

Figure 4-28

<FirstName> <Middle> <LastName>
<Company>
<Address1>
<City>, <State> <PostalCode>

5. View the document as it will appear when merged, and check for any mistakes.
6. Format the label merged document with Arial 8 point font.
7. Merge the labels.
8. Save the merged label document as S4NAPTLB.DOC.
9. Marilyn needs the mailing labels in postal code order, alphabetically by last name, then by first name. Use Word Help to find out how the Query option on the Mail Merge Helper dialog box can help you solve this problem. Then create and print the mailing labels for the data records in P4NAPT.DOC in the correct order.
10. Close all documents.

3. A Cover Letter for Your Résumé

Complete the following:

1. Gather application information for three job openings in which you are interested.
2. Open a new document to serve as the main document, then save it as S4COVLET.DOC.
3. Attach a data source with the following field names in its header row and others you feel are appropriate: Title, FirstName, LastName, JobTitle, Company, Address1, City, State, and PostalCode.
4. Save the data source as S4JOBDAT.DOC.
5. Insert the data you collected for your jobs into the appropriate field, one job to a record.
6. Switch to the main document.
7. Enter the date field code.
8. Insert three blank lines.
9. Enter the appropriate merge field codes for the inside address and salutation.
10. Write a short, three-paragraph cover letter describing your qualifications for the job. In the first paragraph mention the reason you are applying and the job for which you are applying. In the second paragraph point out that you have enclosed your résumé, and mention a few pertinent details about your qualifications or experience. In the final paragraph, express your enthusiasm for the job or the company and your willingness to come in for an interview.
11. Spell check the letter.
12. Format the letter as appropriate, taking into consideration placement on the page.
13. Save the changes to the main document.
14. Check the main document for merging errors.
15. Merge the document to the screen.
16. Correct the main document, if necessary.
17. Print the three merged documents.
18. Close all documents.

Creating Reports

Writing a Report with a Table of Contents

OBJECTIVES

In this tutorial you will:

- Use Word's Thesaurus
- Check grammar
- Assign bookmarks
- Insert section breaks
- Align a page vertically
- Insert headers and footers in a multi-section document
- Define, apply, and redefine styles
- Transfer data between documents
- Create a preface page with a table of contents and a table of figures
- Create a customized document template

CASE

Connolly/Bayle and Associates   Jessica Pangiana is a research assistant with Connolly/Bayle and Associates of San Francisco, a marketing research and analysis firm specializing in investigating economic development opportunities for municipalities. One of the firm's current clients, the Research Division of the Greater San Juan Economic Development Foundation, has contracted with Connolly/Bayle to develop a demographic and industrial profile of the greater San Juan area. The foundation will use the information to apply for grants from the federal and state governments for job training programs and to attract new businesses to the San Juan area.

Henry Santiago is Jessica's manager. He has asked her to create a preliminary report of the demographic and industrial staffing patterns in the San Juan area based on the data she has gathered. He will then use the information in this preliminary report to create a more extensive final report, which will go to the client.

Jessica will follow the productivity strategy to complete her task. In her report document, she has already created a title page, a page for the table of contents, and a third page with the body of her report—unedited and unformatted (Figure 5-1). She separated the three pages with hard page breaks. The body of the report contains three major sections: Methodology, Summary of Major Findings, and Conclusion. Both the Methodology and Summary of Major Findings sections are divided into smaller sections to help the reader digest the information. Jessica has printed the first draft of her report and indicated the changes to be made.

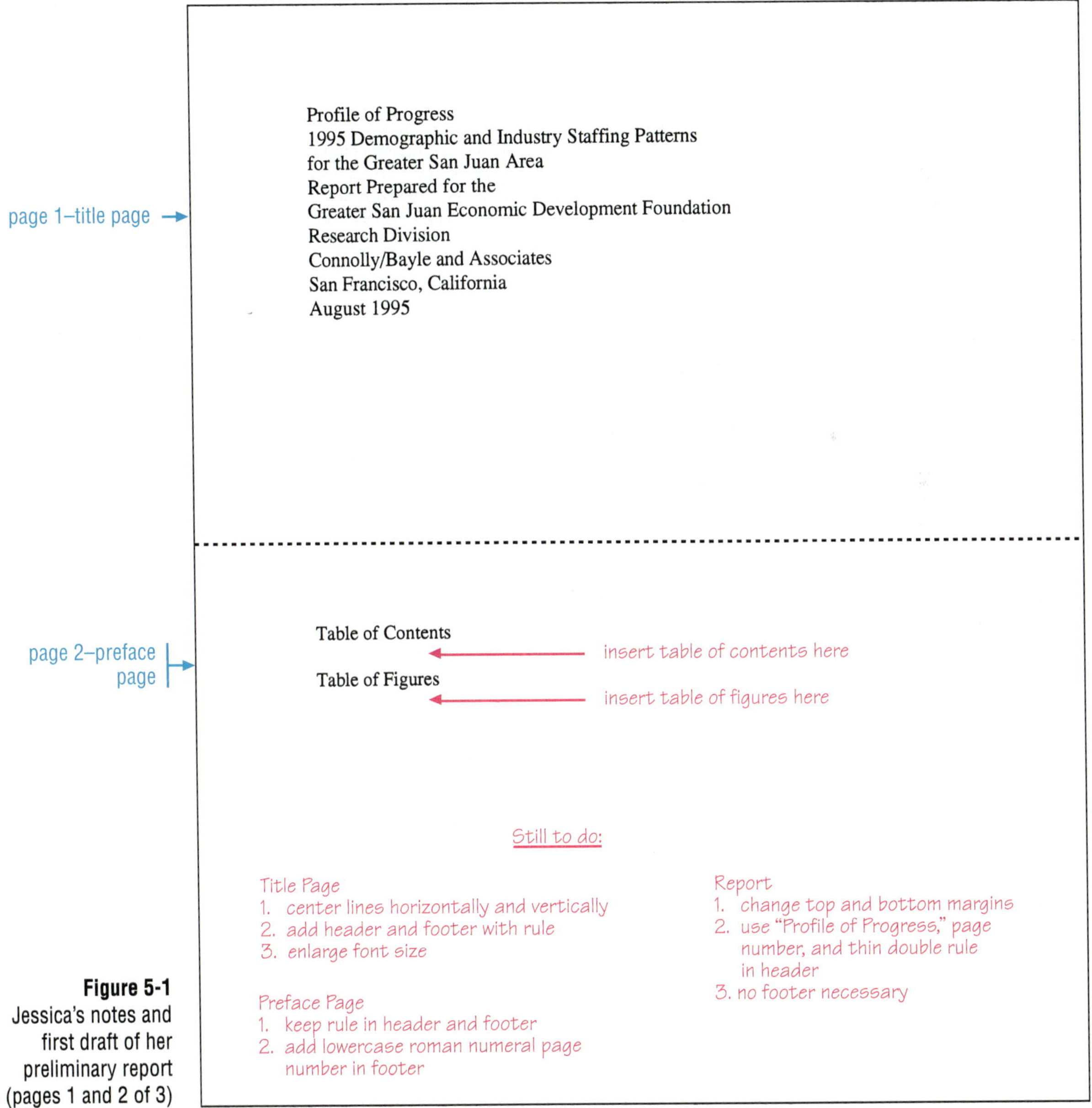

Figure 5-1
Jessica's notes and first draft of her preliminary report (pages 1 and 2 of 3)

Introduction

The Profile of Progress is a compilation of industrial data designed to give the reader an overview of the population, job base, and job growth trends of the Greater San Juan area. The region, which encompasses San Juan, Bellville, Santa Maria, and Williston, continues to lead the way in California's recovery from the economic slump during the early '90s. The following report discusses both the data collection methodology and a summary of the findings.

Methodology

The Sample

The sample for this study was selected from the first quarter 1995 Employment and Wages report submitted to the California Department of Labor by the region's employers. The universe was stratified by standard industrial classification codes. Procedures involved all certainty cases.

Collection Procedures

The majority of the data was colected by mail. Each selected establishment received a structured schedule for there specific industry. The survey from included the following: instructions, occupational titles and definitions, business identification, and a standard industrial classification code. Survey procedures included three follow-up mailings to non-respondents. The telephone was used extensively to clarify data and to canvas critical non-respondents. The demographic statistics for the region was extracted from the 1990 census data.

Summary of Major Findings

Population

The 1995 Profile of Progress presents a growth statistic that continues to display the dynamic growth of the San Juan region. In 1990, the total population of the San Juan region was 192,457. This represents an increase of 48 percent over the 1980 figures and an increase of 150 percent increase over the 1970 figures. Greater numbers of jobs in the defense and computer industries accounted primarily for the population increases. Figure 1 depicts this dramatic growth.

Diversifying San Juan

Diversification, induced in part by natural forces, along with the ingenuity of area business leaders is largely responsible for the continued growth in the San Juan area. Figure 2 shows the makeup of the employing community.

Job Openings

According to our survey of the region's employers, on average, the occupational groups requiring the most education will also see the fastest job growth opportunities. Figure 3 lists the projected job openings during the next five years, including those due to replacement needs and those due to employment increases.

Conclusion

Current population growth trends indicate that the Greater San Juan area will provide a steady job force for the next five to ten years. The diversity of the area's industries will continue to provide 4,000 to 5,000 new jobs over the next five years if current trends continue. These jobs will be largely in the professions, administrative support, and service industries. The San Juan region is a vital area that has grown rapidly over the past two decades and will continue to grow well into the twenty-first century.

Figure 5-1
Jessica's notes and first draft of her preliminary report (page 3 of 3)

page 3–report →

insert chart 1

insert chart 2

insert chart 3

Jessica will edit the report, proofreading the document using Word's Thesaurus and Grammar tools. She will also transfer charts, which she created in another Word document using Microsoft Graph, from the chart document to her report. Next she will format the report. Then she'll create a table of contents and a table of figures before printing the document. Finally Jessica will create a customized document template from the existing document that she can use for other reports she might develop in the future.

To start Word and open the document that Jessica created:

❶ Start Word then conduct the screen check as described in Tutorial 1.

❷ Insert your Student Disk in the disk drive, then open the file C5SJPRPT.DOC from your Student Disk. Scroll through the document to become familiar with it. Compare your document to Figure 5-1. Notice that the document contains three pages.

❸ Click **File** then click **Save As...**, and save the document to your Student Disk as S5SJPRPT.DOC.

❹ Click **OK** or press [**Enter**]. The title bar changes to reflect the new document name.

Now Jessica is ready to start the editing phase of the productivity strategy. She begins by looking up an alternative meaning for a word she has used in her report.

Using Word's Thesaurus

You have used one of Word's proofreading tools, the Spelling command, to spell check a document for errors. Another proofreading tool that facilitates the editing process is the Thesaurus. Word's **Thesaurus** command provides synonyms and some antonyms for a selected word. Once you have looked up an alternative meaning for a word, you can immediately replace the selected word in the document with its synonym.

Jessica notices that she used the term "economic slump" in the first paragraph of the report text to describe the conditions of the local economy. She thinks that "slump" might be too negative, so she decides to use the Thesaurus command to find a synonym with a more positive meaning.

To look up a synonym for "slump" using the Thesaurus command:

❶ Move to page 3 then select the word "slump" (Pg 3, Ln 5).

❷ Click **Tools** then click **Thesaurus...**. The Thesaurus dialog box appears with the word "slump" inserted in the Looked Up list box and three alternative choices in the Meanings list box. See Figure 5-2.

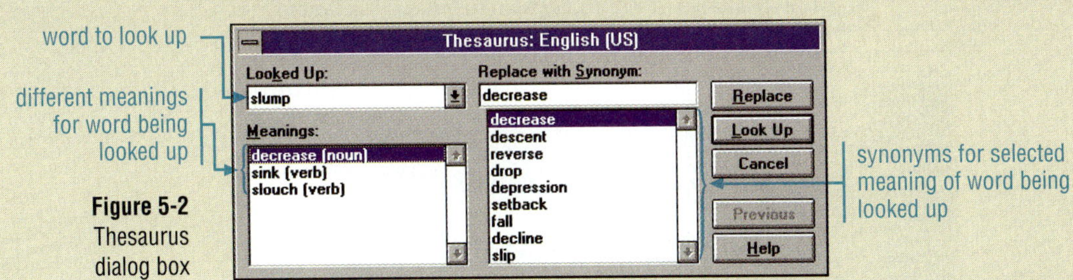

Figure 5-2
Thesaurus dialog box

The highlighted choice "decrease (noun)" in the Meanings list box is the appropriate meaning given the context of the word "slump" in her report, but Jessica doesn't like the choice of synonyms provided by Word. She decides to look up additional meanings for one of the listed synonyms, "depression."

❸ Click **depression** in the Replace with Synonym list box, then click **Look Up** or press [**Enter**]. The choices in the Meanings list box change to reflect options for the word "depression"; an option for antonyms also appears. The most appropriate meaning given the context in Jessica's report is "recession (noun)," not the highlighted choice "hollow (noun)."

❹ Click **recession (noun)** in the Meanings list box, then click **Look Up** or press **[Enter]**. Two meanings for recession appear in the Meanings list box, as well as an entry for Related Words.

"Economic slump (noun)" is the appropriate meaning, given the context. Jessica decides that "slowdown" is the synonym that seems most positive.

❺ Click **slowdown** in the Replace with Synonym list box, then click **Replace**. The selected word, "slowdown," replaces the original word, "slump," in the document.

❻ Save the changes you have made.

Next, Jessica will check her report for grammatical errors.

Checking Grammar

Another proofreading tool available in Word is the Grammar command. The **Grammar** command checks your document for proper grammar usage and style, in addition to checking for spelling errors.

Jessica added the Methodology section after she had checked the other sections for spelling and grammar errors, so she needs to check the grammar in just that part of her document.

To check the grammar in the Methodology section:

❶ Scroll through the document, then select the Methodology section of your document (Pg 3, Ln 8). See Figure 5-3.

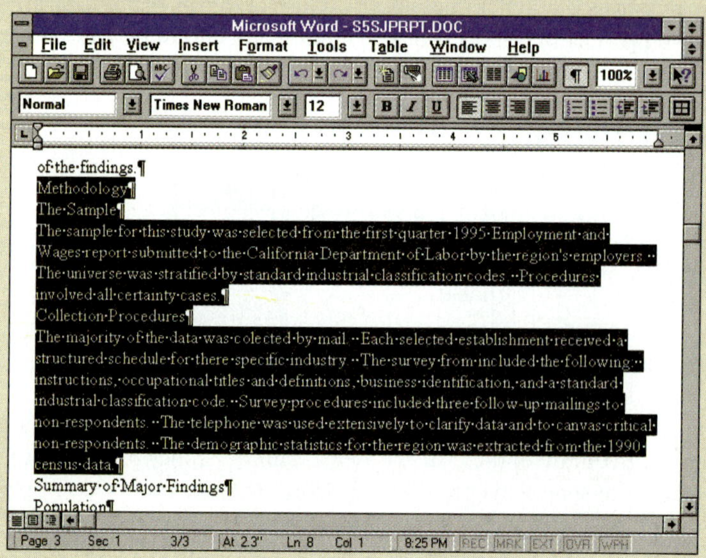

Figure 5-3
Document after selecting Methodology section

TROUBLE? Don't worry if your line endings differ from those shown here; continue with the tutorial.

❷ Click **Tools** then click **Grammar.…** Word stops and highlights the sentence containing the first instance of a grammar usage or style problem. The Grammar dialog box also appears. See Figure 5-4. The sentence containing the flagged error appears in the Sentence box of the dialog box with the "problem" word or words printed in red. Word's suggestions to solve the problem appear in the Suggestions box.

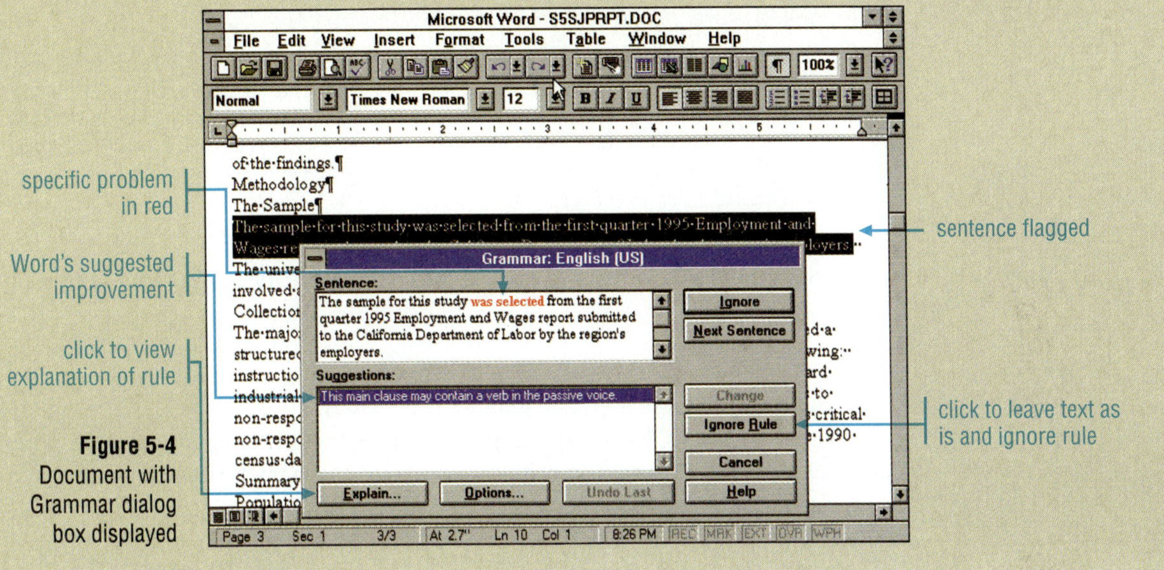

Figure 5-4
Document with
Grammar dialog
box displayed

Jessica needs further explanation of the problem and Word's suggested improvement.

To view the rule for the flagged grammatical error:
❶ Click **Explain.…** An explanation of the grammar rule that applies to this sentence is displayed. See Figure 5-5.

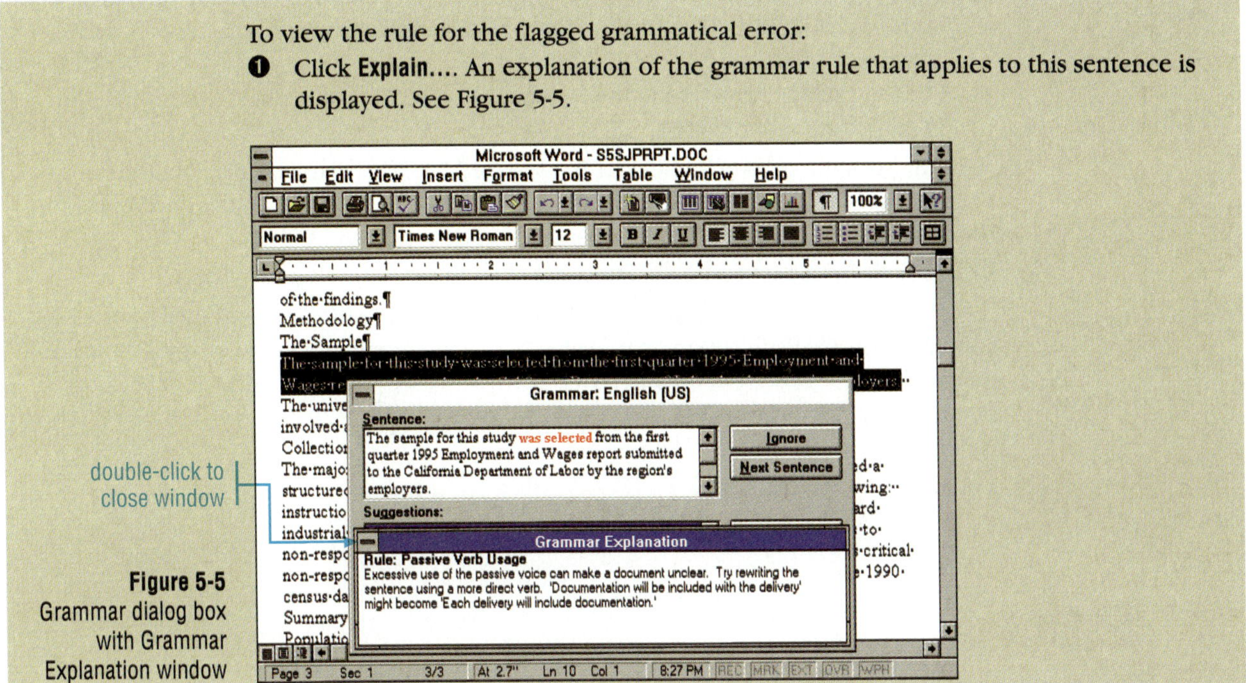

Figure 5-5
Grammar dialog box
with Grammar
Explanation window

❷   After reading the explanation, double-click the **Control menu box** of the Grammar Explanation window to close it.

Although active voice is often preferable to passive voice, Jessica thinks that it is acceptable for a report of this nature, and she decides to ignore the rule for the flagged error.

❸   Click **Ignore Rule**. Word continues the grammar check process and stops at an incorrectly spelled word, "colected."

   TROUBLE? If Word did not find the misspelled word "colected," someone has deactivated the Spelling feature for the Thesaurus command. Click Cancel to close the Grammar dialog box. To activate the feature, click Tools then click Options.... In the Options dialog box, click the Grammar tab, then click the Check Spelling check box. Click OK or press [Enter], then repeat the grammar check procedure described above in this and the preceding set of steps.

As mentioned before, Word also checks for spelling errors at the same time it checks for grammatical errors.

To correct the remaining spelling and grammatical errors:

❶   Click **Change** to accept Word's spelling of "collected." Word next stops at the potential misuse of "there." Read the problem sentence and Word's suggested change.

   TROUBLE? If Word stops at errors other than those discussed in this section, click Ignore Rule and continue with the tutorial.

❷   Click **Change** to accept Word's suggestion. Word next stops at the potential misuse of the word "from." Read the problem sentence and Word's suggested change.

❸   Click **Change** to accept Word's suggestion. Word next stops at the potential misuse of the word "canvas." Read the problem sentence and Word's suggested change.

❹   Click **Change** to accept Word's suggestion. Word next stops at the potential misuse of the word "statistics." This time Word offers two solutions to this subject/verb agreement problem.

❺   Click the **second suggestion** in the Suggestions box (for changing the word "was" to "were"), then click **Change**.

Word finishes the grammar check of the selected block of text, and displays the following message: "Word finished checking the selection. Do you want to continue checking the remainder of the document?"

❻   Click **No** because you needed to check only the Methodology section.

Next Word calculates the readability of the selected text and displays statistics about its content in the Readability Statistics dialog box. This dialog box contains data about various counts, averages, and criteria that measure how easy your document or selected text is to read. See Figure 5-6.

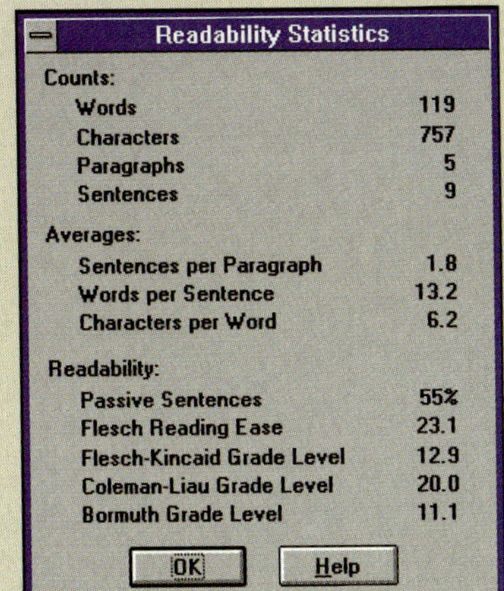

Figure 5-6
Readability Statistics
dialog box

Jessica isn't sure how to interpret the statistics so she decides to use Word Help.

❼ Click **Help** in the Readability Statistics dialog box. Read the information in the Help topic, then close the Word Help window.

❽ After looking over the readability statistics for the selected text, click **OK**, then deselect the text.

❾ Save the changes you have made.

Jessica has one more editing change to make before she moves on to the formatting phase of her task. To help her move quickly to the locations in her report where she needs to insert the three charts, she decides to mark those locations with bookmarks.

Assigning Bookmarks

You can assign a **bookmark** to mark the location of the insertion point, selected text or graphics, or other items that you need to move to quickly. You simply select the location, text, or graphics that you want to mark, then choose the Bookmark command from the Edit menu. You then give the bookmark a name. A bookmark name must begin with a letter, cannot contain more than 40 characters, and cannot contain spaces.

Jessica wants to mark the locations for the charts she must transfer to the report document (Figure 5-1).

To assign bookmarks to the three chart locations:

❶ Place the insertion point in the Population section after the sentence "Figure 1 depicts..." (Pg 3, Ln 29), then press [**Enter**]. This will be the location of Figure 1, which will show one of the charts.

❷ Click **Edit** then click **Bookmark...**. The Bookmark dialog box appears.

❸ Type **figure1** in the Bookmark Name text box. See Figure 5-7.

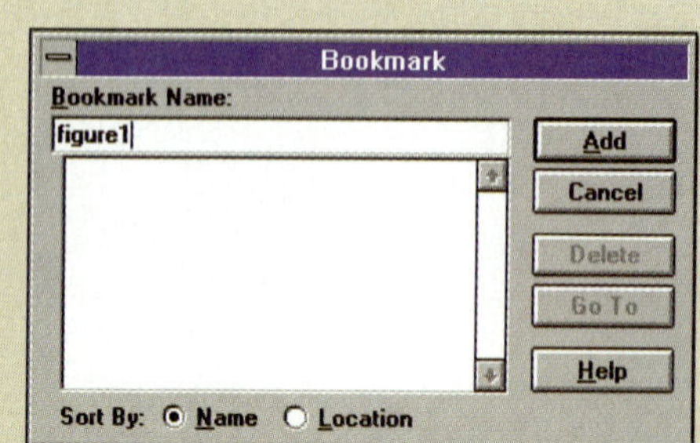

Figure 5-7
Bookmark
dialog box

④   Click **Add** or press **[Enter]**. You return to the document.

Jessica wants to be able to view the bookmark locations in her document.

⑤   Click **Tools**, click **Options…**, then click the **View tab** (if necessary).

⑥   Click the **Bookmarks check box** in the Show section to select the option, then click **OK** or press **[Enter]**. The figure1 bookmark is now visible as a large I-beam. If you had marked text instead of a location, then the marked text would appear enclosed in square brackets.

TROUBLE? If the Bookmarks check box is already selected, do not clear it.

⑦   Save the changes you have made.

⑧   Place the insertion point in the Diversifying San Juan section after the sentence "Figure 2 shows…" (Pg 3, Ln 34), press **[Enter]**, then repeat Steps 2 through 4, naming the bookmark **figure2**. The figure2 bookmark is now visible.

⑨   Place the insertion point in the Job Openings section after the sentence "Figure 3 lists…" (Pg 3, Ln 40), press **[Enter]**, then repeat Steps 2 through 4, naming the bookmark **figure3**. See Figure 5-8. Note that you might need to scroll the window to see all three bookmarks at one time.

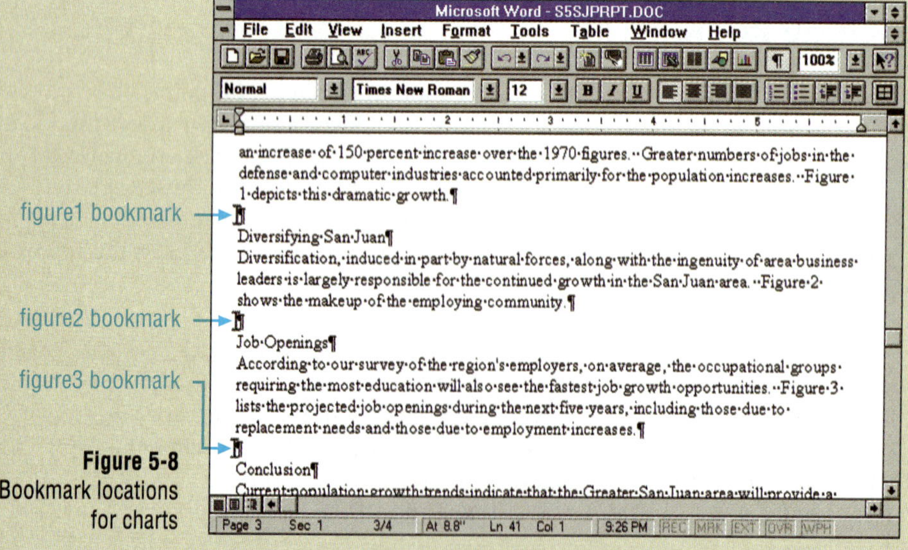

Figure 5-8
Bookmark locations
for charts

⑩   Save the changes you have made.

Jessica has finished the editing phase of the productivity strategy. Now she is ready to format the document.

Formatting Sections in a Document

Jessica's report poses some interesting formatting challenges. In consulting her notes (Figure 5-1), Jessica sees that she needs to align the title page vertically, change the top and bottom margins for the report pages, and create headers and footers for the title page and the table of contents that are different from the headers and footers for the report. Each of these formatting changes—adjusting vertical alignment, changing margins, and inserting different headers and footers—are page-level, or document-level, decisions. As such, they cannot be confined to specific pages as Jessica needs. In addition to these changes, she must make paragraph and font formatting changes to the title page, table of contents page, and the report.

Word's solution to situations like Jessica's is to divide a document into mini-documents called sections, each with its own page-level formatting options. A **section** is a portion of a document in which you can change page setup options, such as page orientation, margins, headers and footers, and vertical alignment. To create a section, you insert a **section break**, a division between sections in a document. When you insert a section break, a double dotted line appears across the page with the words "End of Section," and the status bar changes to reflect an increase in the number of sections in the document. You can either insert a section break using the Break command on the Insert menu, then make the necessary page-level changes, or you can use the Page Setup command on the File menu to insert section breaks as well as apply page-level formatting changes.

When Jessica created her document, she inserted a *page break* between the title page and table of contents page, and between the table of contents page and the text of the preliminary report. She wants to format the title page differently from the table of contents page and from the rest of the document, so she needs to delete the page breaks and insert *section breaks* in their place. Then Jessica can make her page-level changes to each section of the document.

Jessica's first step in making her formatting changes is to insert a section break between pages 1 and 2.

To insert a section break between pages 1 and 2:

❶ Place the insertion point at the top of page 2, directly before the "T" in Table of Contents, then press **[Backspace]** to remove the page break. The title page and table of contents page are combined temporarily. Notice that the status bar indicates that the insertion point is on page 1 of section 1. Until you insert a section break, your entire document is considered one section.

❷ Click **Insert** then click **Break....** The Break dialog box appears. See Figure 5-9.

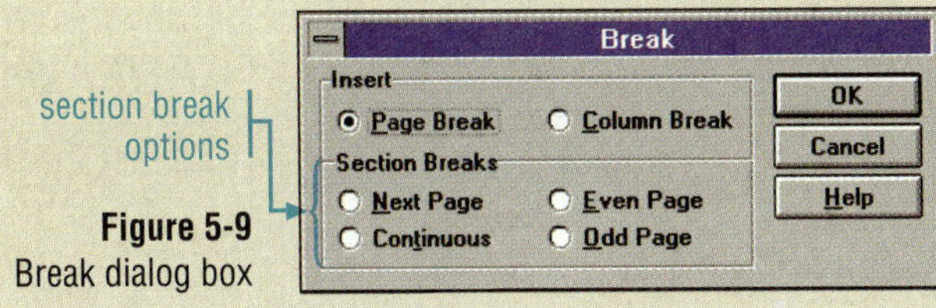

section break options

Figure 5-9
Break dialog box

Jessica wants to insert a section break, and she wants the text after the break to start on a new page.

❸   Click the **Next Page radio button** in the Section Breaks section, then click **OK** or press **[Enter]**. A double dotted line and the words "End of Section" are inserted across the page to indicate that a section break has been inserted. Notice that the status bar now indicates that the document has two sections and that the insertion point is on page 2 of section 2. See Figure 5-10.

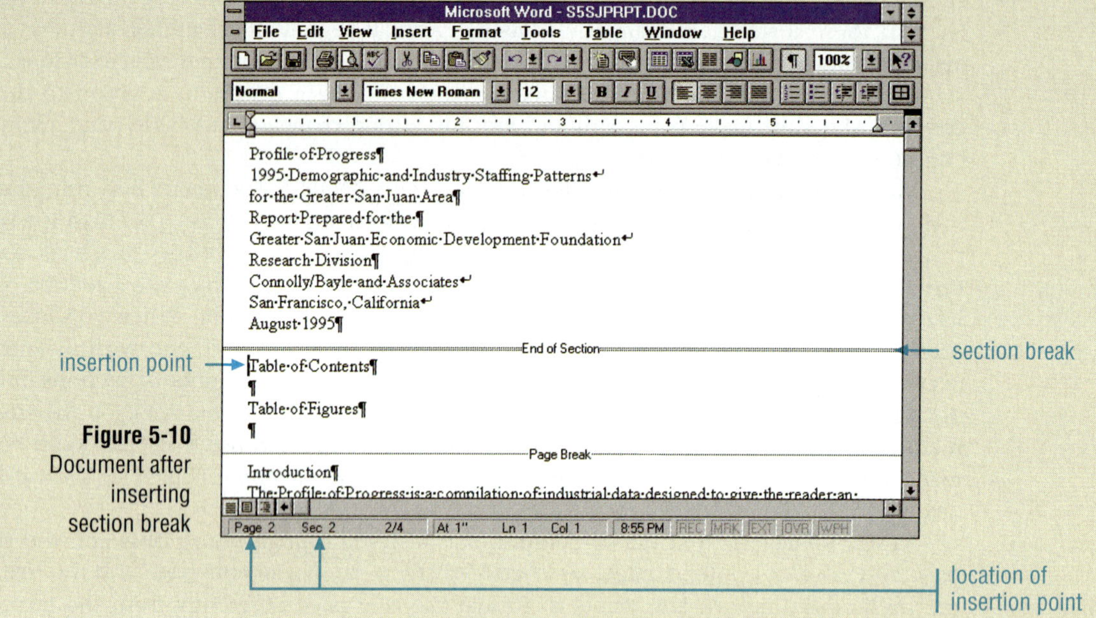

insertion point

section break

Figure 5-10
Document after inserting section break

location of insertion point

❹   Save the changes you have made.

Jessica wants to insert another section break between pages 2 and 3, and she wants the text after the break to start on a new page. She wants 0.75" top and bottom margins for just the text portion of the report.

To insert a section break between pages 2 and 3 then format the sections:

❶   Place the insertion point at the top of page 3, directly before the "I" in Introduction, then press **[Backspace]** to remove the page break.

❷   Click **File** then click **Page Setup....** The Page Setup dialog box appears, with the Margins tab displayed.

❸   Change the top and bottom margins to 0.75", click the **Apply To list box down arrow**, then click **This Point Forward**. This option inserts a section break before the insertion point and applies the changes you just made to the margins from the section break to the end of the document. See Figure 5-11.

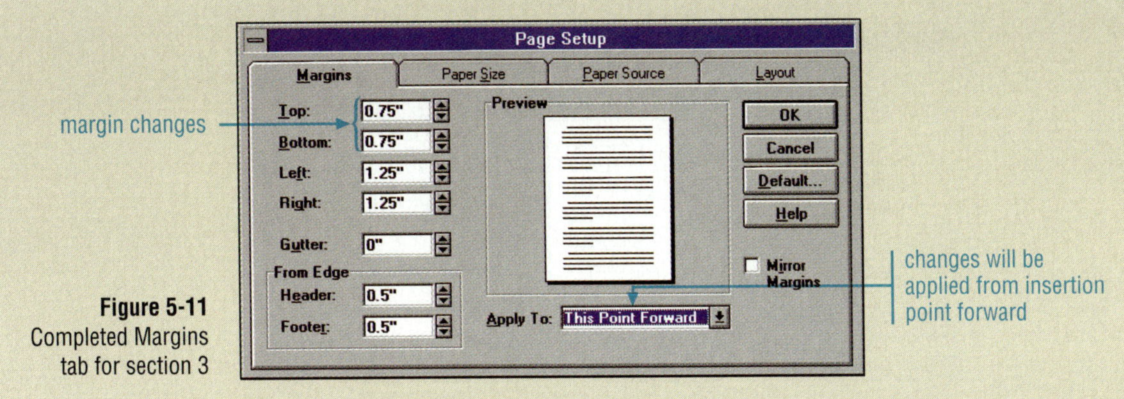

Figure 5-11
Completed Margins tab for section 3

❹ Click **OK** or press **[Enter]**. You return to your document. Notice that a section break is inserted between pages 2 and 3, and the status bar indicates that the insertion point is in section 3 of the document.

❺ Save the changes you have made.

Now that each part of the document—the title page, the table of contents page, and the body of the report—is in its own section, Jessica can format each section individually.

To start, Jessica can align the title page vertically without affecting the rest of the document. When you align text vertically on a page, you align it between the top and bottom margins.

Before changing the vertical alignment option, Jessica must first move the insertion point into the section to be affected by the change. You can use the Go To command [F5] to move quickly between sections.

To change the vertical alignment of the title page:

❶ Press **[F5]**. The Go To dialog box appears.

❷ Click **Section** in the Go To What list box, press **[Tab]** to move to the Enter Section Number text box, type **1**, then click **Go To** or press **[Enter]**. The insertion point moves to section 1.

❸ Click **Close** in the Go To dialog box.

Now that Jessica has moved the insertion point into section 1, she can change the appropriate page-level options.

❹ Click **File** then click **Page Setup...**. The Page Setup dialog box appears.

❺ Click the **Layout tab**, click the **Vertical Alignment list box down arrow**, then click **Justified**. See Figure 5-12.

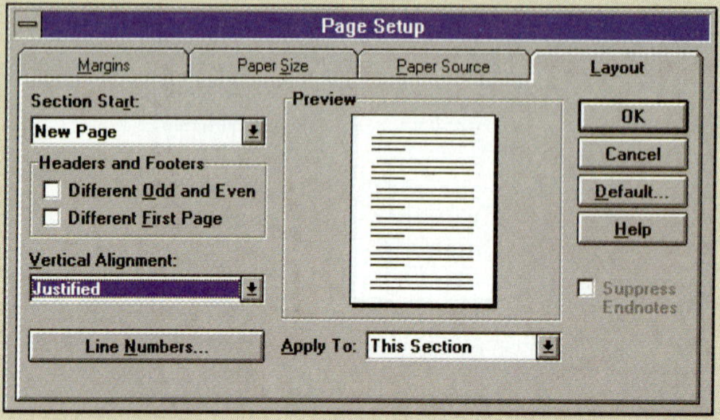

Figure 5-12
Completed Layout
tab for section 1

Notice that the Apply To list box indicates that the selected option applies only to the current section. The default Top alignment option in the Vertical Alignment list box places the contents of a page at the top margin; the Center option centers paragraphs between the top and bottom margins; and the Justified option increases the space between paragraphs on a page so that the first line is even with the top margin and the last line is even with the bottom margin.

❻ Click **OK** or press **[Enter]**.

Looking at the document in normal view, Jessica cannot tell if the title page is justified. She decides to switch to print preview.

❼ Click the **Print Preview button** 🔍 on the Standard toolbar (or click **File** then click **Print Preview**). Notice that the title page is justified between the top and bottom margins. The change in the vertical alignment of a page is a document-level option, but it affects only the section in which it is applied.

TROUBLE? If you do not see all three pages side by side in print preview, click the Multiple Pages button 🔲 on the Print Preview toolbar, then drag across the grid to display three pages.

❽ Click the **Close button** on the Print Preview toolbar.

❾ Save the changes you have made.

Inserting Headers and Footers in a Multi-Section Document

Jessica indicated that she wanted to have headers and footers in all sections of her document, but, as she noted in Figure 5-1, she wants the title page and table of contents page to have both a header and a footer, and the rest of the document to have a slightly different header from the title page and no footer. Unlike other page-level formatting options applied to a section, changes to headers or footers in a section are connected to one another; that is, the header or footer in the first section becomes the default for the entire document. In addition, changes to the headers or footers in any section are reflected in all sections.

Jessica begins by inserting a header and footer in section 1.

To insert a header and footer in section 1:

❶ Place the insertion point in section 1, click **View**, then click **Header and Footer**. The Header text area, now labeled Header -Section 1, appears along with the Header and Footer toolbar.

Jessica wants the header and footer on the title page to be a $^3/_4$ point double rule across the page.

❷ Click the **Borders button** ⊞ on the Formatting toolbar, click the **Line Style list box down arrow**, then click the **$^3/_4$ pt double rule**.

Jessica wants the rule to appear at the bottom of the line space in the header.

❸ Click the **Bottom Border button** ⬓ on the Borders toolbar. The double rule appears across the line space.

Next Jessica wants to place the same type of rule at the top of the line space in the footer for section 1.

❹ Click the **Switch Between Header and Footer button** ⧉ on the Header and Footer toolbar. The insertion point moves into the Footer text area, which is labeled Footer -Section 1.

The $^3/_4$ pt double rule is already selected on the Borders toolbar, so Jessica must only specify its placement.

❺ Click the **Top Border button** ⬒ on the Borders toolbar to place the double rule at the top of the line space in the footer.

❻ Click the **Close button** on the Header and Footer toolbar.

Jessica wants to see how the changes to the title page appear.

❼ Click the **Print Preview button** ▣ on the Standard toolbar (or click **File** then click **Print Preview**). See Figure 5-13.

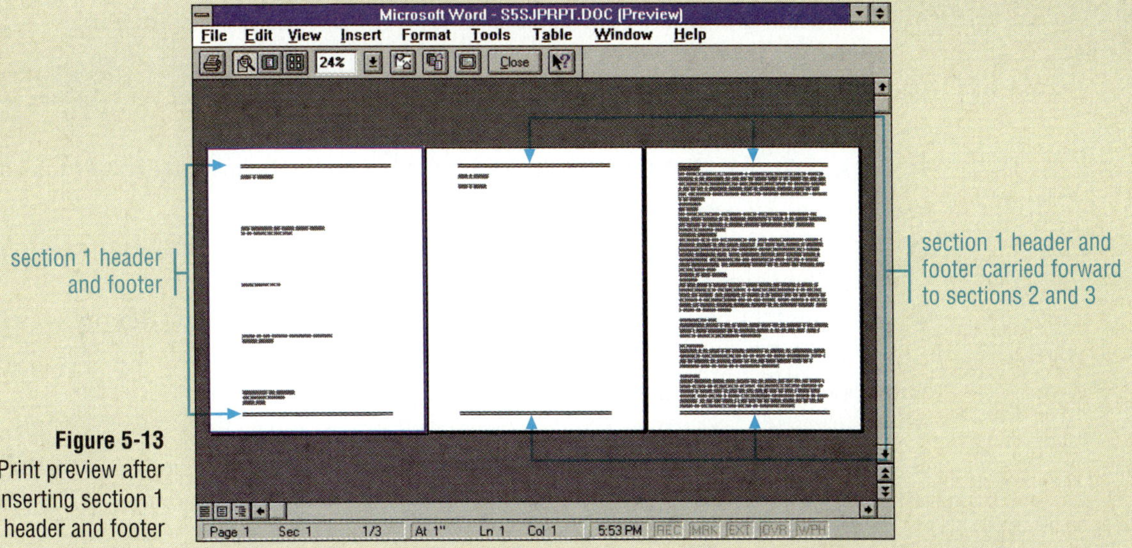

Figure 5-13
Print preview after inserting section 1 header and footer

Notice that the header and the footer appear on all pages of the document, even the pages in sections 2 and 3. Header and footer changes carry forward through the next sections of a document unless they are changed.

TROUBLE? If you do not see all three pages side by side in print preview, click the Multiple Pages button ▦ on the Print Preview toolbar, then drag across the grid to display three pages.

8 Click the **Close button** on the Print Preview toolbar to return to your document.

9 Save the changes you have made.

Jessica wants the same type of rule in both the header and footer of section 2, which is the table of contents page, but she also wants the page number to appear at the center bottom of this page as a lowercase roman numeral. She must, therefore, change the format of the page number. Furthermore, she doesn't want a page number to appear in section 1.

To change the page number format:

1 Place the insertion point in section 2, click **View**, then click **Header and Footer**. Notice that the label "Same as Previous" appears at the right of the Header text area and that the Same as Previous button 🔲 on the Header and Footer toolbar is highlighted. This indicates that, unless you specify otherwise, the header for this section will be the same as the header of the previous section (in this case, section 1).

Jessica wants the double rule to appear in the section 2 header, so she can now move to the footer.

2 Click the **Switch Between Header and Footer button** 🔲 on the Header and Footer toolbar. The Footer -Section 2 text area appears with Same as Previous displayed on the right.

Jessica does *not* want the section 2 footer connected to the section 1 footer because she does not want a page number to appear in section 1.

3 Click the **Same as Previous button** 🔲 on the Header and Footer toolbar to deselect that option for this footer. The Same as Previous label disappears from the Footer -Section 2 text area.

Next Jessica wants to insert a page number at the center of the footer, and she needs to change the number format to lowercase roman numerals.

4 Press [Tab] then click the **Page Numbers button** 🔲 on the Header and Footer toolbar.

Jessica wants the page number to be a lowercase roman numeral.

5 Select the page number, click **Insert**, then click **Page Numbers…**. The Page Numbers dialog box appears.

6 Make sure the Show Number on First Page check box is selected. This option will place the page number on the first page *of the section*.

Now Jessica needs to change the format of the page number.

7 Click **Format…**. The Page Number Format dialog box appears.

8 Click the **Number Format list box down arrow**, then click **i, ii, iii, …**. See Figure 5-14.

lowercase
roman numeral
format selected

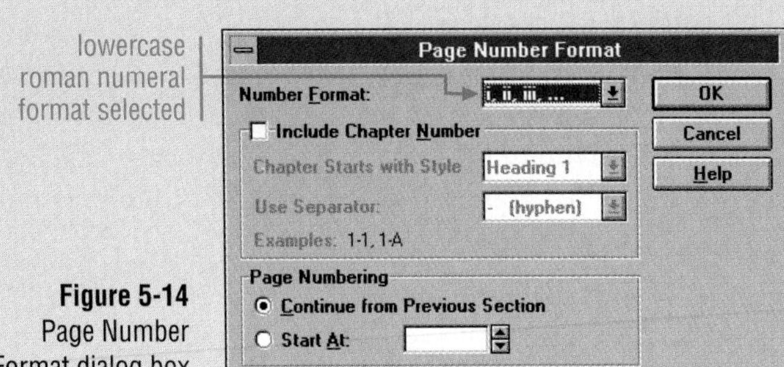

Figure 5-14
Page Number
Format dialog box

9 Click **OK** or press **[Enter]**. You return to the Page Numbers dialog box. Click **OK** or press **[Enter]**. The page number format is changed to a lowercase roman numeral.

10 Close the Header and Footer toolbar, then save the changes you have made.

Jessica now needs to format the header and footer for section 3 of her document. Recall from Figure 5-1 that she wants to keep the ¾ point double rule in the section 3 header and add the name of the report and the page number. She wants to eliminate the footer altogether in section 3, because she'll include the page number in the header in this section.

To create different headers and footers in section 3 of the document:

1 Place the insertion point in section 3, click **View**, then click **Header and Footer**. The Header -Section 3 text area opens. Notice that the Same as Previous label appears on the right and that the Same as Previous button on the Header and Footer toolbar is highlighted, indicating that the header in this section is connected to the previous section. Also notice that the double rule doesn't appear completely because the header is too close to the text of the report.

Jessica doesn't want the header in the previous section of the document to be the same as the header in this section.

2 Click on the Header and Footer toolbar to deselect it. The double rule remains at the bottom of the line space, but the changes you are about to make to this header will not be reflected in the section 2 header.

3 Type **Profile of Progress**, then press **[Tab]** twice. Type **Page**, press **[Spacebar]**, then click the **Page Numbers button** on the Header and Footer toolbar. Select **Profile of Progress** then change its font formatting to **14 pt**, **Bold**, and **Italic**. Select **Page 3** then change its font formatting to **Bold**. Deselect the text.

Next Jessica wants to insert a blank line after the header so that it is not so close to the body of the report.

4 Click the **right mouse button** on the header text to open the shortcut editing and formatting menu, click **Paragraph...** (or click **Format** then click **Paragraph...**), then increase the Spacing After option to **12 pt**. Click **OK** or press **[Enter]**. The additional space inserted below the double rule in the header makes the double rule completely visible now.

5 Click the **Switch Between Header and Footer button** on the Header and Footer toolbar. Notice that the Footer text area is labeled Footer -Section 3, that the Same as Previous label appears on the right, and that the button is again highlighted.

Jessica wants to delete the footer in section 3 completely.

❻ Click ▣ on the Header and Footer toolbar to deselect the button, then click the **No Border button** ▣ on the Borders toolbar.

❼ Drag across the page number in the footer to select the number, then press **[Del]**.

❽ Click the **Close button** on the Header and Footer toolbar to return to your document.

Jessica wants to see how the headers and footers look.

❾ Click the **Print Preview button** ▣ on the Standard toolbar (or click **File** then click **Print Preview**). Notice that the footer has been eliminated from section 3.

❿ Click the **Close button** on the Print Preview toolbar, then save the changes you have made.

If you want to take a break and resume the tutorial at a later time, you can close the current document then exit Word by double-clicking the Control menu box in the upper-left corner of the screen. When you want to resume the tutorial, start Word, place your Student Disk in the disk drive, then complete the screen check procedure described in Tutorial 1. Open the document S5SJPRPT.DOC, then continue with the tutorial.

■   ■   ■

Jessica has finished inserting headers and footers into the different sections of her document. Now she is ready to add paragraph-level and font-level formatting, which will also enhance her report's appearance.

Defining Styles

In Tutorial 3, you learned to apply Word's predefined styles. If you do not want to use any of the styles in Word's predefined templates, you can define your own. Word provides two ways to define a new style. You can define a style by **example**—that is, by basing it on an existing paragraph that already contains the formatting options you want. You can also use the Style command on the Format menu to define a style by specifying each formatting option. Unless you indicate otherwise, user-defined styles are automatically added to the NORMAL template and, therefore, are available globally to all documents.

Jessica used the Style Gallery to preview the styles in Word's existing templates, but she did not find a template that contained the styles to fit her needs exactly. She decides to define her own styles, then save them in a customized document template, which she can use again if she needs to format a similar report.

Defining a New Style by Example

Jessica wants to apply a variety of paragraph and font formats to each line of text on the title page to improve its appearance. She wants some lines to be Arial, bold, 24 point, with centered alignment, a 72 point line space before, and a 36 point line space after. She wants other lines to be Arial, bold, 18 point, with centered alignment, and a 36 point line space before and after. Rather than apply each formatting option individually to each line, Jessica decides to define two new styles to contain the set of formats she wants to use, then apply the appropriate style to each line on the title page.

One way to define a new paragraph style is by example—that is, by using a paragraph that already has all the formats you want.

Defining a New Style by Example

- Select the example paragraph.
- Click the Style list box on the Formatting toolbar to highlight the name of the current style.
- Type a name for the new style.
- Press [Enter].

Jessica wants to define a new style for those lines on the title page that will be Arial, bold, 24 point, with centered alignment, a 72 point line space before, and a 36 point line space after the paragraph. She must first create an example paragraph with these formats, then define the style by example. Because she will be accumulating these styles eventually in a customized document template and doesn't want these new styles to be available globally, Jessica must also prevent Word from automatically saving them to the NORMAL template, thus altering the NORMAL template.

To define a new style by example:

1. Click **Tools** then click **Options…**. The Options dialog box appears.
2. Click the **Save tab**.

Jessica wants to make sure that the styles she creates and modifies will not affect the NORMAL template.

3. Click the **Prompt to Save Normal.dot check box**, then click **OK** or press [Enter]. When you select this setting, Word will display a message box asking you to confirm any changes to the NORMAL template when you exit Word. This will allow you to avoid changing the NORMAL template inadvertently.

   TROUBLE? If the check box is already activated, skip to Step 4 below.

4. Move to page 1 then select the first line, **Profile of Progress**. Notice that the Normal style is in effect for the selected text.
5. Change the font formatting of the selected text to **Arial, 24 pt, Bold**; then change its paragraph formatting options to a **72 pt** line space before, a **36 pt** line space after, and **Centered** alignment.

Now that you have created your "example," you will use it as the basis for your new style. The text should still be selected.

6. Click the style named **Normal** in the Style list box on the Formatting toolbar. This highlights the Normal style.

   TROUBLE? Do not click the Style list box arrow and choose Normal from the list of styles. Simply select (highlight) the word Normal in the Style list box on the Formatting toolbar.

Next Jessica names the new style by typing a name to replace the highlighted word, Normal. A style name can be up to 253 characters in length and can contain spaces.

Style names are case sensitive so "*T*itle 1" and "*t*itle 1" can be the names given to two different styles. Make sure that names of new styles are unique and are not used by Word in its own predefined styles. Jessica wants to name this style "Title 1."

❼ Type **Title**, press **[Spacebar]**, then type **1**. "Title 1" replaces "Normal" in the Style list box.

❽ Press **[Enter]** then deselect the text.

Jessica next wants to see if the new style has been added to the Style list.

❾ Click the **Style list box down arrow** to display the Style list. The style name Title 1 is added to the Style list. The style in effect for the current location of the insertion point is highlighted. See Figure 5-15.

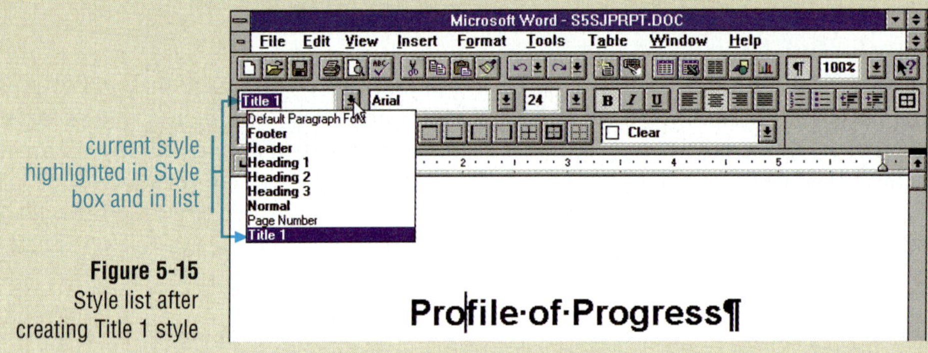

current style highlighted in Style box and in list

Figure 5-15
Style list after creating Title 1 style

❿ Press **[Esc]** to close the Style list.

Jessica will apply this newly defined style to other parts of the title page later, but now she needs to define another style for use on her title page.

Defining a New Style Using the Style Command

The second method for defining a new style is to use the Style command on the Format menu. Essentially you build the style from scratch by specifying all the formatting options you want the style to contain.

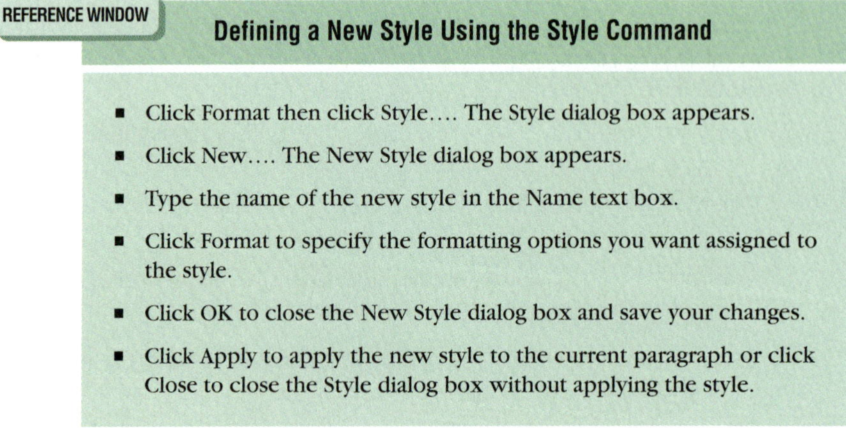

REFERENCE WINDOW

Defining a New Style Using the Style Command

- Click Format then click Style…. The Style dialog box appears.
- Click New…. The New Style dialog box appears.
- Type the name of the new style in the Name text box.
- Click Format to specify the formatting options you want assigned to the style.
- Click OK to close the New Style dialog box and save your changes.
- Click Apply to apply the new style to the current paragraph or click Close to close the Style dialog box without applying the style.

Jessica wants to name her second new style "Title 2" and to define it with the following attributes: Arial, bold, 18 point, centered alignment, and a 36 point line space before and after the paragraph. She decides to define this new style by using the Style command on the Format menu.

To define the new title style using the Style command:

❶ Select the paragraph "1995 Demographic and Industry Staffing Patterns for the Greater San Juan Area," click **Format**, then click **Style…**. The Style dialog box appears with Normal highlighted and checked in the Styles list box. See Figure 5-16. The Styles list includes only those styles that have been used in the current document. The two Preview sections show the current paragraph and character styles. The Description section describes the formatting characteristics of the style applied to the selected paragraph.

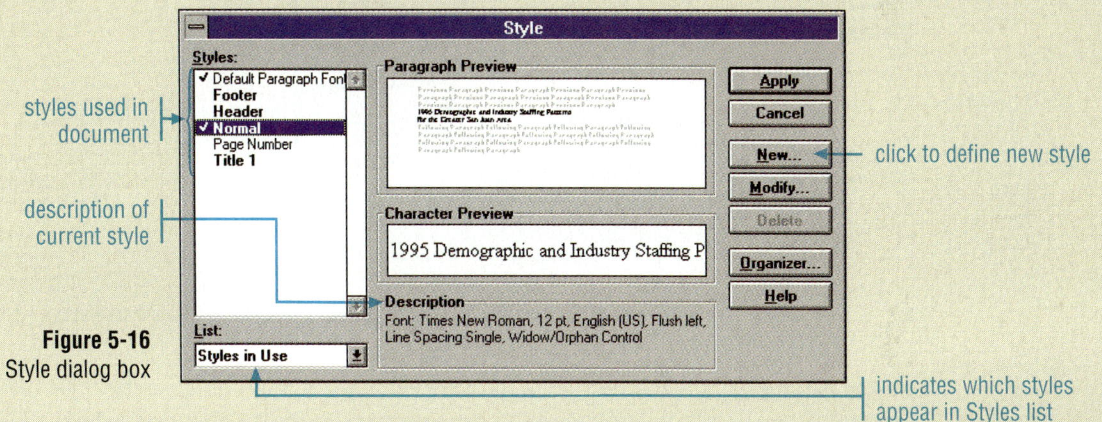

styles used in document

description of current style

Figure 5-16
Style dialog box

click to define new style

indicates which styles appear in Styles list

TROUBLE? If your Styles list includes more styles than shown in Figure 5-16, click the List box down arrow then click Styles in Use.

Jessica needs to define a new style.

❷ Click **New…**. The New Style dialog box appears, with the suggested style name "Style1" highlighted in the Name text box.

Now Jessica needs to replace the style name supplied by Word with "Title 2."

❸ Type **Title 2** in the Name text box to name the new style. You can specify whether the new style is a paragraph style or a character style, which style the new style is based on, and even which style is in effect after you create a new paragraph with the new style then press [Enter]. Unless otherwise specified, new styles are based on the style applied to the paragraph currently selected.

"Normal +" appears in the Description section, signifying that the new style is based on the Normal style but could also contain additional features specifically defined for the new style. The name of the base style Normal also appears in the Based On list box.

Next Jessica specifies the formatting characteristics of the new style.

❹ Click **Format** then click **Font…**. The Font dialog box appears.

❺ Change the font formatting options to **Arial**, **Bold**, **18 pt**.

❻   Click **OK** or press [Enter]. The selected font options are previewed and added to the description in the New Style dialog box.

Now Jessica is ready to add the paragraph formatting options to the Title 2 style definition.

❼   Click **Format** then click **Paragraph....** The Paragraph dialog box appears.

❽   Increase the Spacing Before and Spacing After options to **36 pt**, then click **Centered** in the Alignment list box. Click **OK** or press [Enter]. You return to the New Style dialog box. Notice that the Description section has been updated to reflect the formatting characteristics of the new style. See Figure 5-17.

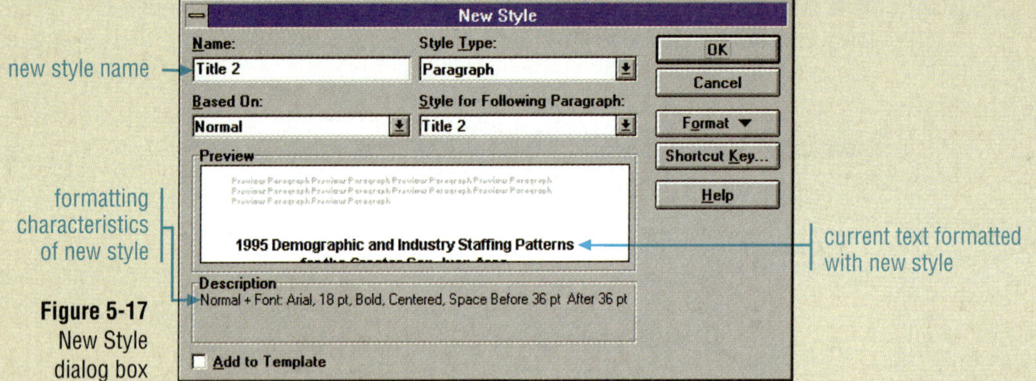

Figure 5-17
New Style
dialog box

❾   Click **OK** or press [Enter]. You return to the Style dialog box. Title 2 has been added to the Styles list.

Jessica can now apply the new style to the selected paragraph or close the Style dialog box. Because she is not going to define any more styles for the title page, she decides to apply the style from the Style dialog box.

❿   Click **Apply** in the Style dialog box or press [Enter]. The new style is applied to the currently selected paragraph.

Jessica is now ready to apply the styles she has defined to the rest of the text on the title page.

Applying Styles

Word provides several methods to apply styles. As you learned in Tutorial 3, the easiest way to apply a style to selected text is to use the Style list box.

Jessica has created two new styles for her title page, and now she is ready to apply those styles to the appropriate paragraphs.

To apply styles on the title page and the table of contents page:

❶   Select the paragraph **Report Prepared for the**. The currently assigned style is Normal.

❷   Click the **Style list box down arrow** on the Formatting toolbar, then click **Title 2**. All the formatting attributes you defined for the Title 2 style are applied to the selected text.

❸ Select the paragraph **Greater San Juan Economic Development Foundation Research Division**, then apply the Title 1 style to it.

❹ Select the paragraph **Connolly/Bayle and Associates, San Francisco, California, August 1995**, then apply the Title 2 style to it.

Jessica decides to use the Repeat command ([F4]) to apply the Title 2 style to the titles on the table of contents page.

❺ Place the insertion point in the title Table of Contents on page 2, then press **[F4]**. Word repeats the steps to apply the Title 2 style to the selected paragraph.

❻ Place the insertion point in the title Table of Figures on page 2, then press **[F4]**. The Title 2 style is applied to the selected text.

Jessica wants to see how the title page and the table of contents page will appear when printed with the new styles applied.

❼ Click the **Print Preview button** on the Standard toolbar (or click **File** then click **Print Preview**). Notice the changes to the first two pages of the document. See Figure 5-18.

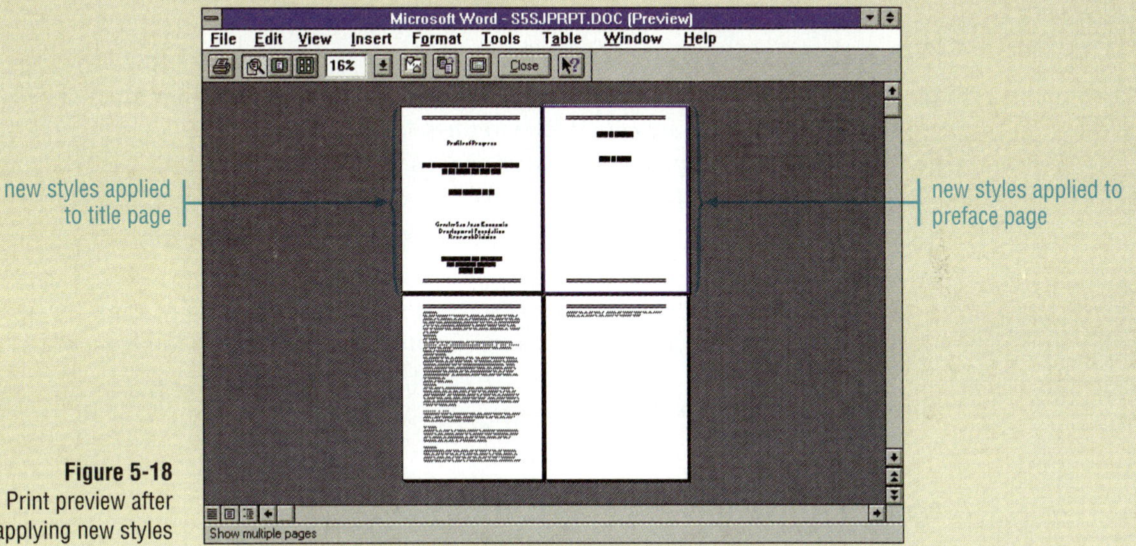

new styles applied to title page

new styles applied to preface page

Figure 5-18
Print preview after applying new styles

TROUBLE? If you do not see all four pages in print preview, click the Multiple Pages button on the Print Preview toolbar, then select four pages.

❽ Click the **Close button** on the Print Preview toolbar.

❾ Save the changes you have made.

Jessica has defined and applied styles to the title page and to the table of contents page. Now she wants to apply the predefined styles Heading 1, Heading 2, and Heading 3 to the headings in her report. Rather than using the Formatting toolbar to apply these styles, she uses the Style command on the Format menu.

To apply the heading styles using the Style command:

❶ Place the insertion point at the beginning of the heading Introduction on page 3.

❷ Click **Format** then click **Style…**. The Style dialog box appears. Notice that only the styles specifically applied to text in the current document appear in the list of styles; the predefined styles Heading 1, Heading 2, and Heading 3 are not available as they are in the Style list box on the Formatting toolbar.

Jessica wants to apply the Heading 1 style to Introduction.

❸ Click the **List box down arrow**, then click **All Styles**. All of the user-defined and predefined styles are listed in the Styles list box.

❹ Scroll through the list of styles, then click **Heading 1**.

❺ Click **Apply** or press **[Enter]**. The Heading 1 style is applied to the heading Introduction.

Next Jessica wants to apply the Heading 2 style to the headings Methodology, Summary of Major Findings, and Conclusion.

❻ Place the insertion point in the heading Methodology, then repeat Steps 2, 4, and 5 except click **Heading 2** in the Styles list.

Jessica uses the Repeat command to apply the Heading 2 style to the other headings.

❼ Place the insertion point in the heading Summary of Major Findings, then press **[F4]**. The Heading 2 style is applied to the selected heading.

❽ Place the insertion point in the heading Conclusion, then press **[F4]**. The Heading 2 style is applied to the selected heading.

Next Jessica wants to apply the Heading 3 style to the remaining headings.

❾ Place the insertion point in the heading The Sample, then repeat Steps 2, 4, and 5 except click **Heading 3** in the Styles list. Use the Repeat command to apply the style to the headings: Collection Procedures, Population, Diversifying San Juan, and Job Openings.

❿ Save the changes you have made.

Applying Styles Using Shortcut Keys

Jessica has applied styles to all elements of her document except to the main text paragraphs of the report. She decides to use one of Word's predefined styles, Body Text Indent, for the main text paragraphs. Because she has so many paragraphs to format with the Body Text Indent style, she decides to define a shortcut key for that style to reduce the amount of time she'll spend formatting the text.

To assign a shortcut key for applying the Body Text Indent style:

❶ Place the insertion point in the first text paragraph on page 3, click **Format**, then click **Style…**. The Style dialog box appears. Because you are going to apply the style after assigning the shortcut key, you need to place the insertion point in a paragraph to which you want to apply the style before choosing the Style command.

❷ Scroll through the Styles list, then click **Body Text Indent**. The Description section identifies the characteristics of the selected style.

❸ Click **Modify…**. The Modify Style dialog box appears. See Figure 5-19.

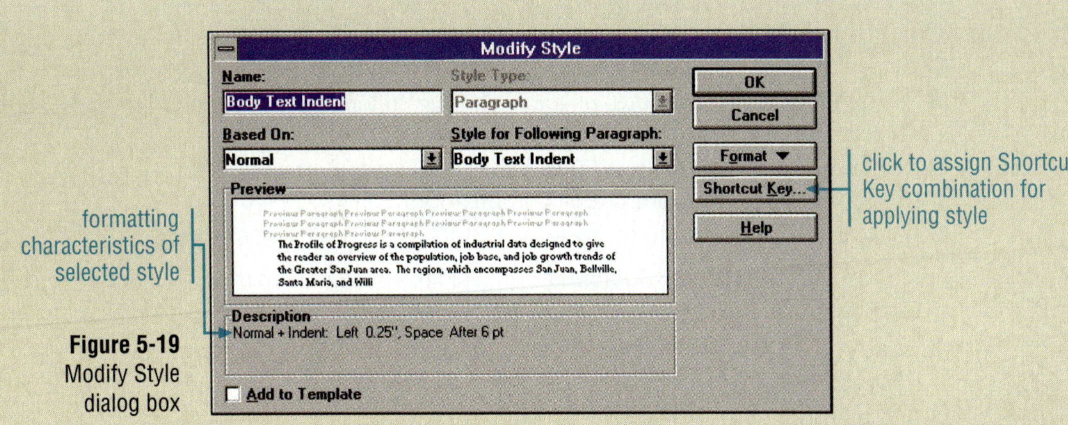

Figure 5-19
Modify Style
dialog box

❹ Click **Shortcut Key…**. The Customize dialog box appears with the Keyboard tab displayed.

Word already has some shortcut keys assigned to options so Jessica must be certain to use a unique combination of keys. She decides to try [Alt][b] as the shortcut key combination.

❺ Press and hold **[Alt]** and press **[b]**. Release both keys. Notice that "Alt+B" appears in the Press New Shortcut Key text box, and a message appears indicating that this key combination is currently unassigned as a shortcut key combination for any other style.

❻ Click **Assign** or press **[Enter]**. The assigned shortcut key appears in the Current Keys list box. See Figure 5-20.

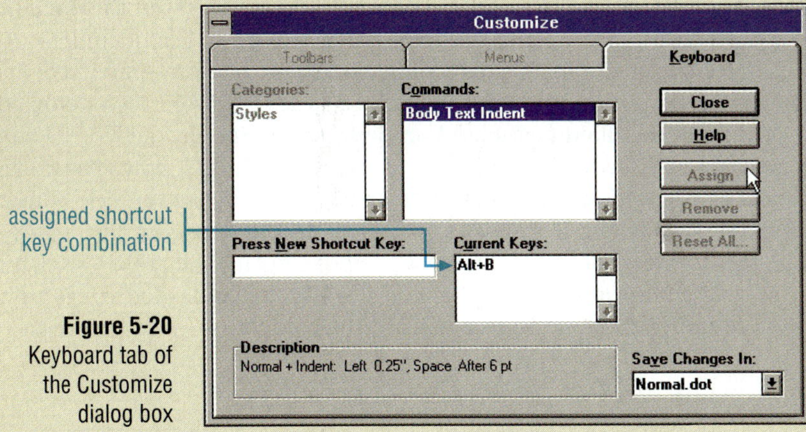

Figure 5-20
Keyboard tab of
the Customize
dialog box

❼ Click **Close** or press **[Enter]**. You return to the Modify Style dialog box.

❽ Click **OK**. You return to the Style dialog box.

❾ Click **Apply** or press **[Enter]**. The attributes of the Body Text Indent style are applied to the selected paragraph.

❿ Save the changes you have made.

Next Jessica needs to apply this style to the remaining text paragraphs in her document.

To apply the Body Text Indent style using the shortcut key:

❶ Place the insertion point in the second text paragraph ("The sample for…").

❷ Press **[Alt][b]**. The attributes of the Body Text Indent style are applied to the selected paragraph.

❸ Continue applying the Body Text Indent style to the remaining text paragraphs using the assigned shortcut key combination.

❹ Save the changes you have made.

Jessica decides to view the document in page layout view so that she can see how it will print.

❺ Click the **Page Layout View button** ▣ in the status bar (or click **View** then click **Page Layout**).

❻ Scroll through the document in page layout view.

❼ Click the **Normal View button** ▤ in the status bar (or click **View** then click **Normal**) to return to normal view.

Jessica has applied styles to all elements of her document, but as she looked at the document in page layout view, she decided that she could further improve its appearance by modifying some of the styles.

Modifying Styles

You can redefine, or modify, any style, either Word's predefined styles or those that you have defined. Word automatically updates any paragraphs previously formatted with the style, thus saving you time and assuring consistent formatting throughout the document.

Jessica isn't satisfied with the appearance of the headings in her document. Rather than making manual changes to each heading in the document, she can simply redefine the formatting characteristics of the styles applied to these headings. Word then automatically updates each heading in the document based on these styles. She decides to redefine the Heading 1, Heading 2, and Heading 3 styles, and the Body Text Indent style. These changes would automatically be stored in the NORMAL template if Jessica had not first chosen the Save option to have Word confirm changes to the NORMAL template. In this way, Jessica can modify the styles for her report document only—the template will remain unchanged.

To make the heading Introduction stand out more, Jessica decides to increase the font size, change it to all uppercase letters, and increase the amount of space before and after the heading.

To modify the Heading 1 style using the Style command:

❶ Move to the top of page 3, then place the insertion point in the heading Introduction. "Heading 1" appears in the Style list box on the Formatting toolbar.

❷ Click **Format** then click **Style…**. The Style dialog box appears.

❸ Click **Modify…**. The Modify Style dialog box appears. Notice that the current definition of the Heading 1 style appears in the Description section.

❹ Click **Format**, click **Font…**, then make the following changes: **24 pt, All Caps**.

❺ Click **OK** or press **[Enter]**. You return to the Modify Style dialog box.

Next Jessica needs to change the paragraph formats for the Heading 1 style.

❻ Click **Format**, click **Paragraph...**, then make the following changes: **Spacing Before 48 pt** and **Spacing After 24 pt**.

❼ Click **OK** or press **[Enter]**. You return to the Modify Style dialog box. Notice the change in the Description section.

❽ Click **OK** or press **[Enter]**. You return to the Style dialog box.

❾ Click **Close**. Notice that the newly defined Heading 1 style is applied to Introduction. This is the only instance of a Heading 1 style in the report.

❿ Save the changes you have made.

You can also redefine a style by example using the Style list box on the Formatting toolbar.

REFERENCE WINDOW

Redefining a Style by Example

- Select a paragraph formatted with the style you want to redefine.

- Make the necessary formatting changes.

- Click the Style list box on the Formatting toolbar to select the style name in effect.

- Press [Enter]. The Reapply Style dialog box appears.

- Click the "Redefine the style using the selection as an example?" radio button, then click OK or press [Enter].

To keep the remaining headings proportional in size to the Introduction heading, Jessica also needs to redefine the predefined styles, Heading 2 and Heading 3. She used each of these styles throughout her document.

To redefine the Heading 2 style by example:

❶ Select the heading **Methodology**. The entire heading must be highlighted. The Style list box on the Formatting toolbar changes to reflect the style applied to Methodology, which is Heading 2.

Jessica wants to change several formatting options.

❷ Click the **right mouse button** on the selected text (or click **Format**), click **Font...**, then make the following changes: **18 pt, All Caps**.

❸ Click **OK** or press **[Enter]**.

❹ Click the **right mouse button** on the selected text (or click **Format**), click **Paragraph...**, then make the following changes: **Spacing Before 24 pt** and **Spacing After 6 pt**.

❺ Click **OK** or press **[Enter]**.

Jessica wants to add a rule to the Heading 2 style definition.

❻ Click the **¾ pt single rule** in the Line Style list box on the Borders toolbar, if necessary, then click the **Top Border button** ▢.

TROUBLE? If the Borders toolbar is not displayed, click the Borders button ⊞ on the Formatting toolbar, then complete Step 6.

Now that Jessica has an example of the way she wants the Heading 2 style to appear, she is ready to redefine the style.

❼   Click the **Style list box** on the Formatting toolbar to select Heading 2, then press **[Enter]**. The Reapply Style dialog box appears for Heading 2. See Figure 5-21.

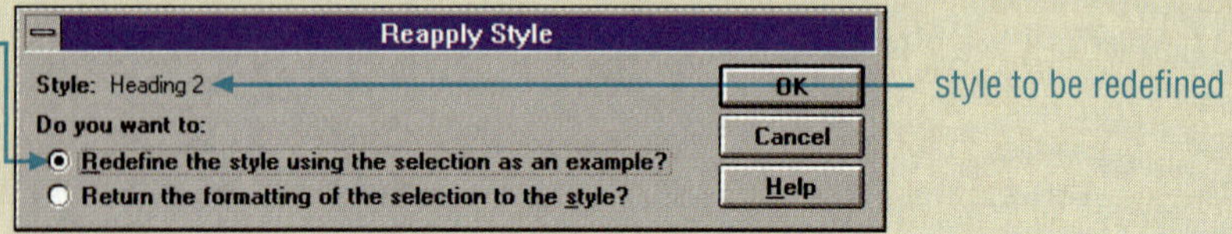

Figure 5-21
Reapply Style
dialog box

❽   Make sure the radio button for the option "Redefine the style using the selection as an example?" is selected, then click **OK** or press **[Enter]**.

❾   Scroll through the document to see that the new formatting characteristics for the Heading 2 style were also applied automatically to the headings Summary of Major Findings and Conclusion.

Next Jessica wants to change the formatting characteristics for the Heading 3 style and for the Body Text Indent style.

To redefine the Heading 3 and Body Text Indent styles by example:

❶   Select the heading **The Sample**. The entire heading must be highlighted. Use the Formatting toolbar to make the following font formatting changes: **Arial, 14 pt**.

❷   Click the right mouse button on the selected text (or click **Format**), click **Paragraph...**, then make the following changes: **Spacing After 12 pt**. (Spacing Before is already set to 12 pt.)

❸   Click **OK** or press **[Enter]**.

❹   Click the **Style list box** on the Formatting toolbar to select Heading 3, then press **[Enter]**. The Reapply Style dialog box appears.

❺   Make sure the radio button for the option "Redefine the style using the selection as an example?" is selected, then click **OK** or press **[Enter]**. Scroll through the document to see that all headings formatted with the Heading 3 style were automatically updated.

Now Jessica modifies the Body Text Indent style.

❻   Place the insertion point anywhere within a main text paragraph, then drag the indent markers on the ruler to the 1-inch mark.

❼   Click the **Justify button** ▤ on the Formatting toolbar.

❽   Repeat Steps 4 and 5 to complete modifying the Body Text Indent style by example. See Figure 5-22.

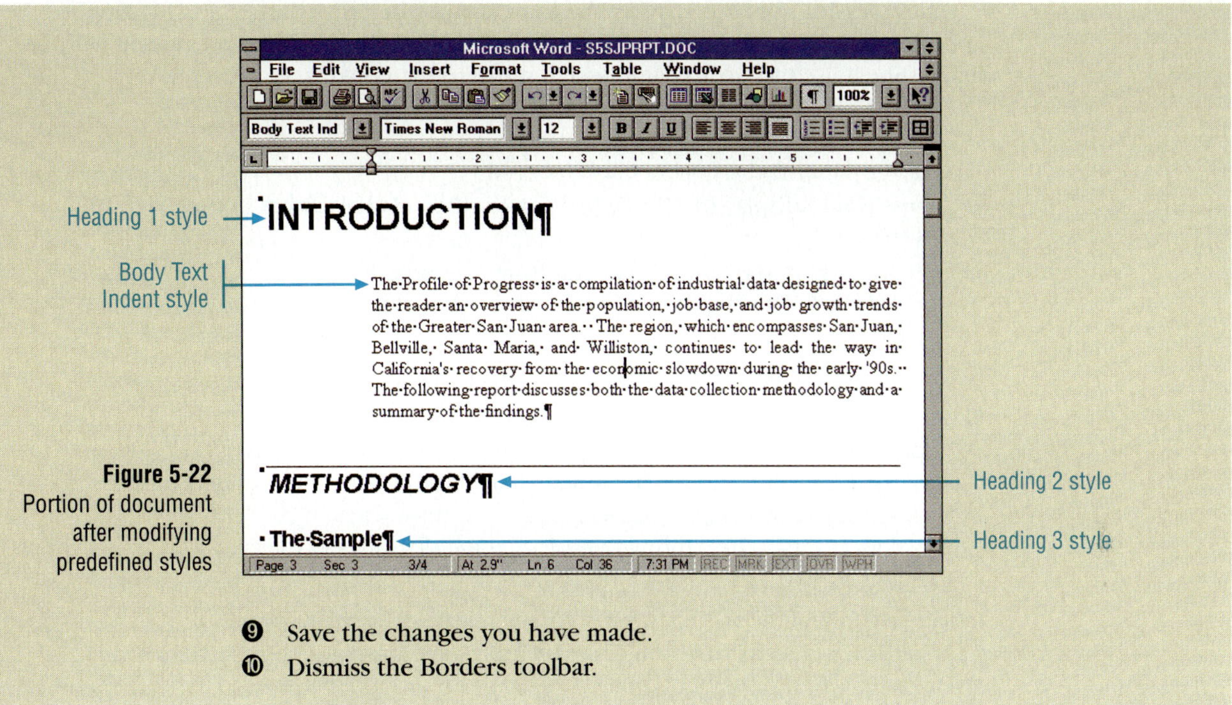

Figure 5-22
Portion of document after modifying predefined styles

⑨ Save the changes you have made.
⑩ Dismiss the Borders toolbar.

Now that she has finished editing and formatting the text of her report, Jessica is ready to transfer the charts she created previously in another document.

Transferring Data Between Documents

One of the hallmarks of the Windows environment is the ease with which you can move or copy information. In previous tutorials, you learned ways to move or copy text *within* a document either by using the Clipboard or by using the drag-and-drop feature. The options for moving or copying information from one Word document to *another* Word document are basically the same as moving and copying text within a document. You can use either the Clipboard or the drag-and-drop feature.

Using the Clipboard to Transfer Data Between Documents

One way to transfer data between documents is by using the Clipboard. You can cut or copy selected text from one document, then paste the contents of the Clipboard in another document. Because the text is on the Clipboard, you can paste the cut or copied text as many times as you need to as many different documents as you need, including documents in other Windows applications.

Jessica thinks that the use of charts will enable the readers of the report to understand more easily the numeric data that she has gathered in her research. A **chart** is a visual display of numerical data in graph form. Jessica used Microsoft Graph to create the charts she needs to insert into the preliminary report and saved them in the file C5SJCHRT.DOC. Microsoft Graph is an **applet**, a small application designed to work with Windows programs such as Microsoft Word or Excel. To learn more about the use of Microsoft Graph, consult the *Microsoft Word User's Guide*.

Now Jessica needs to transfer the three charts she created in C5SJCHRT.DOC to their appropriate locations in S5SJPRPT.DOC. She marked the locations previously with bookmarks. She'll use the Go To command to move to the bookmarks.

To transfer the first chart using the Clipboard:

❶ Press **[F5]** to display the Go To dialog box, then click **Bookmark** in the Go to What list box.

❷ Click **figure1** in the Enter Bookmark Name list box, if necessary, then click **Go To** or press **[Enter]**. The insertion point moves to the selected bookmark. Close the Go To dialog box.

Now Jessica must open the document that contains the three charts she created.

❸ Open the file C5SJCHRT.DOC from your Student Disk. S5SJPRPT.DOC remains open, but it is not visible. Scroll through the chart document to view the three charts Jessica created: a 3-D column chart of population growth data for the area, a 3-D pie chart showing the different types of businesses in the area, and a 2-D stacked column chart showing projected job openings in the area. Each chart is on a separate page.

Jessica will follow the "select, then do" principle to copy the first chart to the Clipboard. To select a chart, you move the mouse pointer over the chart, then click. *Selection handles*, resembling small boxes, appear around the chart to indicate that it is selected. A selected chart is just as susceptible to change as selected text, *so be careful*.

❹ Move the mouse pointer over the 3-D Population column chart.

❺ Click the chart. Selection handles appear around the chart to indicate that it is selected. See Figure 5-23.

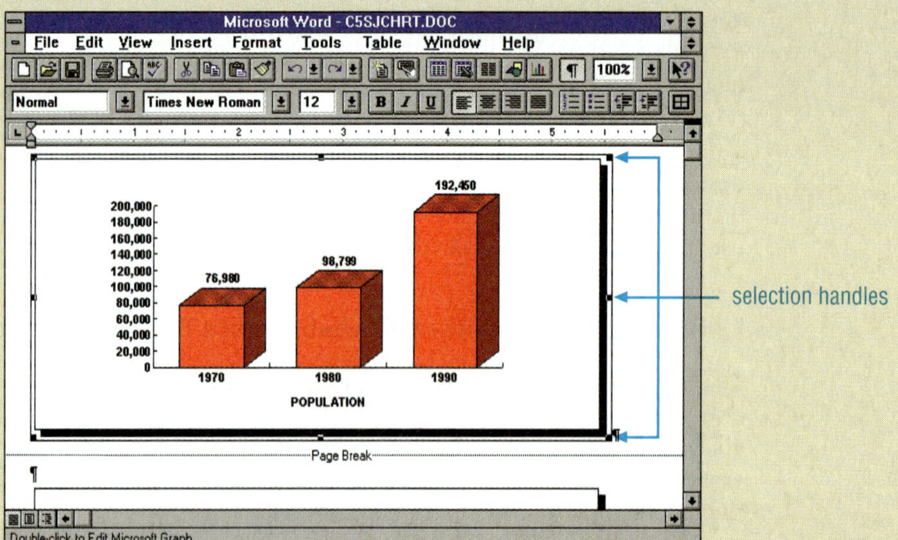

Figure 5-23
Selected
Population chart

TROUBLE? If you accidentally delete a chart, click the Undo button ↶ on the Standard toolbar (or click Edit then click Undo Delete).

Now that the chart is selected, Jessica can copy it to the Clipboard.

❻   Click the **Copy button** on the Standard toolbar (or click **Edit** then click **Copy**).

Next Jessica will paste the copied chart from the Clipboard to its appropriate location in S5SJPRPT.DOC, but first she must make it the active document.

❼   Click **Window** then click **S5SJPRPT.DOC** to make it the active document. Notice that the insertion point is in the same location (figure1 bookmark) as it was before you switched. C5SJCHRT.DOC is still open, just not visible.

❽   Click the **Paste button** on the Standard toolbar (or click **Edit** then click **Paste**). The Population chart is pasted from the Clipboard to the report document. Notice that the bookmark has increased in size to match the size of the chart. See Figure 5-24. Press [↓] to see the entire chart.

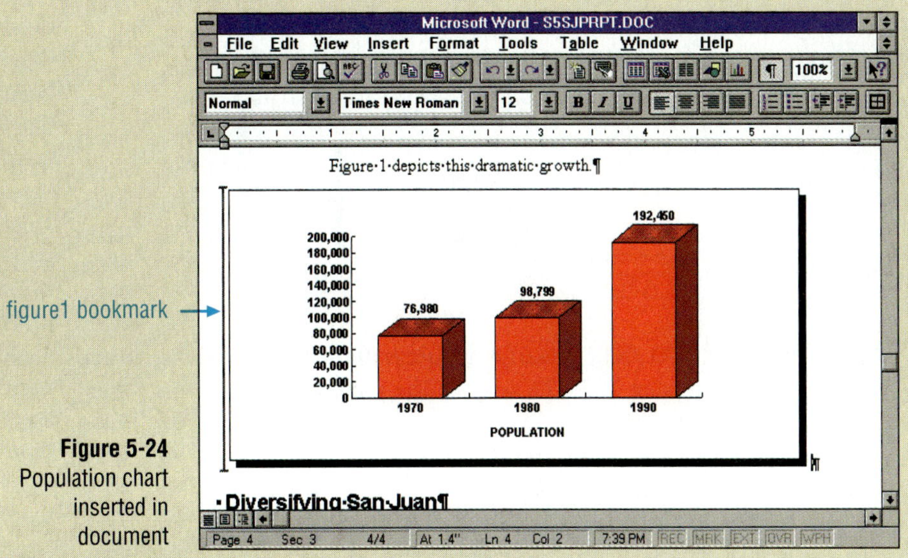

figure1 bookmark →

Figure 5-24
Population chart inserted in document

❾   Save the changes you have made.

Jessica next wants to transfer the pie chart from the chart document to the report document, but she decides to view both documents at once rather than switching between the two.

To arrange open documents on the screen:

❶   Go to the location of the figure2 bookmark in the report document, then close the Go To dialog box.

Rather than switch to the chart document, Jessica now arranges the screen so that both the chart document and the report document are visible at the same time.

❷   Click **Window**. Notice that C5SJCHRT.DOC and S5SJPRPT.DOC are the only two documents open.

   TROUBLE? If other documents are listed, select them, then close them.

❸ Click **Arrange All**. Each document appears in its own document window, and S5SJPRPT.DOC is the active document. Notice also that the active document has its own document Control menu box and sizing buttons. See Figure 5-25.

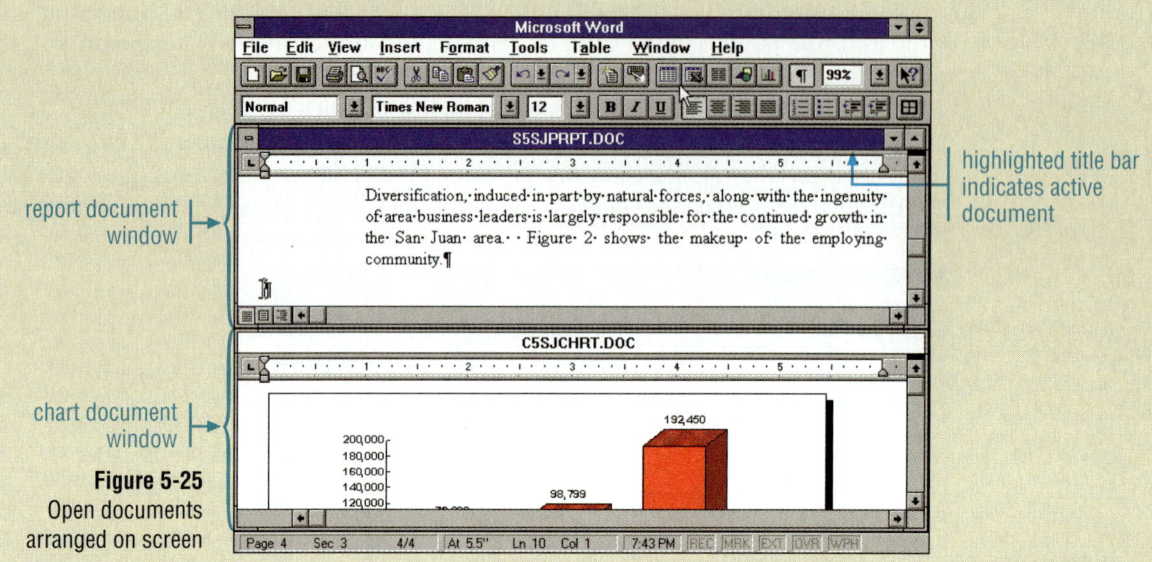

report document window

highlighted title bar indicates active document

chart document window

Figure 5-25
Open documents arranged on screen

❹ Click in the C5SJCHRT.DOC window (or press **[Ctrl][F6]**) to make it the active window, then move to page 2, the location of the pie chart.

❺ Click the pie chart to select it.

❻ Click the **Copy button** on the Standard toolbar (or click **Edit** then click **Copy**). The selected chart is copied to the Clipboard.

Next Jessica must paste the copied chart from the Clipboard to the report document.

❼ Click in the S5SJPRPT.DOC window (or press **[Ctrl][F6]**) to make it the active document. The insertion point is located at the figure2 bookmark.

❽ Click the **Paste button** on the Standard toolbar (or click **Edit** then click **Paste**). The pie chart is copied to its new location in the report document.

❾ Save the changes you have made.

Jessica has one more chart to copy to the report document. She decides to use the drag-and-drop feature to transfer the stacked column chart.

Using Drag-and-Drop Between Documents

In Tutorial 2 you learned to use drag-and-drop to move text within a document. With Word, you can also use drag-and-drop to *copy* text within a document simply by holding down the Control key as you drag the selected text. If you have the screen arranged so that two documents are visible at once, you can even use drag-and-drop to transfer data *between* documents.

To copy the third chart between the two documents using drag-and-drop:

❶ Go to the location of the figure3 bookmark in the report document, then close the Go To dialog box. The insertion point moves to the location of the figure3 bookmark.

❷ Click in the C5SJCHRT.DOC window (or press **[Ctrl][F6]**) to make it the active window, then move to page 3.

❸ Scroll until part of the stacked column chart is visible, then select the chart.

❹ Move the mouse pointer over the selected chart. Notice that the pointer changes to ⌖ just as it does when it is over selected text.

❺ Press and hold **[Ctrl]** and hold down the **left mouse button**. The pointer changes to ⌖ to indicate that you are *copying* rather than *moving* the chart. See Figure 5-26. Do not release [Ctrl] until the copy is complete.

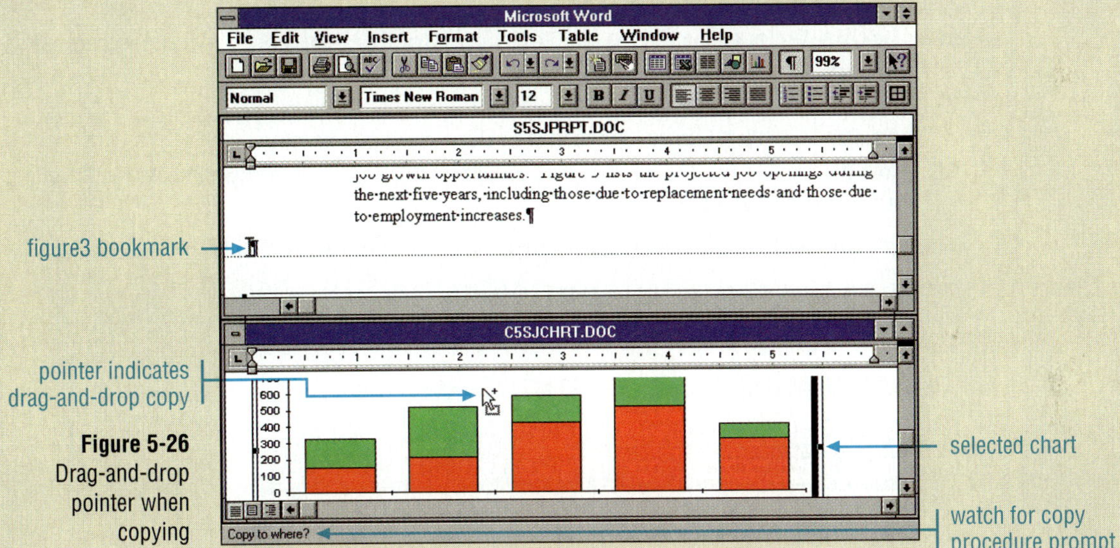

figure3 bookmark

pointer indicates drag-and-drop copy

Figure 5-26 Drag-and-drop pointer when copying

selected chart

watch for copy procedure prompt

❻ Drag the selected chart from the chart document over the title bar of C5SJCHRT.DOC until the dashed insertion point of the pointer is after the figure3 bookmark, then release [Ctrl] and the mouse button. The stacked column chart is copied from the chart document to the report and is still selected.

❼ Deselect the chart. Remember that when using the drag-and-drop procedure, the selected data is *not* placed on the Clipboard.

   TROUBLE? If you notice that the selected chart was moved instead of copied, you released [Ctrl] too soon. Click the Undo button ↶ on the Standard toolbar (or click Edit then click Undo Move), then repeat Steps 3 through 7.

Jessica no longer needs to see both documents at the same time.

❽ Click anywhere in the C5SJCHRT.DOC (or press **[Ctrl][F6]**), then close it without saving changes.

S5SJPRPT.DOC is still open but needs to be maximized.

❾ Click the **Maximize button** for the S5SJPRPT.DOC window.

❿ Save the changes you have made.

Now that Jessica has transferred the charts to the report document, she needs to format them by centering them and adding captions.

Adding Captions to Charts

Jessica formatted the charts when she created them in Microsoft Graph, but she thinks she can improve their appearance by centering them horizontally and adding an identifying caption.

To center the first chart and add a caption:

❶ Go to the figure1 bookmark, then click the chart to select it. If you use the Go To dialog box to move to the bookmarks in the steps, make sure you close the dialog box before continuing.

❷ Click the **Center button** 🖹 on the Formatting toolbar. The chart is centered across the page.

❸ With the chart still selected, click **Insert** then click **Caption....** The Caption dialog box appears with Figure 1 inserted in the Caption text box.

❹ After Figure 1, type : (a colon), press **[Spacebar]** twice, then type **Population Growth in the Greater San Juan Area**.

The Position list box indicates that the caption is to be inserted below the selected chart.

❺ Click **OK** or press **[Enter]**. The caption is centered below the chart. See Figure 5-27.

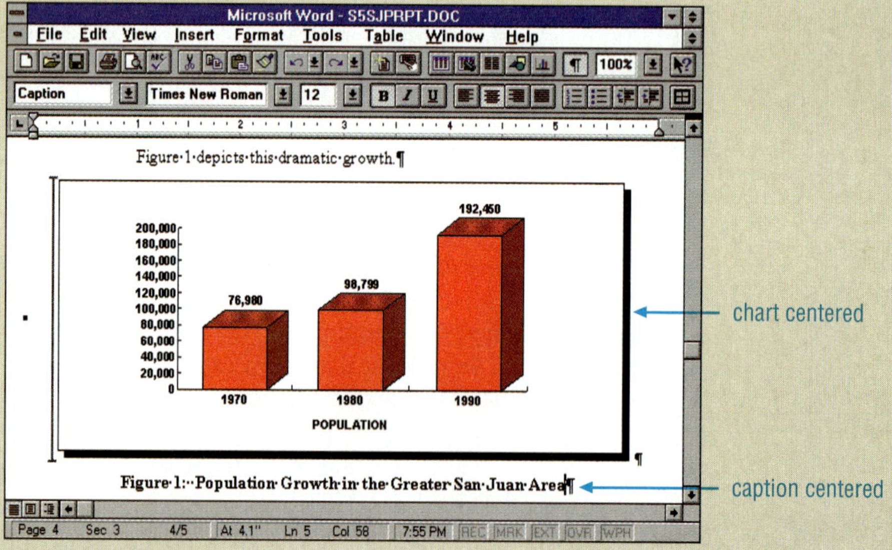

Figure 5-27
Formatted
Population chart

❻ Go to the figure2 bookmark, then select the pie chart. Repeat Steps 2 through 5, except insert the caption **Figure 2: Industrial Mix in the Greater San Juan Area**.

❼ Go to the figure3 bookmark, then select the stacked column chart. Repeat Steps 2 through 5, except insert the caption **Figure 3: Projected Job Openings**.

❽ Save the changes you have made.

Jessica wants to see how the pages split now that she has finished formatting her charts.

❾ Click the **Print Preview button** 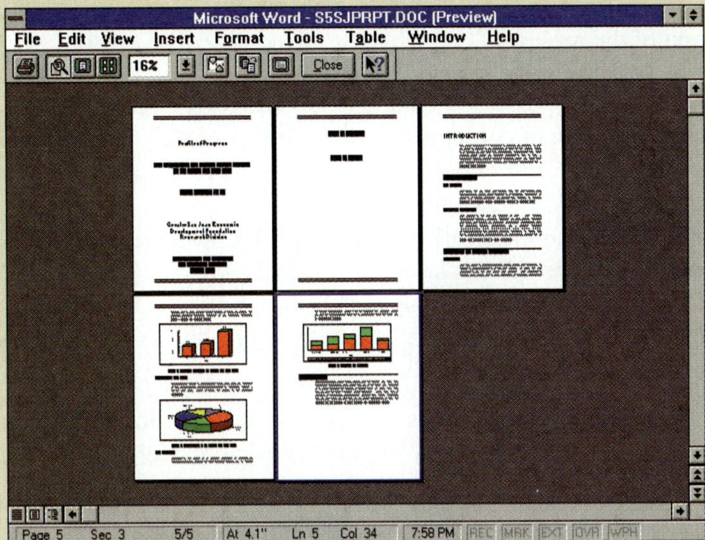 on the Standard toolbar (or click **File** then click **Print Preview**). Notice the location of the charts on pages 4 and 5. See Figure 5-28.

Figure 5-28
Formatted text
and charts in
print preview

TROUBLE? If you do not see all five pages, click the Multiple Pages button ▦ on the Print Preview toolbar, then select five pages.

❿ Click the **Close button** on the Print Preview toolbar.

Jessica no longer needs to see the bookmarks for the charts because she has inserted all three charts in her document. She can now deactivate the bookmarks.

To deactivate the bookmarks:

❶ Click **Tools**, click **Options...**, then click the **Bookmarks check box** on the View tab to deselect this option.

❷ Click **OK** or press **[Enter]**.

Jessica has finished formatting her report, and now she is ready to insert the table of contents.

Creating the Preface Page

In business reports, particularly long business reports, it's customary to include one or more preface pages immediately following the title page. The **preface pages** typically provide a list of the main topics so that a reader can go quickly to that topic without having to read the whole report. This list of main topics is called a **table of contents**. Word allows you to create a table of contents quickly, as well as a table of figures or a table of tables, if you have consistently applied styles to the various levels of topic headings or captions within a document.

Creating a Table of Contents

Jessica wants to insert a table of contents on the preface page between the title page and the text of the report.

To insert the table of contents for the report:

❶   Move to page 2, then place the insertion point immediately before the blank paragraph below the title Table of Contents.

❷   Click **Insert** then click **Index and Tables…**. The Index and Tables dialog box appears with the Index tab displayed.

❸   Click the **Table of Contents tab**.

Word provides a variety of formats for the Table of Contents page, but Jessica prefers the Formal style.

❹   Click **Formal** in the Formats box. Notice that the sample text in the Preview section changes to reflect the new formats. See Figure 5-29.

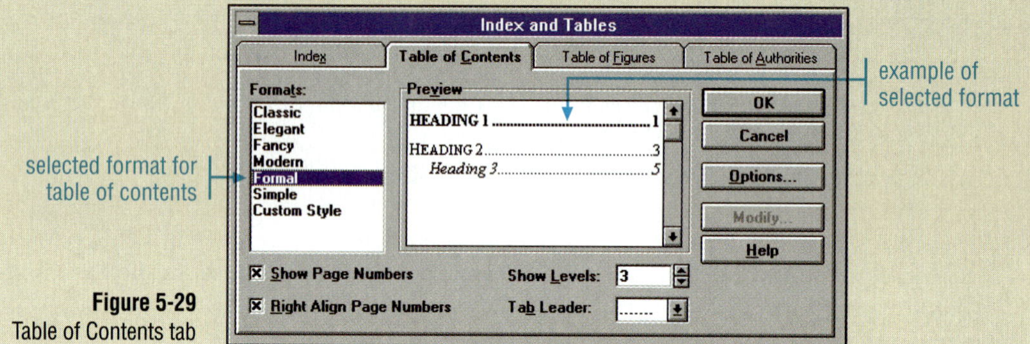

Figure 5-29
Table of Contents tab

Word will look for any text labeled with Heading 1, Heading 2, or Heading 3 styles, then display the text along with its corresponding page number in the Table of Contents.

❺   Click **OK** or press **[Enter]**. The Table of Contents based on text labeled with Heading 1, 2, or 3 styles appears at the insertion point. Recall that the title page used the styles Title 1 and Title 2, therefore, the text labeled with those styles was not included in the Table of Contents.

❻   Save the changes you have made.

Creating a Table of Figures

Next Jessica wants to insert a table of figures, which will list the names of the charts and their locations within the report. She will put the table of figures on the same page as the table of contents.

To insert a table of figures:

❶ Place the insertion point before the blank paragraph below the title Table of Figures on page 2.

❷ Click **Insert** then click **Index and Tables…**.

❸ Click the **Table of Figures tab**.

Jessica wants the table of figures to appear in a format similar to the table of contents.

❹ Click **Formal** in the Formats list box. See Figure 5-30.

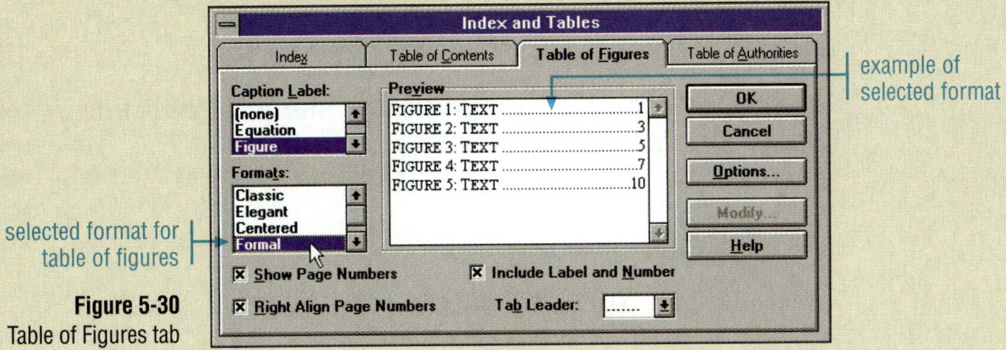

Figure 5-30
Table of Figures tab

❺ Click **OK** or press **[Enter]**. Word builds a table of figures based on the captions inserted below each chart.

❻ Save the changes you have made.

❼ Dismiss the Borders toolbar, if necessary.

Printing the Report

With her report complete, Jessica is anxious to print the document, but she decides to spell check it one more time because she has inserted text since she conducted the grammar check. After spell checking, she'll preview then print her document.

To spell check, preview, then print the document:

❶ Click the **Spelling button** on the Standard toolbar (or click **Tools** then click **Spelling…**) to spell check the document. If additional spelling errors are found, correct them, then save the changes.

❷ Click the **Print Preview button** on the Standard toolbar (or click **File** then click **Print Preview**). Jessica is satisfied with the appearance of her report.

❸ Click the **Print button** on the Print Preview toolbar. The printed document should be similar to Figure 5-31 on the following pages.

❹ Click the **Close button** on the Print Preview toolbar.

Profile of Progress

1995 Demographic and Industry Staffing Patterns for the Greater San Juan Area

Report Prepared for the

Greater San Juan Economic Development Foundation Research Division

Connolly/Bayle and Associates
San Francisco, California
August 1995

Figure 5-31
Jessica's completed
report (page 1 of 5)

Table of Contents

Table of Figures

Figure 5-31
Jessica's completed
report (page 2 of 5)

INTRODUCTION

The Profile of Progress is a compilation of industrial data designed to give the reader an overview of the population, job base, and job growth trends of the Greater San Juan area. The region, which encompasses San Juan, Bellville, Santa Maria, and Williston, continues to lead the way in California's recovery from the economic slowdown during the early '90s. The following report discusses both the data collection methodology and a summary of the findings.

METHODOLOGY

The Sample

The sample for this study was selected from the first quarter 1995 Employment and Wages report submitted to the California Department of Labor by the region's employers. The universe was stratified by standard industrial classification codes. Procedures involved all certainty cases.

Collection Procedures

The majority of the data was collected by mail. Each selected establishment received a structured schedule for their specific industry. The survey form included the following: instructions, occupational titles and definitions, business identification, and a standard industrial classification code. Survey procedures included three follow-up mailings to non-respondents. The telephone was used extensively to clarify data and to canvass critical non-respondents. The demographic statistics for the region were extracted from the 1990 census data.

SUMMARY OF MAJOR FINDINGS

Population

The 1995 Profile of Progress presents a growth statistic that continues to display the dynamic growth of the San Juan region. In 1990, the total population of the San Juan region was 192,457. This represents an increase of 48 percent over the 1980 figures and an increase of 150 percent

Figure 5-31
Jessica's completed
report (page 3 of 5)

Profile of Progress Page 4

increase over the 1970 figures. Greater numbers of jobs in the defense and computer industries accounted primarily for the population increases. Figure 1 depicts this dramatic growth.

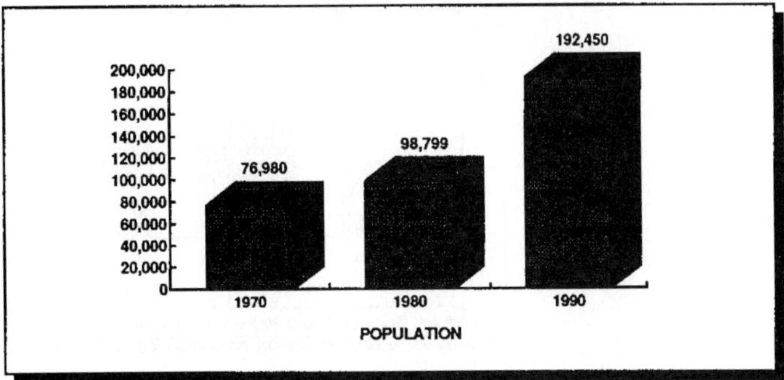

Figure 1: Population Growth in the Greater San Juan Area

Diversifying San Juan

Diversification, induced in part by natural forces, along with the ingenuity of area business leaders is largely responsible for the continued growth in the San Juan area. Figure 2 shows the makeup of the employing community.

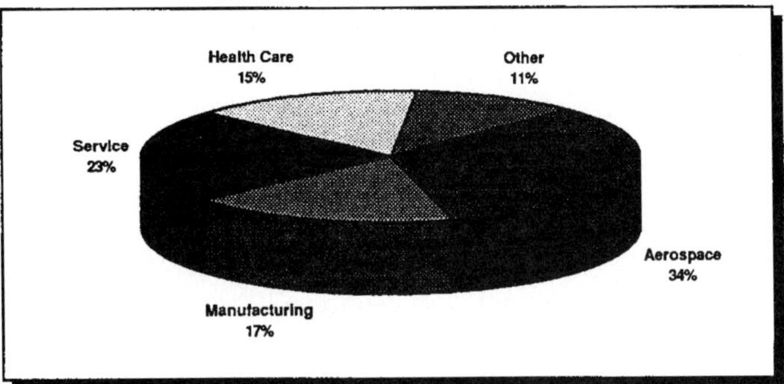

Figure 2: Industrial Mix in the Greater San Juan Area

Job Openings

According to our survey of the region's employers, on average, the occupational groups requiring the most education will also see the fastest

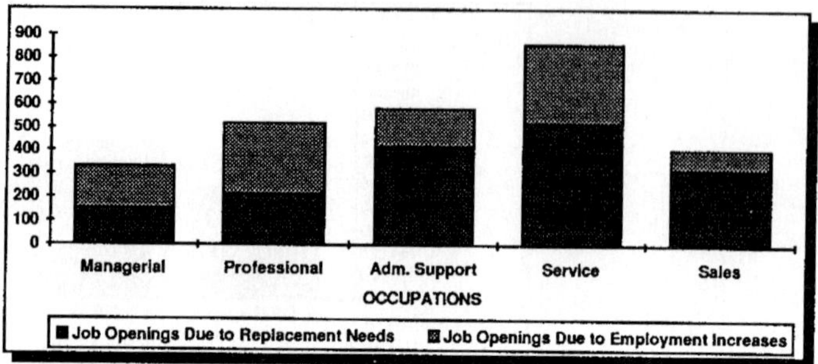

Figure 5-31
Jessica's completed
report (page 5 of 5)

Jessica has printed her document, but before she quits Word she wants to create a customized document template that will contain all the formatting and styles she has worked so hard to define in this report.

Creating a Customized Document Template

While Word's predefined document templates are indeed powerful, they might not exactly fit your needs, so you can create your own customized document templates. Once created, you use the user-defined document templates in the same way you use the predefined templates. Word provides you with several ways to create a customized document template, but the easiest way is to create a template from an existing document.

Jessica divided the original report document into three sections, each with its own specific formats such as headers and footers, margins, and vertical alignment. Although the formats and the styles she defined will be the same for future reports she might create, the text is likely to be different. Thus, her customized report template needs only to contain the styles and the section breaks. She must first prepare her document to be saved as a document template.

To prepare the document as a template:

❶ Make sure you have saved your most recent changes to S5SJPRPT.DOC.

Jessica wants to preserve the formatting in each of the three sections that she has created so she cannot delete any of the section breaks. She does not need any of the text in the document, however.

❷ Move to page 1, then select all the text on page 1 up to, but not including, the section break between pages 1 and 2. By not deleting the section break, the page-level changes made specifically for this section will be preserved.

❸ Press **[Del]**. Word deletes the text, but the styles applied to the text are still available.

Next Jessica moves to the page containing the table of contents. She does not want to delete the section break between pages 2 and 3.

❹ Move to page 2. Select the table of contents that you inserted, but *do not include* the title "Table of Contents" or the blank paragraph below the inserted table of contents.

❺ Press **[Del]**.

❻ Select the table of figures that you inserted, but *do not include* the title "Table of Figures" or the blank paragraph below the inserted table of figures.

❼ Press **[Del]**. The section break between pages 2 and 3 should not be deleted.

Finally, Jessica needs to delete all of the text in the report itself.

❽ Place the insertion point at the top of page 3, then press **[Ctrl][Shift][End]** to select all text and charts from the insertion point to the end of the document.

❾ Press **[Del]**.

Now Jessica is ready to save her prepared document as a customized document template.

To save the document as a template.

❶ Click **File** then click **Save As...**. The Save As dialog box appears.

❷ Click the **Save File as Type list box down arrow**, then click **Document Template**.

Ordinarily you would save your document templates to the Template subdirectory of the Winword directory along with Word's predefined document templates, but you will need to save this template to your Student Disk.

❸   Type **a:\s5report** in the File Name text box. Word will automatically add the template extension "DOT" to the filename. See Figure 5-32.

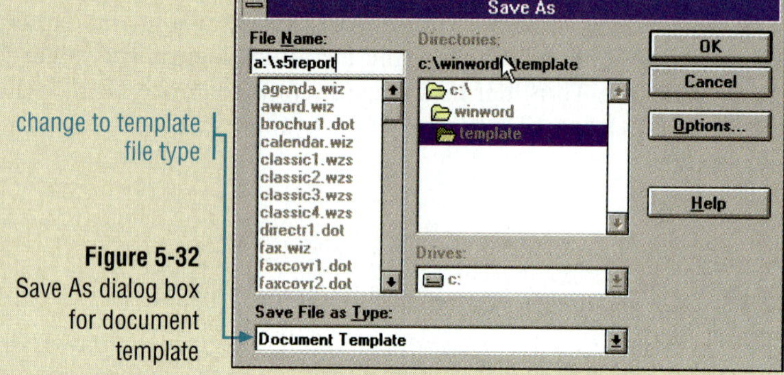

change to template file type

Figure 5-32
Save As dialog box for document template

❹   Click **OK** or press **[Enter]**. Notice the change in the title bar.

For future reference, Jessica wants to print the style sheet, which is a list of the formats defined for each style, for her customized document template.

❺   Click **File** then click **Print...**.
❻   Click the **Print What list box down arrow**, then click **Styles**.
❼   Click **OK** or press **[Enter]**. The style sheet is printed.
❽   Close the document and exit Word. A message box appears asking if you want to save the changes you made to NORMAL.DOT. Recall that, at the beginning of this tutorial, you selected the option that displays this dialog box as a precaution. See Figure 5-33.

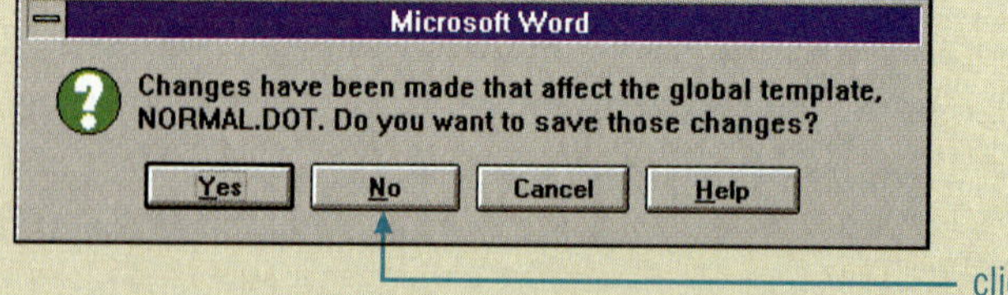

Figure 5-33
Microsoft Word message box

click No

Jessica does *not* want these changes to affect the NORMAL template.
❾   Click **No**. The following message appears: "You placed a large amount of text in the Clipboard. Do you want this text to be available to other applications after Word quits?"
❿   Click **No**.

Jessica submits the preliminary report to Henry. He is pleased with the report and is anxious to incorporate it into the final report.

Questions

1. What is the purpose of the Thesaurus feature?
2. What is the purpose of the Grammar feature?
3. What is the purpose of the Bookmark feature?
4. Under what circumstances would you want to insert a section break into a document?
5. What are two methods for inserting section breaks in a document?
6. What is the command sequence to go to section 3 in a document?
7. Describe the procedure for justifying a page vertically.
8. What is the significance of the Same as Previous indication in a header or footer?
9. How do you change page number formats within sections of a document?
10. Describe two procedures for defining a new style.
11. Describe three procedures for applying a new style.
12. Describe two procedures for redefining a style.
13. Describe the procedure for transferring information from one Word document to another Word document using the Clipboard.
14. Describe the procedure for transferring information from one Word document to another Word document using drag-and-drop.
15. Describe the procedure for arranging open documents on the screen so that they are all visible at the same time.
16. How do you know if a chart within a Word document is selected?
17. Describe the procedure for creating a document template from an existing document.
18. What is the procedure for inserting a table of contents in a document?
19.  In the Print dialog box, how would you specify that you want to print only pages 3 through 5 in section 2 of a document?

Tutorial Assignments

Start Word, if necessary, and conduct a screen check. Open T5PROFIL.DOC from your Student Disk, then complete the following:

1. Save the document as S5PROFIL.DOC.
2. Use the Thesaurus to substitute an appropriate synonym for the word "variety" in the first paragraph on page 2.
3. Proofread the document for grammar and spelling errors, then save your changes.
4. Insert three bookmarks in the document to mark the appropriate locations of the three referenced charts. Make sure you place the bookmarks on the blank line following the figure references. Use the Tools Options command to display the bookmark symbol in your document, if necessary. Name the bookmarks Chart1, Chart2, and Chart3.
5. Substitute a Next Page section break for the page break between pages 1 and 2.
6. Insert a header into section 2 only. The header is to display on all pages except the first page of section 2. Section 1 should not contain a header at all.
7. Center the title page vertically.
8. Click Tools, click Options..., then click the Save tab, and make sure the Prompt to Save Normal.dot option is selected.
9. On the title page, apply the Heading 1 style to the following paragraphs: Profile of Progress and Greater San Juan Economic Development Foundation. Apply the Heading 2 style to the remaining headings on the title page. Save the changes.
10. Define a new style named "Main Text" for the main text paragraphs in section 2 of the document with the following paragraph formatting options: First Line Indentation set to 0.5" and Line Spacing set to double. Apply the style to the four text paragraphs in the Executive Summary.

11. In the Executive Summary, apply the Title style to the title Executive Summary; apply the Heading 3 style to the headings Population, Diversifying San Juan, and Job Openings.

12. Modify the Heading 3 style so that the Spacing After option is increased to 12 pt. Save the changes.

13. As header text for page 2, and all subsequent pages of section 2, insert the header "Executive Summary" at the left margin and the word "Page" plus the page number code at the right margin. Bold the entire header. Increase the Spacing After option for the header to 12 pt. Save the changes.

14. Open T5ESCHRT.DOC from your Student Disk, then copy the chart on page 1 to the Chart1 bookmark in S5PROFIL.DOC.

15. Copy the chart on page 2 of T5ESCHRT.DOC to the Chart2 bookmark in S5PROFIL.DOC.

16. Copy the chart on page 3 of T5ESCHRT.DOC to the Chart3 bookmark in S5PROFIL.DOC.

17. Close T5ESCHRT.DOC without saving any changes, center Figure 1 across the page, then insert the following caption above it: Figure 1: Population Growth in the Greater San Juan Area.

18. Center Figure 2 across the page, then insert the following caption above it: Figure 2: Industrial Mix in the Greater San Juan Area.

19. Center Figure 3 across the page, then insert the following caption above it: Figure 3: Job Openings. Save the changes.

20. Check the spelling in the document. Preview the document, making adjustments if necessary. (If the heading "Diversifying San Juan" appears as the last line on page 2, insert a hard page break before the heading to force it to the top of page 3.) Print the document.

21. Use Word Help to determine how to specify in the Header text area that page numbers are to start at page 1 of section 2. Make the change in your document, then save the changes as S5EXSUM.DOC. Preview the document then print just section 2.

22. Close the document. Do *not* save any changes to NORMAL.DOT.

Case Problems

1. Reporting on Printers at Buffington Engineering

Clinton Williams works as a hardware specialist in the Internal Information Technology Consulting Group of Buffington Engineering, a large consulting firm specializing in traffic engineering, urban planning, and engineering design of roadways, drainage, and structures. Buffington needs to upgrade the printers used by its staff, and Clinton's supervisor, Lyn Follmar, has assigned him to investigate the alternatives. After his initial investigation, Clinton wrote a memo to Lyn explaining his findings. He is now ready to insert a chart illustrating the data he gathered on printer sales.

Open P5PSALES.DOC from your Student Disk, then complete the following:

1. Save the document as S5BUFENG.DOC.

2. Check grammar usage and spelling in the document.

3. Attach the MEMO2 template to the document.

4. Apply the Title style to the heading Memorandum; apply the Message Header style to the paragraphs beginning "TO:..." through "...1995"; apply the Body Text Indent style to the memo text.

5. Open P5PSCHRT.DOC from your Student Disk, then copy the chart and place it a double space below the memo text in S5BUFENG.DOC.

6. Center the chart across the page.

7. Insert the following caption below the chart: Figure 1: Printer Sales.

8. Save the changes to the document.

9. Preview the document, then print it.

10. Use Word Help to find out how to select vertical blocks of text. Select just the memo headings TO:, FROM:, RE:, and DATE:, then bold the vertical block of selected text. Save the document as S5VERT.DOC.

11. Print then close the document.

2. Informational Handout on Inter-Tran Translation Services

Minh Vuong owns a language translation business, Inter-Tran, in Washington, D.C. She has prepared the basic text of a two-page informational handout about the services her company provides. She brings the document to you and asks you to help her improve the appearance of the handout.

Open P5INTRAN.DOC from your Student Disk, then complete the following:

1. Review the document then save it as S5INTRAN.DOC.

2. Insert a Next Page section break between pages 1 and 2.

3. Center page 1 vertically.

4. Change the top margin of section 2 to 2" and the left and right margins to 1.75".

5. Insert appropriate headers and footers in sections 1 and 2.

6. Save the changes.

7. Click Tools, click Options..., then click the Save tab, and make sure the Prompt to Save Normal.dot option is selected.

8. Define attractive styles for the various elements of the handout, including at least two different styles for page 1 and two additional styles for page 2, one for the headings and one for the main text.

9. Apply the styles to the document. Save the changes.

10. Preview the document then print it.

11. Create a document template from S5INTRAN.DOC. Save it to your Student Disk as S5STYLES.DOT.

12. Print a style sheet for the styles used in your document.

13. Close the document. Do *not* save any changes to NORMAL.DOT.

3. Report on Career Opportunities

Write a double-spaced, two- to three-page report on the career opportunities in your major. Base your report on at least two sources, one of which should be the *Occupational Outlook Quarterly*. Consult your school's career counselor or reference librarian for other possible sources. Include in your report a discussion of potential job titles, salary expectations, academic preparation, and job mobility.

Complete the following:

1. Type your report, including a title page. Use different levels of headings to break your report into subtopics. Save the document as S5CAREER.DOC.

2. Edit the report. Check for correct grammar and spelling, but also proofread the report very carefully on your own.

3. Format the report. Center the title page vertically. Insert appropriate headers and footers. Use the standard heading styles in Word or redefine them to fit your preferences. Save the changes.

4. Insert a Table of Contents.

5. Preview the report then print it. Also print the style sheet for the report.

6. Close the document. Do *not* save any changes to NORMAL.DOT.

Desktop Publishing with Word

Creating a Newsletter for Enviro-Disk

OBJECTIVES

In this tutorial you will:

- Identify desktop publishing design elements
- Import text and clipart
- Use WordArt
- Use Organizer to copy styles
- Use outline view to reorganize a document
- Apply a newspaper-style column format
- Insert, size, and position frames
- Create a banner and drop caps
- Insert a masthead and a pull quote
- Layer text and graphics

CASE

Enviro-Disk   Al Wakefield, president of Wakefield Enterprises, is a new breed of entrepreneur: committed to saving the environment but also grounded in the realities of the free enterprise system. He has started a variety of companies, all with one common theme—to capitalize on the business opportunities becoming available with the nation's shift to a sound environmental policy. For instance, several years ago he realized that he was becoming inundated with old computer disks. He also knew that the cost of new disks was prohibitive for some people. He saw a business opportunity in recycling old disks by reformatting them, checking for and cleaning viruses, removing the old labels, then reselling the reclaimed disks at a greatly reduced price. To seize this business opportunity, Al founded the Enviro-Disk Company, just one of his many environmentally based companies.

Several months ago Al began publishing a local newsletter, called *Enviro-Newsletter*, to inform his customers of other companies in the burgeoning environmental business sector. His own efforts at desktop publishing were rather amateurish, so he decided to turn over the task of creating the newsletter to Keisha Beyah, currently in charge of marketing for Enviro-Disk, because of her past experience working on her college newspaper.

In this tutorial you will complete Keisha's task of creating the March issue of *Enviro-Newsletter*.

The finished newsletter will be a large file, requiring a significant amount of disk space. To ensure that your Student Disk will have enough space for the newsletter file, you'll first delete all the files you saved in Tutorial 1. (*Note*: If you do not want to delete these files, copy the files to another disk or directory. Once the files are copied to another location, delete the old files from your Student Disk.) Keep in mind that you might encounter storage problems if you choose not to delete some files from your Student Disk. Ask your instructor or technical support person for assistance, if necessary.

To delete the necessary files from your Student Disk:

❶ Turn on your computer, then insert your Student Disk in the disk drive.

❷ Using the Windows Program Manager, delete all files beginning with "s1" from your Student Disk.

❸ Start Word then complete the screen check as described in Tutorial 1.

Introduction to Desktop Publishing

Publishing a professional-looking brochure, newsletter, program, advertisement, annual report, or any other marketing material previously took a great deal of effort by several people and could easily become quite expensive. With advances in computer technology and more sophisticated software, you can now typeset text, create graphics, layout a professional-looking publication, and get it ready for the printer right at your desktop computer—hence **desktop publishing** (DTP) was born.

DTP Design Elements

The trick to successful desktop publishing is to make your publications look as though they were done professionally. Before you can create your own desktop published documents, you must first know what design elements professionals use to make their documents look "professional." Figure 6-1 shows Keisha's final copy of the March issue of *Enviro-Newsletter* and illustrates some of the design elements that professionals typically include in their documents, which you can also accomplish using Word.

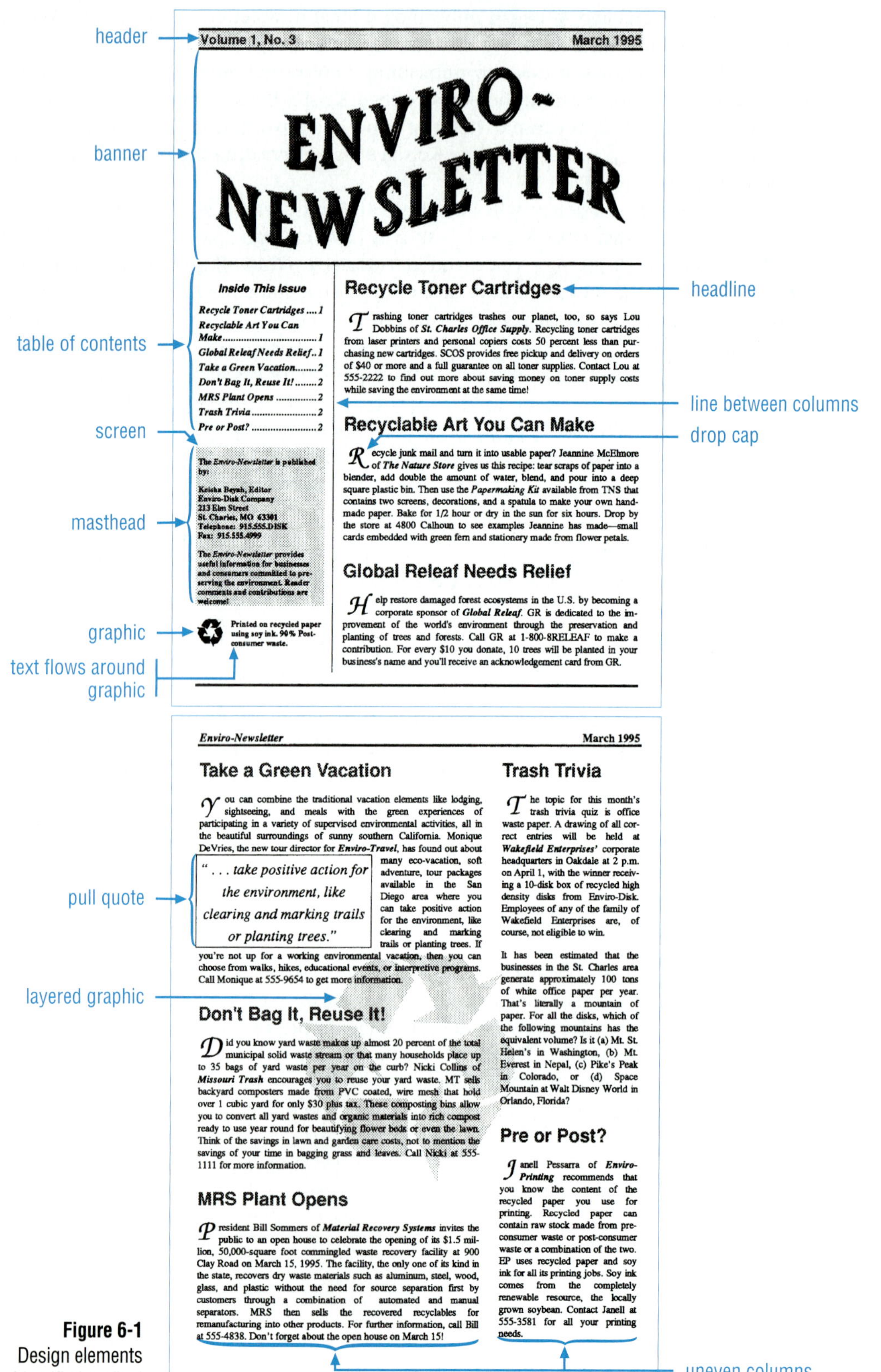

Figure 6-1
Design elements identified on final version of newsletter

Figure 6-2 defines the design elements that you have not used so far in this book.

Element:	Definition:
Banner	The title of the newsletter, usually placed on the front page
Masthead	A list of the newsletter's address, phone number, subscription information, publication staff members, and other appropriate information
Screen	A shaded box appearing behind text to set it off and attract the reader's attention
Graphic	A photograph, drawing, chart, diagram, clipart, etc., used to enhance associated text and add visual interest
Headline	An article title, usually as brief as possible, that identifies the contents of the article and encourages the reader to continue reading the article
Drop Cap	A large uppercase letter, usually set in a different font, applied to the first character of a paragraph to add visual interest
Columns	Text formatted in two or more vertical columns of even or uneven width, creating shorter lines of text, which facilitate reading
Pull Quote	A phrase or quotation extracted from text in the document and formatted in a larger point size to attract the reader's attention
Layered Graphic	A graphic that appears dimmed behind text, so that it does not obscure the text, to add visual interest

Figure 6-2
Description of
design elements

Keisha has been given disks containing all eight articles for the newsletter. Although the articles take up the bulk of the newsletter, Keisha still has to create the banner, the table of contents, and the masthead. She is not ready to create the banner yet, and she can't create the table of contents until she is sure how the articles are best organized. She starts with the masthead information.

Inserting a Masthead

A **masthead** provides information about the publisher and a short mission statement. Typically, this information appears in a smaller font size than the text in the body of a newsletter. As shown in Figure 6-1, the masthead Keisha will create contains text on a screened background.

Keisha has not designed the banner for the name of the newsletter yet, but she does want to leave blank paragraphs as placeholders for the banner and for the table of contents. Therefore, before she types the text of the masthead, she'll insert some blank paragraphs.

To insert the masthead information:

❶ Press **[Enter]** three times to leave placeholders for the eventual placement of the banner and the table of contents and to allow for one blank line after the table of contents.

❷ Type the masthead information as it appears in Figure 6-3.

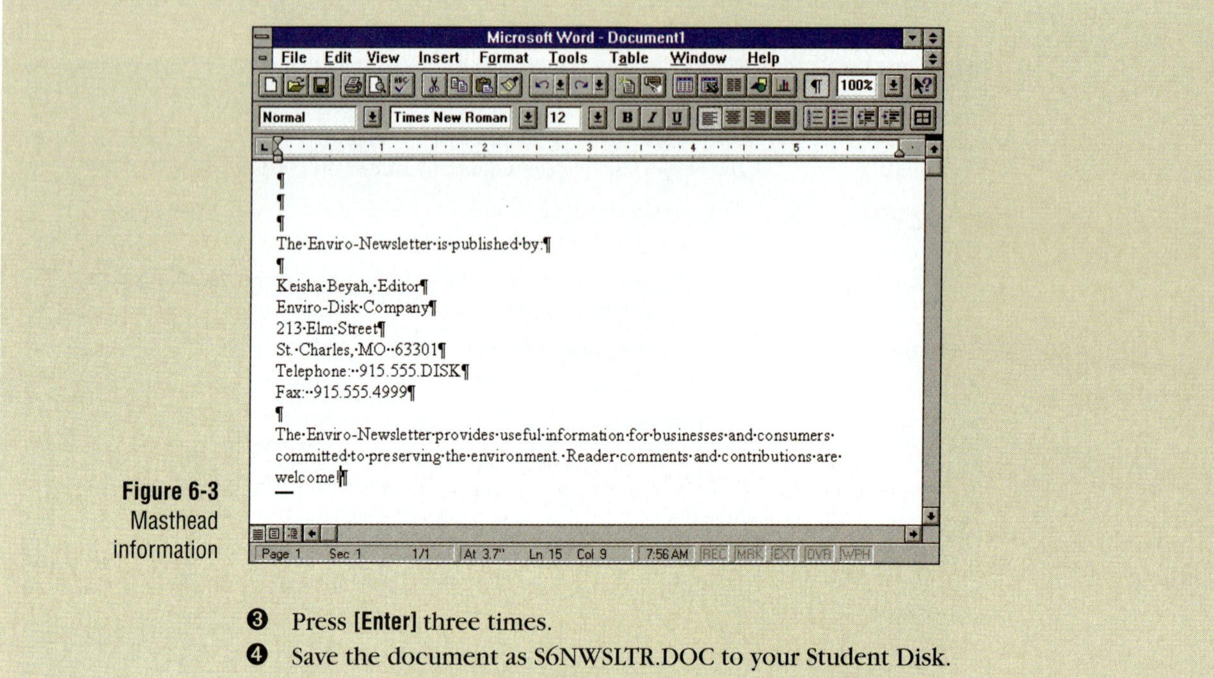

Figure 6-3
Masthead
information

❸ Press **[Enter]** three times.
❹ Save the document as S6NWSLTR.DOC to your Student Disk.

Now Keisha is ready to import the text for the articles in the newsletter.

Importing Text

You have learned several ways to transfer data within and between Word documents. You can also transfer data from a non-Word document into a Word document. To **import** a document means to insert either a non-Word document or a Word document file into another Word document. If you have installed the necessary conversion filters, you will notice no difference between importing a Word document and importing a **foreign-file** (non-Word) document. (See the *Microsoft Word User's Guide* for a list of conversion filters.) To insert a document into a Word document, you choose File from the Insert menu.

The newsletter readers have contributed eight articles to Keisha on disk: five in Word format, the rest in other formats. Rather than copying and pasting the text from the other documents into her newsletter document, she decides to import them using the File command on the Insert menu. She begins with the five Word articles. Let's import those now.

To import the five Word documents into the newsletter document:
❶ Make sure the insertion point is in the last blank paragraph at the end of the document (Ln 18).
❷ Click **Insert** then click **File…**. The File dialog box appears.
❸ Switch to the drive containing your Student Disk, if necessary, then click **c6lou.doc** in the File Name list box. See Figure 6-4.

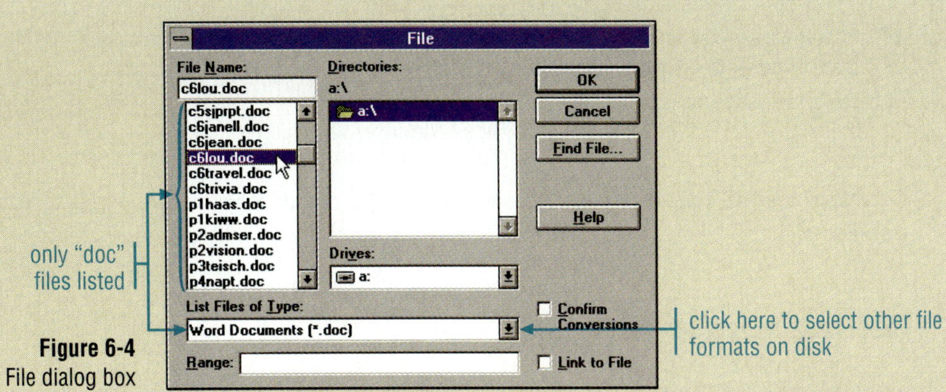

Figure 6-4
File dialog box

❹ Click **OK** or press **[Enter]**. The C6LOU.DOC document appears in the newsletter at the location of the insertion point. Notice that the formatting of the original document stays with the document.

❺ Repeat Steps 2 through 4 to import the files C6JEAN.DOC, C6TRAVEL.DOC, C6JANELL.DOC, and C6TRIVIA.DOC (in that order) into your document immediately following C6LOU.DOC. *Do not press [Enter] between articles.*

❻ Save your changes.

Next Keisha needs to insert those documents created using other word processing applications: C6NICKI.WP (a WordPerfect 5.1 document), C6RELEAF.M5 (a Word 5.0 for Macintosh document), and C6BILL.WRI (a Microsoft Write document).

To insert the foreign-format documents into the newsletter document:

❶ Click **Insert** then click **File....** The File dialog box appears. The File Name list box currently displays only those documents in Word format.

❷ Click the **List Files of Type list box down arrow**, then click **All Files (*.*)**. All files on your Student Disk are now listed in the File Name list box.

❸ Click **C6NICKI.WP**, then click **OK** or press **[Enter]**. A message appears briefly in the status bar indicating that Word is converting the file. The text of the WordPerfect file is inserted seamlessly into the newsletter document, as though it were a Word document. Notice that the formatting from the original document is transferred to the Word document. The WordPerfect code {PRIVATE} appears next to the article title as a result of the conversion, but it will not appear in the printed document.

TROUBLE? If the Convert File dialog box appears, click Cancel. Then click Insert, click File..., and click the Confirm Conversions check box to deselect it. Then repeat Step 3.

Next Keisha needs to insert the remaining documents that were created using other word processing applications.

❹ Repeat Steps 1 and 3 above to insert the files C6RELEAF.M5 and C6BILL.WRI into your document. Make sure that you have inserted all eight articles in the order specified. *Do not press [Enter] between articles.*

Even though the code after the heading of the WordPerfect document will not print, Keisha decides to delete it because it's distracting.

⑤ Scroll up to the Don't Bag It, Reuse It article, select **{PRIVATE}** (make sure to include the braces), then press **[Del]**. The code is deleted from the document.

⑥ Save your changes.

Now that all the text for the newsletter is in place, Keisha can begin to format the document.

Setting Mirror Margins

Attractive formatting is particularly important for desktop-published documents. Formatting should proceed in the same order for desktop-published documents as for other documents—page-level changes, paragraph-level changes, then font-level changes.

Page setup for a publication-style document is not necessarily as straightforward as with typical business communications. Consideration must be given early on as to how the document will be printed, whether the document will be duplexed (printed on both sides of the paper), whether the document will be printed in landscape or portrait orientation, whether the printed document will be bound, and whether it will be printed in color.

Word's Page Setup dialog box provides options for making these document-level decisions. The Mirror Margins option must be selected when you want to print duplexed pages. With **mirror margins**, the margins on facing pages "mirror" each other—that is, the inside margins are the same width and the outside margins are the same width. If a document is to be bound, you must also adjust the **gutter margin**, the additional space allowed on the inside margin of duplexed pages, to accommodate a binding.

Keisha wants the final newsletter to be printed with duplexed pages in portrait orientation. In addition, she wants the top, bottom, and right margins of the newsletter to be .75" and the left margin to be 1". Let's make these changes now.

To set the margins for the newsletter:

❶ Click **File** then click **Page Setup....** The Page Setup dialog box appears. Click the **Margins tab**, if necessary.

Keisha wants the final newsletter to be duplexed, or printed on both sides of the paper.

❷ Click the **Mirror Margins check box**. Notice that the Left option changes to Inside and the Right option changes to Outside, and that two facing pages appear in the Preview section.

❸ Change the Top, Bottom, and Outside margins to **.75"** and change the Inside margin to **1"**. See Figure 6-5.

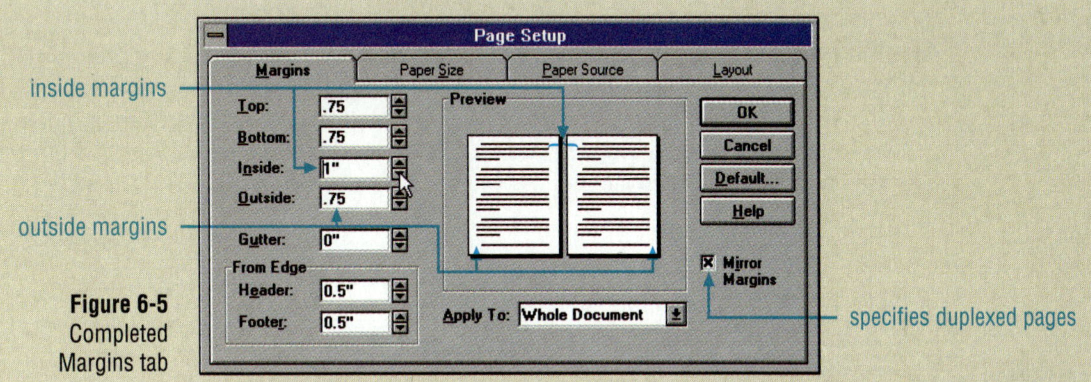

Figure 6-5
Completed
Margins tab

❹ Click **OK** or press **[Enter]**.

❺ Save your changes.

With the change in the margins, the entire width of the document is no longer visible on the screen. In order to see the entire width on the screen, Keisha decides to change the Zoom Control option to Page Width.

❻ Click the **Zoom Control list box down arrow** on the Standard toolbar, then click **Page Width** (or click **View**, click **Zoom…**, click the **Page Width button**, then click **OK** or press **[Enter]**).

The magnification percentage is reduced to 89% so that now the entire page width is visible on the screen.

TROUBLE? If the magnification percentage does not change to 89%, check the margins you just set in the Page Setup dialog box. Make sure you set them correctly, then repeat Step 6.

Now Keisha is ready to insert the banner, which is the name of the newsletter, at the top of the document.

Creating a Banner Using WordArt

Keisha wants the name of the newsletter in the banner to be impressive, so she decides to use **WordArt**, another applet like Microsoft Graph, provided with Word. WordArt allows you to create special effects with text—that is, create curved text or text that is turned on its side, angled, or even turned upside down.

When you choose Microsoft WordArt, you are no longer working in Word. Word is still running in the background, however. The process of running more than one application program at the same time is known as **multitasking**. Keisha will start Microsoft WordArt and use it to create the banner for her newsletter. When she is finished, she will exit WordArt and return to her Word document. The WordArt image she created will be inserted automatically into her document.

To start WordArt:

❶ Press **[Ctrl][Home]** to move the insertion point quickly to the top of the document. The insertion point should be in the first blank paragraph at the top of the document.

❷   Click **Insert** then click **Object….** The Object dialog box appears.

❸   In the Object Type list box, click **Microsoft WordArt 2.0**, then click **OK** or press **[Enter]**. WordArt starts and the Enter Your Text Here dialog box opens on top of your Word document. In your Word document the WordArt image, Your Text Here, appears surrounded by a crosshatched border. The WordArt menu bar and WordArt toolbar, used to choose the special effects to add to the text, also appear. See Figure 6-6.

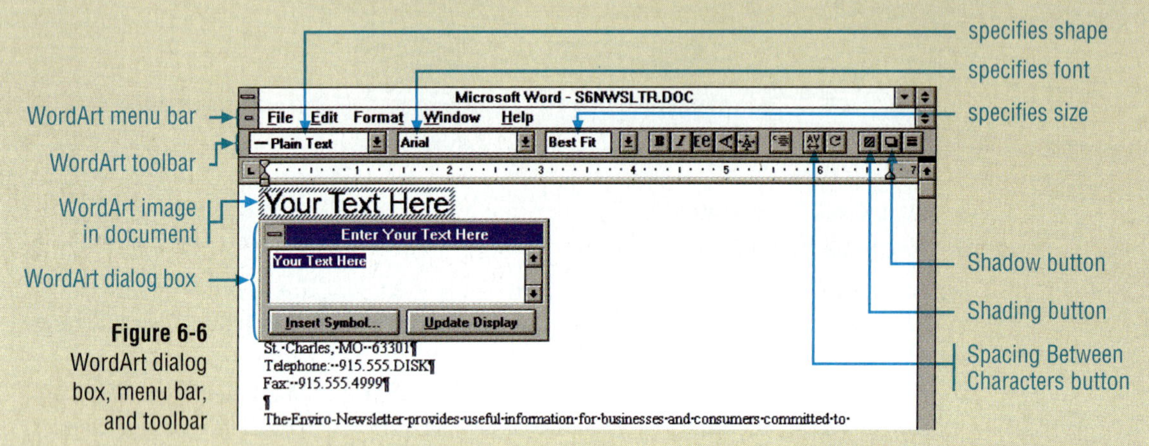

Figure 6-6
WordArt dialog box, menu bar, and toolbar

Keisha knows that she wants the banner to include the newsletter name, *Enviro-Newsletter*, but she's not sure of the special effects to add.

To create the WordArt image for the newsletter name:

❶   Type **ENVIRO-NEWSLETTER** (in all capital letters).

Keisha decides to use WordArt Help to look up a description of the special effects available in WordArt.

❷   Press **[F1]**. The Microsoft WordArt 2.0 Help window opens.

❸   Click the hot topic, **A Description of WordArt Special Text Effects**, then read the contents of the topic. Close the WordArt Help window.

Keisha decides to use the shape Wave2, the font Footlight MT Light, and the font size 50 pt for the banner.

❹   Click the **down arrow** next to Plain Text on the WordArt toolbar, then click the **Wave2 style** (row 4, last option). Click the **Font list box down arrow**, then click **Footlight MT Light**. Click the **Size list box down arrow**, then click **50**. The selected WordArt special effects are applied to the text.

Next Keisha decides to experiment with adding color, shading, and a shadow to the text.

❺   Click the **Shading button** ▨ on the WordArt toolbar. The Shading dialog box appears. Keisha wants the lettering to remain a solid pattern, but she wants to change the foreground color.

❻   Click the **Foreground list box down arrow** in the Color section, scroll through the list of colors, then click **Teal**. See Figure 6-7.

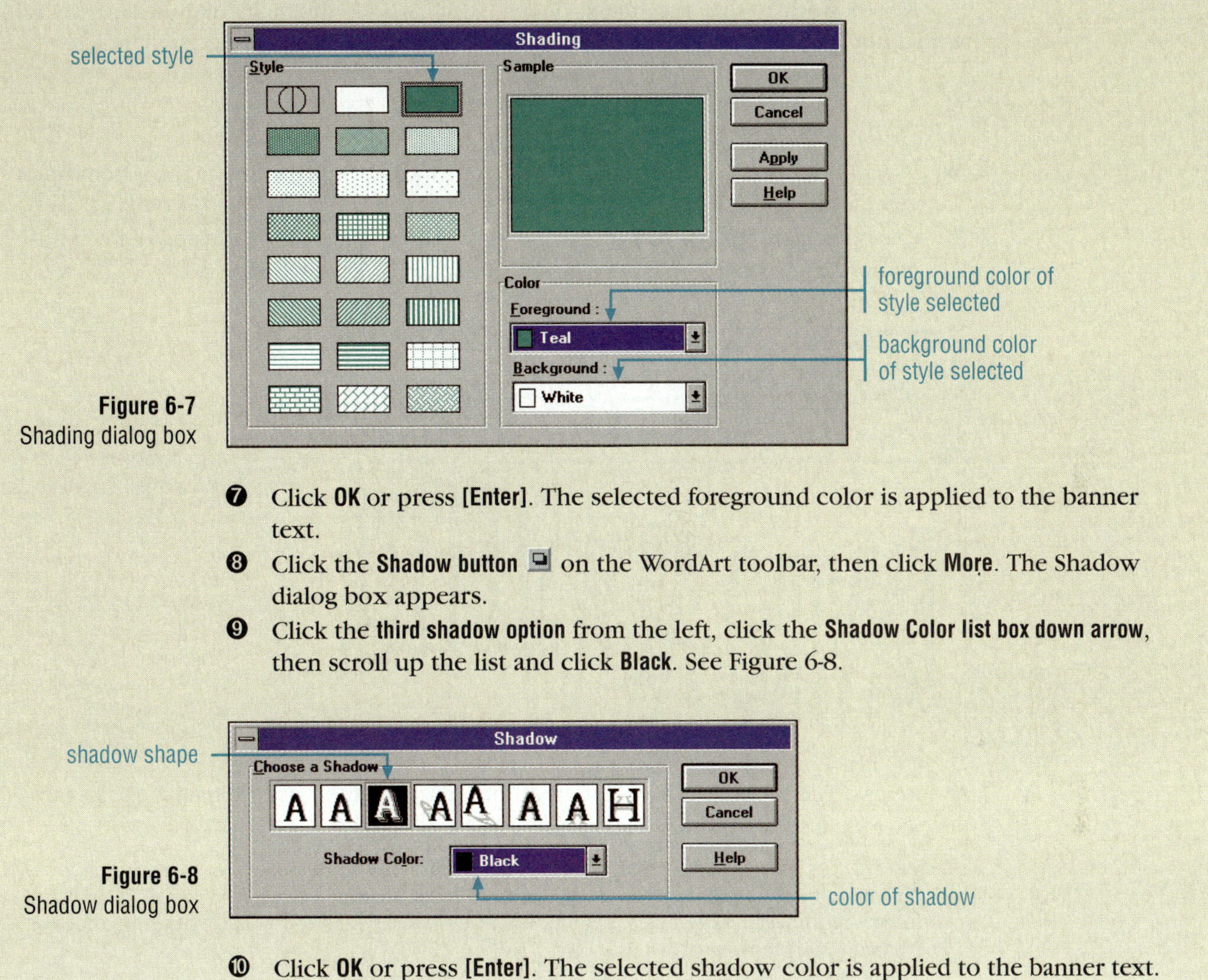

Figure 6-7
Shading dialog box

❼   Click **OK** or press **[Enter]**. The selected foreground color is applied to the banner text.

❽   Click the **Shadow button** 🔲 on the WordArt toolbar, then click **More**. The Shadow dialog box appears.

❾   Click the **third shadow option** from the left, click the **Shadow Color list box down arrow**, then scroll up the list and click **Black**. See Figure 6-8.

Figure 6-8
Shadow dialog box

❿   Click **OK** or press **[Enter]**. The selected shadow color is applied to the banner text.

Keisha is ready to insert the WordArt image into her document.

Embedding an Object into a Word Document

After creating an image with WordArt, you can insert it into your document. The inserted image is considered an embedded object. An **embedded object** is an image, graphic, chart, or spreadsheet created and edited in another application, such as WordArt, but stored in a Word document. Keisha needs to embed the banner into her document.

To embed the WordArt image in the newsletter document:

❶   Click anywhere within the visible part of the document but outside the WordArt image and the dialog box. The WordArt image is updated in the document and appears surrounded by a border with selection handles, indicating it is selected.

Notice that the first paragraph mark now appears on the right side of the document, below the last letter of the banner.

Keisha notices that the image doesn't quite reach the right margin and, therefore, would not be balanced across the page. She decides to resize it using the handles.

To resize the WordArt image:

❶ Place the pointer on the middle handle on the right side of the image. The pointer changes to ↔.

❷ Click and drag the handle until it is even with the right margin, using the ruler as a guide. As you drag, the mouse pointer changes to +. See Figure 6-9.

Figure 6-9
Resizing the
WordArt image

❸ Release the mouse button. Note that the first paragraph mark moves back to the left side of the screen.

   TROUBLE? If the first paragraph mark still appears on the right side of your screen, you did not resize the image far enough to the right. Repeat Step 2, making sure you drag the handle to the right margin. The first paragraph mark will move back to the left margin if you have resized the image correctly.

Keisha wants to switch to print preview to see how the banner looks in relation to the rest of the page.

❹ Click the **Print Preview button** 🔍 on the Standard toolbar (or click **File** then click **Print Preview**).

❺ Click the **Close button** on the Print Preview toolbar.

❻ Save your changes.

After viewing the document in print preview, Keisha decides to make some changes to the banner.

Editing an Embedded Object

Keisha decides that the text "ENVIRO" needs to be emphasized, so she decides to split the title after the hyphen in ENVIRO-NEWSLETTER, dropping "NEWSLETTER" to the next line. Then, she must edit the embedded image. To edit an embedded WordArt object, you double-click the object to start the application, or select the object then choose WordArt Object from the Edit menu.

To edit the WordArt image:

❶ Double-click the **WordArt image** (or select the WordArt image, click **Edit**, click **WordArt Object**, then click **Edit**) to start WordArt.

❷ Place the insertion point after the hyphen (-) in the Enter Your Text Here dialog box, then press **[Enter]**. "NEWSLETTER" moves to the next line.

Now that the banner text is on two lines, Keisha decides that rather than force the size of the font to 50 pt, she will let Word choose the best font size to fit the current image area.

❸ Click the **Font Size list box down arrow**, scroll up the list then click **Best Fit**.

Because of the black shadow behind the letters of the banner, some letters appear to be touching one another. Keisha thinks the letters in the name would look better if they weren't so close together. She decides to add more space between the letters.

❹ Click the **Spacing Between Characters button** ⬚ on the WordArt toolbar. The Spacing Between Characters dialog box appears.

❺ Click the **Loose radio button**. This setting will increase the spacing to be 120% of the original image size, as indicated in the Custom box.

❻ Click **OK** or press **[Enter]**. Extra space is inserted between each character.

❼ Click anywhere within the visible part of the document to embed the edited WordArt image in the Word document. The image appears selected in the document.

Keisha wants to separate the banner from the rest of the newsletter with a rule across the page.

To place a rule below the banner:

❶ Place the insertion point in the blank paragraph immediately below the banner (Ln 2).

❷ Activate the Borders toolbar, insert a 2¼ pt single rule at the bottom of the line space, then dismiss the Borders toolbar. See Figure 6-10.

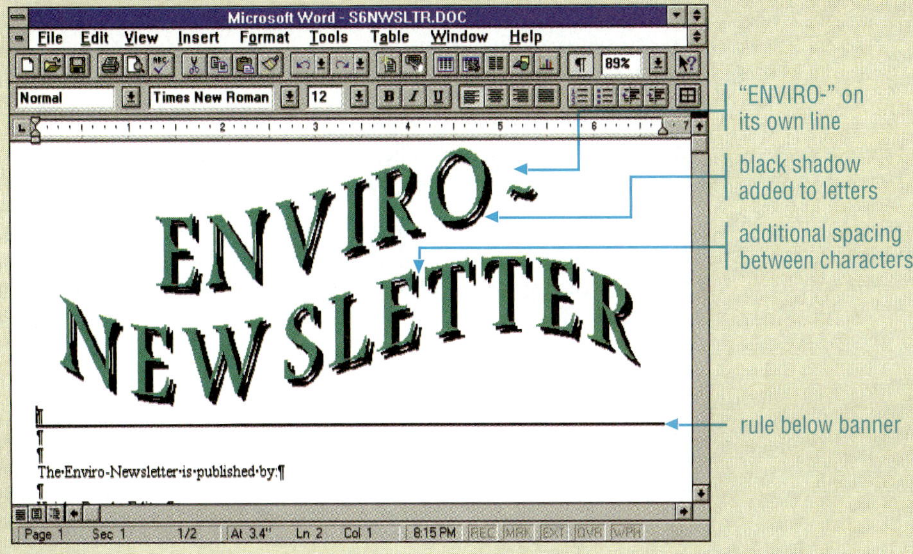

Figure 6-10
Newsletter banner completed

❸ Save your changes.

To save time formatting the *Enviro-Newsletter*, Keisha decides to use the styles she saved in a template for another newsletter. She wants to copy only the paragraph and character styles, not the other text and formatting features of the template. Keisha can use the Organizer to copy the necessary styles.

Copying Styles Using the Organizer

Once you have defined styles for a document or template, you can share those style definitions with any other Word document or template without having to recreate them, thus saving production time. You can use Word's **Organizer** dialog box to copy styles between other documents or templates. You can also use the Organizer to delete or rename styles.

The styles Keisha wants to use are stored in a template named C6OLDNEW.DOT. She'll use the Organizer to copy the styles from this template. Before she does, however, she needs to prevent Word from automatically saving any style changes to the NORMAL template. As you learned in Tutorial 5 when defining styles, style changes can alter the NORMAL template.

To prevent changes to the NORMAL template:

❶ Click **Tools** then click **Options**.... The Options dialog box appears.

❷ Click the **Save tab**.

❸ Make sure the Prompt to Save Normal.dot check box is selected. If it is not, click it to select it. With this setting activated, Word will display a message box asking you to confirm any changes to the NORMAL template.

❹ Click **OK** or press **[Enter]**.

Now Keisha is ready to copy the styles she needs.

To copy styles using the Organizer:

❶ Click **Format** then click **Style**.... The Style dialog box appears. The Styles list box displays only those styles currently in use in the document.

   TROUBLE? If the List box indicates All Styles, you are seeing a complete list of predefined styles. Click the List box down arrow, then click Styles in Use.

❷ Click **Organizer**.... The Organizer dialog box appears with the Styles tab displayed. The styles in use currently for S6NWSLTR.DOC appear on the left side of the Organizer dialog box, and the styles for the NORMAL template appear on the right. See Figure 6-11.

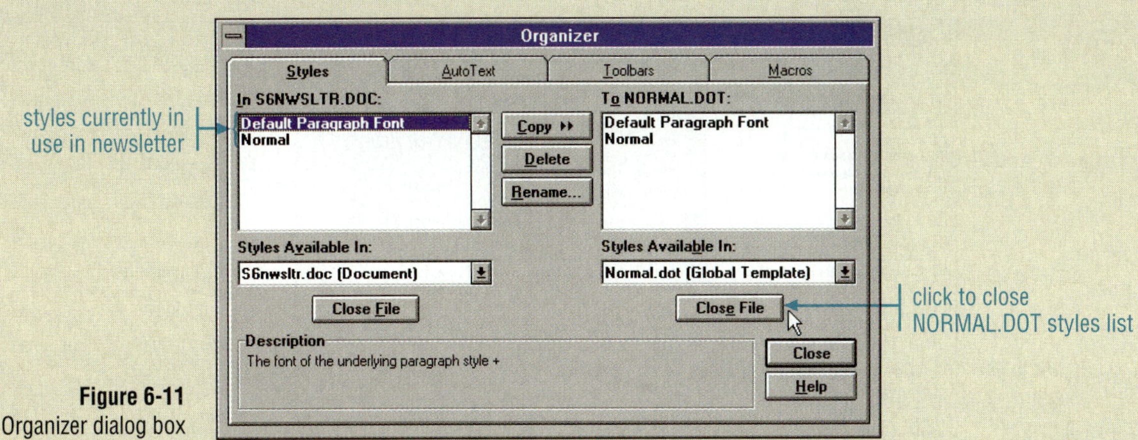

Figure 6-11
Organizer dialog box

Keisha needs to display the styles for the C6OLDNEW template instead of those for the NORMAL template.

❸ Click **Close File** below the NORMAL template list of styles. (See Figure 6-11.) The Close File button changes to the Open File… button.

❹ Click **Open File…**. The Open dialog box appears with all file types displayed.

   TROUBLE? If all files are not listed, select All Files (*.*) from the List Files of Type list box in the Open dialog box.

❺ Select the drive containing your Student Disk, click **C6OLDNEW.DOT**, then click **OK** or press **[Enter]**.

   The right side of the Organizer dialog box now lists the styles for C6OLDNEW.DOT. You can select multiple styles at one time, rather than selecting and copying each style individually. To select consecutive styles in a range, click the first name in the range to be selected, hold down [Shift], then click the last style name in the range. To select non-adjacent styles, click the first style to be selected, then press [Ctrl] while clicking the remaining style names to be selected. To deselect individual styles, press and hold [Ctrl] then click the style name to be deselected.

❻ Click **Article Text**, hold down **[Shift]**, scroll to the bottom of the list, click the last name in the list, **Recycle**, then release [Shift]. All the names in the list are selected. Notice that the arrows on the Copy button now point to the left, indicating that the styles will be copied *from* the C6OLDNEW.DOT template to the current document.

   TROUBLE? All style names for C6OLDNEW.DOT should be highlighted. If not, repeat Step 6.

Keisha decides that she doesn't want to overwrite the Normal style or the Default Paragraph Font style with those same style names from the C6OLDNEW template. She must deselect those two styles from the list.

❼ Press and hold **[Ctrl]** while you click **Normal**, then click **Default Paragraph Font** in the C6OLDNEW.DOT styles list. The two styles are deselected while the remaining styles are still selected.

❽ Click **Copy**. The selected style names now appear in the style list for S6NWSLTR.DOC. See Figure 6-12.

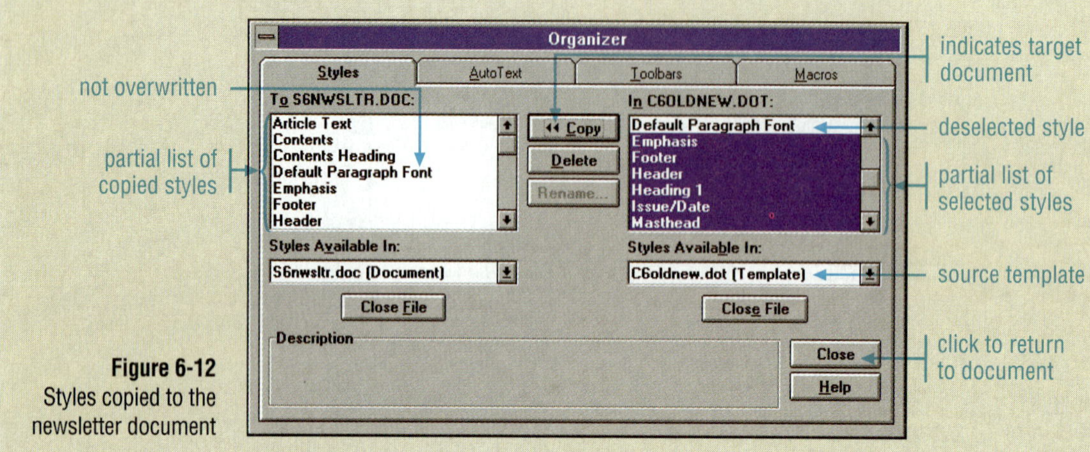

Figure 6-12
Styles copied to the
newsletter document

❾   Click **Close** in the lower-right corner of the dialog box (*do not click either of the Close File buttons*).

Keisha wants to make sure that the styles from the C6OLDNEW.DOT template have been transferred to her current document.

❿   Click the **Style list box down arrow** on the Formatting toolbar. The new styles are listed. Press [**Esc**] to close the Style list without making a selection, then save your changes.

Now that she has copied the styles, Keisha is ready to apply them to the appropriate elements of her newsletter.

Displaying the Style Area

To make sure that you apply the correct style to different parts of your documents, you can display the style area along the left margin. The **style area** displays the name of the style applied to the adjacent paragraph. The style area is usually hidden, but you can display it by specifying a style area width on the View tab of the Options dialog box. The style area can be seen only in normal or in outline view.

Keisha decides to display the style area to help ensure that she applies the appropriate styles to her document. Let's do that now.

To display the style area:
❶   Click **Tools** then click **Options....** The Options dialog box appears.
❷   In the Window section of the View tab, increase the Style Area Width option to **0.5"**.
❸   Click **OK** or press [**Enter**].
Keisha still wants to be able to see the full width of the document on the screen.
❹   Click the **Zoom Control list box down arrow**, then click **Page Width**. Notice that the style area is now visible and that only the Normal style has been used so far in the document. See Figure 6-13.

Figure 6-13
Style area displayed

Now that the style area is displayed, Keisha can apply appropriate styles to the various design elements of the newsletter.

Applying Styles Using Shortcut Keys

Keisha had assigned shortcut keys to the paragraph and character styles that she copied into the current document from the old newsletter template. Figure 6-14 lists the style names and their assigned shortcut keys.

Style Name:	Shortcut Key:	Style Name:	Shortcut Key:
Article Text	[Alt][t]	Heading 1	[Alt][Shift][1]
Contents	[Alt][n]	Issue/Date	[Alt][i]
Contents Heading	[Alt][c]	Masthead	[Alt][m]
Emphasis	[Ctrl][Shift][e]	Recycle	[Alt][r]

Figure 6-14
Shortcut keys for
copied styles

Let's apply these styles now.

To apply the paragraph styles using shortcut keys:

❶ Select the masthead information, beginning with the blank paragraph (Ln 4) above the words "The Enviro-Newsletter is published…" through "…welcome!", then press **[Alt][m]**. The formats defined for the Masthead style are applied to the selected text. Notice the change in the Style list box and in the style area in the left margin. See Figure 6-15.

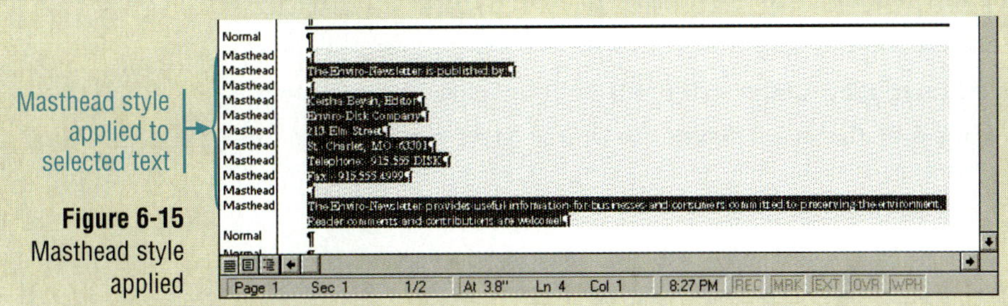

Masthead style
applied to
selected text

Figure 6-15
Masthead style
applied

TROUBLE? If the shortcut keys do not work as described in these steps, apply the styles to the appropriate text by selecting the styles from the Style list box on the Formatting toolbar.

Keisha wants to check the attributes of the Masthead style using Reveal Formats.

❷ Click the **Help button** 🅚 on the Standard toolbar, move the mouse pointer over the masthead text, then click. The attributes assigned to the Masthead style are displayed in the Reveal Formats box. Press **[Esc]** to dismiss the Reveal Formats box.

❸ Place the insertion point in the headline for the first article, Recycle Toner Cartridges, then press **[Alt][Shift][1]**. The Heading 1 style is applied to the headline. Notice the change in the Style list box and in the style area. Use the Reveal Formats feature to view the attributes for the newly applied style.

❹ Place the insertion point in the text of the first article, then press **[Alt][t]**. The Article Text style is applied to the text. Notice the change in the Style list box and in the style area. Use the Reveal Formats feature to view the attributes for the applied style.

❺ Apply the Heading 1 style to the headlines and apply the Article Text style to the text paragraphs for the remaining articles. Notice that the document now extends to three pages.

❻ Save your changes.

Keisha also created a character style, called Emphasis, for words that need to be emphasized in the newsletter. The character attributes for the style are italics and bold. Keisha decides to apply the Emphasis style to the first occurrence of the specific company's name in each article using the shortcut key combination, [Ctrl][Shift][e].

To apply the character style to selected text in the newsletter:

❶ In the Recycle Toner Cartridges article, select **St. Charles Office Supply** then press **[Ctrl][Shift][e]** to apply the Emphasis character style.

❷ In the next article, select **The Nature Store** then press **[F4]** (Repeat) to apply the Emphasis style again.

❸ In the remaining articles, select the first instance of each company's name— Enviro-Travel, Enviro-Printing, Wakefield Enterprises', Missouri Trash, Global Releaf, and Material Recovery Systems—then press **[F4]** to apply the Emphasis character style. Then save your changes.

Keisha notices that the name of the newsletter, Enviro-Newsletter, should appear in italics as well as bold in the masthead. The text is already bold, as specified by the Masthead style. Therefore, she cannot apply the Emphasis style to this text because doing so would remove the bolding from it. Keisha simply needs to italicize the text.

❹ Italicize both occurrences of **Enviro-Newsletter** in the masthead.

Keisha has applied all the styles and can now close the style area.

❺ Click **Tools** then click **Options…**. On the View tab, decrease the Style Area Width option to **0"**.

❻ Click **OK** or press **[Enter]**.

Keisha wants to be able to see as much of the document as possible.

❼ Click the **Zoom Control list box down arrow**, then click **Page Width**.

Next, Keisha needs to format the newsletter in columns. To do so, she'll work in page layout view.

Activating Paste-Up Tools

The traditional means of arranging the text of a publication is called creating a **dummy**, or a **paste-up**, of the page layout of the document. It is essential to be able to see how a document will fit best within the allotted pages. You can approximate this step electronically with some of Word's view options. Page layout view, which you used previously in Tutorials 3 and 5, gives you the most accurate What-You-See-Is-What-You-Get (WYSIWYG) display of text as it will print, a capability essential for "pasting up" dummy documents. Unlike normal view, page layout view displays headers and footers and, more importantly for desktop publishing projects, newspaper-style columns and how text will wrap around graphics. Another essential tool available in page layout view is the vertical ruler, which enables you to judge the placement of objects more accurately. Also, you can see two pages side by side when you use page layout view in combination with the Zoom Control command.

During the paste-up process, you also need to differentiate the various text areas within your document. Word considers the main text of a document, graphics, headers, footers, frames, and footnote reference marks each to be different text areas. By activating the **Text Boundaries** option, you can display dotted boxes around the different text areas and crop marks at the corners. In traditional typesetting, **crop marks**—the notations at the top, bottom, and side margins—were used to indicate the limits of the print area.

Before Keisha formats the newsletter for newspaper-style columns and adds the graphics, she needs to change to page layout view so she can see the effect of these changes as she is working. Text boundaries are visible only in page layout view. She also wants to be able to distinguish the different text areas in the document.

To activate Word's paste-up tools:

❶ Press [Ctrl][Home].

❷ Click the **Page Layout View button** ▣ in the horizontal scroll bar (or click **View** then click **Page Layout**).

❸ Click the **Zoom Control list box down arrow**, then click **Two Pages**. You should see the first two pages of the newsletter.

Now Keisha wants to display text boundaries so that she can see the different text areas.

❹ Click **Tools** then click **Options...**. The Options dialog box appears.

❺ Click the **View tab**, if necessary, then click the **Text Boundaries check box** (if it is not already selected) in the Show section.

❻ Click **OK** or press [Enter]. The document is now displayed with crop marks at the margins on the four corners of the page, and the document text area is outlined with a dashed border. See Figure 6-16.

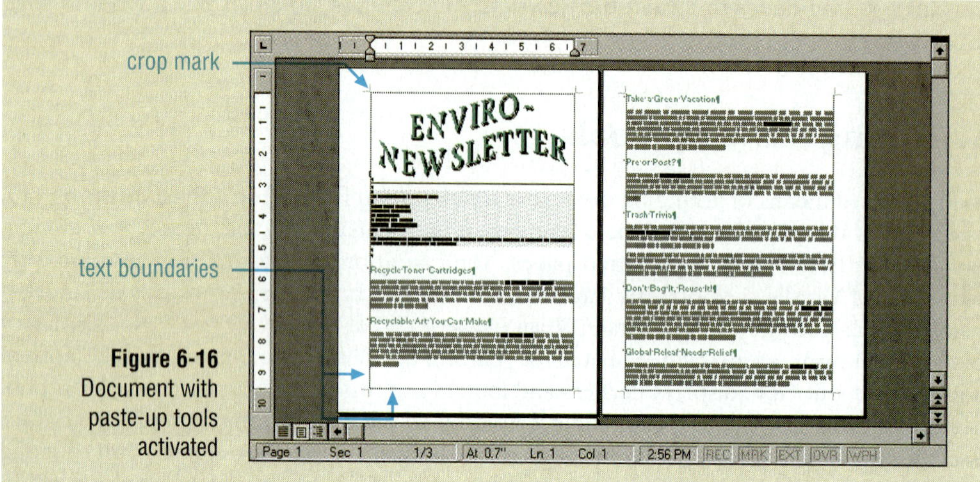

Figure 6-16
Document with
paste-up tools
activated

Next Keisha will insert the headers and footers for the newsletter document.

Inserting Alternating Headers and Footers

Headers and footers are essential design elements for desktop-published documents. They not only provide the reader with valuable information, but can also be used to add visual interest to the appearance of the page. One way to add interest to the headers and/or footers is to alternate the information on the odd and even pages of a document, putting one piece of information on the inside margins and another on the outside margins.

Keisha wants to insert alternating headers to contain the volume number and month issued, and the newsletter name and month issued. She also wants to insert a footer containing the page number on every page but the first.

To insert alternating headers into the newsletter document:

❶ Click **View** then click **Header and Footer**. The Header and Footer toolbar appears.

❷ Click the **Page Setup button** 📖 on the Header and Footer toolbar. The Page Setup dialog box appears. If necessary, click the **Layout tab**.

Keisha wants different headers and footers on the first page, on all even pages, and on all odd pages.

❸ Click the **Different Odd and Even check box**, then click the **Different First Page check box** in the Headers and Footers section.

❹ Click **OK** or press **[Enter]**. The insertion point moves into the First Page Header text area. See Figure 6-17.

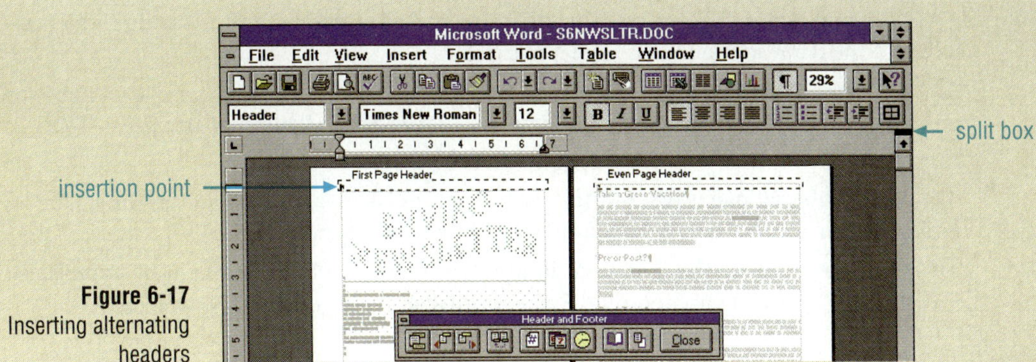

Figure 6-17
Inserting alternating
headers

Keisha wants to insert the volume number and month issued on all odd pages, and the newsletter title and month issued on all even pages, but first she needs to split the window so that she can see what she is typing. Word allows you to split the document window into two *panes* by double-clicking the split box (see Figure 6-17).

❺ Double-click the **split box** above the vertical scroll bar. The window splits into two panes, showing two views of the same document.

❻ Click in the lower pane, then switch to **75%** Zoom view. The top pane remains in Two Pages view, but the magnification of the lower pane is increased so that you can see the text more clearly. See Figure 6-18.

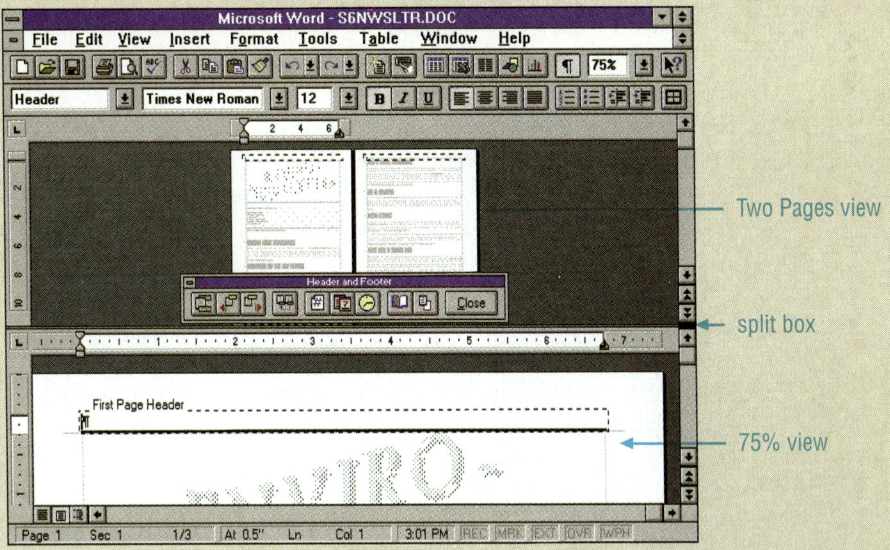

Figure 6-18
Document split in
page layout view

❼ Make sure the First Page Header text area is visible, type **Volume 1, No. 3** and press **[Tab]**, then type **March 1995**. The Header style specifies bold text and provides only one tab in the ruler, located at the right margin.

Keisha wants to use the additional attributes of the Issue/Date style for this text.

❽ With the insertion point anywhere in the First Page Header text area, press **[Alt][i]**, the shortcut key to apply the Issue/Date style. The attributes of the style are applied to the text.

On even-numbered pages, Keisha wants the newsletter name on the outside (left) margin and the date on the inside (right) margin.

9 Click the **Show Next button** on the Header and Footer toolbar to move to the Even Page Header text area at the top of page 2. Type **Enviro-Newsletter** and press **[Tab]**, then type **March 1995**. Italicize Enviro-Newsletter.

On odd-numbered pages (except the first page), Keisha wants the date on the inside (left) margin and the newsletter name on the outside (right) margin.

10 Click to move the insertion point to the Odd Page Header text area. Type **March 1995** and press **[Tab]**, then type **Enviro-Newsletter**. Italicize Enviro-Newsletter.

Now Keisha is ready to insert the footers into her document. For the footer on all pages, except page 1, Keisha wants a 2¼ pt rule at the top of the line space and the page number centered. The style for the footer in the OLDNEW template overwrote the predefined footer style, so a rule has already been added to all footers. Keisha just needs to insert a page number code in both the even and odd page footers.

To insert the footers into the newsletter document:

1 Click the **Switch Between Header and Footer button** on the Header and Footer toolbar. The insertion point moves to the Odd Page Footer text area.

2 Press **[Tab]** then click the **Page Numbers button** on the Header and Footer toolbar.

3 Click the **Show Previous button** on the Header and Footer toolbar to move the insertion point to the Even Page Footer text area.

4 Press **[Tab]** then click.

5 Close the Header and Footer toolbar.

6 Double-click the split box between the two panes to remove the split screen.

Keisha wants to see all three pages at one time.

7 Click the **Print Preview button** on the Standard toolbar. The document appears in print preview. See Figure 6-19.

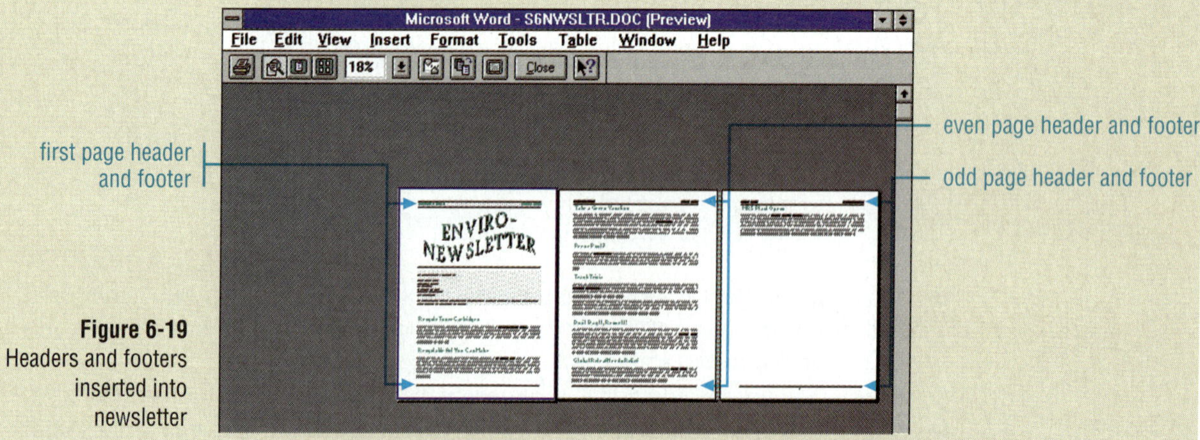

first page header and footer

Figure 6-19
Headers and footers inserted into newsletter

TROUBLE? If you do not see all three pages of the newsletter, click the Multiple Pages button on the Print Preview toolbar, then drag across two pages. Because the Mirror Margins option is activated, each page in print preview is actually two facing pages.

TROUBLE? If you cannot see the rule in the footer on page 1, close print preview, display the First Page Footer text area, place the insertion point in the First Page Footer text area, then press [Tab]. This will fix the problem and display the rule in the footer. Then repeat Step 7.

❽ Click the **Close button** on the Print Preview toolbar.

❾ Save your changes.

Applying a Newspaper-Style Column Format

Another design element of desktop-published documents is the use of **newspaper-style columns**, where the text flows down one column to the bottom of the page, then begins at the top of the next column and continues down that column, until all columns are filled on a page. Newspaper-style columns are popular because text set in narrow columns is easier to read and understand than text set in longer line lengths.

There are two ways to create columns. You can click the Columns button on the Standard toolbar and highlight the number of columns that you want, or for more layout choices you can select the Columns command on the Format menu. Because formatting in columns is a document-level formatting decision, if you want only a part of the document formatted in columns, you must insert a section break between the different parts of the document.

Now Keisha wants to format the copy text into multiple columns. She wants the banner and the rule below it to extend across the entire width of the page (in one column), however, so she must insert a section break between the rule and the copy text. She's not sure how many columns will look good, so she decides to begin with three even-width columns with a vertical line between each column.

To apply a newspaper-style column format to the newsletter document:

❶ Place the insertion point in the first blank paragraph below the rule between the banner and the masthead (Ln 3).

TROUBLE? If it is difficult to move the insertion point to the correct location in Two Pages Zoom view, then return to Page Width Zoom view. If you do switch to Page Width Zoom view, return to Two Pages Zoom view after completing Step 8.

❷ Click **Format** then click **Columns....** The Columns dialog box appears.

❸ In the Presets section, click the **Three icon**, then click the **Line Between check box**. Notice the changes in the Preview section.

Keisha wants these changes to affect only the text from the insertion point to the end of the document, so she needs to insert a section break.

❹ Click the **Apply To list box down arrow**, then click **This Point Forward**. This option inserts a section break at the insertion point. See Figure 6-20.

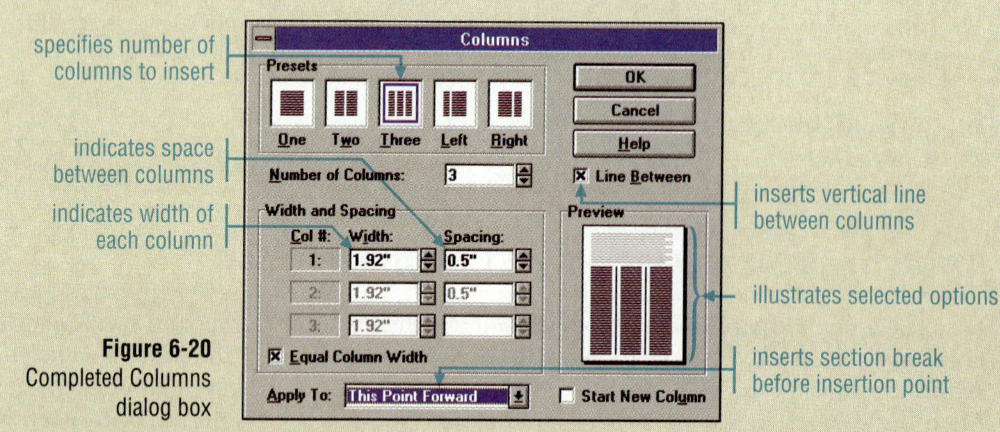

Figure 6-20
Completed Columns
dialog box

⑤ Click **OK** or press **[Enter]**. Notice that the text below the banner flows into three columns, the length of the document is reduced to two pages, and the insertion point is now in section 2. A section break is indicated below the banner.

Keisha thinks the page layout would look better with just two columns in section 2, and the first column narrower than the second column.

⑥ With the insertion point in section 2, click **Format** then click **Columns...**.

⑦ In the Presets section, click the **Left icon**, then decrease the Spacing option for column 1 to **0.3"**. Notice the change in the Preview section. These changes will affect only the current section—section 2.

⑧ Click **OK** or press **[Enter]**. See Figure 6-21.

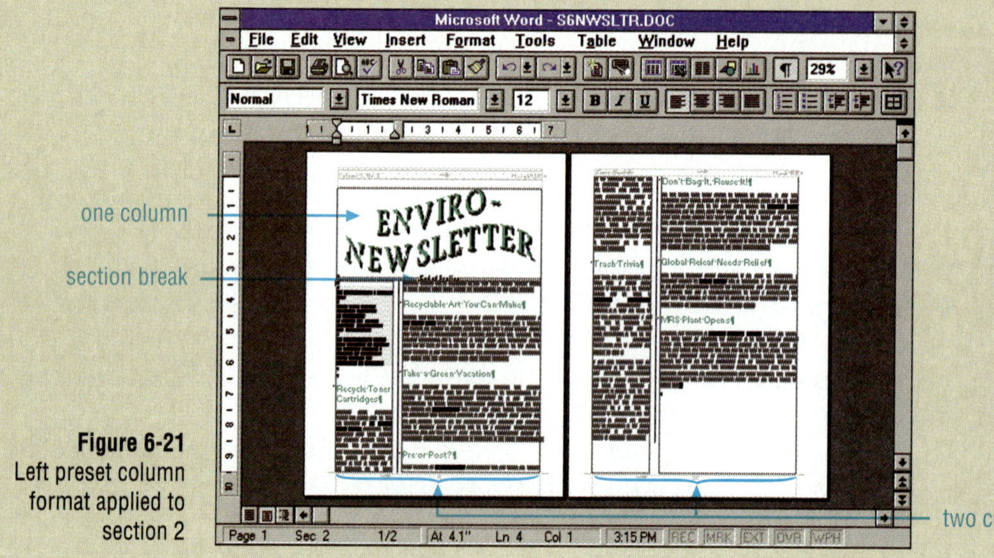

Figure 6-21
Left preset column
format applied to
section 2

⑨ Save your changes.

Next Keisha decides to rearrange the order of the articles in the newsletter.

The article is forced to the top of the second column and the text of all subsequent articles reflows through the columns. See Figure 6-23.

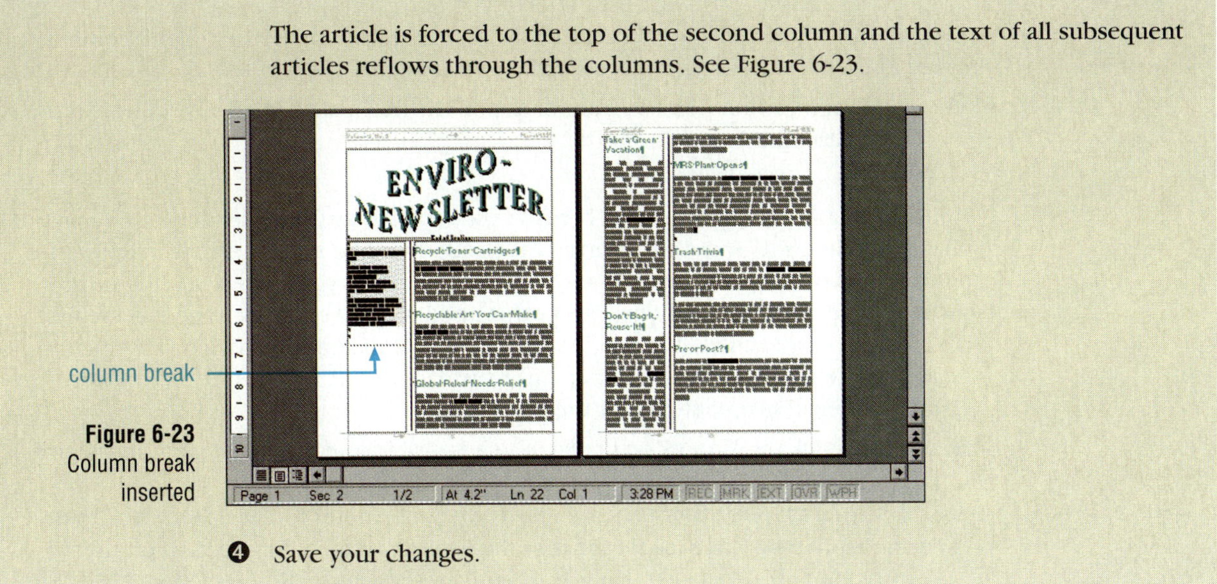

column break

Figure 6-23
Column break
inserted

❹   Save your changes.

Keisha wants to add some variety to her newsletter layout, so she decides to change the column formatting for page 2.

Changing Column Formatting

You might want to change the layout of the columns from page to page. Because the columns feature is a document-level formatting decision, you must first remember to insert a section break at the point where you want to change the column arrangement.

Keisha wants to vary the column arrangement on the second page of the newsletter by making the right column narrower than the left column, and by removing the line between columns. She doesn't want this change to affect the column arrangement on page 1, however.

To modify the column formatting:
❶   Place the insertion point in front of the "T" in Take a Green Vacation, at the top of page 2.
❷   Click **Format** then click **Columns…**. The Columns dialog box appears.

Keisha wants this change to affect the document only from the insertion point to the end of the document. She must insert a section break as well as make the necessary column formatting changes.

❸   In the Presets section, click the **Right icon**, click the **Line Between check box** to deselect it, decrease the Spacing option for column 1 to **0.3"**, click the **Apply To list box down arrow**, then click **This Point Forward**.
❹   Click **OK** or press **[Enter]**. Notice that the text on page 2 is reformatted to fit the new arrangement of columns. Also notice that the insertion point is in section 3, indicating that a section break has been inserted at the bottom of page 1.

Keisha wants the Trash Trivia article always to start at the top of the second column (page 2) even if she makes changes to the preceding text.

❺ Place the insertion point in front of the "T" in Trash, click **Insert**, click **Break...**, then click **Column Break**.

❻ Click **OK** or press **[Enter]**.

When Keisha inserted the section break at the top of page 2, the header for the page changed. When she originally inserted the headers and footers for her newsletter, she decided to have different headers and footers on the first page. Now that the document contains multiple sections, this option applies to *all* sections. Page 2 is the first page for the new section, and the header changed to match the previous first page header, showing the volume number and issue date for the newsletter. Keisha needs to change the Page Setup options for the new section.

❼ Double-click the Header text area, which is visible in page layout view, at the top of page 2 to display the Header and Footer toolbar.

❽ Click the **Page Setup button** 📖 on the Header and Footer toolbar, then click to deselect the **Different First Page check box** in the Headers and Footers section on the Layout tab. This change will apply to only the current section—section 3. Click **OK** or press **[Enter]**.

❾ Close the Header and Footer toolbar. See Figure 6-24.

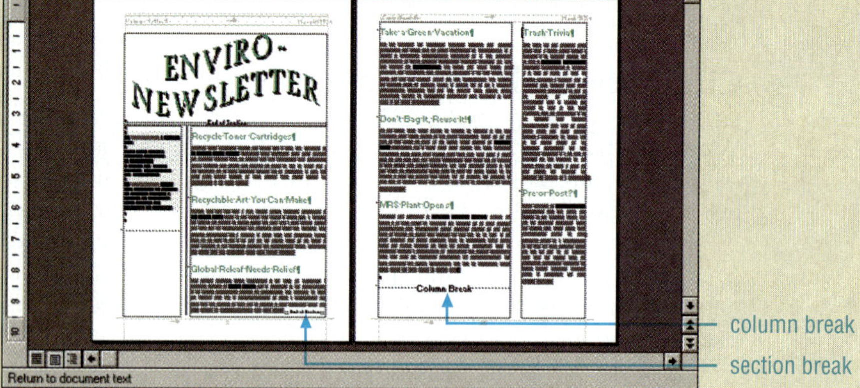

Figure 6-24
Newsletter after modifying column format

Keisha is satisfied with the arrangement of the columns and the text in the columns. She no longer needs to view both pages at one time in page layout view.

❿ Click the **Zoom Control list box down arrow**, then click **Page Width**.

Now that Keisha has finalized the text and the arrangement of the articles, she is ready to insert the table of contents at the top of column 1 in section 2 on page 1. Besides providing information about the articles and their locations in the newsletter, a table of contents can be designed to provide another point of visual appeal to the reader.

To insert a table of contents into the newsletter document:

❶ Place the insertion point in the first blank paragraph on page 1 (Ln 4) below the section break and the rule, then type **Inside This Issue** as the contents heading.

❷ With the insertion point in the contents heading, click the **Style list box down arrow**, then click **Contents Heading**.

❸ Place the insertion point after the "e" in Issue, then press **[Enter]**. You need a blank paragraph before you generate the table of contents.

Because Keisha assigned the Heading 1 style to all the headlines of the articles, the headlines can be used to create the table of contents.

❹ Click **Insert** then click **Index and Tables…**. The Index and Tables dialog box appears.

❺ Click the **Table of Contents tab**.

Keisha has several choices of formats for the table of contents, but she decides that the Elegant format is most appropriate for the newsletter.

❻ In the Formats section click **Elegant**, click the **Tab Leader list box down arrow**, then select the dot leader style.

❼ Click **OK**.

The table of contents is inserted, but it is formatted incorrectly for the column; the page numbers do not fit in the first column.

TROUBLE? If the text for the first article is forced to page 2, then the table of contents will reflect the wrong page numbers. Delete the table of contents. Then check to make sure you have only two blank paragraphs above the masthead and only two blank paragraphs below the masthead in column 1 of page 1. Delete any extra blank paragraphs then repeat Steps 4 through 7.

Keisha needs to apply the table of contents style that she used in the previous newsletter.

❽ Select the table of contents from the title for the first article, Recycle Toner Cartridges, through Pre or Post, click the **Style list box down arrow**, then click **Contents**. Notice the addition of a right-aligned tab stop in the ruler as a result of applying the style. Deselect the table of contents. See Figure 6-25.

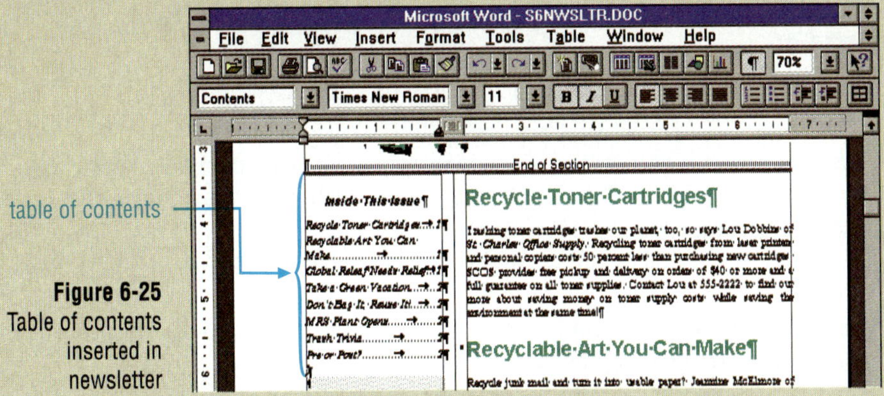

Figure 6-25
Table of contents
inserted in
newsletter

table of contents

TROUBLE? If the format of the entire table of contents did not change, you did not select the entire table of contents. The table of contents automatically turns a dark gray shade when the insertion point is within it, but it is not selected unless it is highlighted.

❾ Save your changes.

Now Keisha is ready to add another design element, a graphic, that will add visual interest to her newsletter.

Inserting Word ClipArt

Graphics add variety to documents, and Word supports a variety of graphic file formats. You can insert a graphic from another Windows application by copying it to the Clipboard, then pasting the image in your document; or you can import a graphic directly by using the Picture command on the Insert menu. Word has its own clipart library, located in a subdirectory named CLIPART, which contains several graphic images in Windows Metafile format (WMF).

Keisha wants to insert a recycle graphic between the masthead and the headline for the first article.

To import the recycle graphic:

❶ Place the insertion point in the second blank paragraph (Ln 30) below the masthead, before the Column Break.

❷ Click **Insert** then click **Picture....** The Insert Picture dialog box appears.

❸ Scroll through the File Name list box, then click **recycle.wmf**.

❹ Click the **Preview Picture check box**, if necessary. The selected graphic file displays in the Preview section. See Figure 6-26.

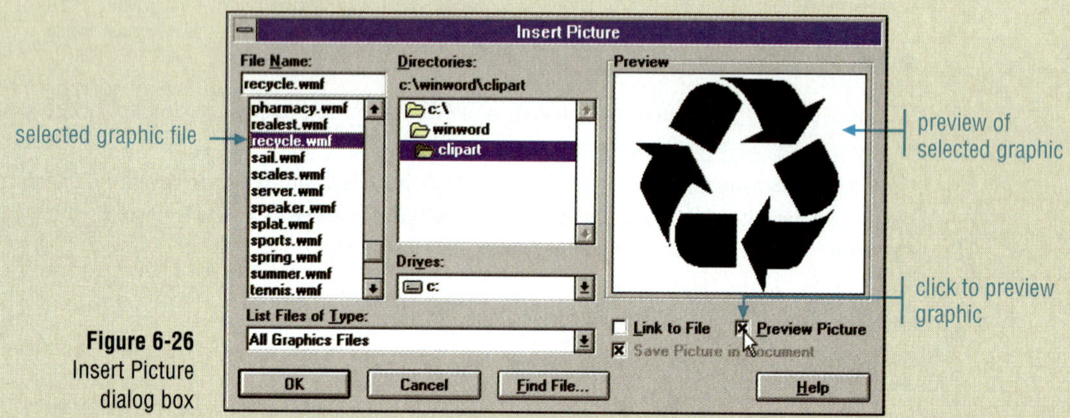

Figure 6-26
Insert Picture
dialog box

❺ Click **OK** or press [Enter]. The recycle graphic appears in the document at the insertion point, but because of its size, it forces the text after it to flow to the next page.

❻ Save your changes.

Keisha must make the graphic smaller so that it will fit in column 1 and the articles will be correctly placed in column 2.

Sizing Graphics

After inserting a picture into a document, you might need to resize it to fit the surrounding text. Word allows you to **scale** a picture, that is, change the picture's proportions, or to **crop** a picture, that is, to cut off any part of the picture. You can scale or crop a picture using either the mouse or the Picture command on the Format menu.

REFERENCE WINDOW

Sizing a Graphic

To use the mouse to scale or crop a graphic:

- Select the graphic to be resized.

- Drag the corner handles to size the graphic proportionally.

- Press and hold [Shift] then drag the center handle on any side of the graphic to crop it.

To use the Picture dialog box to scale or crop a graphic:

- Click Format then click Picture.... The Picture dialog box appears.

- To scale a selected picture, indicate the percentage to increase or decrease the width or height in the Scaling section of the Picture dialog box.

- To crop a selected picture, choose the side or sides to crop, then indicate the exact measurement to cut from the picture.

- Click OK or press [Enter].

Keisha wants to resize the recycle graphic to be .4 x .4-inch square so that it will fit in the first column.

To resize the recycle graphic using exact measurements:

❶ Click the **recycle graphic** to select it, if necessary. Selection handles appear around the graphic.

Keisha could use the selection handles to size the graphic, but she wants a more precise measurement.

❷ Click **Format** then click **Picture**.... The Picture dialog box appears.

❸ Decrease the Width option in the Size section to **0.4"**. Notice that the options in the Scaling section change as well.

❹ Decrease the Height option in the Size section to **0.4"** also. See Figure 6-27.

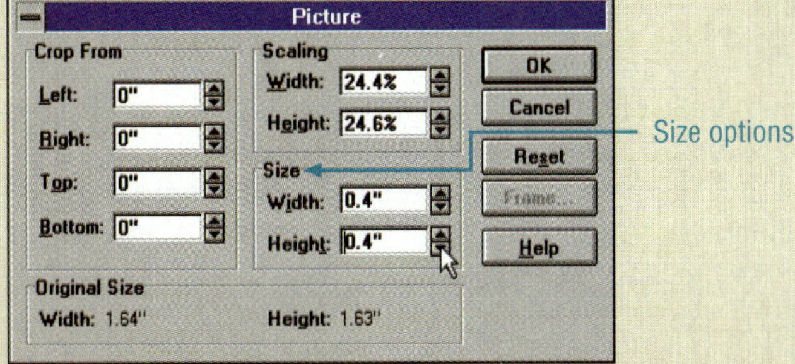

Figure 6-27
Completed Picture dialog box

❺ Click **OK** or press [Enter] then deselect the graphic. The graphic now fits in the first column. See Figure 6-28.

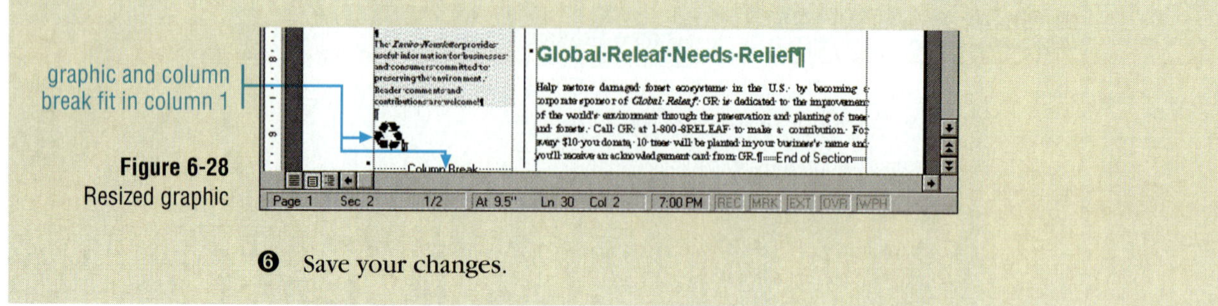

graphic and column break fit in column 1

Figure 6-28
Resized graphic

❻   Save your changes.

Keisha is pleased with the size of the graphic; now she can insert the appropriate text next to it.

Wrapping Text Around a Picture

Another design element that adds interest to a document is to have text wrap around an object on a page. You can create this effect with Word by inserting a frame around the selected text, graphic, or table. A **frame** is a container or enclosure for an object. When working with frames, it is recommended that the document be in page layout view so that you can see the exact location of the frame.

You use frames to position text, graphics, tables, or other objects in your documents. You can either insert a blank frame then insert text or graphics in the frame at a later time, or you can insert a frame around existing text or graphics so that they can be repositioned.

Keisha wants to insert informational text beside the recycle graphic explaining to the reader that the newsletter was printed on recycled paper and describing the specific content of the recycled paper.

To wrap text around the recycle graphic:
❶   With the insertion point in front of the paragraph mark to the right of the recycle graphic (Ln 30), type **Printed on recycled paper using soy ink. 90% Post-consumer waste.** As you type, the recycle graphic and the text move to the top of the second column. Notice also that the typed text does not appear directly next to the recycle graphic.

Keisha must insert a frame around the graphic so that the text will flow beside the picture.

❷   Click the **recycle graphic** to select it.
❸   Click **Insert** then click **Frame**. A frame is inserted around the graphic. A framed object appears to have a crosshatched border. Notice that the text now flows next to the framed graphic, and the text and graphic now appear at the bottom of the first column.

TROUBLE? If a message appears asking whether you want to switch to page layout view, click Yes.

Now Keisha needs to apply the Recycle style to the text.
❹   Place the insertion point anywhere within the paragraph text next to the graphic, click the **Style list box down arrow**, then click **Recycle**. The Recycle style is applied to the selected text. See Figure 6-29.

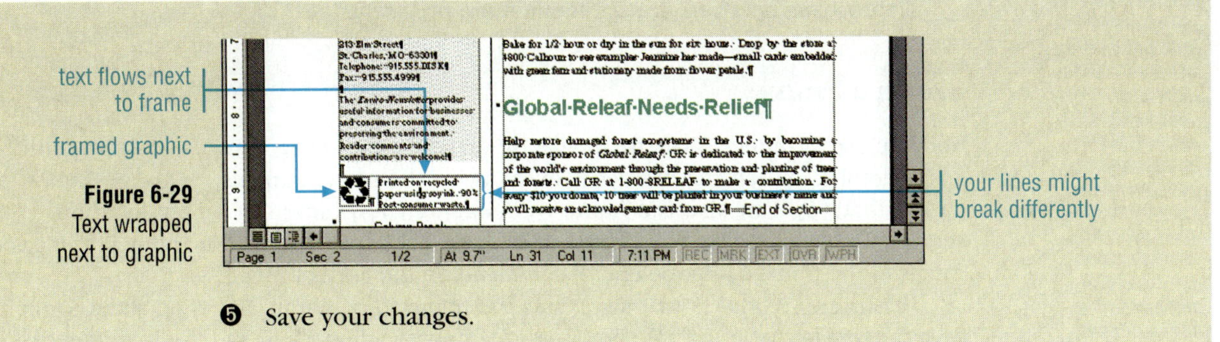

Figure 6-29
Text wrapped next to graphic

❺ Save your changes.

Next Keisha adds several design elements to page 2 of the newsletter.

Inserting a Pull Quote

Keisha wants to insert a pull quote into the newsletter to draw attention to the text in one of the articles. A **pull quote** is a phrase or quotation formatted in a larger point size and/or with a border or extra space between lines. Keisha wants to emphasize part of the text in the article, Take a Green Vacation. To achieve this effect she must insert an empty frame first, then copy the text for the quotation from the article into the frame.

To insert an empty frame for the pull quote:

❶ Place the insertion point in the Take a Green Vacation article text on page 2.

❷ Click **Insert** then click **Frame**. The pointer changes to +.

❸ Place the pointer in the center of the article, below the third line of the article, then press and drag the mouse to insert an empty frame approximately 1" square. You will size the frame more precisely later.

❹ Release the mouse button. See Figure 6-30. Notice that the text of the article wraps around the blank frame and that the frame is outlined with a crosshatched border. Word automatically inserts a thin border around an empty frame. An anchor symbol also appears to the left of the first line of the paragraph to which the frame is "anchored." Both the horizontal and vertical rulers indicate the size of the frame. The adjacent text is underlined but will not appear so when printed.

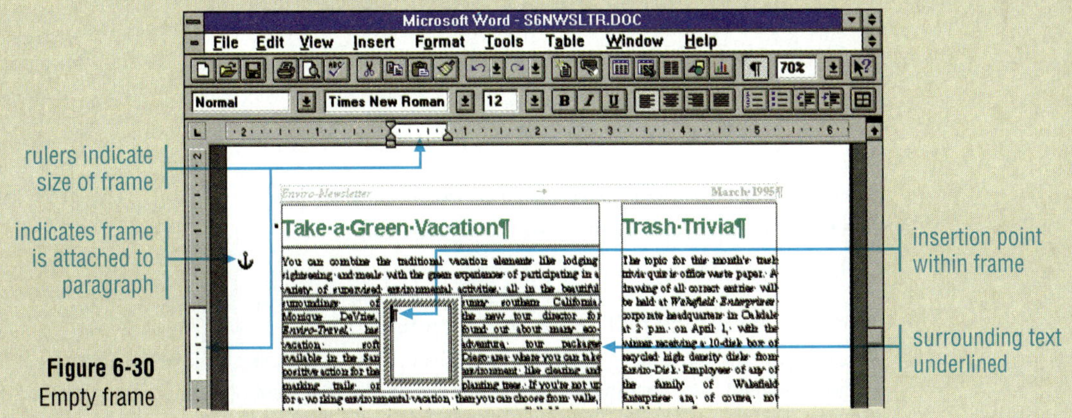

Figure 6-30
Empty frame

Now Keisha needs to size the frame more precisely.

Sizing a Frame

You can size a frame using the mouse by dragging the sizing handles—just as you do to size a graphic. When the pointer is over one of the sizing handles, it changes to ↔ indicating that you can size the frame by dragging the pointer to a new location. If you require a more precisely sized frame, you can specify the exact width and height measurements of the frame using the Frame command on the Format menu.

Keisha approximates that she wants the frame to be about 2.5" wide and 1.5" high to hold the text for the pull quote in this article. She can adjust the frame size later, if necessary.

To size the frame for the pull quote:

❶ Point to the crosshatched border of the empty frame. The pointer changes to ⬚.

❷ Click the crosshatched border of the frame to select it. The selection handles appear.

❸ Click **Format** then click **Frame…**. The Frame dialog box appears. Notice that Around is the default Text Wrapping option.

❹ In the Size section, increase the Width option to **Exactly** At **2.6"** and the Height option to **Exactly** At **1.4"**. See Figure 6-31.

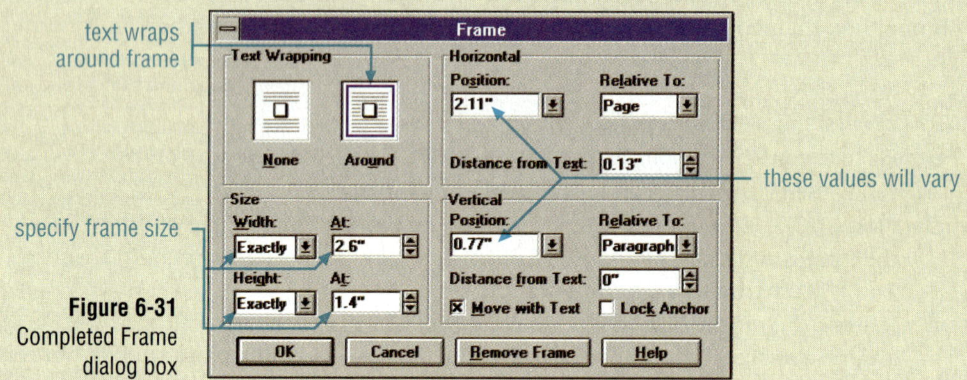

Figure 6-31
Completed Frame dialog box

TROUBLE? Your values in the Horizontal and Vertical Position list boxes will most likely be different; continue with the tutorial.

❺ Click **OK** or press **[Enter]**. The frame becomes the size specified in the Frame dialog box. The text in the second column temporarily moves to page 3.

TROUBLE? If the text in the second column does not move to page 3, just continue with the tutorial.

Now Keisha can insert text into the empty frame. She could type the text, but she decides to copy it instead to prevent typing errors.

To insert the text for the pull quote in the frame:

❶ Select the following text in the Take a Green Vacation article: **take positive action for the environment, like clearing and marking trails or planting trees.** (include the period).

❷ Click the **Copy button** 📇 on the Standard toolbar (or click **Edit** then click **Copy**).

❸ Place the insertion point in the empty frame, then click the **Paste button** 📋 on the Standard toolbar (or click **Edit** then click **Paste**). The copied text appears in the frame.

Keisha decides to add an ellipsis (. . .) to indicate that the copied text is a partial quotation.

❹ Place the insertion point in the frame in front of the "t" in "take."

❺ Type " . . . press **[Spacebar]**, move the insertion point to the end of the quotation after the period, then type ". Make sure you press [Spacebar] to separate the points of the ellipsis.

❻ Save your changes.

Now Keisha needs to format the pull quote so that it will stand out.

Formatting Text in a Frame

Text in a frame is formatted in the same manner as regular text. If you want the formats to apply to all the contents of the frame, click the outside of the frame to select it; otherwise, select just that portion of the text within the frame to be formatted.

Keisha wants to format all the text in the frame.

To format the text in the frame:

❶ Click the crosshatched border of the frame to select it.

❷ Click **Format** then click **Font**.... The Font dialog box appears.

❸ In the Font Style list box, click **Italic**, then in the Size list box click **16**.

❹ Click **OK** or press [Enter]. The text in the frame is formatted with the selected font attributes.

Keisha wants the line spacing to be set at exactly 1.5 times the applied font size (16 pt).

❺ Click **Format** then click **Paragraph**.... The Paragraph dialog box appears. If necessary, click the Indents and Spacing tab.

❻ Click the **Line Spacing list box down arrow**, then click **Exactly**.

❼ Click the **At up arrow** to **24 pt** (16 x 1.5).

❽ Click the **Alignment list box down arrow**, then click **Centered**.

❾ Click **OK** or press [Enter]. See Figure 6-32.

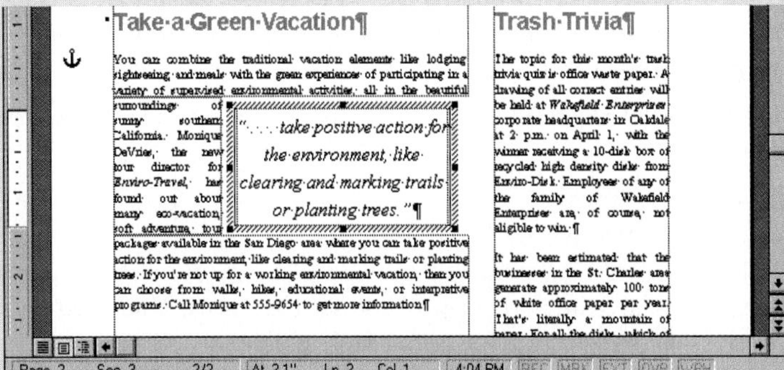

Figure 6-32
Formatted pull quote

❿ Save your changes.

Keisha doesn't like the position of the pull quote; she decides to position it more precisely.

Positioning a Frame

You can use the mouse to drag a frame to any location on the page. To position a frame with the mouse, you must first select it. The pointer changes to ⊹ when it is over the edge of the frame, indicating that the frame can be moved. Then you simply drag the frame to a new location.

To position a frame more precisely, you can use the Frame command on the Format menu, which allows you to specify the frame's horizontal and vertical position, as well as a reference point—page, column, margin, paragraph—for each position. Keisha wants to position the framed pull quote at the left edge of the first column, approximately halfway down the article.

To position the framed pull quote using the Frame command:

❶ Click the framed pull quote to select it, if necessary, click **Format**, then click **Frame**…. The Frame dialog box appears.

❷ In the Horizontal section, click the **Position list box down arrow**, then click **Left**.

❸ In the Horizontal section, click the **Relative To list box down arrow**, then click **Column**.

❹ In the Position box of the Vertical section, type **1"**.

❺ In the Vertical section, click the **Relative To list box down arrow**, then click **Paragraph**, if necessary. See Figure 6-33.

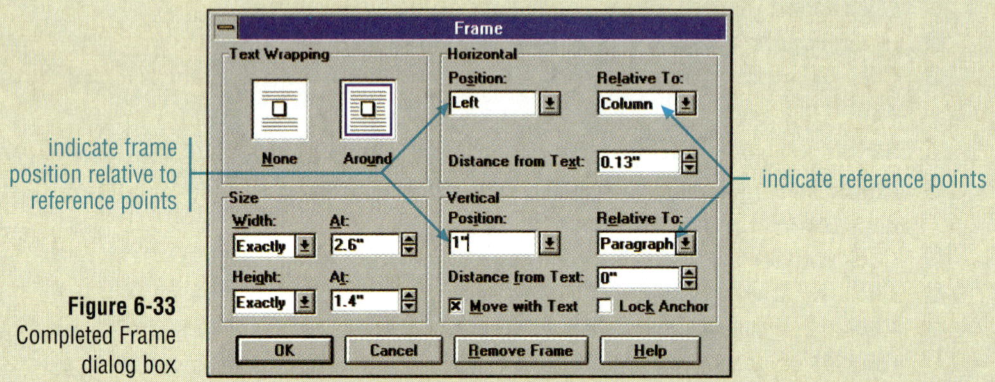

indicate frame position relative to reference points

indicate reference points

Figure 6-33
Completed Frame dialog box

❻ Click **OK** or press **[Enter]**. The pull quote moves to the left side of the column and is also adjusted vertically.

TROUBLE? If the Trash Trivia article still appears on page 3, reduce the size of the frame around the pull quote until the article moves back to page 2.

❼ Save your changes.

Next Keisha wants to apply one of the more traditional design elements to her newsletter—a stylized first letter for each article.

Creating Drop Caps

Another special text effect you can create with frames is a drop cap. A **drop cap** is a large, uppercase character applied usually to the first character of a paragraph with the top part of the drop cap even with the top of the line and the rest of the drop character extending downward into the paragraph below. The surrounding text wraps around the drop cap. With Word, you can also specify that the selected text be displayed as a drop cap in the left margin.

Keisha wants the first character of the first paragraph of each article to begin with a drop cap. She wants the character to extend down into the next line.

To insert drop caps in the articles:

❶ Place the insertion point anywhere in the text paragraph of the article, Recycle Toner Cartridges.

❷ Click **Format** then click **Drop Cap…**. The Drop Cap dialog box appears.

Keisha wants the character to be dropped within the paragraph rather than in the margin, and she wants to use a more stylish font for the drop cap.

❸ Click the **Dropped icon** in the Position section.

❹ Click **Monotype Corsiva** in the Font list box.

> **TROUBLE?** If Monotype Corsiva is not available in your Font list, choose Brush Script MT.

Keisha wants the drop cap to extend downward through two lines of text, and to be set off .05" from the surrounding text.

❺ Decrease the Lines to Drop option to **2**.

❻ Increase the Distance from Text option to **.05"**. Make sure you type .05 and not .5. See Figure 6-34.

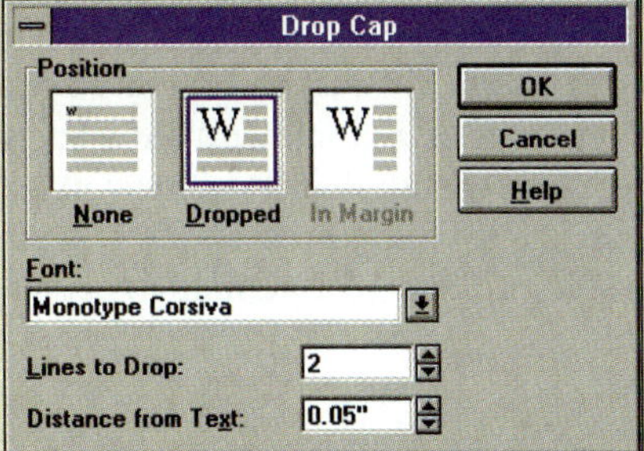

Figure 6-34
Completed Drop Cap
dialog box

❼ Click **OK** or press **[Enter]**. Word automatically formats the first character of the paragraph containing the insertion point as a drop cap with the specified attributes. Notice that a frame has been inserted around the character. See Figure 6-35.

frame inserted around first letter

letter spans two lines

Figure 6-35
Drop cap in first article

Now Keisha inserts drop caps into the remaining articles.

8   Place the insertion point in the first text paragraph of the next article, then press **[F4]**.

9   Repeat Step 8 for the remaining articles.

10   Save your changes.

Keisha notices that her document has several areas with large gaps of space between words; this is caused by the justified text. She decides to correct this problem by hyphenating the document.

Hyphenating a Document

One of the hazards of formatting text in narrow columns and then justifying the text is that Word often inserts noticeable white space in order to accommodate the justified paragraphs. By hyphenating a document, you can eliminate some of the large gaps of space between words. Word's **Hyphenation** command allows you to hyphenate a document automatically with Word making all the decisions for you or manually where Word allows you to accept, reject, or change the suggested word division.

Keisha decides to hyphenate her document to eliminate as many of the large gaps of space between words as possible.

To hyphenate the document:

1   Make sure you have saved your most recent changes.

2   Place the insertion point in the blank paragraph directly before the beginning of the masthead.

3   Click **Tools** then click **Hyphenation…**. The Hyphenation dialog box appears.

Keisha wants as much of a word as possible to fit on a line, so she needs to make the hyphenation zone narrower. She also wants to limit the number of consecutive hyphenated words to 3.

4   Decrease the Hyphenation Zone option to **0.1"**.

5   Change the Limit Consecutive Hyphens To option to **3**. See Figure 6-36.

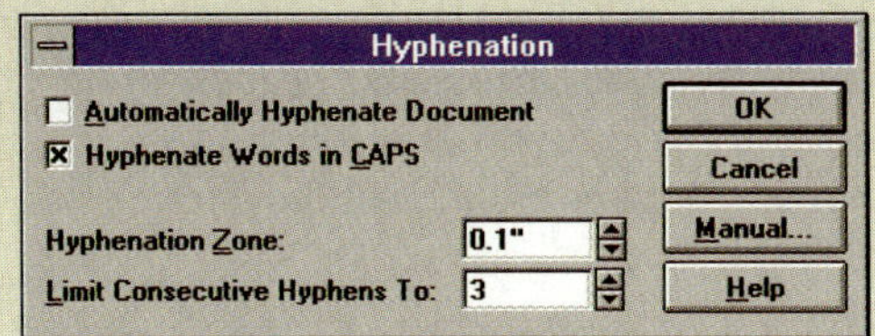

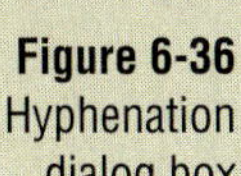
Figure 6-36
Hyphenation
dialog box

Keisha could have Word automatically hyphenate the newsletter but she wants to make each decision.

❻ Click **Manual…**. Word stops at the first instance of the need for a hyphenated word, and displays the Manual Hyphenation dialog box. See Figure 6-37.

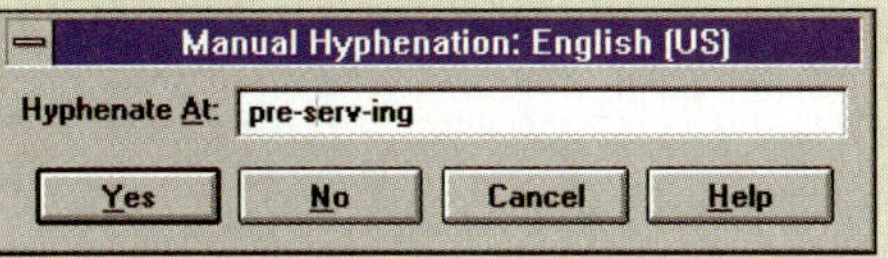

Figure 6-37
Manual Hyphenation
dialog box

TROUBLE? Depending on the type of printer you're using, the word identified in your Manual Hyphenation dialog box might be different. Continue with the steps.

Keisha can decide to either accept Word's suggestion for hyphenation, move the hyphenation point to another syllable in the word, or not hyphenate the word at all. She decides to accept Word's suggestion.

❼ Click **Yes** or press **[Enter]**. Word hyphenates the word and moves to the next instance of a word that needs hyphenating.

❽ Continue accepting all suggestions by Word for hyphenation *except* for proper nouns and words in headlines.

TROUBLE? If the hyphenation process stalls at the end of first page, press [Esc] to cancel the option. Move the insertion point to the top of page 2, then repeat Steps 2, 3, and 6. If the process stalls at any other point, press [Esc], then repeat Steps 2, 3, and 6 beginning at the last stalled location.

❾ Click **OK** or press **[Enter]** in the Word message box that indicates the hyphenation process is complete. Then save your changes.

For a final design element, Keisha wants to insert the same recycle graphic she used below the masthead. This time, however, she wants to layer the graphic so that it appears behind the text on page 2.

Layering Text and Graphics

Another design element that provides a great deal of visual interest in a document is the layering of a graphic behind text, such that a drawing or text on a lower layer shows through to the upper layers. In the past only the most sophisticated desktop publishing packages could accomplish this effect, but now you can do so with Word.

As illustrated in Figure 6-38, every Word document is made up of four layers. The header/footer layer is on the bottom and can include header/footer text, as well as drawings, that appears on every page. You access the header/footer layer through the View menu, whereas you access the background and foreground drawing layers through the Drawing toolbar. The text layer contains the text of the document.

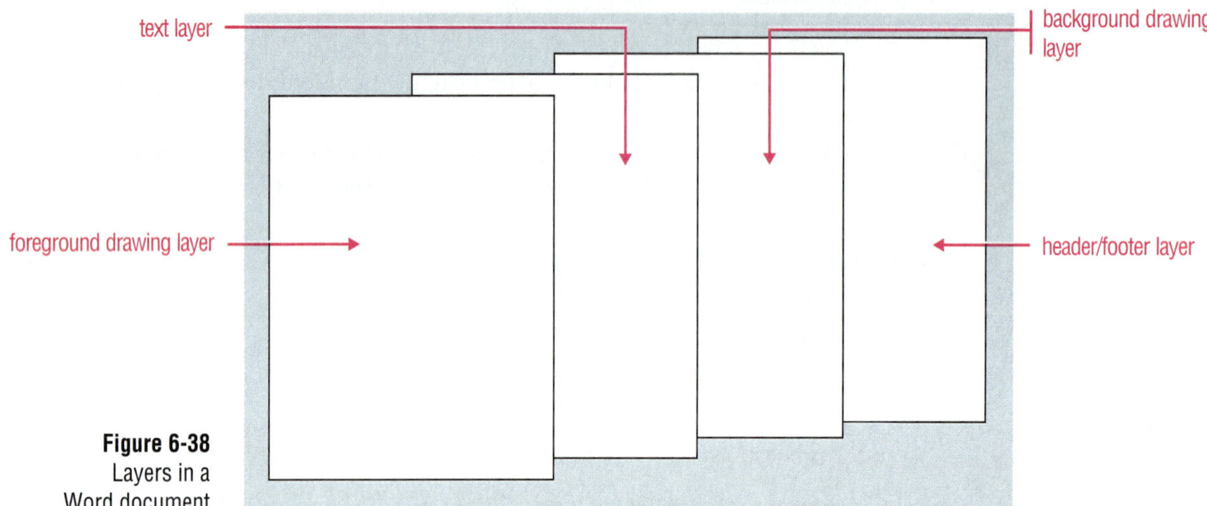

Figure 6-38
Layers in a
Word document

In Word, a drawing object is different from a picture. A **drawing object** is a graphic that you create using the Drawing toolbar; a **picture** is an existing graphic that you import from a graphics program. Another distinction concerns the placement of the graphic itself. You can add *drawings* to *any* layer of a document, but you can add *pictures* only to the *text* layer. Drawings are visible only in page layout view or print preview.

Keisha wants to add the recycle symbol to the center of the last page, but she doesn't want it to obscure any text nor does she want to use a frame to flow text around the symbol; she wants it to show through the text. A graphic, such as the recycle symbol, can be placed on one of the drawing layers only if it is first changed to a drawing object. You can change a graphic to a drawing object by surrounding it with a text box. Keisha must convert the recycle picture to a drawing object in order to accomplish the layered effect.

To layer the recycle symbol behind the text on page 2:

❶ Place the insertion point on page 2, if necessary.

❷ Click the **Drawing button** 🔲 on the Standard toolbar. The Drawing toolbar appears at the bottom of the screen. See Figure 6-39.

❸ Click the **Text Box button** 🔲 on the Drawing toolbar. The pointer changes to + when you move it into the document.

As in Windows Paintbrush, to create a perfect shape with a drawing tool, hold down the Shift key while dragging the mouse.

❹ In the approximate center of page 2, press and hold [Shift], then drag to insert a text box about 3.5" by 3.5". You will adjust the size of the text box more precisely later. Release [Shift] and the mouse button. An empty text box appears. See Figure 6-39.

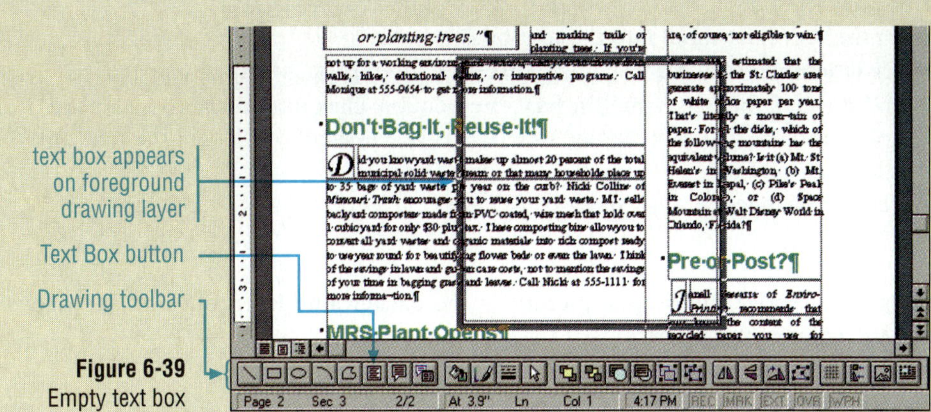

Figure 6-39
Empty text box

Because the empty text box is inserted on the foreground drawing layer, it does not interfere with the text on the layer below, which is the text layer. Even though the text box is inserted as a framed object, the document text does not wrap around it because the text and the text box are on different layers.

As with an empty frame, Word automatically adds a border to a text box. Keisha doesn't want a border around the text box, however.

❺ Move the mouse pointer over the border of the text box. The pointer changes to ⬆. Click to select the object.

❻ Click **Format** then click **Drawing Object…**. The Drawing Object dialog box appears.

❼ Click the **Line tab**, then click the **None button** in the Line section to select the option (if it is not already selected).

Next Keisha must size and position the text box to a more precise location on the page.

❽ Click the **Size and Position tab** in the Drawing Object dialog box, then make the changes shown in Figure 6-40.

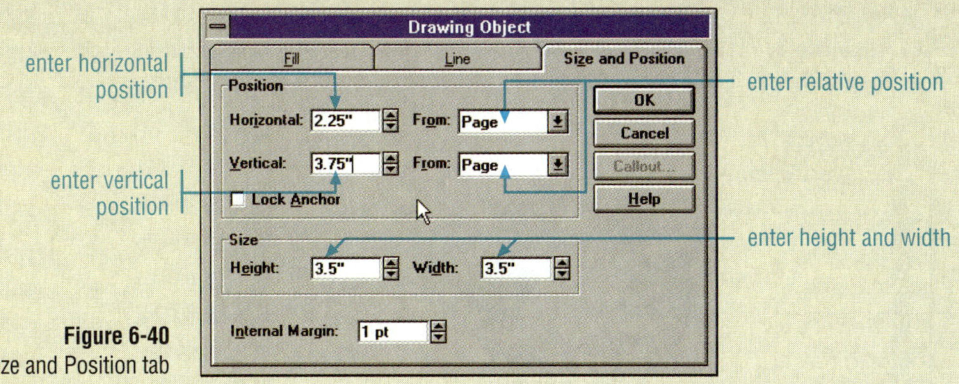

Figure 6-40
Size and Position tab

❾ Click **OK** or press [**Enter**]. The text box is repositioned according to your specifications.

Now Keisha is ready to insert the recycle symbol into the empty text box.

To insert the recycle symbol into the text box:

❶ Click **Insert** then click **Picture….** The Insert Picture dialog box appears.

❷ Scroll through the File Name list box, then double-click **recycle.wmf** to insert the graphic into the text box. Notice that the recycle symbol blocks out the text on the layer behind it.

❸ Save your changes.

Keisha will move the recycle picture to the background layer, but first she needs to change the color of the picture.

Adding Color to a Graphic

Keisha must edit the color of the picture because the black of the image will obscure the text even when she moves the picture to the background layer. To edit a picture, you use the Picture toolbar.

To change the color of the recycle graphic:

❶ Double-click the **recycle graphic** (or click the graphic with the *right* mouse button, then click **Edit Picture**). The Picture toolbar and the recycle graphic are now the only objects on the screen. Word changes the magnification of the screen to 100%.

Keisha reduces the screen magnification so she can bring more of the graphic into view.

❷ Click the **Zoom Control list box down arrow**, then click **Page Width**.

❸ Scroll down the screen until the entire graphic is in view.

You cannot change the color of a WMF file, but you can change the color of a Word drawing object. Keisha must convert the picture to a Word drawing object in order to change its color.

❹ Click the **Select Drawing Objects button** on the Drawing toolbar, then click and drag to insert a selection box around the recycle graphic. See Figure 6-41.

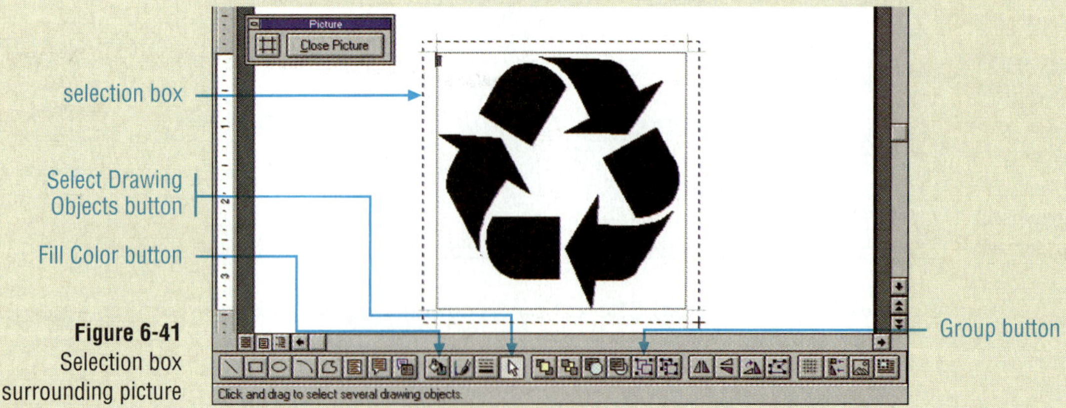

Figure 6-41
Selection box
surrounding picture

❺ Release the mouse button. Selection handles appear around every individual piece of the WMF object.

❻ Click the **Group button** 🔲 on the Drawing toolbar to transform the WMF object into a Word drawing object.

Now Keisha is ready to change the fill color from black to light gray so that text on the text layer will show through.

❼ Click the **Fill Color button** 🔳 on the Drawing Toolbar. The Fill Color palette appears. See Figure 6-42.

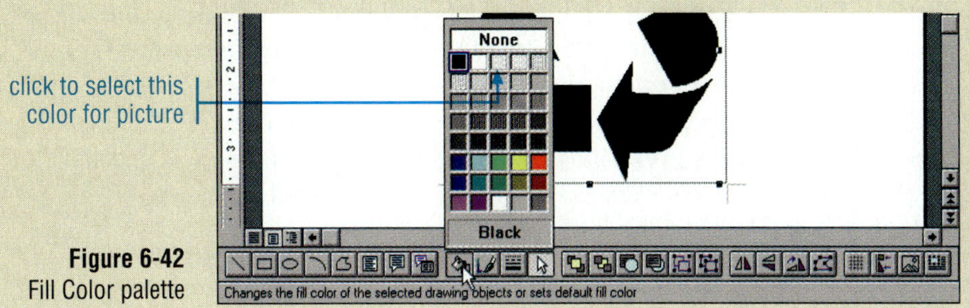

Figure 6-42
Fill Color palette

❽ Click the **light gray color** (first row, third option). The color of the recycle graphic changes to light gray.

❾ Click the **Close Picture button** on the Picture toolbar.

Now Keisha is ready to send the drawing object to the background drawing layer; that is, the layer behind the text.

Moving an Object to the Background Drawing Layer

Even though the color of the picture is lighter, it still blocks the text of the newsletter. Keisha must move the object to the background drawing layer.

To move the recycle graphic to the background drawing layer:
❶ Select the **recycle graphic**, if necessary. Make sure selection handles appear around the outside of the graphic.
❷ Click the **Send Behind Text button** 🔳 on the Drawing toolbar. The recycle graphic moves behind the text layer.
❸ Click outside the graphic to deselect it.
❹ Click the **Drawing button** 🔳 to dismiss the Drawing toolbar.
❺ Turn off the Text Boundaries option on the View tab of the Options dialog box.
❻ Save your changes.

Keisha will electronically transmit her completed newsletter file to Janell at Enviro-Printing, but she needs to print a hard copy for her records. She will spell check then preview the document one more time before she prints it.

To spell check, preview, then print the newsletter document:

❶ Click the **Spelling button** on the Standard toolbar (or click **Tools** then click **Spelling...**) to spell check the document.

❷ Click the **Print Preview button** on the Standard toolbar (or click **File** then click **Print Preview.**)

❸ Click the **Print button** on the Print Preview toolbar. The document might take a while to print. Your printed document should look like Figure 6-1.

❹ Click the **Normal View button** on the horizontal scroll bar to return to normal view. Scroll through the document to see how the newsletter looks in normal view.

❺ Close any supplementary toolbars.

❻ After the newsletter prints, close the document, then exit Word.

❼ Click **No** in the message box asking if you want to save changes to NORMAL.DOT.

Keisha reviews her printed newsletter then electronically distributes it to Janell for printing.

Questions

1. Define the term desktop publishing.
2. Define the following design elements:
   a. banner
   b. masthead
   c. newspaper-style columns
   d. drop cap
   e. pull quote
3. Describe the procedure for importing an entire Word document into the current Word document.
4. Describe the procedure for importing an entire foreign-format file into the current Word document.
5. When do you activate the Mirror Margins option?
6. Explain the purpose of WordArt.
7. Describe the procedure for copying styles from one document or template to another document or template using the Organizer.
8. Describe the procedure for displaying the style area of the Word screen.
9. What features can be displayed while in page layout view?
10. What is the purpose of the Text Boundaries option?
11. Describe the procedure for inserting columns into a document.
12. What are two uses of outline view?
13. Describe the procedure for inserting a column break.
14. Describe the procedure for importing a graphic from Word's CLIPART subdirectory.
15. Describe the procedure for sizing a selected graphic.
16. Define the term "frame."
17. Describe the procedure for making text wrap around a selected picture.
18. Describe the procedure for sizing a selected frame.
19. Describe the procedure for precisely positioning a selected frame.

20. Describe the procedure for creating drop caps.
21. Describe the procedure for hyphenating a document.
22. Explain each of Word's four layers.
23. Explain the difference between a drawing object and a picture.

24. Using a newsletter you've received, identify the design elements of the newsletter. List the procedures for recreating the newsletter using Word. Submit your annotated newsletter and your list of procedures.

Tutorial Assignments

Start Word, if necessary, and conduct a screen check. Open a new document window in preparation for creating the newsletter shown in Figure 6-43.

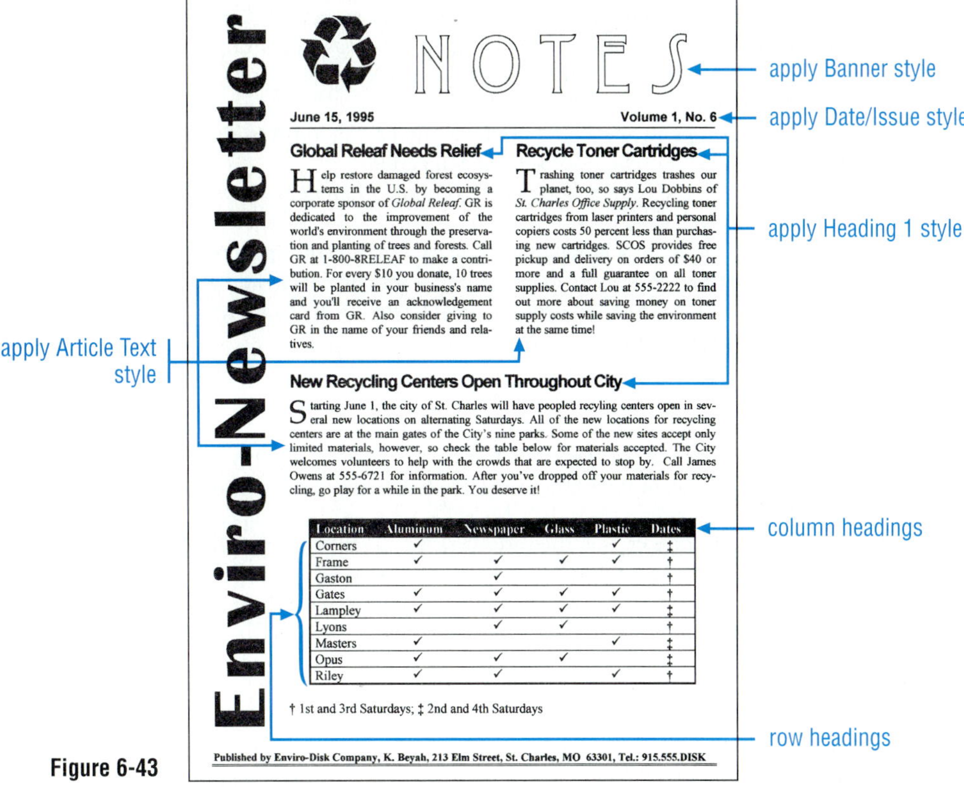

Figure 6-43

Complete the following:

1. Switch to page layout view, start WordArt, then create the following image:
   a. Type "Enviro-Newsletter" as the text for the banner.
   b. Format the banner with the Bottom to Top pattern (first row, last option) in the Style list box, and with the Brittanic Bold font in 72 points.
   c. Click the Spacing Between Characters button, then click the Loose radio button.
   d. Embed the WordArt image in the document.
2. Save the document as S6NOTES.DOC.
3. Insert a frame around the WordArt image, then format the position of the frame using the following options. (Note that you need to type the setting 1" for both position options.)
   a. Horizontal section: Position 1"; Relative To Page; Distance from Text .25"
   b. Vertical section: Position 1"; Relative To Page
4. Save the document.

5. Insert the following text into the document:
   a. Type "Notes" then press [Enter].
   b. Type "June 15, 1995" then press [Tab]; type "Volume 1, No. 6" then press [Enter].
   c. Import the following article files (in order): T6RELEAF.M5, T6LOU.DOC, T6SITES.DOC.
6. Make the following document-level formatting changes:
   a. Left Margin: 2"; Right Margin: 1"
   b. Footer, type: Published by Enviro-Disk Company, K. Beyah, 213 Elm Street, St. Charles, MO 63301, Tel.: 915.555.DISK (*Note:* The footer text will be formatted automatically when you copy styles in the next step.)
7. Copy the styles from T6NOTES.DOT to S6NOTES.DOC without overwriting the Default Paragraph Font style or the Normal style. Click Yes to All to overwrite all other existing style entries.
8. Apply the styles as indicated in Figure 6-43.
9. Insert section breaks so that articles 1 and 2 appear in two-column format with the Spacing option set at .3" and the last article appears in one column.
10. Place the insertion point at the top of the document in front of the "N" in Notes, then insert the recycle graphic. Resize the graphic so that it is exactly 1" square.
11. Insert a space between the graphic and the "N" in Notes.
12. Save the document.
13. Place the insertion point at the end of the document, then press [Enter] once.
14. Insert a 10 x 6 table with the following specifications:
    a. Type the text for the column headings—Location, Aluminum, Newspaper, Glass, Plastic, Dates. See Figure 6-43.
    b. Type the text for the row headings in the table as shown in Figure 6-43.
    c. Insert the checkmark symbol (✓) from the Wingdings character set, and the symbols (†) and (‡) from the (normal text) character set to indicate acceptable materials and open dates.
    d. Select the completed table, then format it using the List 4 table format.
    e. Center align the cells containing symbols.
    f. Select the table then center the entire table horizontally.
    g. Place the insertion point below the table, press [Enter], then type the note indicating the meaning of the symbols used in the Dates column of the table.
    h. Save the document.
15. Insert appropriate drop caps in the three articles. Specify that the drop caps extend to 2 lines, and use a distance from text of .05".
16. Hyphenate the newsletter using a hyphenation zone of .1" and a limit of 3 consecutive hyphenations. Perform a manual hyphenation.
17 Save the document.
18. Preview then print the newsletter.
19. **E** Create a new template for the Notes newsletter saving it to your Student Disk as S6NOTES2.DOT.
20. **E** Delete appropriate text so that just the skeleton document template is displayed. Save the changes to the template.
21. Print the remaining document template and its style sheet.

Case Problems

1. Cerfing The Internet Newsletter

James Dougherty, the director of Technological Services for the Commonwealth of Massachusetts board of higher education, began an electronic bulletin board service for the state's faculty and students concerning the uses of technology in the classroom. It became so popular that he decided to publish a monthly newsletter with worldwide distribution focused on the applications of the information superhighway, the Internet, in the educational environment. You'll create the monthly newsletter, called *Cerfing The Internet*, shown in Figure 6-44.

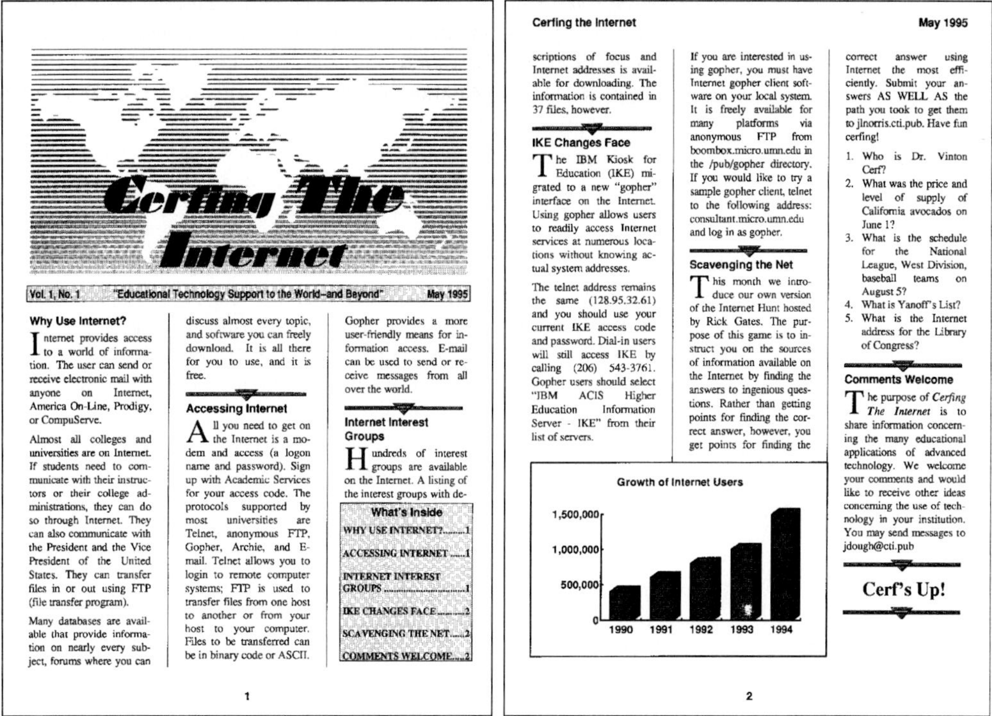

Figure 6-44

Open a new document window, then complete the following:

1. Save the document as S6NETNEW.DOC.
2. Change the left and right margins to 1".
3. At the top of the document, insert CONTINEN.WMF, a Word clipart picture.
4. Resize the graphic so that it is even with the right margin.
5. Place the insertion point in the blank paragraph below and to the right of the graphic, then press [Enter] to insert a blank paragraph mark.
6. Type "Vol. 1, No. 1" then press [Tab]; type the following text *including* the quotation marks: "Educational Technology Support to the World—and Beyond" then press [Tab]; type "May 1995" then press [Enter].
7. Insert the article P6WHY.DOC. Delete the WordPerfect code, {PRIVATE}, after the article title.
8. Place the insertion point in the blank paragraph at the end of the document, insert DIVIDER2.WMF, a Word clipart picture, then press [Enter].
9. Insert the following files (in order): P6ACCESS.MCW, P6GROUPS.WRI, P6IKE.DOC, P6HUNT.DOC, P6COMMEN.DOC, and P6CERFUP.DOC. Make sure your file list shows all types of files. After inserting each file, insert the DIVIDER2.WMF clipart picture, pressing [Enter] after inserting each divider except the last.
10. Save your changes.
11. Insert the following header and footer:
    a. Header: No header on the first page; for subsequent pages, type "Cerfing The Internet" press [Tab]; then type "May 1995." (The text will align properly after you copy styles in Step 12.)
    b. Footer: To appear on all pages, insert a page number code at the center tab.
    c. Save your changes.

12. Copy the styles from P6INET.DOT to S6NETNEW.DOC, without overwriting the Default Paragraph Font style or the Normal style. Click Yes to All to overwrite all other existing style entries.

13. Apply the Issue/Date style to the issue/date information; apply the Heading 1 style to all article titles; apply the Article Text style to all paragraphs; apply the Hunt Questions style to the numbered list. (Note that after you apply the Hunt Questions style to the paragraphs formatted as a numbered list, you must reformat the text as a numbered list.)

14. Switch to page layout view, then format the articles below the issue/date information in three columns with the Line Between option selected.

15. Switch to Two Pages view, then insert frames as placeholders as indicated below.
    a. Bottom of column 3 on page 1—Size section: Width set Exactly At 1.9"; Height set Exactly At 2.3". Horizontal section: Position 5.65"; Relative To Page. Vertical section: Position 7.6"; Relative To Page.
    b. Bottom of column 1 (and extending to the bottom of column 2) on page 2— Size section: Width set Exactly At 4.4"; Height set Exactly At 3". Horizontal section: Position .99"; Relative To Page. Vertical section: Position 7"; Relative To Page. Remove the border from the frame.
    c. Save the document.

16. Insert a table of contents using the following steps:
    a. Place the insertion point in the empty frame at the bottom of the third column on the first page, then type "What's Inside." Press [Enter] twice. Apply the Contents Title style to the text you typed.
    b. Place the insertion point at the last blank paragraph mark under the contents title. Insert a table of contents. Select the Formal style. If necessary, delete the blank paragraph mark below the table of contents after it is generated.
    c. Save your changes.

17. Select the empty frame at the bottom of page 2. Insert the file P6NETCHT.DOC into the selected frame. Save the document.

18. Insert a $1\frac{1}{2}$ pt single line border around the chart.

19. With the chart selected, click Format then click Picture.... Select the following options in the Size section: Width 4.4"; Height: 2.8"

20. Save your changes.

21. Insert drop caps in the first paragraph of all articles. Drop the cap to 2 lines, and increase the distance from text to .05". Save the document.

22. Hyphenate the newsletter using a hyphenation zone of .1" and a limit of 3 consecutive hyphens. Save the document.

23. Insert text on top of the banner graphic using the following steps.
    a. Place the insertion point at the top of the document, then display the Drawing toolbar.
    b. Draw a text box at the center bottom of the graphic, then format the drawing object so that it is positioned as follows: Position section: Horizontal 1" From Page; Vertical 2.7" From Page. Size section: Height 1.6"; Width 6.5".
    c. Type "Cerfing The Internet" then apply the Banner style.
    d. Change the font size of the letters "C," "T," and "I" to 48 pt.
    e. Save the changes.

24. Print the newsletter and its style sheet.

25. Use the microcomputer symbol in the Wingdings character set to indicate the following locations on the banner graphic:
    a. Cambridge, Massachusetts
    b. Houston, Texas
    c. Buenos Aires, Argentina
    d. London, England
    e. Toronto, Ontario
    f. Cairo, Egypt

    g. Moscow, Russia

    h. Sydney, Australia

26. Save the document as S6NET2.DOC, then print page 1 of the document.

2. Butterfly World Parents Newsletter

Elaine Kozinski is the director of the Butterfly World Educational Center in Evanston, Indiana. Butterfly World is a nationally syndicated childcare day school. She has asked the leaders of the pre-kindergarten (Caterpillars) and the kindergarten (Butterflies) to submit articles for inclusion in the September parents' newsletter. You'll create the parents' newsletter, shown in Figure 6-45.

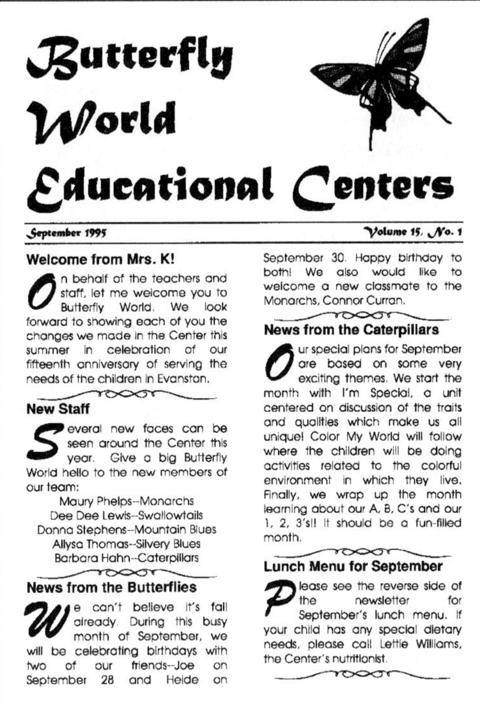

Figure 6-45

Open a new document window and complete the following:

1. Save the document as S6BWNEWS.DOC.
2. At the top of the document, insert BUTTRFLY.WMF, a Word clipart picture, then insert it in a frame. Format the frame's position with the following attributes:
   a. Size section: Width set Exactly At 1.88"; Height set Exactly At 1.82"
   b. Horizontal section: Position 5.1"; Relative To Page. Vertical section: Position 0.1"; Relative To Paragraph
3. Place the insertion point at the top of the document, type the banner text "Butterfly World Educational Centers," then press [Enter].
4. Type the date/issue text "September 1995" then press [Tab]; type "Volume 15, No. 1" then press [Enter]. Save the document.
5. Insert the article P6MRSK.DOC.
6. Insert DIVIDER3.WMF, a Word clipart picture, then press [Enter].
7. Insert the following articles (in order): P6STAFF.DOC, P6BUTTER.MCW, P6PIL-LAR.DOC, and P6LUNCH.WRI, each followed by the DIVIDER3.WMF picture. Press [Enter] after each DIVIDER3.WMF picture, except the one after the last article. Save your changes.
8. Copy the styles from P6BWNEWS.DOT to S6BWNEWS.DOC without overwriting the Default Paragraph Font style or the Normal style. Overwrite any other existing style entries.

9. Apply the Banner style to the newsletter title; apply the Date/Issue style to the date/issue information; apply the Heading 1 style to all article titles; apply the Article Text style to all paragraphs. If necessary, adjust the position of the framed banner graphic so that it appears even with the right margin, and so that the words "Educational Centers" in the banner wrap to the line below the graphic. Save your changes.

10. Insert a section break so that the articles appear in two-column format.

11. Place the insertion point at the end of the document, then insert another section break to begin on the next page. Make the following adjustments to the new section:
    a. Change the page orientation to landscape.
    b. Change the top and bottom margins to 1".
    c. Format in one-column format.
    d. Change the vertical alignment to centered.
    e. Save your changes.

12. Insert the file P6MENU.DOC.

13. Insert a drop cap in the first paragraph of all articles with the following attributes:
    a. Change the font to Brush Script MT.
    b. Drop the cap 3 lines.
    c. Save your document.

14. Center the teachers' names in the New Staff article, as well as each of the DIVIDER3.WMF pictures. Save the document.

15. Print the newsletter and its style sheet.

16. Use the Rectangle drawing tool to draw a border around the entire first page with the following formatting specifications for the drawing object:
    a. A 2 pt line with rounded corners.
    b. Position section: Horizontal -.5" From Margin; Vertical -.4" From Margin.
    c. Size section: Height 10"; Width 7".
    d. Send the drawing object behind the text.
    e. Save the document.

17. Change the issue number to 2, save the document as S6BORDER.DOC, then print the first page of the newsletter.

18. Dismiss the Drawing toolbar.

3. Word Help Desk Newsletter

Create a newsletter that could be used by co-workers and/or clients as a source of up-to-date information about Word. Include in the newsletter articles covering four to six features of Word that you feel are the most useful, along with the purpose and procedures to use each feature correctly. Also consider including a "tips and techniques" section, as well as your most often used shortcut keys.

Complete the following:

1. Create the articles to include in the newsletter, saving each one in a separate file.

2. Decide on a general layout for your newsletter.

3. Create a banner for the newsletter, using WordArt. Save the document as S6HELPDK.DOC.

4. Import the articles into S6HELPDK.DOC.

5. Insert a masthead, using your name as editor.

6. Insert appropriate headers and/or footers.

7. Create or copy styles for the newsletter, then apply them where appropriate. Save the document.

8. Insert attractive design elements to enhance the appearance of your newsletter, including graphics, drop caps, pull quotes, multiple columns, text wrapped around graphics, a table of contents, shading, and, if you have access to a color printer, color. Save the document.

9. Print the newsletter and its style sheet.

Customizing Word

Creating a Customized Interoffice Memo Template

OBJECTIVES

In this tutorial you will:

- Describe the customization strategy
- Modify a predefined document template
- Change margins using the ruler
- Add boilerplate text to a template
- Create and insert an AutoText entry
- Insert, display, and update field codes
- Create, edit, and save macros
- Customize a toolbar, menu structure, and keyboard shortcuts
- Create an automatic macro
- Print template documentation

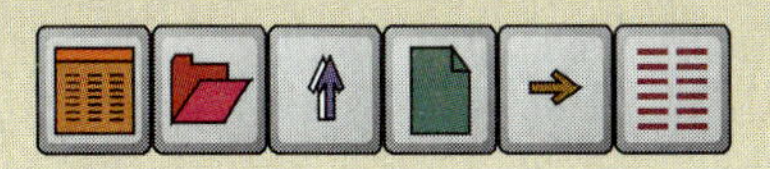

CASE

RoadMasters International   One month ago, Jay Calamari joined the Nashville office of RoadMasters International (RMI), after graduating with a business administration degree in decision support systems. RMI provides contract road managers for gigs (entertainment events) in venues throughout the world. RMI has two other offices, one in London and the other in Rio de Janeiro. Armed with his recently earned degree and his college work experience as the road manager for a college country western band, Jay is primed to set the entertainment world on fire. Unfortunately, he is getting bogged down in all the paperwork he has to do. Jay has decided to automate as much of his work as possible by creating customized templates for the different types of documents he has to produce. Because the templates provided by Word don't fit his working style, Jay decides to customize a template to meet his needs.

In this tutorial you will complete Jay's task of creating a customized document template for one type of document—memos—which he creates frequently. You will also learn an efficient strategy for creating a customized document template.

Customizing the Work Environment

The goal of using the advanced technologies available to business today is to increase the productivity of the workforce and to enable workers "to work smarter, not harder." To take advantage of the potential of technology, you must be able to match the working environment provided by the technology with the work you have to complete; that is, you must be able to customize the technology to fit your needs.

Word provides several time-saving features that allow you to customize your work environment—you have already used some of these; others are presented in this tutorial. These customizations can be divided into two categories—those that affect the text and appearance properties of the document, and those that affect the properties of the Word interface. The following customization features help you to automate the production of a document:

- boilerplate text—text that is the same in every document based on that template
- styles—character and paragraph styles that can be specifically designed for a particular type of document
- AutoText entries—repeatedly used text or graphics that can be inserted automatically as needed in a document
- fields—placeholders that allow you to insert text that varies from document to document
- customized menus, toolbars, and keyboard shortcuts—features that allow you to determine how Word should operate
- macros—series of recorded keystrokes and commands that are included in a template to automate certain procedures necessary to create, edit, format, or print a document

When you customize a template with one or more of these features, they become available to all documents you create based on that template. You can also choose to save customizations in the NORMAL template to make the features available to *all* new documents you create, instead of just the documents you create with a particular template. Creating customized templates with special features designed to fit your work style and preferences greatly increases your productivity.

You need a structured approach to customization just as you need the structured approach to document production provided by the productivity strategy. In this tutorial you will use the customization strategy to help you personalize Word's working environment to your work needs.

Using the Customization Strategy

Not all the documents that you produce deserve to have their own specialized document template. You must first analyze your work patterns and document production process to reveal classes of documents that you create routinely and that would lend themselves to a customized template.

Once you have determined which types of documents you create repeatedly, you should follow the **customization strategy** to plan the features to be included in the template; to create the text template features; to create the interface template features; to evaluate and revise, if necessary, the template features assigned to your new template; and finally, to print the template documentation.

During the **planning** phase of the customization strategy, you analyze the structure of a class of documents you create repeatedly to determine what they have in common. You must also decide on the interface properties you want to include; that is, how you want Word to operate. You determine the customization features to include in the customized template.

The next step is **creating text features** that you assign to the template. Decisions concerning the text properties of a customized document template include those default text characteristics assigned to a document when you create it. These decisions include margin settings, page orientation, page size, and styles designed specifically for the template so that every document based on that template will have the same appearance.

The next phase of the customization strategy involves **creating interface template properties**, which affect how Word operates during the document production process. Decisions concerning Word's interface can include creating customized toolbars, menus, or keyboard shortcuts.

The next phase involves **testing**, or evaluating, the template to determine whether it works correctly. If it does, the template is ready to use. If not, you need to revise those features that are not working properly and test the template again. Once the template is working satisfactorily, you can use it to create documents.

The final phase involves **printing documentation** for the template. This is an important task to complete because the documentation provides a record of the features included in the template and instructions for operating it.

In this tutorial you will complete Jay's task of developing a customized document template for producing interoffice memos for RMI, similar to the memo shown in Figure 7-1. This template will contain several customization features that fit Jay's work style. After developing the customized template, Jay will be able to produce future documents based on the template more efficiently.

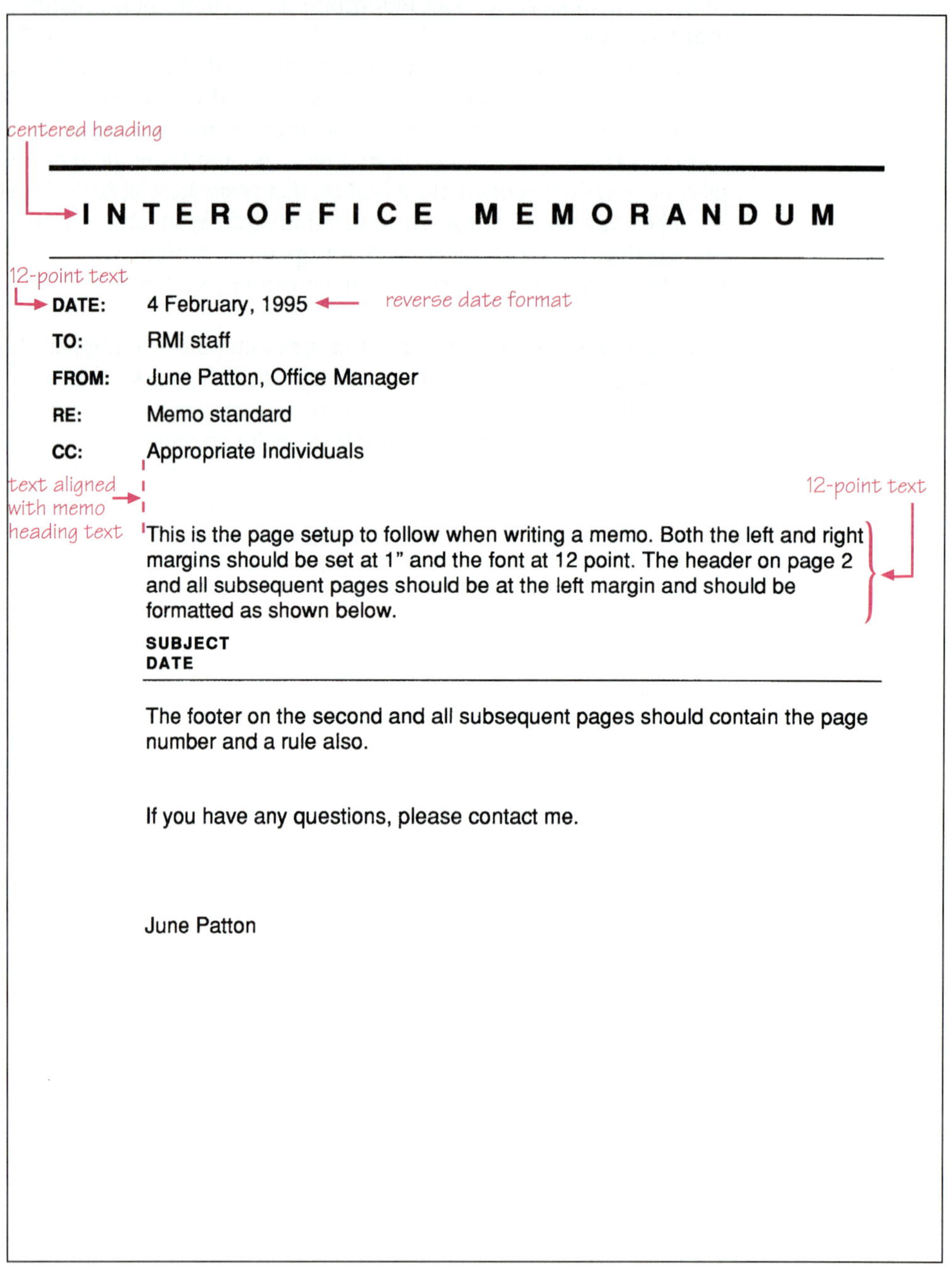

Figure 7-1
Features needed in
Jay's memo template

Planning the Template Features

The first phase of the customization strategy is to plan the features of the template based on the specialized text and operational needs of the specific class of documents. At his new employee orientation, Jay received a procedures manual describing the company's standards for all types of business communications. Figure 7-1 shows RMI's requirements for an interoffice memo.

Jay has completed some preliminary groundwork on his template. He determined that the MEMO2 template provided with Word could be modified to fit the formatting requirements of RMI, but he would have to add several features to automate the document creation process. He'll also need to organize Word's working environment to suit his working style. Figure 7-2 shows Jay's plan for modifying the MEMO2 template.

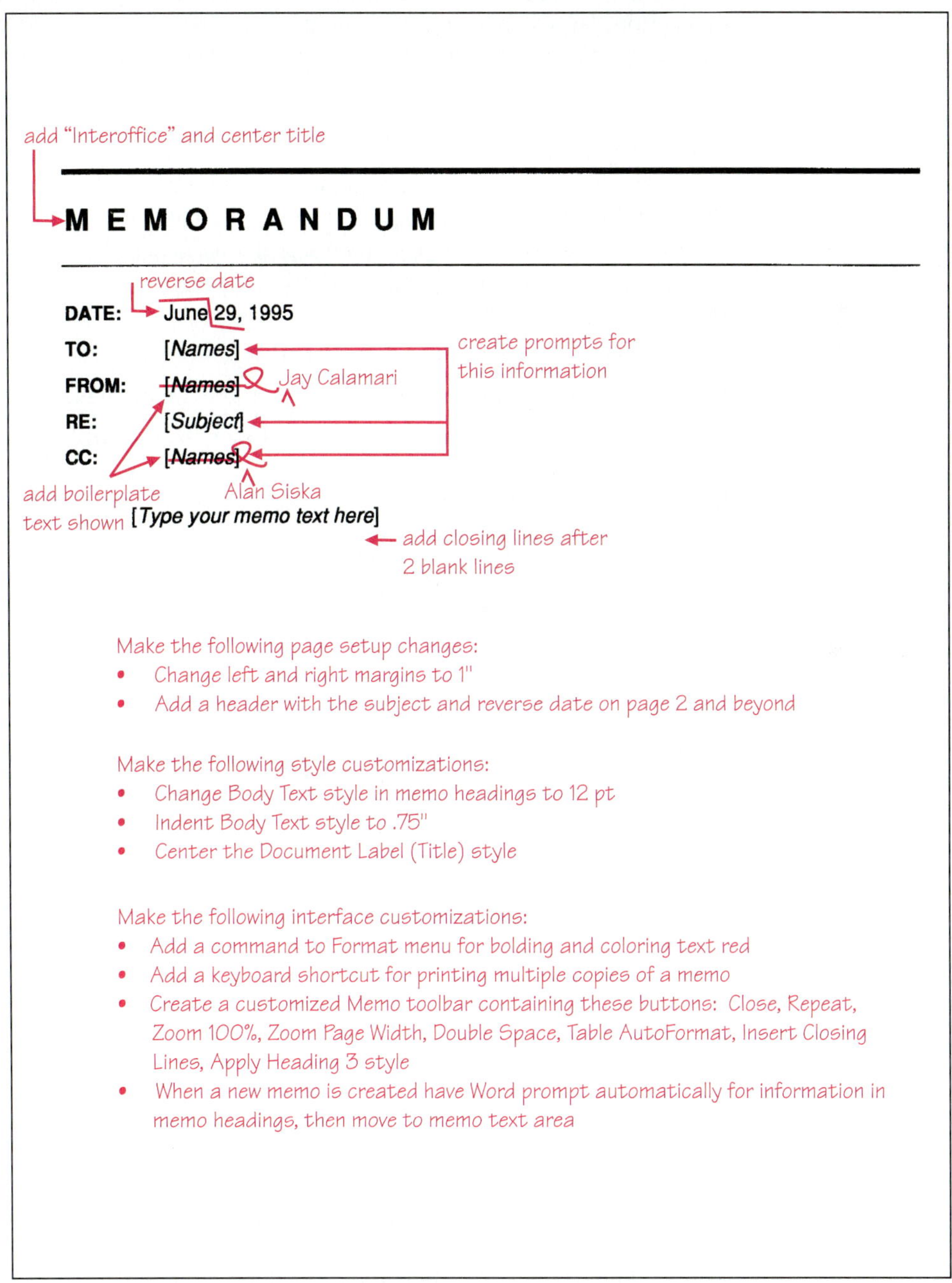

Figure 7-2
Jay's plan for modifying the MEMO2 template

Now that Jay has planned the features of his template, he is ready to move to the next phase of the customization strategy—creating the template's text and interface properties.

Customizing a Predefined Template

Word provides you with several ways to create document templates. As you learned in Tutorial 5, you can create a template from an existing document. You can also modify an existing template or create a template from scratch.

Jay is now ready to create his new document template for interoffice memos. As a precaution, Jay will activate the option to confirm changes to NORMAL.DOT so that the changes he makes will affect only his new template and not the NORMAL template.

To create a new template:

❶   Start Word, if necessary, and conduct the screen check as described in Tutorial 1.

❷   Click **Tools** then click **Options…**. The Options dialog box appears.

❸   Click the **Save tab** then click the **Prompt to Save Normal.dot check box** to activate it. Do not clear the check box if it is already selected.

❹   Click **OK** or press **[Enter]**.

❺   Click **File** then click **New…**. The New dialog box appears.

Jay wants to base his customized template on the MEMO2 template.

❻   Click **Memo2** in the Template list box. Notice the description of the template at the bottom of the dialog box.

❼   Click the **Template radio button** in the New section of the dialog box. *Do not press [Enter]*. See Figure 7-3.

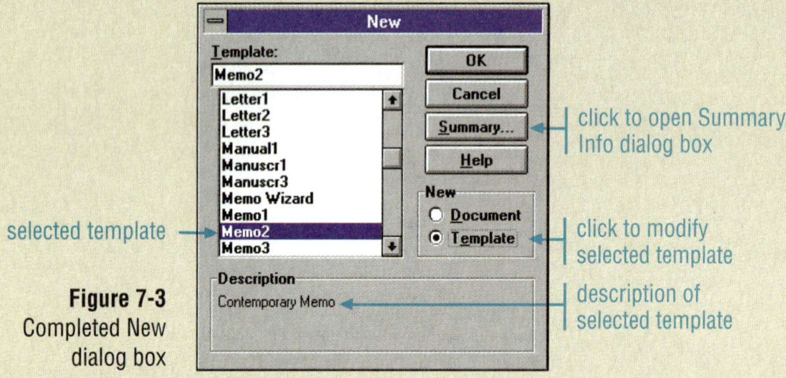

Figure 7-3
Completed New dialog box

Jay wants a description of the new template to appear at the bottom of the New dialog box. To do this, he must complete the Summary Info dialog box with the appropriate description.

Completing the Summary Info Dialog Box

Word summarizes information about a document for reference purposes in the Summary Info dialog box. You can also type information that contains pertinent data about the document for future reference. You open the Summary Info dialog box either from the New dialog box by clicking Summary, or by choosing Summary Info from the File menu. You can change Word's options to display the Summary Info dialog box automatically each time you save a document for the first time by selecting the Prompt for Summary Info check box on the Save tab of the Options dialog box.

Jay wants a description of the purpose of the new template to appear at the bottom of the New dialog box. This will be useful information for other RMI employees who might use the template. Jay must add the description to the Summary Info dialog box in order for it to appear in the New dialog box when the template is selected.

To complete the Summary Info dialog box:

❶ In the New dialog box, click **Summary....** The Summary Info dialog box appears.

> **TROUBLE?** If you closed the New dialog box in the previous steps, click File then click Summary Info... to display the Summary Info dialog box.

❷ In the Title text box, type **RMI's Interoffice Memo**. This text will appear as a description in the New dialog box when the template is selected in the future. See Figure 7-4.

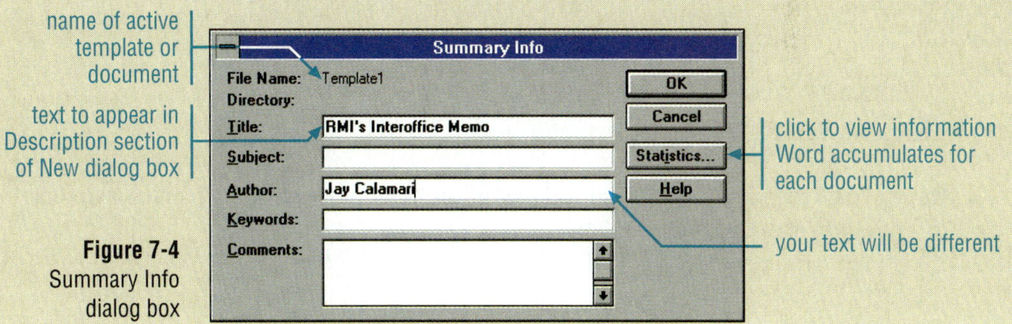

Figure 7-4
Summary Info dialog box

Jay wants to see the statistics that Word records for each document.

❸ Click **Statistics....** The Document Statistics window appears. Read the information that Word maintains for each document, then click **Close** or press **[Enter]**. You return to the Summary Info dialog box.

❹ Click **OK** or press **[Enter]**. The title bar changes to indicate that a template window is open rather than a document window. The rest of the template window appears the same as a document window.

> **TROUBLE?** If the title bar does not read "Template 1," you did not select Template from the New dialog box. Close this document, repeat the previous set of steps, then repeat Steps 1 through 4.

Jay decides to save his template immediately even though he has just begun to work on it. Usually, you save document templates to the WINWORD\TEMPLATES directory. However, you need to save this template to your Student Disk.

To save the document template to your Student Disk:

❶ Make sure your Student Disk is in the disk drive.

❷ Click the **Save button** 🖫 on the Standard toolbar (or click **File** then click **Save As...**). The Save As dialog box appears. Note that the file list contains only the filenames of Word's predesigned document templates and that all the options are dimmed.

To save a template to a directory other than WINWORD, you must type the full path name in the File Name text box.

❸   In the File Name text box, type **a:\s7intmem** to indicate that you want to save the document template to your Student Disk. If necessary, substitute the letter of the appropriate drive that contains your Student Disk. Word automatically adds the extension "DOT" to the template name. See Figure 7-5.

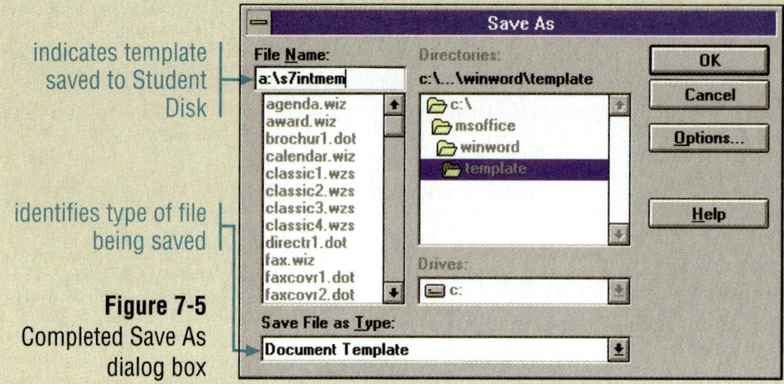

indicates template saved to Student Disk

identifies type of file being saved

Figure 7-5
Completed Save As dialog box

❹   Click **OK** or press [**Enter**]. The title bar in the template window changes to indicate the new name of the template.

Customizing Text Properties in a Template

As part of the customization strategy, Jay is now ready to customize the text properties in his template, including page setup, styles, and boilerplate text. These features, once assigned to the S7INTMEM template, will be part of every new document based on this template. The first change Jay wants to make is to adjust the margins.

Changing Margins Using the Ruler

The purpose of a template is to reduce the amount of time spent in setting up frequently used documents. For example, changes to margins, page orientation, and page size are some of the page setup customizations you can make to a document template.

In earlier tutorials you changed margin settings through the Page Setup dialog box on the File menu. However, you can easily make adjustments to the left and right margins or the top and bottom margins by using the ruler when the document is in page layout view.

Jay wants to change the left and right margins for his memos from 1.25 inches to 1 inch, and he decides to use the ruler to change them. He must change to page layout view first. Let's do that now.

To change the left margin using the ruler:
❶   Click the **Page Layout View button** ▤ in the horizontal scroll bar (or click **View** then click **Page Layout**).
❷   Move the mouse pointer over the left margin in the ruler so that the pointer straddles the dark and light areas. The pointer changes to ↔.

❸ Click and drag the pointer to the left until the "1" in the *dark* area of the ruler is immediately at the beginning of the ruler, on the left. See Figure 7-6.

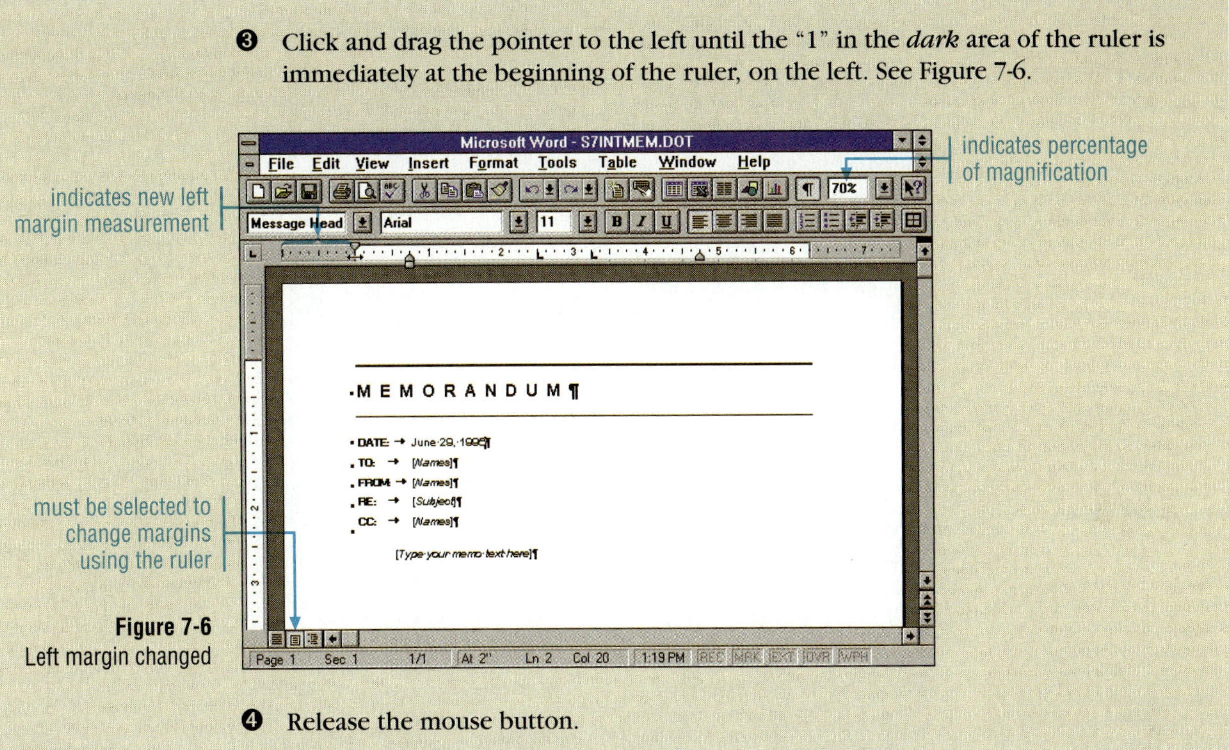

Figure 7-6
Left margin changed

❹ Release the mouse button.

Next Jay wants to change the right margin using the ruler.

To change the right margin using the ruler:
❶ Move the mouse pointer over the right margin in the ruler so that the pointer straddles the dark and light areas. The pointer changes to ↔.
❷ Click and drag the pointer to the right until the scale in the light area of the ruler is at the 6.5-inch mark. See Figure 7-7.

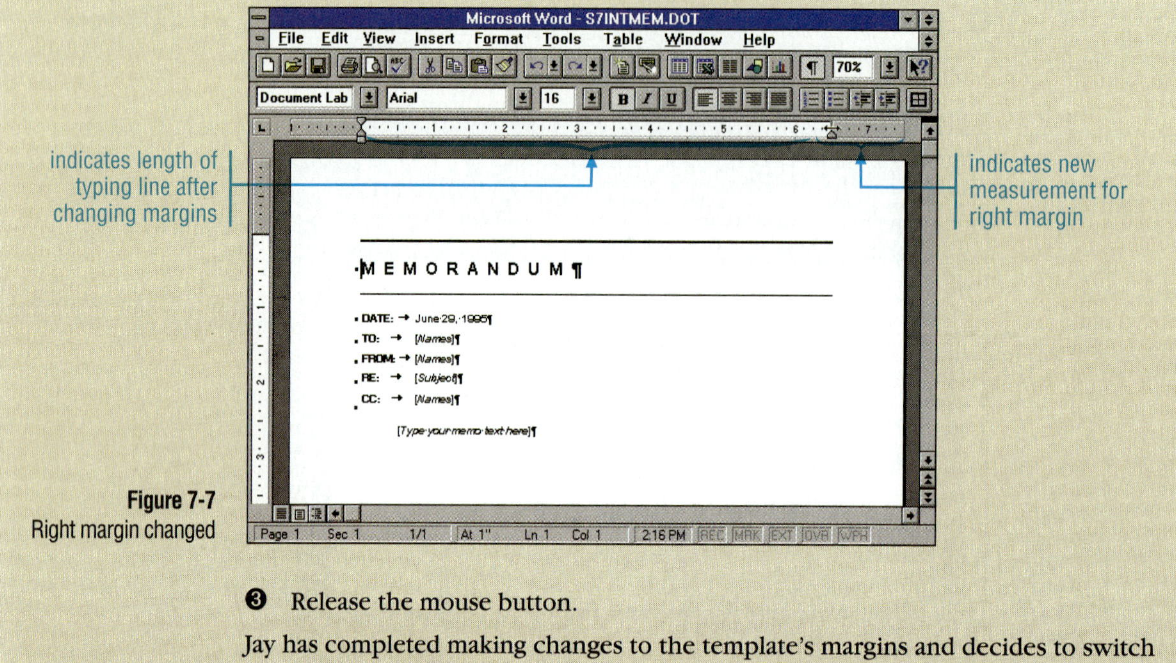

Figure 7-7
Right margin changed

❸ Release the mouse button.

Jay has completed making changes to the template's margins and decides to switch back to normal view.

❹ Click the **Normal View button** in the horizontal scroll bar (or click **View** then click **Normal**). The screen changes to normal view, but stays in Page Width Zoom view (92%).

> **TROUBLE?** If your screen is in 100% view, click the Zoom Control arrow, then click Page Width.

❺ Save your changes. In the future, when you use the template to create a new document, the document will appear in Page Width Zoom view, with the specified margins.

Using Styles to Customize Word

Creating custom styles for use in templates is essential for quick formatting of documents. In Tutorials 3 and 5, you learned how to apply Word's predefined styles and how to define and apply your own styles. By planning the structure of a template according to the *sequence* of the styles to be used, you can further increase your efficiency in producing documents.

Two features to consider when planning styles are the base style for a group of styles, and the style for the paragraph following the current paragraph. A **base style** is simply a paragraph style upon which other paragraph styles are based. You specify the base style using the Based On option in the New Style or Modify Style dialog box. As illustrated in Figure 7-8, you can quickly modify the attributes shared by styles when you modify the base style. For instance, a change in the Heading base style ripples through all other styles based on it, eliminating the need to modify each individual style.

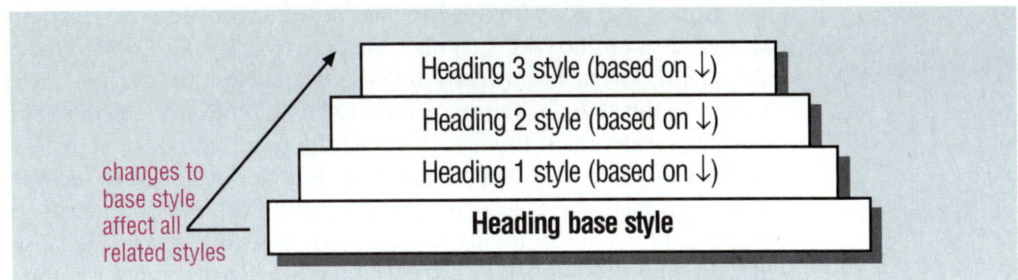

Figure 7-8
How the base
style works

The Style for Following Paragraph option in the New Style or Modify Style dialog box governs the style applied to the paragraph that *comes after* the current paragraph style; that is, when you press [Enter] and create a new paragraph. Using the Style for Following Paragraph option when defining a style eliminates the need for you to apply styles individually to each new paragraph.

Jay is not sure which styles have been applied to the visible elements of the template. He decides to display the style area so that he can see the applied styles.

To display the style area:
1. Click **Tools** then click **Options…**. The Options dialog box appears.
2. Click the **View tab**, if necessary, then increase the Style Area Width option to **1.5"**.
3. Click **OK** or press **[Enter]**.

Jay uses the Style dialog box to look up the style definitions of the Message Header styles and finds out that they are based on the Body Text style. Figure 7-9 shows the definitions for the other styles used in the template.

Style Name	Based On	Additional Attributes	Style for Following Paragraph
Body Text	Normal	Space After 6 pt	
Message Header	Body Text	Indent: Hanging 0.75" Right 1.5", Keep Lines Together, Tab stops: 2.5", 3.25"	
Message Header First	Message Header	Space Before 6 pt	Message Header
Message Header Label (character style)	Font for underlying paragraph style	Font: 10 pt, Bold, All Caps	
Message Header Last	Message Header	Space After 18 pt	Body Text
Normal		Font: Arial 11pt, Indent: Left 0.5" Flush left, Line Spacing Single, Widow/Orphan Control	

Figure 7-9
S7INTMEM template
style definitions

Notice that Body Text is the base style for the Message Header styles and that the font size is 11 point, not the 12 point required by RMI. Also notice that the Style for Following Paragraph option has already been activated for the current styles in this template; for example, the style for the paragraph following Message Header Last is Body Text.

Jay doesn't need to change any of the base style or next style options that were originally defined for the MEMO2 template, but he does need to modify some of the attributes of the template styles to make them conform to RMI's standards. Jay needs to change the font for the memo headings and the body text to 12 point. Because the affected styles are all based on the Body Text style, Jay needs to change only the font in the Body Text style (the base style for the Message Header styles) to make the necessary changes in the styles based on it. He also needs to modify the Body Text style so that it will align with the text after the memo headings. He will redefine the Body Text style by example.

To modify the Body Text style by example:

❶ Move the insertion point to the end of the document into the Body Text style area, then select the entire line beginning **[Type your memo text here]**, including the paragraph mark at the end of the line. Notice that the Font Size list box indicates 11 pt.

❷ Click the **Font Size list box down arrow** on the Formatting toolbar, then click 12.

Jay also wants the body text of the memo to align with the text after the memo headings.

❸ With the text still selected, drag the rectangle under the left indent marker to .75 inches on the ruler so that the body text aligns with the text after the memo headings.

Now that Jay has changed the paragraph Body Text style to match RMI's standard for memo body text, he can redefine the Body Text style by example.

❹ Click **Body Text** in the Style text box on the Formatting toolbar to select the style name, then press **[Enter]**. The Reapply Style dialog box appears.

❺ Make sure the option for redefining the style is selected, then click **OK** or press **[Enter]**. The Body Text style is redefined with the new font size and left margin, and the Message Header styles are redefined automatically with the new font size because they're based on the Body Text style.

To make sure that the font for the Message Header lines has changed, Jay moves the insertion point up.

❻ Place the insertion point after the TO: memo heading. Notice that the Font Size list box now shows 12. By changing the base style for a group of related styles, you also change all related styles, thus saving production time.

Jay must also change the alignment of the memo title MEMORANDUM to centered, as specified by RMI's standards. Therefore, he needs to change the Document Label style to centered alignment for his template.

To modify the Document Label style:

❶ Place the insertion point in the title MEMORANDUM, then click the **Center button** on the Formatting toolbar. The title is now centered.

Now Jay needs to redefine the Document Label style by example.

❷   Click **Document Label** in the Style text box on the Formatting toolbar to select the style, then press **[Enter]**. The Reapply Style dialog box appears.

❸   Make sure the option for redefining the style is selected, then click **OK** or press **[Enter]**.

Jay no longer needs to view the style names.

❹   Click **Tools** then click **Options**.... The Options dialog box appears. Decrease the Style Area Width option to **0"**.

❺   Click **OK** or press **[Enter]**.

❻   Save your changes.

Next Jay will insert another text customization feature—boilerplate text—into his template.

Using Boilerplate Text to Customize Word

As you learned earlier in the book, boilerplate text is text that stays the same from document to document. When considering whether to add boilerplate text to a document template, you must determine which text is common to every document in the same class of documents. After you insert it into a template, boilerplate text appears in every new document based on the template, saving time in the document production process.

The memo already contains some boilerplate text—the title MEMORANDUM and the memo headings TO:, FROM:, RE:, DATE:, and CC:. Jay must add the word INTEROFFICE to the title, per RMI memo standards, and the name of his boss, Alan Siska, as one recipient of a copy. Jay will also add his name after the FROM: memo heading. Let's add this boilerplate text now.

To add boilerplate text to the template:

❶   Place the insertion point in front of MEMORANDUM, type **INTEROFFICE** then press **[Spacebar]**.

Jay doesn't want to spend time typing his name after the FROM: memo heading each time he creates a memo, so he decides to insert his name as boilerplate text.

❷   Select **[Names]** after the FROM: memo heading. Do *not* include the paragraph mark.

❸   Type **Jay Calamari**. [Names] is replaced with Jay Calamari.

   TROUBLE?   If you selected [Names] after the TO: memo heading instead of after FROM:, click the Undo button 🗘 on the Standard toolbar (or click Edit then click Undo Typing), then repeat Steps 2 and 3.

Jay must send a copy of every memo to his boss, Alan Siska. From time to time, he might also need to send copies to other people.

❹   Select **[Names]** after the CC: memo heading, then type **Alan Siska**.

Jay wants the insertion point to move under the "A" in Alan so that he can type the name of anyone else who needs to receive a copy, and this text will align with Alan's name. However, the style in effect now, Message Header, includes a Style for Following Paragraph option. If he inserts a paragraph mark, the Body Text style will be applied automatically to the next paragraph, which would be incorrect. Jay must insert a new

line mark instead of a paragraph mark so that the Style for Following Paragraph option
won't take effect.

❺   Press **[Shift][Enter]**. A new line mark is inserted, and the insertion point moves
below the name.

❻   Save your changes.

Next, Jay needs to insert text for the closing lines of his memo. Rather than inserting
this text as boilerplate text, he decides to create an AutoText entry for these lines.

Creating AutoText Entries

An **AutoText entry** is a block of text or graphics—such as the closing signature lines of a
letter or memo, special characters or symbols like a company name or logo, paragraphs of
extended text, or graphics—that is used repeatedly without revision. An AutoText entry
can be a single character or multiple pages of text. You select the text or graphic to be
stored as an AutoText entry, then you assign it a short name using either the Edit AutoText
button or by selecting the AutoText command from the Edit menu. An AutoText name can
contain up to 31 characters, including spaces. You must also decide whether you want
the AutoText entry to be available to all documents or just to documents based on a particular template.

REFERENCE WINDOW

Creating an AutoText Entry

■   Select the block of text or the graphics you want to store as an
AutoText entry.

■   Click the Edit AutoText button on the Standard toolbar, or click Edit
then click AutoText.... The AutoText dialog box appears.

■   In the Name text box, type a name for the AutoText entry.

■   Click Add.

After defining an AutoText entry, you can insert the text stored in the entry at any
location in a document. To insert an AutoText entry, place the insertion point at the location where you want the stored text to appear, type the short name of the AutoText entry,
then click the Insert AutoText button (the same button as the Edit AutoText button) or
press the Insert AutoText key ([F3]), then select the AutoText entry name.

Once he has finished writing a memo, Jay wants to be able to quickly insert the closing
lines required by RMI. He decides to create an AutoText entry for the closing lines so that he
can control when they are inserted. According to RMI standards, the layout of the closing
lines requires two blank lines after the last line of a memo, and then the writer's name.

To create an AutoText entry for the closing lines:

❶ Press **[Ctrl][End]** to move the insertion point to the end of the document (Ln 10). Note that line numbers are given for reference only; depending on your monitor, the line number might be different.

❷ Press **[Enter]** three times then type **Jay Calamari**.

Now that Jay has created the AutoText entry, he is ready to store it. Jay will store the AutoText entry in the S7INTMEM template rather than in the NORMAL template because he wants to use it only when creating memo documents.

To store the AutoText entry:

❶ Select the closing lines of text you just typed, including the three paragraph marks above Jay's name and the one following. See Figure 7-10.

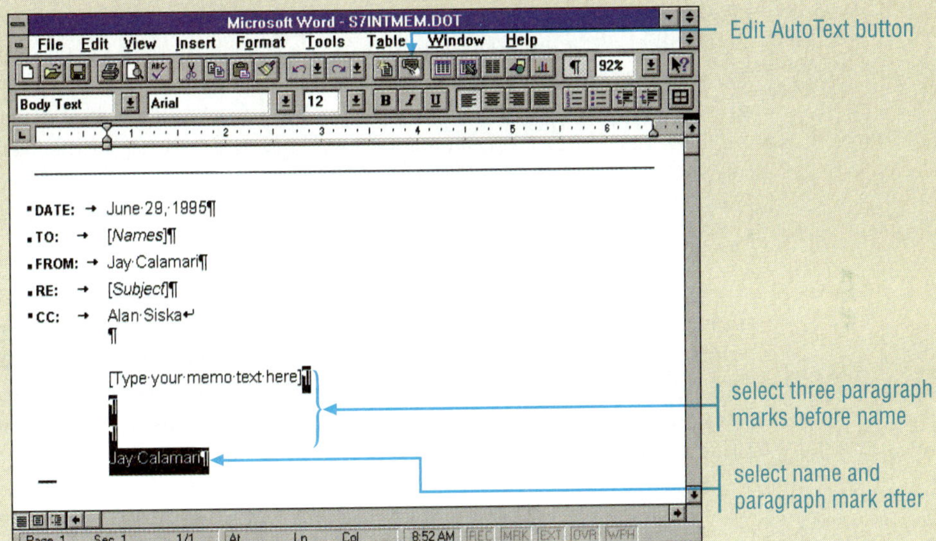

Figure 7-10
Selected text for AutoText entry

❷ Click the **Edit AutoText button** on the Standard toolbar (or click **Edit** then click **AutoText...**). The AutoText dialog box appears.

❸ Type **Closing** in the Name text box as the name for the AutoText entry. *Do not press [Enter]*.

Jay wants the AutoText entry stored with this template only, not in the NORMAL template.

❹ Click the **Make AutoText Entry Available To list box down arrow**, then click **Documents Based On S7intmem.dot**. See Figure 7-11.

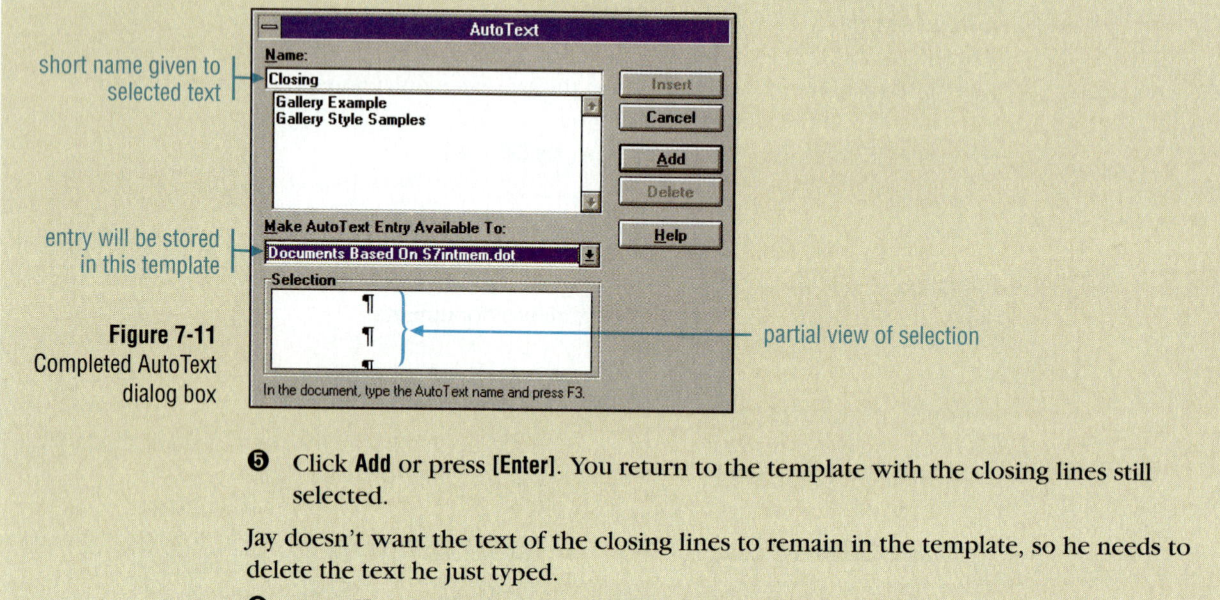

Figure 7-11
Completed AutoText
dialog box

❺ Click **Add** or press **[Enter]**. You return to the template with the closing lines still selected.

Jay doesn't want the text of the closing lines to remain in the template, so he needs to delete the text he just typed.

❻ Press **[Del]** to delete the selected text.

❼ Save your changes.

Jay will test this AutoText entry by inserting it in a test document later.

If you want to take a break and resume the tutorial at a later time, close the document and exit Word. Do not save any changes to the NORMAL template. When you want to resume the tutorial, start Word then conduct the screen check described in Tutorial 1. Open the S7INTMEM template from your Student Disk, activate the Prompt to Save Normal.dot check box on the Save tab of the Options dialog box, if necessary, then continue with the tutorial.

Next Jay wants to customize the template further by creating ways to insert variable text in the documents he will create using the memo template.

Inserting Variable Text

In addition to including boilerplate text, which does not change, in a template, you'll often want Word to automatically insert variable text into documents based on your custom template. For instance, the date or the person receiving the document is variable text because it can change from document to document. To instruct Word to insert this type of text automatically, you need to insert fields that contain instructions representing the type of information you want Word to display.

In Tutorial 4 you used merge field codes to insert variable information from a data source into your merged documents. You also inserted a date field code that was automatically updated to the current date as determined by your computer's clock. You also inserted a page field code when you clicked the Page Number button on the Header and Footer toolbar to have Word automatically number the pages of your documents.

Word supports a total of 68 field types that can help you automate many tasks. Usually, when you insert a field you see the *field results* (for example, 29 June, 1995) rather than the *field code* (for example, {DATE}). **Field results** can be text, graphics, or numbers. By default, Word shades inserted fields—either results or codes—so that you will not mistakenly delete them while editing.

After you insert a field in a document, the displayed results won't change until you instruct Word to **update**, or evaluate, the field. Word evaluates the field based on the current values in the document. Some fields, such as the date and time, are updated automatically when you print a document, but you must update most fields manually. However, you can also have Word update all fields automatically when you print a document.

Because of the importance of fields, Word provides several shortcut keys and key combinations to make working with them easier. Figure 7-12 lists these shortcut keys.

Shortcut Keys	Purpose
[Shift][F9]	Toggle the display of individual fields between results or codes
[F9]	Update a field
[F11]	Move to the next field and select it
[Shift][F11]	Move to the previous field and select it
[Ctrl][F9]	Insert a field
[Ctrl][F11]	Lock a field
[Ctrl][Shift][F11]	Unlock a field
[Ctrl][Shift][F9]	Unlink a field

Figure 7-12
Keyboard shortcuts for fields

Understanding Field Code Syntax

A field code can include one or more of the following components: field characters, a field name, and field instructions (Figure 7-13). **Field characters** are the curly braces that mark the beginning and end of the field. The **field name**, or **field type**, describes what the field does. Some fields require **field instructions** that specify the general action of a field. **Switches**, which must be preceded by a backslash (\), are optional instructions that alter the format of the field's results. Each field code has its own **syntax**, the arrangement of the field name, instructions, and switch options for a field within the field characters.

Figure 7-13
Elements of a field code

Inserting Field Codes

The easiest way to insert field codes is to use the Insert Field command, and then choose the appropriate field from the list displayed in the Field dialog box. The various fields are divided into nine broad categories based on function (Figure 7-14).

Category	Associated Fields
Date and Time	CreateDate, Date, EditTime, PrintDate, SaveDate, Time
Document Automation	Compare, GoToButton, If, MacroButton, Print
Document Information	Author, Comments, FileName, FileSize, Info, Keywords, LastSavedBy, NumChars, NumPages, NumWords, Subject, Template, Title
Equations and Formulas	=(Formula), Advance, Eq, Symbol
Index and Tables	Index, RD, TA, TC, TOA, TOC, XE
Links and References	AutoText, IncludePicture, IncludeText, Link, NoteRef, PageRef, Quote, Ref, StyleRef
Mail Merge	Ask, Compare, Database, Fill-in, If, MergeField, MergeRec, MergeSeq, Next, NextIf, Set, SkipIf
Numbering	AutoNum, AutoNumLgl, AutoNumOut, BarCode, Page, RevNum, Section, SectionPages, Seq
User Information	UserAddress, UserInitials, UserName

Figure 7-14
Field categories

If you know the name of the field you want to insert, you can scroll through the list of field names in the Field dialog box to select it. The dialog box also displays the correct syntax for the selected field, as well as any optional instructions available for the field. By using the Field dialog box to help you build field codes, you don't have to remember all the different field names, their correct syntax, and the various options. You can also insert a field code by pressing [Ctrl][F9] to insert the pair of field characters, then typing the correct syntax for the field you want to insert. You cannot use the curly braces on the keyboard as field characters, however. For an explanation of the function of each field code, see the References section at the end of this book.

Jay is not sure which field code was inserted originally in the MEMO2 template to produce the date shown. He must view the field code for the field.

You can either view the results of a field, or you can view the field code itself. You can toggle between the two types of display for a single field or selected fields by using the Toggle Field key, [Shift][F9], or by clicking the right mouse button while pointing to either the selected field result or the field code, then clicking Toggle Field Codes in the shortcut menu.

Let's view the field code for the date field in the template.

To display the field code for the date:
❶ Click the **date** with the right mouse button. The shortcut menu appears. Note that the menu is context-sensitive; because you clicked a field code, options for working with fields appear in the menu. See Figure 7-15.

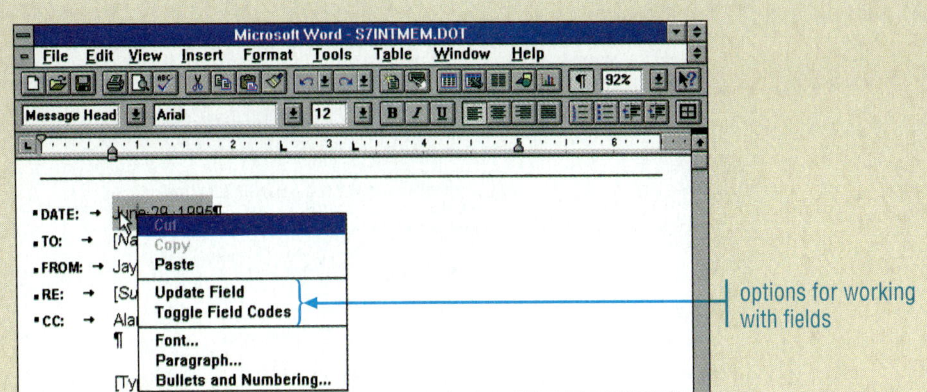

Figure 7-15
Shortcut menu

❷   Click **Toggle Field Codes**. The field code that produces the date is displayed rather than the field results. This code specifies the date format "Month Day, Year."

Jay decides to switch back to the field results display.

❸   Press **[Shift][F9]**. The results are again displayed.

Jay needs to change the field code for the date to conform to RMI's standards.

Inserting a Date and Time Category Field Code

The Date and Time field category enables you to insert the system date or time as well as other information that Word creates for each document, such as the date created, the date last saved, the date printed, and the total editing time. You can view this information in the Statistics window of the Summary Info dialog box. The syntax for each of the field codes that produce these results (except for the EDITTIME field code) is:

{FIELDNAME [\@ "Date-Time Picture"]}

The \@ tells Word to insert either the system date or time, depending on the field name, but to format the result as specified by the Date-Time Picture instruction. The **Date-Time Picture** is a special instruction that tells Word how to format the inserted date or time. You can type a custom Date-Time Picture, or you can select from the available Date-Time options. Figure 7-16 describes the symbols used in the date format options. The Date-Time Picture instruction is inserted in quotation marks because this instruction is longer than one word. Word reads each group of characters followed by a space as one instruction, so each instruction longer than one word must be enclosed in quotation marks; otherwise Word would misinterpret your intentions and an error would occur.

Character	Purpose	Example
M (capital only)	Month in numeric format	6
MM	Month in numeric format with a leading zero in front of single digit months	06
MMM	Month abbreviated as three letters	Jun
MMMM	Month spelled out	June
d	Day in numeric format, 1-31	29
dd	Day in numeric format with a leading zero in front of single digit months	29
ddd	Day of week abbreviated as three letters	Mon
dddd	Day of week spelled out	Monday
y	Last two digits of year	95
yy	Year	1995

Figure 7-16
Date format options

Jay wants the current date to appear every time he creates a document based on his memo template, but he doesn't want the date changed if he prints the same memo at a later date. Rather than use the current field code, which would be updated to the system date each time he prints the document, Jay wants to restrict the date printed to the document creation date. He must replace the current field code with a CREATEDATE field code. Also, Jay needs to change the date format in the template to the reverse date format, which is the company's standard, so he will use d MMMM, yyyy as the Date-Time Picture.

To insert a CREATEDATE field code:

❶ Click the **date** after the DATE: memo heading. Notice that Word shades fields—either results or codes—to make them identifiable.

Next Jay must select the field. A field is not selected unless it is highlighted with a dark gray shading and the text in the field is white.

❷ Double-click the **date** to select the field. Dark gray shading appears behind the field.

❸ Click **Insert** then click **Field…**. The Field dialog box appears.

❹ Click **Date and Time** in the Categories list box. Notice that the various field names associated with this category appear, and the CreateDate field name is selected by default. Notice also that its syntax appears as a guideline for you next to Field Codes, and the code CREATEDATE is added to the Field Codes text box. A description of the selected field also appears in the Description section. You might want to click each different Date and Time field name and read its description.

❺ With CreateDate selected in the Field Names list box, click **Options…**. The Field Options dialog box appears. Several date and time formats are listed in the Date-Time Formats list box.

Next Jay needs to specify the reverse date format.

❻ Click the third date format (d MMMM, yyyy), then click **Add to Field** or press **[Enter]**. The Date-Time Picture instruction is added to the Field Codes text box in quotation marks. See Figure 7-17.

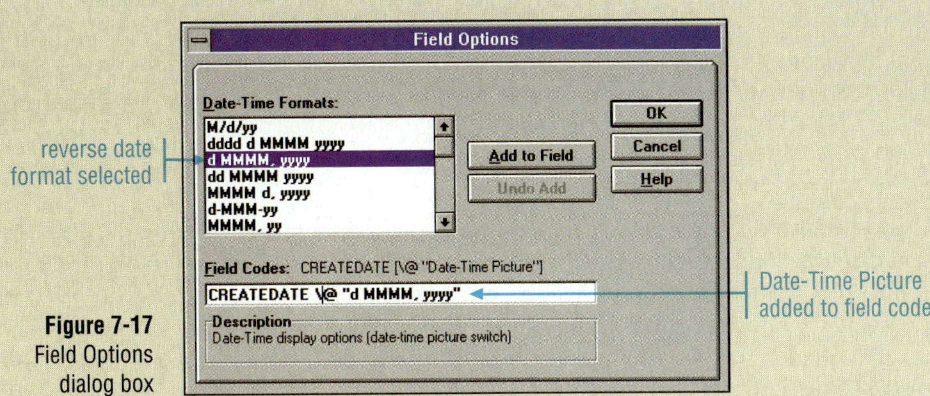

reverse date format selected

Date-Time Picture added to field code

Figure 7-17
Field Options
dialog box

❼ Click **OK** or press **[Enter]**. The completed field code appears in the Field dialog box. Notice that the Preserve Formatting During Updates check box is selected by default in the Field dialog box. With this option selected, any formatting directly applied to the field code will be preserved during updates; if the option is deselected, any direct formatting will be lost during subsequent updates of the field. See Figure 7-18.

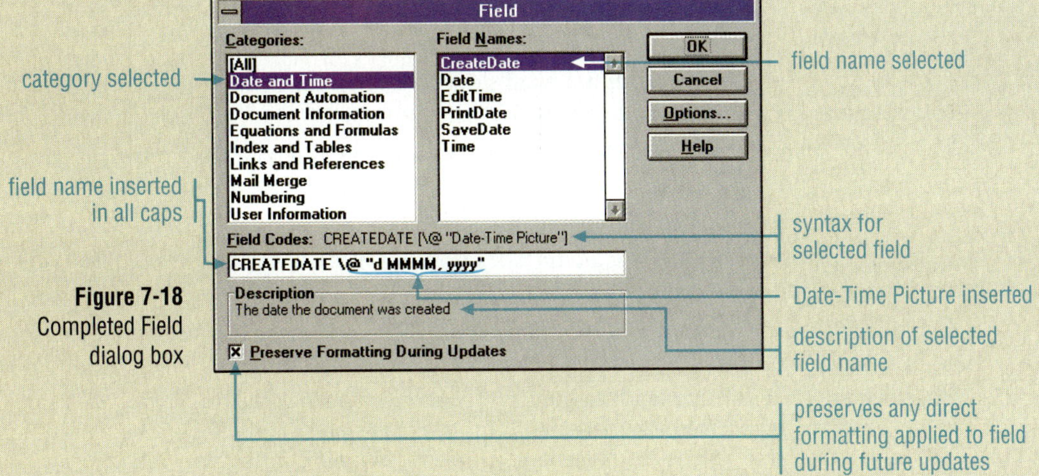

category selected

field name selected

field name inserted in all caps

syntax for selected field

Date-Time Picture inserted

description of selected field name

preserves any direct formatting applied to field during future updates

Figure 7-18
Completed Field
dialog box

❽ Click **OK** or press **[Enter]**. The CREATEDATE field is inserted in the template with the results displayed. Also the date now appears in the reverse date format.

TROUBLE?   If the field code appears instead of the results, click Tools, click Options..., click the View tab, then click the Field Codes check box to deselect it.

TROUBLE?   If you inserted the field code in the wrong location, delete it by selecting the entire field code then pressing [Del]. Repeat Steps 1 through 8. Or, if a second date appears, you did not have the original date selected first. Click the Undo button ↰ on the Standard toolbar (or click Edit then click Undo Insert Field), then repeat Steps 1 through 8.

❾ Save your changes.

Jay has several more field codes to insert that will help him automate the completion of the memo headings. He doesn't want to have to switch between viewing field results and field codes for each field he inserts to see if the code inserted produces the results he wants. Therefore, he decides to display only the field codes.

Viewing All Field Codes

If you want to display the field codes throughout a document rather than the field results, you can toggle the screen view by selecting the Field Codes check box on the View tab of the Options dialog box. If you will be working with field codes extensively, you can split the window into two panes using the split box, and then toggle one of the panes to view the field codes so that you can see both the field codes and the field results simultaneously. With both field views displayed, you can determine immediately if the codes you inserted produce the results you expected.

Jay decides to turn on field codes for the entire document and also to split the template window into two panes so he can see both the field results and the field codes.

To toggle between field views:

❶ Click **Tools**, click **Options...**, then click the **View tab** if necessary.

❷ Click the **Field Codes check box** in the Show section of the View tab, then click **OK** or press **[Enter]**. The field code that Jay inserted for the date is displayed instead of the results of the field.

Jay wants to be able to see both the results of the fields he inserts as well as the field codes so that he will not have to toggle between views.

❸ Double-click the **split box**. The template window splits into two panes with the insertion point flashing in the bottom pane. Scroll the bottom pane up so that the boilerplate text appears in both panes.

Next Jay must turn off the View Field Codes option for the bottom pane so that it will display the results of any fields inserted.

❹ Place the insertion point in the bottom pane, if necessary, click **Tools**, then click **Options...** to display this dialog box again.

❺ Click the **Field Codes check box** in the Show section of the View tab to deselect it, then click **OK** or press **[Enter]**. The screen is now split into two panes, the bottom pane showing results and the top pane showing field codes. Notice that the * MERGEFORMAT instruction is added to the field code because the Preserve Formatting During Updates check box was selected in the Field dialog box. See Figure 7-19.

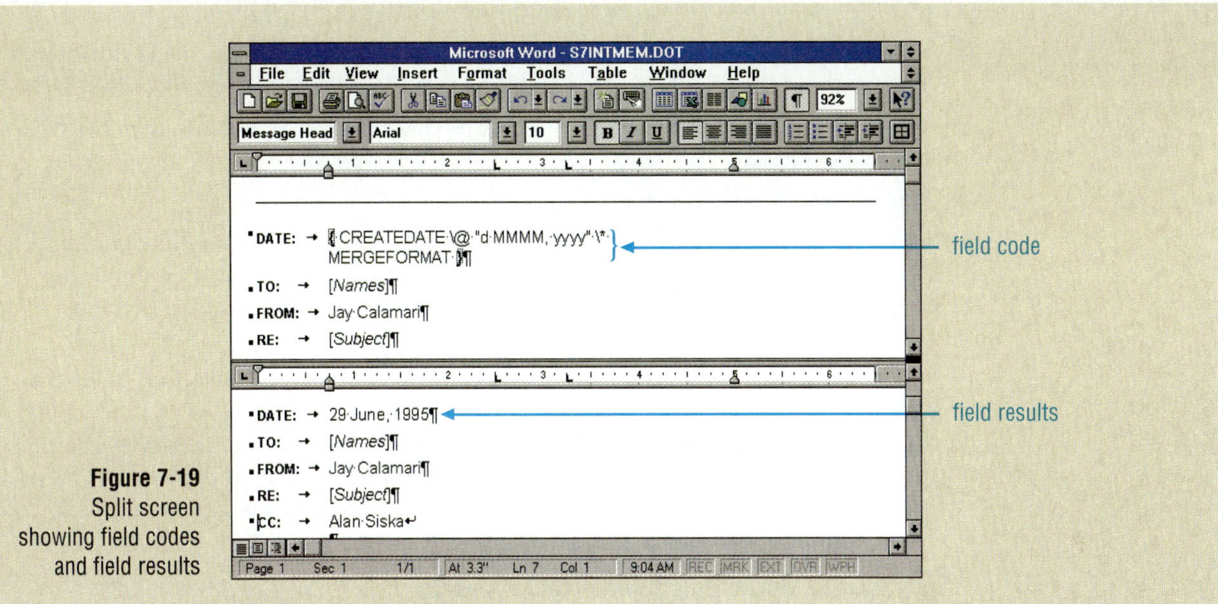

Figure 7-19
Split screen
showing field codes
and field results

Now that Jay has arranged his screen so that he can view both field results and field codes at the same time, he can continue inserting fields into his template that will help him automate the document production process.

Inserting FILLIN Field Codes

Several of Word's fields allow you to request input from the user. Once the user responds to Word's request for information, Word inserts the information in the appropriate location. The FILLIN and ASK fields prompt the user through a dialog box. Because these fields are used most often during the mail merge process, both are considered Mail Merge category fields.

Jay wants Word to prompt him to type the name of the recipient of his memos. He then wants Word to insert the recipient's name in the correct location after the TO: memo heading. Jay wants to be prompted with the question "Who is to receive this memo?" in a dialog box. To create this type of prompt, he must insert a FILLIN field.

To insert the FILLIN field:

❶ With the bottom pane still active, select **[Names]** after the TO: memo heading in this pane. Do not include the ending paragraph mark. Click **Insert** then click **Field....** The Field dialog box appears.

❷ Click **Mail Merge** in the Categories list box, then click **Fill-in** in the Field Names list box. Notice that the syntax guide for the FILLIN field code is displayed, the FILLIN field name is inserted in the Field Codes text box, and the Description box changes. Also notice that the Preserve Formatting During Updates check box is selected.

❸ Click **Options....** The Field Options dialog box appears.

Jay is not sure how to proceed so he decides to get help on the FILLIN field.

❹   Click **Help** in the dialog box. Word Help opens to the topic FILLIN. Read the information about the FILLIN field code, then close the Help window.

After reading the Help topic, Jay decides that he doesn't need to add any switches to the FILLIN field code.

❺   Click **Cancel**. You return to the Field dialog box.

Jay doesn't want to add any switches, but according to the field code syntax guide, Jay needs to type, in quotation marks, the prompt he wants to be displayed in the dialog box. He must include the quotation marks because the prompt is likely to be longer than one word.

❻   Click in the Field Codes text box, then press **[End]** to move the insertion point one space past the field name.

❼   Type **"Who is to receive this memo?"** (make sure you include the surrounding quotation marks). If you forget to include the quotation marks around the prompt, Word will display only the first word of the prompt in the dialog box. See Figure 7-20.

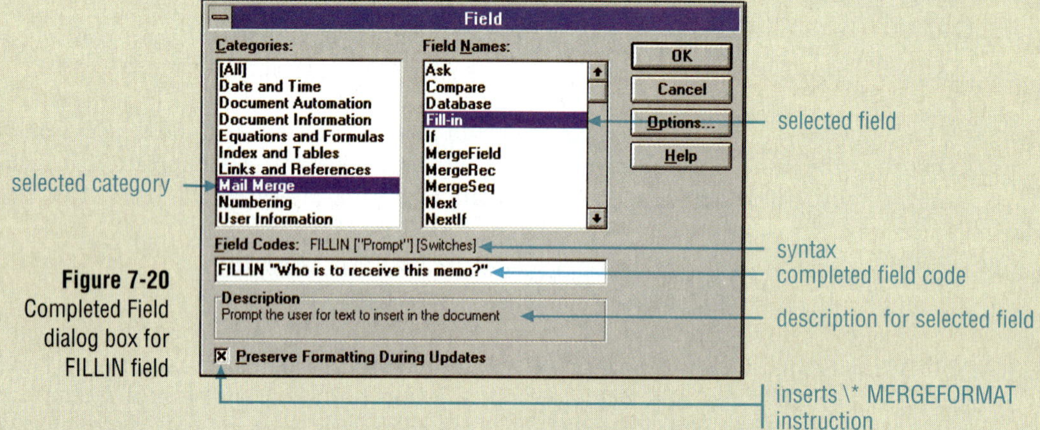

Figure 7-20
Completed Field dialog box for FILLIN field

❽   Click **OK** or press **[Enter]**. The prompt that Word will display each time the field is updated appears in a dialog box. See Figure 7-21.

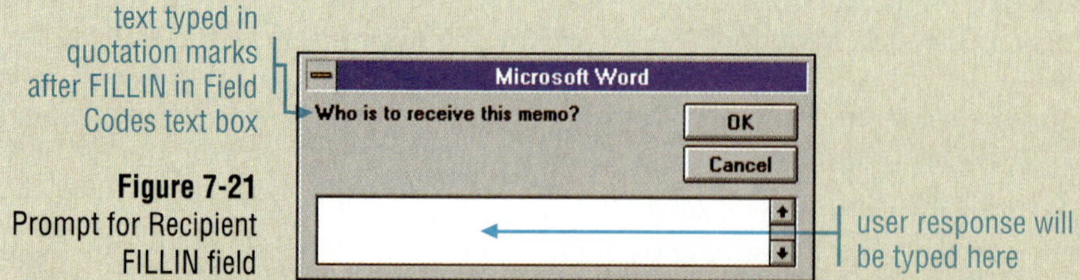

text typed in quotation marks after FILLIN in Field Codes text box

Figure 7-21
Prompt for Recipient FILLIN field

TROUBLE?   If you did not surround the prompt in quotation marks, the correct prompt will not appear in the dialog box. Click Cancel, then select the Recipient field code in the top pane and delete it. Repeat Steps 1 through 8.

Jay decides to enter some descriptive text to be inserted into his template as default text.

❾   Type **Recipient's Name** then click **OK**. The Recipient FILLIN field code is displayed in the top pane of the template window and the results—that is, the text typed into the dialog box—are displayed in the bottom pane. Notice that the * MERGEFORMAT instruction is added to the FILLIN code. See Figure 7-22.

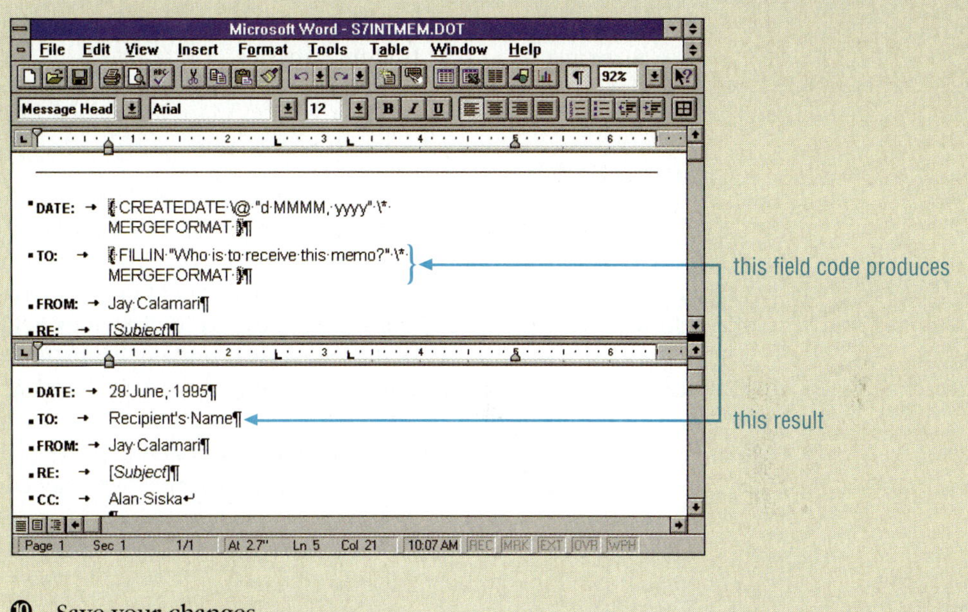

Figure 7-22
FILLIN field code
and results

⑩   Save your changes.

Next Jay wants to insert a FILLIN field code for the Subject heading.

To insert the Subject FILLIN field code:
❶   With the bottom pane still active, select **[Subject]** after the RE: memo heading in this pane. Do not include the ending paragraph mark.
❷   Click **Insert** then click **Field…**. The Field dialog box appears.
❸   Click **Mail Merge** in the Categories list box, if necessary, then click **Fill-in**.
❹   Click in the Field Codes text box, then press **[End]** to move the insertion point one space past the field name.
❺   Type "**What is the subject of this memo?**" (make sure you include the quotation marks).
❻   Click **OK** or press **[Enter]**. The dialog box appears with the prompt displayed.
❼   Type **Subject of Memo** to serve as default text, then click **OK**.
❽   Save your changes.

Next Jay needs to insert a FILLIN field code for the CC: memo text, but he must type additional instructions to remind him of what to do if he needs to send copies.

To insert a FILLIN field code for the CC: text:
❶   In the bottom pane, place the insertion point in the empty paragraph below Alan Siska (Ln 10). Repeat the previous steps for inserting a FILLIN field code so that

the following prompt appears: **"Who is to receive a copy of this memo? Press [Enter] after each name, except the last; otherwise press [Backspace], then click OK."**

❷ Type **Copy2** to serve as default text when Word prompts you for a response, then click **OK**. The FILLIN field code for the CC: heading is inserted in the top pane; the results are inserted in the bottom pane.

❸ Save your changes.

Updating Fields

The prompt for a FILLIN field appears only when the field is subsequently updated. A FILLIN field, like most Word fields, is updated when you select the field then press the Update Field key, [F9], or when you click Update Field in the shortcut menu after clicking the field with the right mouse button. To move to the previous field in a document and to select it at the same time, press the Previous Field key, [Shift][F11] or [Alt][Shift][F1]. To advance to the next field in a document and select it at the same time, press the Next Field key, [F11] or [Alt][F1].

Jay wants to check to see if the dialog box containing the prompt for the Recipient FILLIN field appears when the field is updated. He must first move to and select that field.

To update the Recipient FILLIN field:

❶ With the insertion point still in the bottom pane, after Copy2 (Ln 12), press **[Shift][F11]** (or **[Alt][Shift][F1]**) three times to move to and select the Recipient FILLIN field.

❷ Click the **right mouse button** on the selected Recipient FILLIN field to display the shortcut menu, then click **Update Field**. The prompt "Who is to receive this memo?" appears in a dialog box with the default text, Recipient's Name, highlighted.

Jay is satisfied that the Recipient FILLIN field works properly so he decides to cancel the dialog box.

❸ Click **Cancel**.

Now Jay wants to make sure the Subject FILLIN field works properly. He must first move to and select that field.

❹ Press **[F11]** (or **[Alt][F1]**) to move to and select the next field in the document, the Subject FILLIN field.

❺ Click the **right mouse button** on the selected Subject FILLIN field, then click **Update Field** to update the field. The prompt "What is the subject of this memo?" appears in a dialog box with the default text, Subject of Memo, highlighted.

❻ Click **Cancel**.

Next Jay wants to see if the CC FILLIN field operates correctly when it is updated.

❼ Press **[F11]** (or **[Alt][F1]**) to move to and select the CC FILLIN field.

Jay decides to use the Update Field key, [F9], to view the prompt.

❽ Press **[F9]** to update the field manually. The prompt "Who is to receive a copy of this memo?…" appears with the default text, Copy2, highlighted.

❾ Click **Cancel**.

❿ Press **[↓]** to deselect the text and move into the memo body text area.

Inserting a Links and References Category Field Code

You might need to insert a field code that inserts a link to part of an existing file or a reference to an element of a document such as an AutoText entry, an existing graphics file, the text from a file, or the text of a bookmark. The fields that produce these results are available when you select the Links and References category in the Field dialog box.

According to RMI's standards, the header for the second and subsequent pages of any memo must include the subject of the memo at the left margin, with the date on the line below. Jay knows that he can easily instruct Word to insert the date automatically by inserting a CREATEDATE field code. But he doesn't want to retype the subject of the memo in the header text area for each memo that he writes. He wants Word automatically to insert in the header whatever text is entered after the RE: memo heading. He has several options to accomplish this effect, but Jay decides to insert a bookmark marking the text after the RE: memo heading, then to insert a REF field code, which references the bookmark and displays the results of the bookmark's contents. You used a bookmark in Tutorial 5 to move quickly to a specified location within a document. With the REF field code, you can also use a bookmark to reference and insert selected text.

Jay must first assign a bookmark to the text after the RE: memo heading. Rather than just mark the location of the beginning of the subject text, this bookmark must select the entire text of the inserted subject.

To insert the bookmark for the subject text:

❶ In the bottom pane, select the default text **Subject of Memo**. Make sure the text is selected, not just shaded.

❷ Click **Edit** then click **Bookmark....** The Bookmark dialog box appears.

❸ Type **Subject** in the Bookmark Name text box, then click **Add** or press **[Enter]**. The bookmark will appear in the document only if the Bookmarks option is selected on the View tab of the Options dialog box (by default, this option is not selected).

Next Jay inserts the REF field code in the header for the second and subsequent pages of the memo template. He must first force the memo to create a second page so he can insert the header for the second page.

To insert a REF field code in the header:

❶ Place the insertion point at the end of the document, press **[Enter]**, then press **[Ctrl][Enter]**. A hard page break appears and the insertion point moves to page 2.

❷ Click **View** then click **Header and Footer**. The insertion point moves into the Header text area of the second page. Per RMI standards, Jay doesn't want a header on the first page.

The bottom pane changes to page layout view so that the header can be displayed. The results of field codes will continue to be displayed in this pane. Jay will be able to insert the REF field code and see the results displayed in the bottom pane, but he will not be able to view the inserted field code in the header because the top pane is not in page layout view.

❸ Click **Insert** then click **Field....** The Field dialog box appears.

❹ Click **Links and References** in the Categories list box, then click **Ref** in the Field
Names list box. Notice the syntax guide and the description for the selected field.

Jay wants Word to insert the Subject bookmark in the field.

❺ Click **Options...**, click the **Bookmarks tab**, click **Subject** in the Name list box, if necessary, then click **Add to Field** or press **[Enter]**. The bookmark name "Subject" is added
to the REF field code in the Field Codes text box. See Figure 7-23.

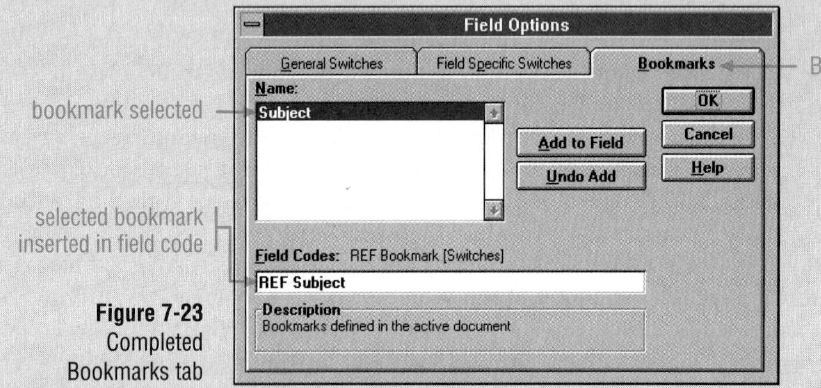

Figure 7-23
Completed
Bookmarks tab

❻ Click **OK** or press **[Enter]**. You return to the Field dialog box.
❼ Click **OK** or press **[Enter]**. You return to the header text area with the results of the
REF field code displayed at the left margin.

Jay can't see the header text area completely so he decides to move the Header and
Footer toolbar to the right.

❽ If necessary, drag the Header and Footer toolbar to the right so that you can see
the results of the REF field code.

Jay also wants to add the CREATEDATE field on the next line, but not in a separate
paragraph, because the Header style adds too much space at the end of a paragraph.

To insert the CREATEDATE field code in the header:
❶ Press **[Shift][Enter]** to insert a new line mark.
❷ Click **Insert** then click **Field....** Click **Date and Time** in the Categories list box, then
click **CreateDate**, if necessary.
❸ Click **Options...** then select the reverse date option.
❹ Click **Add to Field** or press **[Enter]**, then click **OK** or press **[Enter]**. You return to the
Field dialog box.
❺ Click **OK** or press **[Enter]**. See Figure 7-24.

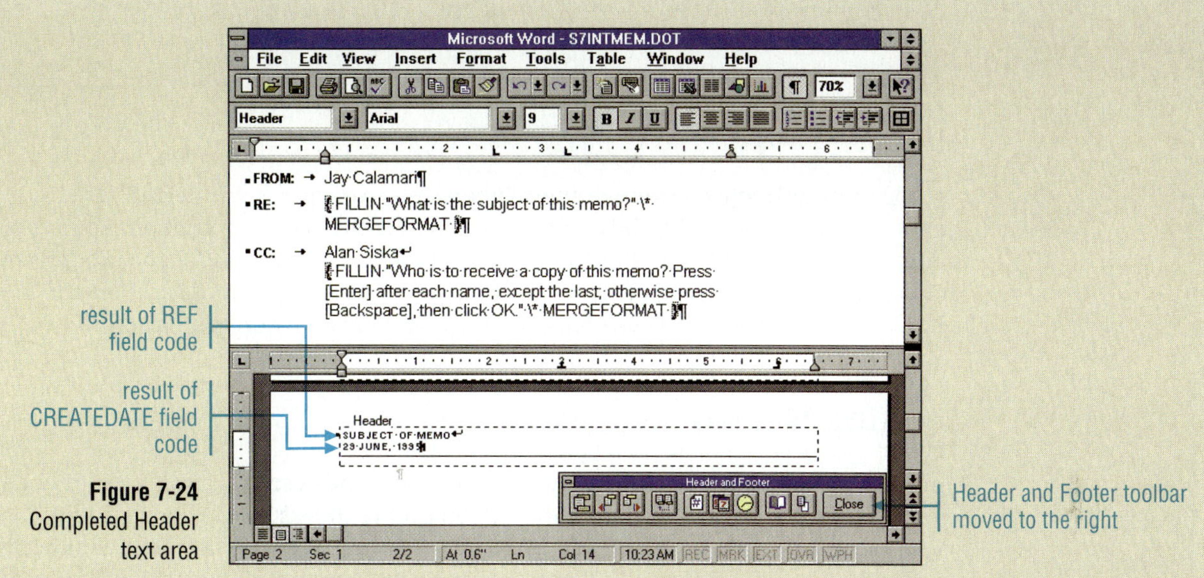

Figure 7-24
Completed Header
text area

result of REF field code

result of CREATEDATE field code

Header and Footer toolbar moved to the right

❻   Click the **Close button** on the Header and Footer toolbar.

Now that he has created the header for page two, Jay no longer needs the page break.

❼   Scroll the bottom pane up until the page break is visible. Press **[Backspace]** twice to delete the hard page break and the paragraph mark. The insertion point returns to page 1.

❽   Double-click the split box to unsplit the window. The top pane containing the displayed field codes fills the entire window.

Jay is finished inserting field codes, so he wants to display field results rather than field codes throughout the document. He must deactivate the Field Codes option.

❾   Click **Tools**, click **Options…**, click the **View tab** if necessary, then click the **Field Codes check box** in the Show section to deselect it. Click **OK** or press **[Enter]**. Now the results of the inserted fields, rather than the field codes, are displayed throughout the document.

❿   Save your changes.

Jay has completed creating the customization features for the text attributes of his memo template. Before he moves to the next phase of the customization strategy—customizing features of Word's interface—Jay decides to take a break.

If you want to take a break and resume the tutorial at a later time, close the document and exit Word. Do not save any changes to the NORMAL template. When you want to resume the tutorial, start Word then conduct the screen check described in Tutorial 1. Open the S7INTMEM template from your Student Disk, activate the Prompt to Save Normal.dot check box on the Save tab of the Options dialog box, if necessary. Make sure your document window is in Page Width Zoom view, then continue with the tutorial.

Jay wants to further customize the template by automating some of the tasks he needs to perform.

Customizing Word's Interface

The most distinctive feature of the Windows environment is its interface; that is, how the user communicates with the computer to operate the active application. You can customize three components of Word's interface—toolbars, menus, and keyboard shortcuts. You customize these interface options through the Customize command on the Tools menu. Another way you can customize these components is by creating macros.

Creating Macros

A **macro** is a series of recorded keystrokes and commands used to automate a frequently repeated task. You create a macro either by recording the series of actions using Word's macro recorder, or by writing macro statements using WordBasic, a programming language. When you run a macro, Word plays back the keystrokes, commands, or options that were recorded. These user-defined macros allow you to build additional commands into Word, thus customizing Word's interface to suit your needs.

Before creating a macro, you should plan what you want the macro to do. Next you start the macro recording process by selecting the Macro command from the Tools menu. Before you actually begin recording a macro, you must name the macro in the Record Macro dialog box. A **macro name** must begin with a letter, can include only letters or numbers, and cannot contain spaces.

After naming the macro, you can assign it to a toolbar, menu, or keyboard shortcut so that you can run the macro more easily. As with other customization features, you also specify the template in which to store the macro.

Once you begin recording a macro, each keystroke, command, and option you choose is added to the macro. You can use either the keyboard or the mouse to choose the commands you want to record, but Word cannot record text selections with the mouse or positioning of the insertion point. Once you have recorded the sequence of commands necessary to complete your task, you stop the macro recorder. If necessary, you can pause the macro recorder and resume recording when ready.

Jay wants to automate the process of printing his memos. He decides to record a macro for this task and assign the macro to a keyboard shortcut.

Recording a Macro and Assigning It to a Shortcut Key

Assigning a shortcut key to a macro involves the same process you used to assign a shortcut key to a style, which you learned in Tutorial 5. The choice of shortcut key combinations for macros is almost limitless. You can use [Ctrl], [Alt], [Ctrl][Shift], [Alt][Shift], or [Alt][Ctrl][Shift] in combination with any letter, any number, the F2 to F12 function keys, [Pg Up], [Pg Dn], [Home], [End], [Ins], [Del], or any arrow key. Once you press the combination of keystrokes you want for the shortcut key, Word will let you know if it is already assigned to another command or if it is currently unassigned.

Jay anticipates that he'll need to print at least three copies of each memo he creates— one for the recipient, one for his boss, Alan Siska, and one for his correspondence file. Rather than having to change the Print dialog box option to print three copies each time he gets ready to print a memo, Jay decides to record the series of tasks as a macro.

Before recording the macro, Jay plans the sequence of commands and options he needs to record:

1. Click File.
2. Click Print….
3. In the Print dialog box, change the Copies option to 3.
4. Click OK or press [Enter].

Jay decides to name the macro PrintMemo, and he wants to assign it to the shortcut key combination [Alt][p]. Also, he wants to save the macro to the S7INTMEM template.

To create a macro to print three copies of the memo:

❶ Click **Tools** then click **Macro…**. The Macro dialog box appears. The StyleMerger macro is already listed because it was assigned to the MEMO2 template originally. Your list might display other macro names as well.

❷ Type **PrintMemo** in the Macro Name text box. *Do not press [Enter].*

Jay wants to save the macro in the S7INTMEM template rather than in the NORMAL template.

❸ Click the **Macros Available In list box down arrow**, then click **S7intmem.dot [Template]**.

❹ Click in the Description text box, then type **Prints copies of a memo**. See Figure 7-25.

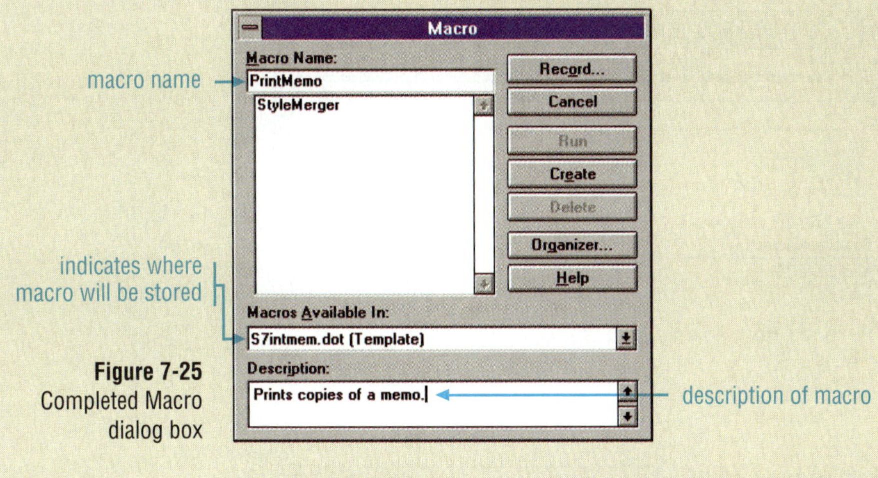

Figure 7-25
Completed Macro
dialog box

❺ Click **Record…**. The Record Macro dialog box appears.

Now Jay is ready to assign the macro to the shortcut key combination, [Alt][p].

To assign the macro to a shortcut key:

❶ Click the **Keyboard icon** in the Assign Macro To section. The Customize dialog box appears with the Keyboard tab displayed. Note that the insertion point is active in the Press New Shortcut Key text box. The macro will be assigned to the key combination you press next.

Jay wants to assign [Alt][p] as the shortcut key combination.

❷ Press **[Alt][p]**. "Alt+P" appears in the Press New Shortcut Key text box. Notice that Jay's choice for the shortcut key is not currently assigned to any other command. Also notice that the Description section contains the macro description you entered earlier, and the Save Changes In list box displays S7intmem.dot.

❸ Click **Assign** or press **[Enter]**. "Alt+P" appears in the Current Keys list box.

Now Jay is ready to record the macro. The easiest way to create a macro is to use the macro recorder. The macro recorder works like a tape recorder, except that it records the commands you give Word through the keyboard or mouse.

To record the macro:

❶ Click **Close** or press **[Enter]**. In the status bar, REC appears darker to indicate that the macro recorder is activated, and the pointer changes to 🖱. Also the Macro Recorder toolbar appears. See Figure 7-26. Every action you perform will be recorded until you either pause or stop the recorder.

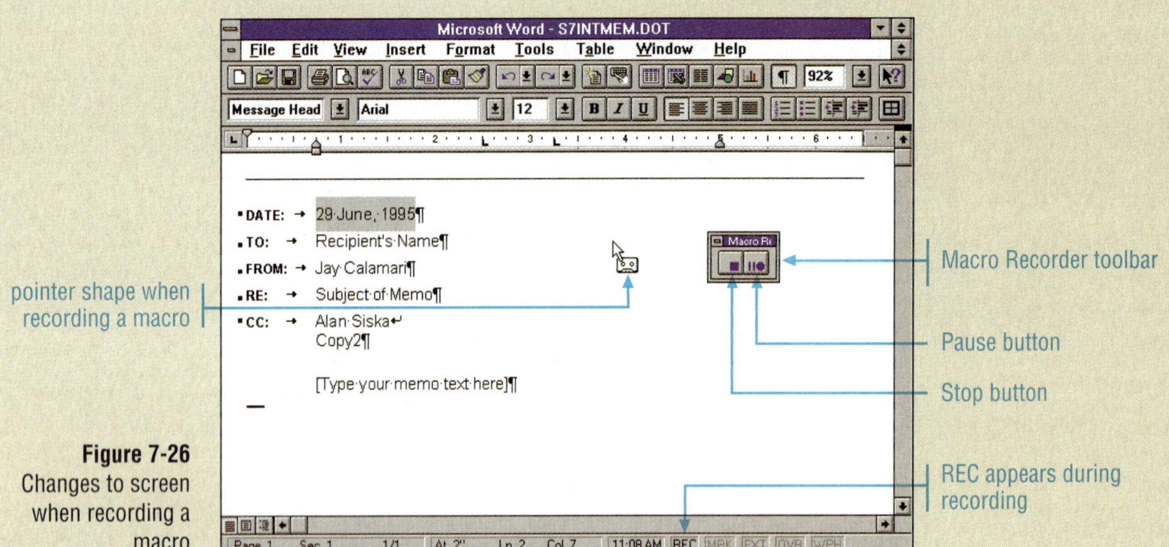

pointer shape when recording a macro

Figure 7-26
Changes to screen when recording a macro

Jay will now follow his plan for recording the PrintMemo macro.

❷ Click **File** then click **Print...**. The Print dialog box appears.

❸ Change the Copies option to **3**.

❹ Click **OK** or press **[Enter]**. The template is sent to print.

TROUBLE?   If the FILLIN field codes are updated when you send the document to print, then the Update Fields check box in the Printing Options section of the Print tab for the Options command has been selected. Click Cancel for each of the FILLIN field prompts, stop the recorder, then deactivate the Update Fields check box. Delete the PrintMemo macro by clicking Tools, clicking Macro..., selecting PrintMemo from the Macro Name list, then clicking Delete. Confirm that you want to delete the PrintMemo macro. Re-record the macro starting with the steps in the previous section, "To create a macro to print three copies of the memo."

Jay is finished recording the commands necessary to print three copies of a memo.

❺   Click the **Stop button** ▪ on the Macro Recorder toolbar. REC appears dimmed once again in the status bar, the Macro Recorder toolbar closes, and the pointer changes to Ɪ.

❻   Save your changes.

Editing a Macro

When you record a macro, Word translates the commands, keystrokes, or options into lines of programming code. The programming language used in Word is **WordBasic**. If you make a mistake while recording a macro, you can either re-record the macro or you can edit the macro programming code. To see the programming code Word writes as you record a macro, you must open the Macro Editor window.

Jay decides that he doesn't need to keep a correspondence file, so he needs to print only two copies of each memo. Rather than re-recording the macro, he decides to edit the macro programming code.

To edit the PrintMemo macro:

❶   Click **Tools** then click **Macro....** The Macro dialog box appears. In addition to opening the Macro Editor window from this dialog box, you can also run or delete a macro.

❷   Click **PrintMemo** in the Macro Name list box, then click **Edit**. The Macro Editor window appears. See Figure 7-27.

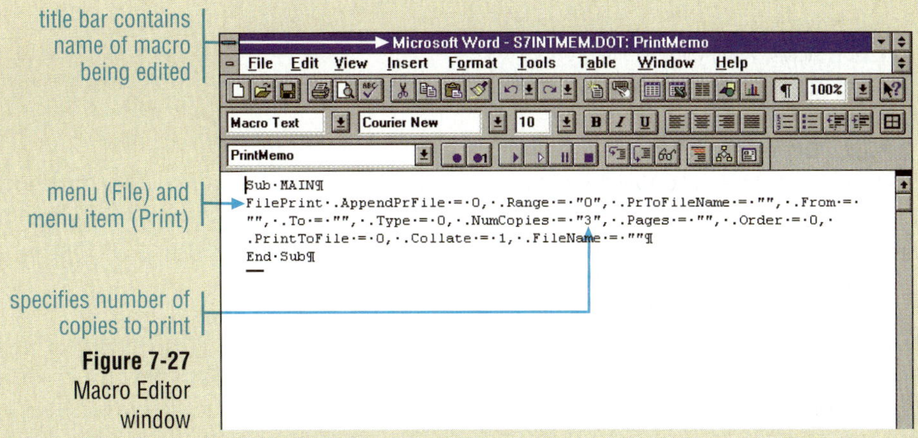

title bar contains name of macro being edited

menu (File) and menu item (Print)

specifies number of copies to print

Figure 7-27
Macro Editor
window

The title bar indicates the macro being edited. The Macro toolbar contains useful commands for editing a macro. The lines of text in the window represent WordBasic programming code. The first line and the last line must be present in every macro. The lines between represent the commands, keystrokes, or options you selected when recording the PrintMemo macro. Notice that the macro begins with the menu and command selected (FilePrint) and each option in the Print dialog box is listed. The only option Jay changed is represented by the .NumCopies = "3" statement.

Jay needs to change the number of copies from 3 to 2.

❸   Select the **3** after .NumCopies =, then type **2**.

Jay has finished editing the PrintMemo macro and needs to save the changes.

❹   Click the **Save button** 🖫 on the Standard toolbar to save the changes to the macro. The following message appears: "Do you want to keep the changes to the macro S7INTMEM.DOT:PrintMemo?"

❺   Click **Yes** or press **[Enter]**.

Jay is now ready to close the Macro Editor window.

❻   Double-click the **Control menu box** for the Macro Editor window (or click **File** then click **Close**). You return to the template window.

❼   Save your changes.

Recording a Macro and Assigning It to a Menu

You can change Word's menu structure by adding, deleting, or changing menu commands. You can add any of Word's built-in commands to a menu, or you can record a macro and assign it to a menu as a command. You can even identify an **accelerator key** for your new command; that is, the keyboard equivalent command that will activate your option.

Jay likes to emphasize certain words by bolding and changing the font color to red. He uses this kind of emphasis for the electronic mail memos he sends to RMI's other two locations. He decides to add a command to the Format menu for bolding and coloring selected text red. Jay first plans his strategy for recording the macro for this command:

1. Select text before turning on the macro recorder.
2. Click Format.
3. Click Font….
4. Click Bold.
5. Click the Color list box down arrow.
6. Click Red.
7. Click OK or press [Enter].

As when assigning the macro to the shortcut key earlier, Jay wants this command to be available only in his memo template. He decides to name the command Red Bold and use the letter "l" as the accelerator key. He wants the command to appear at the bottom of the Format menu as "Red Bold."

To create a macro that changes the font color to red and bolds selected text:

❶   Move the insertion point to the end of the document, then select the word **here**.

Jay decides to use a different way of starting the macro recorder.

❷   Double-click **REC** in the status bar. The Record Macro dialog box appears.

❸   Type **RedBold** in the Record Macro Name text box (no spaces). *Do not press [Enter].*

Jay wants to save the macro with his custom-designed template, S7INTMEM.DOT, rather than with the NORMAL template.

❹   Click the **Make Macro Available To list box down arrow**, then click **Documents Based On S7intmem.dot**.

❺ Click in the Description text box, then type **Bolds and colors red selected text.** This description will appear in the status bar when the Red Bold menu command is selected. See Figure 7-28.

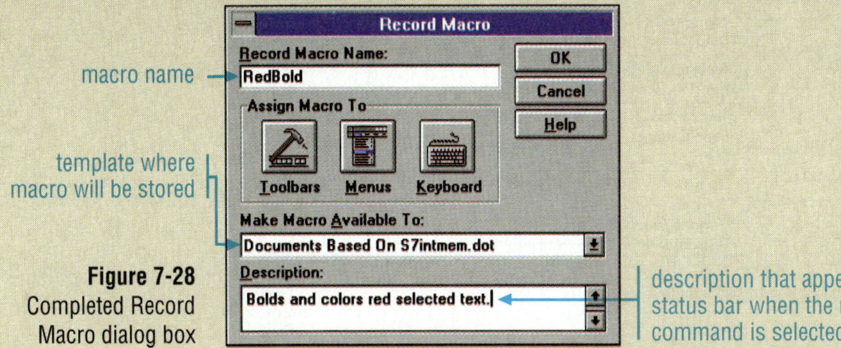

macro name

template where macro will be stored

Figure 7-28
Completed Record
Macro dialog box

description that appears in status bar when the menu command is selected

❻ Click the **Menus icon** in the Assign Macro To section. The Customize dialog box appears with the Menus tab displayed.

Now Jay is ready to assign the RedBold macro to the Format menu.

To assign the RedBold macro to the Format menu:
❶ Click the **Change What Menu list box down arrow**, then click **F&ormat**. The ampersand (&) in front of the "o" in Format indicates that the letter "o" is the accelerator key for displaying this menu.

Jay wants the new command for the RedBold macro positioned at the bottom of the Format menu.

❷ Click the **Position on Menu list box down arrow**, then click **(At Bottom)**.

Jay wants the command name on the menu to be Red Bold with the letter "l" underlined, indicating it is the accelerator key for the command. He must type an ampersand (&) in front of the "l."

❸ Press **[Tab]** to move to the Name on Menu text box, then type **Red Bo&ld** in the text box. Make sure to insert a space between the two words of the menu command.
❹ Click **Add** or press **[Enter]**. The command Red Bold is added to the Format menu.

Jay is ready to record the RedBold macro.

To record the RedBold macro:
❶ Click **Close** or press **[Enter]**. REC appears darker in the status bar to indicate that the macro recorder is activated, and the pointer changes to ▨. Also the Macro Recorder toolbar appears.
❷ Click **Format**. Notice that the command Red Bold has been added to the bottom of the Format menu, and that the "l" in Bold is underlined. See Figure 7-29.

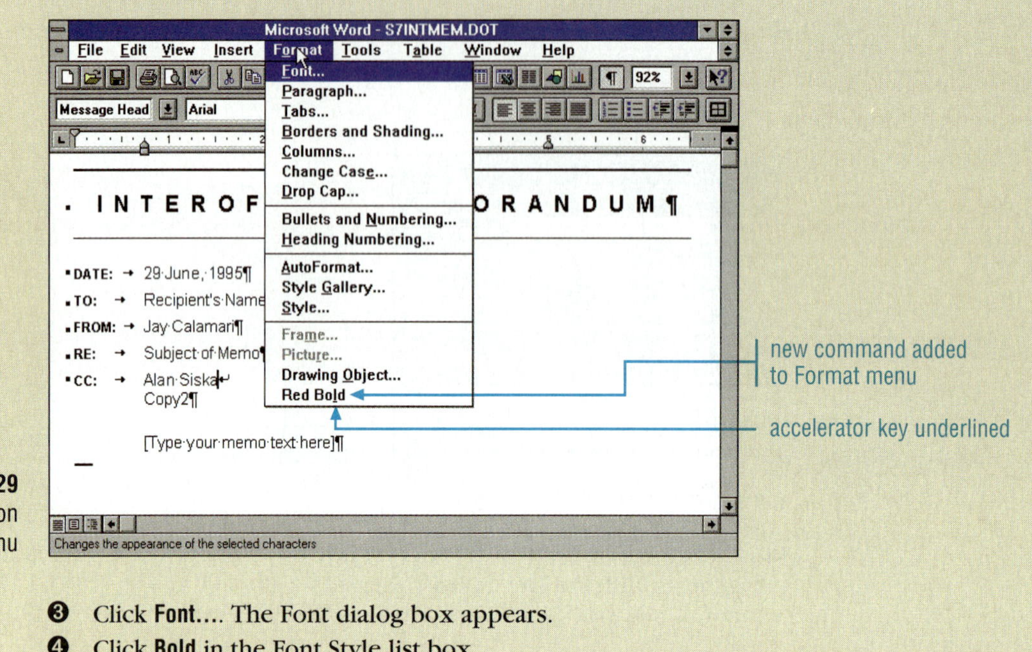

Figure 7-29
New command on
the Format menu

❸ Click **Font...**. The Font dialog box appears.

❹ Click **Bold** in the Font Style list box.

❺ Click the **Color list box down arrow**, then click **Red**.

❻ Click **OK** or press **[Enter]**.

Jay is finished recording the commands necessary to bold and color red the selected text.

❼ Double-click **REC** in the status bar to stop recording.

Jay needs to remove the emphasis from his template text.

❽ With the word "here" still selected, click the **Undo button** ↶ on the Standard toolbar (or click **Edit** then click **Undo Font Formatting**). The formatting is removed from the selected text.

❾ Deselect the text, then save your changes.

Now Jay is ready to customize another interface property—a toolbar—that will enable him to create his memos quickly.

Customizing a Toolbar

The buttons on the default Standard and Formatting toolbars perform 37 of Word's most often used commands. In addition to these default toolbars, Word provides several specialized toolbars such as the Database toolbar, the Borders toolbar, and the Drawing toolbar. Word, however, contains over 350 built-in commands, any of which you can assign to a toolbar. You can customize the buttons that are displayed on these toolbars, or you can create your own toolbar containing the commands you need for a special type of document or the commands you use most frequently. In addition to assigning Word's built-in commands to toolbars, you can also assign AutoText entries, user-defined macros, fonts, and styles to toolbars.

According to Jay's plan, he wants to create a customized toolbar to use when he creates documents based on the S7INTMEM template. This toolbar, which he decides to name the Memo toolbar, will contain buttons for the commands and tasks Jay completes most often when writing memos.

To create the Memo toolbar:

❶ Click **View** then click **Toolbars…**. The Toolbars dialog box appears.

❷ Click **New…**. The New Toolbar dialog box appears.

❸ Type **Memo** in the Toolbar Name text box.

As with his other customizations, Jay wants the Memo toolbar to be stored in the S7INTMEM template, not in the NORMAL template.

❹ If necessary, click the **Make Toolbar Available To list box down arrow**, then click **Documents Based On S7intmem.dot**. See Figure 7-30.

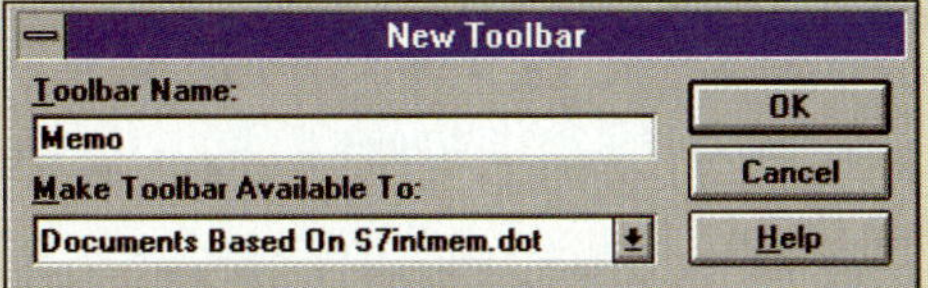

Figure 7-30
Completed New
Toolbar dialog box

❺ Click **OK** or press **[Enter]**. The Customize dialog box appears with the Toolbars tab displayed. Also, a toolbar labeled "Memo" appears to the left of the dialog box on the screen. See Figure 7-31.

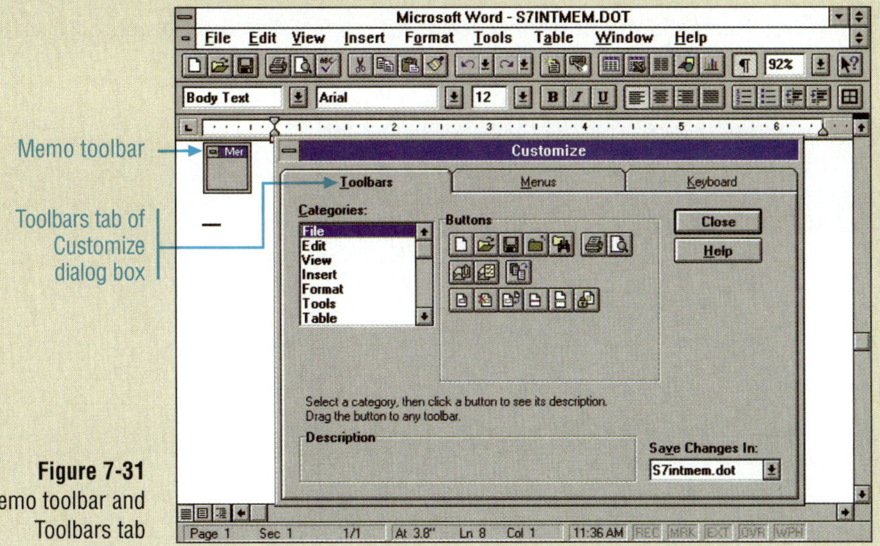

Figure 7-31
Memo toolbar and
Toolbars tab

Next Jay wants to add buttons to his new toolbar for the commands he'll use most frequently when creating memos.

Adding Buttons to a Custom Toolbar

Microsoft creates toolbars and places buttons on the toolbars based on research that indicates which Word commands are used most often. Once you become familiar with Word, however, you might use different commands more often than those provided on the default toolbars. You can add or delete buttons from the default toolbars, or, if you would rather not change the default arrangement, you can create your own toolbar and add buttons to it. Word provides buttons for additional commands not found on its default or specialized toolbars; you can add any of these buttons to any toolbar as well, including your custom toolbar. You can even create your own images for buttons.

Jay wants to add buttons to his Memo toolbar as specified in his plan (Figure 7-2). He wants to make sure that the changes to the Memo toolbar appear only in the S7INTMEM template.

To add buttons for built-in commands to the Memo toolbar:

❶ If necessary, click the **Save Changes In list box down arrow** in the Customize dialog box, then click **S7intmem.dot**.

❷ Click **File** in the Categories list box, if necessary. Buttons associated with some of the commands for the File menu appear in the Buttons section.

Jay recognizes some of the button images in the Buttons section—New, Open, Save, Print, and Print Preview—but he is not familiar with the rest. He wants to see which Word built-in commands are associated with the other buttons provided for the File menu in the Buttons section.

❸ Click each button in the Buttons section and read its description in the Description box at the bottom of the dialog box. See Figure 7-32.

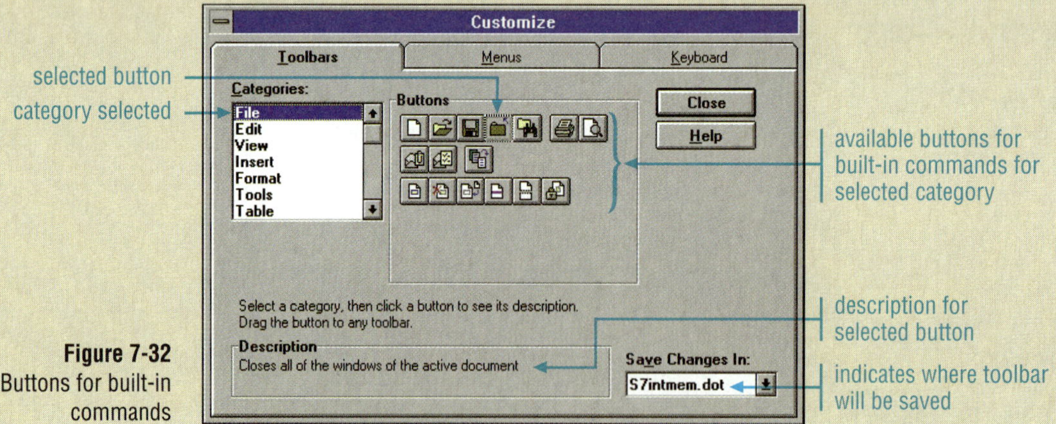

Figure 7-32
Buttons for built-in
commands

Jay wants to add the Close button, which closes all windows of the active document, to the Memo toolbar.

❹ Click the **Close button** in the Buttons section, then drag it to the Memo toolbar *between the boundaries* of the toolbar. As you drag the button, it appears in a dashed box. See Figure 7-33.

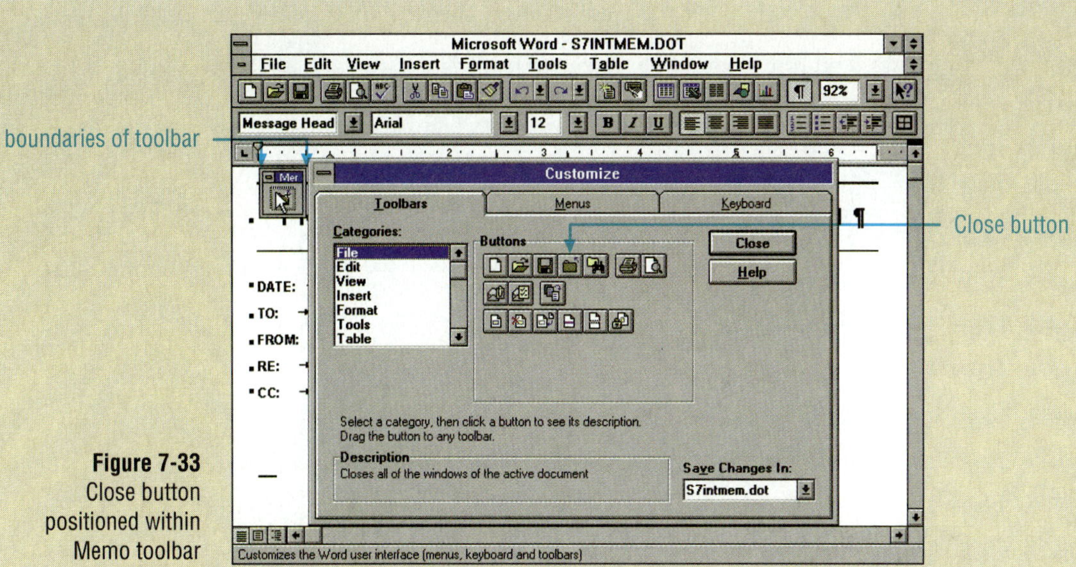

Figure 7-33
Close button
positioned within
Memo toolbar

⑤ Release the mouse button when the pointer is between the boundaries of the Memo toolbar. If you pause over the newly placed button, the appropriate ToolTip appears.

⑥ Repeat the above steps to add the buttons for the following built-in commands to the Memo toolbar:

Edit menu—Repeat button

View menu—Zoom 100% button and Zoom Page Width button

Format menu—Double Space button

Table menu—Table AutoFormat button

Make sure that you stay within the boundaries of the Memo toolbar when you drag a button to the toolbar. Word will automatically adjust the width of the toolbar to make room for each additional button.

Jay wants to add a button to the Memo toolbar for the AutoText entry he created to insert the closing lines and a button for a style he uses quite often. He must add custom buttons for these items.

To add custom buttons to the Memo toolbar:
❶ Scroll to the bottom of the Categories list box in the Toolbars tab, click **AutoText**, then click **Closing** in the AutoText list box, if necessary.
❷ Drag the Closing AutoText title to the Memo toolbar. The Custom Button dialog box appears. Notice that the Text Button is selected. This button specifies that the text in the Text Button Name text box will appear on the button (instead of an image or graphic). Notice also that the name of the AutoText entry, Closing, appears in the Text Button Name text box. See Figure 7-34.

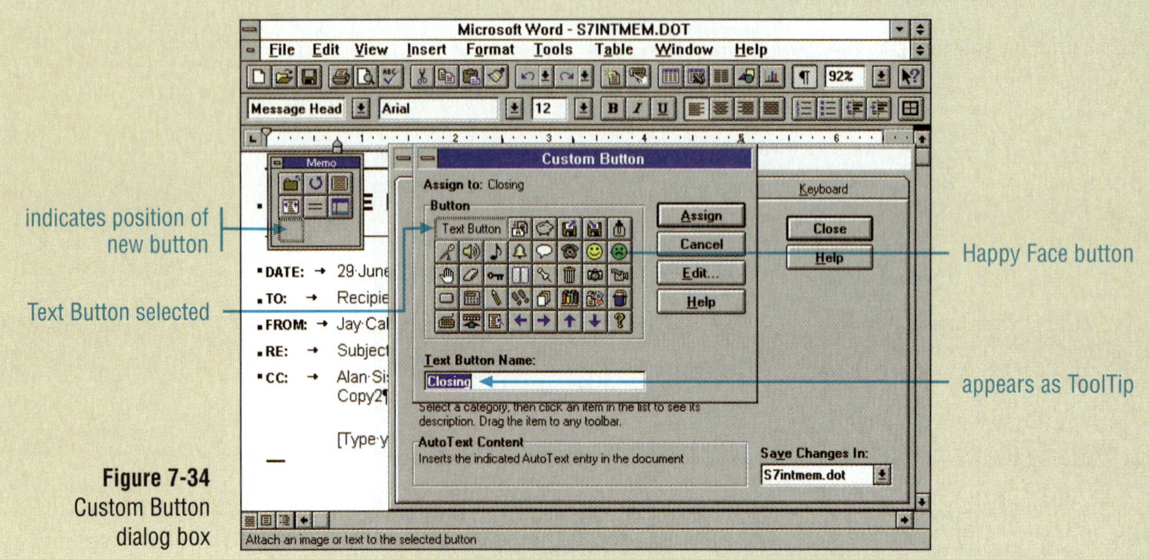

Figure 7-34
Custom Button
dialog box

Jay decides that the Happy Face image would be appropriate for this button, instead of the text "Closing." In this case, the entry in the Text Button Name text box (Closing) will appear as a ToolTip for this button.

❸ Click the **Happy Face button** 🙂, then click **Assign** or press **[Enter]**. The Happy Face button is assigned to the Memo toolbar.

Jay thinks that he will be using the Heading 3 style frequently so he decides to assign it to the Memo toolbar also.

❹ Click **Styles** in the Categories list box, then click **Heading 3** in the Styles list box.

❺ Drag the selected Heading 3 style name to the Memo toolbar. The Custom Button dialog box appears.

Jay decides to assign text to the button for the style rather than an image because none of the image buttons available in the Custom Button dialog box relate to the style name.

❻ Click the **Text Button button**, if necessary, then type **H3 Style** in the Text Button Name text box. The text "H3 Style" will appear on the button itself (not as a ToolTip).

❼ Click **Assign** or press **[Enter]**. The H3 Style button appears on the Memo toolbar.

Jay is finished assigning buttons to the Memo toolbar.

❽ Click **Close** or press **[Enter]**.

Jay wants to make sure the ToolTips for the buttons on his new toolbar work properly.

❾ Move the mouse pointer slowly over each button on the Memo toolbar. The H3 Style button does not have a ToolTip because it is a text button rather than an image button.

❿ Save your changes.

Moving a Toolbar

Another way to customize Word's interface is to change the location of its toolbars. You can move an entire toolbar to a new location. Simply click and hold the mouse pointer on the title bar, if available, or any empty space in a toolbar, then drag it to the left, right, top, or bottom of the screen to anchor it in position. You can even move a toolbar to the middle of the screen, in which case it is called a **floating toolbar**. You can also move or remove a button from any toolbar. To move a button, press [Alt], then click and drag the button to its new location. To remove a button, press [Alt], then drag the button off the toolbar.

Jay wants to anchor the floating Memo toolbar. He decides to move it to the bottom of the screen rather than the top because the screen would look too cluttered with three toolbars.

To move the Memo toolbar:

❶ Point to the title bar or any empty space of the Memo toolbar, then click and drag it to the bottom of the screen, above the status bar (but below the view buttons). As you drag the toolbar, a square dashed box appears; then as you near the bottom of the screen, the box changes to a rectangle.

❷ Release the mouse button when the toolbar is in the center of the screen at the bottom. See Figure 7-35.

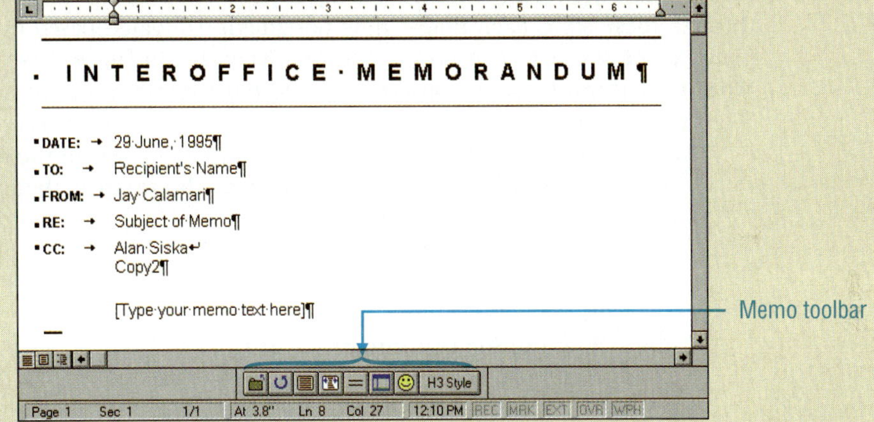

Figure 7-35
Memo toolbar in
new location

❸ Arrange the buttons on your toolbar to fit the arrangement shown in Figure 7-35. If necessary, press [Alt] and drag a button to its correct location. Also, drag the Memo toolbar border, if necessary, so that all buttons fit next to each other in a row.

❹ Save your changes.

Now Jay is ready to create the final customization feature for his template—automating document creation.

Using Word's AutoMacros

Word provides five **automatic macros** that control what happens when Word performs its most basic operations—starting Word, creating a new document, opening an existing document, closing a document, and exiting Word. Figure 7-36 lists the names and functions of these five automatic macros. To use these automatic macros, you simply need to use the proper AutoMacro name when recording a macro.

AutoMacro Name	Purpose
AutoExec	Runs when you first start Word
AutoNew	Runs when you create a new document
AutoOpen	Runs each time you open a previously created document
AutoClose	Runs when you close a document
AutoExit	Runs when you quit Word

Figure 7-36
Word's AutoMacros

To make the production of memo documents as efficient as possible, Jay wants to build more automation into the operation of the template. When he creates a new document based on the S7INTMEM template, Jay wants Word to prompt him automatically to insert the information for the memo heading text areas. To accomplish these tasks, Word must update all fields. Then he wants Word to move the insertion point to the beginning of the memo text area, which he'll mark with a bookmark. In order to get Word to go through these steps each time a new document is created based on the S7INTMEM template, Jay must create a macro named AutoNew that includes these steps. In order to get Word to perform these actions at once, he must record a macro and name it AutoNew. Word will execute these commands whenever a new document is created.

The plan for the AutoMacro that Jay must create consists of the following steps:
1. Prior to recording the macro, insert a bookmark that selects the existing memo text.
2. Click Edit then click Select All.
3. Press [F9] to update all fields.
4. Click OK at the Recipient prompt.
5. Click OK at the Subject prompt.
6. Click OK at the CC prompt.
7. Press [F5].
8. In the Go To dialog box, click Bookmark, click BeginMemoHere, click Go To, then click Close.

Jay is ready to insert a bookmark to mark the memo body text. He will name the bookmark BeginMemoHere.

To insert a bookmark that selects the current memo text:
❶ Place the insertion point at the end of the document. Make sure that the Style list box in the Formatting toolbar displays the style name Body Text.

Jay wants the current text in the memo text area to be deleted when he starts typing.

❷ Select the text **[Type your memo text here]** (include the brackets in the selection, but *not* the ending paragraph mark).
❸ Click **Edit** then click **Bookmark…**. The Bookmark dialog box appears.
❹ Type **BeginMemoHere** (all one word) in the Bookmark Name text box.
❺ Click **Add** or press **[Enter]**. Deselect the text.
❻ Save your changes.

Now Jay is ready to create the macro that will start automatically each time he creates a document based on the S7INTMEM template. He must name the macro AutoNew so that Word will know to execute it when a new document is created. He must store it in the S7INTMEM template so that Word will know to execute the AutoNew macro when a new document is based on S7INTMEM. Because it will run automatically at startup, Jay doesn't need to assign the macro to a toolbar, menu, or shortcut key.

To create the AutoNew macro:

❶ Click **Tools** then click **Macro...**. The Macro dialog box appears.

❷ Type **AutoNew** in the Macro Name text box. Using the name AutoNew specifies that this macro will run every time a new document is created based on the indicated template.

❸ If necessary, click the **Macros Available In list box down arrow**, then click **S7intmem.dot [Template]**.

❹ In the Description text box, type **Prompts user for memo heading information then moves the insertion point to the beginning of the memo body text and selects existing text.**

❺ Click **Record...**. The Record Macro dialog box appears.

Jay does not need to assign the AutoNew macro to a toolbar, menu, or keyboard. It will run only at the startup of a new document. Jay wants the macro stored in the S7INTMEM template not in the NORMAL template.

❻ Click the **Make Macro Available To list box down arrow**, then click **Documents Based On S7intmem.dot**, if necessary. See Figure 7-37.

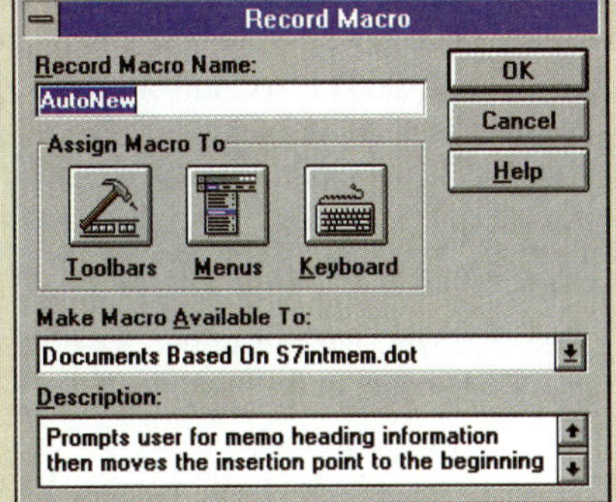

Figure 7-37
Completed Record Macro dialog box for AutoNew macro

Now Jay is ready to record the commands to be stored in the AutoNew macro.

To record the AutoNew macro:

❶ Click **OK**. REC appears darker in the status bar to indicate that macro recording is activated.

Jay wants all fields to be updated, but first he must select the entire document so that all the fields will be selected at once.

❷ Click **Edit** then click **Select All**. The entire document is selected.

Next Jay updates the fields in the document.

❸ Press **[F9]**. All the fields in the template are updated.

❹ When the prompts for the Recipient, Subject, and CC FILLIN fields appear, click **OK**.

After he completes the prompts for the memo heading information, Jay wants the insertion point to move to the beginning of the memo body text where he placed the BeginMemoHere bookmark. The text [Type your memo text here] will also be selected.

❺ Press **[F5]**. The Go To dialog box appears.

❻ Click **Bookmark** then click **BeginMemoHere** in the Enter Bookmark Name list, if necessary.

❼ Click **Go To** or press **[Enter]**. The text of the bookmark BeginMemoHere is selected. Click **Close** to close the Go To dialog box.

Jay has completed all the commands he needs for this macro.

❽ Click the **Stop button** ▪ on the Macro Recorder toolbar. REC appears dimmed again in the status bar. Deselect the text.

❾ Save your changes.

❿ Close the template. You return to the Nil menu.

Jay is now ready to test his template to make sure it works properly.

Testing the Template

After creating a custom template, the next phase of the customization strategy is to test the template to make sure all the features and options work as intended.

Now that his customized template is complete, Jay is ready to create a new document based on the S7INTMEM template. He will send it to Stan Angkor, and the subject will be "Increasing Office Productivity." Only Alan Siska will receive a copy of this memo.

To create a test document based on the S7INTMEM template:

❶ Click **File** then click **New…**. The New dialog box appears. Ordinarily, the custom template would appear in the list with the other templates, but you saved S7INTMEM to your Student Disk.

❷ Type **a:\s7intmem** to tell Word to base the new document on the template on your Student Disk. Notice that the description you typed in the Summary Info dialog box appears at the bottom of the New dialog box.

❸ Click **OK** or press **[Enter]**. A new document opens. As a result of the AutoNew macro, which runs automatically when a new document is created based on the S7INTMEM template, all the fields are updated, with the Recipient FILLIN prompt appearing first. Also notice that the Memo toolbar appears at the bottom of the screen and that the document opens in Page Width Zoom view.

❹ Type **Stan Angkor** when prompted for the memo recipient's name, then click **OK**.

❺ Type **Increasing Office Productivity** when prompted for the subject of the memo, then click **OK**.

Jay isn't sending a copy of this memo to anyone but Alan.

❻ Press **[Backspace]** when prompted for copy recipients to delete the default text, then click **OK**. Notice that the insertion point moves immediately into the memo body text area and selects the displayed text. This is a result of the last instruction you entered in the AutoNew macro—to move to the bookmark BeginMemoHere after completing the CC dialog box.

❼ Type the following as the text of the memo:

I have developed a template for use with Word to create documents designed specifically for RMI memo standards. If you think it would be worthwhile, I could create templates for the rest of the staff and/or provide instructions for installing, modifying, and using the template.

Jay wants to see if the REF and CREATEDATE fields in the second page header work properly.

❽ Press [Enter] then press [Ctrl][Enter]. A hard page break is inserted into the document, and the insertion point moves to page 2.

❾ Type the following text on page 2 of the memo:

Page 2 Features

As you can see, the template even inserts the appropriate header on page 2 and all subsequent pages.

❿ Save the document as S7TEMTST.DOC to your Student Disk.

Next Jay wants to test the interface features that he created for the S7INTMEM template.

To test the interface features:

❶ Select the words **appropriate header** in the paragraph on page 2, click **Format**, then click **Red Bold**. The selected text is colored red and bolded.

❷ Select the phrase **all subsequent pages** in the same paragraph, then click the **Repeat button** on the Memo toolbar. The previous action is repeated.

❸ Place the insertion point in the heading "Page 2 Features," then click the **H3 Style button** on the Memo toolbar. The heading is formatted with the Heading 3 style.

❹ Click anywhere within the paragraph of text on page 1 of the memo to select the paragraph, then click the **Double Space button** on the Memo toolbar. The selected paragraph becomes doubled-spaced.

❺ Place the insertion point at the end of the document (on page 2), then click the **Closing button** on the Memo toolbar. The closing lines created by the Closing AutoText entry are inserted.

❻ Change to page layout view to see if the header has been inserted properly. The subject is inserted on the first line of the header and the date is inserted in reverse date format.

Next Jay wants to see if the Zoom 100% and Zoom Page Width view buttons work.

❼ Click the **Zoom 100% button** on the Memo toolbar. The magnification percentage increases to 100%, and the screen changes to normal view.

❽ Click the **Zoom Page Width button** on the Memo toolbar. The magnification percentage returns to 92%.

❾ Spell check the document then save your changes.

Jay is ready to print his document.

⑩ Press **[Alt][p]** to print two copies of the test document. Figure 7-38 shows one printed copy.

I N T E R O F F I C E   M E M O R A N D U M

DATE: 29 June, 1995

TO: Stan Angkor

FROM: Jay Calamari

RE: Increasing Office Productivity

CC: Alan Siska

I have developed a template for use with Word to create documents designed specifically for RMI memo standards. If you think it would be worthwhile, I could create templates for the rest of the staff and/or provide instructions for installing, modifying, and using the template.

Figure 7-38
Jay's test document
(page 1 of 2)

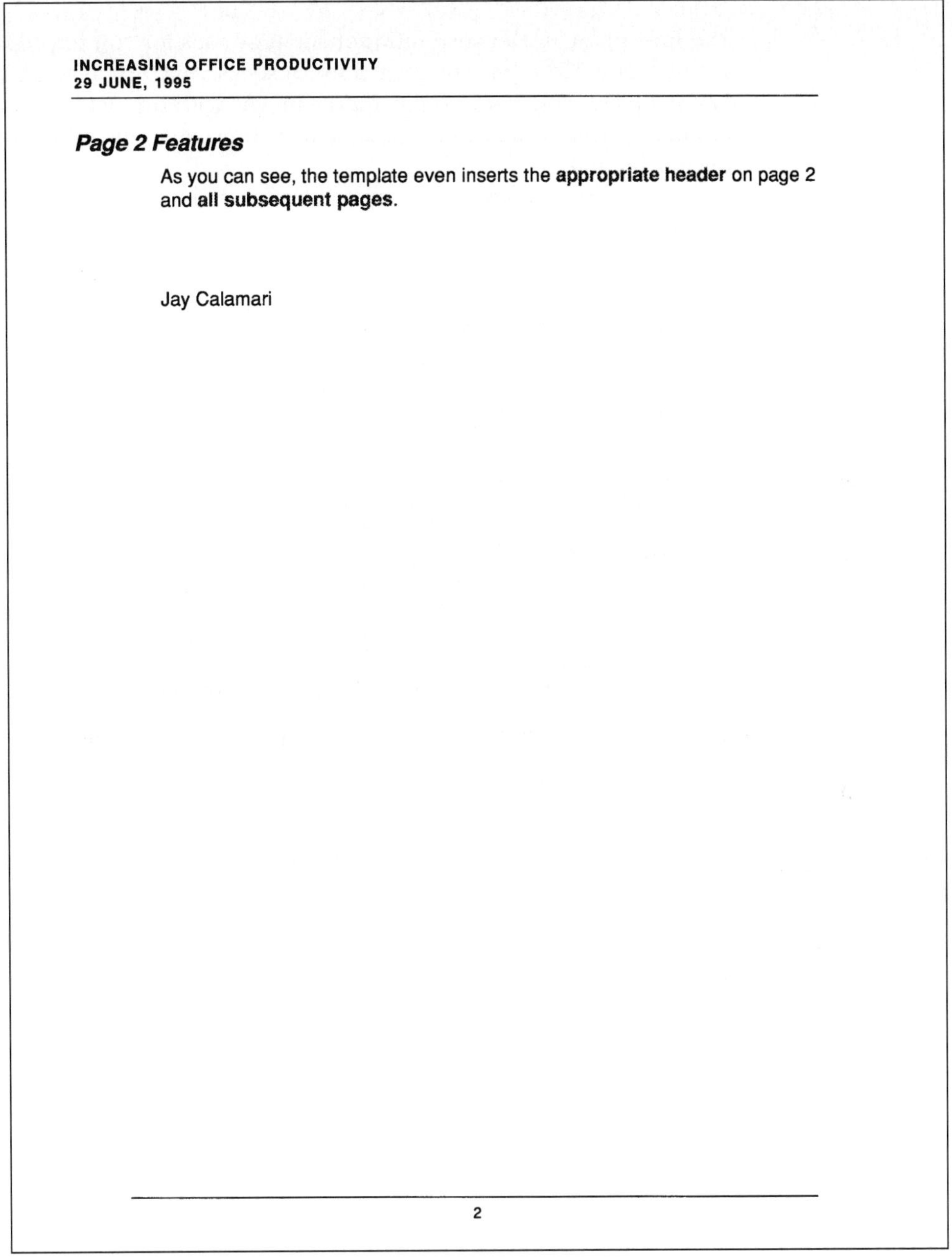

Figure 7-38
Jay's test document
(page 2 of 2)

Jay has completed creating and testing his custom template, and he is satisfied with
the way it works. Now he decides to print the documentation for the new template.

Printing Template Documentation

The final phase of the customization strategy calls for you to prepare documentation for the template. Word lets you print a list of styles, AutoText entries, and shortcut keys used in a template. You can also print a document with the field codes displayed. Each piece of output must be sent to print separately, however. This information serves as template documentation.

Jay wants to complete the customization process by printing the documentation for this template.

To print the documentation for the S7INTMEM template:

❶ Click **File** then click **Print....** The Print dialog box appears.

❷ Click the **Print What list box down arrow** to reveal the various types of output Word can print. See Figure 7-39.

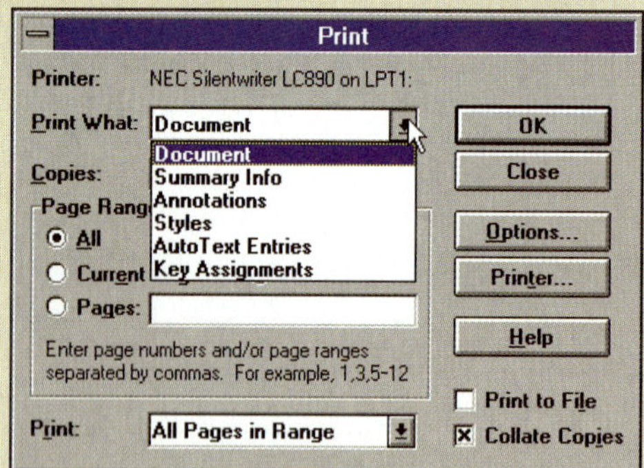

Figure 7-39
Print dialog box

❸ Click **Styles** then click **OK** or press [Enter]. Word prints the styles available in the template along with a description of their attributes.

❹ Click **File** then click **Print....** Click the **Print What list box down arrow**, click **AutoText Entries**, then click **OK** or press [Enter].

❺ Repeat Step 3 to print the **Key Assignments**.

Jay now wants to print the test document with the field codes displayed, including those in the header.

To print the test document with field codes displayed:

❶ Click **File** then click **Print....**

❷ Click **Options....** The Options dialog box appears with the Print tab displayed.

❸ Click the **Field Codes check box** in the Include with Document section of the dialog box. See Figure 7-40.

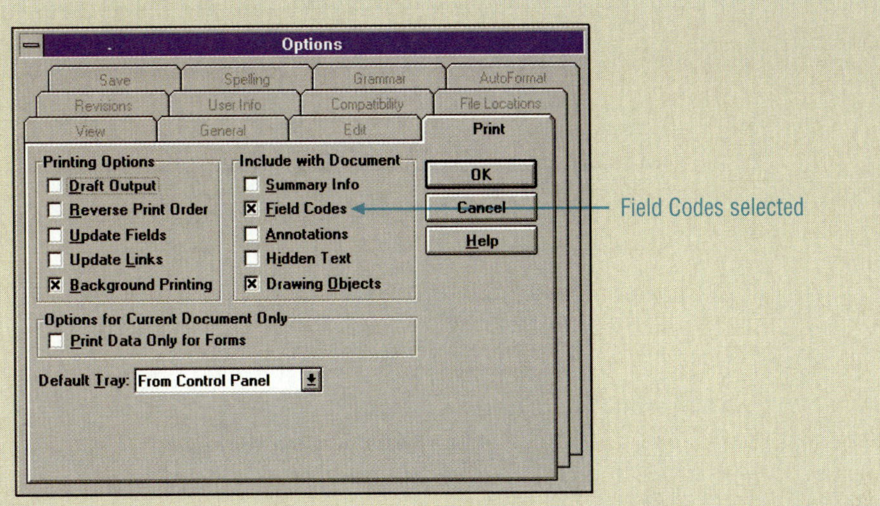

Figure 7-40
Print tab

❹ Click **OK** or press **[Enter]** in the Print tab, then click **OK** or press **[Enter]** in the Print dialog box. The document prints with field codes displayed. See Figure 7-41.

I N T E R O F F I C E   M E M O R A N D U M

DATE: { CREATEDATE \@ "d MMMM, yyyy" *
MERGEFORMAT }

TO: { FILLIN "Who is to receive this memo?" *
MERGEFORMAT }

FROM: Jay Calamari

RE: { FILLIN "What is the subject of this memo?" *
MERGEFORMAT }

CC: Alan Siska
{ FILLIN "Who is to receive a copy of this memo? Press
[Enter] after each name, except the last; otherwise press
[Backspace], then click OK." * MERGEFORMAT }

I have developed a template for use with Word to create documents

designed specifically for RMI memo standards. If you think it would be

worthwhile, I could create templates for the rest of the staff and/or provide

instructions for installing, modifying, and using the template.

Figure 7-41
Jay's test document
with field codes
displayed
(page 1 of 2)

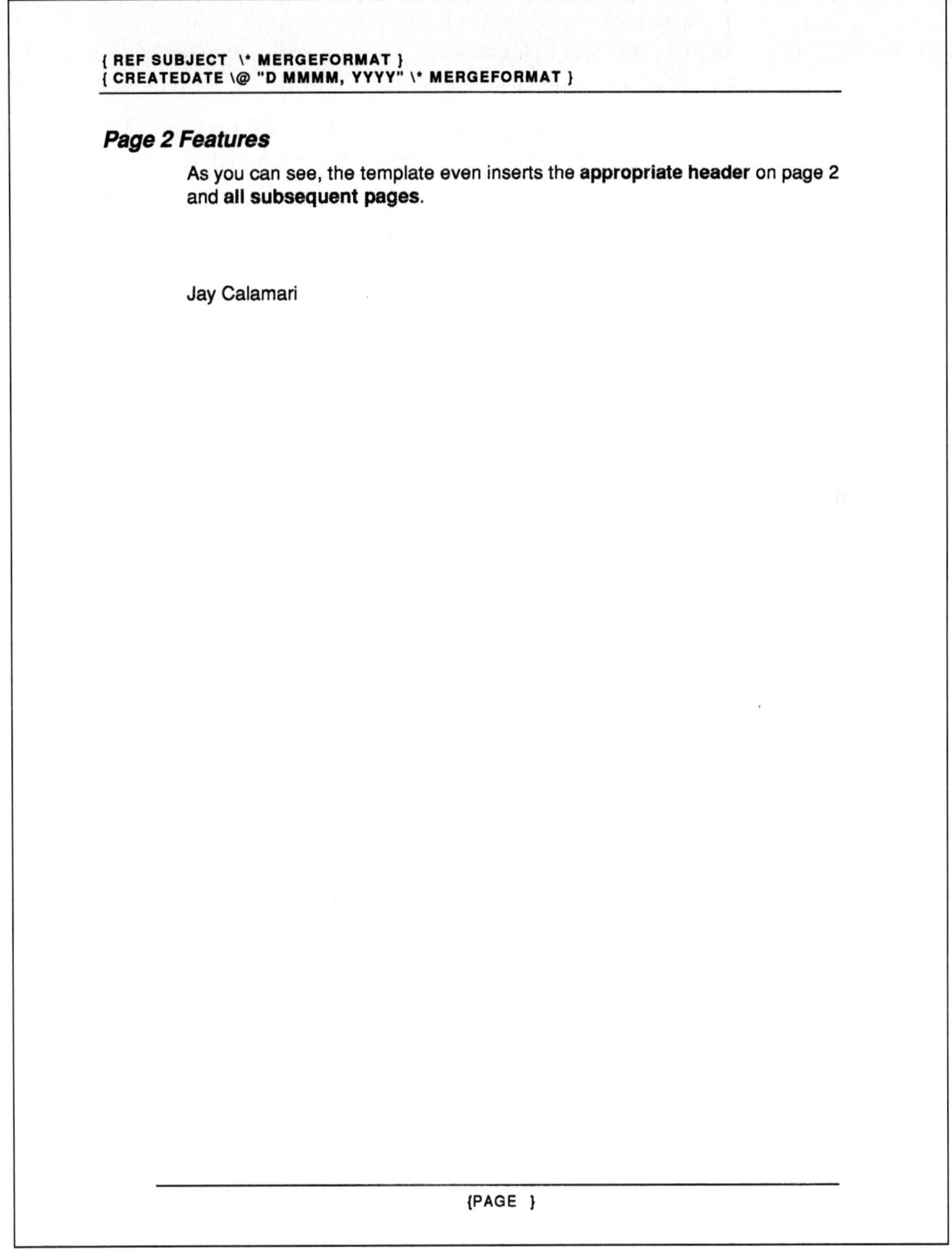

Figure 7-41
Jay's test document
with field codes
displayed
(page 2 of 2)

Now Jay needs to deactivate the Field Codes option so that future printouts will not be affected.

To deactivate the Field Codes option:

❶ Click **Tools**, click **Options…**, then click the **Print tab**, if necessary.

❷ Click the **Field Codes check box** to deselect it, then click **OK** or press **[Enter]**.

Jay is finished printing the documentation for his template, so he decides to use his customized memo toolbar to close this document.

❸ Click the **Close button** on the Memo toolbar to close the document. At the prompt, click **No** because you don't need to save the test document. You return to the Nil menu.

❹ Exit Word without saving any changes to the NORMAL template.

Jay can now use his new template to catch up on all the internal correspondence he must write.

Questions

1. Describe the phases of the customization strategy.
2. What are the three methods for creating a document template?
3. What is the purpose of the Summary Info dialog box? How do you open the Summary Info dialog box?
4. What are the text properties that can be assigned to a template?
5. Describe the procedure for changing the margins using the ruler.
6. Describe the purpose of the Based On style option.
7. Describe the purpose of the Style for Following Paragraph option.
8. What is boilerplate text?
9. Describe the purpose of an AutoText entry.
10. Describe the procedure for defining an AutoText entry.
11. Describe two procedures for inserting an AutoText entry.
12. Describe the difference between saving customization features to a particular template and saving features to the NORMAL template.
13. Describe the difference between field results and field codes.
14. What are the shortcut keys for performing the following operations?
    a. Toggle between field results and field codes
    b. Update a field
    c. Move to the next field and select it
    d. Move to the previous field and select it
15. What are the possible components of a field code?
16. Define field code syntax and give an example.
17. How are field codes inserted into a document?
18. Describe the procedures for displaying field codes individually and all at once.
19. What is a date/time picture instruction?
20. What is the purpose of the CREATEDATE field code?
21. What is the purpose of the FILLIN field code?
22. Describe the procedure for updating fields manually.
23. What is the purpose of a REF field code? How does it work?
24. What are the interface properties that can be assigned to a template?

25. Describe the procedure for using the macro recorder to record a macro.
26. Describe the procedure for customizing the menu structure.
27. What types of items can be assigned to a toolbar?
28. Describe the procedure for assigning items to a toolbar.
29. Describe the procedure for moving a toolbar.
30. Describe the procedure for moving a button on a toolbar.
31. Describe Word's five automacros.
32. Describe the procedure for printing a style sheet, AutoText entries, and key assignments.
33. How do you print a document with field codes displayed?

E 34. What is the syntax for the AutoText field?

E 35. How would you create a macro that involves selecting the text from the insertion point to the end of a word? (Hint: You can't use the mouse to select text when recording a macro.)

Tutorial Assignments

Start Word, if necessary, and conduct a screen check. Open the template T7SERCON.DOT from your Student Disk and complete the following:
1. Save the document as S7SERCON.DOT to your Student Disk.
2. Insert field codes for the bracketed items shown in Figure 7-42.

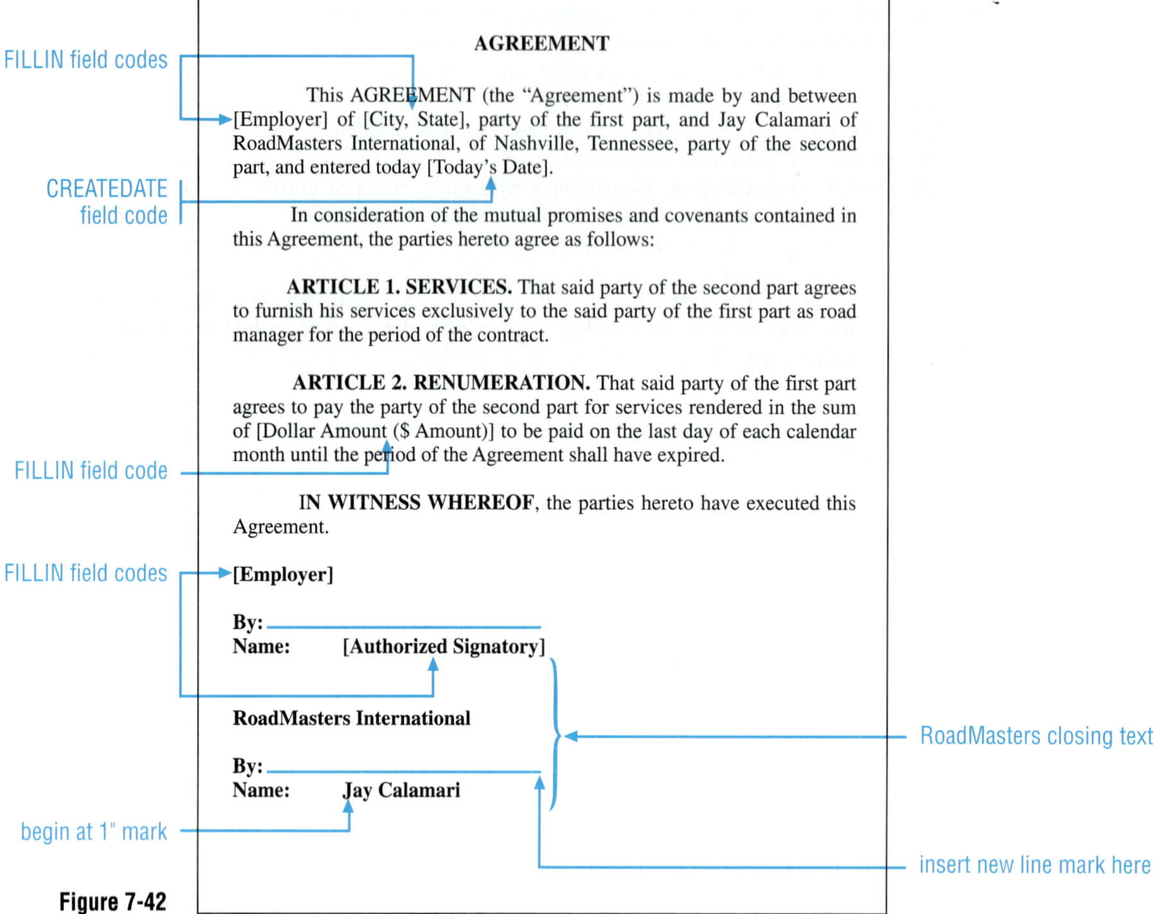

Figure 7-42

    a. Select the text [Employer] in Ln 3, then insert a FILLIN field code that prompts you with "Employer?". Enter "Employer" as the default text in the dialog box.

    b. Select the text [City, State] in Ln 3, then insert a FILLIN field code that prompts you with "City, State?". Enter "City, State" as the default text in the dialog box.

    c. Select the text [Today's Date] in Ln 5, then insert a CREATEDATE field code using the date-time picture MMMM d, yyyy.

    d. Select the text [Dollar Amount ($ Amount)] in Ln 11, then insert a FILLIN field code that prompts you with "Dollar Amount ($ Amount)?". Enter "Dollar Amount ($ Amount)" as the default text in the dialog box.

    e. Select the text [Employer] in Ln 16, then insert a FILLIN field code that prompts you with "Employer?". Enter "Employer" as the default text in the dialog box.

    f. Select the text [Authorized Signatory] in Ln 18, then insert a FILLIN field code that prompts you with "Authorized Signatory?". Enter "Authorized Signatory" as the default text in the dialog box.

3. Create an AutoText entry named "Closing."

    a. Move to the end of the document, then type the closing text for Roadmasters International as indicated in Figure 7-42. Insert a new line mark to move to the next line after typing the underscore for the signature.

    b. Select the closing text for Roadmasters International, including the paragraph mark before RoadMasters International and the paragraph mark after Jay Calamari.

    c. Click Edit then click AutoText.... Name the AutoText entry "Closing" and save it to S7SERCON.DOT.

    d. Delete the selected text.

4. Customize the Standard toolbar by adding a button for the Closing AutoText entry.

    a. Click Tools then click Customize.... Click the Toolbars tab, if necessary.

    b. Click AutoText in the Categories list of the Toolbars tab.

    c. Drag the Closing AutoText label to the Standard toolbar to the space between the Insert AutoText button and the Insert Table button.

    d. Assign the Happy Face image to the button.

5. Record a macro named AutoNew and save it to the S7SERCON.DOT template. Type the following as a description: "Selects the document, updates all fields, then moves to the end of the document." Do not assign the macro to a toolbar, menu, or shortcut key. Record the steps below:

    a. Select the command Select All from the Edit menu.

    b. Update the fields.

    c. Move the insertion point to the end of the document.

6. Save the changes, then close the template.

7. Test the S7SERCON.DOT template by creating a new document based on S7SERCON.DOT, then insert the following information into the test document:

Employer:	Rocky and Poindexter
City, State:	Eden, Kansas
Monthly Pay:	Three Thousand Dollars ($3,000.00)
Authorized Signatory:	Rocky Burke

8. Save the test document as S7BURKE.DOC to your Student Disk.

9. Use the Closing button on the Standard toolbar to insert the Closing AutoText entry.

10. Save the changes.

11. Preview then print the test document, both with and without field codes displayed.

12. Deactivate the Field Codes option on the Print tab of the Options dialog box.

13. Close the S7BURKE.DOC document.

E 14. Open the S7SERCON.DOT template, then edit the CREATEDATE field code so that it is in reverse format (d MMMM, yyyy).

15. Save the template as S7REVRSE.DOT to your Student Disk.

16. Print then close the template.

Case Problems

1. SynFeuls International

Joy Barrett, the receptionist for SynFeuls International of Des Moines, Iowa, wants you to create an electronic message pad, like the one shown in Figure 7-43, for her to use to take messages on-line instead of writing them down.

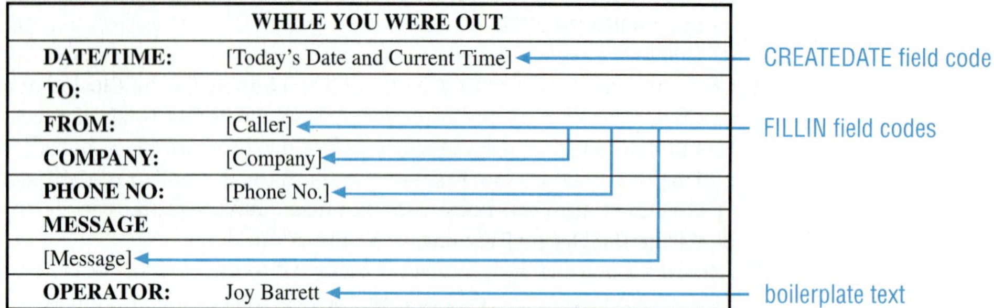

<table>
<tr><td colspan="2" align="center">WHILE YOU WERE OUT</td></tr>
<tr><td>DATE/TIME:</td><td>[Today's Date and Current Time]</td></tr>
<tr><td>TO:</td><td></td></tr>
<tr><td>FROM:</td><td>[Caller]</td></tr>
<tr><td>COMPANY:</td><td>[Company]</td></tr>
<tr><td>PHONE NO:</td><td>[Phone No.]</td></tr>
<tr><td>MESSAGE</td><td></td></tr>
<tr><td colspan="2">[Message]</td></tr>
<tr><td>OPERATOR:</td><td>Joy Barrett</td></tr>
</table>

Figure 7-43

Open P7MSGPAD.DOT from your Student Disk and complete the following:

1. Save the template as S7MSGPAD.DOT to your Student Disk.
2. Create AutoText entries for use in the cell after TO: for the following employees of SynFeuls, including you. Save each AutoText entry to the S7MSGPAD template. Delete any remaining text in the cell after the TO: label when you are done.

ml	Marguarite Lawson
jc	James Cloninger
ch	Christopher Hopkins
mk	Matt Kyle
your initials	your name

3. Insert field codes for the bracketed items shown in Figure 7-43.
   a. Select the text [Today's Date and Current Time] in Ln 2, then insert a CREATEDATE field code using the date-time picture MM/dd/yy h:mm AM/PM.
   b. Select the text [Caller] in Ln 4, then insert a FILLIN field code that prompts you with "Caller?". Enter "Caller" as the default text in the dialog box.
   c. Select the text [Company] in Ln 5, then insert a FILLIN field code that prompts you with "Company?". Enter "Company" as the default text in the dialog box.
   d. Select the text [Phone No.] in Ln 6, then insert a FILLIN field code that prompts you with "Phone No.?" Enter "Phone No." as the default text in the dialog box.
   e. Select the text [Message] in Ln 8, then insert a FILLIN field code that prompts you with "Message?". Enter "Please return call." as the default text in the dialog box.
4. Insert Joy Barrett as boilerplate text in the cell after the OPERATOR label.
5. Save your changes.
6. Place the insertion point in the message pad, if necessary, then record a macro named NewMessage and save it to the S7MSGPAD.DOT template. Type the following as a description: "Copies the message pad to a new page, then updates all fields."
   a. Assign the macro to a toolbar.
   b. Drag the NewMessage label to the space between the Save button and the Print button on the Standard toolbar.
   c. Assign the Telephone image to the new button.
   d. Place the insertion point in the message pad, if necessary, then select the table.
   e. Copy the table to the Clipboard.
   f. Deselect the table, then move to the end of the document, if necessary.
   g. Insert a hard page break.
   h. Paste the contents of the Clipboard to the new page.
   i. Place the insertion point in the new message pad, then select the table.
   j. Update the fields.
   k. Deselect the message pad, then move the insertion point into the table.
   l. Stop the macro recorder.
   m. Delete the page break and second message pad.
7. Save your changes.

8. Record a macro named AutoClose that prints one copy of the current file before clos-ing the document. Save the macro to the S7MSGPAD template. Type the following as a description: "Prints one copy of the current file before closing the document." Do not assign the macro to a toolbar, menu, or shortcut key. Record the following steps:
   a. Click File.
   b. Click Print....
   c. Click OK or press [Enter].
9. Save the changes to the S7MSGPAD.DOT template, then close the template.
10. Test the S7MSGPAD.DOT template.
    a. Open a new document based on S7MSGPAD.DOT.
    b. Save the test document as S7MSGPAD.DOC.
    c. Place the insertion point in the cell after the label TO:, type your initials, then click the Insert AutoText button on the Standard toolbar. Your full name should appear.
    d. Select the message pad, then update the fields, using your instructor's name as the caller and an appropriate telephone number and message.
    e. Deselect the message pad.
11. Place the insertion point in the message pad, then click the NewMessage button on the Standard toolbar.
    a. Enter "Andy Southern" as the caller's name and "Commerce Transportation" as the company name. Insert an appropriate telephone number and message.
    b. Save the changes.
12. Close the document. Make sure that the document is sent automatically to print.
13. Customize the File menu by inserting a command for the built-in macro FileSendMail.
    a. Open the S7MSGPAD.DOT template from your Student Disk.
    b. Display the Customize dialog box from the Tools menu, then display the Menus tab.
    c. Click All Commands in the Categories list, then click FileSendMail in the Commands section.
    d. Place the command at the bottom of the File menu with the "e" in Send serving as the accelerator key.
    e. Save the changes to the template.
14. Place a copy of the window with the File menu open on the Clipboard.
    a. Press and hold [Alt], then press [F], then without releasing [Alt], press [Print Screen]. This places an image of the screen on the Clipboard.
    b. Click the New button on the Standard toolbar, then paste the contents of the Clipboard on the screen. Close the File menu without making a selection.
    c. Save the document as S7MENU.DOC to your Student Disk.
    d. Print the document. This will take several minutes.
    e. Close the document.
15. Print the AutoText entries for the S7MSGPAD.DOT template and print a copy of the document with field codes displayed, then deactivate the Field Codes option on the Print tab of the Options dialog box.
16. Close the document.

2. Newman, Hurley & Strauss

Daniel Cohen is a registered sales representative with the investment firm of Newman, Hurley & Strauss in Rochester, Minnesota. He recently received a request to give a presentation to the Rochester Society of Certified Public Accountants, whose members want to learn about starting an investment club. Daniel decides to use Word's Present1 template, with slight modifications, to create three overheads to use during his presentation. Figure 7-44 shows the first overhead.

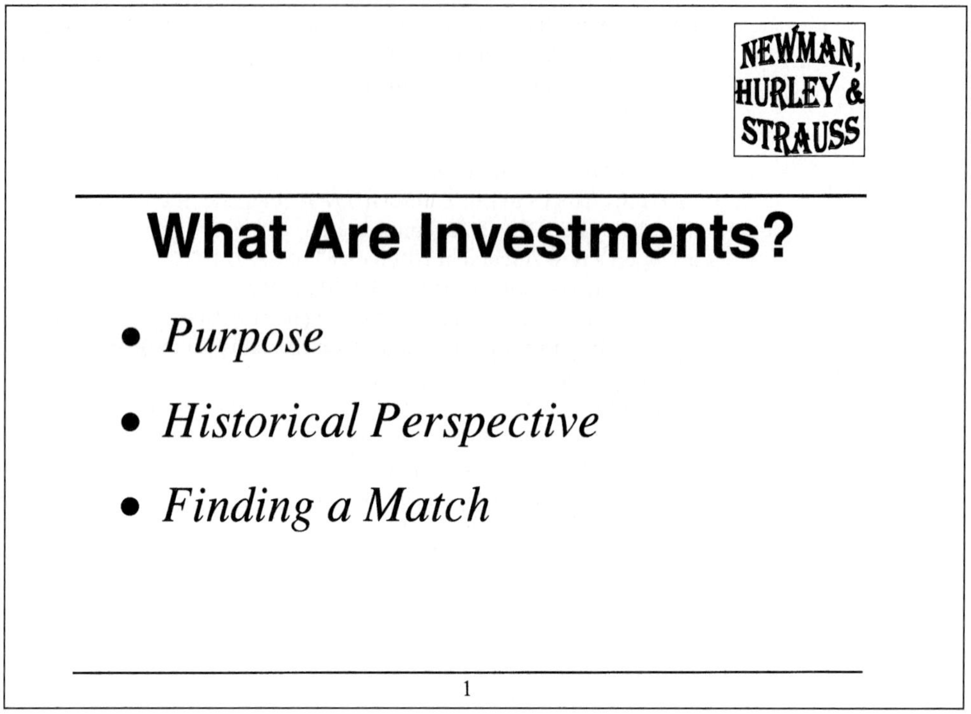

Figure 7-44

Complete the following:

1. Open a new template file based on the PRESENT1 template. In the Summary Info dialog box, type "NHS Overhead Transparency Master" in the Title text box; in the Author text box type "Daniel Cohen."

2. Save the template as S7OVRHD.DOT to your Student Disk.

3. Switch to page layout view, then select Whole Page from the Zoom Control list box, if necessary. Your screen should display the full page of the overhead slide in landscape orientation.

4. Open the Header text area, press [Tab] twice, then insert a WordArt 2.0 image of the company name at the right margin of the header. Specify the following attributes for the WordArt image:

   a. Type each partner's name on a separate line: Newman, (Line 1), Hurley & (Line 2), Strauss (Line 3).

   b. Click the Format down arrow on the WordArt menu bar, then select the Inflate format (fifth row, first symbol).

   c. Click the Font down arrow on the WordArt menu bar, then select the Algerian font.

   d. Embed the WordArt image in the document at the right margin of the Header text area.

5. After embedding the WordArt image at the right margin of the header, scale the picture to 75% of its original size and place a 1 1/2 pt border around it. Close the Header and Footer toolbar. Save your changes.

6. Modify the styles of the S7OVRHD.DOT template according to the specifications indicated in Figure 7-45.

Style	Based On	Style for Following Paragraph	Paragraph
Heading 1		Heading 2	Page Break Before (Text Flow option)
Heading 2	List Bullet	Heading 2	Spacing Before 12 pt; Spacing After 6 pt
Header			Spacing After 6 pt

Figure 7-45

7. To make sure that each document created with this template opens with a Heading 1 style at the top of the document, apply the Heading 1 style to the blank paragraph at the top of the document.
8. Use the Borders toolbar to add a 2 1/4 pt rule to the top of the line space (refer to Figure 7-44).
9. Make sure the insertion point is in the Heading 1 paragraph at the top of the page, then redefine the Heading 1 style by example to include the rule you just created.
10. Open the Footer text area, then use the Borders toolbar to add a 1 1/2 pt rule to the top of the footer line space (refer to Figure 7-44).
11. Make sure the insertion point is in the footer, then redefine the Footer style by example to include the rule.
12. Save the changes.
13. Create a new toolbar called Presentations. Save it to the S7OVRHD.DOT template. Add text buttons for the Heading 1 and Heading 2 styles to the Presentations toolbar.
14. Save the changes, then close the template.
15. Create a test document based on the S7OVRHD.DOT template, then save it as S7RSCPA.DOC to your Student Disk. Type the text shown in Figure 7-46, applying the Heading 1 style to the lines indicated, using the Presentations toolbar. A new page should begin each time you apply the Heading 1 style to a heading.

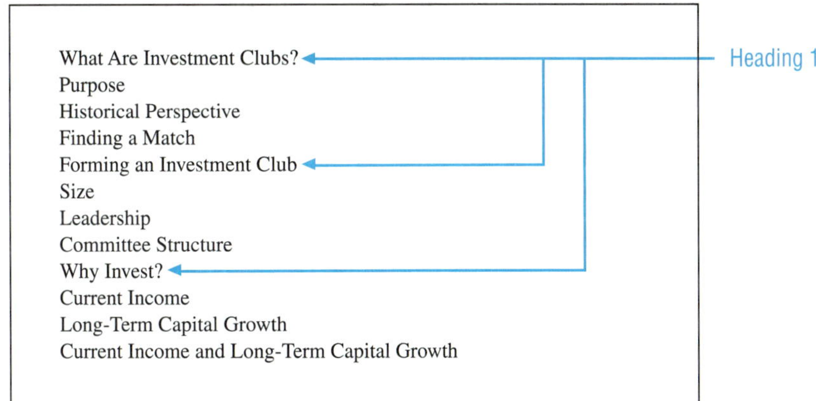

Figure 7-46

16. Spell check the document.
17. Save the changes.
18. Preview then print the document.
19. Switch to outline view, then view only the Level 1 headings. Reorder the transparencies so that the information on page 3 (Why Invest?) moves to page 2 and the information on page 2 (Forming an Investment Club) moves to page 3.
20. Switch back to page layout view, then save the document as S7RSCPA2.DOC to your Student Disk.

E
21. Open the Summary Info dialog box, then type "Investment Clubs" in the Subject text box.

E
22. Open the Footer text area, then insert a field at the left margin that inserts the text of the Subject text box from the Summary Info dialog box. Choose the Uppercase option also.

23. Move the existing page number in the footer to the right margin.
24. Save the changes.
25. Print pages 2 and 3 only.
26. Dismiss the Borders toolbar, switch to normal view, then close the document.

3. Title Page Template

Create a template that produces a title page for reports, research papers, or assignments that you must turn in for your courses. Figure 7-47 shows a sample of a document created with the title page template. The title page has three parts: the title, the Prepared For section, and the Prepared By section. Each part should be one paragraph. Use a new line mark to force a new line to start within a paragraph, where appropriate.

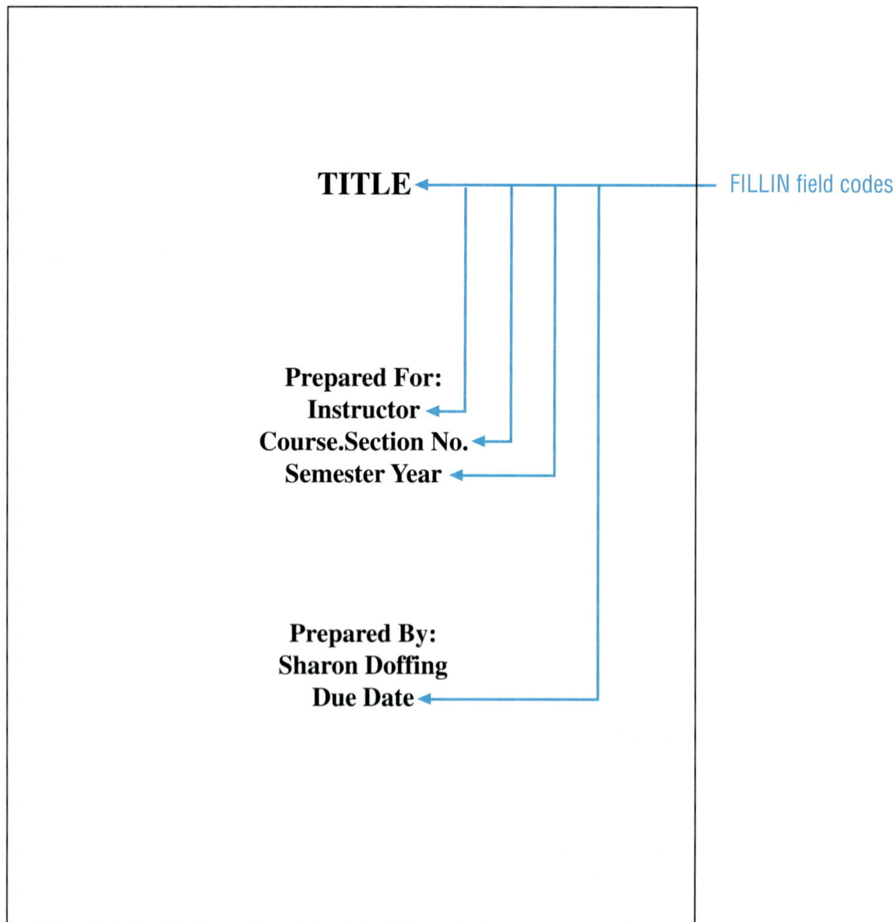

Figure 7-47

Complete the following.

1. Create a new template based on the NORMAL.DOT template. Type "Cover Page" in the Title box of the Summary Info dialog box.
2. Save the template as S7TITLPG.DOT to your Student Disk.

3. Press [Enter] to create a placeholder for the title (part 1), then type "Prepared For:".
4. Press [Shift][Enter] five times, then press [Enter] (end of part 2).
5. Type "Prepared By:", press [Shift][Enter], then type your name, press [Shift][Enter], then press [Enter] (end of part 3).
6. Save your changes.
7. Use the Page Setup command on the File menu to change the top margin of the template to 2" and to align the title page vertically, selecting justified alignment (Layout tab).
8. Modify the Heading 1 and Heading 2 styles using the attributes shown in Figure 7-48.

Style	Font	Paragraph
Heading 1	Century Schoolbook, Bold, 24 pt, All Caps	No spacing before or after; centered alignment
Heading 2	Century Schoolbook, Bold, 18 pt	No spacing before or after; centered alignment

Figure 7-48

9. Apply the Heading 1 style to the empty paragraph mark at the top of the page (part 1), then apply the Heading 2 style to the remaining lines on the page.
10. Insert field codes for the items shown in Figure 7-47.
    a. Place the insertion point in Ln 1, then insert a FILLIN field code that prompts you with "Title?". Enter "Title" as the default text in the dialog box.
    b. Place the insertion point in Ln 3, then insert a FILLIN field code that prompts you with "Instructor?". Enter "Instructor" as the default text in the dialog box.
    c. Place the insertion point in Ln 4, then insert a FILLIN field code that prompts you with "Course and Section No.?". Enter "Course and Section No." as the default text in the dialog box.
    d. Place the insertion point in Ln 5, then insert a FILLIN field code that prompts you with "Semester and Year?". Enter "Semester and Year" as the default text in the dialog box.
    e. Place the insertion point in Ln 10, then insert a FILLIN field code that prompts you with "Due Date?". Enter "Due Date" as the default text in the dialog box.
11. Save the changes.
12. Record a macro named AutoNew and save it to the S7TITLPG.DOT template. Type the following as a description: "Selects the document, updates all fields, then deselects the text." Do not assign the macro to a toolbar, menu, or shortcut key. Record the steps below:
    a. Select the command Select All from the Edit menu.
    b. Update the fields.
    c. Press [↓].
13. Save the changes.
14. Preview the document, then print the template with field codes displayed.
15. Deactivate the Field Codes option on the Print tab of the Options dialog box, then close the template.
16. Test the S7TITLPG.DOT template by creating a new document that produces a title page for this assignment (Tutorial 7, Case Problem 3).
17. Save the document as S7COVER.DOC.
18. Preview then print the title page.
19. Close the document and exit Word.

Using the Master Document Feature to Manage Long Documents

OBJECTIVES

In this tutorial you will:

- Set up a master document containing subdocuments
- Mark, review, accept, and reject revisions in a document
- Insert, find, view, and delete annotations in a document
- Lock and unlock subdocuments
- Include chapter numbers in captions and page numbers
- Create cross-references
- Create an index

Creating a Training Manual

Solomon Technical Communications

Solomon Technical Communications (STC) specializes in creating training manuals developed to meet specific client needs. Morgan Taylor, one of the editors at STC, has been assigned to work on the recently acquired project for Spectrum Engineering Associates. Spectrum has made the transition to the Windows environment, with Word 6.0 as its corporate standard word processing package. STC developed manuals on the upgrade to Word 6.0 for Spectrum, and now Spectrum wants STC to produce a manual on three advanced Word topics: Find File and two of Microsoft's applets, Microsoft Equation and Microsoft Graph. Morgan assigned the project to two technical writers in her group—the Find File lesson to Carla Covington and the Microsoft Equation and Microsoft Graph lessons to Connie Rodriquez. Morgan has received a file from each writer containing the first draft of each topic. She will edit their drafts on-line, then return the edited drafts to the writers electronically for their acceptance or rejection of her suggested revisions. At the same time Morgan will send the material to Matt Wurzbach, the index compiler, so that he can begin the process of indexing the training manual according to STC specifications. The writers will return the final versions of their topics to Morgan, then she will combine them to create the finished product—complete with cross-references, an index, a table of contents, and a table of figures.

Morgan has set deadlines for each phase of the production process. Now that she has received the finished lessons from the technical writers, she can begin to assemble the various elements of the training manual. Each training manual must contain a front matter section, which includes the title page, acknowledgments page, table of contents, and table of figures. STC uses a standard front matter for its manuals; Morgan only needs to customize the front matter for the particular manual she's producing.

A training manual template, C8STCTM.DOT, has already been created and transmitted by STC's Production Department for the editors and writers to use. Using this template, Morgan will edit the topics submitted by the technical writers to make sure that all the text conforms to STC specifications, then she will return the edited documents to the writers for their review—all editing being done on-line. Once the writers have accepted or rejected her revisions, she will format the training manual according to STC specifications and complete the manual. The training manual will then be transmitted to the Printing Department for reproduction and binding.

Using Word with Workgroups

With the increasing use of local area networks in organizations, it is also becoming commonplace for organizations to establish workgroups to complete projects more quickly. A **workgroup** is a team of people working together to complete a project. In a workgroup setting, documents used by the project team are stored on a network file server, enabling the team members to exchange files easily.

Word provides several features for sharing, exchanging, and editing documents, and for managing long documents that are typically the result of workgroup projects. These features include setting up a master document, inserting revision marks and annotations, and creating cross-references.

Master Documents

A **master document** is a long document made up of individual files that are linked together. These individual files are known as **subdocuments**. See Figure 8-1. A master document gives you the convenience of working in smaller files, which require less in terms of computer speed and performance, while providing you with the capability to create cross-references, an index, and tables of contents and figures for the entire document. The master document feature is extremely valuable in a workgroup setting. One person can set up a master document and the subdocuments on the network server, then individual members of the workgroup can open and work on any subdocument by opening the master document.

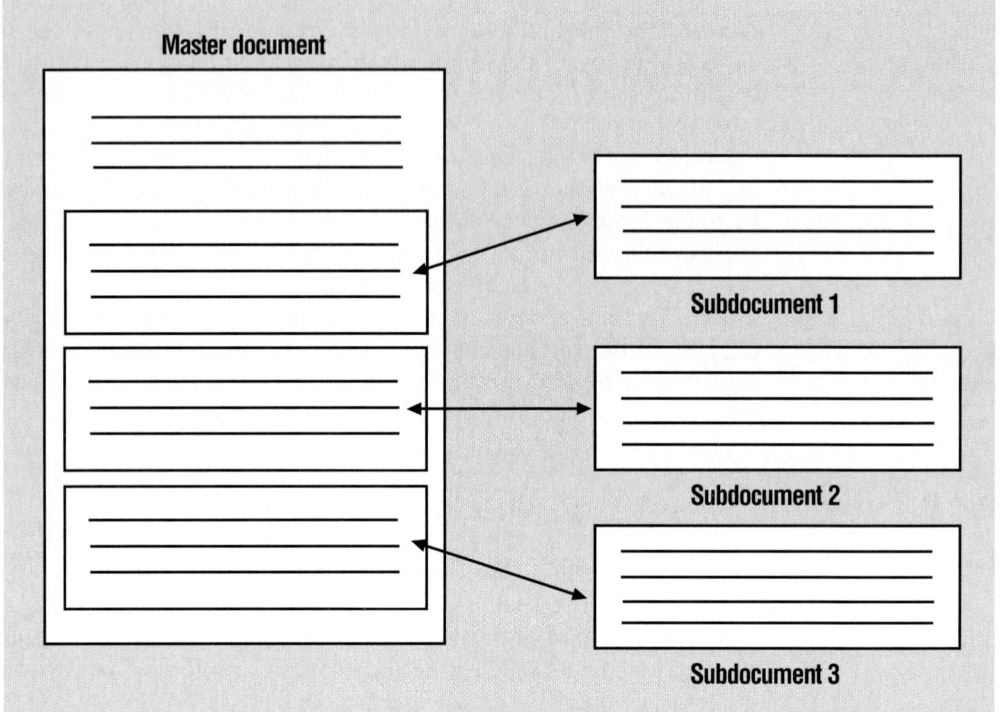

Figure 8-1
Master document
and subdocuments

Setting Up a Master Document

Word provides you with several ways to create a master document, each requiring that you switch to master document view first. **Master document view** is similar to outline view, except that it displays multiple documents instead of just one. You use master document view to link the individual files. You can switch to master document view by selecting Master Document from the View menu or by clicking the Outline View button, then clicking the Master Document button on the Outline toolbar. Once in master document view, the Outline View button in the horizontal scroll bar becomes the Master Document button so that you can easily switch between normal and master document view.

You can create a master document from scratch, or you can convert an existing document into a master document by telling Word to divide a long document into smaller subdocuments based on heading levels. After you have generated a master document, you can also convert existing documents into subdocuments of the master document. Once the subdocuments are set up, you can return to normal view and work on the entire document or open one of the subdocuments. All changes made in the master document are also made in the subdocuments, and vice versa.

Morgan has received the two files from the technical writers assigned to the project. According to STC's specifications, the completed training manual must have consistent formatting among the topics, a table of contents and a table of figures with references to the lesson number and page, and an index of entries at the end of the document.

To begin, Morgan will open a new document, insert the standard front matter file, and customize it for the training manual she's producing.

Note: In order to complete the procedures in this tutorial, you will have to change the User Info settings of the Options dialog box at different times to simulate another person using the computer (thus creating the workgroup setting).

To change the User Info settings:

❶ Start Word and conduct the screen check described in Tutorial 1.

❷ Click **Tools** then click **Options....** The Options dialog box appears.

❸ Click the **User Info tab**.

❹ Select the current entry in the Name text box, then type **Morgan Taylor**.

❺ Press **[Tab]** to move to and select the current entry in the Initials text box, then type **MT**.

Note: You must complete Steps 4 and 5, or the procedures in the remainder of the tutorial will not work properly.

❻ Click **OK** or press **[Enter]**. This establishes ownership of the master document (in this case, Morgan Taylor owns the document).

Now Morgan is ready to open the front matter file and customize it as necessary.

To open and customize the front matter file:

❶ Open the file C8STCPRE.DOC from your Student Disk, then save it as S8WWADV.DOC.

❷ Click the **Page Layout View button** 🗏 on the horizontal scroll bar (or click **View** then click **Page Layout**). Scroll through the document, noticing the styles that have been applied to various paragraphs, and the format of the headers and footers. The document consists of 7 pages. Notice that the page number in the status bar indicates the number format assigned to that section; for example, section 1 contains the preface pages and is formatted with lowercase roman numerals.

Next Morgan needs to insert the name of the training manual—Word 6.0 for Windows: Advanced Features—on the title page, the acknowledgments page, and the table of contents page.

❸ Click the **Normal View button** ☰ on the horizontal scroll bar, place the insertion point in the blank paragraph at the top of the document, then type **Word 6.0 for Windows: Advanced Features**. Note that the word "Features" drops to the next line.

❹ Place the insertion point at the top of page ii, select the text *[Training Manual Name]*, then type **Word 6.0 for Windows: Advanced Features**. The text appears in italics.

❺ Place the insertion point in the blank paragraph at the top of page iii, then type **Word 6.0 for Windows: Advanced Features**.

❻ Save your changes.

Now Morgan is ready to convert the current document into a master document. She will simply open the document in master document view.

To set up the master document from the front matter document:

❶ Press **[F5]**, click **Section** in the Go to What list box, then type **3** in the Enter Section Number text box. Click **Go To** or press **[Enter]**. The status bar should read "Page 1, Sec 3, 5/7."

> **TROUBLE?** Because of the complexity of this document, throughout the tutorial you will be given status bar references for page and section numbers. Use these references as a guide only; the references you see might be different, depending on the type of monitor you're using.

❷ Close the Go To dialog box.

❸ Click **View** then click **Master Document**. The document is displayed in master document view. The Master Document toolbar contains many of the same buttons that appear on the Outline toolbar, plus buttons that are specific to working with master documents and subdocuments. See Figure 8-2.

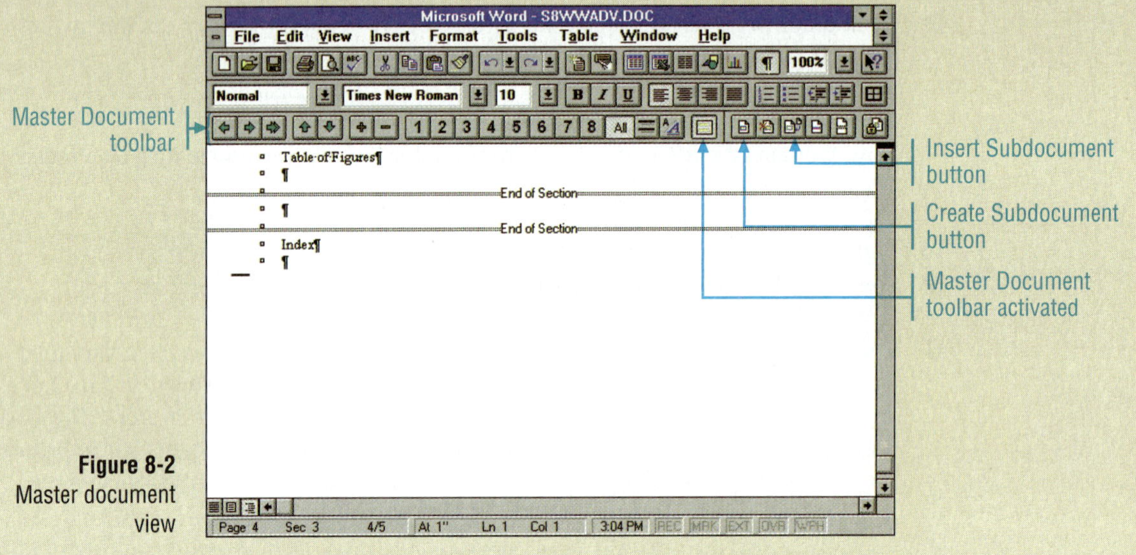

Figure 8-2
Master document view

> **TROUBLE?** If the headings appear formatted, click the Show Formatting button on the Master Document toolbar to deactivate this feature.

Now Morgan is ready to insert the files from the technical writers as subdocuments.

Inserting Subdocuments

A master document can contain up to 80 subdocuments, but the maximum number depends on your computer's memory and storage capacities. Breaking up a long document into smaller parts makes it less cumbersome to work with. To create subdocuments from an existing document that has been converted to a master document, specify the heading level for Word to use as the beginning of each subdocument, select the entire master document, then click the Create Subdocument button on the Master Document toolbar. Word creates and saves the text between the specified heading levels as separate subdocuments (Figure 8-3).

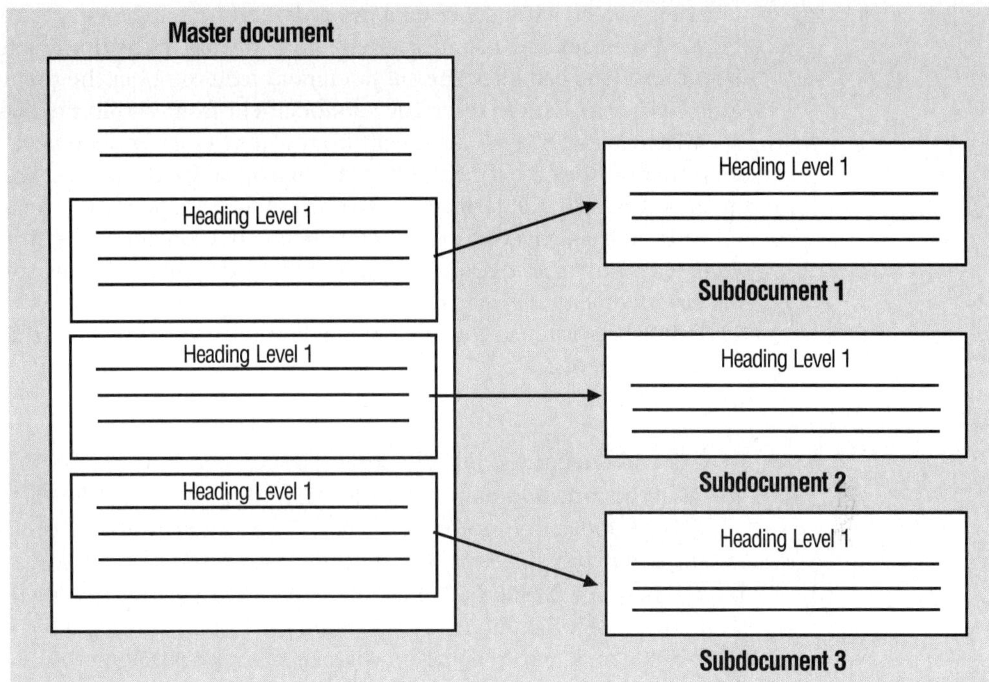

Figure 8-3
Creating subdocuments from a master document

Word also lets you add existing documents to a master document by using the Insert Subdocument button on the Master Document toolbar (Figure 8-4). You move the insertion point to the location in the master document where you want to insert the subdocument, click the Insert Subdocument button, then select the document you want from the Insert Subdocument dialog box.

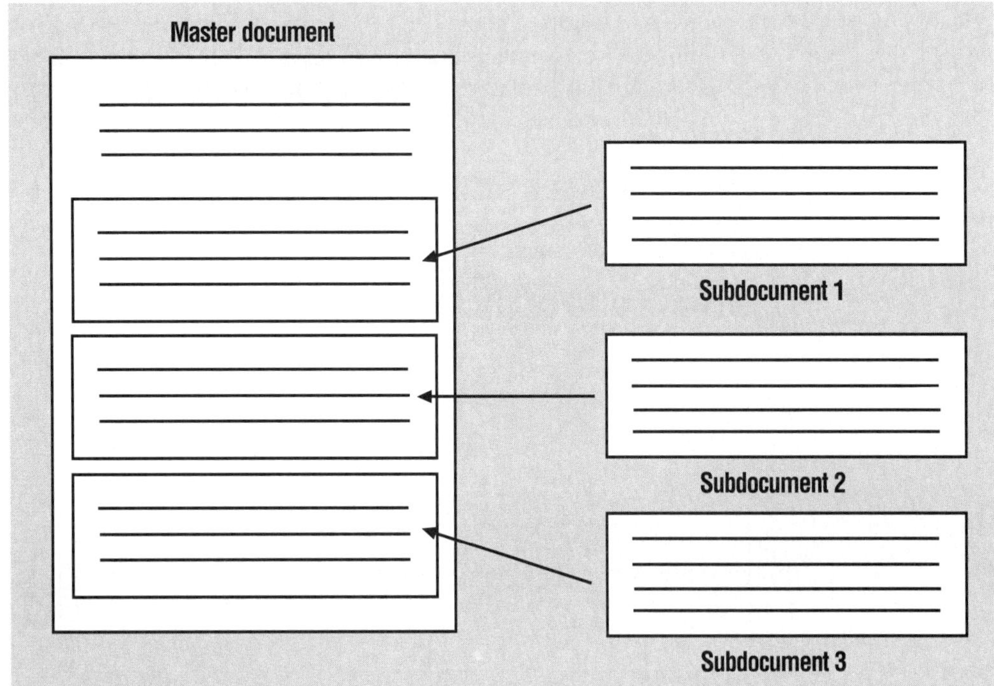

Figure 8-4
Inserting subdocuments into a master document

After you create a subdocument, a dashed box appears around the text belonging in the subdocument and a subdocument icon appears in the upper-left corner of the subdocument text. You can click the subdocument icon to select the text of the subdocument or double-click the icon to open the subdocument from within the master document.

When you open a subdocument from within a master document, the master document's template overrides the formatting of the individual subdocument. When you open a subdocument individually, the formatting attached to the subdocument's template takes effect.

Morgan has converted an existing document (containing the front matter) into a master document. Now she is ready to insert existing document files as subdocuments within the master document. The files submitted by the technical writers were also based on the C8STCPRE template, so the attributes will be the same for both the master document and the subdocuments.

To insert subdocuments into the master document:

❶ With the insertion point in section 3, click the **Insert Subdocument button** 🗐 on the Master Document toolbar. The Insert Subdocument dialog box appears. Make sure the dialog box displays the list of files on your Student Disk.

❷ Double-click **C8FIND.DOC**. The following message appears: "Style 'Address' exists in both the subdocument you are adding (C8FIND.DOC) and the master document. Would you like to rename the style in the subdocument?" Because a master document's template overrides the attributes of a subdocument's template, Word gives you a chance to rename styles sharing the same name, if you don't want a style in a subdocument to be overridden.

The master document and each file from the technical writers were created using the same template, so many of the styles are duplicates. Morgan doesn't need to rename any of the styles in the subdocument.

❸ Click **No to All**. Word inserts a subdocument icon and a box around the text of the inserted subdocument. The subdocument also appears in its own section (subdocuments are essentially sections in Word). Notice that not all of the text of the subdocument is displayed because the Show All button on the Master Document toolbar is not selected. See Figure 8-5. (If necessary, scroll your screen.)

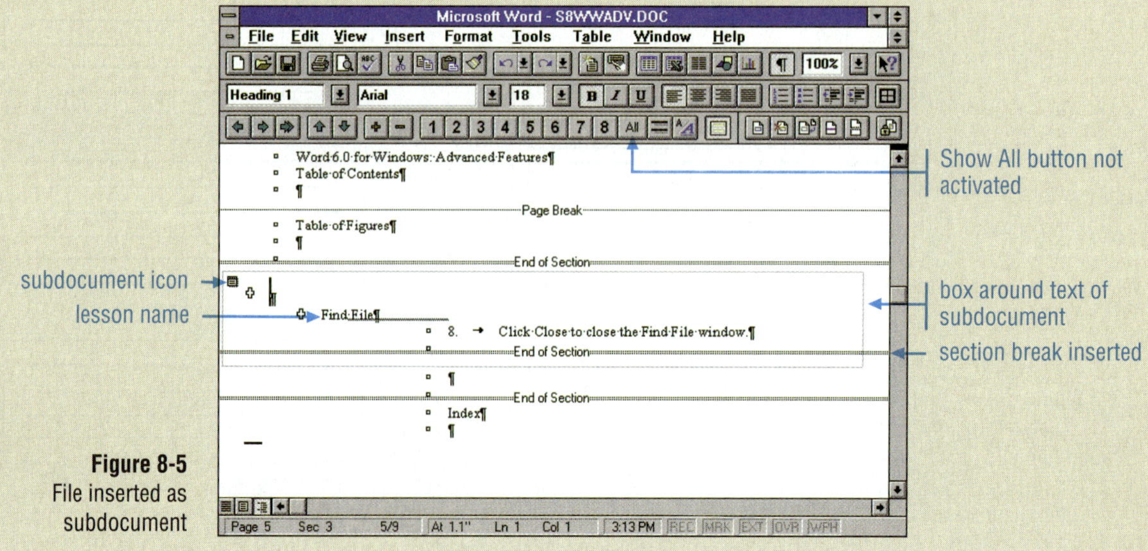

subdocument icon

lesson name

Show All button not activated

box around text of subdocument

section break inserted

Figure 8-5
File inserted as subdocument

Morgan wants the subdocument containing the lessons on the two applets to be inserted in section 4.

④ Place the insertion point in the blank paragraph in section 4, click 🗐 on the Master Document toolbar, then double-click **C8APPLET.DOC**. The same message regarding styles appears.

⑤ Click **No to All**. The file is inserted as a subdocument in the master document. Now the master document consists of 8 sections and 17 pages.

Morgan wants to view just the level 1 and level 2 headings of the master document to make it easier to view the major parts of the document on one screen.

⑥ Click the **Show Heading 2 button** 2 on the Master Document toolbar. The lesson names appear as level 2 headings, with a line beneath them, indicating that text is associated with the headings but is just not visible. See Figure 8-6.

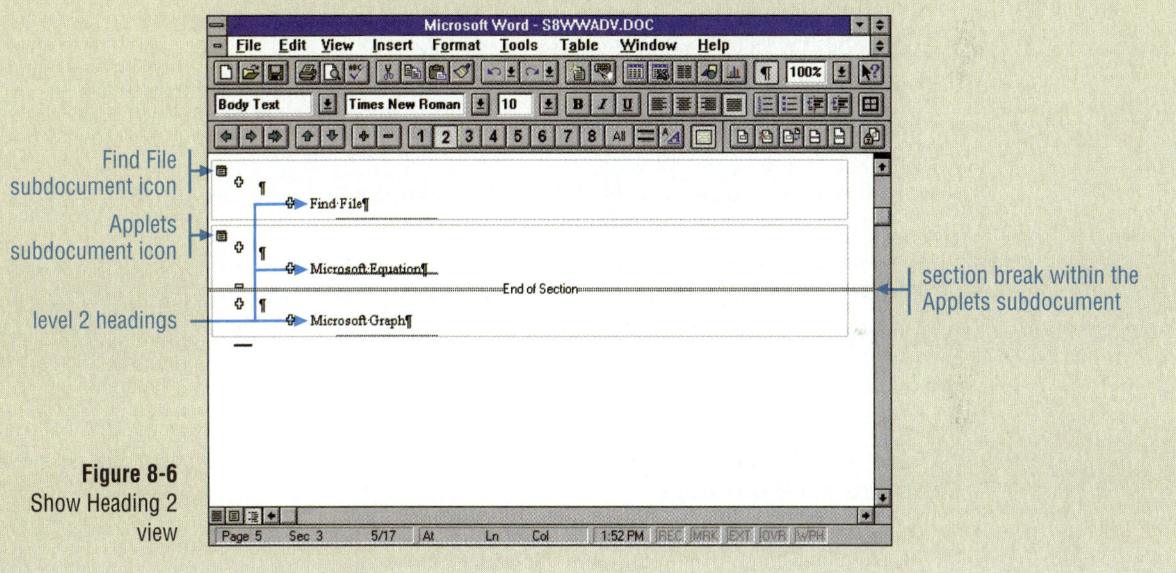

Figure 8-6
Show Heading 2 view

Notice that the first line of each subdocument is blank. The technical writers were told to leave the first line of each lesson blank and to apply the Heading 1 style to it. The blank line serves as a placeholder for the eventual addition of the lesson number (Lesson 1, Lesson 2, and Lesson 3). The title of each lesson, for example Find File, follows, formatted with the Heading 2 style. Also notice that the Applets subdocument consists of two lessons, separated by a section break.

Morgan wants to save each subdocument under a new name so that the original files will remain intact.

Saving a Subdocument

Once a master document is saved with inserted subdocuments, the subdocuments are linked to the master document. Even if you open one of the subdocuments without first opening the master document, changes to the subdocument will be reflected in the master document. If you do not want the original files to be linked to the master document, save the subdocuments under new names *before* you save the master document.

Because the writers might need to use these same files in training manuals for other clients, Morgan wants to rename the subdocuments so that changes to the writers' original files will not be reflected in the master document for Spectrum. She will then work in the renamed subdocuments.

To save a subdocument with a different name:

❶ Double-click the **Find File subdocument icon** (see Figure 8-6 for the location of this icon). C8FIND.DOC opens as a separate document in normal view. S8WWADV.DOC is still open, just not visible.

❷ Click **File**, click **Save As…**, then save the document as S8FIND.DOC to your Student Disk.

❸ Close S8FIND.DOC. You return to the master document.

❹ Double-click the **Applets subdocument icon** (see Figure 8-6 for the location of this icon). C8APPLET.DOC opens as a separate document in normal view. S8WWADV.DOC is still open, just not visible.

❺ Click **File**, click **Save As…**, then save the document as S8APPLET.DOC to your Student Disk.

❻ Close S8APPLET.DOC. You return to the master document.

Morgan is now ready to save the master document and, by doing so, link the subdocuments to the master document.

❼ Save the master document. The master document S8WWADV.DOC now contains two subdocuments, S8FIND.DOC and S8APPLET.DOC. Any changes you make to the master document will be reflected in these two subdocuments, and vice versa.

Inserting the subdocuments added extra section breaks to the master document, which will interfere with the eventual formatting of the document. Morgan must delete these extra section breaks.

To review and delete additional section breaks:

❶ Switch to normal view.

❷ Press [F5], then go to section 3 of the master document. Close the Go To dialog box. Notice that only one section break appears between the Find File lesson and the section above (for the Table of Figures).

❸ Scroll down to the end of Section 3 (Pg 7) of the Find File lesson. Two section breaks appear together.

❹ Delete the second section break by placing the insertion point on it and pressing [Del].

   TROUBLE?   If you deleted the first section break by mistake, click the Undo button 🔙 on the Standard toolbar, then repeat Step 4. You need to delete the second section break because the first one contains formatting related to the previous section.

❺ Move to the end of the Microsoft Graph lesson in the Applets subdocument (Pg 4, Sec 5).

Morgan no longer needs the placeholder (blank paragraph mark) between sections 5 and 6 so she will delete it as well as the second section break.

❻ Delete the blank paragraph mark and the second section break.

Next, Morgan must make sure that each lesson and the index begin on an odd-numbered (right-hand) page, according to STC's specifications.

To change the type of section breaks in the master document:

❶ Go to section 3.

❷ Click **File**, click **Page Setup…**, then click the **Layout tab**.

Morgan wants all lessons and the index—that is, all sections from the insertion point forward—to begin always on an odd-numbered page, even if text is moved later.

❸ Click the **Section Start list box down arrow**, then click **Odd Page**.

❹ Click the **Apply To list box down arrow**, then click **This Point Forward**. All sections from section 3 forward will now be forced to start on an odd-numbered page. If necessary, Word will insert a blank page between sections to force this page numbering. See Figure 8-7.

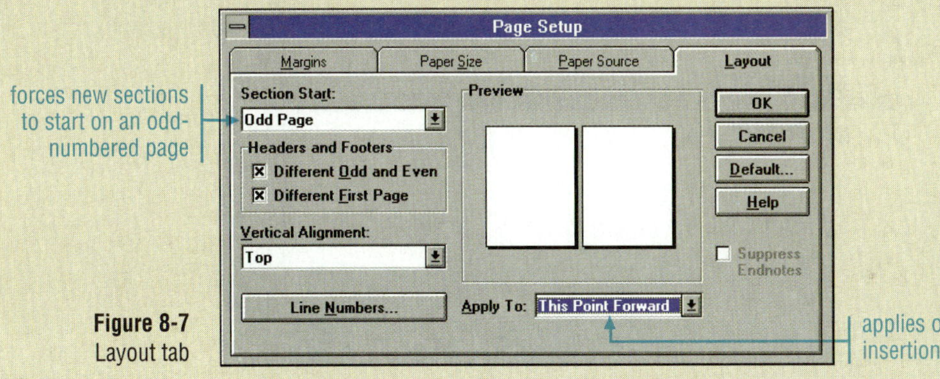

Figure 8-7
Layout tab

❺ Click **OK** or press **[Enter]**.

❻ Save your changes. This might take a few minutes. Notice the status bar as the master document is saving. Word also saves the changes to each of the subdocument files at the same time.

Using the Heading Numbering Feature

Word's **Heading Numbering** feature automatically numbers a series of items that are assigned one of the predefined heading styles (Headings 1 through 9). You could use this feature, for instance, to create a numbered outline. You can customize the numbering scheme to include text such as Chapter, Topic, or Lesson to precede a number (as in "Lesson 1"). This feature is particularly useful in long documents. If you use the Heading Numbering feature to indicate chapter numbers of a book, for instance, and you decide to restructure the order of the chapters, Word can renumber the chapters for you. Furthermore, if you have referenced the chapter number in page numbers (for example, Page 2-1) or figure captions (for example, Figure 2-1) and you subsequently reorder the chapters, Word automatically renumbers the chapter references also.

The technical writers were instructed to insert a blank paragraph mark at the beginning of each lesson to serve as a placeholder for the eventual insertion of a lesson number. Morgan is not sure of the final order of the lessons in the training manual. She decides to use the Heading Numbering feature to format the lesson numbers so that, if she reorders the lessons later, the lesson numbering and any references to lesson numbers will be updated with the new numbers.

To activate the Heading Numbering feature:

❶ Click the **Master Document View button** ⬛ on the horizontal scroll bar (or click **View** then click **Master Document**) to switch to master document view.

❷ Click the **Show Heading 2 button** 2 on the Master Document toolbar, if necessary.

❸ Select the two subdocuments. See Figure 8-8.

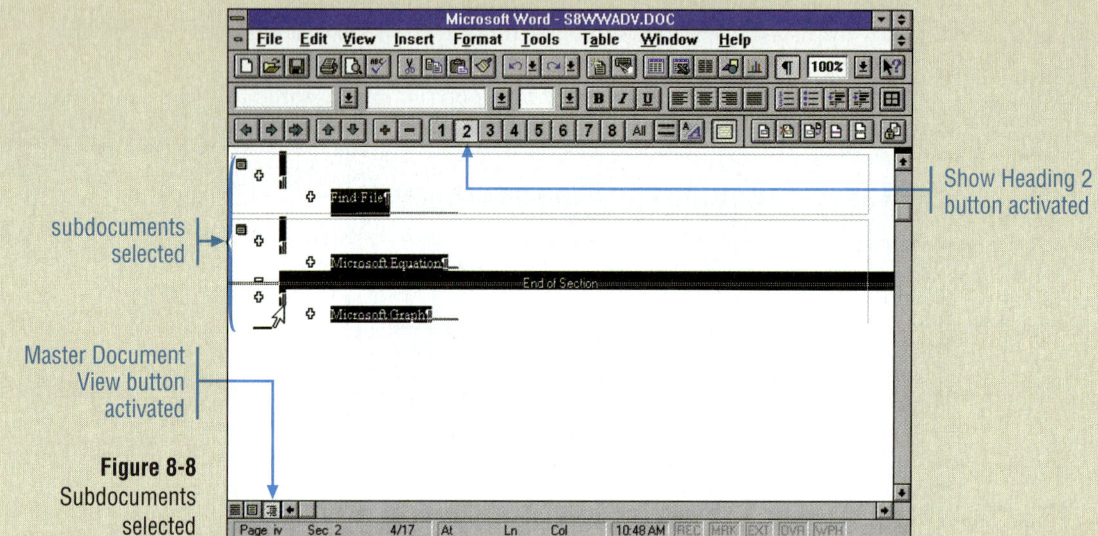

Figure 8-8
Subdocuments
selected

❹ Click **Format** then click **Heading Numbering....** The Heading Numbering dialog box appears.

Morgan wants the text of the lesson numbers to appear as the word "Lesson" followed by the appropriate number—1, 2, or 3. She must change the current selection in the Heading Numbering dialog box.

❺ Click the **Chapter 1 icon**, then click **Modify....** The Modify Heading Numbering dialog box appears.

❻ Double-click **Chapter** in the Text Before text box to select it, type **Lesson** to replace the default text, then press **[Spacebar]** to insert a space between the word "Lesson" and the number that will follow. As indicated in the dialog box, this specification applies only to Level 1 headings. Also, notice the sample text in the Preview section. See Figure 8-9.

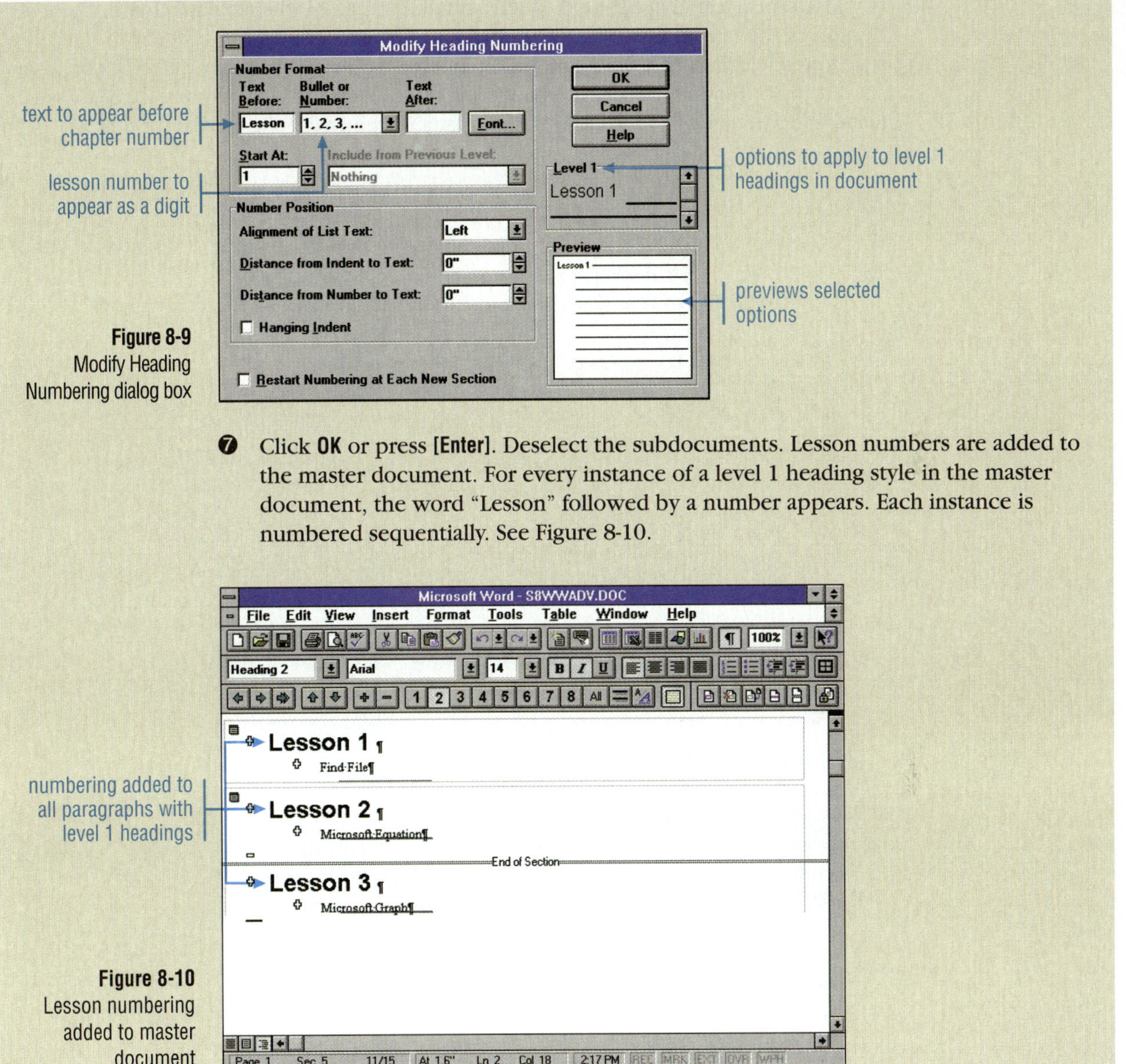

Figure 8-9
Modify Heading
Numbering dialog box

❼   Click **OK** or press **[Enter]**. Deselect the subdocuments. Lesson numbers are added to the master document. For every instance of a level 1 heading style in the master document, the word "Lesson" followed by a number appears. Each instance is numbered sequentially. See Figure 8-10.

Figure 8-10
Lesson numbering
added to master
document

Double Numbering Captions

In long documents, it is helpful to double number figures or tables within a document. To **double number** means to include the chapter number as well as the figure or table number when numbering captions (for example, Figure 2-4 is the fourth figure in chapter 2) rather than using only a continuous numbering scheme for all figures throughout the document. To achieve this effect in Word, you must first apply a unique style to the heading levels containing the chapter number, and then number the chapter headings using the Heading Numbering feature. Then, when you add captions to figures or tables in a document, the chapter number will also appear. If you subsequently rearrange the chapters, Word will automatically update the chapter numbering in the captions.

STC's specifications require the lesson number as well as the table number in every table caption, in the format "Table 1.1, Table 2.1," and so on. Morgan already applied the Heading 1 style to the headings containing the lesson numbers—Lesson 1, Lesson 2, and Lesson 3—and she already activated the Heading Numbering feature. Morgan decides to use the Go To command to move quickly to the tables in the master document so she can format them.

To include lesson numbers in the table captions:

❶ Switch to normal view, then place the insertion point at the top of the document.

❷ Press **[F5]**. The Go To dialog box appears. Click **Table** in the Go to What list box, then click **Next** or press **[Enter]**. The insertion point moves to the first cell of the table in the Find File lesson.

❸ Close the Go To dialog box.

❹ Select the table, click **Insert**, then click **Caption....** The Caption dialog box appears.

❺ Click **Numbering....** The Caption Numbering dialog box appears.

Morgan must specify that she wants the lesson number to be included in the caption label.

❻ Click the **Include Chapter Number check box**.

Morgan must specify which heading level she based the heading formatting on. She assigned lesson numbering to all paragraphs formatted with the Heading 1 style. Heading 1 is the default text in the Chapter Starts with Style text box so she doesn't need to change it. Next she needs to specify the separator character she wants to appear between the lesson number and the table number in each caption.

❼ Click the **Use Separator list box down arrow**, then click **. (period)**. See Figure 8-11.

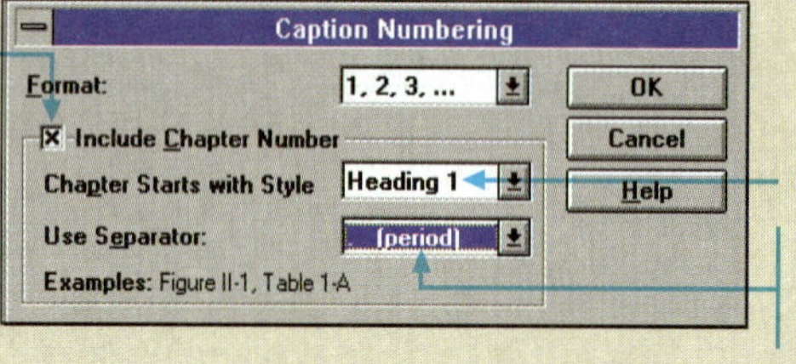

Figure 8-11
Completed Caption Numbering dialog box

❽ Click **OK**. The Caption Numbering dialog box closes. The lesson number is added to the caption label.

Morgan is now ready to type the caption for the table in Lesson 1.

❾ In the Caption text box, press **[Spacebar]** then type **File Management Commands**. Click the **Position list box down arrow**, then click **Below Selected Item** (if necessary). This specifies that the table caption will appear below the table. See Figure 8-12.

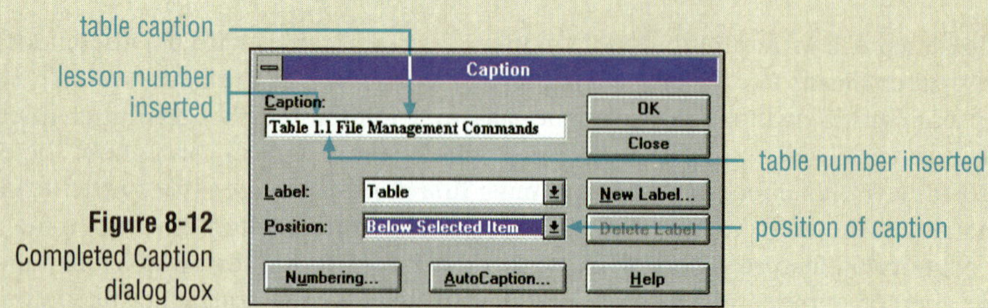

Figure 8-12
Completed Caption dialog box

⑩ Click **OK**. The Caption dialog box closes. The lesson number and the table number appear in the caption below the table. The Caption style has been applied to the caption.

TROUBLE?   If the number of the caption "1.1" does not appear to be italicized, select the caption then apply the Caption style to the paragraph.

Morgan wants the caption to be centered below the table.

To center the table caption:

❶ Click the **Center button** ▤ on the Formatting toolbar. See Figure 8-13.

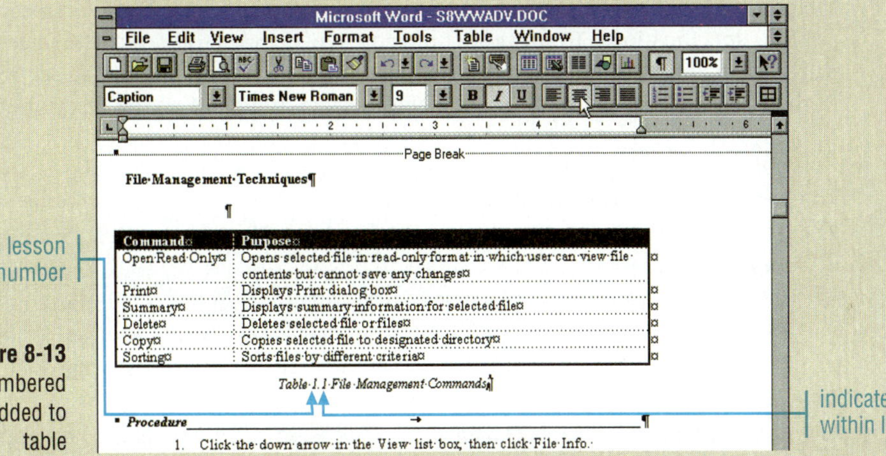

Figure 8-13
Double-numbered caption added to table

❷ Save your changes (this might take a few minutes). Remember Word saves the subdocuments as well as the master document.

Next Morgan must insert a caption for the table in Lesson 2. She will use the Repeat Go To command ([Shift][F4]), which moves the insertion point to the next item specified in the Go To dialog box (in this case, the next table) to move quickly to the table in the Microsoft Equation lesson.

To insert a caption for the table in the Microsoft Equation lesson:

❶ Press [**Shift**][**F4**] to go to the table in the Microsoft Equation lesson.

Morgan wants to double number this table also.

❷ Select the table, click **Insert**, then click **Caption….** The Caption dialog box appears with Table 2.1 already displayed in the Caption text box.

❸ Press [**Spacebar**] then type **Equation Palettes**.

❹ Click **OK** or press [**Enter**]. The caption for Table 2.1 appears below the table.

❺ Click the **Center button** ▤ on the Formatting toolbar to center the caption.

Now Morgan needs to insert a caption for the table in the Microsoft Graph lesson.

To insert a caption for the table in the Microsoft Graph lesson:
1. Press **[Shift][F4]** to go to the table in the Microsoft Graph lesson.
2. Select the table, click **Insert**, then click **Caption…**. The Caption dialog box appears with the lesson number and table number displayed.
3. Press **[Spacebar]** then type **Types of Charts**.
4. Click **OK** or press **[Enter]**. The caption for Table 3.1 appears below the table.
5. Click the **Center button** to center the caption.
6. Save your changes. This might take a few minutes.

Double Numbering Page Numbers

Morgan notices that the page numbering for Lesson 1 (section 3) does not start with page 1, per STC specifications. To prevent confusion, she decides to correct the page numbering for this section and to double number the page numbers in the footers for sections 3, 4, and 5. Both tasks require the use of the Page Numbering command on the Insert menu.

To double number page numbers:
1. Go to section 3, click **View**, then click **Header and Footer**. The Header and Footer toolbar appears.
2. Click the **Switch Between Header and Footer button** on the Header and Footer toolbar to move the insertion point into the First Page Footer - Section 3 text area. You might need to move the Header and Footer toolbar out of the way.
3. Select the page number **5** in the footer.
4. Click **Insert** then click **Page Numbers…**. The Page Numbers dialog box appears.
5. Click **Format…**. The Page Number Format dialog box appears.

Morgan wants the lesson number to be included, a hyphen to separate the lesson number and the page number, and the page numbers to start over with each lesson.

6. Click **1, 2, 3…** in the Number Format list box, if necessary, then click the **Include Chapter Number check box**. By default, Heading 1 appears in the Chapter Starts with Style list box and - (hyphen) appears in the Use Separator list box.

Each lesson is in its own section so Morgan wants the page numbering to start over with 1 for each new section.

7. Click the **Start At radio button** in the Page Numbering section. By default, 1 appears in the text box. See Figure 8-14.

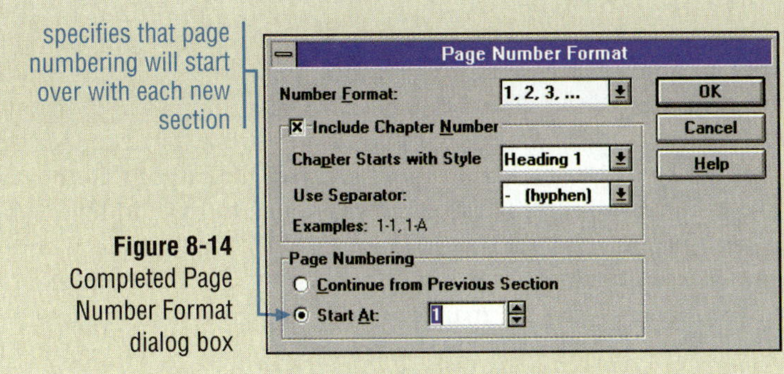

Figure 8-14
Completed Page
Number Format
dialog box

❽   Click **OK** or press **[Enter]**. The Page Number Format dialog box closes.

❾   Click **OK** or press **[Enter]**. The Page Numbers dialog box closes. The page number 1-1 appears in the footer. Also notice the page number in the status bar now reads "Page 1, Sec 3." See Figure 8-15.

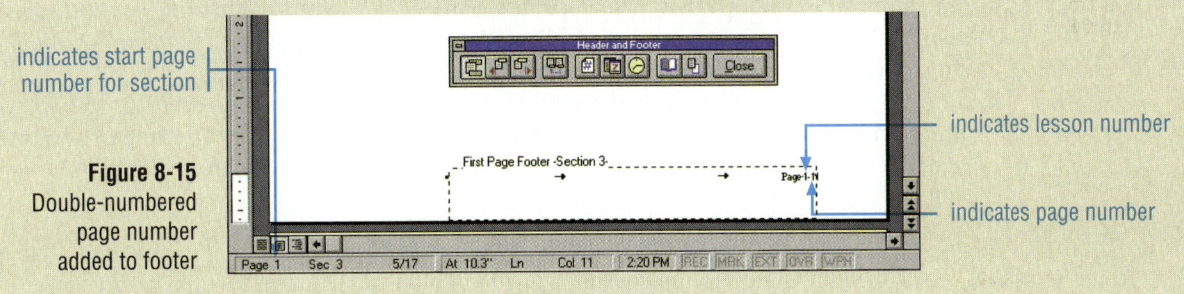

Figure 8-15
Double-numbered
page number
added to footer

Morgan must double number the page numbers in sections 4 and 5.

To double number the page numbers in sections 4 and 5:

❶   Click the **Show Next button** 🔲 on the Header and Footer toolbar until the insertion point moves into the First Page Footer - Section 4 text area.

❷   Repeat Steps 3 through 9 in the previous section to double number the page numbers in the footers in section 4. The page number 2-1 appears.

❸   Click 🔲 on the Header and Footer toolbar until the insertion point moves into the First Page Footer - Section 5 text area.

❹   Repeat Steps 3 through 9 in the previous section to double number the pages in section 5. The page number 3-1 appears.

Morgan has finished inserting double numbered page numbers in sections 3, 4, and 5.

❺   Close the Header and Footer toolbar.

❻   Save your changes.

Morgan is now ready to edit the files submitted by the technical writers.

Marking Revisions in a Document

When a document is reviewed and edited by more than one person, it is necessary to keep track of not only the revisions to the document but also who made the revisions. Word's **Revisions** feature provides such a way of marking a document that is edited by more than one person—with all revisions tracked in the document file rather than on different printed copies of the document. Each reviewer can mark added text and text to be deleted. Each reviewer can also be assigned a different color for revision marks to identify who made which revisions. Once a document is marked for revision, the revisions can be reviewed individually by the author or project manager, who can accept or reject revisions as appropriate. Or, the author or project manager can choose to accept or reject all revisions in one step.

You activate the Revisions feature by choosing the Revisions command from the Tools menu or by double-clicking MRK in the status bar. If you want to mark revisions to a document, you must activate the Revisions feature *prior* to the editing process. You can choose options for marking the revisions while editing and for displaying the revision marks on the screen. If you plan to print a hard copy of your document, you can choose to print it with the revision marks indicated. You can also specify the format for the revision marks so that each reviewer's initials appear with their comments.

Morgan is now ready to begin editing the lessons submitted by the technical writers. She wants her edits to stand out so that the writers can decide whether to accept or reject her suggestions; therefore, she'll use the Revisions feature to mark her edits.

To activate revision marks for the master document:

❶   Click **Tools** then click **Revisions**…. The Revisions dialog box appears, with two options selected.

Morgan wants the revisions to be marked and displayed on the screen while she is editing. She won't be printing a hard copy of the document with her revisions, so she will deselect the check box for that option.

❷   Click the **Mark Revisions While Editing check box** to select it. Make sure the Show Revisions on Screen check box is selected.

❸   Click the **Show Revisions in Printed Document check box** to deselect it. See Figure 8-16.

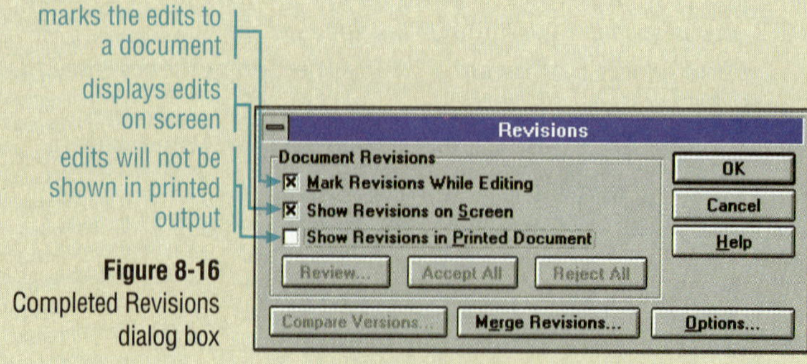

Figure 8-16
Completed Revisions dialog box

❹   Click **Options…** in the Revisions dialog box. The Options dialog box appears with the Revisions tab displayed.

Morgan decides to keep the default marks for revisions, which specify that inserted text will be marked with an underline, deleted text will be marked with a strikethrough line, and all revision lines indicating where edits have occurred will appear on the outside border of each page. Also, each reviewer's revisions and comments will appear in a different color, as specified by the By Author color option.

❺ Click **OK** or press **[Enter]**. The Options dialog box closes.

❻ Click **OK** or press **[Enter]**. The Revisions dialog box closes. Notice that MRK appears darker in the status bar, indicating that revision marks are in effect.

Morgan is now ready to make revisions to the individual subdocuments. She could switch to normal view and make the revisions within the master document, but she decides to open each subdocument individually. Because she will no longer be working in the master document but in separate subdocuments, she must also activate the revision marks for the two subdocuments before she makes any changes. She'll start with the Find File lesson.

To activate the Revisions feature for the Find File subdocument:

❶ Switch to master document view.

❷ Double-click the **Find File subdocument icon**. S8FIND.DOC opens and the window changes to normal view. S8WWADV.DOC is still open but is not visible. Any changes made in the subdocument S8FIND.DOC will be reflected in the master document S8WWADV.DOC. Notice that "Lesson 1" is not displayed on the first line of the subdocument. The Heading Numbering feature applies to the level 1 headings in the master document only, not in subdocuments.

Morgan needs to activate revision marks for this subdocument.

❸ Click **Tools** then click **Revisions…**. The Revisions dialog box appears.

❹ Click the **Mark Revisions While Editing check box** to select it, then click the **Show Revisions in Printed Document check box** to deselect it. Make sure the Show Revisions on Screen check box is selected.

❺ Click **OK** or press **[Enter]**. The Revisions dialog box closes.

Morgan is now ready to edit the Find File lesson, which was submitted by Carla Covington.

To edit and mark revisions in the Find File subdocument:

❶ Press **[F5]** then go to page 3 of the document. Close the Go To dialog box.

❷ Delete the word **which** in the second sentence of step 1 (Ln 14). Notice that Word strikes through the revision with the color blue but does not actually delete the word. A revision line appears in the left margin to indicate that an edit has occurred at this location in the document.

Morgan sees that some text is missing from step 5 of the current set of procedures.

❸ Place the insertion point at the end of step 5 (Ln 22), then type **sort files, choose the Commands button.** Word inserts the new text in blue and underlines it; a revision mark appears in the left margin. See Figure 8-17.

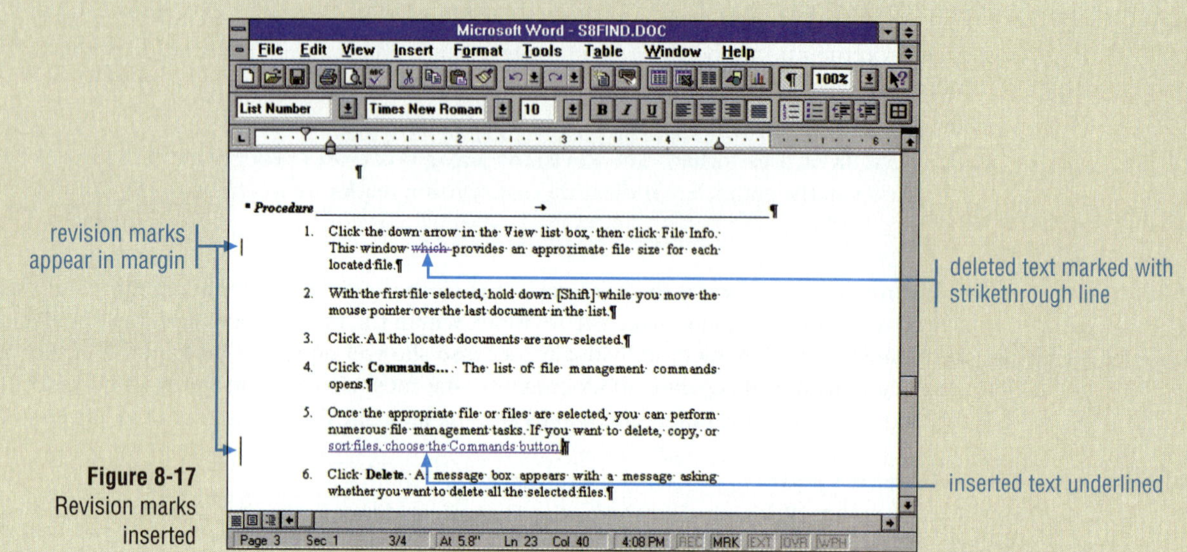

Figure 8-17
Revision marks
inserted

❹ Save your changes to S8FIND.DOC. Notice the status bar as the document is saving. The master document S8WWADV.DOC is not saved. The changes made in the subdocument are reflected now in the master document, but the changes aren't saved to the master document—only to the subdocument.

Morgan is finished making revisions to this subdocument so she decides to deactivate the Revisions feature for the subdocument. When Carla reviews Morgan's edits later, she'll need to activate the Revisions feature when she opens S8FIND.DOC so that she can see where Morgan made changes.

❺ Double-click **MRK** in the status bar (or click **Tools** then click **Revisions...**). The Revisions dialog box appears.

❻ Deselect both the Mark Revisions While Editing check box and the Show Revisions on Screen check box.

❼ Click **OK** or press **[Enter]**. The revision marks are no longer activated.

Morgan wants to make sure that the changes she made in the subdocument are reflected in the master document.

❽ Click **Window** then click **S8WWADV.DOC** to return to the master document. Notice that a padlock icon 🔒 now appears next to the Find File subdocument, and the Lock Document button 🔏 on the Master Document toolbar is activated. See Figure 8-18. These indicate that the subdocument is locked, which prevents others from opening and editing the file. The subdocument is still open and will remain locked and unavailable to other users until Morgan closes it.

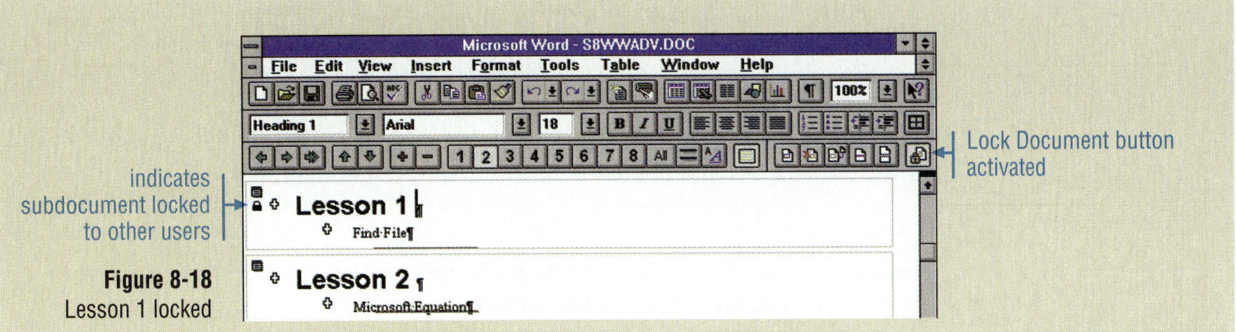

Figure 8-18
Lesson 1 locked

Morgan did not turn off the Revisions feature for the master document, just the sub-document. She should still be able to see the changes she made in the Find File subdocument reflected in the master document.

❾ Switch to normal view then scroll down through the master document into the Find File lesson. Notice that the changes you made in the subdocument also appear in the master document.

Now Morgan will revise the second subdocument, S8APPLET.DOC, which contains two lessons—one on Microsoft Equation and one on Microsoft Graph.

To edit and mark revisions in the second subdocument from within the master document:

❶ Scroll down into Lesson 3, Microsoft Graph, then select the text of step 2, beginning with "Click the Zoom Page..." (Pg 2, Sec 5, Ln 41). Do *not* include the ending paragraph mark.

❷ Type **Click the Zoom Control down arrow, then click Page Width so that the entire width of the table is in view.** The typed text appears as inserted text; the selected text appears as deleted text.

To be consistent with STC specifications, Morgan must also bold the name of the button and the command in this step.

❸ Select the text **Zoom Control down arrow** then click the **Bold button** B on the Formatting toolbar.

❹ Select the text **Page Width** then click B . Deselect the selected text. See Figure 8-19.

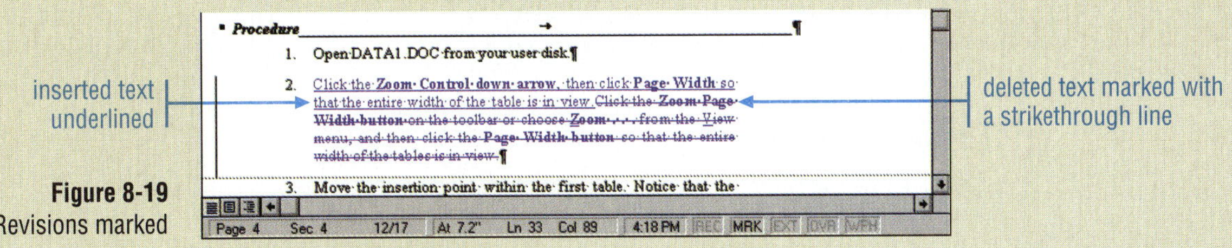

Figure 8-19
Revisions marked

Morgan realizes that she is working in the master document rather than the subdocument. She decides to switch to the subdocument so that the performance of her computer won't be slowed by the length of the master document.

❺ Switch to master document view, then double-click the **Applets subdocument icon** to open the subdocument S8APPLET. You might have to scroll up to view the Applets subdocument icon.

❻ Scroll through the subdocument to notice that the change you made in Lesson 3 while in master document view is reflected in the subdocument.

Morgan can now make the remaining changes to the S8APPLET subdocument. She must turn on the revision marks for this subdocument.

To edit and mark revisions in the S8APPLET subdocument:

❶ Click **Tools** then click **Revisions…**. The Revisions dialog box appears.

❷ Click the **Mark Revisions While Editing check box** to select it, then click the **Show Revisions in Printed Document check box** to deselect it. Make sure the Show Revisions on Screen check box is selected.

❸ Click **OK** or press **[Enter]**. The Revisions dialog box closes.

❹ Select the entire paragraph below step 5 in the Creating a Standard Column Chart section beginning with "Microsoft Graph starts and opens…" (Pg 3, Sec 2) (including the ending paragraph mark), then click the **Cut button** ✂ on the Standard toolbar. Word strikes through the paragraph to indicate a deletion.

❺ Place the insertion point in front of the heading Editing Graphs, then click the **Paste button** 🗐 on the Standard toolbar. Word underlines the paragraph in its new location to indicate inserted text. Deselect the paragraph. See Figure 8-20.

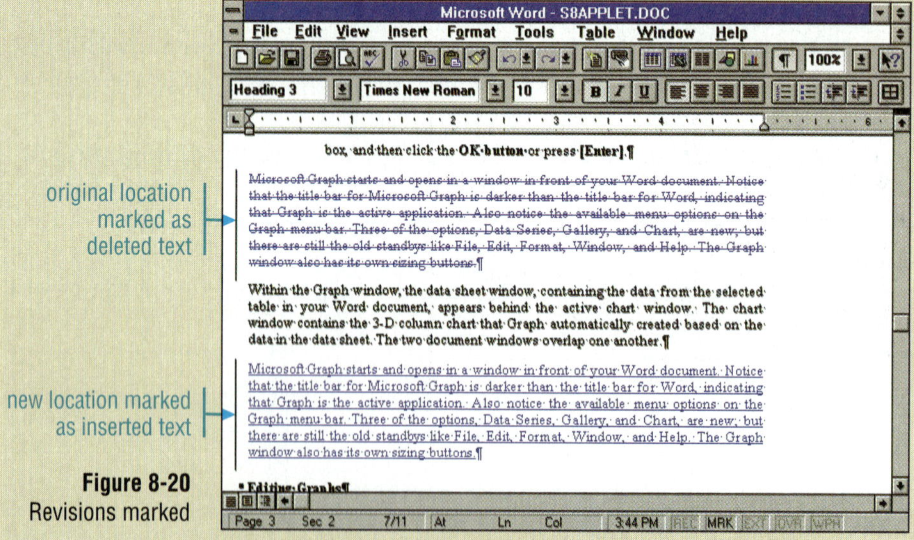

original location marked as deleted text

new location marked as inserted text

Figure 8-20
Revisions marked

❻ Save your changes to S8APPLET.DOC.

Morgan has no more changes to make. She decides to turn off the option for marking revisions, but she wants the revisions she just made to still be visible.

❼ Double-click **MRK** in the status bar (or click **Tools** then click **Revisions…**). The Revisions dialog box appears.

❽ Deselect the Mark Revisions While Editing check box, then click **OK** or press **[Enter]**. The existing revisions can still be seen in the document.

❾ Click **Window** then click **S8WWADV.DOC** to return to the master document. A padlock icon appears next to the Applets subdocument, and the Lock Document button is activated, indicating that this subdocument is still open and locked to other users.

Next, Morgan wants to add comments explaining her edits so that the writers will know why she made them.

Inserting Annotations

During the editing process, reviewers typically provide explanations, called **annotations**, for their suggested revisions to a document. Word's **Annotation** feature allows you to insert such comments in the document file. If you have the necessary hardware, you can even insert voice or light pen annotations rather than on-line annotations. These reviewer comments appear in an annotation pane so that the text of the document is not interrupted. Each annotation is numbered and preceded by the reviewer's initials, if the reviewer's initials have been entered in the User Info tab of the Options dialog box. You can copy, move, and delete annotations. You can also print a separate listing of the annotations in a document.

Morgan wants to insert annotations explaining her revisions so that the writers will understand her suggested changes.

To insert an annotation in the Find File subdocument:

❶ Click **Window** then click **S8FIND.DOC**.

Because she didn't make major changes to this document, Morgan just wants to congratulate Carla on a job well done.

❷ Place the insertion point at the top of the document, click **Insert**, then click **Annotation**. The Annotations pane opens at the bottom of the screen. Notice that Morgan's initials and the annotation number [MT1] appear at the point of the inserted annotation in the document and in the Annotations pane.

❸ Type **Nothing major to change. You did a great job. Thanks.** Word inserts the annotation. See Figure 8-21.

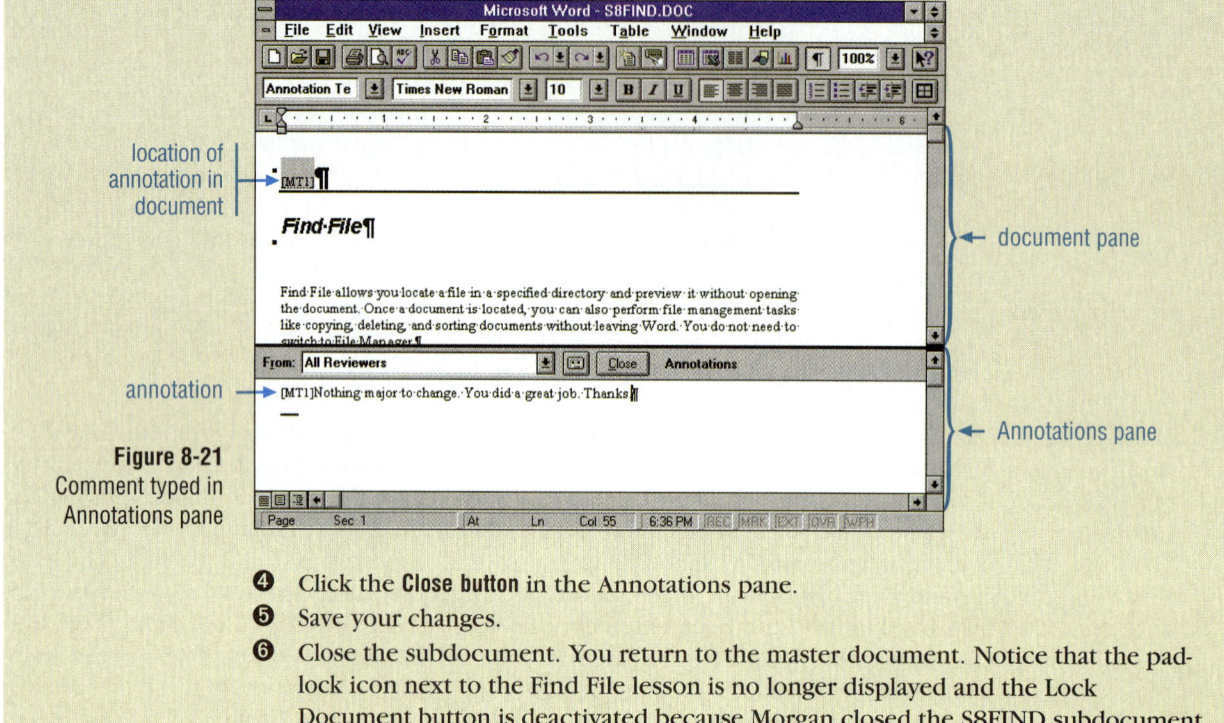

location of annotation in document

document pane

annotation

Annotations pane

Figure 8-21
Comment typed in
Annotations pane

❹ Click the **Close button** in the Annotations pane.

❺ Save your changes.

❻ Close the subdocument. You return to the master document. Notice that the padlock icon next to the Find File lesson is no longer displayed and the Lock Document button is deactivated because Morgan closed the S8FIND subdocument. Other users can now access this file.

Next Morgan wants to insert comments about the revisions she made to the Applets subdocument written by Connie Rodriquez.

To insert multiple annotations within a document:

❶ Click **Window** then click **S8APPLET.DOC**. S8APPLET.DOC opens in normal view.

❷ Scroll up to section 2 (Pg 2, Ln 41), then click in front of the text of step 2, where Morgan made the first revision in the Applets subdocument ("Click the Zoom...").

❸ Click **Insert** then click **Annotation**. The Annotations pane opens.

❹ Type **I'm not sure, but I think you used Word 2.0 rather than Word 6.0 commands. Please check my changes.**

Morgan also wants to insert a comment about the revision she made in the order of the paragraphs below this set of steps. She doesn't have to close the Annotations pane to insert the next annotation mark.

❺ Press **[F6]** to switch to the document pane, then place the insertion point in front of the text "Within the Graph..."

❻ Click **Insert** then click **Annotation**. Annotation number [MT2] appears.

❼ Type **I think this section flows better with the "Within the Graph window" paragraph before the "Microsoft Graph" paragraph. What do you think?** See Figure 8-22.

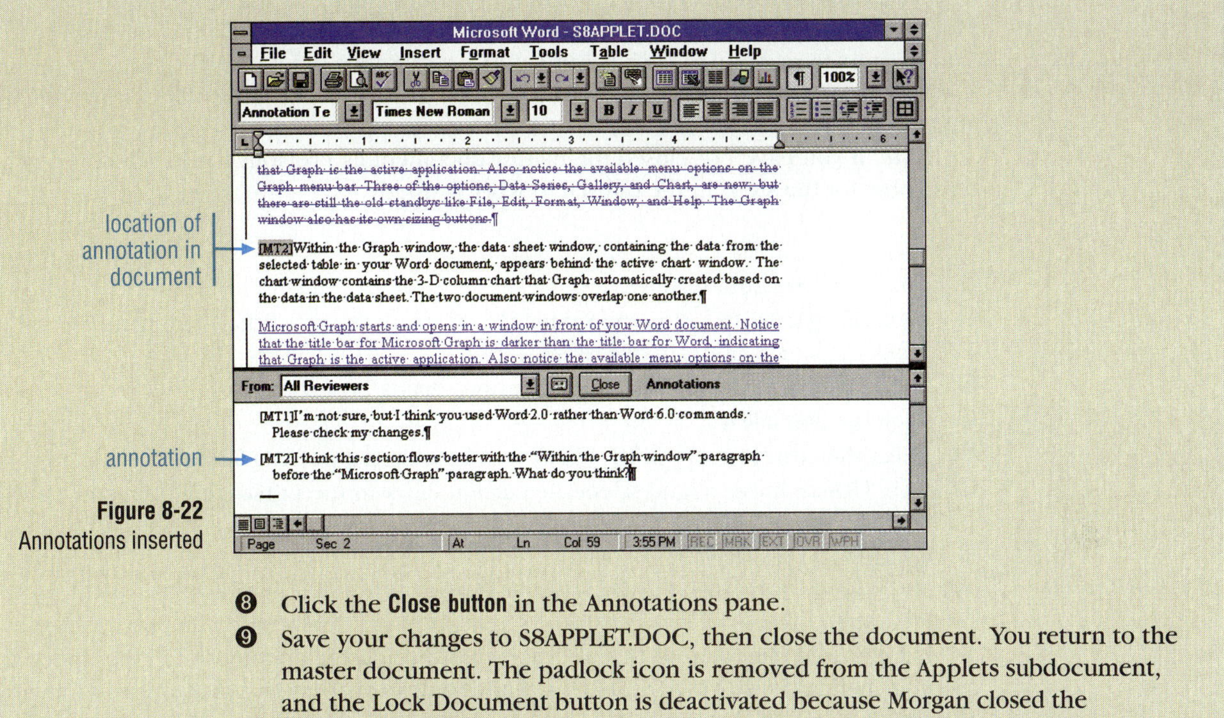

⑧   Click the **Close button** in the Annotations pane.

⑨   Save your changes to S8APPLET.DOC, then close the document. You return to the master document. The padlock icon is removed from the Applets subdocument, and the Lock Document button is deactivated because Morgan closed the S8APPLET subdocument.

⑩   Save your changes to the master document, then close the master document.

If you want to take a break and resume the tutorial at a later time, exit Word. If you are prompted to save changes to NORMAL.DOT, click No. When you want to resume the tutorial, start Word and place your Student Disk in the disk drive. (Do *not* open S8WWADV.DOC until instructed to do so.) Remember to complete the screen check procedure described in Tutorial 1. Then continue with the tutorial.

Morgan sends an electronic mail message to the technical writers explaining that she has finished her revisions and would like them to read the revisions and annotations by the next day. She also sends a message to the index compiler, Matt Wurzbach, indicating that he can begin the indexing process. She also tells everyone the name of the master document assigned to the training manual.

Document Protection

Sharing a document with others poses some interesting document protection problems. You need to be able to read documents and often revise documents created by others. Word provides a special file-locking feature that initially prevents you from having read-write privileges to master documents and subdocuments not "owned" (created) by you. If you need to make changes to a master document or a subdocument created by someone else, however, you only need to toggle off the Lock Document feature, and you will be able to access and edit that document. Word determines who "owns" a document by analyzing the information in the User Info tab of the Options dialog box.

Carla Covington received Morgan's electronic mail message and wants to read Morgan's annotations before viewing the actual revisions. The standard procedure at STC is for writers to respond to each comment by a reviewer.

First, you need to change the User Info settings to simulate that Carla is now working at her computer.

Note: If you have not closed the master document as previously instructed, you must do so now for the steps in the tutorial to work properly.

To change the User Info settings:

❶ Click the **New button** 🗋 on the Standard toolbar to display all the Word menus in the document window, if necessary.

❷ Click **Tools** then click **Options....** The Options dialog box appears.

❸ Click the **User Info tab**.

❹ Select the current entry in the Name text box, then type **Carla Covington**.

❺ Press **[Tab]** to move to and select the current entry in the Initials text box, then type **CC**.

❻ Click **OK** or press **[Enter]**.

Morgan told the writers that the name of the master document for the Spectrum training manual is S8WWADV.DOC. Carla decides to open that document to review Morgan's comments.

To open the master document then unlock the subdocument:

❶ Open the file S8WWADV.DOC from your Student Disk, then switch to master document view, if necessary.

❷ Click the **Show Heading 2 button** 2 on the Master Document toolbar. Notice that the title bar displays "(Read-Only)" next to the title of the document, indicating that the person who opened the document does not own the document. The person opening the document can read the document, but any changes that a non-owner makes to the document cannot be saved. See Figure 8-23.

indicates that the person who opened the document does not own the document

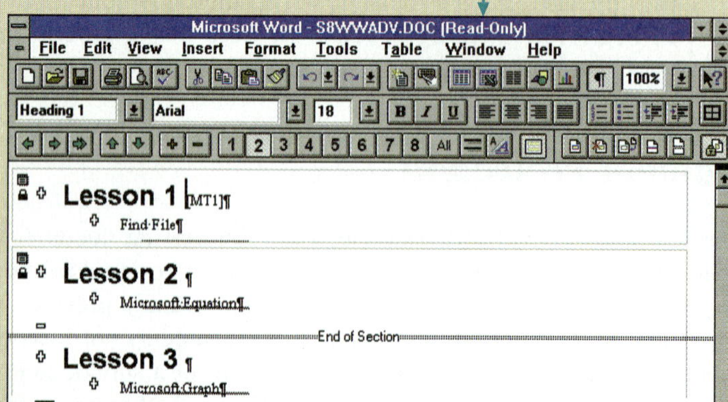

Figure 8-23
Master document protection

Carla must be able to view the changes that Morgan made to the Find File lesson and respond to them. She must change her privileges from read-only to read-write.

❸ Place the insertion point at the end of the line containing the text "Lesson 1."

❹ Click the **Lock Document button** 🔒 on the Master Document toolbar to deselect it. The padlock icon disappears from the Find File subdocument.

Now Carla can open the subdocument that she wrote and save changes to it.

❺ Double-click the **Find File subdocument icon**. S8FIND.DOC opens. Notice that it is not in read-only format.

Now Carla wants to review the comments Morgan made in her annotations.

Finding and Reviewing Annotations

Annotation marks are displayed throughout a document if the Show/Hide ¶ option is activated so you could just scroll through a document looking for any annotation marks. To open the Annotations pane, simply double-click an annotation mark. You can find annotations in a document quickly just as you find other document elements such as specific page numbers, sections, tables, or bookmarks—with the Go To command. You can also view all annotations by choosing Annotations from the View menu. If you want Word to display just one reviewer's comments, click the From list box down arrow in the Annotations pane, then select the appropriate reviewer's initials.

Carla wants to review Morgan's annotations for the Find File lesson.

To view the annotations for the Find File lesson:

❶ Double-click [MT1] at the top of the document (or click **View** then click **Annotations**). Morgan's comment to Carla appears in the Annotations pane.

Carla reads Morgan's comment and sees that no other comments appear in the Annotations pane so she decides to review Morgan's revisions. She needs to turn on revision marks so that she can see the revisions in the document.

❷ Double-click **MRK** in the status bar (or click **Tools** then click **Revisions...**), then click the **Show Revisions on Screen check box** in the Revisions dialog box. Click **OK** or press [**Enter**].

❸ Scroll through the document to see the revisions Morgan made.

Carla is now ready to type her response to Morgan's comment. She will put her comment directly after Morgan's comment.

❹ Click [MT1] in the Annotations pane, then click after the annotation mark in the document pane representing Morgan's first comment [MT1].

❺ Click **Insert** then click **Annotation**. An annotation reference mark appears with Carla's initials and a number, [CC2]. Notice that the annotation number increases by 1. The annotation number represents the total number of annotations in the subdocument.

TROUBLE? The initials displayed in the figures throughout this tutorial will be different from those that appear on your screen unless you change the User Info settings when indicated.

❻ Type **Thanks for the opportunity to work on this project with you. Find File has some terrific features.** See Figure 8-24.

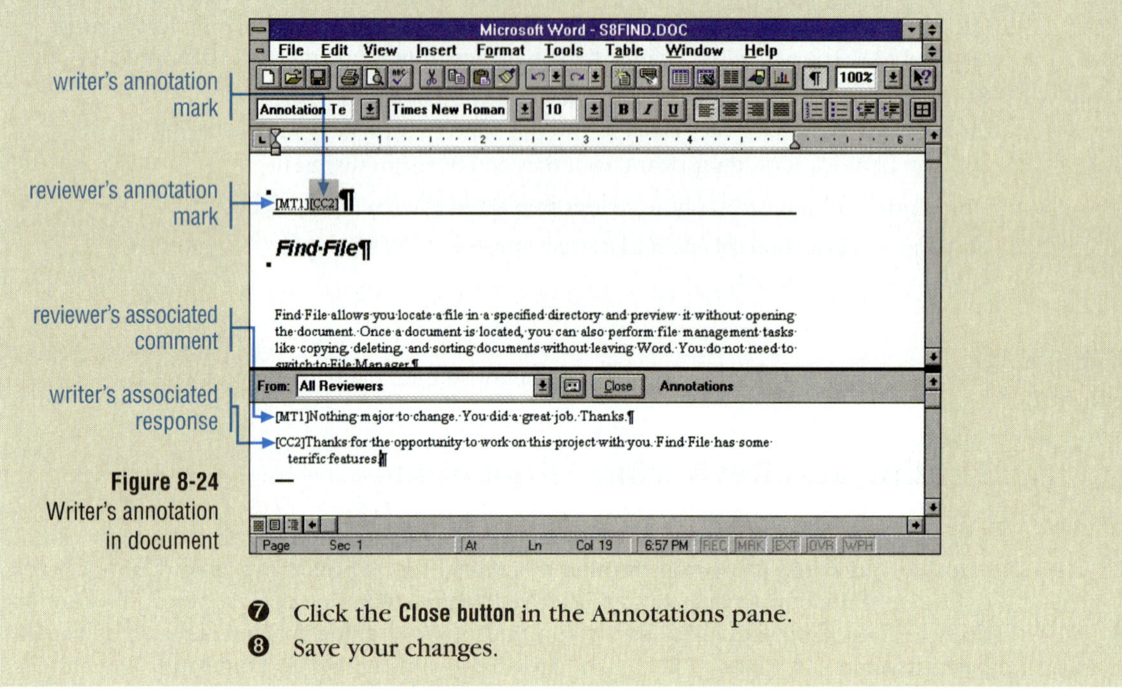

Figure 8-24
Writer's annotation
in document

❼ Click the **Close button** in the Annotations pane.

❽ Save your changes.

Accepting or Rejecting All Revisions

Once revisions have been marked in a document, decisions must be made whether to accept or reject the changes. You can either accept or reject all of the revisions for a document or a selection, or you can review and accept or reject each revision individually. To review revisions, select the Revisions command from the Tools menu.

Carla reviewed Morgan's revisions as she was scrolling through the document. Rather than reviewing the revisions again, she decides to accept all the revisions at once.

To accept all the revisions to the Find File subdocument:

❶ Move to the top of the document, if necessary.

❷ Double-click **MRK** in the status bar (or click **Tools** then click **Revisions...**). The Revisions dialog box appears.

❸ Click **Accept All**. The following message appears: "Do you want to accept all revisions in S8FIND.DOC?"

❹ Click **Yes** or press **[Enter]**. You return to the Revisions dialog box.

❺ Click **Close**. You return to the document.

❻ Scroll through the document. Notice that no revisions remain marked. All of Morgan's suggested revisions have become part of Carla's document.

❼ Save your changes to S8FIND.DOC. The changes made in the subdocument will also be reflected in the master document.

❽ Close the subdocument. You return to the master document.

❾ Close the master document, without saving changes.

TROUBLE? If you attempt to save the master document, the following message appears: "This file is read-only. (A:\S8WWADV.DOC)." Click OK or press [Enter]. The changes to the subdocument will be incorporated without saving changes to the master document. Close the master document.

Carla sends an electronic mail message to Morgan indicating that she has finished reviewing the revisions.

Accepting or Rejecting Revisions Individually

During the review process of a document, you are not likely to accept or reject all revisions at one time; usually you must make decisions on each revision individually. Word allows you to find and then accept or reject individual revisions in the Review Revisions dialog box.

The writer of the Microsoft Equation and Microsoft Graph lessons, Connie Rodriquez, received Morgan's message and decides to review Morgan's annotations before reading each revision.

First, you need to change the User Info settings to simulate that Connie is now working at her computer.

To change the User Info settings:

❶ Click the **New button** ☐ on the Standard toolbar to display all the Word menus in the document window, if necessary.

❷ Click **Tools** then click **Options…**. The Options dialog box appears.

❸ Click the **User Info tab**, if necessary.

❹ Select the current entry in the Name text box, then type **Connie Rodriquez**.

❺ Press **[Tab]** to move to and select the current entry in the Initials text box, then type **CR**.

❻ Click **OK** or press **[Enter]**.

Connie is ready to review the annotations to her part of the master document. She must open the master document.

❼ Open S8WWADV.DOC. Notice that the title displays "(Read-Only)" next to the title of the document, indicating that the person who opened the document does not own the document.

❽ Switch to master document view, if necessary, then click the **Show Heading 2 button** ☐2 on the Master Document toolbar.

Connie must unlock the subdocument she needs to review.

❾ Place the insertion point at the end of the line containing the text "Lesson 2," then click the **Lock Document button** ☐ on the Master Document toolbar to deselect it. The padlock icon disappears from the Applets subdocument.

❿ Double-click the **Applets subdocument icon**. S8APPLET.DOC opens in normal view.

Now that the Applets subdocument is open, Connie will first review the annotations Morgan made, then make decisions about whether to accept or reject Morgan's revisions.

To review multiple annotations:

❶ Click **View** then click **Annotations**. Word moves to the first annotation, shades the mark in the document pane, and opens the Annotations pane.

Connie reads Morgan's comments to the first revision and decides to type a response.

❷ Press [F6] to move to the document pane, then click after the annotation mark in the document pane indicating Morgan's comment, [MT1].

❸ Click **Insert**, then click **Annotation**. An annotation mark for Connie's comment is inserted ([CR2]).

❹ Type **You're right. My mistake.** Word changes the numbering of all the remaining annotations to indicate the total number of annotations in this document.

Connie needs to move to the location of the next annotation, read Morgan's comment, then type a response.

❺ Click [MT3] in the Annotations pane. The document pane changes so that the location of Morgan's next comment is in view.

Connie reads Morgan's comment to the next revision and types a response indicating that she doesn't agree with Morgan's change.

❻ Press [F6] then click after the annotation mark in the document indicating Morgan's second comment [MT3].

❼ Click **Insert**, click **Annotation**, then type **The features of the new window are discussed in the "Microsoft Graph" paragraph. Since the users have not seen the Microsoft Graph window before, I think it's best to leave the order of the paragraphs as originally written.**

❽ Click the **Close button** in the Annotations pane.

❾ Save your changes to the subdocument.

Because Connie is not going to accept all the revisions Morgan made to her document, Connie must review the revisions individually.

To review the revisions to the Applets subdocument:

❶ Place the insertion point at the top of the document, double-click **MRK** in the status bar, then click **Review...** in the Revisions dialog box. The Review Revisions dialog box appears.

Connie wants Word to find the next revision automatically each time she accepts or rejects a revision.

❷ Click the **Find Next After Accept/Reject check box** to select it, if necessary, then click **Find ⇒** or press [Enter]. Word finds the first revision in the document and highlights it. Notice that the reviewer's name and the date and time of the revision are displayed in the Description section.

Connie agrees with this revision for changing the instructions in step 2.

❸ Click **Accept**. Word makes the revision, removes the revision marks, and moves to the next revision.

Connie doesn't agree with Morgan's change to the order of the paragraphs.

❹ Click **Reject**. The revision marks are removed from the original paragraph; that is, the text is no longer deleted. Word moves to the next revision—the location change of the original paragraph.

❺ Click **Reject** or press [Enter]. The revision marks are removed, and the paragraph is removed from its new location. The following message appears: "Word reached the end of the document. Do you want to continue searching from the beginning of document?"

❻ Click **Cancel**.
❼ Click **Close** in the Review Revisions dialog box.
❽ Save your changes then close S8APPLET.DOC. You return to the master document.
❾ Close the master document.

Printing Annotations

As part of the documentation of a project, you should keep copies of correspondence (that is, annotations) between all members of the project team. Word lets you print the annotations inserted into a document as a separate output page from the document itself.

Morgan needs to delete all the annotation marks from the training manual so that they will not show in the final document. She decides to print a copy of the annotations first so that she will have a record of the comments made concerning the development of the training manual.

First, you need to change the User Info settings to simulate that Morgan is now working at her computer.

To change the User Info settings:
❶ Click the **New button** ☐ on the Standard toolbar to display all the Word menus in the document window, if necessary.
❷ Click **Tools** then click **Options...**. The Options dialog box appears.
❸ Click the **User Info tab**, if necessary.
❹ Select the current entry in the Name text box, then type **Morgan Taylor**.
❺ Press [Tab] to move to and select the current entry in the Initials text box, then type **MT**.
❻ Click **OK** or press [Enter].

Now Morgan is ready to print the annotations in the master document.

To print the annotations in the master document:
❶ Open the file S8WWADV.DOC from your Student Disk. Notice that it doesn't open in read-only format because Morgan Taylor is the owner of the document.
❷ Click the **Normal View button** ≣ on the horizontal scroll bar, if necessary.

Morgan wants to make sure the agreed-upon edits were made to the master document.

❸ Scroll through the document and notice that the revisions accepted by the writers are included in the master document.
❹ Click **File** then click **Print...**. The Print dialog box appears.
❺ Click the **Print What list box down arrow**, then click **Annotations**.
❻ Click **OK** or press [Enter]. All the annotations are listed on the printout.

Now Morgan can remove the annotation marks and their associated comments from the master document.

Removing Annotations

Although the annotation comments will not print within the text of a document, the annotation marks will. Morgan needs to remove the annotation marks as well as the text of the annotation comments. To delete an annotation mark and its associated comment, you must select the annotation mark in the document, then press [Del]. Morgan must turn off revision marks for the master document before she deletes the annotations to prevent Word from marking the deleted annotations as revisions.

To remove the annotation marks and annotation text from the master document:

❶ Double-click **MRK** in the status bar (or click **Tools** then click **Revisions...**). The Revisions dialog box appears.

❷ Deselect both the **Mark Revisions While Editing check box** and the **Show Revisions on Screen check box**. Click **OK** or press **[Enter]**.

❸ Place the insertion point at the top of the document, if necessary, click **View**, then click **Annotations**. Word moves to the first annotation, shades the mark in the document pane, and opens the Annotations pane. The annotation mark in the document, however, is not selected.

Morgan decides to select both annotations [MT1] and [CC2] so she can delete them at the same time.

❹ Press **[F6]** to move the insertion point into the document pane.

❺ Drag across both the **[MT1]** and **[CC2]** annotation marks in the document pane to select them (the shading turns to black, and the text turns to white), then press **[Del]**. Word deletes the annotation marks in the document and the accompanying comments in the Annotations pane, changing the annotation numbering for the remaining annotations.

Morgan needs to move to the next annotation in the document.

❻ Press **[F6]** then click **[MT1]** in the Annotations pane. The document window changes to display the location of the next annotation mark in the document pane. Select the next two visible annotation marks in the document, then press **[Del]**.

❼ Repeat Step 6 until all annotations have been removed.

❽ Click the **Close button** in the Annotations pane.

❾ Save your changes.

If you want to take a break and resume the tutorial at a later time, you can do so now. Close the document and exit Word. If you are prompted to save changes to NORMAL.DOT, click No. When you want to resume the tutorial, start Word, open a new document window, conduct a screen check, then change the appropriate User Info settings in the Options dialog box to Morgan Taylor and MT *before* you open S8WWADV.DOC from your Student Disk. Then continue with the tutorial.

■   ■   ■

Morgan can now begin putting the finishing touches on the master document.

Creating a Cross-Reference

Cross-references are used to refer to related information in other parts of a document, such as text in other sections, figures, tables, or footnotes. For instance, you might want to make a reference to text (as in, "See Inserting Captions"), or to a page number (as in, "See Inserting Captions on page 219"), or to a table or figure (as in, "See Figure 2-1"). In the past, cross-references were bothersome to insert manually in a document because the editing process could cause the cross-references to become inaccurate. Word's **Cross-reference** feature allows you to insert all types of cross-references within the same document or even across documents in a master document. Because the Cross-reference feature involves the use of fields, editing changes no longer cause the references to become inaccurate. You simply update the fields, and the field results reflect the changes.

A cross-reference consists of two parts: the introductory text you type in the document (such as the word "See") and the cross-reference field, which indicates the type of reference (for example, a reference to text or a page number).

The text in the Microsoft Graph section refers to Graph as an applet. Morgan thinks that users might need to be reminded of the definition of an applet, which was explained previously on page 2-1 of the lesson on Microsoft Equation. Morgan wants to insert a cross-reference from the Microsoft Graph lesson back to the Microsoft Equation lesson. She must first insert a bookmark in the Microsoft Equation lesson to mark the element that she wants to refer to. Then, Morgan will return to the Microsoft Graph lesson, type the introductory text to the cross-reference, and insert the cross-reference back to the Microsoft Equation lesson.

Morgan decides that she wants to use a page number cross-reference to the applet definition; that is, she wants to refer the users to the page where the definition first appears. She begins by marking the location of the definition in the Microsoft Equation lesson with a bookmark.

To insert a cross-reference to the Microsoft Equation lesson:

❶ Go to the first page of the Microsoft Equation lesson (Pg 1, Sec 4), then click in front of the bolded instance of "applet" in the first paragraph (Ln 4).

❷ Click **Edit** then click **Bookmark**.... The Bookmark dialog box appears.

❸ Type **applet** in the Bookmark Name text box, then click **Add** or press **[Enter]**.

Now that Morgan has inserted a bookmark in the Microsoft Equation lesson, she can insert a cross-reference to it in the Microsoft Graph lesson. She types the introductory text in Lesson 3.

❹ Go to the first page of the Microsoft Graph lesson (Pg 1, Sec 5), then click at the end of the first paragraph ("...within your documents" Ln 7).

❺ Press **[Spacebar]**, type **For more information on applets, see page** then press **[Spacebar]**.

Now that she has typed the introductory text, Morgan must insert the cross-reference to the page number of the Microsoft Equation lesson that contains the definition of applet.

❻ Click **Insert** then click **Cross-reference**.... The Cross-reference dialog box appears.

Morgan wants to refer to the bookmark she created.

❼ Click **Bookmark** in the Reference Type list box. Notice that the choices in the Insert Reference To list box changed when you selected a reference type.

Morgan wants the page number where the bookmark is located to be inserted rather than the text of the bookmark or the paragraph number.

❽ Click **Page Number** in the Insert Reference To list box, then click **applet** in the For Which Bookmark list box, if necessary. See Figure 8-25.

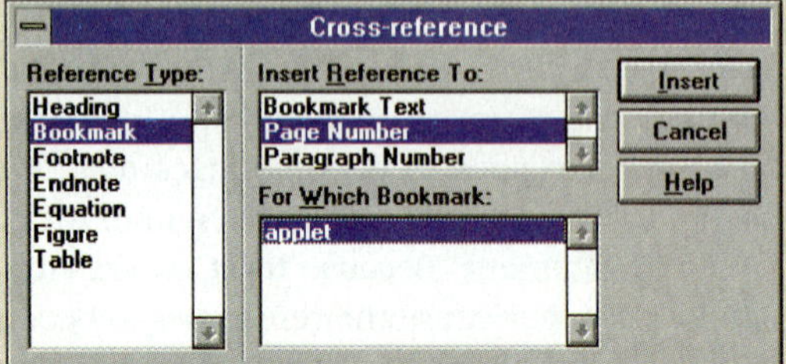

Figure 8-25
Cross-reference
dialog box

❾ Click **Insert** or press **[Enter]**, then click **Close** or press **[Enter]**. The correct page number (2-1) for the referenced information is inserted. If the location of the referenced text changes, you can update the cross-reference.

❿ Type **.** (a period) to end the sentence containing the cross-reference, then save your changes.

Using Style References in Headers and Footers

Headers and footers are extremely important in long documents because they help the reader to locate text more easily in the document. Typically the scheme for the headers and footers in the various parts of a long document is somewhat complicated, with lowercase roman numerals in the preface pages, cross-references to major headings in the document, and double numbering of the page numbers. If a long document is set up as a master document, creating headers and footers is not as time consuming as if you had to set up the headers and footers for each individual document.

STC's specifications for headers and footers is rather complicated, so Morgan refers to her notes as she prepares to add headers and footers to the master document (Figure 8-26).

Element	Specifications
All footers in lessons	Page "Lesson number-Page Number"; flush outside margin
All first page headers	Empty
All even page headers	On separate lines, title and subtitle of manual; rule between; flush outside margin
All odd page headers	Reference to Heading 3 text on current page; flush outside margin; rule below

Figure 8-26
STC's header and
footer specifications

The writers were told to insert headers and footers in the documents they submitted; however, the production department recently changed the specifications for the odd-page headers in documents. Morgan will implement this specification for the Spectrum document herself rather than sending all the documents back to the writers to change. First she wants to review the headers and footers in the document.

To review the headers and footers in the master document:

❶ Place the insertion point at the top of the document, click **View**, then click **Header and Footer**. Use the down arrow on the vertical scroll bar to move through the pages of the master document in page layout view, comparing the text of the current headers and footers with the STC specifications. Note the following:

- No headers or footers appear on the Title or Acknowledgments pages.
- The first page footer for section 2 includes the page number in lowercase roman numerals, per STC specifications.
- The even page header of section 2, as well as the remaining sections, includes the title and subtitle of the training manual.
- The first page header of section 3 (Lesson 1) contains no text. Per STC standards no first page header of any section should contain text.
- The first page footer of section 3 contains the word "Page" followed by the lesson number and the page number flush at the right margin. The footers in sections 4 and 5 are the same.

After reviewing the headers and footers, Morgan must now insert odd page headers for sections 3, 4, and 5 according to STC's latest specifications. She must include the text of the first Heading 3 paragraph on any odd page, except page 1.

Style reference fields can be used to insert the entire text of a paragraph in a document to which a specific paragraph or character style has been applied. Word searches for the nearest paragraph or text to which the specific style has been applied. In headers and footers in a multi-section document, Word inserts the first paragraph or block of text that it finds with the specified style in the current section. The STYLEREF field code is considered a type of Links and References field code, which you learned about in Tutorial 7.

Morgan wants to include the text of any Heading 3 style paragraph in the header of odd-numbered pages except the first. She decides to use the STYLEREF field code.

To insert a style reference field in the header:

❶ Place the insertion point in the Odd Page Header - Section 3 text area. Notice that the header is bold.

❷ Press [Tab] twice, click **Insert**, then click **Field…**. The Field dialog box appears.

❸ Click **Links and References** in the Categories list box, then click **StyleRef** in the Field Names list box. Notice the syntax guide and the description for the selected field code.

Morgan must specify the style for Word to look for, in this case Heading 3.

❹ Click **Options…** then click the **Styles tab**.

❺ Scroll to and click **Heading 3** in the Name list box, then click **Add to Field** or press [Enter]. Heading 3 is added to the field code. See Figure 8-27.

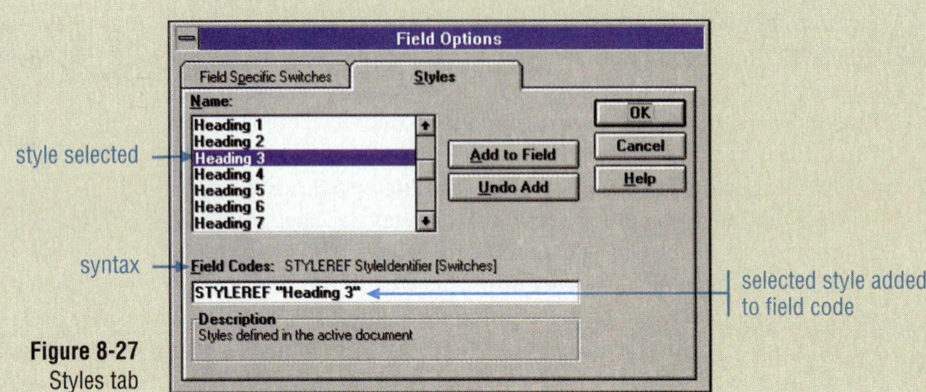

Figure 8-27
Styles tab

❻ Click **OK** or press **[Enter]**. You return to the Field dialog box. Click **OK** or press **[Enter]**. You return to the header pane. The first heading formatted with the Heading 3 style on the current page—File Management Techniques—is inserted in the header.

Now Morgan must insert a rule at the bottom of the line space to comply with STC's specifications.

❼ Add a ³/₄ pt rule at the bottom of the line space using the Borders toolbar. Refer to Tutorial 2 if you do not recall how to insert a rule using the Borders toolbar. Dismiss the Borders toolbar. See Figure 8-28.

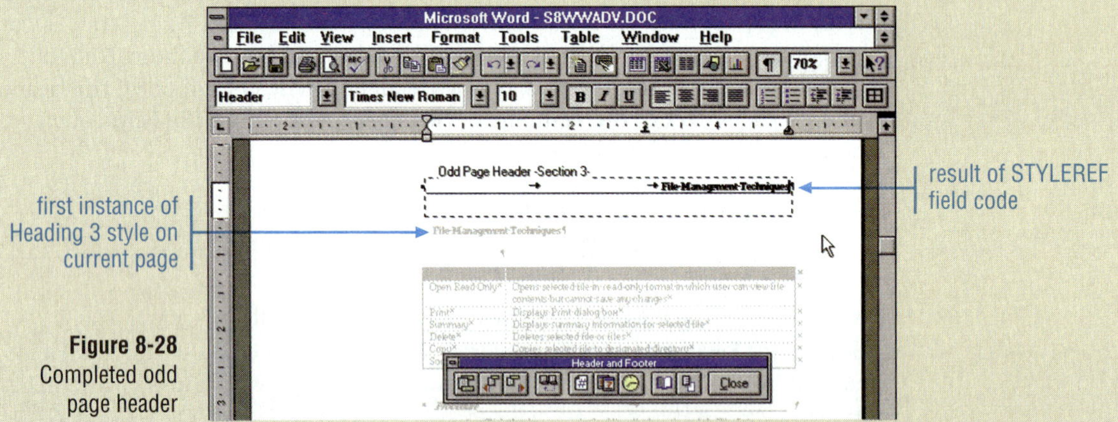

Figure 8-28
Completed odd
page header

Now Morgan must create similar headers for all odd-numbered pages in the remaining sections.

❽ Click the **Show Next button** on the Header and Footer toolbar until you reach the Odd Page Header text area for section 4.

❾ Click the **Same as Previous button** on the Header and Footer toolbar. The following message appears: "Do you want to delete this header/footer and connect to the header/footer in the previous section?" Click **Yes** or press **[Enter]**.

❿ Repeat Steps 8 and 9 for section 5, close the Header and Footer toolbar, then save your changes.

Now that Morgan has finished formatting the headers and footers, she can create the index for the master document.

Creating an Index

An **index** is a reference tool that lists topics and their corresponding page numbers. An index typically appears at the end of a document. Figure 8-29 illustrates several types of index entries, including main entries, subentries, single page references, range of page references, and a cross-reference.

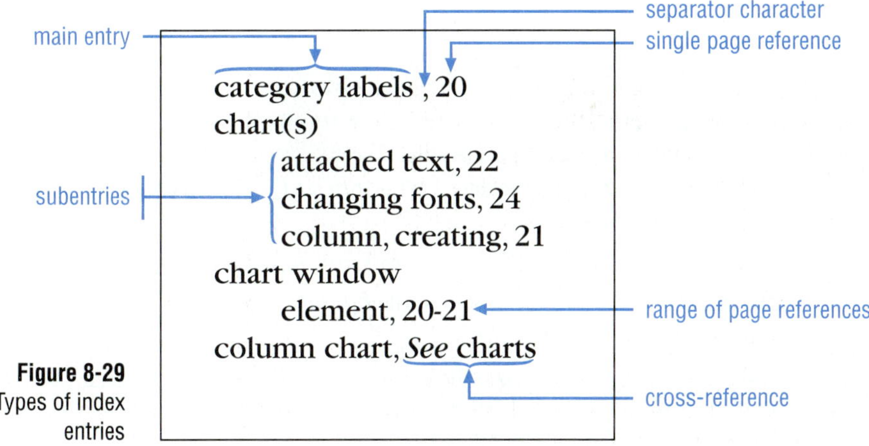

Figure 8-29
Types of index entries

To create an index with Word, you must first decide which items you want to appear in the index. You must choose which main entries, subentries, sub-subentries, and cross-references you want to display in the index. You can make the index as detailed or as simple as you want. Just remember that the more detailed the index is, the more helpful it will be to the reader. Most businesses that require indexes in their documents will contract with an index compiler who specializes in creating indexes.

After you have planned the entries for your index, you must insert an INDEX ENTRY (XE) field code for each entry. The field code includes the main entry, subentry (if appropriate), and cross-references (if appropriate). The field codes for the various index entries are shown in Figure 8-30.

Field Code	Example
{XE "main entry"}	category labels
{XE "main entry:subentry"}	charts column
{XE "main entry:subentry"\t"See"}	chart elements, *See* charts

Figure 8-30
Index entry field codes

Although Word provides several features that facilitate creating an index, you must still insert an index entry field code for each item you want to appear in the index, *and* you must insert an index entry for each instance of each item that you want to appear in an index. Once each item is designated in the document, you can then instruct Word to compile the index using the Insert Index and Tables command.

Marking a Main Index Entry

Morgan hasn't heard from Matt Wurzbach, the index compiler, today. She leaves a message for him to send his suggested index entries as soon as possible. In the meantime, Morgan decides to try her hand at indexing just in case Matt doesn't get her message. She wants to create a main entry for the word "files" and the following subentries for this word: copying, deleting, sorting, and finding. She also wants to create a cross-reference for the main entry "documents" to the main entry "files."

To mark index text and insert an index entry manually:

❶ Switch to normal view, if necessary, then go to the Find File lesson (Pg 1, Sec 3). Select the word **file** in the first paragraph (Ln 3).

❷ Click **Insert** then click **Index and Tables**.... The Index and Tables dialog box appears with the Index tab displayed.

Morgan wants to mark the word "file" as a main entry in the index.

❸ Click **Mark Entry**.... The Mark Index Entry dialog box appears with the selected text inserted in the Main Entry text box.

Morgan wants the index entry to read "files" instead of "file." She must edit the main entry text. Note that Word will mark all occurrences of the word "file" as well as the word "files." The index entry will be "files."

❹ Place the insertion point after the word "file" in the Main Entry text box, then type **s**. See Figure 8-31.

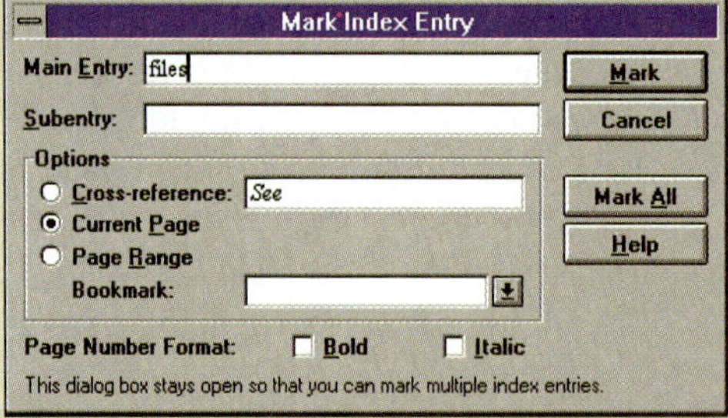

Figure 8-31
Mark Index Entry
dialog box

Morgan knows there are several instances of the word "files" throughout the master document, so she decides to let Word mark them all for her.

❺ Click **Mark All**. Word searches throughout the master document and marks all instances of the word "files." Notice that Word inserts index entry field codes (XE) next to each instance of the word "file" and the word "files" in the document. The Mark Index Entry dialog box remains open. See Figure 8-32.

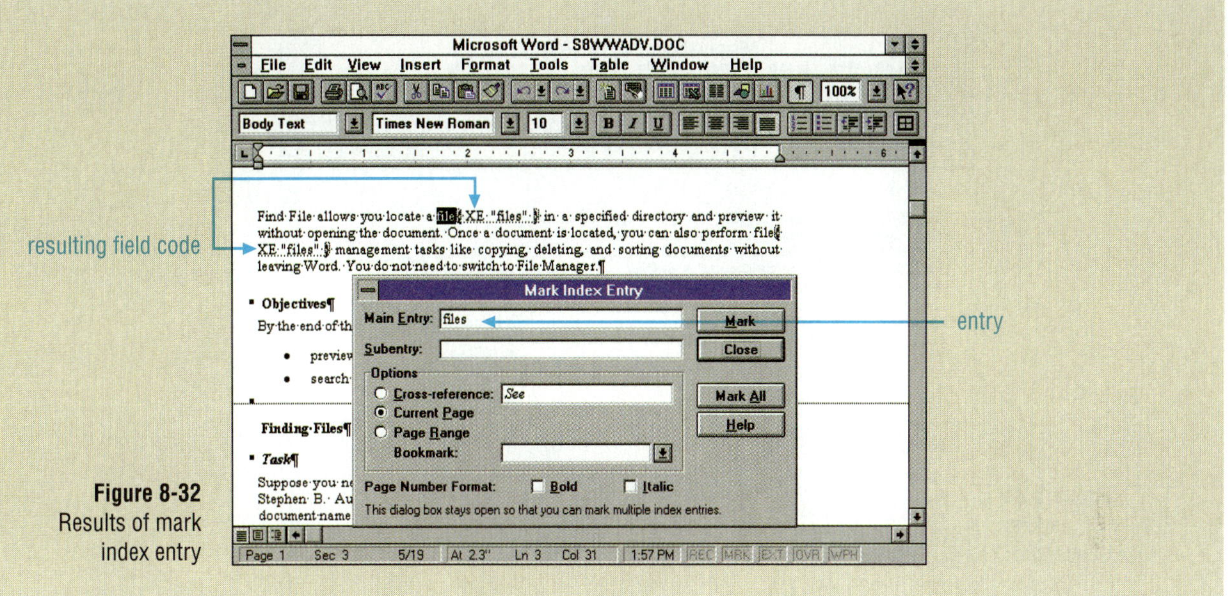

Figure 8-32
Results of mark
index entry

Marking Subentries

Next Morgan wants to create index subentries for the "files" main entry. She will create subentries for copying, deleting, sorting, and finding—all referenced to the same page in the document.

To create subentries for the "files" main entry:

❶ Click twice in the first paragraph on page 1 after the word "copying," then click in the Mark Index Entry dialog box to make it active.

❷ Type **files** in the Main Entry text box, press [**Tab**], then type **copying** in the Subentry text box.

❸ Click **Mark** or press [**Enter**]. The Mark Index Entry dialog box remains open, allowing you to mark additional entries. Notice the index entry that Word inserts for the "copying" subentry.

Next Morgan wants to create a subentry for "deleting."

❹ Double-click in the Subentry text box to select its contents, then type **deleting**. Click **Mark** or press [**Enter**].

❺ Repeat Step 4 to mark subentries for "sorting" then "finding." See Figure 8-33. The Main Index Entry dialog box remains open.

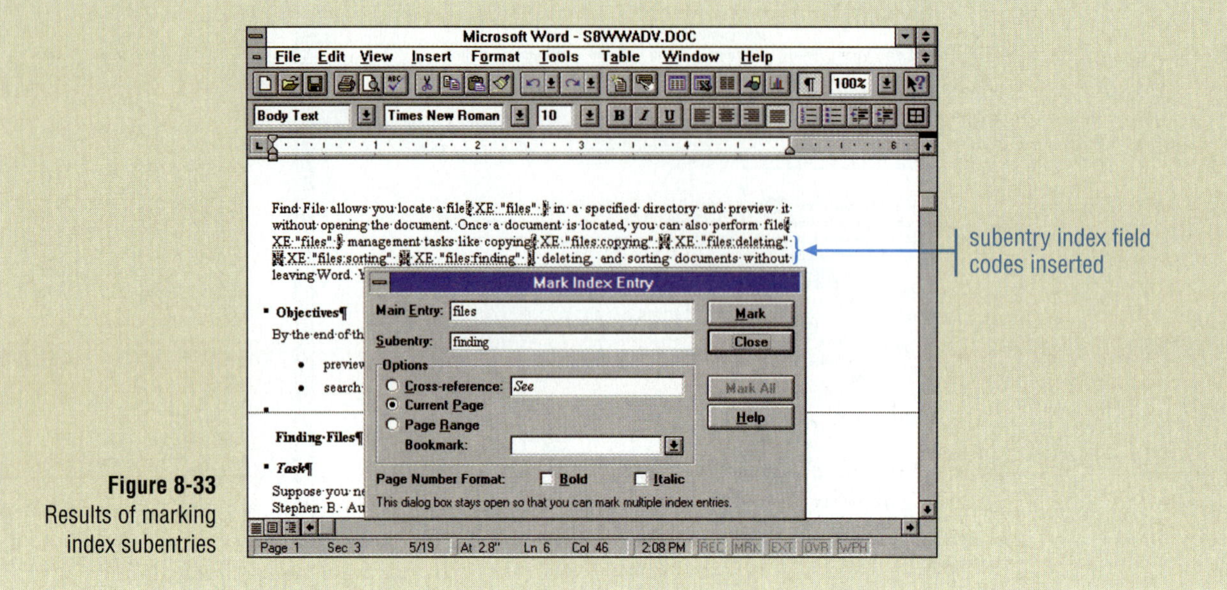

Figure 8-33
Results of marking
index subentries

Creating Cross-Referenced Index Entries

Next Morgan wants to create a cross-reference from the main entry "documents" to the main entry "files."

To create a cross-reference to the "files" main entry:

❶ Select the word **documents** in the first paragraph of the Find File lesson (Ln 6).

❷ Click in the Mark Index Entry dialog box to make it active. The word "documents" appears in the Main Entry text box.

❸ Click the **Cross-reference radio button** in the Options section, then type **files** after *See*. See Figure 8-34.

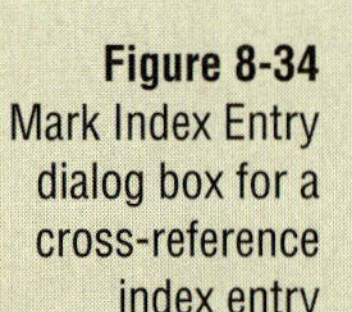

Figure 8-34
Mark Index Entry
dialog box for a
cross-reference
index entry

❹ Click **Mark** or press **[Enter]**.

❺ Click **Close** or press **[Enter]**. Notice the index field code that Word inserts for a cross-reference index entry.

Creating an Index Entry for a Page Range Reference

Morgan wants to create an index entry for the topic "Creating Standard Column Charts." This topic covers two pages in the Microsoft Graph lesson. To refer to the range of pages that the topic covers rather than just the first page of the discussion, Morgan must first mark the entire text of the topic with a bookmark, then refer to the bookmark in the index entry field code.

To create an index entry that references a range of pages:

❶ Move the insertion point to the Microsoft Graph lesson (Pg 2, Sec 5, Ln 32). Select the entire section, Creating a Standard Column Chart (up to the heading "Editing Graphs"). Notice that the selection includes two pages.

Now Morgan must create a bookmark for the selected text.

❷ Click **Edit** then click **Bookmark….** The Bookmark dialog box appears.

❸ Type **chart** in the Bookmark Name text box.

❹ Click **Add** or press **[Enter]**. Deselect the text.

Morgan decides to use the shortcut key combination to open the Mark Index Entry dialog box, [Alt][Shift][X].

❺ Place the insertion point after "chart" (Ln 33), then press **[Alt][Shift][X]** to display the Mark Index Entry dialog box.

❻ Type **chart** in the Main Entry text box, press **[Tab]**, type **creating a column chart** in the Subentry text box.

❼ Click the **Page Range Bookmark radio button** in the Options section.

❽ Click the **Page Range Bookmark list box down arrow** in the Options section, then click **chart**. See Figure 8-35.

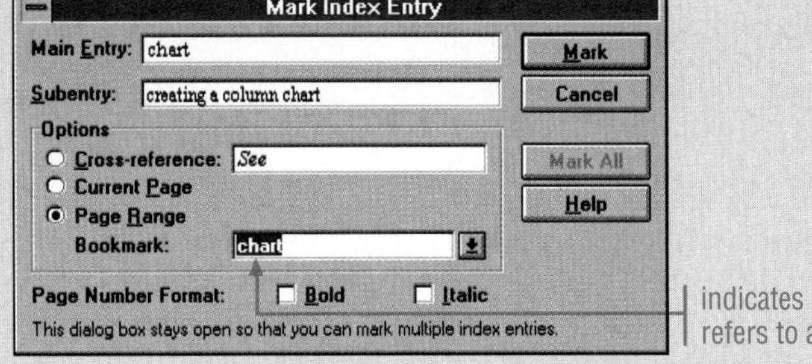

Figure 8-35
Page range bookmark index entry

❾ Click **Mark** or press **[Enter]**, then click **Close** or press **[Enter]**. Notice the field code that Word inserts to reference a range of pages in an index entry.

❿ Save your changes.

Morgan receives a message from Matt that he has transmitted the file containing his suggestions for the index of the training manual—C8WWCON.DOC.

Marking Index Entries Automatically

Word provides an alternative to marking every index entry or subentry manually. You can create a separate file containing the entries and subentries. This file is called a **concordance file**. Word's concordance files can take the form of a one- or two-column table. In a two-column table the first column contains the entry that Word is to search for and the second column contains the exact text that Word is to insert into the XE field code if it finds an instance of the entry. Within the document to be indexed, you select the AutoMark command in the Index and Tables dialog box, then specify the name of the concordance file. Word then searches the document for the items listed in the concordance file, inserting XE entries for all instances that it finds. The AutoMark feature is case-sensitive so only those items that match both uppercase and lowercase letters will be marked.

Matt sent Morgan the entries he suggested for the training manual in the document C8WWCON.DOC. This document is in the form of a two-column table, so Morgan can use it as a concordance file to complete the index.

To mark index entries automatically using a concordance file:
❶   Click **Insert** then click **Index and Tables…**. The Index and Tables dialog box appears.
❷   Click **AutoMark…**. The Open Index AutoMark File dialog box appears. Make sure this dialog box displays the drive containing your Student Disk.
❸   Double-click **C8WWCON.DOC**. Word begins searching the master document for the words listed in the concordance file. The status bar keeps track of the number of entries marked.
❹   Scroll through the master document noticing the additional index entries Word inserts (approximately 115).
❺   Save your changes.

Now that Morgan has marked all the items she wants included in the index, she can compile the index.

Compiling an Index

After you have inserted all the index entries, you must compile the index. First you place the insertion point at the location in the document where you want the index to appear. Word then compiles the index automatically for you based on the index entries that were marked in the document.

Morgan is now ready to insert the index into the master document.

To compile the index:
❶   Place the insertion point at the end of the document (Sec 6) in the blank paragraph below the heading Index.
❷   Click **Insert** then click **Index and Tables…**. The Index and Tables dialog box appears with the Index tab displayed.

Morgan wants to use the Indented type (the default) and the Classic format. She wants the index to appear in two columns (the default).

❸   Click **Classic** in the Formats list box, if necessary. See Figure 8-36.

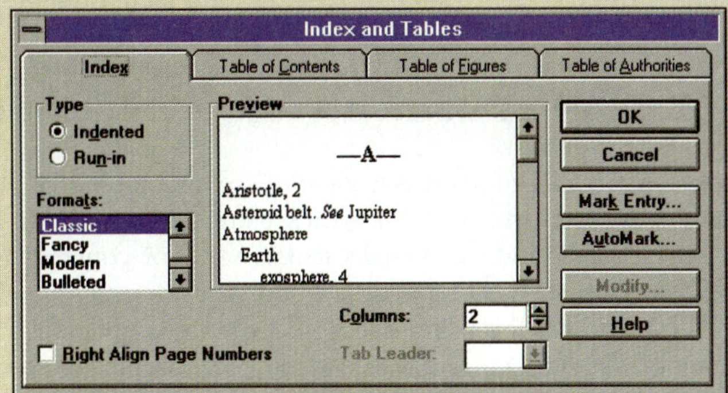

Figure 8-36
Index tab

❹ Click **OK** or press **[Enter]**. Word inserts the index at the insertion point, surrounded by section breaks. You can see the index in two columns only if you change the screen to page layout view or print preview.

Morgan wants to check the subentries and cross-reference she inserted.

❺ Switch to page layout view, then scroll through the index noticing the cross-reference for the main index entry "documents" and the subentries for "files"; also notice the range of pages reference inserted for the "creating a column chart" subentry under "charts."

TROUBLE? The first column of the index might break at a different point than shown in Figure 8-37. Just continue to the next step.

Morgan doesn't like the way that Word splits the index within the -F- section.

❻ Place the insertion point in front of the first hyphen (-) in the label for the -F- section. See Figure 8-37.

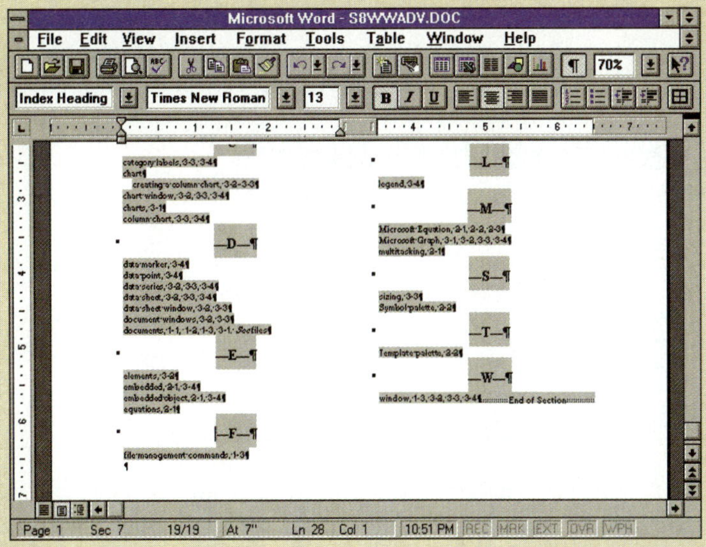

Figure 8-37
Formatting the index columns

❼ Click **Insert** then click **Break…**. The Break dialog box appears.

❽ Click the **Column Break radio button** in the Insert section, then click **OK** or press **[Enter]**. A column break is inserted, and the -F- section of the index starts at the top of column 2.

❾ Switch to normal view.

❿ Save your changes.

Now Morgan can create the table of contents and table of figures.

Creating a Table of Contents and a Table of Figures

Before the capability to link files was available, creating a table of contents for a multi-file document had to be done manually. If topics were then reordered in the document, you had to make the corresponding changes to the table of contents manually. With Word's Master Document feature, creating a table of contents across several files is as easy as creating the table of contents for a single file. In addition, if the page numbers have been formatted to include chapter numbers, the table of contents will also reflect that format. Like a table of contents for a single file, a table of contents for a master document can be updated easily if changes are made to the structure of the document. You can also create a table of figures as easily as a table of contents.

Morgan wants to create both a table of contents and a table of figures. Each will go on a separate page in section 2.

To insert a table of contents and a table of figures in the master document:

❶ Place the insertion point in section 2 (page iii) in the blank paragraph below the heading Table of Contents.

❷ Click **Insert** then click **Index and Tables....** The Index and Tables dialog box appears with the Index tab displayed.

❸ Click the **Table of Contents tab**, then click **Elegant** in the Formats box.

According to STC's specifications, the text of only Heading 2 and Heading 3 style paragraphs should be included in the table of contents.

❹ Click **Options....** The Table of Contents Options dialog box appears.

❺ Scroll through the Available Styles list box until the Heading 1 style is displayed.

❻ Drag across the **1** in the TOC Level text box for Heading 1 to select it, then press **[Del]**. The checkmark in front of Heading 1 is removed. See Figure 8-38.

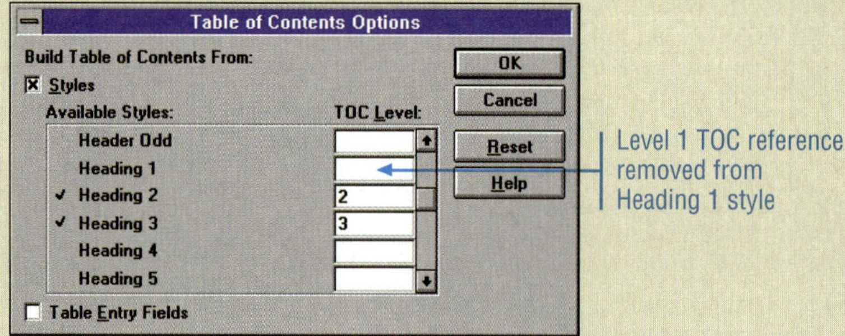

Figure 8-38
Table of Contents
Options dialog box

❼ Click **OK** or press **[Enter]**. You return to the Table of Contents tab. Notice the change in the Preview section—Heading 1 is no longer shown as an example.

❽ Click **OK** or press **[Enter]**. The table of contents is inserted in the document, and the page numbers include the lesson number references. Notice that the headings Lesson 1, Lesson 2, and Lesson 3 are not included in the table of contents.

Next Morgan needs to insert the table of figures on page iv. The table of figures contains the captions for each table, including the lesson number reference. The page number for each table will also be double-numbered.

To insert a table of figures in the master document.

❶ Place the insertion point in the blank paragraph below the heading Table of Figures on page iv.

❷ Click **Insert** then click **Index and Tables…**. The Index and Tables dialog box appears with the Table of Contents tab displayed.

❸ Click the **Table of Figures tab**, then click **Table** in the Caption Label list box.

❹ Click **Elegant** in the Formats list box, if necessary.

❺ Click **OK** or press **[Enter]**. The Table of Figures is inserted in the document and the page numbers include lesson number references.

❻ Save your changes.

Printing Sections of a Document

If you need to print a range of pages within a document that has been divided into sections, you must specify which section and which page *within that section* you want to print. For instance, if you needed to print pages 2 through 4 of section 3, in the Print dialog box you specify p2s3-p4s3 in the Pages text box where "p" stands for page and "s" stands for section. You can also specify printing an entire section, nonadjacent sections, or a range of pages across sections, provided that you specify the section and correct page number within the section, where appropriate.

Morgan needs to provide the client with a listing of the topics to be covered in the training manual. The client wants to review just the table of contents, the index, and Lesson 1. When the index was compiled, Word inserted a continuous section break around the index so the title "Index" is in section 6 with the index itself in section 7.

To print nonadjacent sections of a document:

❶ Click **File** then click **Print…**. The Print dialog box appears.

❷ Click the **Pages radio button** in the Page Range section.

Morgan wants to print just the table of contents and the table of figures (section 2), Lesson 1 (section 3), and the Index (sections 6 and 7).

❸ Type **s2-s3,s6-s7** (no spaces) in the Pages text box. See Figure 8-39.

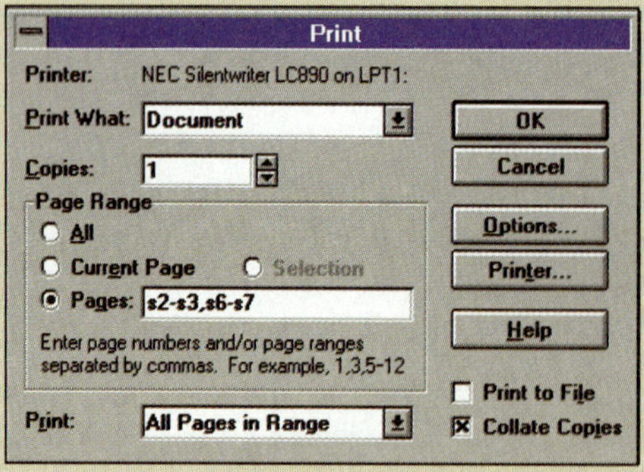

Figure 8-39
Print dialog box

❹ Click **OK** or press **[Enter]**. Sections 2, 3, 6, and 7 are printed. See Figure 8-40.

❺ Save your changes then exit Word.

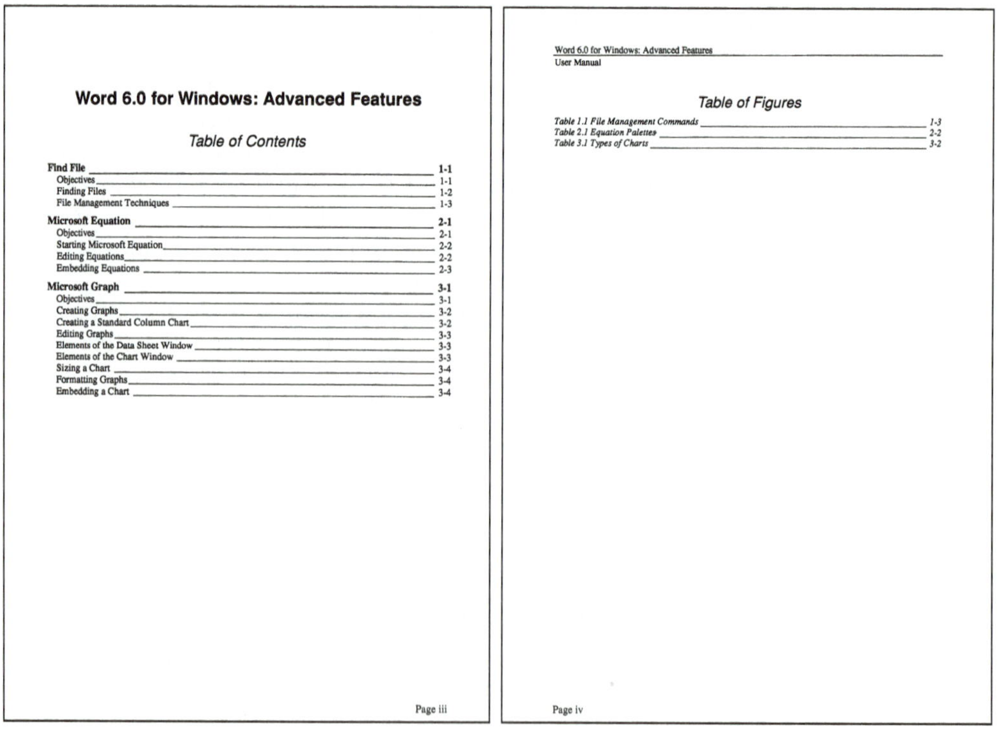

Figure 8-40
Printed sections
2, 3, 6, and 7
(two of six pages)

Word 6.0 for Windows: Advanced Features

Table of Contents

Page iii

Word 6.0 for Windows: Advanced Features
User Manual

Table of Figures

Page iv

Lesson 1

Find File

Find File allows you locate a file in a specified directory and preview it without opening the document. Once a document is located, you can also perform file management tasks like copying, deleting, and sorting documents without leaving Word. You do not need to switch to File Manager.

Objectives

By the end of this lesson, you will:

- preview documents using Find File.
- search for documents using Find File.

Word 6.0 for Windows: Advanced Features
User Manual

Finding Files

Task

Suppose you need to locate a file containing a document you wrote to Stephen B. Austin and, when possible, you include the recipient's initials in the document name. You want to find all files that begin with SBA.

Procedure

1. Click **File**, then click **Find File...**. The Find File dialog box appears.

2. To locate all the files that start with "sba" on your disk, you can include wildcards in your search string so that Word will find all instances of the search text.

3. Type **sba*.doc** in the File Name text box of the Search For section.

4. Click the down arrow in the Location text box, then select the location directory you want to search..

5. Click **OK** or press **[Enter]**. Word searches the designated drive and directory for the specified search text and previews the first located document in the Preview section. The first document found is previewed in the Preview section of the Find File dialog box. To preview other located documents, just click the document's name in the list.

File Management Techniques

File Management Techniques

Command	Purpose
Open Read Only	Opens selected file in read-only format in which user can view file contents but cannot save any changes
Print	Displays Print dialog box
Summary	Displays summary information for selected file
Delete	Deletes selected file or files
Copy	Copies selected file to designated directory
Sorting	Sorts files by different criteria

Table 1.1 File Management Commands

Procedure

1. Click the down arrow in the View list box, then click File Info. This window provides an approximate file size for each located file.

2. With the first file selected, hold down [Shift] while you move the mouse pointer over the last document in the list.

3. Click. All the located documents are now selected.

4. Click **Commands...**. The list of file management commands opens.

5. Once the appropriate file or files are selected, you can perform numerous file management tasks. If you want to delete, copy, or sort files, choose the Commnds button.

6. Click **Delete**. A message box appears with a message asking whether you want to delete all the selected files.

7. Click **Yes** or press **[Enter]**. The selected files are deleted from the specified directory.

8. Click **Close** to close the Find File window.

Index

—A—

applet, 2-1
application window, 3-2

—B—

button, 1-3, 2-2, 3-3

—C—

category labels, 3-3, 3-4
chart
   creating a column chart, 3-2–3-3
chart window, 3-2, 3-3, 3-4
charts, 3-1
column chart, 3-3, 3-4

—D—

data marker, 3-4
data point, 3-4
data series, 3-2, 3-3, 3-4
data sheet, 3-2, 3-3, 3-4
data sheet window, 3-2, 3-3
document windows, 3-2, 3-3
documents, 1-1, 1-2, 1-3, 3-1. *See* files

—E—

elements, 3-2
embedded, 2-1, 3-4
embedded object, 2-1, 3-4
equations, 2-1

—F—

file management commands, 1-3
files, 1-1, 1-2, 1-3
   copying, 1-1
   deleting, 1-1
   finding, 1-1
   sorting, 1-1
Find File, 1-1, 1-2

—G—

Graph, 3-1, 3-2, 3-3, 3-4
Graph button, 3-2, 3-3

—L—

legend, 3-4

—M—

Microsoft Equation, 2-1, 2-2, 2-3
Microsoft Graph, 3-1, 3-2, 3-3, 3-4
multitasking, 2-1

—S—

sizing, 3-3
Symbol palette, 2-2

—T—

Template palette, 2-2

—W—

window, 1-3, 3-2, 3-3, 3-4

Figure 8-40
Printed sections
2, 3, 6, and 7
(four of six pages)

Morgan has finished the training manual and is ready to transmit the file to the Printing Department.

Questions

1. Define workgroup.
2. Define master document.
3. Define subdocument.
4. What are three ways to switch to master document view?
5. How do you create a subdocument?
6. How to you insert a subdocument?
7. How is a subdocument indicated in a master document?
8. What is the purpose of an odd-page section break?
9. What is the purpose of the Heading Numbering feature?
10. Define double numbering.
11. What is the procedure for including chapter numbers in captions?
12. What is the procedure for including chapter numbers in page numbers?
13. What is the function of [Shift][F4]?
14. What is the purpose of the Start At option in the Page Numbering Format dialog box?
15. What is the purpose of the Revisions feature?
16. What are two methods of activating the Revisions feature?
17. What is the purpose of the Annotations feature?
18. How do you find annotations in a document?
19. How do you view annotations in a document?
20. How do you remove annotations from a document?
21. How does Word determine who owns a document?
22. What is the purpose of the Cross-Reference feature?
23. What is the syntax for the STYLEREF field code?
24. Define index.
25. Describe four types of index entries.
26. What is the purpose of a concordance file?
27. What is the procedure to compile an index?
28. How do you specify in the Print dialog box that you want to print from page 3 of section 2 through page 5 of section 4 in a document?

E   29. What is the purpose of the Compare Versions feature in the Revisions dialog box?

E   30. Make a copy of one or two pages of an index from a book, then label one example of each of the following: main entry, subentry, cross-reference, multiple page reference, single page reference.

E   31. Switch to File Manager from Word, then look at the size of the following files: S8WWADV.DOC, S8FIND.DOC, S8APPLET.DOC. Why is the size of S8WWADV.DOC smaller than the total of S8FIND.DOC and S8APPLET.DOC? Switch back to Word.

Tutorial Assignments

Start Word and complete the following:

1. Change the User Info tab by entering "Morgan Taylor" in the Name text box and "MT" in the Initials text box.

2. Open the file T8STCPRE.DOC from your Student Disk, then save the document as
   S8OUTLIN.DOC.
3. Type the training manual name "Using Outline View" in the following locations:
   a. in the blank paragraph at the top of the title page
   b. in place of *[Training Manual Name]* at the top of the acknowledgments page
       (page ii)
   c. in the blank paragraph at the top of the table of contents page (page iii)
   d. Save the changes.
4. Insert subdocuments into the master document:
   a. Switch to master document view.
   b. Go to Section 3, then insert the subdocument T8OUTCRE.DOC. Do not rename
       any styles in the subdocument.
   c. Go to Section 4, then insert the subdocument T8OUTED.DOC. Do not rename
       any styles in the subdocument.
   d. Go to Section 6, then insert the subdocument T8OUTFP.DOC. Do not rename
       any styles in the subdocument.
5. Rename the individual subdocuments:
   a. Click the Show Heading 2 button on the Master Document toolbar, then dou-
       ble-click the Lesson 1 subdocument icon, save the subdocument as S8OUT-
       CRE.DOC to your Student Disk, then close the document. You return to the
       master document.
   b. Double-click the Lesson 2 subdocument icon, save the subdocument as
       S8OUTED.DOC to your Student Disk, then close the document. You return to
       the master document.
   c. Double-click the Lesson 3 subdocument icon, save the subdocument as
       S8OUTFP.DOC to your Student Disk, then close the document. You return to
       the master document.
   d. Save the master document.
6. Delete and review section breaks:
   a. Switch to normal view, go to section 3, scroll to the end of the section, then
       delete the second section break.
   b. Go to section 4, scroll to the end of the section, then delete the second section
       break.
   c. Go to section 5, scroll to the end of the section, then delete the blank para-
       graph mark and the second section break.
   d. Save your changes.
7. Format the headers and footers of the document:
   a. Go to the First Page Footer text area for Section 3, then use the Page Numbers
       command on the Insert menu to start the page numbering at 1. All subsequent
       pages in the remaining lessons should be numbered consecutively.
   b. Go to the Even Page Header text area of Section 3, then connect the header to
       the previous section.
   c. Go to the Even Page Header text area of Section 4, then connect the header to
       the previous section.
   d. Go to the Even Page Header text area of Section 5, then connect the header to
       the previous section.
   e. Go to the Odd Page Header text area of section 3, tab to the right margin, then
       insert a STYLEREF field code for the title of the lesson (Heading 2 style).
   f. Go to the Odd Page Header text area of section 4, then connect the header to
       the previous section.
   g. Go to the Odd Page Header text area of section 5, then connect the header to
       the previous section.
   h. Save your changes.
8. Mark entries for an index:
   a. Mark all instances of the main index entry "outline" (Pg 1, Sec 3, Ln 1) in the
       master document.

b. Mark the subentry "typing" (Pg 2, Sec 3, Ln 2) for the main entry "outline."

c. Mark the subentry "editing " (Pg 5, Sec 4, Ln 2) for the main entry "outline."

d. Mark the subentry "promoting and demoting headings" (Pg 6, Sec 4, Ln 1) for the main entry "outline."

e. Mark the subentry "collapsing and expanding" (Pg 9, Sec 4, Ln 3) for the main entry "outline."

f. Mark the subentry "formatting" (Pg 13, Sec 5, Ln 3) for the main entry "outline."

g. Mark the subentry "printing " (Pg 15, Sec 5, Ln 13) for the main entry "outline."

h. Create a cross-reference index entry from the main entry "Outline view" (Pg 2, Sec 3, Ln 3) to the main entry "outline."

i. Create a bookmark named PD for the section "Promoting and Demoting Headings" (Pg 6-8, Sec 4) in the lesson, then insert a Page Range Bookmark entry to that section after the heading.

j. Use the concordance file T8OUTCON.DOC to mark additional entries for the master document.

k. Save your changes.

9. Go to section 6, place the insertion point in the blank paragraph after the title Index, then compile the index using Run-in type, Classic format, and 4 columns.

10. Insert a table of contents:

a. Go to section 2, then place the insertion point in the blank paragraph after the title Table of Contents.

b. Use the Classic format and dot leaders.

c. Remove the references to Heading 1 style from the table of contents.

d. Save your changes.

11. Delete the page break below the table of contents, delete the text Table of Figures, delete the blank paragraph mark on page iv, then save your changes.

12. Print the sections containing the table of contents, Lesson 1, and the index.

13. Close the document.

Case Problems

1. P. K. Sparks and Associates

P. K. Sparks is the founder and principal partner in the architectural firm of P. K. Sparks and Associates of Honolulu, Hawaii. He has decided that, as part of any future proposals made to clients for building designs, several sections be devoted to how his firm carries out the design process. He thinks this material will help to educate potential clients to the details involved in designing and constructing a building. He asked various junior members of the firm to create the different sections of the material. P. K. wrote the introduction to the document, but Marie Nakamura will set up the master document inserting her document at the end of the master document. Then George Makai will review the master document, making annotations and revisions, and insert his document at the end of the master document. Finally Marie will review George's document, making revisions and annotations, then print the document with revisions displayed.

Complete the following:

1. Change the User Info tab of the Options dialog box by typing "Marie Nakamura" in the Name text box and "MN" in the Initials text box.

2. Open the file P8SPARKS.DOC from your Student Disk, then save it as S8SPARKS.DOC.

3. Insert and rename the subdocument P8PS.DOC.

a. Switch to master document view.

   b. Place the insertion point at the end of the document, then insert P8PS.DOC as a subdocument at the end of the master document. Do not rename any styles in the subdocument.

   c. Open the Professional Services subdocument, then save it as S8PS.DOC to your Student Disk.

   d. Close S8PS.DOC. You return to the master document.

   e. Save the master document.

   f. Close the master document.

4. Change the User Info tab of the Options dialog box by typing "George Makai" in the Name text box and "GM" in the Initials text box.

5. Insert an annotation in the Professional Services subdocument:

   a. Open the file S8SPARKS.DOC.

   b. Unlock the Professional Services subdocument, then open it.

   c. Place the insertion point before the heading Construction Administration (Ln 31), then insert the following as an annotation for George Makai.

     You mention bidding and negotiation as step 4, but you left it out of the discussion. Inserted a couple of points. Change at will.

   d. Close the Annotations pane.

6. Make revisions to the Professional Services subdocument:

   a. Activate the Mark Revisions While Editing and Show Revisions on Screen options in the Revisions dialog box.

   b. Place the insertion point before the Construction Administration heading, if necessary, then type the following text:

Bidding and Negotiation
Assist in obtaining bids or negotiated proposals from a selected list of general contractors
Assist in reviewing and awarding the construction contract

   c. Apply the Heading 2 style to the text Bidding and Negotiation.

   d. Apply the List style to the next two paragraphs.

   e. Number the listed items.

   f. Turn off the revision mark options for the subdocument.

   g. Save George's changes to Marie's document.

   h. Close the subdocument. You return to the master document.

7. Insert and rename the P8OVER.DOC subdocument:

   a. Place the insertion point in section 3, then unlock it.

   b. Insert P8OVER.DOC as a subdocument. Do not rename any styles in the subdocument.

   c. Open the Overview subdocument, then save it as S8OVER.DOC to your Student Disk.

   d. Close the subdocument.

   e. Save the master document.

   f. Close the master document.

8. Change the User Info tab of the Options dialog box by typing "Marie Nakamura" in the Name text box and "MN" in the Initials text box.

9. Make revisions to the Overview subdocument:

   a. Open S8SPARKS.DOC, then unlock the Overview subdocument.

   b. Open the Overview subdocument.

   c. Activate the Mark Revisions While Editing and Show Revisions on Screen options in the Revisions dialog box.

   d. Move the second paragraph of the Conceptual and Schematic Design section (beginning "What is design?") so that it becomes the first paragraph in the section.

   e. In the Construction Observation section, delete the word "his" on page 2, Ln 23, and insert the word "these."

    f. In the Construction Observation section, delete the word "him" on page 2, Ln 24 and insert the words "our firm."

    g. Turn off the Mark Revisions While Editing option only.

10. Insert annotations in the Overview subdocument:

    a. Insert the following annotation on Ln 13 in front of the first revision:

       This is a great statement. We need to have it at the beginning of the section.

    b. Move to the location of the second revision (Pg 2, Ln 23), then insert the following annotation:

       We need to make the text gender neutral. Changed in the next line also.

    c. Save the changes to S8OVER.DOC.

    d. Close the subdocument.

    e. Save the master document.

11. Format the footers of the document:

    a. Switch to normal view, then delete the second section break at the end of section 2.

    b. With the insertion point at the beginning of section 2, use the Page Setup option to insert a New Page section break for sections 2 and 3.

    c. Insert a page number in the footer of the first page of the document at the center.

    d. Number the pages so that you can continue page numbering from the previous section.

    e. Save the changes.

12. Print the annotations for the document.

13. Print S8SPARKS.DOC with the revisions marks displayed.

14. Switch back to master document view, then turn on revision mark options for the master document.

E 15. Move the Overview subdocument before the Professional Services subdocument, but below the section break for section 1.

16. Use the Page Setup option to insert a New Page section break in the Overview of the Design Process heading.

17. Insert a page number in the footer at the center.

18. Switch to normal view, then print page 2 of the document.

19. Save the document as S8SDMOVE.DOC to your Student Disk.

20. Close the document.

2. Record Storage Systems Procedures Manual

Frank Tillman is the vice president of Record Storage Systems (RSS), the largest and most experienced business records storage center in Utah. The company is expanding its operations into the active records management market, and Frank has been asked to write one chapter of a records management procedures manual for use by clients who contract for RSS's services. He has completed the writing and editing of his chapter, and he is now ready to put the finishing touches on it before transmitting it to the others who are writing the remaining chapters for their review. He must insert appropriate headers and footers that meet the standards set for the procedures manual, as well as mark his chapter for index entries. He must also include a table of contents for review by the project manager.

    Open the file P8FILES.DOC and complete the following:

1. Save the document as S8FILES.DOC to your Student Disk.

2. Format the document's headers and footers:

    a. Place the insertion point in section 2, then add chapter numbering to the blank paragraph mark at the top of section 2.

    b. Apply the Chapter 1 format to this blank paragraph, but modify it so that the chapter numbering starts at 5.

  c. Insert page numbers at the center of the footer for section 2 only. Footers are not to appear in the table of contents (section 1) or the index (section 3).

  d. Specify that the page numbers include the chapter number separated by a hyphen (that is, 5-1).

  e. The page numbering should begin with the number "1" in section 2.

  f. In the headers in all pages of section 2, except the first, use a STYLEREF field code to insert the chapter name (Filing Procedures) at the left margin. No headers are to appear in sections 1 and 3.

  g. Bold the contents of the header.

3. Mark and compile an index for the document:

  a. Create a main index entry for the term "records" (Pg 1, Sec 2, Ln 4). Mark all instances.

  b. Mark the subentry "filing" (Ln 9, Pg 1, Sec 2) for the main entry "records."

  c. Mark the subentry "classifying" (Ln 20, Pg 1, Sec 2) for the main entry "records."

  d. Mark the subentry "sorting " (Ln 24, Pg 1, Sec 2) for the main entry "records."

  e. Mark the subentry "placing " (Ln 27, Pg 1, Sec 2) for the main entry "records."

  f. Mark the subentry "restricted access filing" (Ln 3, Pg 2, Sec 2) for the main entry "records."

  g. Mark the subentry "charge-out" (Ln 7, Pg 2. Sec 2) for the main entry "records."

  h. Place the insertion point in the blank paragraph mark after the title Index in section 3, then compile the index for the marked entries. Use the Indented type, Classic format, and 1 column.

4. Compile the table of contents:

  a. Place the insertion point in the blank paragraph mark after the title Table of Contents in section 1.

  b. Use the Classic format and dot tab leaders.

  c. Delete references to the TOC level 1 heading style, Heading 1, in the table of contents.

  d. Add references for a TOC level 1 heading to the style Title.

5. Save the changes.

6. Preview then print the document.

E 7. Create a concordance file by completing the following:

  a. Open a new document, then save it as S8FILCON.DOC to your Student Disk.

  b. Create the table shown in Figure 8-41.

communications
reference materials
duplicate
emergency outguide

Figure 8-41

  c. Save the changes, then close the document.

8. Use S8FILCON.DOC to automatically mark additional entries in S8FILES.DOC.

E 9. Update the current index:

  a. Select the index.

  b. Click the right mouse button, then update the fields.

  c. Place the insertion point in front of the "I" in Index in section 3, then use the Page Setup option to insert a New Page section break.

10. Save the document as S8AUTOIN.DOC to your Student Disk.

11. Print just the index (sections 3 and 4).

12. Close the document.

3. Collaborative Workgroup Project

Form a collaborative workgroup with two other members of your class to create a two-
to three-page research paper on Group Decision Support Software (GDSS). The paper
should consist of the following topics: Introduction, Overview of Group Decision
Support Software, Review of a Commercially Available GDSS, and Conclusion. Appoint
one member to write the Introduction and Conclusion of the paper, along with being
the "owner" of the master document; another group member to write the overview
section; and the third group member to write the software review section. Base each
document on REPORT2.DOT. Each group member should save his or her section of the
research paper to a separate file, making sure that each writer is the owner of his or
her document.

Once the separate documents are written, complete the following:

1. Save all three files to one disk.
2. The writer of the Introduction and Conclusion should insert the other two documents as subdocuments.
3. Each writer should review and make annotations throughout the document.
4. Print the master document with revision marks displayed, then print the
   annotations.
5. After all group members have reviewed and commented on the other members'
   sections, the owners should accept or reject the revisions for their individual
   subdocuments, inserting a comment for each revision.
6. Print the master document, including annotations, without revision marks
   displayed.

Creating On-line Forms

Creating an Expense Report

CASE

CyberPark Development   Pierre Bodine is a staff accountant with CyberPark Development. CyberPark develops theater complexes for immersive reality rides, better known as simulation rides. CyberPark executives believe there is a market for rides that allow the rider to travel through and interact with a cyberspace world that is as enveloping as the real world, but without the real world's uncontrollable risks. Another company actually creates the rides, and CyberPark creates the theater complexes to house them. The complex is a cross between a movie theater and a theme park.

Although the mission of the company is futuristic, Pierre still has to deal with the mundane realities of accounting for expenses. Because the company is relatively new, it needs to create all the forms necessary to run a business. Pierre is responsible for designing, creating, and managing forms for CyberPark. He has already adapted Word's INVOICE and PURCHORD templates to create invoice and purchase order forms for the company. His next priority is to create an expense report form for use by employees who travel and must keep track of their expenses for eventual reimbursement.

Pierre wants to encourage traveling employees to maintain their expense reports daily, so he decided to create an on-line form that employees can access with their portable laptop computers from wherever they are traveling. Pierre wants to create a system to get the traveling employees to fill out the form for the previous day's expenses while the expenses are fresh in their minds and the receipts warm in their pockets.

The productivity strategy for creating a form is much the same as for a regular document, except more time should be spent in planning a form's design. Pierre received input from potential users of the expense report and also talked with employees who must analyze the data on the expense report. He wants to ensure that the expense report he creates meets the needs of those who must fill out the form and those who must use the form's data. He diagrammed the preliminary design of the form and is now ready to create the form's structure. He will use the same basic design he used for the invoice and purchase order forms he already created, saving the expense report form as a template so that employees will not be able to change the form except for entering variable information. After he creates and formats the expense report form template, he will test the template by filling in typical data. Figure 9-1 shows Pierre's completed expense report template.

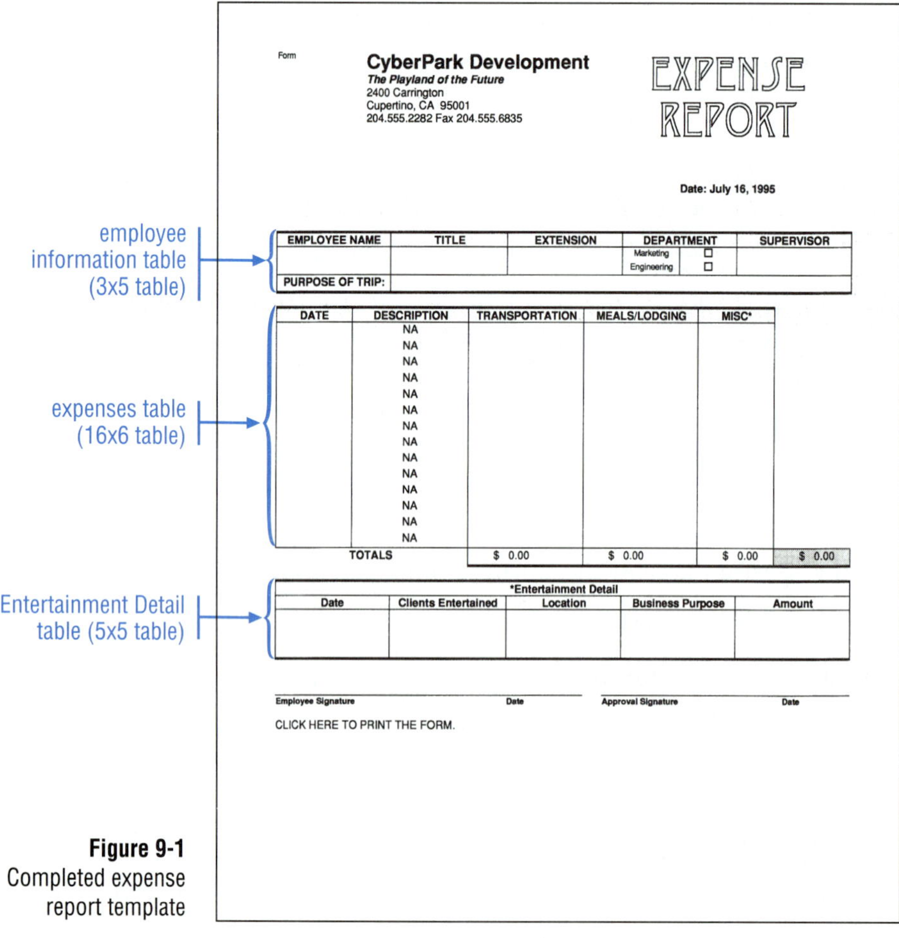

Figure 9-1
Completed expense report template

Creating Forms

Forms are used to collect, format, and record information. To be useful, they must be easy to complete and easy to analyze. The items on the form should flow in a logical sequence and the contents should be separated into well-defined areas. A good form must also accommodate different types of data—some data will require a fill-in-the-blank format whereas other data might need only a check box format. Much like the main document used in merging, a form contains fixed information, that is, information that does not vary from instance to instance, and it also contains variable information, which does change. Word provides two types of forms: text forms and grid forms. You use text forms when you have boilerplate text that is interspersed with blank areas (as in a contract). You use grid forms when the information fits a table format, laid out in rows and columns.

Word provides several features that make it easy to create forms. The Table feature is useful for grid forms and, along with the Borders and Shading feature, allows you to create professional-looking forms. You can create forms as templates rather than documents so that users cannot change the basic structure of the form. Furthermore, you can use the Form Field feature to create forms for users to complete on-line. You can also add Help messages to any form field to give instructions on the type of information to be inserted.

Creating a Form Template

Pierre created a basic form that he used with the invoice and purchase order forms. So that all the forms will have a consistent look, he will use the same basic form but adapt it for the expense report form.

To create a new document template for the expense report form:

❶ Start Word and conduct the screen check procedure described in Tutorial 1.

❷ Click **File** then click **New...**.

Pierre wants to base the new expense report form on the basic form template he already created (which is stored on your Student Disk).

❸ Type **a:\c9cpform** in the Template text box.

❹ Click the **Template radio button** in the New section to signify that you are creating a new template. See Figure 9-2.

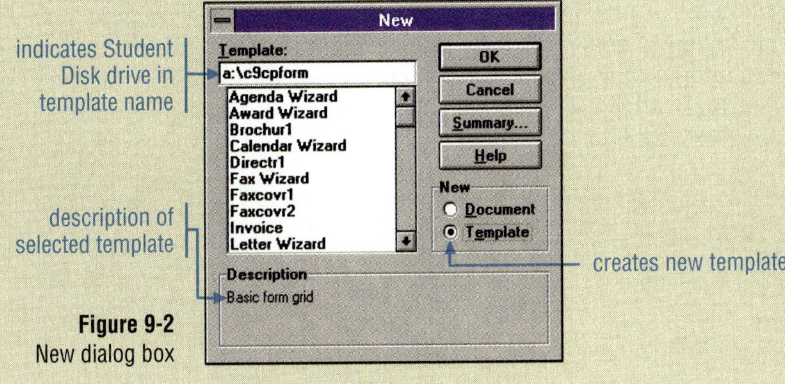

Figure 9-2
New dialog box

❺   Click **Summary....** The Summary Info dialog box appears.

Pierre wants to include a description for the template so that employees will know they've chosen the correct form.

❻   In the Title text box, type **Expense Report** then click **OK** or press **[Enter]**. The title bar now reads "Template 1." The basic form appears in Page Width Zoom view.

 TROUBLE? If the title bar does not read "Template 1," close the current document without saving changes. Then repeat Steps 2 through 6.

 TROUBLE? If the basic form does not appear in Page Width Zoom view, click the Zoom Control list box down arrow, then click Page Width.

 TROUBLE? If gridlines do not appear, click Table then click Gridlines.

Pierre wants to save the new expense report form with a different template name in order to keep the original structure of the basic form template intact.

❼   Click the **Save button** 🖫 on the Standard toolbar (or click **File** then click **Save As...**). Word defaults to the WINWORD\TEMPLATE subdirectory, where you ordinarily would save a template. Here, you'll save the template to your Student Disk.

❽   Type **a:\s9exprep** in the File Name text box, then click **OK** or press **[Enter]**. The title bar now reads "S9EXPREP.DOT."

Now Pierre is ready to adapt the basic form he created to fit the needs of the company for an expense report form.

Creating a Form Grid Structure

Word's Table feature allows you to create a form laid out as a grid of rows and columns. A **form grid** consists of labels (descriptions of information needed) and blank areas to be filled in or, if you are creating an on-line form, to insert form fields. The structure of the form grid must include a column for each label and piece of information that is needed in a row within a grid. It is easy enough, however, to change the structure of the form grid by adding or deleting columns or rows. You can then use the Table AutoFormat command and the AutoFit option to enhance the appearance of the form grid. The form grid should consist of several different parts, each a separate table.

Pierre's basic form template already contains three parts—an area at the top of the form for the company information and form title, a table to contain the specific employee information in the middle of the form, and a table to contain the approval signatures at the bottom of the form. Pierre created these three parts of the basic form grid using Word's Table feature (Figure 9-3).

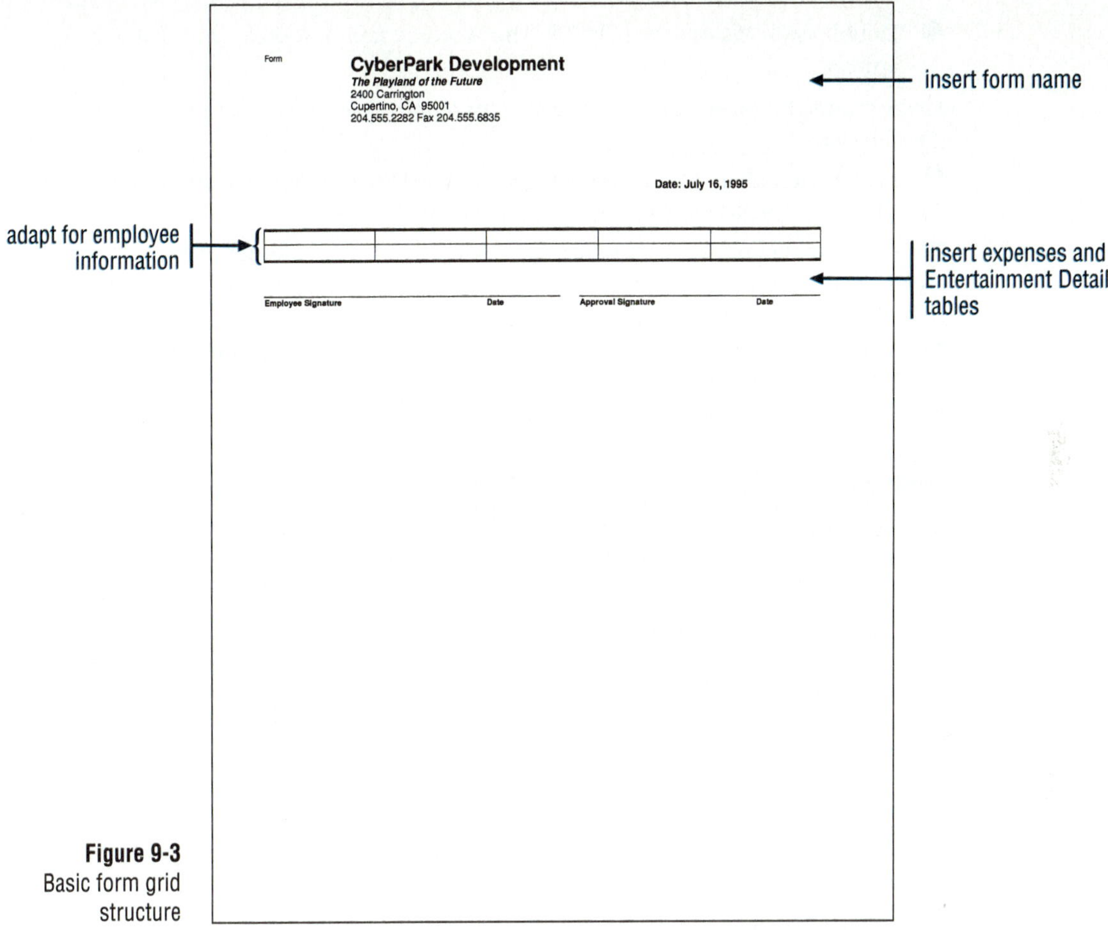

Figure 9-3
Basic form grid structure

Pierre needs to add two more parts to his basic form grid—a table to record the actual expenses for the traveling employee and a table to record the details for any entertainment expenses incurred by the employee. He also has to adapt the current parts 1 and 2 for the expense report form.

Pierre will begin adapting the basic form grid structure by inserting the form name at the top of the form. He decides to create a WordArt image for the name to enhance the form's appearance.

Inserting a WordArt Image into a Form

Pierre will add the form name "Expense Report" as a WordArt image. The image will become part of the background text of the form template.

To insert a WordArt image for the name of the expense report:
1. Place the insertion point at the top right of the form grid structure, in the cell to the right of the company name, click **Insert**, then click **Object…**. The Object dialog box appears.

❷ Double-click **Microsoft WordArt 2.0**. The WordArt menu, toolbar, and dialog box appear.

Pierre wants the form name to appear on two lines, and he wants to use the font Desdemona.

❸ In the Enter Your Text Here dialog box, type **Expense**, press [**Enter**], then type **Report**.

❹ Click the **Font list box down arrow**, then click **Desdemona**.

❺ Click anywhere outside the dialog box to embed the WordArt image in the cell.

Pierre wants the image aligned more evenly with the company information in the cell to the left, so he must insert extra space before the WordArt image.

❻ With the image selected, click **Format**, click **Paragraph...**, then change the Spacing Before option to **6 pt**.

❼ Click **OK** or press [**Enter**]. See Figure 9-4.

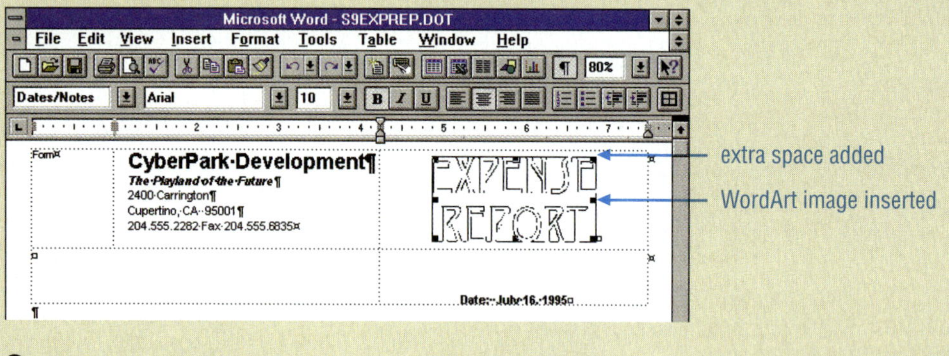

Figure 9-4
Form name inserted

❽ Save your changes.

Creating the Expense Report Form

Next Pierre needs to adapt the second table in the form, which provides information about the employee. He needs to type labels in the first row, but he also needs to add a third row to contain the label "PURPOSE OF TRIP:" and space for an explanation of the trip's purpose.

To modify the employee information table:

❶ Place the insertion point in row 1, cell 1 of the employee information table, type **EMPLOYEE NAME**, press [**Tab**], type **TITLE**, press [**Tab**], type **EXTENSION**, press [**Tab**], type **DEPARTMENT**, press [**Tab**], then type **SUPERVISOR**. Notice that the ColumnHead style is applied automatically to the column headings. See Figure 9-5.

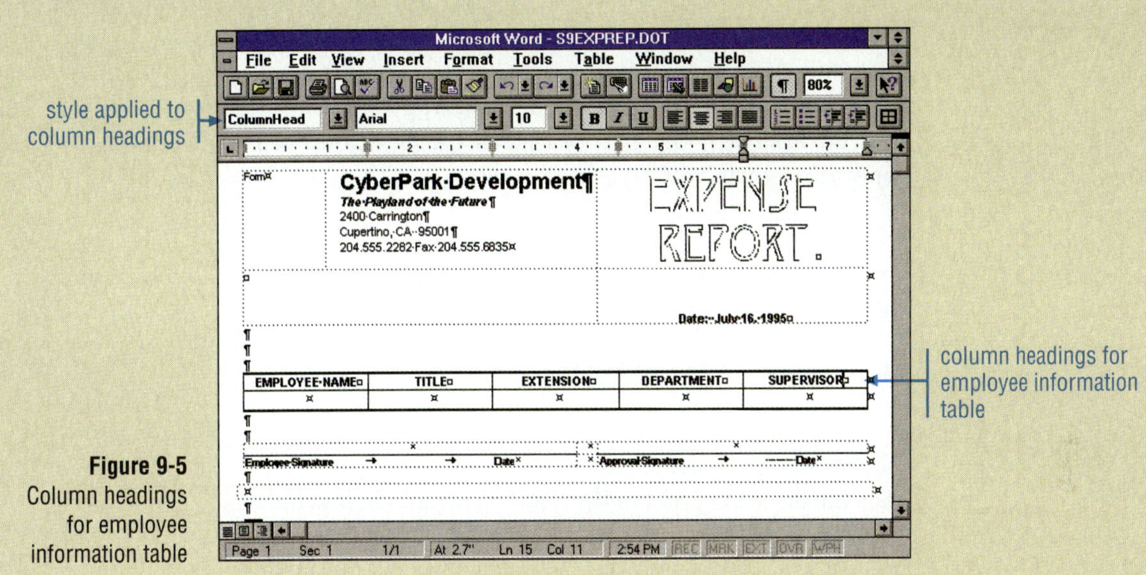

Figure 9-5
Column headings
for employee
information table

Pierre now must add another row to contain the label "PURPOSE OF TRIP:" and an area for an extended explanation.

❷ Press [↓] to place the insertion point in row 2, cell 5, then press **[Tab]**. A third row is added to the employee information table.

❸ Type **PURPOSE OF TRIP:** in row 3, cell 1, then apply the ColumnHead style to the text in the cell.

❹ Save your changes.

Next Pierre will create the table for the specific expense information for the employee. Pierre needs to create a six-column table, even though the bulk of the information in this table will be contained in just the first five columns. He needs to enter the following column headings in the first row: DATE, DESCRIPTION, TRANSPORTATION, MEALS/LODGING, and MISC*. The asterisk (*) after the column heading MISC refers the employee to the Entertainment Detail table.

To create the expenses table:

❶ Place the insertion point in the blank paragraph (Ln 18) below the employee information table, then press **[Enter]**.

❷ Click the **Insert Table button** on the Standard toolbar (or click **Table** then click **Insert Table...**), then insert a 16-row by 6-column table.

Pierre is ready to type the column headings. As shown in Figure 9-1, the last column will remain empty except for one cell, which will eventually contain the grand total of expenses the employee incurred while traveling for the company.

❸ With the insertion point in row 1, cell 1, type **DATE**, press **[Tab]**, type **DESCRIPTION**, press **[Tab]**, type **TRANSPORTATION**, press **[Tab]**, type **MEALS/LODGING**, press **[Tab]**, then type **MISC***.

Don't worry about the titles wrapping within the cells. You will adjust the column widths later.

❹   Select row 1 then apply the ColumnHead style.

❺   Place the insertion point in row 16, cell 1, then type **TOTALS**.

❻   Apply the ColumnHead style to the cell.

Now Pierre is ready to add the Entertainment Detail table to the form grid structure (see Figure 9-1). Employees must complete this table if they entertain clients while traveling for the company. The asterisk (*) in the column heading MISC of the expenses table refers the employee to this part of the form.

To create the Entertainment Detail table:

❶   Place the insertion point in the blank paragraph below the expenses table (Ln 21), then press **[Enter]**.

❷   Repeat Step 2 in the preceding set of steps, except insert a 5-row by 5-column table.

❸   Place the insertion point in row 1, cell 1 of the new table, if necessary, then type ***Entertainment Detail**.

❹   Place the insertion point in row 2, cell 1, type **Date**, press **[Tab]**, type **Clients Entertained**, press **[Tab]**, type **Location**, press **[Tab]**, type **Business Purpose**, press **[Tab]**, then type **Amount**.

❺   Select rows 1 and 2 of the Entertainment Detail table, apply the Dates/Notes style, then click the **Center button** ▤ on the Formatting toolbar. Deselect the rows. See Figure 9-6.

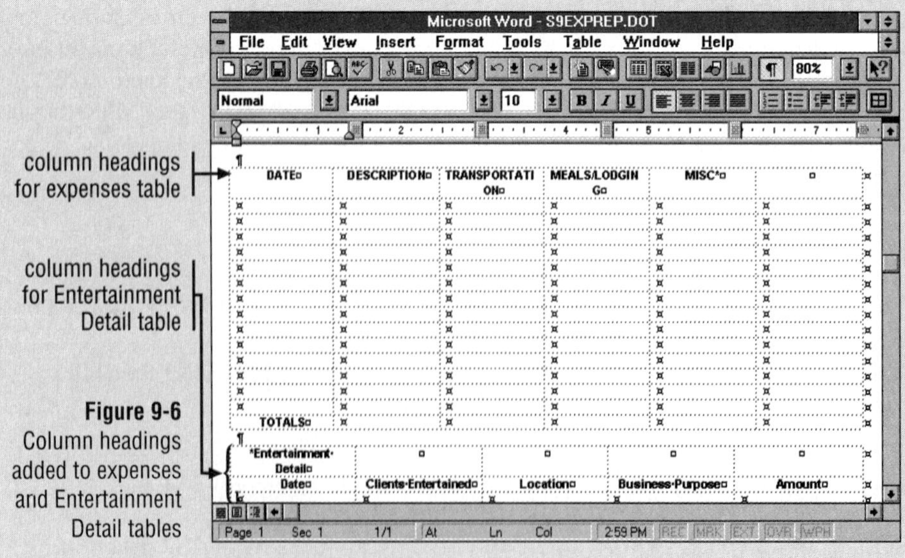

Figure 9-6
Column headings added to expenses and Entertainment Detail tables

❻   Save your changes.

Widening Columns Precisely

Pierre needs to adjust the column widths of the two tables he just inserted. If he uses AutoFit, the overall width of the table will decrease. Pierre wants to maintain the same overall width of the tables on the form grid.

You can use the ruler to adjust the width of columns; but to adjust the width of the columns and the space between columns precisely, you must specify options on the Column tab of the Cell Height and Width dialog box, which you access from the Table menu.

The expenses table structure specifies columns that are 1.5 inches wide with no space between columns, for a total of 7.5 inches. Pierre can maintain this same overall table width by making columns 1 (DATE), 5 (MISC), and 6 (for total amounts) only 1 inch wide, and making columns 2 (DESCRIPTION), 3 (TRANSPORTATION) and 4 (MEALS/LODGING) 1.5 inches wide, without inserting any extra space between columns.

To adjust the column widths precisely:

❶ Select column 1 (the DATE column) of the expenses table, click **Table**, then click **Cell Height and Width…**. The Cell Height and Width dialog box appears. Click the **Column tab**, if necessary.

❷ Type **1"** in the Width of Column 1 text box, then change the Space Between Columns text box to **0"**. See Figure 9-7.

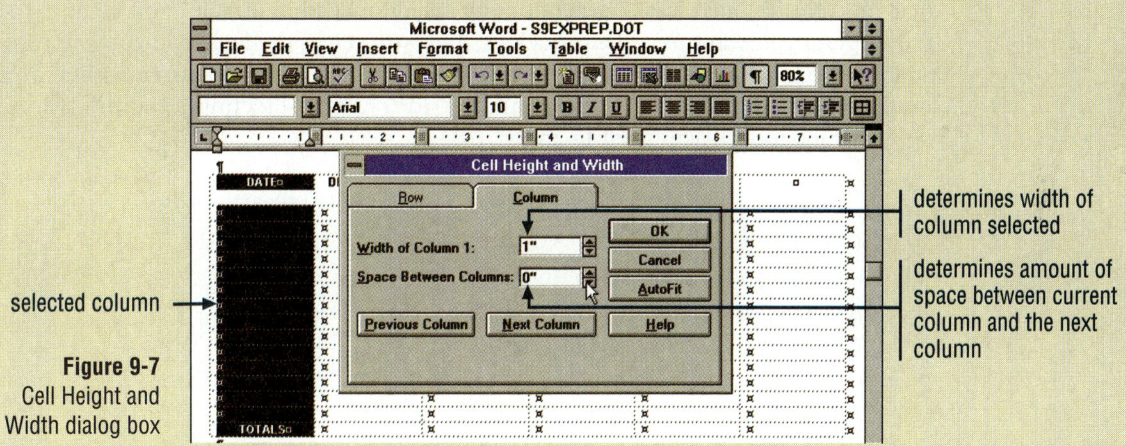

Figure 9-7
Cell Height and Width dialog box

❸ Click **Next Column**. Word adjusts column 1, then selects column 2 (DESCRIPTION).

❹ Type **1.5"** in the Width of Column 2 text box. The Space Between Columns option remains set at 0".

❺ Click **Next Column**.

❻ Repeat Steps 4 and 5 for columns 3 and 4 (TRANSPORTATION and MEALS/LODGING).

❼ With column 5 selected, type **1"** in the Width of Column 5 text box, then click **Next Column**.

❽ With column 6 selected, type **1"** in the Width of Column 6 text box.

❾ Click **OK** or press **[Enter]**.

Next Pierre must adjust the width of the columns in the Entertainment Detail table. He needs to set the width of all five columns to 1.5 inches with no space allowed between columns.

To adjust the column widths in the Entertainment Detail table:

❶ Select the Entertainment Detail table, click **Table**, then click **Cell Height and Width…**. Click the **Column tab**, if necessary.

❷ Type **1.5"** in the Width of Columns 1-5 text box, then change the Space Between Columns text box to **0"**.

❸ Click **OK** or press **[Enter]**.

❹ Deselect the table.

❺ Save your changes.

Custom Formatting a Table

The Table AutoFormat command enables you to give tables a professional look. However, the formats provided might not fit your needs. You can create custom formatting for your tables by using the Table Borders and Shading dialog box to add borders to the selected table or selected cells within a table. You can choose to place a border around the outside of the selected table and around each cell with the preset formats available in the Table Borders and Shading dialog box. You can see the effect of your choices in the Borders section of the dialog box, which provides a diagram of the borders in the selected table.

The Borders section also allows you to control the top, bottom, left, right, inside vertical, and inside horizontal borders of any selection within a table. You click the side of the diagram you want to add a border to, then you select the line style you want from the Style list box. To apply the same line style to multiple sides, click one side, then press and hold [Shift] while clicking the remaining sides. After selecting all appropriate sides, choose the line style you want to apply.

REFERENCE WINDOW

Setting Borders in a Table

- Select the table or cells within a table to which you want to add a border.

- Click Format then click Borders and Shading…. The Table Borders and Shading dialog box appears.

- To select one edge of an outside border, click the border diagram in the Border section. Arrows appear at either end of the border to indicate that it is selected.

- To select an inside vertical border, click the vertical gutter in the middle of the border diagram; to select an inside horizontal border, click the horizontal gutter in the middle of the border diagram. Arrows appear at either end of the border to indicate that it is selected.

- To select multiple borders, click one border in the diagram, press and hold [Shift], then click other borders.

- Apply a line style to the selected borders by choosing an option from the Style list box.

- Apply a color to the selected borders by choosing an option from the Color list box.

- Click OK or press [Enter].

Pierre needs to customize the appearance of the tables he inserted to match the appearance of the employee information table; that is, he needs a $2^1/_4$ pt rule at the top and bottom borders, a $^3/_4$ pt rule at the left and right borders, and a $^3/_4$ pt rule on the inside vertical border.

To custom format the borders in the expenses table:

❶ Place the insertion point anywhere in the expenses table, click **Table**, then click **Select Table**. The entire expenses table is selected.

❷ Click **Format** then click **Borders and Shading….** The Table Borders and Shading dialog box appears. See Figure 9-8.

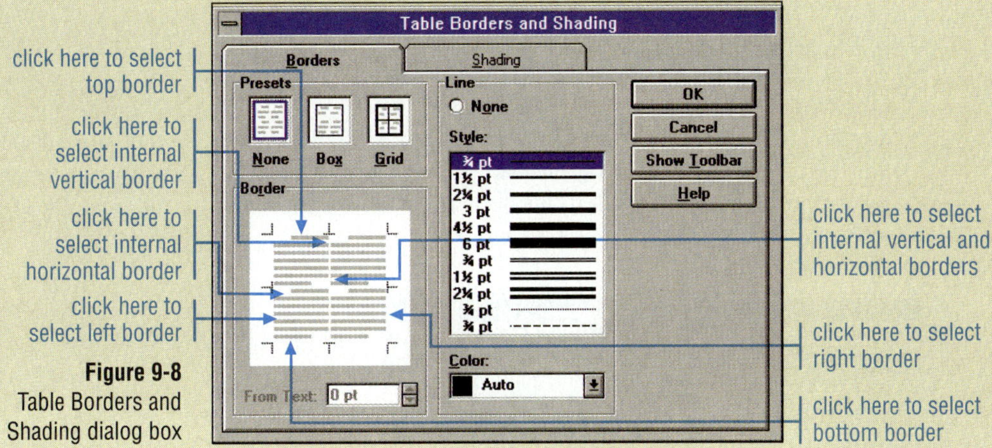

Figure 9-8
Table Borders and Shading dialog box

Pierre wants a $2\,^1/_4$ pt line style for the top and bottom borders, and a $^3/_4$ pt line style for the left, inside vertical, and right borders. He does not want any horizontal borders to appear in the table. He can use the shift-click technique to keep multiple borders selected in the Border section of the Table Borders and Shading dialog box at the same time.

❸ Click the **top border** of the diagram in the Border section, (arrows appear to the left and right of the top border indicating that the top border is selected), press and hold **[Shift]**, then click the **bottom border** of the diagram (arrows appear to the left and right of the bottom border and the arrows remain to the left and right of the top border).

❹ In the Line section, under Style, click **2 $^1/_4$ pt**. The line style is applied only to the selected borders. See Figure 9-9.

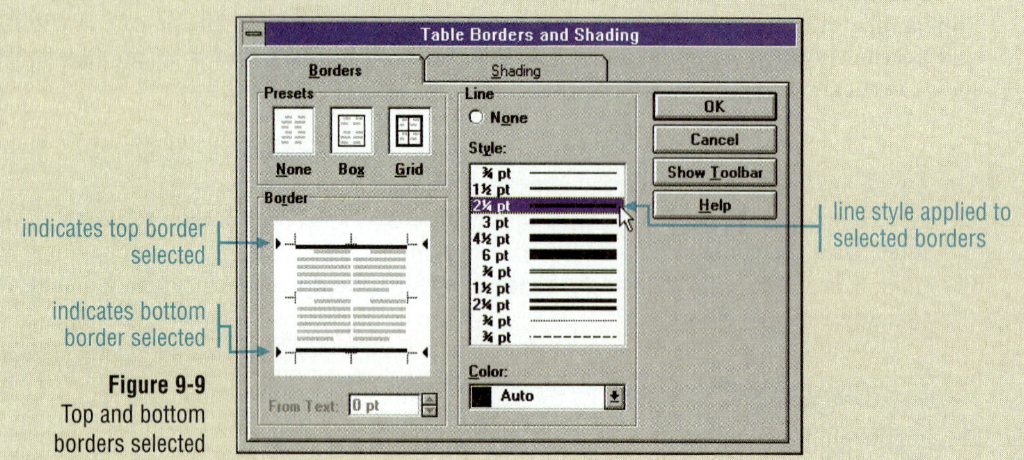

indicates top border selected

indicates bottom border selected

line style applied to selected borders

Figure 9-9
Top and bottom borders selected

❺ Click the **left border** of the diagram, press and hold **[Shift]**, click the **inside vertical gutter** of the diagram, click the **right border**, (arrows disappear from the top and bottom borders, and appear on the left, inside vertical, and right borders), then click ³/₄ **pt**. See Figure 9-10.

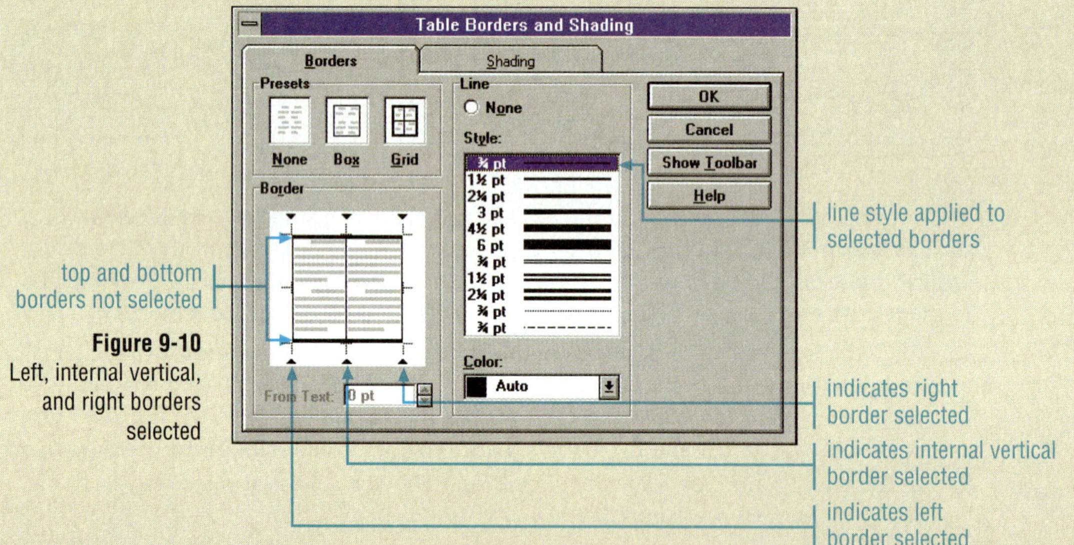

top and bottom borders not selected

line style applied to selected borders

Figure 9-10
Left, internal vertical, and right borders selected

indicates right border selected

indicates internal vertical border selected

indicates left border selected

TROUBLE? If the horizontal internal border is also selected, press and hold [Shift], then click the horizontal gutter in the diagram to deselect it.

❻ Click **OK** or press **[Enter]**. Deselect the table. Notice that the selected line styles are applied to the appropriate borders.

Next Pierre wants to format the Entertainment Detail table with the same border attributes.

❼ Place the insertion point anywhere in the Entertainment Detail table, then repeat Steps 1 through 6 to format the table. Deselect the table. See Figure 9-11.

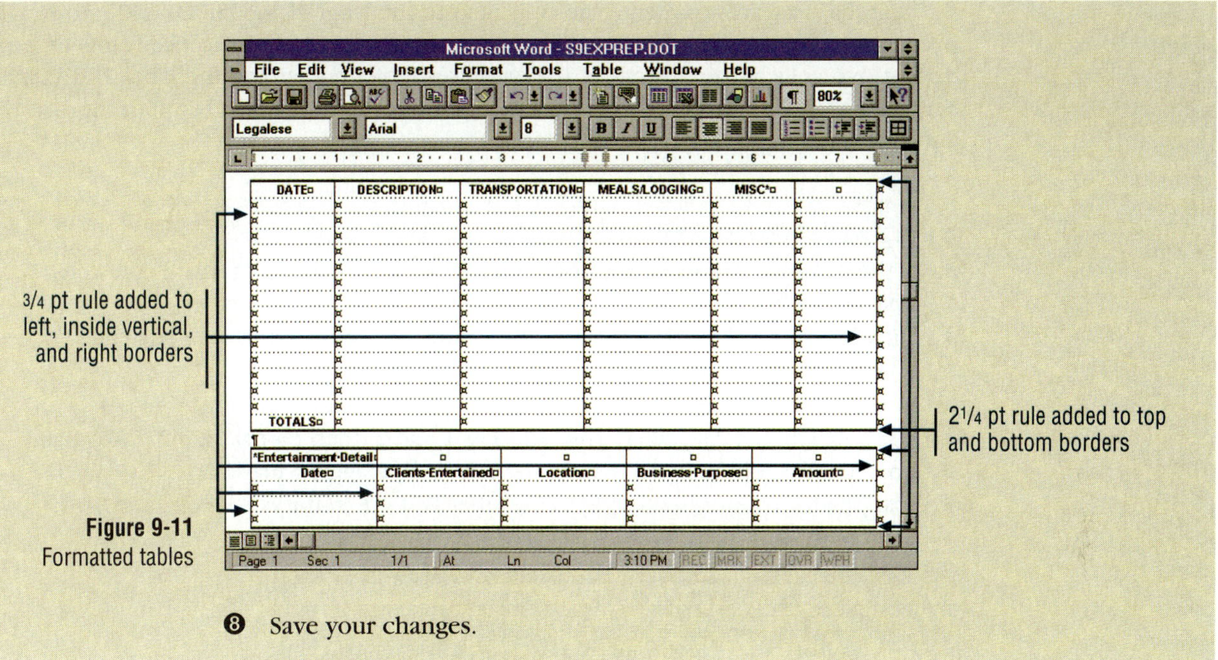

Figure 9-11
Formatted tables

❽   Save your changes.

Merging and Splitting Cells

You can change the structure of a table easily with Word by inserting or deleting rows or columns. You can also change the structure of a table by merging adjacent cells to create one larger cell, and by splitting a cell into two or more cells to create smaller cells in the same space. You can only merge adjacent cells in a row horizontally, not in a column vertically.

As shown in Figure 9-1, Pierre needs to split the cell below the column DEPARTMENT in the employee information table into two cells: the first cell will contain the names of the two most likely departments in which traveling employees work; the second cell will contain check boxes for employees to use to indicate the department.

To split the cell below the DEPARTMENT heading into two cells:
❶   Select row 2, cell 4 of the employee information table (below DEPARTMENT).
❷   Click **Table** then click **Split Cells…**. The Split Cells dialog box appears.

Pierre wants this one cell split into two cells. Currently the Number of Columns option specifies 2; this means that the cell will be split into two cells.

❸   Click **OK** or press **[Enter]**, then deselect the cells. The two cells fit in the space that was previously taken up with one cell.

Pierre wants to insert the most likely choices of departments as labels in the left cell of the split cell.

❹   In the left cell of the split cell, type **Marketing**, press **[Enter]**, then type **Engineering**.
❺   Select both the left and right cells of the split cell, then change the font size to **8 pt**. See Figure 9-12.

Pierre will add the check boxes in the right cell of the split cell later on.

Next, Pierre wants to merge the cells next to the label PURPOSE OF TRIP: to provide space for employees to insert an extended explanation, if needed. He also wants to merge the first two cells at the bottom of the expenses table, containing the label TOTALS, and merge all the cells in row 1 of the Entertainment Detail table (containing the title *Entertainment Detail) to improve the appearance of these two tables.

To merge cells in the two tables:

❶ In the employee information table, select cells 2, 3, 4, and 5 of row 3 (the cells next to PURPOSE OF TRIP:).

❷ Click **Table** then click **Merge Cells**. Cells 2 through 5 are merged into one cell. Notice that the TableText style is applied to the text.

❸ Deselect the cells.

❹ In the expenses table, select row 16, cells 1 and 2, then repeat Step 2. Cells 1 and 2 are merged into one cell. Delete the inserted paragraph mark.

❺ Reapply the ColumnHead style to the label TOTALS in the cell. See Figure 9-12.

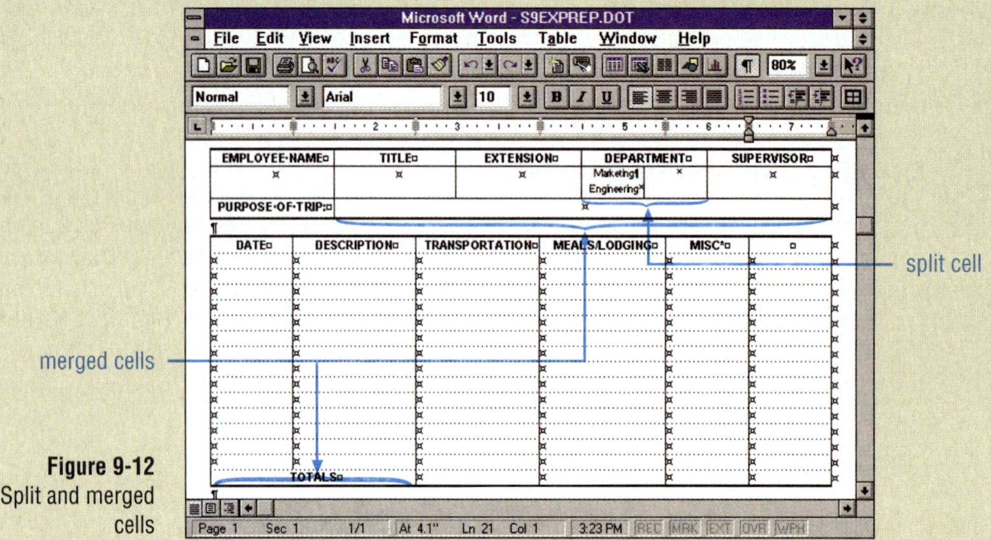

Figure 9-12
Split and merged cells

❻ In the Entertainment Detail table, select all the cells in row 1, then repeat Step 2. Delete the inserted paragraph mark.

❼ Save your changes.

Adding Custom Borders and Rules

All lines used in a form should serve a purpose. You might need to add borders, rules, or shading to distinguish different areas of the form. On the other hand, if a line doesn't serve any purpose, you should delete it. With Word, you can selectively add and remove borders, rules, and shading to cells or sides of cells to improve the appearance of a form. You can use either the Table Borders and Shading dialog box or the Borders toolbar to achieve the effects you want, but it is usually easier to add or remove borders to individual cells using the buttons on the Borders toolbar. The Borders toolbar indicates which borders are activated for the selected line style.

Pierre decides to use the Borders toolbar to create a customized form design by inserting and removing borders from some of the rows and cells of the form grid structure.

To insert and remove borders from the expenses table using the Borders toolbar:

❶ Click the **Borders button** 🔲 on the Formatting toolbar. The Borders toolbar appears.

Pierre wants to add a rule below the column headings in the expenses table.

❷ In the expenses table, select row 1, cells 1 through 5, click the **Line Style list box down arrow**, then click **³/₄ pt**, if necessary. Notice that the selected buttons on the Borders toolbar indicate those borders of the selection that have the $^3/_4$ pt line style applied to them—in this case the left, right, and inside borders. See Figure 9-13.

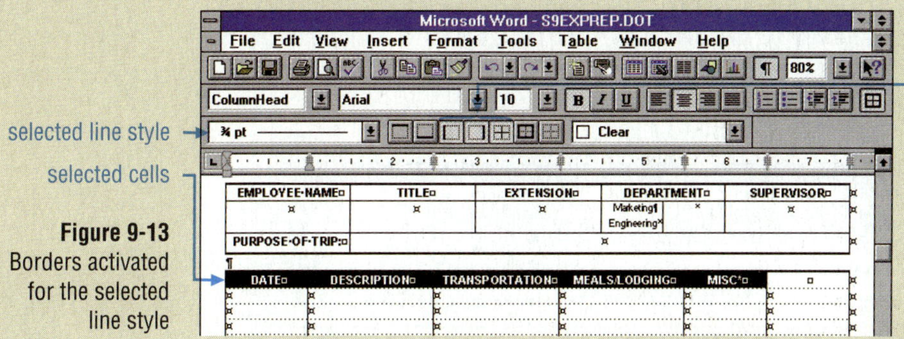

selected line style → (label)

selected cells → (label)

selected buttons indicate borders activated for the selected line style (label)

Figure 9-13
Borders activated for the selected line style

❸ Click the **Bottom Border button** 🔲 on the Borders toolbar. Deselect the cells. A $^3/_4$ pt border is added to the bottom of the selection.

Pierre also wants to add a border at the bottom of row 15 in the expenses table to indicate that the following row contains the results of calculations (the totals).

❹ Select row 15 then click 🔲. Deselect the cells. A $^3/_4$ pt border is added to the bottom of the selection.

Next Pierre wants to remove the left and bottom borders from cell 1 of row 16, because they are not needed.

❺ Select row 16, cell 1. Notice that the Left Border and Right Border buttons are activated on the Borders toolbar, indicating that a $^3/_4$ pt border is in effect for the left and right borders of the selection.

❻ Click the **Left Border button** 🔲 on the Borders toolbar to deselect that border style for the cell.

Now Pierre wants to remove the $2^1/_4$ pt rule from the bottom border of the selected cell.

❼ Click the **Line Style list box down arrow**, then click **2¹/₄ pt**. Notice that the Borders toolbar changes to reflect the border in the selected cell that has a $2^1/_4$ pt border applied to it—in this case, the bottom border.

❽ Click 🔲 on the Borders toolbar to deactivate the button.

Pierre needs to remove the outside border from rows 1 through 15 of column 6 as well as the top border of the top cell of column 6.

❾ Select the top cell in column 6, click the **Line Style list box down arrow**, then click **2 ¹/₄ pt**, if necessary. Click the **Top Border button** 🔲 on the Borders toolbar to deactivate it.

⑩ Select column 6, rows 1 through 15, click the **Line Style list box down arrow**, then click ³/₄ pt. The Bottom, Left, and Right Border buttons become activated to indicate that a ³/₄ pt border is currently in effect for these borders in the selected cells. Click the **Right Border button** 🔲 on the Borders toolbar to deactivate it. Deselect the cells. The gridlines still appear to mark the cells of the table, but they will not print on the final form.

Pierre decides to add shading to the grand total cell to make it stand out.

To add shading to the grand total cell:
❶ Select **row 16, cell 5** of the expenses table (the last cell in the row).
❷ Click the **Shading list box down arrow** on the Borders toolbar, then click **5%**. Shading is added to the cell. See Figure 9-14.

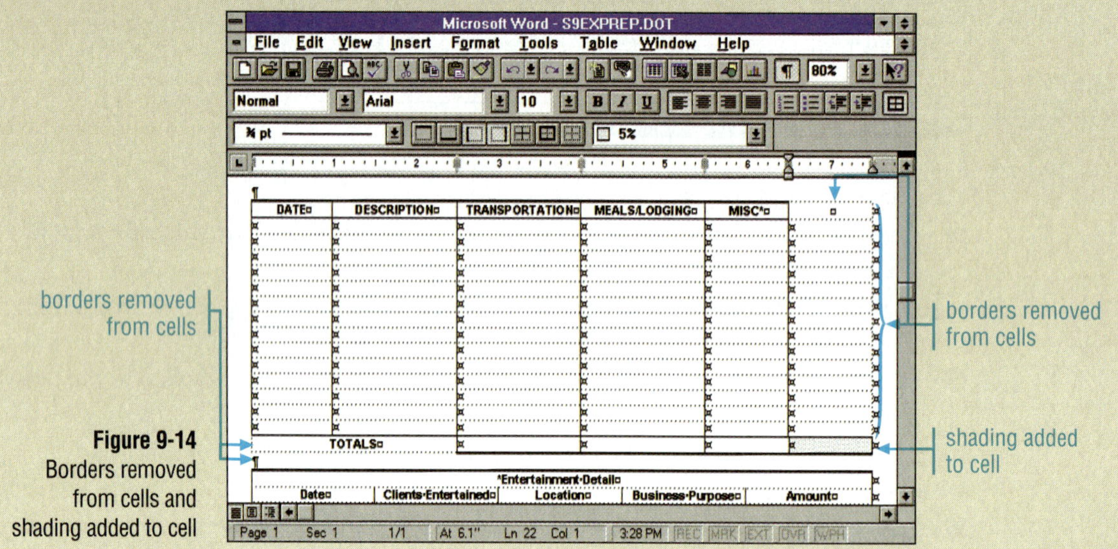

borders removed from cells

borders removed from cells

shading added to cell

Figure 9-14
Borders removed from cells and shading added to cell

Pierre is now ready to customize the borders for the Entertainment Detail table. He must add a border to the bottom of rows 1 and 2. He can accomplish this by selecting just row 2.

To add borders to the Entertainment Detail table using the Borders toolbar:
❶ In the Entertainment Detail table, select row 2, click the **Line Style list box down arrow**, then click ³/₄ **pt**, if necessary. Notice the Borders toolbar.
❷ Click the **Top Border button** 🔲 on the Borders toolbar, then click the **Bottom Border button** 🔲 on the Borders toolbar. Deselect the cells. See Figure 9-15.

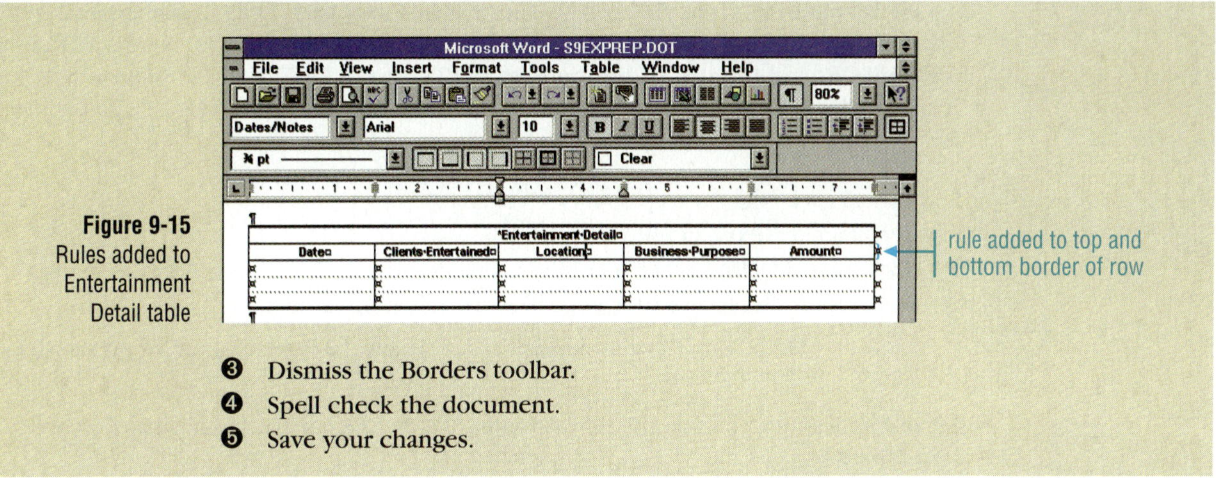

Figure 9-15
Rules added to
Entertainment
Detail table

❸ Dismiss the Borders toolbar.
❹ Spell check the document.
❺ Save your changes.

If you want to take a break and resume the tutorial at a later time, close the document and exit Word. Do not save any changes to the NORMAL template. When you want to resume the tutorial, start Word, conduct a screen check as described in Tutorial 1, then open the S9EXPREP template from your Student Disk so you can continue with the tutorial.

■   ■   ■

As the form grid now stands, Pierre has created a useable expense report form. He could use the template to print a completed form for employees to fill out manually. Pierre thinks he can make the form easier for employees to complete on-line by adding Word's form fields to the template.

Using Form Fields

Word allows you to create three types of form fields—text, check box, and drop-down—each with its own set of attributes. You can insert form fields by using either the Form Field command on the Insert menu or the Forms toolbar. After you insert form fields into a form template and protect the form, others using the template to create a new document can move only to form fields—they cannot change the underlying structure of the form.

Inserting Text Form Fields

A **text form field** is included in an on-line form in situations where the user must type in information. Word provides six types of text form fields: Regular Text, Number, Date, Current Date, Current Time, and Calculation—each with its own set of display options. To insert a text form field, click the Text Form Field button on the Forms toolbar, then click the Form Field Options button to set the options for a particular type of text form field.

Inserting Regular Text Form Fields

A **Regular Text form field** provides a fill-in-the-blank format in an on-line form. You can specify default text for a Regular Text form field, which the user can change if necessary. You can also specify the case format to be used.

Pierre wants to insert Regular Text form fields in several cells in the expense report form. In the employee information table, the cells below EMPLOYEE NAME, TITLE, and SUPERVISOR, and the cell to the right of PURPOSE OF TRIP: will be Regular Text form fields. He does not want to specify any default text for the form fields. Pierre decides to use the Forms toolbar to insert the form fields.

To insert Regular Text form fields:

❶　Click the **right mouse button** on either visible toolbar to display the Toolbars menu.

❷　Click **Forms**. The Forms toolbar appears as a floating toolbar.

　　TROUBLE?　If the Forms toolbar appears directly below the Formatting toolbar, as shown in Figure 9-16, skip to Step 4.

Pierre decides to reposition the Forms toolbar below the Formatting toolbar to move it out of the way.

❸　Point to the Forms toolbar title bar, then drag it below the Formatting toolbar. Release the mouse button. See Figure 9-16.

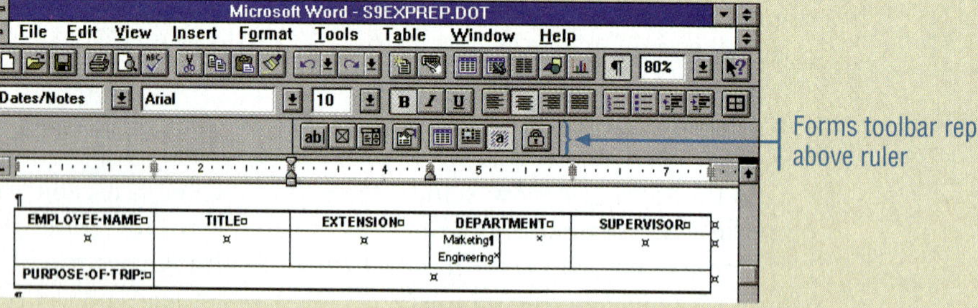

Figure 9-16
Forms toolbar

Pierre is now ready to insert the first Regular Text form field.

❹　Place the insertion point in row 2, cell 1 of the employee information table (below EMPLOYEE NAME).

❺　Click the **Text Form Field button** abl on the Forms toolbar. Shading appears in the cell, and the Form Field Shading button ⓐ on the Forms toolbar is activated.

❻　Click the **Form Field Options button** 🖺 on the Forms toolbar. The Text Form Field Options dialog box appears. Regular Text appears by default in the Type list box.

Pierre wants the text to be formatted in uppercase no matter what the user types.

❼　Click the **Text Format list box down arrow**, then click **Uppercase**. This format will be applied when the insertion point leaves the field as the user is completing the form. See Figure 9-17.

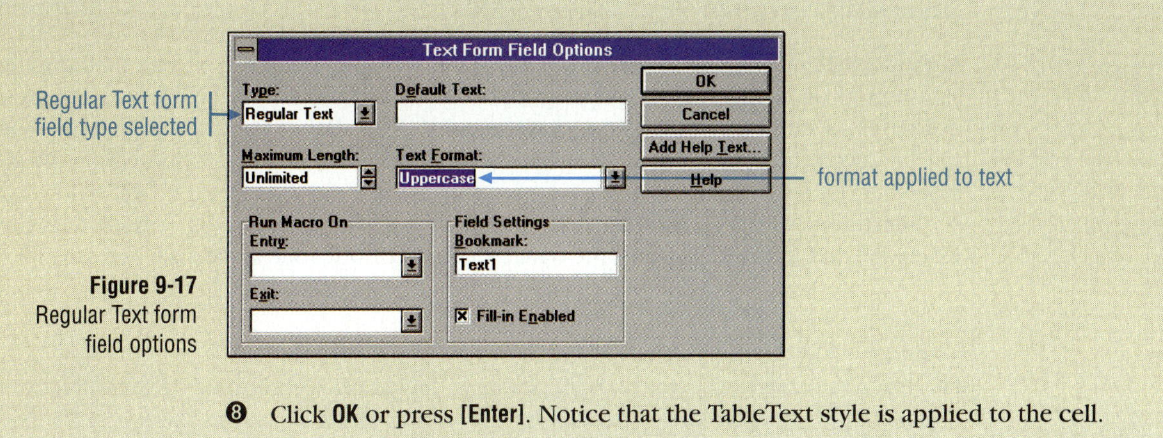

Regular Text form field type selected

format applied to text

Figure 9-17
Regular Text form field options

❽   Click **OK** or press **[Enter]**. Notice that the TableText style is applied to the cell.

Inserting Form Fields with Similar Formatting

You can use Word's Copy and Paste commands to insert form fields with similar formatting into various places on a form. This decreases the amount of time necessary to create an on-line form. If you have applied a style to a cell that contains a form field, the entire cell must be selected (including the end-of-cell mark) if you want to copy both the form field and the style applied to the cell.

Pierre wants to insert Regular Text form fields in six other cells on his form. He decides to use a combination of the Copy and Paste commands along with the Repeat command (**[F4]**). He wants to insert a Regular Text form field in the TITLE, SUPERVISOR, and PURPOSE OF TRIP: cells in the employee information table, and in the Clients Entertained, Location, and Business Purpose cells in the Entertainment Detail table.

To copy and paste Regular Text form fields in the tables:

❶   In the employee information table, select row 2, cell 1 (including the end-of-cell mark), then click the **Copy button** on the Standard toolbar. The formatting applied to the Regular Text form field is copied to the Clipboard.

❷   Place the insertion point in row 2, cell 2 of the employee information table (below TITLE), then click the **Paste button** on the Standard toolbar.

❸   Place the insertion point in row 2, cell 5 of the employee information table (below SUPERVISOR), then press **[F4]**.

❹   Place the insertion point in row 3, cell 2 of the employee information table (next to PURPOSE OF TRIP:), then press **[F4]**.

❺   In the Entertainment Detail table, repeat Step 4 for row 3, cells 2, 3, and 4.

❻   Save your changes.

Rather than copying the contents of these cells to the cells in the rest of the column, Pierre will wait until he inserts and formats all the cells in one complete row, then he'll copy the row to the remaining rows in the table.

Inserting Number Text Form Fields

A **Number text form field** is used for any type of numeric entry in a form, including dollar amounts or measurements. Word accepts only numbers in this type of form field. If the user tries to enter any other type of data, such as regular text or a date, the field will remain highlighted until the user inserts a number. Word provides options for different types of number formats.

Pierre must insert a Number text form field in the cell for the employee's telephone extension and in the cells for all the dollar amounts throughout the form.

To insert a Number text form field for the employee's extension:

❶ Place the insertion point in row 2, cell 3 of the employee information table (below EXTENSION), then click the **Text Form Field button** abl on the Forms toolbar.

❷ Click the **Form Field Options button** 🖼 on the Forms toolbar. The Text Form Field Options dialog box appears.

❸ Click the **Type list box down arrow**, then click **Number**.

The extension numbers for CyberPark are four digits in length. Pierre decides to set the maximum length for this field at 4 to prevent the user from entering more numbers, indicating a typing mistake.

❹ Change the Maximum Length to **4**. See Figure 9-18.

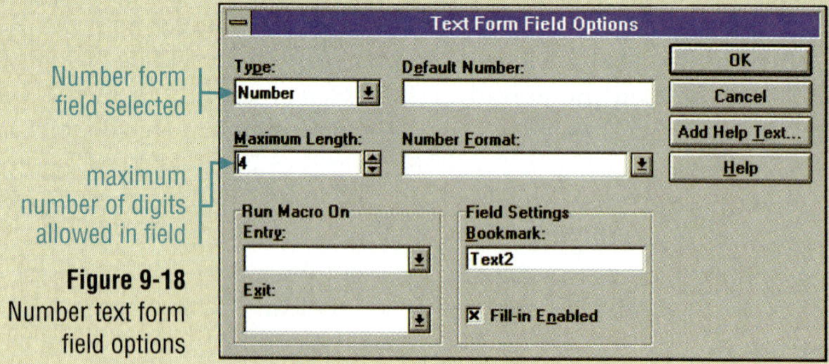

Number form field selected

maximum number of digits allowed in field

Figure 9-18
Number text form field options

❺ Click **OK** or press **[Enter]**.

❻ Select the entire cell (including the end-of-cell mark), then apply the TableData style to the cell.

Pierre doesn't need another Number text form field limited to only 4 digits in this form, but he does need to insert several dollar amount Number form fields.

To insert Number text form fields for dollar amounts:

❶ In the expenses table, place the insertion point in row 2, cell 3 (below TRANS-PORTATION), then click the **Text Form Field button** abl on the Forms toolbar. The form field is inserted.

❷ Click the **Form Field Options button** 🖼 on the Forms toolbar. The Text Form Field Options dialog box appears.

❸ Click the **Type list box down arrow**, then click **Number**.

Pierre wants the dollar amounts to be formatted properly.

❹ Click the **Number Format list box down arrow**, then click **$#,##0.00;($#,##0.00)** (this is the fifth option in the list). See Figure 9-19.

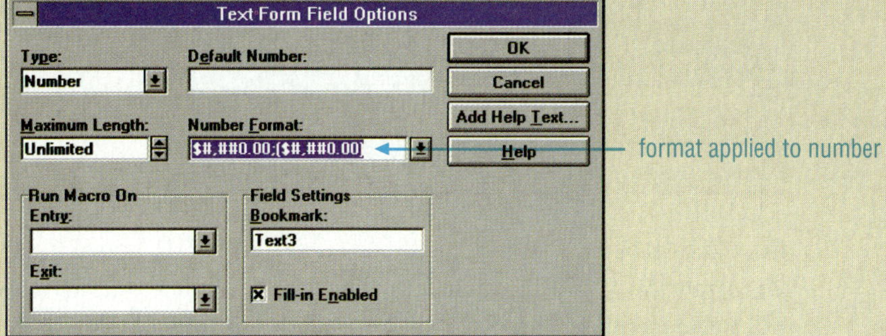

❺ Click **OK** or press **[Enter]**.

Pierre wants to copy the Number form field, including the TableData style.

❻ Select the entire cell (including the end-of-cell mark), then apply the TableData style to the cell.

❼ With the entire cell still selected, copy the Number form field for the dollar amount format to row 2, cells 4 and 5 in the expenses table (below MEALS/LODGING and MISC*), and to row 3, cell 5 in the Entertainment Detail table (below Amount).

❽ Save your changes.

Inserting Date Text Form Fields

A **Date text form field** is used when the form requires a date entry. Word checks the date entered by the user to see if it is a valid date. If not, the insertion point remains in the Date form field until a valid date is inserted.

Pierre needs to insert two Date text form fields into the form grid structure—one in the expenses table and the other in the Entertainment Detail table.

To insert the Date text form fields:

❶ Place the insertion point in row 2, cell 1 of the expenses table (below DATE), then click the **Text Form Field button** abl on the Forms toolbar.

❷ Click the **Form Field Options button** 🖼. The Text Form Field Options dialog box appears.

❸ Click the **Type list box down arrow**, then click **Date**.

Pierre wants slashes to appear between the numbers in the date.

❹ Click the **Date Format list box down arrow**, then click **M/d/yy**. See Figure 9-20.

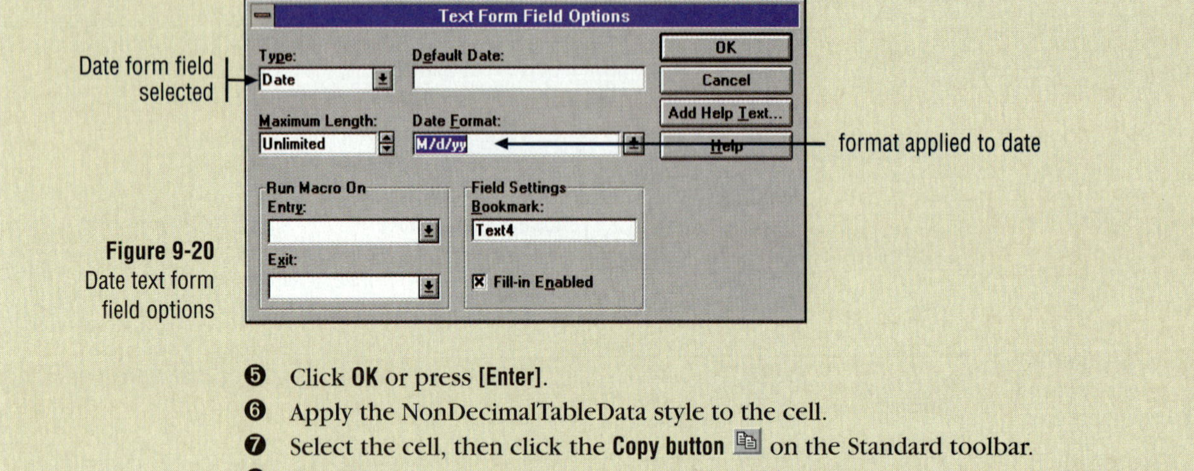

Date form field selected →

format applied to date

Figure 9-20
Date text form field options

❺　Click **OK** or press **[Enter]**.
❻　Apply the NonDecimalTableData style to the cell.
❼　Select the cell, then click the **Copy button** on the Standard toolbar.
❽　Place the insertion point in row 3, cell 1 of the Entertainment Detail table (below Date), then click the **Paste button** on the Standard toolbar.
❾　Save your changes.

Inserting Calculation Text Form Fields

A **Calculation text form field** is used for cells in which a calculation, such as adding a row or column of numbers, must be completed. Word inserts the Formula field code, = (the equal sign), to calculate a formula. As you learned in Tutorial 3, Word's calculation capabilities are suitable for simple calculations only.

As with a spreadsheet, you can insert a formula or a function to calculate. Also, each cell in a Word table has its own reference ID with a letter representing a column and a number representing a row (Figure 9-21). To designate a range of cells, you use a colon to separate the first and the last cell in the range.

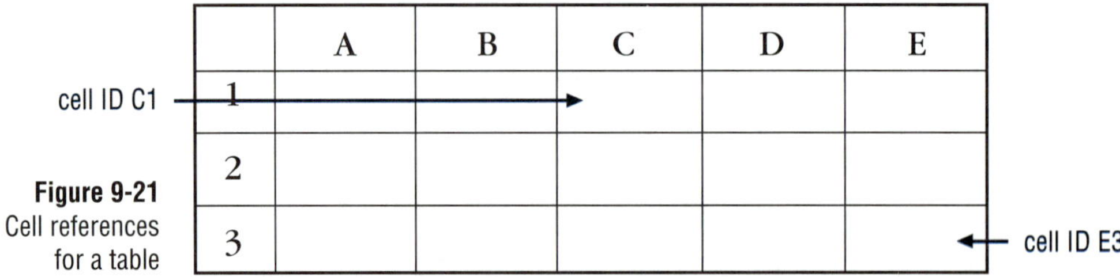

cell ID C1

Figure 9-21
Cell references for a table

cell ID E3

Pierre wants to insert Calculation form fields to sum the TRANSPORTATION, MEALS/LODGING, and MISC columns. He also wants to add a Calculation form field for the grand total.

To insert the Calculation text form fields for the expenses table:
❶　Place the insertion point in row 16, cell 2 of the expenses table (to the right of the TOTALS cell), click the **Text Form Field button** on the Forms toolbar, then click the **Form Field Options button**.
❷　Click the **Type list box down arrow**, then click **Calculation**.

In the Expression text box, Pierre needs to insert a formula that will total all the numbers in the TRANSPORTATION column. He decides to use the cell references in the formula. The TRANSPORTATION column is considered column C and the rows with amounts to be added are rows 2 through 15.

❸ Click in the Expression text box after = (the equal sign), then type **sum(c2:c15)** (no spaces).

Pierre wants the Calculation form field to be formatted in the same way as the amounts in the cells in the column above.

❹ Click the **Number Format list box down arrow**, then click **$#,##0.00;($#,##0.00)**. See Figure 9-22.

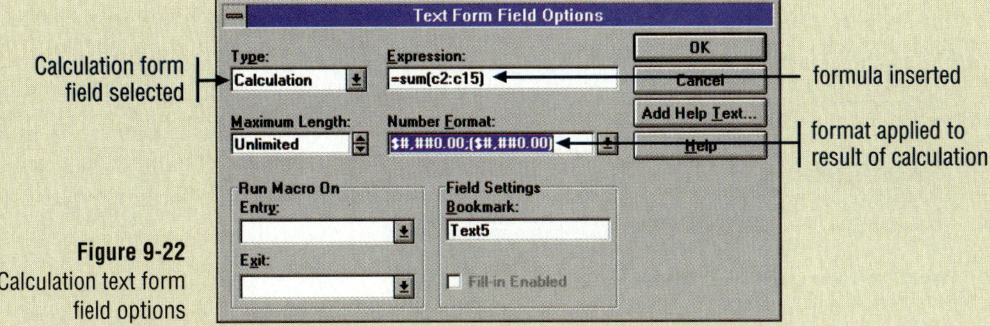

Calculation form field selected

formula inserted

format applied to result of calculation

Figure 9-22
Calculation text form field options

❺ Click **OK** or press **[Enter]**.

Pierre next needs to insert a Calculation form field that will sum the numbers in the MEALS/LODGING column—column D.

❻ Place the insertion point in row 16, cell 3, then repeat Steps 1 through 5 except type **sum(d2:d15)** in the Expression text box after the equal sign.

Pierre must now insert a Calculation form field that will sum the numbers in the MISC column—column E.

❼ Place the insertion point in row 16, cell 4, then repeat Steps 1 through 5 except type **sum(e2:e15)** in the Expression text box.

Finally, Pierre must insert a Calculation form field to calculate the grand total of all the expense totals. This formula will total the values resulting from all the formulas in the TOTALS row, row 16.

❽ Place the insertion point in row 16, cell 5, then repeat Steps 1 through 5 except type **sum(b16:d16)**.

❾ Select row 16, cells 2 through 5 (the cells containing the formulas you just entered), then apply the TableData style.

❿ Deselect the cells then save your changes.

Inserting Check Box Form Fields

A **Check Box form field** enables the user to indicate a yes or no response to a question. In the Form Field Options dialog box for check box form fields, you can specify if a check box should appear selected by default, and you can also specify the size of the check box.

The user of an on-line form can toggle the check box selection on or off by pressing [Spacebar] or by pressing [Enter] for a selected check box.

Pierre wants to insert two Check Box form fields in the employee information table—one next to Marketing and one next to Engineering—to give employees a quick way to indicate which department they are assigned to.

To insert a Check Box form field:

❶   Move to the split cell in row 2 of the employee information table (below DEPART-MENT), then click in the right cell of the split cell.

❷   Click the **Check Box Form Field button** ⊠ on the Forms toolbar, then click the **Form Field Options button** 🖾. The Check Box Form Field Options dialog box appears.

Pierre wants the size of the check box to match the point size he applied to the labels in the split cell—8 pt.

❸   In the Check Box Size section, click the **Exactly radio button**, then select **8 pt**. See Figure 9-23.

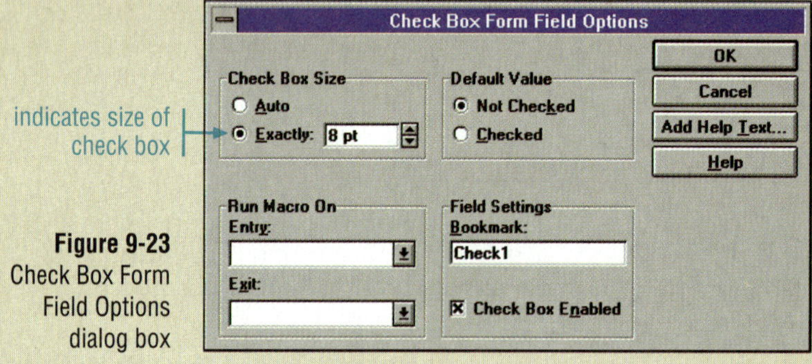

indicates size of check box →

Figure 9-23
Check Box Form
Field Options
dialog box

❹   Click **OK** or press **[Enter]**. The check box appears for the Marketing label.

Pierre needs to copy the check box for the next label—Engineering.

❺   Drag across the check box to select it, then click the **Copy button** 🖹 on the Standard toolbar.

❻   Press **[→]** to deselect the check box, then press **[Enter]**.

   TROUBLE? If the insertion point moved into the cell below SUPERVISOR, you selected the entire cell instead of just the check box. Repeat Steps 5 and 6.

❼   Paste the check box next to the label Engineering.

❽   Save your changes.

Inserting Drop-Down Form Fields

A **Drop-Down form field** is used when you want to specify a list of options from which the user must choose. A drop-down arrow appears when the user moves the insertion point into a cell containing a Drop-Down form field.

Pierre knows that traveling employees have a limited number of choices for the DESCRIPTION column. Rather than taking up a lot of room on the form with check boxes, he decides to insert a Drop-Down form field containing a list of options for the description.

To insert a Drop-Down form field for the DESCRIPTION column:

❶ Place the insertion point in row 2, cell 2 of the expenses table (below DESCRIP-TION), then click the **Drop-Down Form Field button** 📇 on the Forms toolbar.

❷ Click the **Form Field Options button** 📄. The Drop-Down Form Field Options dialog box appears.

Pierre will type the name of an expense item, then click Add until all the expense items have been listed. He begins with the expense item Fare.

❸ Type **Fare** in the Drop-Down Item text box, then click **Add** or press **[Enter]**. The item "Fare" moves to the Items in Drop-Down List box.

   TROUBLE? If you add the wrong item to the drop-down list, select the item in the list box, then click Remove.

Pierre has several more items to add to the drop-down list.

❹ Repeat Step 3 to add the following items: **Taxi/Limo, Rental Car, Parking/Tolls, Hotel, Breakfast, Lunch, Dinner, Entertainment, NA**.

Pierre wants to rearrange the order of the items on the drop-down list so that the most frequently used items are at the top of the list.

❺ Click **Parking/Tolls** in the Items in Drop-Down List box, then click the **Move Up button** twice so that the item appears after Fare.

❻ Move **Rental Car** after Parking/Tolls, then move **NA** to the top of the list so that it appears above Fare. See Figure 9-24.

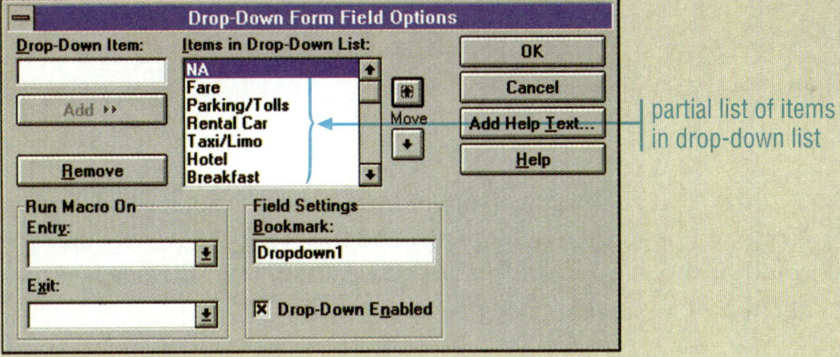

Figure 9-24
Drop-Down Form
Field Options
dialog box

❼ Click **OK**. NA, the item at the top of the drop-down list, appears in the cell. The drop-down arrow will appear to users when they select the cell. Then they click the drop-down arrow to make a selection from the list of expense items.

❽ Apply the TableText style to the cell.

❾ Save your changes.

Inserting Help for Form Fields

Word allows you to create Help messages to assist users as they complete an on-line form. You can either set up instructions to appear in the status bar or to appear in a dialog box when the user presses [F1]. The instructions appear only when the insertion point enters the specific form field and after the form template has been protected. (You learn how to protect a form template in the next section.)

Pierre wants to provide a reminder to users to complete the Entertainment Detail table for any entertainment amounts entered in the MISC column. He'll insert a Help message in the cell below the MISC heading.

To insert Help for the form field in the MISC column:

❶ Double-click the **Number text form field** in row 2, cell 5 of the expenses table (the cell below MISC). The Text Form Field Options dialog box appears.

❷ Click **Add Help Text....** The Form Field Help Text dialog box appears.

Pierre wants the instructions to appear in the status bar. If necessary, click the Status Bar tab.

❸ Click the **Type Your Own radio button**, then, in the text box below, type **Complete the Entertainment Detail section also if Misc. expense involves client entertainment**. See Figure 9-25.

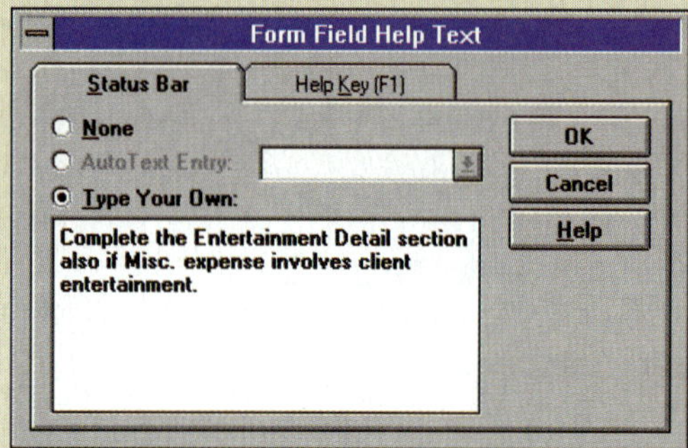

Figure 9-25
Form Field Help
Text dialog box

❹ Click **OK**, then click **OK** or press [Enter].

❺ Save your changes.

Now that the first row containing fields in the expenses table is formatted correctly, Pierre can paste the contents of the entire row to the remaining rows in the table—or he could create a macro to do the same thing. He decides to create a macro because he might have to do this same procedure again.

To create a macro to copy cell contents to the remaining rows in the table:

❶ In the expenses table, select row 2, cells 1 through 5 (the row immediately below the column headings). Do not include cell 6 in the selection.

❷ Click the **Copy button** 📋 on the Standard toolbar, press [↓] to place the insertion point in the row below, then click the **Paste button** 📋 on the Standard toolbar.

Pierre will create a macro that moves the insertion point down one row, then repeats the last action.

❸ Click **Tools** then click **Macro....** The Macro dialog box appears.

❹ Type **RowFill** in the Macro Name text box, then assign the macro to the S9EXPREP.DOT template.

❺ In the Description text box, type **Moves the insertion point down one line, then repeats the last action**.

❻ Click **Record....** The Record Macro dialog box appears.

Pierre wants to create a keyboard shortcut for this macro.

❼ Click the **Keyboard icon**, then press **[Alt][I]** as the shortcut key for the macro. Notice that [unassigned] appears in the Currently Assigned To section.

❽ Click **Assign** or press **[Enter]**, then click **Close** or press **[Enter]**. The Macro Recorder toolbar appears.

Now Pierre is ready to record the keystrokes for the macro.

❾ Press **[↓]** then press **[F4]**. The fields now appear in the third row below the column headings.

❿ Click the **Stop button** ■ on the Macro Recorder toolbar.

Pierre is now ready to use the macro he just created to fill in the rest of the expenses table and to complete the Entertainment Detail table.

To use the macro to complete the tables in the form:

❶ Press **[Alt][I]**.

❷ Repeat Step 1 for the remaining rows in the expenses table (through row 15).

❸ In the Entertainment Detail table, select row 3, cells 1 through 5 only (the row below the column headings; do not include the end-of-row mark).

❹ Click the **Copy button** 🗐 on the Standard toolbar.

❺ Press **[↓]** to place the insertion point in the next row, then click the **Paste button** 🗐 on the Standard toolbar.

❻ Press **[Alt][I]** to complete the last row in this table.

❼ Save your changes.

Assigning a Macro to a Form Field

In addition to adding a Help message for any form field, Word allows you to run a macro when a user either enters a form field or exits a form field.

Pierre wants employees to have a hard copy of the form once they complete it. He decides to create a form field that will run the macro PrintForm, which prints one copy of the form. Pierre created this macro for the basic form, but he needs to insert a form field that will run it automatically when the field is selected by the employee. To indicate the location of the field, he will type the text "Click here to print the form."

To run the PrintForm macro from a form field:

❶ Move the insertion point to the end of the document, then click in the blank paragraph below the signature lines.

❷ Click the **Text Form Field button** abl on the Forms toolbar, then click the **Form Field Options button** 🗐. The Text Form Field Options dialog box appears.

❸ Type **Click here to print the form.** in the Default Text box.

❹ Click the **Text Format list box down arrow**, then click **Uppercase**.

❺ In the Run Macro On section, click the **Entry list box down arrow**, then click **PrintForm**. See Figure 9-26.

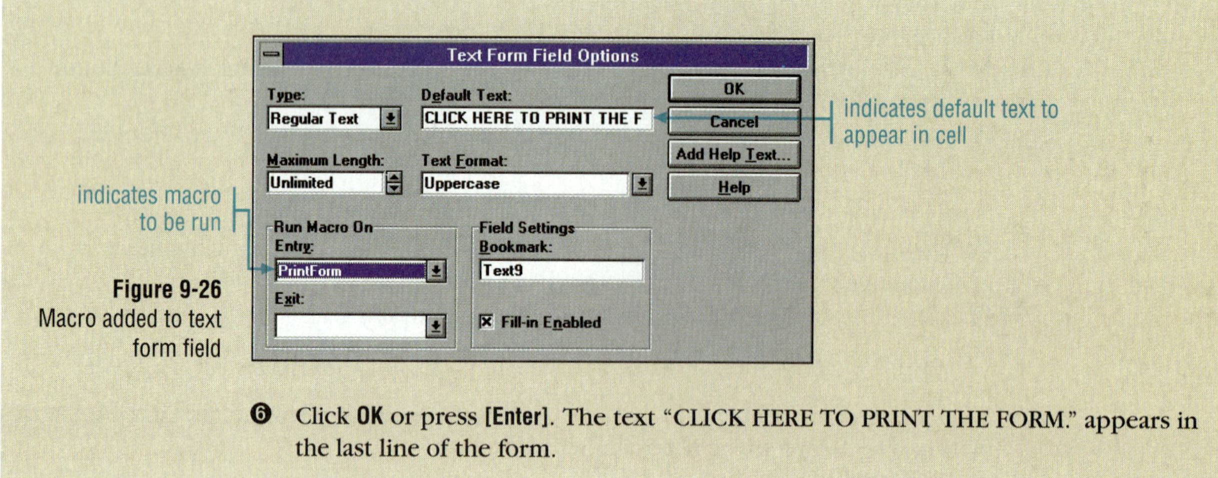

Figure 9-26
Macro added to text
form field

❻   Click **OK** or press **[Enter]**. The text "CLICK HERE TO PRINT THE FORM." appears in the last line of the form.

Pierre has now completed the expense report template. He must protect the form to prevent users from changing the basic structure of the form.

Protecting a Form Template

You protect a form template to prevent users from changing the underlying structure of the form. Also if the form includes form fields and will be completed on-line, protecting the form template allows users to move quickly from form field to form field. Word prevents users from selecting any other cell on the form. Also, when you protect a form template, most commands on Word's default menus are not available for use.

Pierre needs to protect the form template so that employees will be able to change only the contents of the form fields on-line.

To protect the expense report form template:
❶   Click **Tools** then click **Protect Document....** The Protect Document dialog box appears.
❷   Click the **Forms radio button** in the Protect Document For section. See Figure 9-27.

Figure 9-27
Protect Document
dialog box

❸   Click **OK** or press **[Enter]**. Notice that the Protect Form button 🔒 on the Forms toolbar is now highlighted.
❹   Dismiss the Forms toolbar.
❺   Save your changes then close the template.
Now Pierre is ready to test the form template by filling in the form on-line.

Filling In an On-line Form

Once you have created your form template, you can distribute it for general use. The users then open a new document based on the form template rather than the template itself. If the form template has been protected, then Word will allow on-line users of the template to move to and change only those form fields that require input from the user. Word does not allow the user to change fields that have been set up to insert information automatically, like date or time fields, or calculation fields. Figure 9-28 shows the methods for filling in various types of form fields.

If You Want To:	Press:
Move to the next form field	[Tab], [Enter], or [↓]
Move to the previous form field	[Shift][Tab] or [↑]
Select or deselect a check box form field	[Spacebar] or [x]
Open a drop-down form field	[F4] or [Alt][↓]
Select an item from a drop-down field	[↑] [↓], then [Enter]
View Help for a form field, if available	[F1]

Figure 9-28
Methods for completing on-line forms

Pierre is now ready to test his expense report form template. He will create a new document based on his template.

To complete the employee information table of the expense report on-line form:

❶ Click **File** then click **New....** The New dialog box appears.

Ordinarily you would choose a template from the Template list, but you must type the complete path for the template that you saved on your Student Disk.

❷ In the Template text box, type **a:\s9exprep** then click **OK** or press [Enter]. The expense report form appears and the first form field to be completed—EMPLOYEE NAME—is selected. The form comes up in Zoom Page Width view. Save the document as **S9TESTER.DOC** to your Student Disk.

❸ Type **Pierre Bodine** then press [Tab] to move to the next field. Notice that the text of the name changes to uppercase format.

❹ Type **Staff Accountant** then press [Tab].

To see if the four-digit limitation of the extension number works, Pierre will type in a five-digit extension number.

❺ Type **24001**. The computer beeps and the last digit was not entered.

   TROUBLE? Your computer might not beep; however, the last digit that you typed will not be inserted in the cell.

❻ Delete the current extension 2400, then type **4001** and press [Tab]. The check box for the Marketing label becomes highlighted.

Pierre wants to select the Engineering label.

❼ Press [Tab] then press [x] or press [Spacebar]. An "x" appears in the check box, indicating it is "checked off," or selected.

❽ Press [Tab] to move to the SUPERVISOR column.

❾ Type **Johnson** then press [Tab] to move to the cell for PURPOSE OF TRIP.

⑩ Type **To meet with MetroPlex officers**, then press **[Tab]**.

Next Pierre will test the expenses table in the form. He first wants to test the date form field.

To complete the expenses table in the expense report form:

❶ In the first cell below the DATE column heading, type **January 5, 1995** then press **[Tab]**. The date is converted to the selected formatting option, the insertion point is now in the cell for DESCRIPTION, and the drop-down arrow appears in the DESCRIPTION cell.

❷ Click the **DESCRIPTION drop-down arrow** to display the list of options, then click **Fare**.

❸ Press **[Tab]** to move to the TRANSPORTATION cell, then type **312**. This entry will convert to the appropriate dollar format after you complete the next step.

Pierre next enters an entertainment expense. He must move to the next line of the expense form.

❹ Click the **DESCRIPTION form field** for the next row, click the **drop-down arrow**, then click **Entertainment**.

❺ Press **[Tab]** three times to move to the MISC column. Notice the Help message that appears in the status bar. See Figure 9-29.

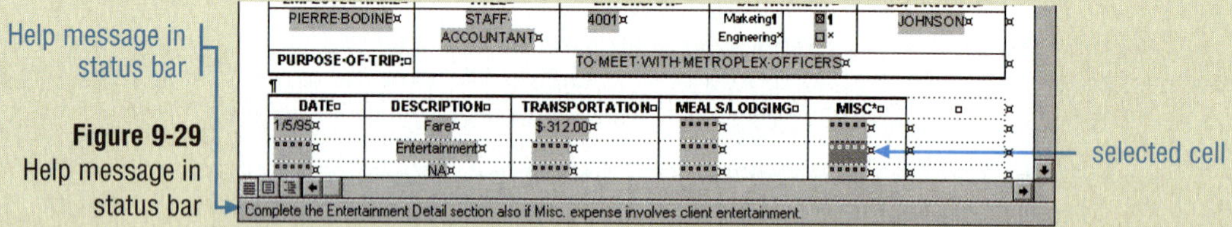

Figure 9-29
Help message in status bar

❻ Type **78.65**.

❼ Complete the form as shown in Figure 9-30.

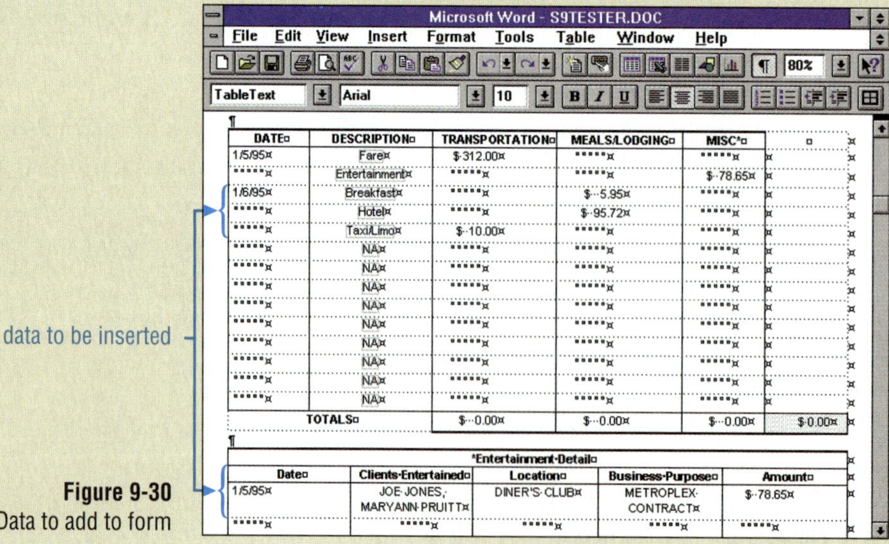

DATE	DESCRIPTION	TRANSPORTATION	MEALS/LODGING	MISC*	
1/5/95	Fare	$ 312.00			
	Entertainment			$ 78.65	
1/6/95	Breakfast		$ 5.95		
	Hotel		$ 95.72		
	Taxi/Limo	$ 10.00			
	NA				
	NA				
	NA				
	NA				
	NA				
	NA				
	NA				
	NA				
	NA				
TOTALS		$ 0.00	$ 0.00	$ 0.00	$ 0.00

*Entertainment Detail				
Date	Clients Entertained	Location	Business Purpose	Amount
1/5/95	JOE JONES, MARYANN PRUITT	DINER'S CLUB	METROPLEX CONTRACT	$ 78.65

Figure 9-30
Data to add to form

data to be inserted

❽ Save your changes.

Next Pierre wants to see if the form is updated—that is, the calculations for the totals are completed—and then is sent to print when he moves into the last cell.

❾ Move to the end of document, then click in the cell "CLICK HERE TO PRINT THE FORM." Notice that the totals are updated and that the form is sent to print. See Figure 9-31.

Form

CyberPark Development
The Playland of the Future
2400 Carrington
Cupertino, CA 95001
204.555.2282 Fax 204.555.6835

EXPENSE
REPORT

Date: July 16, 1995

EMPLOYEE NAME	TITLE	EXTENSION	DEPARTMENT		SUPERVISOR
PIERRE BODINE	STAFF ACCOUNTANT	4001	Marketing	☒	JOHNSON
			Engineering	☐	
PURPOSE OF TRIP:		TO MEET WITH METROPLEX OFFICERS			

DATE	DESCRIPTION	TRANSPORTATION	MEALS/LODGING	MISC*
1/5/95	Fare	$ 312.00		
	Entertainment			$ 78.65
1/6/95	Breakfast		$ 5.95	
	Hotel		$ 95.72	
	Taxi/Limo	$ 10.00		
	NA			
	NA			
	NA			
	NA			
	NA			
	NA			
	NA			
	NA			
	NA			
TOTALS		$ 322.00	$ 101.67	$ 78.65	$ 502.32

*Entertainment Detail				
Date	Clients Entertained	Location	Business Purpose	Amount
1/5/95	JOE JONES, MARYANN PRUITT	DINER'S CLUB	METROPLEX CONTRACT	$ 78.65

Employee Signature   Date   Approval Signature   Date

CLICK HERE TO PRINT THE FORM.

Figure 9-31
Completed test expense report form

Saving Form Data

You can save the entire form document or you can save just the form data; that is, the variable data entered by a user on-line. You save the form data to a text file, which can then be imported to a database file, for example.

Pierre wants to save just the data from the form he completed.

To save the form data:
❶   Click **Tools** then click **Options....** The Options dialog box appears.
❷   Click the **Save tab,** then click the **Save Data Only for Forms check box** in the Save Options section. See Figure 9-32.

select to save
data only

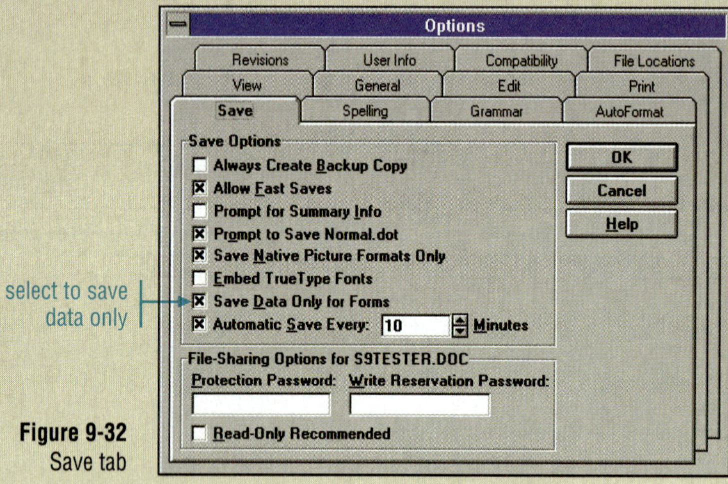

Figure 9-32
Save tab

❸   Click **OK** or press [Enter].
❹   Click **File.** Notice that the Save As command is replaced with the Save Copy As command.
❺   Click **Save Copy As....**
❻   Save the form data as **S9EXPREP** to your Student Disk. Word will add a .TXT extension to the file.

Pierre is satisfied with the form and is ready to distribute the template to the rest of the company.

❼   Click **Tools** then click **Options....** Click the **Save tab,** if necessary.
❽   Deselect the Save Data Only for Forms check box.
❾   Close the document and exit Word without saving any changes to the NORMAL template.

Pierre distributes the template to the appropriate employees for use in recording their travel expenses.

Questions

1. What is the purpose of a form?
2. What are two types of forms?
3. What is the procedure for precisely changing column widths?
4. What is the procedure for setting individual borders using the Table Borders and Shading dialog box?
5. What is the procedure for splitting cells in a table?
6. What is the procedure for merging cells in a table?
7. What are two methods for inserting form fields into a document?
8. List and briefly describe the different types of form fields.
9. Where can Help messages for form fields be located?
10. What is the procedure for assigning a macro to a form field?
11. What is the purpose of protecting a form template?

 12. What is the purpose of the Bookmark option in the Form Field Options dialog box?

Tutorial Assignments

Start Word, if necessary, and conduct a screen check. Complete the following:

1. Open a new template based on T9CPFORM.DOT from your Student Disk. In the Title text box of the Summary Info dialog box, type "Employee Review."
2. Save the template as S9EMPREV.DOT to your Student Disk.
3. Insert a WordArt image in the top right of the form grid structure.
   a. Type the form name "Employee Review" so that it appears on two lines.
   b. Apply the font Desdemona.
   c. Embed the WordArt image into the form.
   d. Use the Paragraph command to insert a 6 pt space before the paragraph.
   e. Save your changes.
4. Insert a table for employee information:
   a. Place the insertion point in the blank paragraph below the row containing the date, then press [Enter].
   b. Insert a 4-row by 4-column table, then type the information shown in Figure 9-33.

Figure 9-33

Employee Name:		Title:	
Employee Number:		Status:	
Department:		Supervisor:	
Reviewer:		Reviewer's Title:	

   c. Apply the Form style to the table.
   d. Adjust the column widths as follows, and specify no space between columns:
      column 1   1.31"
      column 2   2.45"
      column 3   1.3"
      column 4   2.45"
   e. Add a $3/4$ pt rule to the bottom of each row of the table.
5. Insert a table for employee traits.
   a. Place the insertion point in the blank paragraph below the employee information table, then press [Enter].
   b. Insert a 14-row by 5-column table, then type the following information as column headings, beginning in row 1, cell 2: Excellent, Good, Fair, Poor.

    c. Apply the ColumnHead style to the column headings.

    d. Type the following information in column 1 beginning in row 2: Integrity, Productivity, Dependability, Technical Skills, Communication Skills, Work Quality, Attendance, Enthusiasm, Punctuality, Cooperation, Attitude, Initiative, Work Consistency.

    e. Apply the Form style to the traits in column 1.

    f. Apply the TableData style to the remaining cells in the table (row 2, cells 2 through 5, through row 14, cells 2 through 5).

    g. Adjust the column widths as follows, and specify no space between columns:

        column 1   3.1"

        columns 2 through 5   1.1"

    h. Save your changes.

6. Insert a table for open-ended comments.

    a. Place the insertion point in the empty paragraph below the employee traits table, then press [Enter].

    b. Insert a 3-row by 1-column table.

    c. Type "Comments:" in the first row at the left margin.

    d. Adjust the Width of Column 1 option to 7.5" and specify no space between columns.

    e. Add a $^3/_4$ pt rule to the bottom of each row of the table.

    f. Save your changes.

7. Replace the word "Authorized" in the signature lines with the word "Reviewer's."

8. Insert Regular Text form fields formatted with the Title Case text format in the cells to the right of the following labels: Employee Name, Reviewer, Title, Status (specify Full-time as the default text), Supervisor, Reviewer's Title.

9. Insert a Number text form field with a maximum of nine characters in the cell to the right of Employee Number.

10. Insert a Drop-Down form field in the cell to the right of Department. Place the following names on the drop-down list: Marketing, Engineering, Human Resources, Real Estate, Administrative Services.

11. Insert 12 pt check boxes in the blank cells in the employee traits table (row 2, cells 2 through 5, through row 14, cells 2 through 5).

12. Spell check the document.

13. Protect the template from changes.

14. Save your changes.

15. Preview, print, then close the template.

16. Test the template by completing a new form document using your name and pertinent information as the employee and your instructor as the reviewer. Save the document as S9TRAITS.DOC to your Student Disk.

17. Print then close the document.

E   18. Open a new template based on T9CPCRED.DOT from your Student Disk. In the Title text box of the Summary Info dialog box, type "Credit Reminder." Save the template as S9CPCRED.DOT to your Student Disk. Substitute appropriate form fields for the bracketed items.

19. Save your changes.

20. Activate the Print Field Codes option, then print the template.

21. Turn off the Print Field Codes option.

22. Close the document.

Case Problems

1. Plank Nautical Services Account Statement Form Template

Tom Plank, Jr. recently took over the running of the family marine services business from his father. Tom has decided to bring the administrative functions of the company into the twentieth century by automating as many tasks as possible, as well as giving the company's image a more professional polish. One way Tom hopes to achieve both objectives is to design and create more professional-looking forms for the jobs the company does. He decides to start with an account statement form.

Complete the following:

1. Open a new template based on P9PNFORM.DOT from your Student Disk. In the Title text box of the Summary Info dialog box, type "Account Statement."
2. Save the template as S9PNSTMT.DOT to your Student Disk.
3. Insert a WordArt image in the top-right cell of the form grid structure.
   a. Type the form name "Account Statement" so that it appears on two lines.
   b. Apply the font Britannic Bold.
   c. Embed the WordArt image into the form.
   d. Save your changes.
4. Place the insertion point after Date, press [Spacebar], then insert a CREATEDATE field code.
5. Insert a table for customer information:
   a. Place the insertion point in the blank paragraph below the row containing the date, then press [Enter].
   b. Insert a 7-row by 3-column table, then type "TO:" in row 1, cell 1; type "Terms:" in row 7, cell 1; and type "Amount Enclosed:$" in row 7, cell 3.
   c. Apply the Date/Notes style to the table.
   d. Adjust the column widths as follows, and specify no space between columns:

      column 1   3.68"

      column 2   .17"

      column 3   3.68"
6. Insert remittance instructions.
   a. Place the insertion point in the blank paragraph below the customer information table, then press [Enter] twice.
   b. Press [↑] once to move the insertion point up one line, then type:
      PLEASE DETACH AND RETURN THIS PORTION WITH YOUR REMITTANCE. MAKE CHECK PAYABLE TO: PLANK NAUTICAL SERVICES.
   c. Change the font to 8 pt Arial, then center the paragraph across the page.
   d. Add a $^3/_4$ pt dashed rule across the bottom of the line space.
   e. Save your changes.
7. Insert a table for account activity.
   a. Place the insertion point in the blank paragraph below the remittance instructions, then press [Enter].
   b. Insert a 15-row by 5-column table, then type the following information as column headings: Date, Description, Charges, Credits, Balance.
   c. Apply the ColumnHead style to the column headings, then apply Solid (100%) shading to row 1.
   d. Apply the TableText style to columns 1 and 2 starting with row 2.
   e. Apply the TableData style to cell 5 of row 2 and to columns 3, 4, and 5 starting with row 3.
   f. Adjust the column widths as follows, and specify no space between columns:

      column 1   1"

      column 2   3.5"

      columns 3 through 5   1"
   g. Merge cells 2, 3, and 4 in row 2 of the account activity table, type "Balance Forward:" then right align the text in the cell.
   h. Save your changes.
8. Create the following custom border formatting scheme for the account activity table:
   a. Row 1: $^3/_4$ pt (solid rule) on all outside borders
   b. Row 2: $^3/_4$ pt on bottom, left, right, and internal vertical borders
   c. Rows 3 through 14: $^3/_4$ pt on bottom, left, right, and internal vertical borders
   d. Save your changes.

9. Insert a closing statement.
   a. Place the insertion point in the empty paragraph below the account activity table, then press [Enter].
   b. Type "Thank You For Your Business!"
   c. Apply the Dates/Notes style, then center the paragraph across the page.
   d. Save your changes.
10. Spell check the form.
11. Preview then print the template.
12. Insert a Number text form field to the right of Account No. with a maximum of 4 digits.
13. Insert Regular Text form fields formatted with Title Case in cell 1 of rows 2 through 5 of the customer information table, and in cell 2, rows 3 through 14 (below DESCRIPTION) of the account activity table.
14. Insert a Drop-Down form field to the right of Terms: in the customer information table. Add the following items to the drop-down list: n/30, 5/10, 3/20, n/60.
15. Insert a Date text form field formatted with slashes between digits in cell 1, rows 2 through 14 (below DATE) of the account activity table.
16. Insert a Number text form field with the format $#,##0.00;($#,##0.00) in cell 5 of row 2 and cells 3, 4, and 5 of rows 3 through 14.
17. Protect the form from changes.
18. Save your changes then print the template.
19. Save the template as S9BALANC.DOT to your Student Disk, then unprotect the form.
20. Remove the Number text form fields from cell 5 of rows 3 through 14.

E 21. Insert Calculation form fields in cell 5 of rows 3 through 14 that will calculate the balance due if charges or credits are made to the beginning balance.

E 22. Assign the macro Update to the Regular Text form field in cell 5, row 15, to be activated when the insertion point enters the cell.
23. Save your changes then close the template.
24. Test the S9BALANC.DOT template by completing a new form document. Save the document as S9ACSTMT.DOC to your Student Disk. Use the following information to complete the account statement form:

> Acct. No. 1003
>
> Customer: Raymond Janik
>
> Coastal Marine
>
> 109 Marina Bay Drive
>
> Seabrook, CT 06121
>
> Terms: 5/10
>
> Balance Forward: $502
>
> Payment Received on 2/19/1995 of $350
>
> Charge for dry dock services on 2/28/95 of $475

25. Save your changes.
26. Run the Update macro to print the form.
27. Close the document.

2. Sugar Mills, Inc., Software Audit Form

Pamela Ivey is the manager of Information Services for Sugar Mills, Inc., a large corporation refining sugar in southern Texas. She has been ordered by upper management to coordinate an audit of the software on all personal computers in the corporate headquarters. Original documentation and disks must exist for each copy of a software product resident on a hard disk, or the cost center will be charged for the purchase price of the software. Pamela decides to develop a form to be distributed to all department heads who will, in turn, distribute the form to each personal computer user in that department.

Complete the following:

1. Open a new template based on P9SMAUDT.DOT from your Student Disk. In the Title text box of the Summary Info dialog box, type "Software Audit."
2. Save the template as S9SMAUDT.DOT to your Student Disk.
3. Type the text "Sugar Mills, Inc." then press [Enter]. Type "Software Audit Work Sheet" then press [Enter] twice.
4. Apply the Title style to the first three lines of the document.
5. Move the insertion point to the end of the document, then type the following:

> Instructions: Use this worksheet to record the software found on the hard disk of each personal computer. You are to provide the following information for each software product: Name and version number, publisher, serial no., and type of license support actually on hand (M=Manual, D=Disks, L=License Agreement, R=Registration Card with Serial No., I=Invoice, and C=Cancelled Check).

6. Press [Enter] twice.
7. Insert a table for computer information:
   a. Place the insertion point at the end of the document, then press [Enter].
   b. Insert a 3-row by 2-column table, then type the following information in cell 1:
      row 1   Computer Serial No.
      row 2   User Name
      row 3   Office Location
   c. Apply the Date/Notes style to the table.
   d. Adjust the column widths as follows, and specify no space between columns:
      column 1   2"
      column 2   5.5"
   e. Put a $^3/_4$ pt border around all sides, internal horizontal and internal vertical borders of the computer information table.
   f. Save your changes.
8. Insert a table for software product information.
   a. Place the insertion point in the blank paragraph below the computer information table, then press [Enter].
   b. Insert a 25-row by 10-column table, then type the following information as column headings: Software Product, Version Number, Software Publisher, Software Serial No., M, D, L, R, I, C.
   c. Apply the ColumnHead style to the column headings.
   d. Adjust the column widths as follows, and specify no space between columns:
      columns 1 through 4   1.4"
      columns 5 through 10   .3"
   e. Apply the TableText style to rows 2 through 25.
   f. Save your changes.
9. Put a $^3/_4$ pt border around all sides, internal horizontal and internal vertical borders of the software product information table.
10. Spell check the form.
11. Save your changes.
12. Preview, print, then close the template.

3. Design Your Own Day Planner

1. Open a new template based on NORMAL.DOT. In the Title text box of the Summary Info dialog box, type "Daily Schedule."
2. Save the template as S9DAYSCH.DOT to your Student Disk.
3. Change the page setup options so that all margins are .5" and the page orientation is landscape.
4. Switch to Page Width Zoom view, if necessary.
5. Save your changes.
6. Insert a table for your daily schedule:
   a. Insert a 37-row by 5-column table.
   b. Adjust the columns widths as follows, and specify no space between columns:
column 1	.5"
column 2	.25"
column 3	2.75"
column 4	3.6"
column 5	2.9"
   c. Merge cells 1, 2, and 3 of row 1.
   d. Merge cells 1, 2, and 3 of rows 33 through 37.
   e. Save your changes.
7. Type your name in cell 1, row 1; format the text with Arial, 12 pt, bold; then press [Enter].
8. Type "Daily Schedule For:"; format the text with Arial 10 pt, bold; then press [Enter].
9. Insert a Date text form field (MMMM d, yyyy).
10. Type the following column headings in row 2, then format the headings with Arial, 10 pt, bold, and centered alignment:
cell 1	Time
cell 2	X
cell 3	Appointments
cell 4	Calls
cell 5	Notes
11. Type "Expenses" in cell 1 of row 33, then format the text with Arial, 10 pt, bold.
12. In row 34, type "Item" in cell 1, "Business Purpose" in cell 2, and "Amount" in cell 3, then format the text with Arial, 10 pt, bold, and centered alignment.
13. Starting in row 3, cell 1 type "7:00," then in each cell below increase the time in 30-minute increments through 9:30 (p.m.).
14. Save your changes.
15. Put a $^3/_4$ pt border around all sides, internal horizontal and internal vertical borders of the form.
16. Spell check the form.
17. Save your changes then close the template.
18. Test the S9DAYSCH template by completing a new form document using your schedule for today. Save the document as S9TODAY.DOC to your Student Disk.
19. Close the document and exit Word.

Using Word with Other Microsoft Applications

Creating Conference Materials

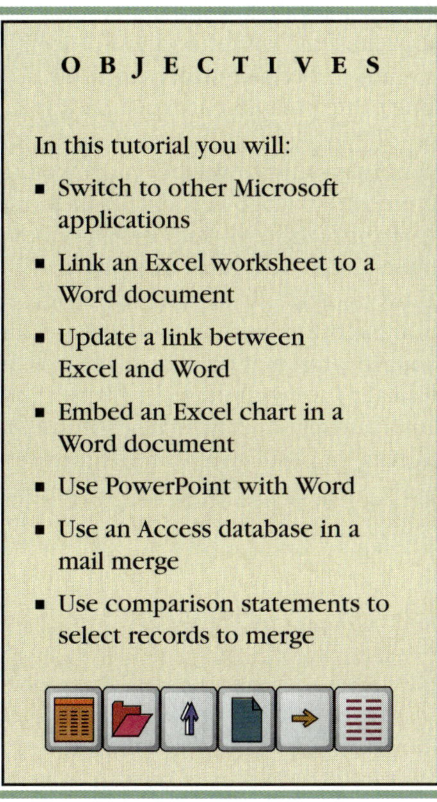

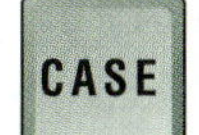

Association of Construction Engineering Educators 4th Annual Conference Nykita Kwan is an associate professor of civil engineering in the College of Technology at Wabash University in Wabash, Ohio. Nykita is making preparations to attend the 4th Annual Conference of the Association of Construction Engineering Educators (ACEE) in Cincinnati. As the previous president of ACEE, she serves on the executive council and is responsible for membership statistics. In addition, Nykita and one of her colleagues at another university submitted a proposal to make a presentation to the Software Tools Special Interest Group (SIG) of ACEE. Their proposal was accepted recently, and now they are collaborating on finalizing the content. Nykita was also asked to send a letter to the new ACEE members who also joined the Software Tools SIG informing them of the field trip to the multimedia instructional lab of Cincinnati College. Nykita sets out a plan of action to accomplish all of these tasks with a minimal duplication of effort.

Note: In order to complete this tutorial, you must have Excel 5.0, PowerPoint 4.0, and Access 2.0 loaded on your computer in addition to Word 6.0. You might encounter "Out of Memory" messages when multitasking if you have less than 8 MB of RAM on your computer.

Windows Environment Revisited

As noted earlier in this book, one of the hallmarks of the Windows environment is its consistent operational features among applications. These features decrease the amount of time required to learn new Windows applications, which enables you to work more efficiently rather than spending time learning the tools necessary to do your job.

Furthermore, overall productivity is increased because of how the various Microsoft applications work together. You'll save time if you remember the principle: *enter data one time, use data multiple times.* Adhering to this principle will cut down on duplication of effort.

Nykita has created the shell of the report she must submit to the executive council concerning membership data, but she used Excel to create a worksheet and chart for the membership enrollment by region for the years 1991 through 1994. Rather than retyping the data into a Word table, Nykita wants to use the Excel worksheet and chart in the membership report. The second task that Nykita must complete is to prepare her presentation for the Software Tools SIG. She has already outlined the presentation in Word, and she wants to use PowerPoint to format this outline in presentation slides. She doesn't want to retype the outline; she wants to simply transfer the Word outline to PowerPoint and let PowerPoint create a presentation for her automatically. Finally, Nykita will use the membership database, which was created using Access, to produce a form letter to send to the new Software Tools SIG members concerning the field trip to the multimedia instructional lab.

Making Connections with Microsoft Applications

Microsoft provides three levels of data-sharing capabilities—copying, linking, and embedding. Making connections efficiently among the various Microsoft applications involves not only knowing *how* to exchange information between applications but also knowing *when* to use which level. Figure 10-1 describes the three levels of data transfer available and some of the circumstances when each would be an appropriate method to use.

Method of Data Transfer	Purpose
Copying	You want to place a static copy of data in another location.
Embedding	You need to be able to edit the copied data in the source application, but source files are potentially not available for updating.
Linking	The copied data has to be the most recent version available and/or data must be shared with more than one document.

Figure 10-1
Data transfer levels

Switching to Other Microsoft Applications

One of the common operational features of the Windows environment is the ability to switch easily between applications. To launch another application you can use [Alt][Tab] to switch to the Program Manager, then double-click the icon of the application you want. The Microsoft toolbar provides another way to switch between Microsoft applications. To display this toolbar, use the Toolbars command on the View menu of any Microsoft application. The Microsoft toolbar lists all of Microsoft's most popular applications so that you can launch another application easily from whichever application is open.

Nykita has already created the text of the memo report to the executive council. Now she needs to switch to Excel to copy the membership summary worksheet to the memo.

To switch to another application:

❶ Start Word and conduct the screen check procedure as described in Tutorial 1.

❷ Open the file C10EC.DOC from your Student Disk. The memo appears. Save the document as **S10EC.DOC** to your Student Disk.

❸ Press **[Ctrl][End]** to move the insertion point to the end of the document.

Nykita needs to switch to Excel, so she decides to display the Microsoft toolbar.

❹ Click **View**, click **Toolbars...**, then click the **Microsoft check box**.

❺ Click **OK** or press **[Enter]**. The Microsoft toolbar appears.

The toolbar is in the way so Nykita decides to move it to the right edge of the window.

❻ Point to the title bar of the Microsoft toolbar, then drag it to the right side of the screen. See Figure 10-2.

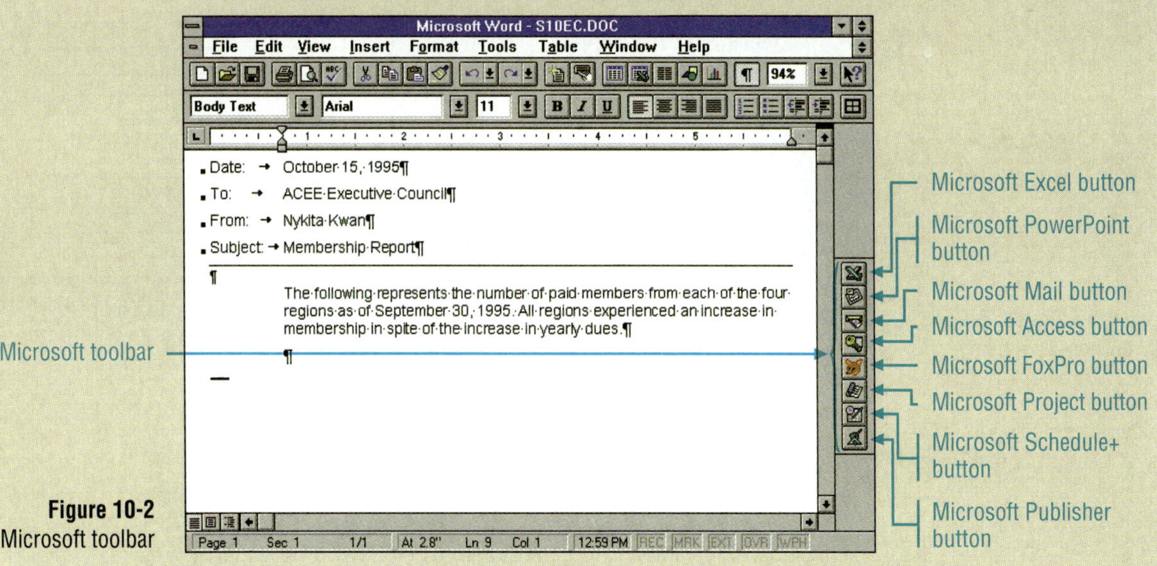

Figure 10-2
Microsoft toolbar

Nykita is now ready to launch Excel.

Exchanging Data with Excel

One of the most popular spreadsheet packages available on the market is Microsoft Excel 5.0. Because of its popularity, you need to know how to exchange information between Word and Excel. Both Word and Excel can serve as either a source application or a destination application during the data exchange process, with Word typically acting as the destination application.

Linking an Excel Worksheet

You might need to insert the same worksheet data in several Word documents. If you link the Excel worksheet (the source document) to the Word documents (destination documents), then the Word documents are automatically updated if changes are made to the worksheet (Figure 10-3). Linking places only a *representation* of the data in the destination document, not the data itself. When two documents are linked, Word actually inserts a LINK field code containing the field code name LINK followed by the exact path to the source application and file.

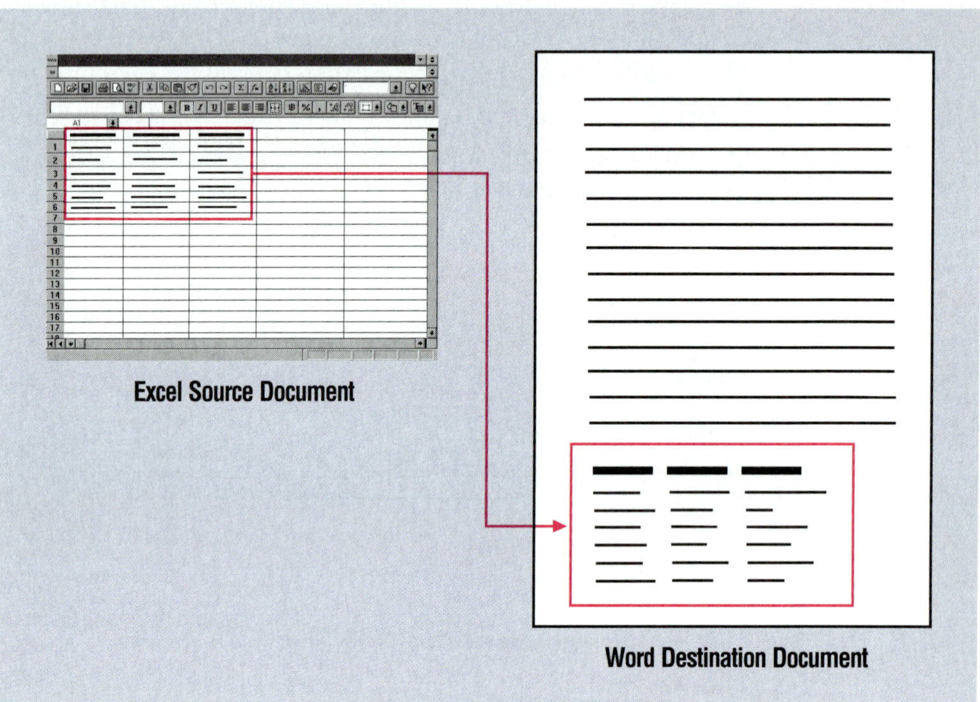

Figure 10-3
Linking documents

REFERENCE WINDOW

Creating a Link Between Word and Another Application

- Open the source application, then copy the selected text, graphics, or sound object to the Clipboard.

- Switch to Word then position the insertion point in the location where you want the information from the source application located.

- Click Edit then click Paste Special…. The Paste Special dialog box appears.

- Click the Paste Link radio button.

- In the As section, select the application to which you want the linked object associated.

- Click OK or press [Enter].

Nykita is still waiting for final membership figures from the Mountain division. Because the Excel data will change, she decides to link the worksheet to her document rather than embed it in the document.

To link the Excel worksheet to the Word document:

❶ Click the **Microsoft Excel button** on the Microsoft toolbar. The Excel application window and workbook window appear. Maximize the application and workbook windows, if necessary.

Nykita has already created the worksheet she wants to include in the membership report to the executive council of ACEE.

❷ Click the **Open button** on the Standard toolbar. The Open dialog box appears.

❸ Switch to the drive containing your Student Disk, then open the file **C10ACEE.XLS**. The C10ACEE.XLS workbook appears.

❹ Save the workbook as **S10ACEE.XLS** to your Student Disk.

Nykita will eventually need to switch back to Word, so she decides to open the Microsoft toolbar available in Excel.

❺ Click **View**, click **Toolbars…**, click the **Microsoft check box** in the Toolbars list box, then click **OK** or press [Enter]. The Microsoft toolbar appears. You can move this toolbar out of the way, if necessary.

Nykita wants to include the entire worksheet in her report, but not the graph. She needs to select only cells A1 through F8. She will use the same techniques to select the cells in the Excel worksheet as she does to select cells in a Word table.

❻ Click **cell A1**, press and drag through **cell F8**, then click the **Copy button** on the Standard toolbar.

Nykita wants to link the worksheet rather than embed it because she still needs some information from one of the regions.

❼ Click the **Microsoft Word button** on the Microsoft toolbar (or press [Alt][Tab]). The memo report appears.

❽ Place the insertion point at the end of the document, if necessary, click **Edit**, then click **Paste Special…**. The Paste Special dialog box appears.

❾ Click the **Paste Link radio button**, then click **Microsoft Excel 5.0 Worksheet Object** in the As section. See Figure 10-4.

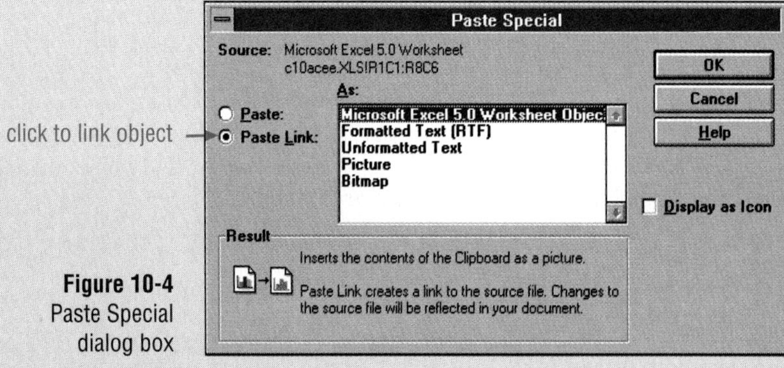

Figure 10-4
Paste Special
dialog box

⑩ Click **OK** or press **[Enter]**. The selected cells of the worksheet appear in the memo document.

When the representative of the Mountain region contacts her, Nykita will update the information in the Excel worksheet, and the same information will be updated automatically in her memo document.

Nykita wants to view the LINK field code for the membership summary to make sure it includes the correct source file information.

To view the LINK field code for the Excel worksheet:

❶ Click **Tools** then click **Options....** The Options dialog box appears.

❷ Click the **View tab**, if necessary, then click the **Field Codes check box** in the Show section.

❸ Click **OK** or press **[Enter]**. The linked cells from the Excel worksheet are replaced by a LINK field code. See Figure 10-5.

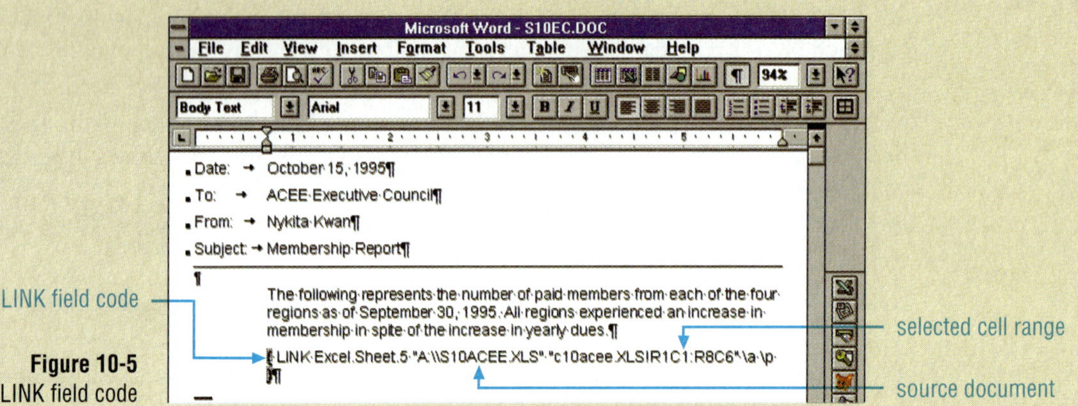

Figure 10-5
LINK field code

Nykita is satisfied that the LINK field code includes the correct path to the source file, as well as the specific cells in the worksheet that she selected.

❹ Click **Tools**, click **Options...**, then click the **Field Codes check box** to deselect it.

❺ Click **OK** or press **[Enter]**.

❻ Save your changes.

Just as she finishes viewing the LINK field code, Nykita receives an electronic mail message from the Mountain region representative. The current membership for the Mountain region is 42. Nykita can now change the Excel worksheet, and her memo document will be updated automatically because the two are linked.

Updating a Link

If you need to edit the data in a linked document, you should return to the source document to make the revisions, particularly if more than one destination document is linked to the same source document.

Nykita needs to revise the data in the membership summary worksheet. Because the memo document to the executive council is linked to this worksheet, the memo will be updated automatically, so Nykita has to make the change only once.

To update the linked Excel worksheet:

❶ Press **[Alt][Tab]** or click the **Microsoft Excel button** ⊠ on the Microsoft toolbar to switch to Excel. The S10ACEE.XLS workbook appears with a dashed box surrounding the selected worksheet. Press **[Esc]** to dismiss the selection box.

❷ Click **cell E5** to select it, then type **42**.

❸ Press **[↓]** or press **[Enter]**. Notice that the worksheet totals and the chart are updated automatically to reflect the new information.

❹ Save the changes to the worksheet.

Nykita wants to make sure that the worksheet was updated in the memo report.

❺ Click the **Microsoft Word button** 𝗪 on the Microsoft toolbar or press **[Alt][Tab]** to display S10EC.DOC. The Mountain region's 1994 membership figure and the total amounts are updated in the Word document. See Figure 10-6.

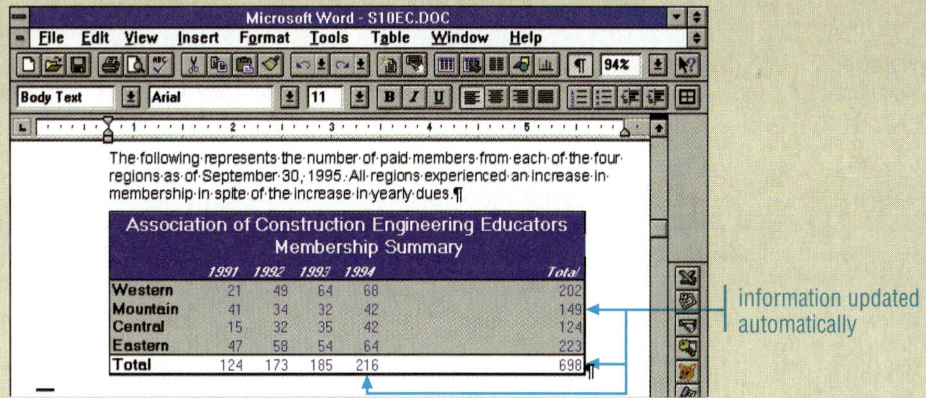

Figure 10-6
Updated linked document

The following table reproduces the linked data shown in the figure:

	1991	1992	1993	1994	Total
Western	21	49	64	68	202
Mountain	41	34	32	42	149
Central	15	32	35	42	124
Eastern	47	58	54	64	223
Total	124	173	185	216	698

❻ Save your changes.

Embedding an Excel Chart

You embed an object from another Microsoft application in the same way as you embed an object from one of Word's applets, such as Microsoft WordArt. After you embed the object, you can double-click it to start the source application so that you can edit the object. As Figure 10-7 illustrates, embedding actually places a copy of the selected data in the destination document. Like linking, embedding inserts a field code, EMBED, in the Word document.

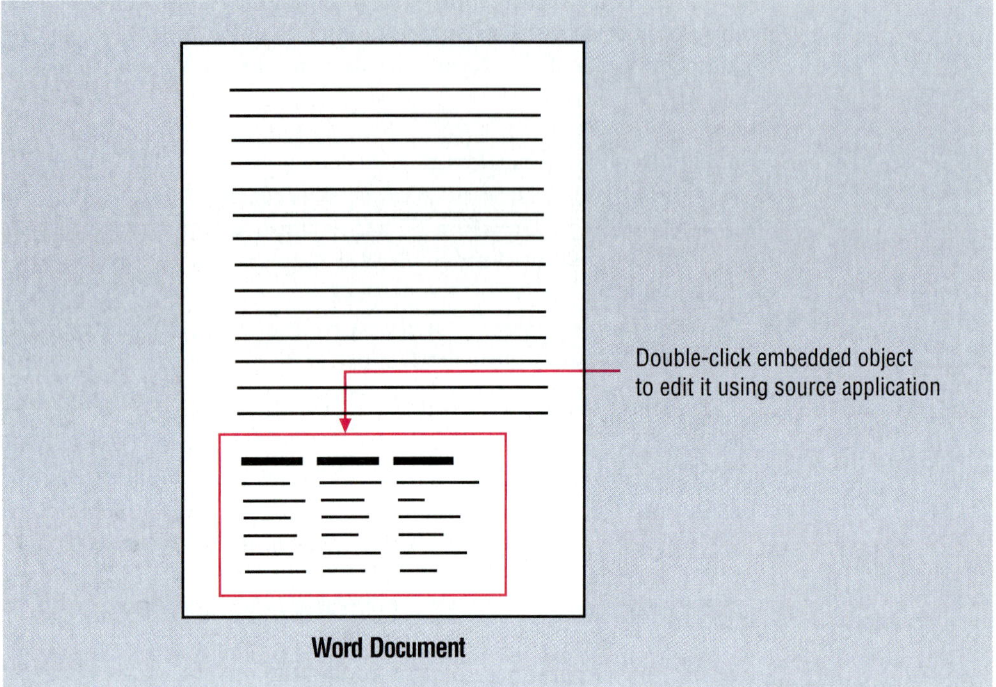

Figure 10-7
Embedded object

Now that she has the most current data, Nykita decides to embed in her Word memo document the Excel chart that displays the membership of each region as a percentage of the total membership.

To embed the Excel chart in the Word memo document:

❶ Place the insertion point at the end of the document, if necessary, then press **[Enter]**.

❷ Type: **The following chart indicates the membership of each region as a percentage of the total.** Press **[Enter]**.

❸ Click the **Microsoft Excel button** ☒ on the Microsoft toolbar to return to Excel and display the S10ACEE.XLS workbook.

❹ Click just inside the border of the **3-D pie chart**. Handles appear around the border of the chart to indicate that it is selected.

❺ Click the **Copy button** 🖺 on the Standard toolbar.

Nykita no longer needs to have Excel open.

❻ Dismiss the Microsoft toolbar in Excel, then double-click the **Excel application control menu box** to exit Excel, saving your changes if prompted to save. You return to S10EC.DOC.

Nykita only wants to embed the chart, not link it; therefore, she'll use the Paste command instead of the Paste Special command.

❼ Click the **Paste button** 🖺 on the Standard toolbar.

Nykita wants the chart to be centered across the page.

❽ Click the **Center button** ≣ on the Formatting toolbar.

❾ Save your changes.

Nykita wants to view the EMBED field code to make sure she embedded the object properly. Then she'll print her completed memo document.

To check the EMBED field code then print the document:

❶ Click **Tools**, click **Options...**, then click the **View tab**, if necessary.

❷ Click the **Field Codes check box**, then click **OK** or press **[Enter]**. The LINK field code specifies the path to the linked worksheet, so changes will be updated automatically. The EMBED field code simply identifies the embedded object and the application used to create it. See Figure 10-8.

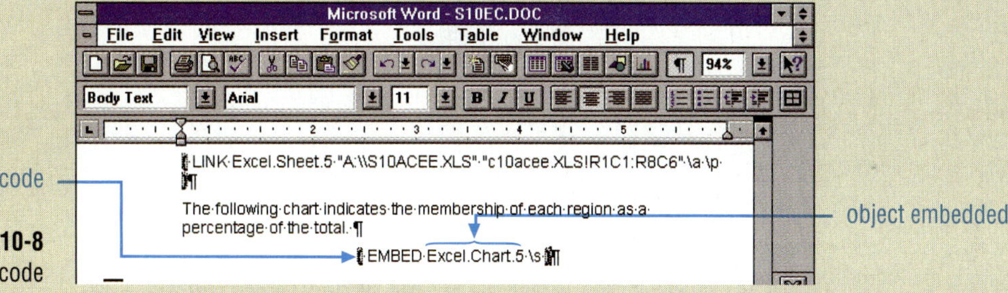

Figure 10-8
EMBED field code

❸ Deactivate the Field Codes option on the View tab.

❹ Save your changes.

Nykita decides to print the document.

❺ Click the **Print button** 🖨 on the Standard toolbar. See Figure 10-9.

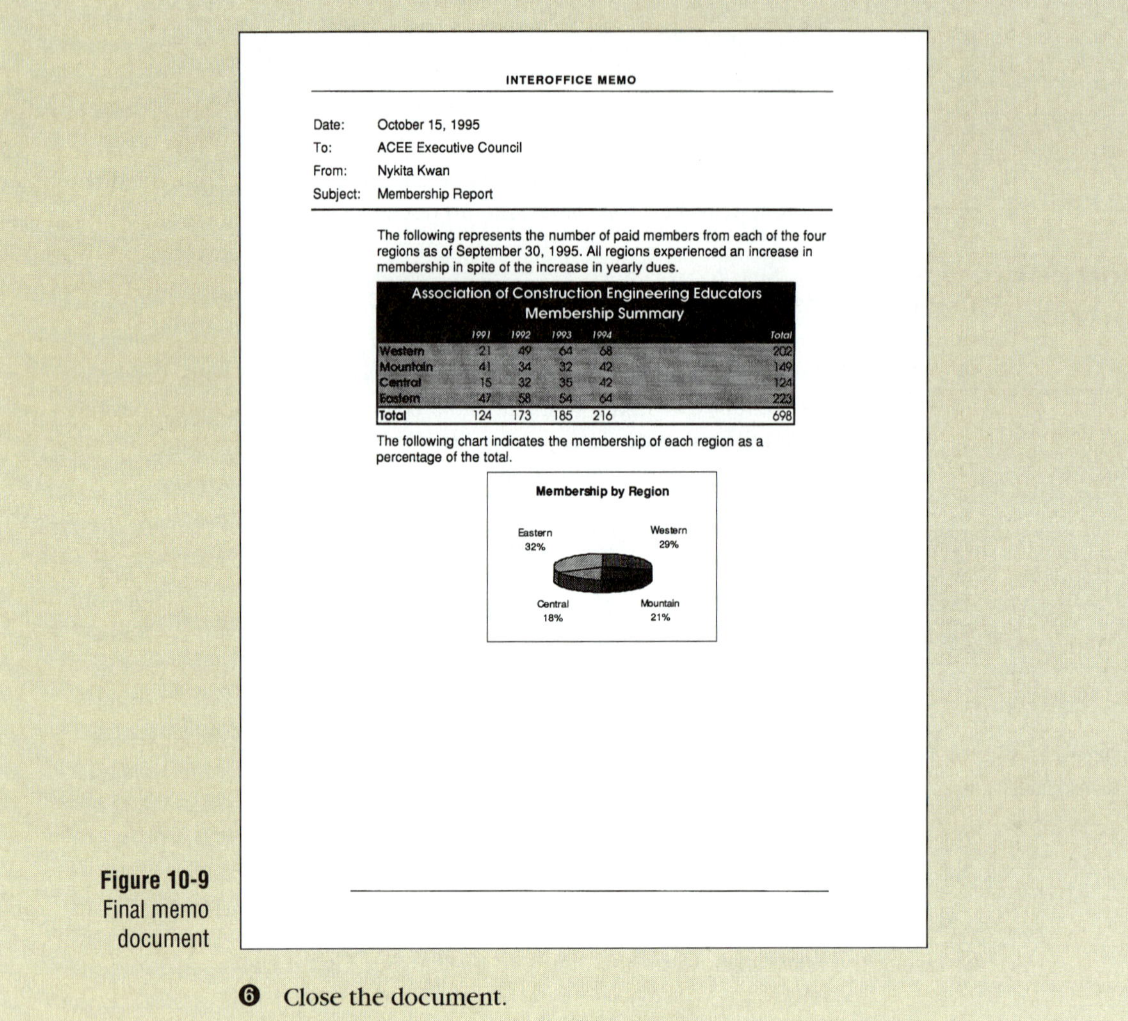

Figure 10-9
Final memo
document

6 Close the document.

If you want to take a break and resume the tutorial at a later time, you can exit Word now. When you want to resume the tutorial, start Word, place your Student Disk in the disk drive, complete the screen check procedure described in Tutorial 1, then continue with the tutorial.

Next Nykita decides to work on her presentation to the Software Tools SIG.

Using PowerPoint with Word

Microsoft PowerPoint 4.0 is used to create professional-looking presentations for viewing on-screen or on an overhead projector. Like Excel and Word, PowerPoint can serve as either a source application or a destination application. PowerPoint is similar to Word in that it has several time-saving document creation features, among them the use of templates and wizards. A **wizard** is a quick way to create a presentation in which you are asked questions about the presentation structure, and then PowerPoint builds a presentation based on your responses.

Both Nykita and her co-presenter have PowerPoint on their computers but have never used it. Nykita has already created an outline of the presentation using Word's Heading styles 1 and 2, and decides to explore PowerPoint based solely on what she already knows about Microsoft applications.

To create a PowerPoint title slide:

❶ Click the **Microsoft PowerPoint button** 🖼 on the Microsoft toolbar. The PowerPoint application and the PowerPoint dialog box appear.

❷ Click the **Blank Presentation radio button** in the PowerPoint dialog box to select it, if necessary, then click **OK** or press **[Enter]**. The New Slide dialog box appears. See Figure 10-10.

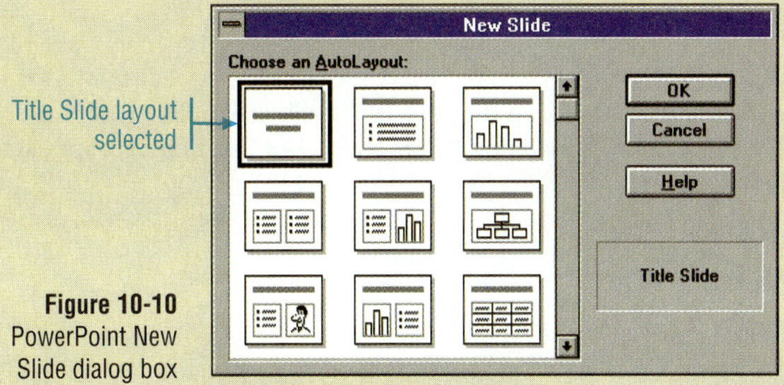

Figure 10-10
PowerPoint New
Slide dialog box

Title Slide layout selected

Nykita needs to create the title slide for the presentation. The Title Slide layout option is already selected.

❸ Click **OK** or press **[Enter]**. A title layout slide appears.

❹ Click the **Save button** 🖫 on the Standard toolbar. Save the document as S10OUT to your Student Disk. PowerPoint will automatically add the extension .PPT to the filename. Click **OK** or press **[Enter]**. The Summary Info dialog box appears.

❺ Type **Nykita Kwan** in the Author text box, then click **OK** or press **[Enter]**.

Nykita wants to type the title of the presentation, Object Linking and Embedding, in the title text area.

❻ Click the **title text area**, then type **Object Linking and Embedding**.

Nykita next wants to enter the name of the presenters—Nykita Kwan and Farouk Hosny.

❼ Click the **subtitle text area**, then type **Nykita Kwan, Wabash University**, press **[Enter]**, then type **Farouk Hosny, Southern Ohio College**.

❽ Save your changes.

Now Nykita is ready to insert the Word outline that she created containing the main points to be covered in her presentation.

To insert the Word outline into the PowerPoint presentation:

❶ With the insertion point still in the subtitle text area, click **Insert** then click **Slides from Outline....** Switch to the drive containing your Student Disk, if necessary.

❷ Click **C10OUT.DOC** in the File Name list box, then click **OK** or press **[Enter]**.

Nykita wants to see if the outline was inserted properly into PowerPoint.

❸ Press **[PgDn]** or click the **double-headed down arrow** in the vertical scroll bar to advance to Slide 2.

❹ Continue to advance through the remaining four slides.

❺ Save your changes.

Nykita wants her presentation to look professionally developed, but she is not sure of her options so she decides to use PowerPoint's Wizard feature.

To use PowerPoint's Wizard feature:

❶ Click the **Pick a Look Wizard button** 🖼 on the Standard toolbar (or click **Format** then click **Pick a Look Wizard...**). The Pick a Look Wizard-Step 1 of 9 dialog box appears. See Figure 10-11.

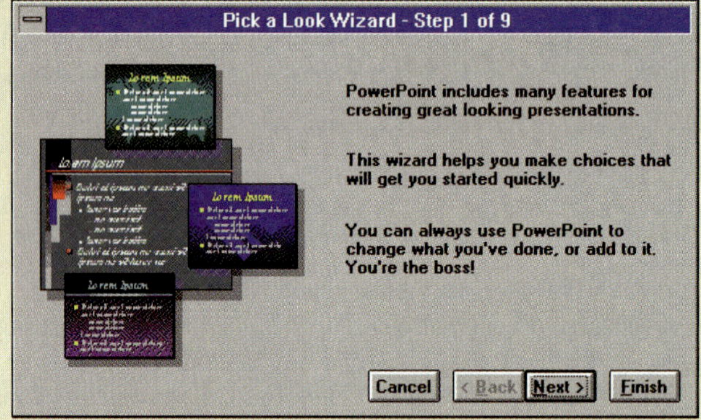

Figure 10-11
Pick a Look Wizard
dialog box

❷ Read the information then click **Next** or press **[Enter]**. The Pick a Look Wizard-Step 2 of 9 dialog box appears.

Nykita wants to use the college's color LCD panel connected to a notebook computer during the presentation.

❸ Click the **On-Screen Presentation radio button**, if necessary, then click **Next** or press **[Enter]**. The Pick a Look Wizard-Step 3 of 9 dialog box appears.

❹ Review each of the listed template design options.

After viewing each of the options, Nykita decides to use the Multiple Bars template.

❺ Click the **Multiple Bars radio button**, if necessary, then click **Next** or press **[Enter]**. The Pick a Look Wizard-Step 4 of 9 dialog box appears. This dialog box provides options for printing your presentation in different ways; for example, you can print a reduced version of each slide with space below for speaker notes, and you can print audience handout pages showing reduced versions of the slides. See Figure 10-12.

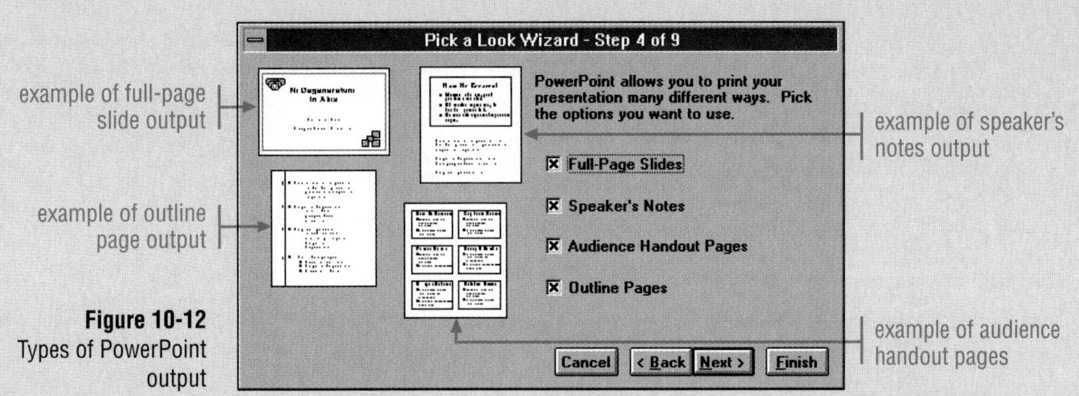

Figure 10-12
Types of PowerPoint output

Nykita eventually wants to print all the different options, so she accepts all the selected print options.

❻   Click **Next** or press **[Enter]**. The Pick a Look Wizard-Slide Options dialog box appears.

Nykita wants the association's initials and the page number to appear on all slides of the presentation.

❼   Type **ACEE** in the text box, click the **Page Number check box**, then click **Next** or press **[Enter]**. The Pick a Look Wizard-Notes Options dialog box appears.

Nykita wants the same information to appear on the Notes Options, Handout Options, and Outline Options printouts.

❽   Click **Next** or press **[Enter]** for each of the next three dialog boxes. The Pick a Look Wizard-Step 9 of 9 dialog box appears.

❾   Click **Finish** or press **[Enter]**.

❿   Save your changes.

Nykita wants to preview the slides as they will project on screen to the audience. During the presentation she wants to control the timing when each slide is advanced rather than letting PowerPoint automatically advance to the next slide.

To view the PowerPoint slide presentation:
❶   Click **View** then click **Slide Show....** The Slide Show dialog box appears.

Nykita wants to view the entire presentation and wants to advance the slides manually.

❷   Click **Show** or press **[Enter]**. The title slide appears. Notice that PowerPoint assigns the features of the Multiple Bars template to Nykita's Word outline and inserts the name of the organization and the slide number in the footer of the slide.

❸   Click the **left mouse button** or press **[PgDn]** to advance to the next slide.

❹   Repeat Step 3 until you return to slide view.

Nykita is satisfied with the first version of the slides for her presentation. So that her co-presenter won't have to use PowerPoint to view the slides, she decides to embed the PowerPoint presentation in a transmittal memo that she has prepared.

To embed the PowerPoint slide presentation in the Word document:

❶   Click **View** then click **Slide Sorter**. Small pictures of the slides appear.

❷   Click **Edit** then click **Select All**. All the slides are selected. See Figure 10-13.

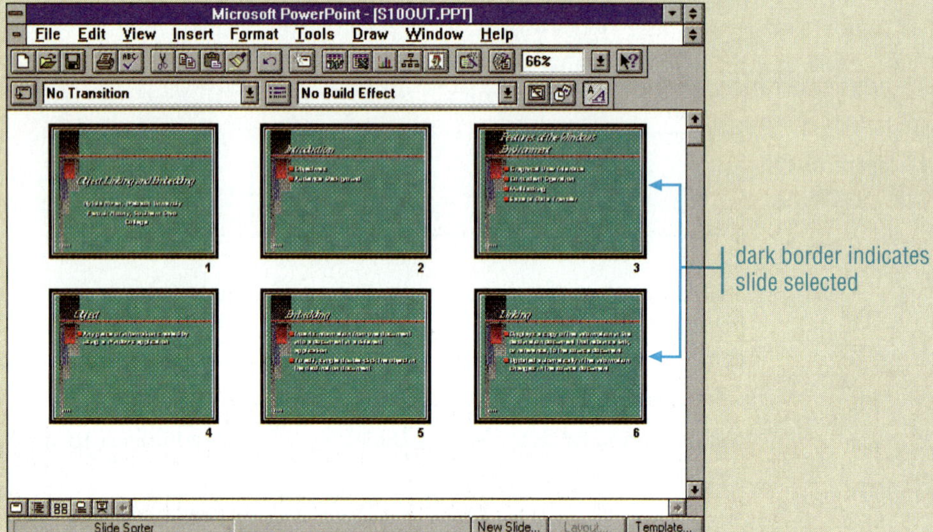

Figure 10-13
Presentation slides selected

❸   Click the **Copy button** on the Standard toolbar.

❹   Exit PowerPoint, saving your changes if prompted to save. You return to Word.

Nykita already started the memo she wants to use to transmit her presentation to her co-presenter.

❺   Click the **Open button** on the Standard toolbar. The Open dialog box appears. Open the file C10OLE.DOC from your Student Disk, then save it as **S10OLE.DOC**.

❻   Move to the end of the document, then type **Double-click the slide below to view the presentation**. Press **[Enter]**.

❼   Click the **Paste button** on the Standard toolbar. The first slide of the presentation appears.

❽   Save your changes.

Nykita wants to make sure that the embedding works.

❾   Double-click the **first slide** of the presentation, then use the left mouse button or [PgDn] to advance the slides. After the last slide, you return to the transmittal memo. See Figure 10-14.

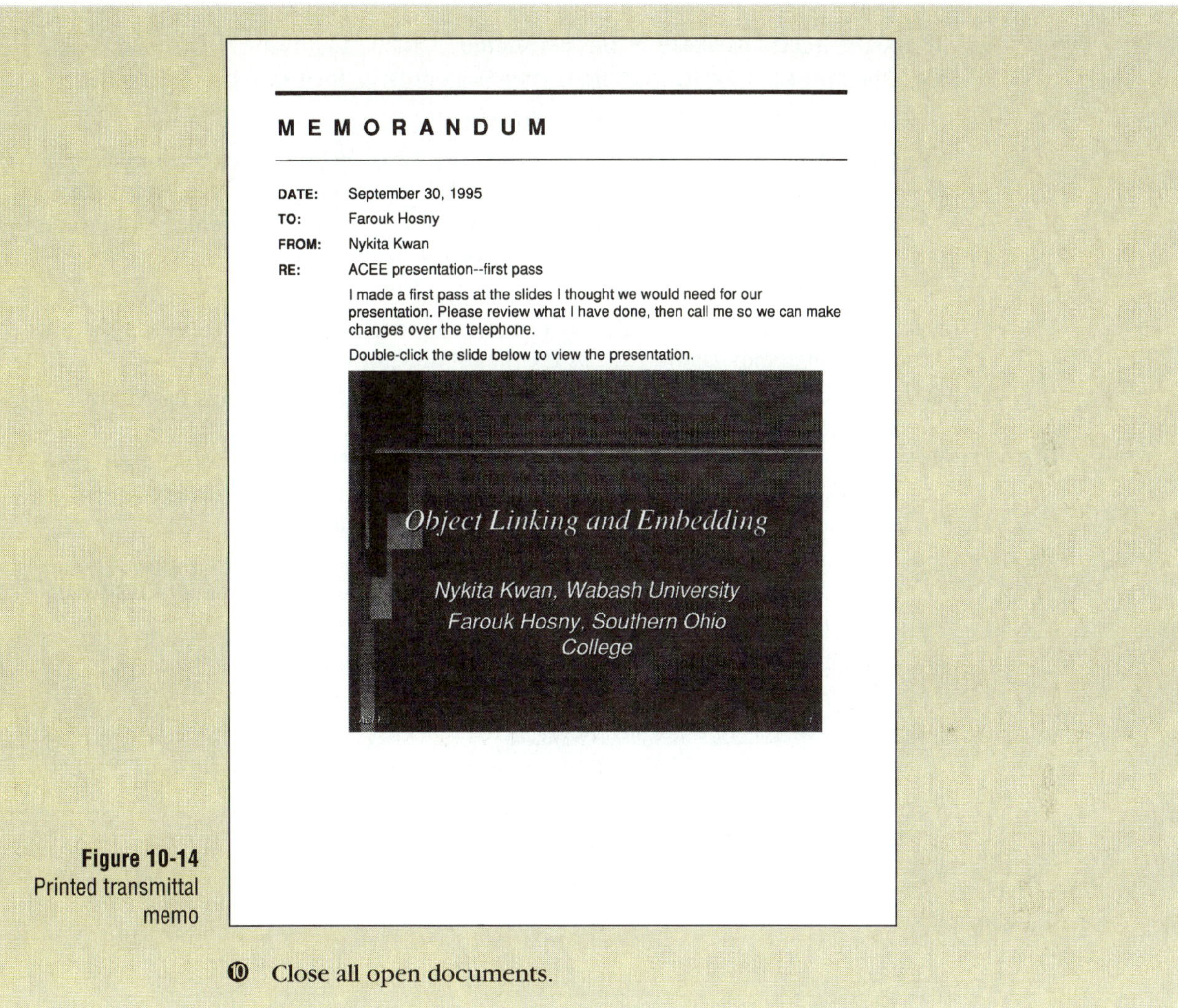

The following document is reproduced within the figure:

M E M O R A N D U M

DATE: September 30, 1995

TO: Farouk Hosny

FROM: Nykita Kwan

RE: ACEE presentation--first pass

I made a first pass at the slides I thought we would need for our presentation. Please review what I have done, then call me so we can make changes over the telephone.

Double-click the slide below to view the presentation.

Figure 10-14
Printed transmittal memo

❿   Close all open documents.

Using an Access Database in a Mail Merge

In Tutorial 4 you used a Word document as the data source—the document containing the information on each individual record—in a mail merge. Word does not limit you to using only documents in Word format as data source documents, however. You can also use external data sources such as spreadsheet applications, like Excel, or database applications like Microsoft Access 2.0, as a data source in a mail merge.

Nykita needs to send a letter to the new members of Software Tools SIG informing them of the group's activities during the conference. The ACEE membership information is maintained in an Access database. She decides to perform a mail merge so that each letter will be personalized. Nykita has already created the text of the letter she wants to send to the new SIG members.

To use the Access database as the data source:

❶ Open the file C10SIG.DOC from your Student Disk, then save it as **S10SIG.DOC**.

Nykita will use this letter as the main document.

❷ Click **Tools** then click **Mail Merge…**. The Mail Merge Helper dialog box appears.

❸ Click **Create** or press **[Enter]** to create the Main Document, then click **Form Letters…**. A dialog box appears with choices for creating the main document. Nykita wants the document in the active window to be the main document.

❹ Click **Active Window** or press **[Enter]**.

Nykita is now ready to attach the data source to the main document. She will use the Access membership database file as the data source for her mail merge.

❺ Click **Get Data** or press **[Enter]** in the Data Source section, then click **Open Data Source…**. The Open Data Source dialog box appears.

❻ Click the **List Files of Type list box down arrow**, click **MS Access Databases (*.mdb)**, then select C10ACEE.MDB from your Student Disk. Click **OK** or press **[Enter]**. Access is launched and the Microsoft Access dialog box appears.

TROUBLE?   If MS Access Databases is not a choice in the List Files of Type list box, then Access 2.0 is not installed on your computer system. Ask your instructor or technical support person for help.

❼ Click the **Tables tab**, if necessary. See Figure 10-15.

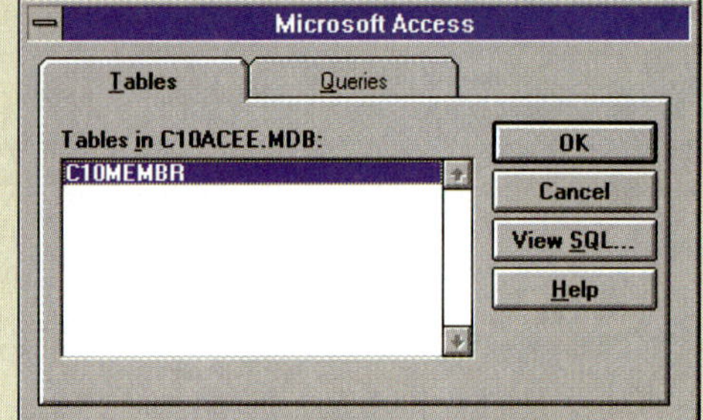

Figure 10-15
Microsoft Access
dialog box

❽ Click **C10MEMBR**, if necessary, then click **OK** or press **[Enter]**. The C10MEMBR database is now attached to the main document S10SIG.DOC.

❾ Click **Edit Main Document** or press **[Enter]**, move the insertion point to Ln 8, then insert the merge fields shown in Figure 10-16, making sure to use new line marks to return to the left margin within the inside address. Refer to Tutorial 4 if you do not remember how to insert merge field codes.

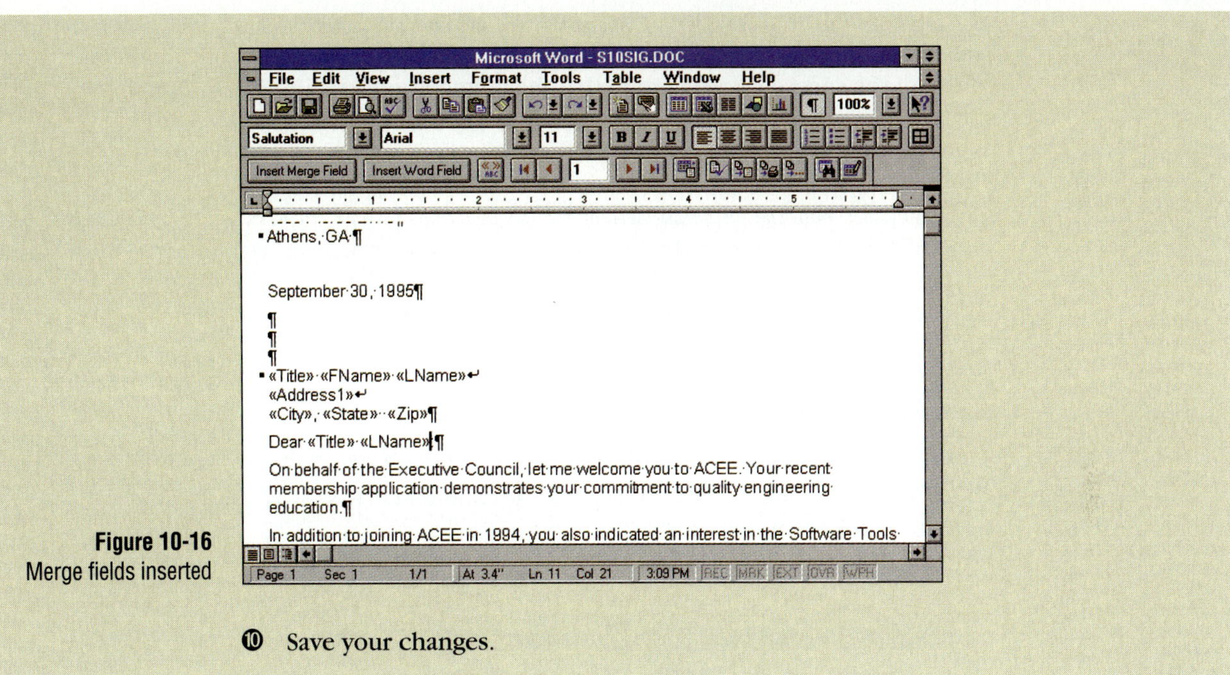

Figure 10-16
Merge fields inserted

⓪ Save your changes.

Now Nykita is ready to merge the data source with the main document, but first she must limit the records to be merged to just those members who joined in 1994 *and* indicated an interest in the Special Tools SIG.

Using Comparison Statements to Select Records to Merge

Word provides you with several options to control the data you output for a mail merge. You can select a specific record or range of records to merge from the Merge dialog box, or you can use Word's Query options to specify criteria for record selection. To set up a comparison statement, you must specify the field or fields Word will base its decision for selection on as well as a comparison rule. Figure 10-17 lists the comparison rules that are available during a mail merge. Word lets you set up more than one comparison statement by joining each rule with "and" or "or."

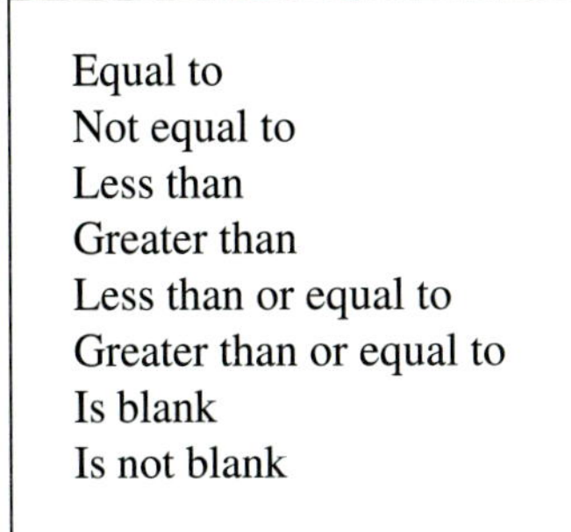

Figure 10-17
Comparison rules

The database provided to Nykita by the former membership chairman contains data for *all* members. Nykita wants to send the letter only to those members who joined in 1994 *and* who also joined the Software Tools SIG because they might not be familiar with the success of the field trips at the previous conferences. The Status field of the membership database contains the year each member joined ACEE, and the SIG field contains the name of the special interest group that the member joined.

To select records to merge:

❶ Click the **Mail Merge Helper button** 📇 on the Mail Merge toolbar, then click **Query Options…** in the Merge the Data with the Document section. The Query Options dialog box appears with the Filter Records tab displayed.

❷ Click the **Field list box down arrow** in the first row, then click **Status**. "Equal to" appears in the Comparison text box.

❸ Type **1994** in the Compare To text box, then press **[Tab]**. "And" appears in the box along the left side of the next row.

Nykita wants to enter the second comparison for record selection—SIG interest.

❹ Press **[Tab]**, click the **Field list box down arrow**, then click **SIG**. "Equal to" appears in the Comparison text box.

❺ Type **ST** (for Software Tools) in the Compare To text box. See Figure 10-18.

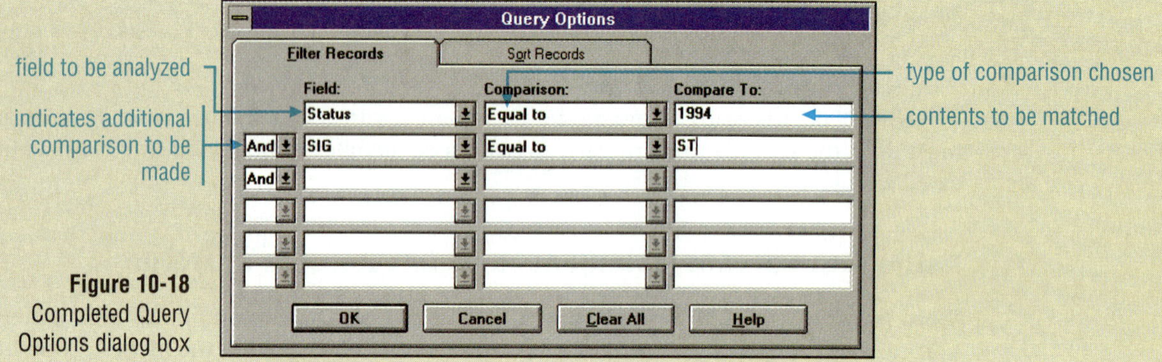

Figure 10-18
Completed Query
Options dialog box

❻ Click **OK** or press **[Enter]**. You return to the Mail Merge Helper dialog box.

❼ Click **Merge…** in the Merge the Data with the Document section or press **[Enter]**. The Merge dialog box appears.

Nykita wants to merge to a new document rather than print all the letters.

❽ Click **Merge** or press **[Enter]**. Four records matching Nykita's specifications are merged.

❾ Save the merged form letters as S10MRG.DOC to your Student Disk, then print just the first letter. See Figure 10-19.

ASSOCIATION OF CONSTRUCTION ENGINEERING EDUCATORS

4800 Pierce Drive
Athens, GA 30601

September 30, 1995

Dr. Margaret Owens
6105 Cypress
El Paso, TX 99074

Dear Dr. Owens:

On behalf of the Executive Council, let me welcome you to ACEE. Your recent membership application demonstrates your commitment to quality engineering education.

In addition to joining ACEE in 1994, you also indicated an interest in the Software Tools Special Interest Group. Since you may not have attended the Annual Conference before, I would like to tell you about the field trip we have planned especially for the Software Tools SIG members. We are fortunate to be able to visit one of the leading engineering colleges in the nation at Cincinnati College. Last year the faculty in the engineering school received a National Science Foundation grant to implement a multimedia instructional laboratory for its students. A panel of engineering faculty and instructional support personnel will be on hand to discuss the planning and implementation of the laboratory. In addition, lunch will be served.

If you plan to attend the Annual Conference this year, please join us on this informative tour. Call me at 999-846-1010 to make a reservation for the bus ride to and from Cincinnati College as well as for the luncheon. Looking forward to meeting you in October.

Sincerely,

Nykita Kwan, Ph.D.
Facilitator, ACEE Software Tools SIG

Figure 10-19
First merged
document

❿ Dismiss the Microsoft toolbar then exit Word.

Nykita has finished all of the tasks she needed to complete in preparation for the ACEE conference.

Questions

1. Explain the three levels of data transfer.
2. Describe two methods for switching between applications.
3. Describe the procedure to link part of document A to document B.

4. Interpret the following field code:
   {LINK Excel.Sheet.5 "A:\\S10ACEE.XLS" "C10acee.XLS!R1C1:R8C6" \a \p}

5. Given the field code above, if the file S10ACEE.XLS is moved to drive H, will the link be updated properly? Why or why not?
6. Interpret the following field code: {EMBED PowerPoint.Slide.4}.
7. Explain the difference between linking document A to document B and embedding document B in document A.
8. Explain the procedure for using an external database in a mail merge.
9. What comparison statements would you use to merge only those records with zip codes between 77001 and 77098?
10. What comparison statements would you use to merge all records *except* those with zip codes between 77001 and 77098?

11. Describe the procedure for breaking a link between documents.

12. Describe the procedure for locking a link between documents.

Tutorial Assignments

Start Word, if necessary, and conduct a screen check. Complete the following:
1. Open the file T10AUDIT.DOC from your Student Disk, then save it as S10AUDIT.DOC.
2. Place the insertion point in the blank paragraph between paragraphs 1 and 3 in the body of the memo.
3. Link the Excel worksheet S10AUDIT.XLS to the Word document S10AUDIT.DOC.
   a. Switch to Excel.
   b. Open the file T10AUDIT.XLS from your Student Disk, then save it as S10AUDIT.XLS.
   c. Select cells A1 through F16, then copy the selection to the Clipboard.
   d. Switch to Word then use the Paste Special command to paste link the Excel 5.0 Worksheet Object to the S10AUDIT.DOC document.
   e. Save the changes.
   f. Print the document.
4. Update the link.
   a. Switch to Excel then press [Esc] to dismiss the copy selection.
   b. Type "5125" in cell C5—the cell containing the total revenue from registration fees. Press [Enter].
   c. Save the changes to S10AUDIT.XLS, then close the worksheet and exit Excel.
   d. Switch to S10AUDIT.DOC, if necessary, then save the document.
   e. Print the document.
   f. Activate the Field Codes option on the Print tab of the Options dialog box, then print the document with field codes displayed.

5. Break the link between the worksheet and document.
   a. Click Edit then click Links….
   b. Click Break Link, then confirm that you want to break the selected link.
   c. Print the document with field codes displayed.
   d. Deactivate the Field Codes option on the Print tab of the Options dialog box, then save the document as S10BREAK.DOC to your Student Disk.
   e. Close the document.
6. Use mail merge to create name tags for members of the Software Tools SIG.
   a. Open a new document, if necessary, then save it as S10NAMES.DOC to your Student Disk.
   b. Select the Mail Merge command from the Tools menu.
   c. Create a mailing label main document in the active window.
7. Attach the external Access database T10MEMBR.MDB to the mailing label main document.

8. Set up the mailing label main document.
    a. Select the C10MEMBR table in the Microsoft Access dialog box.
    b. Select Product Number 5383–Name Tag in the Label Options dialog box.
    c. In the Create Labels dialog box, insert the FName field code, press [Spacebar], then insert the LName field code.
9. Edit the main document, S10NAMES.DOC.
    a. Select the entire document, then change the font to Brush Script MT, 28 point.
    b. Center the contents of each cell vertically and horizontally. Deselect the document.
    c. Save the changes.
10. Merge only the records for members of the Software Tools SIG.
    a. Switch to the Mail Merge Helper dialog box, then select the Query Options button.
    b. Select the Filter Records tab, if necessary, then set up the comparison statement so that the contents of the SIG field equal ST.
    c. Merge the selected records to a new document.
    d. Save the merged label document as S10TAGS.DOC to your Student Disk.
11. Print the merged document.
12. Close all documents.
13. Use the Object command on the Insert menu to embed a PowerPoint slide into a Word document.
    a. Open a new document, if necessary, then save it as S10EMBED.DOC to your Student Disk.
    b. Select the Object command from the Insert menu, then select MS PowerPoint 4.0 Slide from the Object Type list box.
    c. Type "Tutorial Assignment 13" in the title text area and your name in the subtitle text area.
    d. Exit PowerPoint and return to S10EMBED.DOC. Confirm that you want to update the slide in the Word document (S10EMBED.DOC).
    e. Save the changes.
14. Print the document with and without the Field Codes option activated on the Print tab.
15. Deactivate the Field Codes option, then save the changes.
16. Close the document.

Case Problems

1. Equipment Rental Quotation

John Rivers is the sales supervisor for Electro-Lease Company in Washington, D. C. John follows up each telephone quote with a confirmation letter that provides a written quotation. He calculates the quotation in an Excel worksheet, then inserts the worksheet into the confirmation letter. If the customer subsequently decides to change the specifications of the quote, John wants to be able to update the confirmation letter easily.

Complete the following:

1. Open the file P10QUOTE.DOC from your Student Disk, then save it as S10QUOTE.DOC.
2. Place the insertion point in the blank paragraph between paragraphs 1 and 3 in the text of the letter.
3. Link the Excel worksheet S10QUOTE.XLS to the Word document S10QUOTE.DOC.
    a. Switch to Excel.
    b. Open the file P10QUOTE.XLS from your Student Disk, then save it as S10QUOTE.XLS.
    c. Select the cells A1 through G6, then copy the selection to the Clipboard.
    d. Switch to Word, then use the Paste Special command to paste link the Excel 5.0 Worksheet Object in the appropriate location.
    e. Save the changes.

   4. Print the document.
   5. Update the link.
      a. Switch to Excel.
      b. Change the quantity ordered for all three items to 2.
      c. Save the changes to the worksheet.
      d. Exit Excel and return to S10QUOTE.DOC.
      e. Save the changes to S10QUOTE.DOC, then print the document.

   6. Lock the link between the two documents.
      a. Select the Links command from the Edit menu.
      b. Click to select the Locked check box, then click OK or press [Enter].
      c. Save the document as S10LOCK.DOC to your Student Disk.
      d. Activate the Field Codes option on the Print tab of the Options dialog box, then
          print the document. Notice the status bar when you send the document to print.
      e. Deactivate the Field Codes option on the Print tab, then save your changes.
      f. Close all documents.

2. Personnel Directory

Curtis Stuart is associate dean of the College of Business Information Systems at
Northern State University. The university maintains a personnel database using Access,
and from time to time must generate reports using the data in the personnel database.
Curtis uses Word to generate most of the important reports because he finds them easier to format in Word rather than Access. Curtis has been asked to format and print a
list of the professors and a list of the associate professors in the college.
   Complete the following:
   1. Create a new document based on the DIRECTR1 template, then save it as
      S10DIR.DOC to your Student Disk.
   2. Select the Mail Merge command from the Tools menu, then create a catalog main
      document in the active window.
   3. Attach the external Access database P10DIR.MDB from your Student Disk as the
      data source for the main document. In the Microsoft Access dialog box, select the
      DATABASE table.
   4. After being prompted to edit the main document, insert the field codes as shown
      in Figure 10-20. Press [Enter] after inserting the PHONE field code.

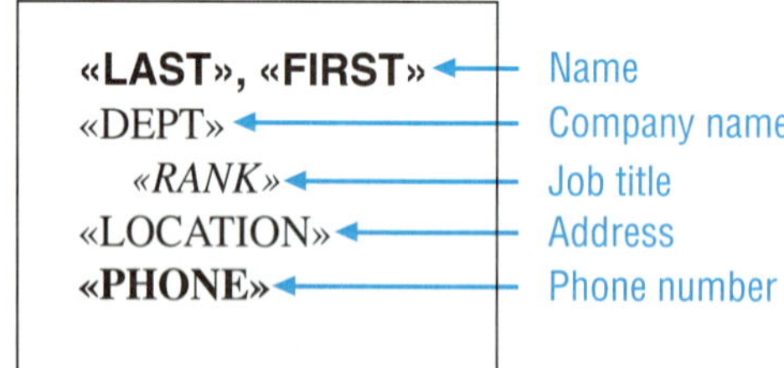

Figure 10-20

   5. Apply the styles shown in Figure 10-20.
   6. Prepare a directory listing of just the faculty with the rank of Professor, sorted by
      last name. Save the merged records as S10PRODR.DOC to your Student Disk.
   7. Format and print the directory listing of professors.
      a. Place the insertion point at the top of the document. Type the title "Listing of
          Professors," press [Enter], type the subtitle "College of Business Information
          Systems," then press [Enter].
      b. Apply the Title style to the first line and the Subtitle style to the second line.
      c. Place the insertion point in front of the first name in the directory, then format
          from the insertion point forward into three columns.
      d. Save your changes.
      e. Preview then print the merged document. Close the merged document.

E

8. Prepare a directory listing of just the faculty with the rank of Associate Professor, sorted by last name, located on the second floor of building M. Save the merged records as S10AP.DOC to your Student Disk. The offices on the second floor are numbered in the 2000's. (*Hint:* The offices in building M are numbered beginning with "M-.")

9. Format and print the directory listing of associate professors.
   a. Place the insertion point at the top of the document. Type the title "Associate Professors To Be Moved," press [Enter], type the subtitle "College of Business Information Systems," then press [Enter].
   b. Apply the Title style to the first line and the Subtitle style to the second line.
   c. Save your changes.
   d. Print the merged document.
   e. Close all documents.

3. A Presentation on Word's Features

Prepare a presentation covering the four features of Word that you feel are the most useful. For each feature, give its purpose and command sequence (and/or step-by-step procedure).

Complete the following:

1. Create an outline of your presentation in outline view of Word. Save the document as S10WWOUT.DOC to your Student Disk.
2. Apply the Heading 1 style to the name of each feature and the Heading 2 style to the feature's purpose and/or command sequence. Save the changes.
3. Switch to PowerPoint then insert the title of your presentation and your name on a blank title presentation slide.
4. Save the PowerPoint presentation as S10WWPRE.PPT to your Student Disk.
5. Insert your presentation outline document, S10WWOUT.DOC, into the PowerPoint presentation. Save your changes.
6. Use the Pick a Look Wizard feature to apply an appropriate background to your presentation. Insert this course name and the slide number in the footer of each slide.
7. Save your changes.
8. Copy all the slides of your PowerPoint presentation to the Clipboard, then exit PowerPoint.
9. Move to the end of the Word document, S10WWOUT.DOC, then embed the PowerPoint presentation S10WWPRE.PPT. Save the document as S10WWALL.DOC to your Student Disk.
10. Print the document S10WWALL.DOC.
11. Close the document and exit Word.

Additional Case 1

Creating a Handout for Items on Sale

OBJECTIVES

In this case you will:

- Import a foreign-file format document
- Convert text to a table, sort a table, insert rows and delete a column in a table, center a table across the page, align columns in a table, and add borders and shading to a table
- Copy and paste text
- Change the page setup options of a document
- Change the row height and column width in a table
- Insert a header and a footer in a document
- Insert and format a frame, and insert a picture
- Move tab stops
- Apply styles to text
- Format a document in newspaper style columns

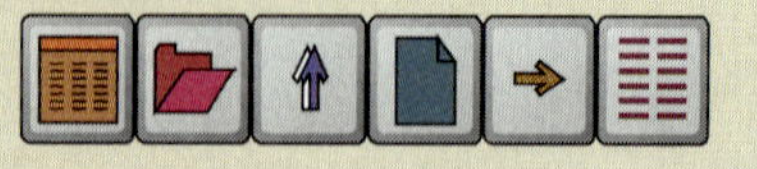

DISK SPACE NOTE: If you have done all the exercises in Tutorial 10, you might not have enough space on your Student Disk to complete these Additional Cases. If you plan to do all the Additional Cases, you might want to copy the Additional Cases files to another formatted disk before you begin.

The Sports Barn Lionel Zargoza is the owner and operator of the Sports Barn in Madison, Wisconsin. He is getting ready for the annual spring supersale where he puts all bike accessories in his store on sale. This year Lionel wants to provide customers with a handout listing all the accessories on sale, the sale price, and the regular price. He has extracted all the bike accessory items from his inventory database, arranged them alphabetically, and saved them in a text file. The text file contains the item name, sale amount, regular price, and accessory category code for each bike item on sale. Lionel wants to import the text file into Word, then convert it to a table so that he can format the handout more easily. The completed handout is shown in Figure 1.

Sports Barn
2945 Clay Boulevard
490-8100

Computers and Heart Rate Monitors

Item	Sale	Regular
Dogtail Dual	19.99	29.99
Opposite Edge HRM	159.99	189.99
Opposite Favor HRM	99.99	119.99
Opposite Pacer HRM	129.99	169.99
Specialized Time Zone	36.99	44.99
Star Sensor Computer	24.99	29.99
Zetta D-40	34.99	44.99

Saddles and Saddle Pads

Item	Sale	Regular
CDX (children)	14.99	24.99
Dricoflex	17.99	22.99
Ovoseat (mtn. bike)	29.99	34.99
Ovoseat (racing)	49.99	79.99

Gloves

Item	Sale	Regular
Aspimonte	11.99	19.99
Setsumi	19.99	29.99

Eyewear

Item	Sale	Regular
Heaters	79.99	99.99
Sweeps	89.99	109.99
Toadskins	31.99	39.99

Car Racks

Item	Sale	Regular
Trans-Gear Child Seat	79.99	119.99
Trans-Gear Security Cable	14.99	17.99
Trans-Gear Shuttle	44.99	49.99
Yokohama Bike Mounts	59.99	79.99
Yokohama Roof Racks	79.99	109.99

Cycling Clothing

Item	Sale	Regular
Ascente Classic Bib Shorts	49.99	65.99
Ascente Padded Briefs	14.99	21.99
Aspimonte 4-Panel Shorts	20.99	29.99
Aspimonte 8-Panel Shorts	29.99	39.99
KoolMan Jerseys	29.99	39.99
Opposite Accurer HRM	219.99	249.99

10% Off All Other Parts and Accessories During the SuperSale on May 4, 5, and 6

Figure 1
Completed handout (page 1 of 2)

Sports Barn
2945 Clay Boulevard
490-8100

Helmets

Item	Sale	Regular
Spiro Hammerhead	59.99	79.99
Star Children's Helmets	24.99	29.99
Star Micro	24.99	29.99
Star Micro Lite	34.99	39.99

Tires/Tubes/Flat Killers

Item	Sale	Regular
Sports Barn Armidillos	19.99	24.99
Sports Barn Off Road	21.99	24.99
Sports Barn Patch Kit	.99	1.99
Hardy Flat Preventer	7.99	9.99
Oozey	4.99	6.99

Pumps

Item	Sale	Regular
Sports Barn Floor Pump	36.99	41.99
Tufal Alloy Road Pump	22.99	31.99
Tufal Floor Pump	22.99	31.99
Tufal Frame Pump	19.99	34.99

Safety

Item	Sale	Regular
Dog's Tail Headlight	12.99	19.99
Horizon Flashing Taillight	12.49	14.99
King First Aid Kit	3.49	4.99

Bags

Item	Sale	Regular
Astro Bar Bags	9.99	15.99
Astro Seat Bags	14.99	19.99
Sports Barn Express Pack 2	14.99	19.99
Trans-Gear Bar End Mirror	11.99	15.99

Cycling Shoes

Item	Sale	Regular
Happy Trails W020	101.99	146.99
Kids Happy Trails C010	35.99	47.99
Yokohama Mtn. M030	46.99	54.99
Yokohama Mtn. M050	94.99	114.99
Yokohama Trg. Shoes R120	114.99	134.99
Yokohama Trg. Shoes T110	62.99	69.99

10% Off All Other Parts and Accessories During the SuperSale on May 4, 5, and 6

Figure 1
Completed handout (page 2 of 2)

Start Word, complete the screen check procedure described in Tutorial 1, then complete the following:

1. Press [Enter] twice to enter two blank paragraphs to serve as placeholders, then save the document as SAC1SALE.DOC to your Student Disk.
2. With the insertion point at the end of the document, insert the text file AC1SALE.TXT from your Student Disk.
3. Select only the inserted text, then convert it to a four-column table.
4. Sort the table in ascending order based on accessory category code in Column 4.
5. Insert two blank rows above the first item in each accessory category.
6. Type the appropriate label in cell 1 of the first inserted blank row for each accessory category, as shown in Figure 2.

Type this category label:	In the first inserted blank row above:
Computers and Heart Rate Monitors	Code 1
Saddles and Saddle Pads	Code 2
Gloves	Code 3
Eyewear	Code 4
Car Racks	Code 5
Cycling Clothing	Code 6
Helmets	Code 7
Tires/Tubes/Flat Killers	Code 8
Pumps	Code 9
Safety	Code 10
Bags	Code 11
Cycling Shoes	Code 12

Figure 2
Category labels

7. Place the insertion point in cell 1 of the blank row below the category label Computers and Heart Rate Monitors, then type the following column headings in the cells indicated:
   Item (cell 1)
   Sale (cell 2)
   Regular (cell 3)
8. Copy just the three column headings (do not copy the entire row) to the remaining blank rows below each category label.
9. Delete the accessory category code column (Column 4) from the table.
10. Save your changes.
11. Change the page orientation to landscape and all margins to 1".
12. Select the table, then change the font to Arial and the font size to 10 pt.
13. Change the row height of just those rows containing items (not category labels or column headings) to Exactly 15 pt.
14. Center the table across the page.
15. Adjust the width of the columns as follows:
    Column 1:   2.48"
    Column 2:   .63"
    Column 3:   .73"
    Space between columns: .15"
16. Save your changes.
17. Insert a header with the following attributes:

    a. Type "Sports Barn," insert a new line mark, type "2945 Clay Boulevard," insert a new line mark, then type "490-8100."

    b. Change the font of the header text to 14 pt, bold.

    c. Insert a $^3/_4$ pt rule at the bottom of the telephone number line space.

    d. Increase the Spacing After option to 12 pt.

    e. Insert a frame at the right margin of the header.

    f. Format the frame as follows:

Width:	Exactly At 1.25"
Height:	Exactly At 1"
Horizontal Position:	Right relative to the margin
Vertical Position:	.3" relative to the page

    g. Select the frame then insert the SPORTS.WMF picture from the WINWORD\CLIPART directory.

18. Insert a footer with the following attributes:

    a. Move the center tab to 4.5" and the right-aligned tab to 9".

    b. At the center tab, type "10% Off All Other Parts and Accessories During the SuperSale on May 4, 5, and 6."

    c. Change the font of the footer text to 18 pt, bold.

    d. Insert a $^3/_4$ pt rule at the top of the line space.

    e. Increase the Spacing Before option to 12 pt.

19. Right-align the amount columns (Columns 2 and 3).

20. Apply the Heading 1 style to the rows containing category labels.

21. Apply the Heading 3 style to the rows containing column headings.

22. Place the insertion point in the second blank paragraph at the top of the document, then format the document in two columns from the insertion point forward.

23. Delete the blank paragraph mark at the top of section 2.

24. Shade the cells containing the Sale amounts with a 5% shading.

25. For each accessory category, select all the rows containing the column headings through the last item in the category, then insert a 2 $^1/_4$ pt border around the selection.

26. Insert a $^3/_4$ pt rule at the bottom of the row containing the column headings for each accessory category.

27. Save your changes, then preview and print the document.

28. Dismiss the Borders toolbar, if necessary, then close the document.

Additional Case 2

Creating a Workshop Training Schedule and Evaluation Forms

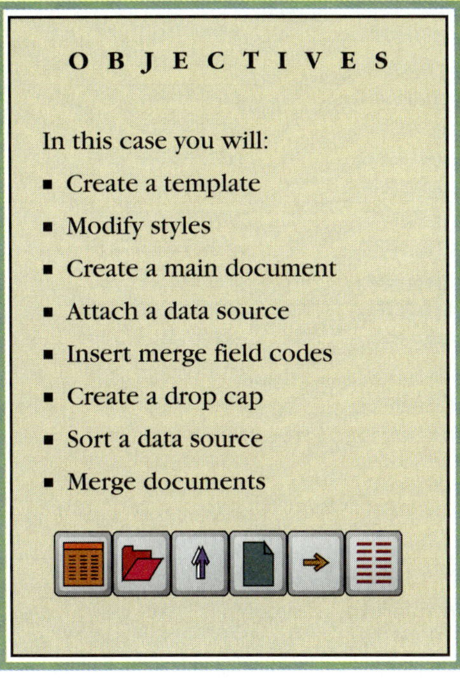

The Source   Niko Giannukos is the director of The Source, a training organization in Houston, Texas. He must create the workshop training schedule for the first quarter of the new year. The schedule will be part of a quarterly catalog that describes all the training classes conducted by The Source. The schedule information has been entered into a table, but Niko wants to adjust the layout and formatting of the text to conform to the rest of the training catalog. He decides to use Word's merge feature to create the document. Figure 3 shows the completed document. After he creates the workshop document, Niko must also create evaluation forms for some of the scheduled workshops.

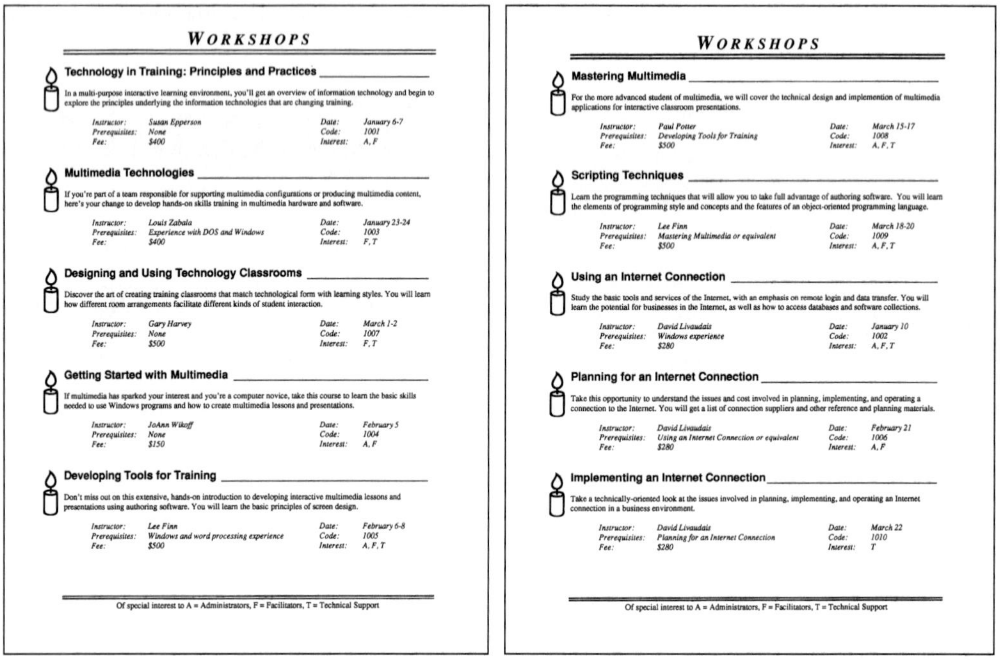

Figure 3
Completed
workshop document

WORKSHOPS

Technology in Training: Principles and Practices

In a multi-purpose interactive learning environment, you'll get an overview of information technology and begin to explore the principles underlying the information technologies that are changing training.

Instructor:	*Susan Epperson*	*Date:*	*January 6-7*
Prerequisites:	*None*	*Code:*	*1001*
Fee:	*$400*	*Interest:*	*A, F*

Multimedia Technologies

If you're part of a team responsible for supporting multimedia configurations or producing multimedia content, here's your change to develop hands-on skills training in multimedia hardware and software.

Instructor:	*Louis Zabala*	*Date:*	*January 23-24*
Prerequisites:	*Experience with DOS and Windows*	*Code:*	*1003*
Fee:	*$400*	*Interest:*	*F, T*

Designing and Using Technology Classrooms

Discover the art of creating training classrooms that match technological form with learning styles. You will learn how different room arrangements facilitate different kinds of student interaction.

Instructor:	*Gary Harvey*	*Date:*	*March 1-2*
Prerequisites:	*None*	*Code:*	*1007*
Fee:	*$500*	*Interest:*	*F, T*

Getting Started with Multimedia

If multimedia has sparked your interest and you're a computer novice, take this course to learn the basic skills needed to use Windows programs and how to create multimedia lessons and presentations.

Instructor:	*JoAnn Wikoff*	*Date:*	*February 5*
Prerequisites:	*None*	*Code:*	*1004*
Fee:	*$150*	*Interest:*	*A, F*

Developing Tools for Training

Don't miss out on this extensive, hands-on introduction to developing interactive multimedia lessons and presentations using authoring software. You will learn the basic principles of screen design.

Instructor:	*Lee Finn*	*Date:*	*February 6-8*
Prerequisites:	*Windows and word processing experience*	*Code:*	*1005*
Fee:	*$500*	*Interest:*	*A, F, T*

Of special interest to A = Administrators, F = Facilitators, T = Technical Support

WORKSHOPS

Mastering Multimedia

For the more advanced student of multimedia, we will cover the technical design and implemention of multimedia applications for interactive classroom presentations.

Instructor:	*Paul Potter*	*Date:*	*March 15-17*
Prerequisites:	*Developing Tools for Training*	*Code:*	*1008*
Fee:	*$500*	*Interest:*	*A, F, T*

Scripting Techniques

Learn the programming techniques that will allow you to take full advantage of authoring software. You will learn the elements of programming style and concepts and the features of an object-oriented programming language.

Instructor:	*Lee Finn*	*Date:*	*March 18-20*
Prerequisites:	*Mastering Multimedia or equivalent*	*Code:*	*1009*
Fee:	*$500*	*Interest:*	*A, F, T*

Using an Internet Connection

Study the basic tools and services of the Internet, with an emphasis on remote login and data transfer. You will learn the potential for businesses in the Internet, as well as how to access databases and software collections.

Instructor:	*David Livaudais*	*Date:*	*January 10*
Prerequisites:	*Windows experience*	*Code:*	*1002*
Fee:	*$280*	*Interest:*	*A, F, T*

Planning for an Internet Connection

Take this opportunity to understand the issues and cost involved in planning, implementing, and operating a connection to the Internet. You will get a list of connection suppliers and other reference and planning materials.

Instructor:	*David Livaudais*	*Date:*	*February 21*
Prerequisites:	*Using an Internet Connection or equivalent*	*Code:*	*1006*
Fee:	*$280*	*Interest:*	*A, F*

Implementing an Internet Connection

Take a technically-oriented look at the issues involved in planning, implementing, and operating an Internet connection in a business environment.

Instructor:	*David Livaudais*	*Date:*	*March 22*
Prerequisites:	*Planning for an Internet Connection*	*Code:*	*1010*
Fee:	*$280*	*Interest:*	*T*

Of special interest to A = Administrators, F = Facilitators, T = Technical Support

Start Word, conduct the screen check described in Tutorial 1, then complete the following:

1. Create a new *template* based on BROCHUR1.DOT. Save the new template as SAC2DESC.DOT to your Student Disk.
2. Make the following page setup changes to the template:
   a. Change the orientation to portrait.
   b. Deselect the Different First Page check box in the Headers and Footers section of the Layout tab.
3. Modify styles with the attributes specified in Figure 4.

Style Name	Style for Next Paragraph	Font	Paragraph	Border	Tabs
Body Text	Heading 9		Spacing After 12 pt; Keep with Next		
Footer		Character Spacing Normal		Top (Double, $1^1/_2$ pt line style)	
Header		24 pt, Bold, Italic, Small Caps	Spacing After 12 pt	Bottom (Double, $2^1/_4$ pt line style)	
Heading 1		14 pt	Spacing Before 24 pt; Spacing After 12 pt		6.5", Right, Leader option 4 (underscore)
Heading 9		No Bold, Italic only	Indent Left .5"; Spacing Before and After 0 pt		Left-aligned at 1.5", 4.5", 5.25"

Figure 4
Styles to modify

4. Save your changes then close the template.
5. Create a new *document* based on SAC2DESC.DOT. Save the document as SAC2MAIN.DOC to your Student Disk.
6. Create a catalog main document in the active window, then attach the data source AC2DATA.DOC from your Student Disk to the main document.
7. As shown in Figure 5, insert the merge field codes, text, and tab characters, then apply the styles indicated.

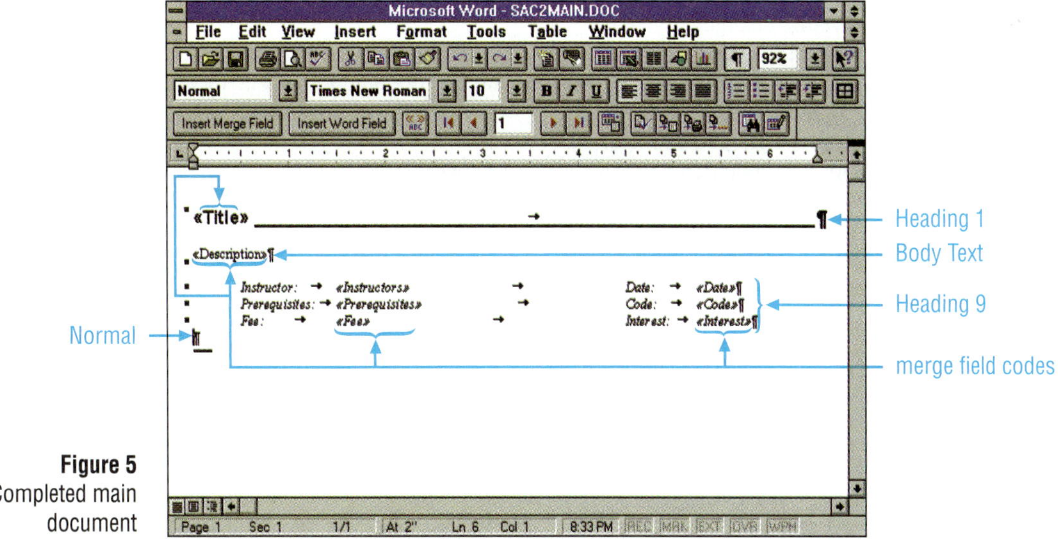

Figure 5
Completed main document

8. Move to the top of the document, then insert the Wingdings candle symbol (row 1, the symbol in the eighth box from the left).
9. Select the inserted symbol, then format it as a drop cap, selecting the In Margin position option. Save your changes.
10. Merge to a new document, then save the merged document as SAC2MRG1.DOC to your Student Disk.

11. Type "Workshops" as the text of the header of the merged document.
12. Type "Of special interest to A = Administrators, F = Facilitators, T = Technical Support" as the text of the footer. Save your changes.
13. Preview, print, then close the merged document (SAC2MRG1.DOC).
14. Sort the attached data source AC2DATA. DOC by the Code field in ascending order.
15. Merge to a new document, then save it as SAC2MRG2.DOC to your Student Disk.
16. Type "Workshops" as the text of the header.
17. Type "Of special interest to A = Administrators, F = Facilitators, T = Technical Support" as the text of the footer. Save your changes.
18. Preview then print the document.
19. Close all documents without saving any changes.
20. Create a new document based on SAC2DESC.DOT. Save it as SAC2EVAL.DOC to your Student Disk.
21. Create a form letter main document in the active window, then attach it to AC2DATA.DOC from your Student Disk.
22. Type "Workshop Evaluation," then press [Enter] twice. Apply the Title Cover style to the first line.
23. Move to the end of the document, then insert a three-row by two-column table. Change the width of column 1 to 2" and the width of column 2 to 4.5". Do not include any space between columns.
24. In row 1, cell 1, type "Workshop Title:"; in row 2, cell 1, type "Workshop Date:"; in row 3, cell 1, type "Workshop Instructor:."
25. In row 1, cell 2, insert the Title merge field code; in row 2, cell 2 insert the Date merge field code; in row 3, cell 2 insert the Instructors merge field code.
26. Apply the Body Text style to all cells of the table, then bold the contents of column 1.
27. Place the insertion point at the end of the document, then press [Enter] four times.
28. Insert the file AC2FORM.DOC from your Student Disk, then center the table across the page.
29. Insert a page break at the end of the document.
30. Save the changes.
31. Merge the documents so that only the records containing 1005 through 1007 in the Code field are merged. Save the merged document as SAC2MRG3.DOC to your Student Disk.
32. Print the merged document.
33. Close all documents without saving changes.

Additional Case 3

Creating a Fall Schedule of Events

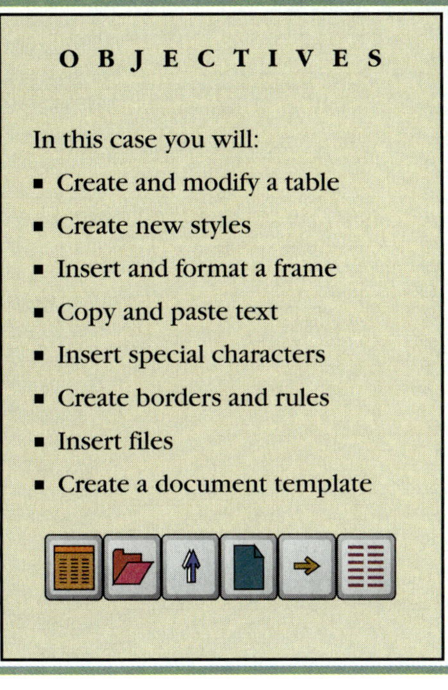

Old Keystone Herb Emporium   Trey Claxton owns and operates the Old Keystone Herb Emporium, one of many stores located in the historic section of Keystone, Pennsylvania. The tourist trade slows down in the fall, so Trey, along with several other store owners in Old Keystone, decided to implement a marketing strategy to increase traffic in the area during the fall. Trey came up with the idea of holding workshops and seminars in his store to create interest in the many uses of herbs to improve the quality of life.

Trey wants to create a flyer listing the dates and course descriptions of the workshops he plans to hold during the fall. The flyer must also contain a registration form for attendees to return to him. To save money on mailing, Trey decides to include a place for the customer's address along with the bulk rate stamp. Trey has already typed the course descriptions and saved them in the file AC3CD.DOC. He decides to create the registration form and the bulk rate stamp each in a separate file, then insert them where appropriate in the course description file. Figure 6 shows the completed flyer.

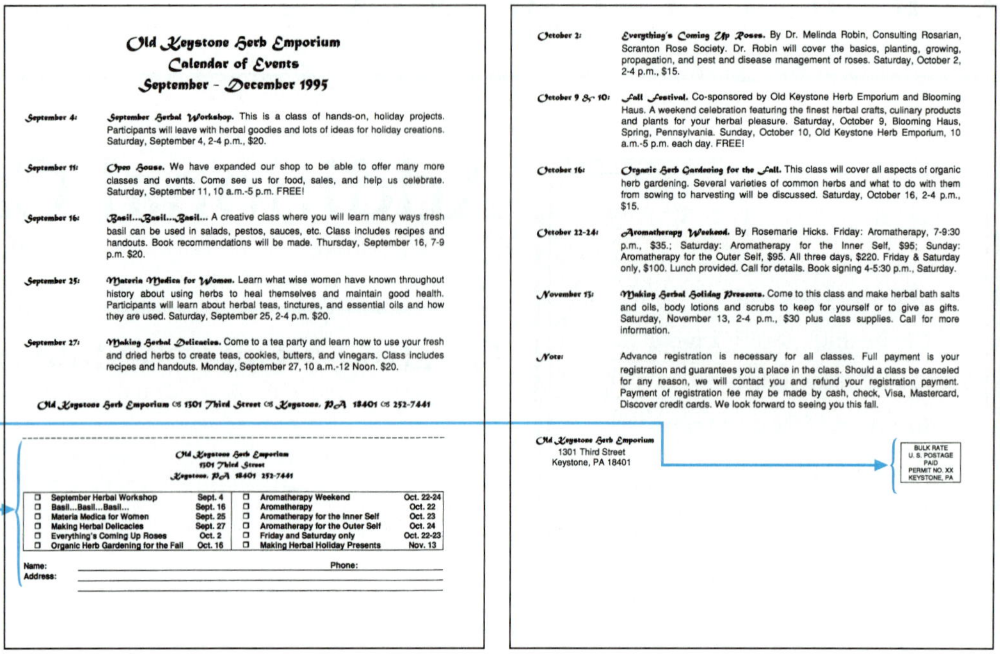

Figure 6 — Completed flyer

Old Keystone Herb Emporium
Calendar of Events
September – December 1995

September 4: **September Herbal Workshop.** This is a class of hands-on, holiday projects. Participants will leave with herbal goodies and lots of ideas for holiday creations. Saturday, September 4, 2-4 p.m., $20.

September 11: **Open House.** We have expanded our shop to be able to offer many more classes and events. Come see us for food, sales, and help us celebrate. Saturday, September 11, 10 a.m.-5 p.m. FREE!

September 16: **Basil...Basil...Basil...** A creative class where you will learn many ways fresh basil can be used in salads, pestos, sauces, etc. Class includes recipes and handouts. Book recommendations will be made. Thursday, September 16, 7-9 p.m. $20.

September 25: **Materia Medica for Women.** Learn what wise women have known throughout history about using herbs to heal themselves and maintain good health. Participants will learn about herbal teas, tinctures, and essential oils and how they are used. Saturday, September 25, 2-4 p.m. $20.

September 27: **Making Herbal Delicacies.** Come to a tea party and learn how to use your fresh and dried herbs to create teas, cookies, butters, and vinegars. Class includes recipes and handouts. Monday, September 27, 10 a.m.-12 Noon. $20.

Old Keystone Herb Emporium ☙ 1301 Third Street ☙ Keystone, PA 18401 ☙ 252-7441

October 2: **Everything's Coming Up Roses.** By Dr. Melinda Robin, Consulting Rosarian, Scranton Rose Society. Dr. Robin will cover the basics, planting, growing, propagation, and pest and disease management of roses. Saturday, October 2, 2-4 p.m., $15.

October 9 & 10: **Fall Festival.** Co-sponsored by Old Keystone Herb Emporium and Blooming Haus. A weekend celebration featuring the finest herbal crafts, culinary products and plants for your herbal pleasure. Saturday, October 9, Blooming Haus, Spring, Pennsylvania. Sunday, October 10, Old Keystone Herb Emporium, 10 a.m.-5 p.m. each day. FREE!

October 16: **Organic Herb Gardening for the Fall.** This class will cover all aspects of organic herb gardening. Several varieties of common herbs and what to do with them from sowing to harvesting will be discussed. Saturday, October 16, 2-4 p.m., $15.

October 22-24: **Aromatherapy Weekend.** By Rosemarie Hicks. Friday: Aromatherapy, 7-9:30 p.m., $35.; Saturday: Aromatherapy for the Inner Self, $95; Sunday: Aromatherapy for the Outer Self, $95. All three days, $220. Friday & Saturday only, $100. Lunch provided. Call for details. Book signing 4-5:30 p.m., Saturday.

November 13: **Making Herbal Holiday Presents.** Come to this class and make herbal bath salts and oils, body lotions and scrubs to keep for yourself or to give as gifts. Saturday, November 13, 2-4 p.m., $30 plus class supplies. Call for more information.

Note: Advance registration is necessary for all classes. Full payment is your registration and guarantees you a place in the class. Should a class be canceled for any reason, we will contact you and refund your registration payment. Payment of registration fee may be made by cash, check, Visa, Mastercard, Discover credit cards. We look forward to seeing you this fall.

Old Keystone Herb Emporium
1301 Third Street
Keystone, PA 18401

BULK RATE
U. S. POSTAGE
PAID
PERMIT NO. XX
KEYSTONE, PA

inserted bulk rate stamp

inserted registration form

Registration form (inserted):

Old Keystone Herb Emporium
1301 Third Street
Keystone, PA 18401 252-7441

❑	September Herbal Workshop	Sept. 4	❑	Aromatherapy Weekend	Oct. 22-24
❑	Basil...Basil...Basil...	Sept. 16	❑	Aromatherapy	Oct. 22
❑	Materia Medica for Women	Sept. 25	❑	Aromatherapy for the Inner Self	Oct. 23
❑	Making Herbal Delicacies	Sept. 27	❑	Aromatherapy for the Outer Self	Oct. 24
❑	Everything's Coming Up Roses	Oct. 2	❑	Friday and Saturday only	Oct. 22-23
❑	Organic Herb Gardening for the Fall	Oct. 16	❑	Making Herbal Holiday Presents	Nov. 13

Name: _______________________   Phone: _______________________
Address: _______________________

After completing the flyer, Trey will have it duplexed printed, then he will fold each flyer in thirds, staple it, and attach a mailing label. He also wants to create a document template from the final flyer document in case he decides to produce a similar flyer in the spring.

Start Word, conduct the screen check procedure described in Tutorial 1, then complete the following.

1. Create the registration form.
    a. Open a new document then save it as SAC3REG.DOC to your Student Disk.
    b Press [Enter], type "Old Keystone Herb Emporium," press [Enter], type "1301 Third Street," press [Enter], type "Keystone, PA," press [Spacebar] twice, type "18401," press [Spacebar] twice, type "252-7441."
    c. Press [Enter] twice.
    d. Change the left and right margins to .5".
    e. Insert a six-row by six-column table.
    f. Change the column widths to the following measurements, with no space between columns:
    Column 1:   .5"
    Column 2:   2.5"
    Column 3:   .75"
    Column 4:   .5"
    Column 5:   2.5"
    Column 6:   .75"
    g. Insert the text as shown in Figure 7, using the Wingdings character ❑ (third row, second symbol from the right) in the cells in columns 1 and 4.

<table>
<tr><td>❒ September Herbal Workshop</td><td>Sept. 4</td><td>❒ Aromatherapy Weekend</td><td>Oct. 22-24</td></tr>
<tr><td>❒ Basil…Basil…Basil…</td><td>Sept. 16</td><td>❒ Aromatherapy</td><td>Oct. 22</td></tr>
<tr><td>❒ Materia Medica for Women</td><td>Sept. 25</td><td>❒ Aromatherapy for the Inner Self</td><td>Oct. 23</td></tr>
<tr><td>❒ Making Herbal Delicacies</td><td>Sept. 27</td><td>❒ Aromatherapy for the Outer Self</td><td>Oct. 24</td></tr>
<tr><td>❒ Everything's Coming Up Roses</td><td>Oct. 2</td><td>❒ Friday and Saturday only</td><td>Oct. 22-23</td></tr>
<tr><td>❒ Organic Herb Gardening for the Fall</td><td>Oct. 16</td><td>❒ Making Herbal Holiday Presents</td><td>Nov. 13</td></tr>
</table>

Figure 7
Text registration form

h   Place the insertion point at the end of the document, then press [Enter].

i.   Insert a three-row by two-column table, with a width of 1" for column 1 and a width of 6.5" for column 2 (with no space between columns).

j.   Type "Name:" in cell 1 of row 1 and "Address:" in cell 1 of row 2.

k.   Split cell 2 of row 1 into two cells, then change the width of the newly split cell 2 by dragging the cell border to 5.5".

l.   Type "Phone:" in cell 3 of row 1.

m. Save your changes.

2. Format the registration form.

a.   Create new paragraph styles with the attributes shown in Figure 8.

Style Name	Font	Paragraph
Registration Title	Matura MT Script Capitals, Bold, 10 pt	Centered
Registration Text	Arial, Bold, 10 pt	

Figure 8
Attributes for new paragraph styles in registration form

b.   Select the first five lines of the document, then apply the Registration Title style.

c.   Select the two tables then apply the Registration Text style.

d.   Center the contents of columns 1, 3, 4, and 6 of the table containing the seminar names.

e.   Insert a $^3/_4$ pt border around the outside of the table containing the seminar names and along the right side of column 3.

f.   Insert a $^3/_4$ pt rule at the bottom of the cells in column 2 and cell 3 of row 1 of the second table.

g.   Spell check the document.

h.   Save the changes.

i.   Close the document.

3. Create the document for the bulk rate stamp.

a.   Open a new document, then save it as SAC3POST.DOC to your Student Disk.

b.   Change the left and right margins to .5".

c.   Insert a center tab at the 1" mark on the ruler.

d.   Type "Old Keystone Herb Emporium," then press [Enter].

e.   Press [Tab], type "1301 Third Street," then press [Enter].

f.   Press [Tab], type "Keystone, PA 18401," then press [Enter].

g.   Create new paragraph styles with the attributes shown in Figure 9.

Style Name	Font
Return Name	Matura MT Script Capitals, 11 pt
Return Address	Arial, 11 pt
Bulk Rate	Arial, 11 pt, All Caps

Figure 9

Attributes for new paragraph styles in bulk rate stamp document

h. Select the store name then apply the Return Name style to the selection.

i. Select the two lines of the return address, then apply the Return Address style to the selection.

j. Place the insertion point at the end of the document, then type the following text:
Bulk Rate
U. S. Postage
Paid
Permit No. XX
Keystone, PA

k. Select the inserted bulk rate text, then apply the Bulk Rate style to the selection.

l. Switch to page layout view, select the bulk rate text, then insert a frame around the selection.

m. Select the frame then format it with the following attributes:
Width: Exactly At 1.2"
Height: Exactly At 1"
Horizontal Position: Right relative to the margin
Vertical Position: 0" relative to the paragraph

n. Center the text within the frame.

o. Spell check the document.

p. Switch to normal view then save the changes.

q. Close the document.

4. Create the flyer.

a. Open a new document then save it as SAC3FALL.DOC to your Student Disk.

b. Insert the flyer title information as shown below:
Old Keystone Herb Emporium
Calendar of Events
September - December 1995

c. Press [Enter].

d. Change the top, bottom, left, and right margins to .5".

e. Create new paragraph styles with the attributes shown in Figure 10.

Style Name	Font	Paragraph
Flyer Title	Matura MT Script Capitals, 20 pt	Centered
Course	Arial, 12 pt	Hanging Indent: 1.5"; Spacing Before: 18 pt, Justified
Divider	Matura MT Script Capitals, Bold, 12 pt	Centered

Figure 10

Attributes for new paragraph styles in flyer document

f. Insert the file AC3CD.DOC from your Student Disk.

g. Select the three flyer title lines, then apply the Flyer Title style to the selection.

     h. Select the remaining text of the document, then apply the Course style to the selection.

     i. In the first course description, select the date and the course title (include the period), then apply the Matura MT Script Capitals font to the selection.

     j. Repeat the previous step (i) for the date and course title in the remaining course descriptions and the note.

     k. Save your changes.

5. Create the divider text.

     a. Place the insertion point at the end of the September 27 course description, then press [Enter] three times.

     b. Place the insertion point in the second blank paragraph (Ln 22), then type "Old Keystone Herb Emporium 1301 Third Street Keystone, PA 18401 252-7441."

     c. Apply the Divider style to the line.

     d. Insert the Wingdings character ↄȝ (row 5, 7th symbol from the left) between the store name and the street address, then press [Spacebar].

     e. Repeat the previous step (d) to insert the symbol between the street address and city and also between the zip code and the telephone number.

6. Insert the registration form into the flyer.

     a. Place the insertion point in front of the "O" in October 2, then insert the file SAC3REG.DOC.

     b. Place the insertion point in the blank paragraph before the registration form title (Ln 24).

     c. Insert a $^3/_4$ pt dashed rule at the top of the line space.

7. Insert the bulk rate stamp document into the flyer.

     a. Place the insertion point at the end of the document (Ln 27).

     b. Press [Enter].

     c. Insert the file SAC3POST.DOC at the insertion point.

     d. Switch to page layout view, then select the frame around the bulk rate stamp.

     e. Format the frame so that it is even with the store name (vertical position 7.2" relative to the margin).

     f. Save the document.

8. Print the document.

9. Create a document template from the flyer document.

     a. Save the document as a template named SAC3FLY.DOT to your Student Disk.

     b. Print the style sheet for the SAC3FLY.DOT template.

10. Close all documents.

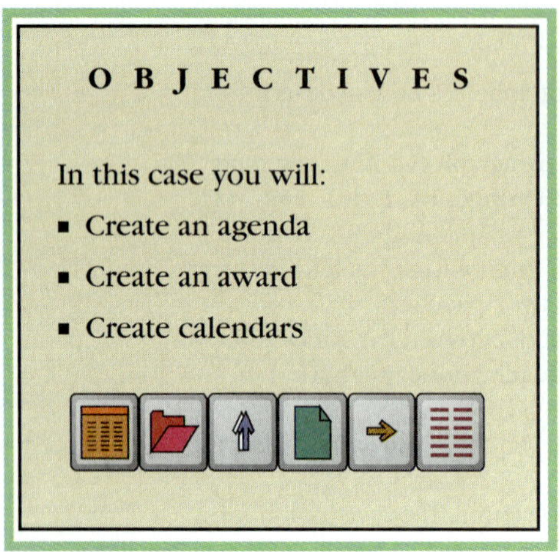

Additional Case 4

Creating Materials for a Quarterly Sales Meeting

CASE

E Tankology, Inc.   Ben Penney has just returned from a road trip and checked his day's schedule. He has a note from his boss welcoming him back and reminding Ben of the quarterly sales meeting for the regional sales managers next week, for which he is responsible. Ben must prepare the agenda, the calendars for the last quarter of the year, and an award certificate for the top salesperson. He must prepare all these documents now so that they can be reproduced and the agenda sent to the attendees. Ben has 45 minutes before his first meeting of the day, then he is booked solid for the rest of the day. Although he has never used them before, Ben decides to use Word's wizards to produce the documents he needs quickly.

Start Word, conduct the screen check procedure described in Tutorial 1, then complete the following:

1. Check the time. You should complete this case problem in 30 minutes.
2. Create an agenda.
   a. Click File then click New.... Select the Agenda Wizard, then click OK or press [Enter].
   b. Choose the following wizard options:

   Style: Standard
   Date: September 6, 1995
   Starting time: 9:00 AM
   Title: Quarterly Sales Meeting
   Location: Hartland Plaza
   Headings to include: Type of meeting, Please bring
   Names on agenda: Note taker, Attendees
   Agenda topics:

Topic	Person responsible	Time allocated in minutes
Meeting Overview	Ben Penney	10
Eastern Region Status Report	Camille Early	15
Northern Region Status Report	Austin Porterfield	15
Southern Region Status Report	Mort Tyler	15
Western Region Status Report	Don Houston	15
New Products	Ben Penney	15
4th Quarter Sales Goals	Ben Penney	15
Schedule for New Customer Database Training	Camille Early	10
Staff Concerns	Ben Penney	15

   Form for recording: Yes
   c. Save the document as SAC4AGND.DOC to your Student Disk.
   d. In the finished agenda, type:

   Type of meeting: Scheduled
   Note taker: Susan Grau
   Attendees: Camille Early, Don Houston, Ben Penney,
                      Austin Porterfield, and Mort Tyler
   Please bring: Quarterly and Year-to-Date Sales Reports

   e. Copy the information in the cells to the notetaking form (pg 2).
   f. Spell check the document.
   g. Save your changes.
3. Print the agenda and notetaking form.
4. Close the document.

Next Ben decides to create the award certificate for the top salesperson of the second quarter. He and the president of Tankology Inc., Judith Miers, will sign the certificate.

5. Create an award certificate.
   a. Click File then click New.... Select the Award Wizard, then click OK or press [Enter].
   b. Choose the following wizard options:

   Style: Jazzy
   Direction: Landscape
   Name of person: Emmett Landry
   Title of award: Million Dollar Club
   Name of persons to sign: Judith Miers, Ben Penney
   Name of group: no presenter's name needed
   Date of award: September 6, 1995
   Additional information: Top Salesperson, 2nd Quarter 1995

     c. Save the document as SAC4AWRD.DOC to your Student Disk.

     d. Spell check the document.

6. Print the award.

7. Close the document.

Ben has one more document to complete—calendars for the months in the last quarter. He wants to include an area on the calendars for notetaking.

8. Create the calendars.

     a. Click File then click New.... Select the Calendar Wizard, then click OK or press [Enter].

     b. Choose the following wizard options:

Direction:	Landscape
Style:	Boxes and borders
Room for picture:	Yes
Starting and Ending Months:	October 1995 through December 1995

9. Save the document as SAC4CAL.DOC.

10. Adapt the calendars for notetaking.

     a. Move the insertion point to the top of the document, if necessary, click the picture to the left of the October calendar to select it, then press [Del].

     b. Select the remaining frame, then press [Del]. Two blank paragraphs remain.

     c. Place the insertion point in the second blank paragraph, then insert a 25-row by 1-column table with the column width equal to 3.5".

     d. Adjust the row height of the table so that each row is at least 20 pt.

     e. Insert a $^3/_4$ pt rule at the bottom of the internal horizontal cells.

     f. Save your changes.

11. Adapt the remaining calendars.

     a. Select the notetaking table in the October calendar, then click the Copy button on the Standard toolbar.

     b. Select the picture to the left of the November calendar, then delete it; delete the remaining frame as well.

     c. Place the insertion point in the second blank paragraph, then paste the notetaking table from the Clipboard.

     d. Repeat steps b and c for the December calendar.

     e. Save your changes.

12. Print the calendars.

13. Close the document.

14. Check the time.

References

1 **Microsoft Word Commands**

2 **Toolbar Buttons**

3 **Field Codes**

R E F E R E N C E 1

Microsoft Word Commands

This section describes the commands available in the Microsoft Word 6.0 for Windows menu bar. For additional information on any command, select Help from the menu bar or the Help button on the Standard toolbar. Keyboard shortcuts for selected commands appear at the right of some menus. If an ellipsis (...) appears after a command, a dialog box will appear when you select the command.

File Commands

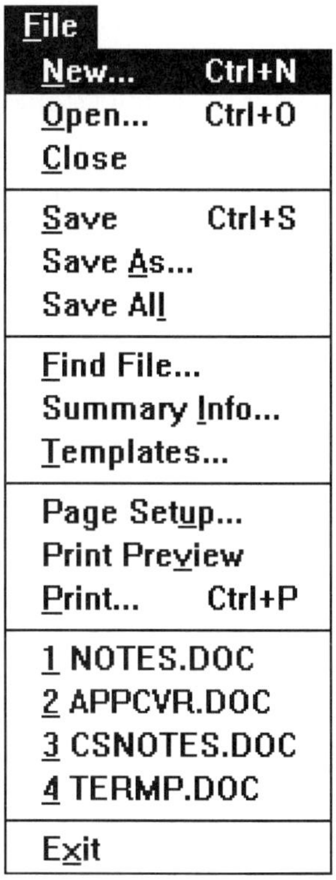
File
New... Ctrl+N
Open... Ctrl+O
Close
Save Ctrl+S
Save As...
Save All
Find File...
Summary Info...
Templates...
Page Setup...
Print Preview
Print... Ctrl+P
1 NOTES.DOC
2 APPCVR.DOC
3 CSNOTES.DOC
4 TERMP.DOC
Exit

New Creates and opens a new document based on the document template you select.

Open Opens an existing Word document, template, foreign or non-Word file. A dialog box will appear, prompting you to indicate the name, directory and drive location, and the type of file.

Close Closes the document that is currently on the screen. If changes have been made in the document, you will be prompted to save the changes.

Save Saves the active document but does not close it. If the document has not been saved before, you will be prompted for a filename and location to save to. If the document has been saved before, the Save command will save the document to the same location, under the same name. When you are editing a macro, Save changes to Save Template.

Save As Saves the current document to the name, directory, drive, and file type you assign. A dialog box will appear, allowing you to enter the new filename, directory and drive, and type of file; the Options button on the right side of the dialog box lets you customize how and when Word will save documents and whether a password will be needed to use the document.

Save All Saves all open documents. If an open document has not been saved before, the Save As dialog box will appear.

Find File Searches for a document by name, date of creation, or date of last modification. If you have information about the document in Summary Info (see Summary Info, below), you can search for a document based on author, title, or key words.

Summary Info Allows you to input and view a summary of information about the document. If Summary Info has been entered, you can then find a file and input field codes based on the information you have entered.

Templates Helps you create memos, faxes, and other documents without extensive formatting by letting you use preset styles that determine the text, graphics, and format of the document.

Page Setup Sets margins, paper size, paper source, and layout for the whole document or a selected section of the document.

Print Preview Displays on your screen how the document will appear when printed. Use the vertical scroll bar to view the document pages. Lets you print directly from the screen by selecting the Print button on the toolbar.

Print Prints the document on the selected printer. The Print What option in the dialog box also allows you to print information associated with the document, such as Summary Info, styles, and key assignments. Lets you select the printer, number of copies, range of pages, and print options for the document.

(File Name) Lists the last documents you used, and lets you open them quickly from the menu without choosing File Open. You can change the number of documents displayed by choosing Options from the Tools menu and adjusting the number on the General tab.

Exit Ends the Microsoft Word session. If a document has been changed since the last time it was saved, you will be prompted to save the changes.

Edit Commands

```
Edit
 Undo Bold      Ctrl+Z
 Repeat Bold    Ctrl+Y

 Cut            Ctrl+X
 Copy           Ctrl+C
 Paste          Ctrl+V
 Paste Special...
 Clear          Delete
 Select All     Ctrl+A

 Find...        Ctrl+F
 Replace...     Ctrl+H
 Go To...       Ctrl+G
 AutoText...
 Bookmark...

 Links...
 Object
```

Undo Reverses your most recent action or command. The name of the command on the menu will change to indicate the action that will be undone (Undo Typing, Undo Cut, Undo Bold, etc.)

Repeat Repeats the last change you made in the document, including typing text, formatting, editing, and making tables. The name of the command on the menu will change to indicate the action that will be undone (Repeat Typing, Repeat Cut, Repeat Bold, etc.)

Cut Deletes the selected text from the document, and places it on the Clipboard.

Copy Copies the selected text from the document, and places it on the Clipboard.

Paste Copies the cut or copied text to the location of the insertion point in the document.

Paste Special Copies the contents of the Clipboard into the document in a specified format, or creates a link between the Word document and a document in another application. If a link is created, information that is updated in another application is automatically updated in Word.

Clear Deletes selected items. You cannot reinsert items that have been removed using the Clear command; you can use the Undo command to retrieve the cleared item.

Select All Selects the entire document.

Find Searches for text or formatting that matches the description you provide. You can specify whether the text should exactly match, or if it is part of a word; you can also specify in which direction you want to search the document.

Replace Searches for specified text and replaces it with the text indicated.

Go To Moves the insertion point to the location you specify. You can specify different types of locations, including page number, line number, table, endnote, footnote, or graphic.

AutoText Creates or inserts an AutoText entry—a block of text or a graphic that can be inserted anywhere in the document.

Bookmark Marks selected text, graphics, tables, or rows within a table in a document. A bookmark can be used to quickly locate items using the Go To command, create cross-references, mark a range of pages for an index entry, or calculate equations based on numbers in the text. Square brackets ([ ]) will indicate the beginning and end of each bookmark.

Links Displays and modifies the link, or connection, between text or graphics in the active document (the destination document) with either a separate Word document or a file from another application (the source document). Once the link has been established, any changes that are made to the source document will also appear in the active document.

Object Opens the application of the item that has been linked (table, graphic, etc.) so that changes can be made to the item.

View Commands

View
• **Normal**
Outline
Page Layout
Master Document
F**u**ll Screen
Toolbars...
√ **R**uler
Header and Footer
Footnotes
Annotations
Zoom...

Normal Shows the formatted text of a document, but not the layout on the page. Use normal view for entering, editing, and formatting most text.

Outline Creates an outline of the document; allows you to hide text and graphics, promote and demote headings, and select the headings you wish to view.

Page Layout Displays the document as would be printed on paper, including headers, footers, footnotes, frames, and graphics.

Master Document Shows the master document as an outline. A master document is composed of several subdocuments; you can work with either the master document or any of the individual subdocuments. The document appears in outline form and can be manipulated in the same way as an outline. When you select this view, the Master Document toolbar will appear (for information on the toolbar, see Master Document toolbar in Reference 2).

Full Screen Removes the menu bar, toolbars, scroll bars, and title bar; only the document appears on the screen.

Toolbars Displays the toolbars that are available, and lets you select which toolbars will appear on your screen. If you use a particular toolbar frequently, select it and it will always appear on the screen in that document.

Ruler Hides or displays the ruler.

Header and Footer Displays the header or footer and allows you to enter text that will appear at the top and/or bottom of each page, including the page number, date, and time.

Footnotes Views the footnotes that have been entered in the footnote pane. (See Footnote under Insert commands.)

Annotations Views the annotations that have been entered into the annotations pane. (See Annotations under Insert commands.)

Zoom Allows you to magnify and reduce the size of the document on the screen.

Insert Commands

Insert
Break...
Page N<u>u</u>mbers...
<u>A</u>nnotation
Date and <u>T</u>ime...
Fi<u>e</u>ld...
<u>S</u>ymbol...
For<u>m</u> Field...

Foot<u>n</u>ote...
Cap<u>t</u>ion...
Cross-<u>r</u>eference...
Inde<u>x</u> and Tables...

Fi<u>l</u>e...
<u>F</u>rame
<u>P</u>icture...
<u>O</u>bject...
<u>D</u>atabase...

Break   Inserts a break in the column, page, or section at the insertion point.

Page Numbers   Inserts page numbers and allows you to select the position of the numbers on the page.

Annotation   Creates an annotation pane and places a note at the insertion point. It allows people who are reviewing the document to make comments instead of changing the document itself. The initials of the reviewer and an annotation mark will appear on the screen when you selected the Show/Hide ¶ button ¶ on the Standard toolbar. You can also print annotations by selecting Annotations from the Print What option in the Print dialog box.

Date and Time   Places the current date and/or time at the insertion point in the format you select.

Field   Inserts a set of codes, known as a field, that instructs the Word program to automatically place text, graphics, or other material at the insertion point. For a list of field codes and their definitions, see Reference 3.

Symbol   Places a symbol or special character such as (α, ©, ™, or $\Rightarrow$) at the insertion point.

Form Field   Creates a field in the document that allows only certain types of text (a text form field, a check box form field, or a drop-down form field) to be entered. The document can then be protected so that only the form fields can be changed. This lets you make a form that will allow changes to only certain parts of the text. You can display the Forms toolbar by selecting Show Toolbar in the Form Field dialog box (for more information on the Forms toolbar, see Reference 2).

Footnote   Creates a footnote or endnote pane and places a footnote or endnote at the insertion point.

Caption   Inserts a text caption above or below a graphic, table, or equation.

Cross-reference   Creates a reference to an item in another part of the document or in another document.

Index and Tables   Creates an index, table of contents, table of figures, or table of authorities, and allows you to select the style in which it will appear.

File   Inserts all or part of the contents of a second document or other application file into the document. A dialog box will prompt you for the name, location, and type of file you wish to insert.

Frame   Creates a box around an area of text. This allows you to easily change the position of the frame (and enclosed text); you can also make other text flow around the frame. For information on formatting a frame, see the Frame command in the Format menu.

Picture   Inserts a graphic from another application; a picture that has been inserted can then be linked to the original application. A dialog box will open that prompts you for the name, location, and type of file you wish to insert.

Object   Embeds the object of another application (table, graph, etc.) in the current document. Embedding an object means that the application the object was written in will become active. *Note: You must have the application installed on your computer in order to embed an object from it.*

Database   Inserts the records from a database into the current document.

Format Commands

Font   Allows you to change the font type, size, and style. The Font command also allows you to use special characters, including strikethrough, superscript, subscript, small caps, all caps, and hidden.

Paragraph   Changes the indentation, spacing, and text flow of the text in the documents.

Tabs   Sets the tab stop position, alignment, and leader character.

Borders and Shading   Draws a box around paragraphs, tables, and pictures, and adds shading and color to the interior of the box.

Columns   Sets the number of columns, their width, and spacing in a document.

Change Case   Changes the capitalization of the selected letters.

Drop Cap   Creates a dropped initial capital letter or word.

Bullets and Numbering   Creates bulleted or numbered lists in either text or a table.

Heading Numbering   Creates a numbered list containing different headings.

AutoFormat   Automatically creates a format based on the existing text in the document.

Style Gallery   Offers the opportunity to see your document with a variety of style templates and to select the template you want.

Style   Allows you to create, apply, and modify a text style.

Frame   Lets you change the placement and size of the frame. Also adjusts the text around the frame.

Picture   Changes the size of the picture. Allows you to crop any or all sides of the picture.

Drawing Object   Allows you to modify the size, placement, color, pattern, and line thickness of objects drawn in Word.

Tools Commands

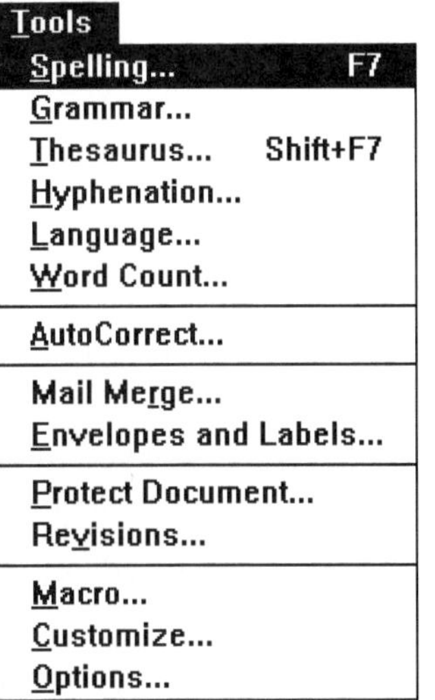

Spelling   Checks the spelling of all text in the document, suggests correct spellings, and allows you to create a dictionary of words that are not included in the Word dictionary. You can also check the spelling of selected text by highlighting the text and then selecting Spelling.

Grammar   Checks the document and highlights possible grammar inconsistencies in the text.

Thesaurus   Offers synonyms and antonyms for selected words or phrases.

Hyphenation   Hyphenates the document. This can be done either manually or automatically.

Language   Lets you specify a different language in order to check spelling and use the thesaurus.

Word Count   Counts the number of pages, words, characters, paragraphs, and lines in the current document or selected text, and displays them in a dialog box.

AutoCorrect Corrects text automatically as you type. You can add words that you frequently type incorrectly that you wish to have automatically corrected. For example, if you spell "document" as "documnet," you can use AutoCorrect to fix the error whenever the incorrect spelling is typed.

Mail Merge Merges a main document with a data source (for example, a mailing list) to create personalized form letters, mailing labels, envelopes, and brochures.

Envelopes and Labels Prints envelopes and mailing labels.

Protect Document Protects a document from changes except those you allow. If you have inserted a form field (see Form Field under Insert commands), you can protect the document and allow changes only to the form field.

Revisions Allows revisions to a document to be marked, reviewed, and accepted or rejected. This is useful when someone else is reviewing your document and you want to see the revisions they made before you decide to accept changes they suggest.

Macro Records, runs, edits, and deletes macros. A macro is a series of word actions and commands that can be recorded and run again without retyping the commands repeatedly.

Customize Creates customized toolbars, menus, and keyboard shortcuts.

Options Changes Word defaults; option tabs include View, General, Edit, Print, Revisions, User Info, Compatibility, File Locations, Save, Spelling, Grammar, and AutoFormat.

Table Commands

Table
Insert Table...
Delete Cells...
Merge Cells
Split Cells...

Select Row
Select Column
Select Table   Alt+Num 5

Table AutoFormat...
Cell Height and Width...
Headings

Convert Text to Table...
Sort Text...
Formula...
Split Table
√ Gridlines

Insert Table Inserts a table at the insertion point. Whenever the insertion point is positioned in an existing table, Insert Table changes to Insert Row, Column, or Cell on the Table menu, allowing you to add rows, columns, and cells to the table.

Delete Cells Removes rows, columns, and cells from a table. If rows, columns, or cells are selected, Delete changes to Delete Rows, Delete Columns, or Delete Cells.

Merge Cells Combines selected horizontal cells into one cell.

Split Cells Splits selected cells into the number of cells you specify.

Select Row Selects the entire row.

Select Column Selects the entire column.

Select Table Selects the entire table.

Table AutoFormat Allows you to review a list of several table designs and to select the format you want for the table.

Cell Height and Width Allows you to change the height of selected rows and width of selected columns.

Headings Places table headings at the top of the page on tables that are more than one page long.

Convert Text to Table   Converts selected text to a table. In order to create a table, the selected text must contain separator characters—a paragraph mark, comma, or tab—that will be used to create the table.

Sort/Sort Text   Sorts paragraphs, lists, or the contents of cells, and arranges them alphabetically, numerically, or by date. If the insertion point is in a table, the command appears as Sort; otherwise, it appears as Sort Text.

Formula   Creates a mathematical formula.

Split Table   Splits the table at the insertion point into two separate tables.

Gridlines   Makes lines separating the contents of the table visible and invisible.

Window Commands

New Window   Opens a new window in the active file. Any changes made to one window will be made in all windows.

Arrange All   Displays all open documents simultaneously.

Split   Splits the screen into two separate panes, allowing you to see different parts of the same file on the screen simultaneously. Prompts you for an insertion point.

(File Name)   Lists the open documents and allows you to switch between them.

Help

Contents   Lists the table of contents for the Help document, and provides information on using Help.

Search for Help on   Lets you look up help by typing the name of the topic.

Index   Provides an alphabetical index of all the help listings; allows you to scroll down the listings.

Quick Preview   Offers a demonstration of Microsoft Word.

Examples and Demos   Provides examples of many Word features; offers automated demonstrations.

Tip of the Day   Displays a dialog box with information about using Word. It can be set to appear whenever you start Word.

WordPerfect Help   Offers help based on WordPerfect commands.

Technical Support   Provides information about receiving technical support from Microsoft.

About Microsoft Word   Displays information about Word and your computer.

Toolbar Buttons

Standard Toolbar Buttons

- Creates and opens a new document
- Opens an existing document
- Saves the active document
- Prints the active document on the current defaults
- Previews how the active document will look when printed
- Checks spelling
- Cuts and moves the current selection to the Clipboard
- Copies the current selection to the Clipboard
- Pastes the contents of the Clipboard at the insertion point in the document
- Copies the format of the Painter selected text to another block of text
- Reverses the last action or command
- Repeats the last action or command that was undone
- Automatically formats a document Format
- Automatically inserts a block of text anywhere in the document
- Creates a table
- Inserts a Microsoft Excel worksheet in the current document
- Changes the number of columns in a section of the document
- Draws an object; displays the Drawing toolbar
- Creates a chart Chart
- Displays or hides nonprinting characters and hidden notes
- Changes how large or small the document appears on the screen

- Displays context-sensitive help about the next item selected

Formatting Toolbar Buttons

- Reviews, creates, or changes a style
- Changes the selected font
- Changes the selected font size
- Adds or removes boldface
- Adds or removes italics
- Adds or removes underlining
- Aligns paragraph to the left
- Centers paragraph
- Aligns paragraph to the right
- Aligns paragraph on both right and left margins
- Creates a numbered list
- Creates a bulleted list
- Decreases indentation of the selected paragraph
- Indents or increases indentation of the selected paragraph
- Adds borders and shading to selected paragraph; displays the Borders toolbar

Borders Toolbar Buttons

- Changes the width of border lines
- Adds a border at the top of selected paragraphs, table cells, or frames
- Adds a border at the bottom of selected paragraphs, table cells, or frames
- Adds a border at the left of selected paragraphs, table cells, or frames
- Adds a border at the right of selected paragraphs, table cells, or frames

Adds a border between selected paragraphs, table cells, or frames

Adds a border around selected paragraphs, table cells, or frames

Removes borders from selected paragraphs, table cells, or frames

Controls the shading for selected paragraphs, table cells, or frames

Database Toolbar Buttons

Creates a data form for each record in a data source

Adds, deletes, or renames fields in a data source

Adds a new record to the database

Deletes the selected record

Sorts the database in ascending order (from A-Z alphabetically, or from smallest to largest number numerically)

Sorts the database in descending order (from Z-A alphabetically, or from largest to smallest number numerically)

Inserts a table containing information from a database or other information source

Instructs Word to follow the commands in the field and to produce the result

Locates a record

Switches between the main document and the data source during a mail merge Main Document

Drawing Toolbar Buttons

Note: Drawings appear only in page layout view

Draws a straight line

Draws a rectangle or box

Draws an ellipse; hold down the Shift key to draw a circle

Draws an arc

Draws a freeform line

Creates a box for text that can be positioned behind or in front of the main text

Creates a text callout that points to an illustration

Formats the text callout

Fills a drawn figure with color

Changes the color of the line

Changes the thickness and type of line

Selects previously drawn objects

Places the selected drawn object in front of all other objects

Places the selected drawn object behind all other objects

Places the selected drawn object in front of text

Places the selected drawn object behind text

Groups a set of drawn objects together; allows you to work with the drawn objects as a single unit

Separates a unit that has been grouped back to the original, separates objects

Flips a drawn object or grouped objects horizontally

Flips a drawn object or grouped objects vertically

Rotates a drawn object or grouped objects

Reshapes a freeform object

Creates an invisible grid that aligns drawn objects

Aligns the selected drawn objects horizontally or vertically on the page or with each other

Creates a picture combining an imported picture and drawn objects

Creates a frame

Forms Toolbar Buttons

Creates a text form field

Creates a checkbox form field

Creates a drop-down menu form field

Modifies form fields

Inserts a table at the insertion point

Inserts a frame at the insertion point

Toggles shading in the form field off and on

Protects the document from changes except in the form field

Microsoft Toolbar Buttons

Note: You must have the Microsoft application installed on your computer to switch to the application.

Switches to the MS Excel application

Switches to the MS PowerPoint application

Switches to the MS Mail application

Switches to the MS Access application

Switches to the MS FoxPro application

Switches to the MS Project application

Switches to the MS Schedule+ application

Switches to the MS Publisher application

Status Bar Buttons

Displays the document in normal view

Displays the layout of the page as it will appear when printed, including headers, footers, and graphics

Displays the text in an outline; allows you to hide text and promote and demote heads

Header and Footer Toolbar

Toggles between the header and the footer Header and Footer

Shows the previous header or footer (if different headers or footers appear in your document)

Shows the next header or footer (if different headers or footers appear in your document)

Reconnects a header or footer with the previous section

Inserts a page number field in the header or footer

Inserts a date field in the header or footer

Inserts a time field in the header or footer

Changes the layout of headers and footers on different pages

Displays or hides the text of the document

Close   Closes the Header and Footer toolbar and returns to document text

Macro Toolbar

Macro1   Lists the name of the current macro; allows you to select other macros

Begins recording the macro

Records the next command

Runs the macro

Highlights each statement as the macro executes it

Continues to run a macro

Stops recording the macro

Executes the macro step by step; does not pause at macros with subroutines

Executes the macro step by step, including subroutines

Shows the variables of the active menu

Adds or removes remarks

Creates, runs, deletes, or revises the macro

Opens the macro dialog editor

Mail Merge Toolbar

Insert Merge Field   Lists the available mail merge fields, and places selected fields at the insertion point

Insert Word Field   Inserts a Microsoft Word field

Toggles between viewing the merge fields and the data

Displays the first record in the data source

Displays the previous record in the data source

1   Displays the specified record in the data source

Displays the next record in the data source

Displays the last record in the data source

Mail Merge Helper Switches to the Mail Merge Helper dialog box

Searches for errors

Creates a separate, mail-merged document

Prints the results of the mail merge

Performs the mail merge

Finds a record in the data source

Makes changes to the data source

Master Document Toolbar

Promotes the text or header to a higher level in the outline

Demotes the text or header to a lower level in the outline

Converts a header to body text

Moves the text or header up in the body of the document

Moves the text or header down in the body of the document

Shows the next level of hidden text in the document

Hides the lowest level of text in the document

1 2 Shows the level of headings through the number selected (for example, clicking **1** will display only the first level and hide any other levels)

All Displays all the levels and the body text in the outline

Shows only the first line of text in the outline; to show all the text, click the button again

A/A Shows the text formatting

Toggles between the master document view and outline view

Creates a subdocument from the selected outline items

Transforms the subdocument into part of the master document

Inserts a Word document as a subdocument

Merges one or more subdocuments into one subdocument

Splits a subdocument into two subdocuments

Locks the subdocument; the user can read the subdocument but cannot make changes to it

Outline Toolbar

Promotes the text or header to a higher level in the outline

Demotes the text or header to a lower level in the outline

Converts a header to body text

Moves the text or header up in the body of the document

Moves the text or header down in the body of the document

Shows the next level of hidden text in the document

Hides the lowest level of text in the document

1 2 Shows the level of headings through the number selected (for example, clicking **1** will display only the first level and hide any other levels)

All Displays all the levels and the body text in the outline

Shows only the first line of text in the outline; to show all the text, click the button again

A/A Shows the text formatting

Toggles between the master document view and outline view

WordArt Toolbar

Normal Changes the line and shape of the text

Arial Changes the font of the text

18 Changes the font size

B Adds or removes boldface

I Adds or removes italics

Ee Makes all the letters of even height

Flips the text

Stretches the text

Justifies the text

Adjusts the spacing between characters

Changes the angle of rotation or arc rotation of the text

Adds shading to the text

Adds shadows to the text

Changes the thickness of the text lines

Field Codes

Field codes allow you to insert information such as the filename, current date, and equations into the document; information is automatically updated when it is changed in an original file, or when the date changes, or when an equation changes. Field codes available in Word are listed below, followed by the correct syntax for each field code and a brief description of the field codes. For more information on a field code, select Field from the Insert menu, select the field code you want, and then press [F1].

Date and Time Field Codes

CreateDate CREATEDATE [\@ "Date-Time Picture"] Displays the creation date of the document

Date DATE [Switch] [\@ "Date-Time Picture"] Displays the current date

EditTime EDITTIME Displays the amount of time spent editing the document

PrintDate PRINTDATE [\@ "Date-Time Picture"] Displays the last time the document was printed

SaveDate SAVEDATE [\@ "Date-Time Picture"] Displays the last time the document was saved

Time TIME [\@ "Date-Time Picture"] Displays the current time

Document Automation Field Codes

Compare COMPARE Expression1Expression2 Operator Compares two values (if the comparison is true, Word prints the number 1; if it is false, Word prints 0)

GoToButton GOTOBUTTON Destination DisplayText Moves the insertion point from one location to a new location

If IF Expression1 Operator Expression2TrueText FalseText Evaluates arguments conditionally (if the argument is true, Word prints the "TrueText"; if false, the "FalseText")

MacroButton MACROBUTTON MacroName DisplayText Automatically runs a macro

Print PRINT "PrinterInstructions" Prints a document

Document Information Field Codes

Author AUTHOR ["NewName"] Displays the name of the author listed in the Summary Info dialog box

Comments COMMENTS ["New Comments"] Displays comments from the Summary Info dialog box

FileName FILENAME [Switches] Displays the name and location of the document

FileSize FILESIZE [Switches] Displays the amount of disk space the document occupies

Info [INFO] Infotype ["NewValue"] Displays all the data in the Summary Info dialog box

Keywords KEYWORDS ["NewKeywords"] Displays the key words listed in the Summary Info dialog box

LastSavedBy LASTSAVEDBY Displays the name of the user who saved the document last

NumChars NUMCHARS Displays the number of characters in the document

NumPages NUMPAGES Displays the number of pages in the document

NumWords NUMWORDS Displays the number of words in the document

Subject SUBJECT ["NewSubject"] Displays the subject in the Summary Info dialog box

Template TEMPLATE [Switches] Displays the name of template that has been attached to the document

Title TITLE ["NewTitle"] Displays the title of the document as listed in the Summary Info dialog box

Equation and Formula Field Codes

= [Formula] = Formula [Bookmark] [\# Numeric-Picture] Calculates the results of the equation

Advance ADVANCE [Switches] Advances the text within a line to the left, right, up, or down

Eq EQ Instructions Creates an equation

Symbol SYMBOL CharNum [Switches] Inserts a special character, such as a copyright symbol, box, or arrow

Index and Table Field Codes

Index INDEX [Switches] Creates an index

RD RD FileName Creates an index, table of contents, table of figures, or table of authorities using multiple documents

TA TA [Switches] Marks an entry for a table of authorities

TC TC "Text" [Switches] Marks an entry for a table of contents

TOA TOA [Switches] Makes a table of authorities

TOC TOC [Switches] Makes a table of contents

XE XE "Text" [Switches] Marks an entry for an index

Link and Reference Field Codes

AutoText AUTOTEXT AutoTextEntry Inserts an existing AutoText entry

IncludePicture INCLUDEPICTURE FileName [Switches] Inserts a picture

IncludeText INCLUDETEXT [Bookmark] [Switches] FileName Inserts text

Link LINK ClassName FileName[PlaceReference] [Switches] Uses object linking and embedding (OLE) toinsert part of a file

NoteRef NOTEREF Bookmark [Switches] Inserts the number of a footnote or endnote

PageRef PAGEREF Bookmark [*Format Switch] Inserts the page number of the specified bookmark

Quote QUOTE "LiteralText" Inserts the specified text

Ref REF Bookmark [Switches] Inserts bookmarked text

StyleRef STYLEREF StyleIdentifier [Switches] Inserts the text from a paragraph with the specified style

Mail Merge Field Codes

Ask ASK Bookmark "Prompt" [Switches] Prompts the user the enter text in a bookmark

Compare COMPARE Expression1 Operator Expression2 Compares two values (if the comparison is true, Word prints the number 1; if it is false, Word prints 0)

Database DATABASE [Switches] Inserts data from an external database

Fill-in FILLIN ["Prompt"] [Switches] Prompts the user to add text to the document

If IF Expression1 Operator Expression2TrueText FalseText Evaluates the argument (if the condition is true, print TrueText; if it is false, print FalseText)

MergeFieldMERGEFIELD FieldName Inserts a mail merge field

MergeRec MERGEREC Inserts the number of the merged record

MergeSeq MERGESEQ Displays the number which represents the order in which the records were merged

Next NEXT Moves to the next record in the mail merge

NextIf NEXTIF Expression1 Operator Expression2 Conditionally continues to the next record in the mail merge

Set SET Bookmark "Text" Assigns new text to a bookmark

SkipI SKIPIF Expression1 Operator Expression2 Conditionally skips a record in a mail merge

Numbering Field Codes

AutoNum AUTONUM Automatically assigns a number to a paragraph

AutoNumLgl AUTONUMLGL Automatically assigns a number to a paragraph in legal outline format

AutoNumOut AUTONUMOUT Automatically assigns a number to a paragraph in traditional outline format

BarCode BARCODE \u "LiteralText" or Bookmark \b[Switch] Inserts a postal bar code

Page PAGE [* Format Switch] Inserts the current page number

RevNum REVNUM Inserts the number of times the document has been saved

Section SECTION Inserts the number of the current section

SectionPages SECTIONPAGES Inserts the total number of pages in the current section

Seq SEQ Identifier [Bookmark] [Switches] Sequentially numbers parts of a document, such as chapters or figures

User Information Field Codes

UserAddress USERADDRESS ["NewAddress"] Displays the mailing address listed in the User Info tab in the Options command of the Tools menu

UserInitials USERINITIALS ["NewInitials"] Displays the initials listed in the User Info tab in the Options command of the Tools menu

UserName USERNAME ["NewName"] Displays the name listed in the User Info tab in the Options command of the Tools menu

Index

TASK	MOUSE	MENU	KEYBOARD
Annotations, Inserting, *W 355*		Click Insert, click Annotation	[Alt][I],[A]
Annotations, Printing, *W 363*		Click File, click Print..., click Print What list box down arrow, click Annotations, click OK	[Alt][F],[P], [Alt][P], choose Annotations, [Enter]
Annotations, Removing *W 364*		Select annotations mark in document, press [Del], press [Y]	
Annotations, Viewing, *W 359*	Double-click any visible annotation mark	Click View, click Annotations	[Alt][V], [A]
Apply or define a style, *W 134*	Click Style box arrow, click style	Click Format, click Style..., choose style options, click Apply	[Alt][O], [S], choose style options, [Alt][A] or [Enter]
Arrange open documents, *W 207*		Click Window, click Arrange All	[Alt][W], [A]
Attach a template, *W 131*		Click File, click Templates..., choose template, click OK	[Alt][F], [T], choose template, [Enter]
AutoCorrect entries, change, *W 107*		Click Tools, click AutoCorrect..., make changes, click OK	[Alt][T], [A], make changes, [Enter]
AutoText entry, creating, *W 286*		Click Edit, click AutoText..., type a name for the entry, click Add	[Alt}[E], [X], type a name for entry, [Enter]
AutoText entry, inserting, *W 286*	Type AutoText name, click Insert AutoText button	Click Edit, click AutoText..., select name, click Insert	Alt][I], [X], choose options, [Enter]
Between character spacing, change, *W 90*		Click Format, click Font..., click Character Spacing tab, change spacing options, click OK	[Alt][O], [F], [Alt][R], change spacing options, [Enter]
Bold selected text, *W 43*	**B**	Click Format, click Font..., click Font tab, click Bold, click OK	[Alt][O], [F], [Alt][N], click Bold, [Enter]
Bookmark, assign, *W 185*		Click Edit, click Bookmark..., enter bookmark information, click Add	[Alt][E], [B], enter bookmark information, [Alt][A] or [Enter]
Border or shading, add to selected paragraphs and tables, *W 85*	, choose border and shading options in Borders toolbar	Click Format, click Borders and Shading..., click appropriate tab, choose border and shading options, click OK	[Alt][O], [B], [B] or [S], choose border and shading options, [Enter]
Bulleted list, create, *W 45*		Click Format, click Bullets and Numbering..., click Bulleted tab, click list format, click OK	[Alt][O], [N], [Alt][B], choose list format, [Enter]
Calculations, perform in tables, *W 124*		Click Table, click Formula..., enter calculation, click OK	[Alt][A], [O], enter calculation, [Enter]
Caption, insert, *W 125*		Click Insert, click Caption..., specify caption and format, click OK	[Alt][I], [I], specify caption and format, [Enter]
Center a selected table, *W 139*		Click Table, click Cell Height and Width..., click Row tab, click Center, click OK	[Alt][A], [W], [Alt][R], [Alt][T], [Enter]

TASK	MOUSE	MENU	KEYBOARD
Center selected text, *W 82*	▤	Click Format, click Paragraph..., click Indents and Spacing tab, click Alignment arrow, click Centered, click OK	[Ctrl][E], or [Alt][O], [P], [Alt][I], [Alt][G], choose Centered, [Enter]
Close a document, *W 19*	Double-click document Control menu box	Click File, click Close	[Alt][F], [C]
Column break, insert, *W 248*		Click Insert, click Break..., click Column Break, click OK	[Alt][I], [B], [Alt][C], [Enter]
Column width, change, *W 136*	Drag boundary between columns using ◄▐►	Click Table, click Cell Height and Width..., click Column tab, change column width options, click OK	[Alt][A], [W], [Alt][C], change column width options, [Enter]
Columns, format into, *W 245*	▦	Click Format, click Columns..., choose column options, click OK	[Alt][O], [C], choose column options, [Enter]
Compile an index, *W 374*		Click Insert, click Index and Tables..., choose options, click OK	[Alt][I], [X], choose options, [Enter]
Continuous section break, insert, *W 187*		Click Insert, click Break..., click Continuous, click OK	[Alt][I], [B], [Alt][T], [Enter]
Convert existing text to a table, *W 110*	▦	Click Table, click Convert Text to Table..., choose table options, click OK	[Alt][A], [V], choose table options, [Enter]
Copy selected text or graphics to Clipboard, *W 113*	▤	Click Edit, click Copy	[Ctrl][C], or [Alt][E], [C]
Copy selected text without using the Clipboard, *W 61*			[Shift][F2], place insertion point in location, [Enter]
Copy styles, *W 236*		Click Format, click Style..., click Organizer..., click Styles tab, choose styles to copy, click Close	[Alt][O], [S], [Alt][O], [Alt][S], choose styles to copy, [Enter]
Crop a selected graphic, *W 253*	Press and hold [Shift], drag any center handle	Click Format, click Picture..., specify cropping dimensions, click OK	[Alt][O], [R], specify cropping dimensions, [Enter]
Cross-reference, creating, *W 365*		Click Insert, click Cross-reference..., select options, click Insert	[Alt][I], [R], choose options, [Enter]
Cut selected text or graphics to Clipboard, *W 114*	✂	Click Edit, click Cut	[Ctrl][X], or [Alt][E], [T]
Date and time, insert, *W 160*		Click Insert, click Date and Time..., click format, click OK	[Alt][I], [T], click format, [Enter]
Decimal tab, insert, *W 73*	⊥	Click Format, click Tabs..., click Decimal, click OK	[Alt][O], [T], [Alt][D], [Enter]

TASK REFERENCE
Microsoft Word 6.0 for Windows

Italicized page numbers indicate the first discussion of each task.

TASK	MOUSE	MENU	KEYBOARD
Double-space text, *W 81*		Click Format, click Paragraph..., click Indents and Spacing tab, click Line Spacing arrow, click Double, click OK	[Ctrl][2], or [Alt][O], [P], [Alt][I], [Alt][N], choose Double, [Enter]
Drawing object, add, *W 262*	🖎		
Drop cap, insert into a selected paragraph, *W 259*		Click Format, click Drop Cap..., choose drop cap options, click OK	[Alt][O], [D], choose drop cap options, [Enter]
Exit Word, *W 26*	Double-click Word Control menu box	Click File, click Exit	[Alt][F4], or [Alt][F], [X]
Field codes, printing, *W 320*		Click Tools, click Options..., click Print tab, click Field Codes, click OK	[Alt][T], [O], [P], [Alt][F], [Enter]
Field codes, viewing, *W 294*		Click Tools, click Options..., click View tab, click Field Codes, click OK	[Alt][T], [O], [V], [Alt][F], [Enter]
Font, change, *W 88*	Click Font list box arrow, click font	Click Format, click Font..., click Font tab, click font, click OK	[Alt][O], [F], [Alt][N], choose font, [Enter]
Form Fields, inserting, *W 403*		Click Insert, click Form Field..., select options, click OK	[Alt][I], [M], choose options, [Enter]
Formats, display, *W 135*	Click 📝 , then click text		
Formatting toolbar, activate/deactivate, *W 14*		Click View, click Toolbars..., click Formatting, click OK	[Alt][V], [T], click Formatting, [Enter]
Frame, insert, *W 254*		Change to page layout view, click Insert, click Frame	Change to page layout view, [Alt][I], [F]
Frame, position selected, *W 258*		Click Format, click Frame..., specify horizontal and/or vertical reference points, click OK	[Alt][O], [M], specify horizontal and/or vertical reference points, [Enter]
Frame, size selected, *W 256*		Click Format, click Frame..., specify frame size, click OK	[Alt][O], [M], specify frame size, [Enter]
Go to a position in a document, *W 76*		Click Edit, click Go To...	[F5], or [Alt][E], [G], or [Ctrl][G]
Grammar, check, *W 183*		Click Tools, click Grammar...	[Alt][T], [G]
Graphic, insert, *W 252*		Click Insert, click Picture..., click graphic name, click OK	[Alt][I], [P], click graphic name, [Enter]
Graphic, size selected, *W 253*		Click Format, click Picture..., specify graphic size, click OK	[Alt][O], [R], specify graphic size, [Enter]
Hard page break, insert, *W 65*		Click Insert, click Break..., click Page Break, click OK	[Ctrl][Enter], or [Alt][I], [B], [Alt][P], [Enter]
Headers and footers, insert, *W 127*		Click View, click Header and Footer, enter headers and footers, click Close	[Alt][V], [H], enter headers and footers, click Close
Help, access, *W 48*	📝	Click Help, click Contents	[F1], or [Alt][H], [C]

TASK	MOUSE	MENU	KEYBOARD
Hyphenate a document, *W 260*		Click Tools, click Hyphenation..., choose hyphenation options, click OK	[Alt][T], [H], choose hyphenation options, [Enter]
Import a document, *W 228*		Click Insert, click File..., click document name, click OK	[Alt][I], [L], click documer name, [Enter]
Indent selected paragraph to next tab stop, *W 70*	⊞		[Ctrl][M]
Insert a field code, *W 289*		Click Insert, click Field..., select field, select options, click OK	[Ctrl][F9] or[Alt][I], [E], choose field, choose options, [Enter]
Italicize text, *W 42*	*I*	Click Format, click Font..., click Font tab, click Italic, click OK	[Ctrl][I], or [Alt][O], [F], [Alt][N], click Italic, [Enter]
Justify text, *W 83*	☰	Click Format, click Paragraph..., click Indents and Spacing tab, click Alignment arrow, click Justified, click OK	[Ctrl][J], or [Alt][O], [P], [Alt][I], [Alt][G], choose Justified, [Enter]
Left-align text, *W 82*	☰	Click Format, click Paragraph..., click Indents and Spacing tab, click Alignment arrow, click Left, click OK	[Ctrl][L], or [Alt][O], [P], [Alt][I], [Alt][G], click Left [Enter]
Left-aligned tab, insert, *W 73*	L	Click Format, click Tabs..., click Left, click OK	[Alt][O], [T], [Alt][L], [Enter]
Lock a field, *W 289,*			[Ctrl][F11]
Mail merge process, start, *W 153*		Click Tools, click Mail Merge...	[Alt][T], [R]
Margins, change, *W 63*		Click File, click Page Setup..., click Margins tab, change margin settings, click OK	[Alt][F], [U], [Alt][M], change margin settings, [Enter]
Mark index entries, automatically, *W 374*		Click Insert, click Index and Tables..., click AutoMark, select concordance file, click OK	[Alt][I], [X], [U], select concordance file, [Enter]
Mark index entries, *W 370*		Click Insert, click Index and Tables..., click Mark Entry, click OK	[Alt][I], [X], choose Mark Entry, [Enter]
Master Document view, switch to, *W 336*		Click View, click Master Document	[Alt][V], [M]
Merge cells, *W 400*		Click Table, click Merge Cells	[Alt][A], [M]
Merged mailing labels, create, *W 170*		Click Tools, click Mail Merge..., click Create, click Mailing Labels...	[Alt][T], [R], [Alt][C], [M]
Move selected text without using the Clipboard, *W 61*			[F2], place insertion poin in location, [Enter]
Move to next field, *W 289*			[F11]
Move to previous field, *W 289*			[Shift][F11]

TASK	MOUSE	MENU	KEYBOARD
Move to previous location in a document, *W 87*			[Shift][F5]
New line mark, insert, *W 78*			[Shift][Enter]
Next Page section break, insert, *W 187*		Click Insert, click Break..., click Next Page, click OK	[Alt][I], [B], [Alt][N], [Enter]
Normal view, change to, *W 12*		Click View, click Normal	[Alt][V], [N]
Number headings, *W 343*		Click Format, click Heading Numbering..., choose options, click OK	[Alt][O], [H], choose options, [Enter]
Numbered list, create, *W 80*		Click Format, click Bullets and Numbering..., click Numbered tab, click list format, click OK	[Alt][O], [N], [Alt][N], choose list format, [Enter]
Open a new document, *W 17*		Click File, click New..., click a template, click OK	[Ctrl][N], or [Alt][F], [N], click a template, [Enter]
Open an existing document, *W 27*		Click File, click Open..., click document name, click OK	[Ctrl][F12], or [Alt][F], [O], click document name, [Enter]
Outline view, change to, *W 12*		Click View, click Outline	[Alt][V], [O]
Overtype mode, activate/deactivate, *W 34*	Double-click OVR in the status bar	Click Tools, click Options..., click the Edit tab, click Overtype Mode, click OK	[Insert] or [Alt][T], [O], click the Edit tab, click Overtype Mode, [Enter]
Page layout view, change to, *W 12*		Click View, click Page Layout	[Alt][V], [P]
Paste text or graphics from the clipboard, *W 113*		Click Edit, click Paste	[Ctrl][V], or [Alt][E], [P]
Point size, change, *W 89*	Click Font Size box arrow, click size	Click Format, click Font..., click Font tab, click size, click OK	[Alt][O], [F], [Alt][N], choose size, [Enter]
Print a document, *W 46*		Click File, click Print..., specify print options, click OK	[Ctrl][P], or [Alt][F], [P], specify print options, [Enter]
Print an envelope, *W 51*		Click Tools, click Envelopes and Labels..., click Envelopes tab, click Print	[Alt][T], [E], [Alt][E], [Alt][P]
Print Preview a document, *W 46*		Click File, click Print Preview	[Alt][F], [V]
Protect a form, *W 414*		Click Tools, click Protect Document..., click Forms, click OK	[Alt][T], [P], [Alt][F], [Enter]
Record a macro, *W 302*	Double-click REC in the status bar, select options, click Record, conduct steps, double-click REC	Click Tools, click Macro..., select options, click Record, conduct steps, click Stop	[Alt][T], [M], choose options, [Alt][O], conduct steps, [Alt][T], [M], [Alt][O]
Redo a previous undone action, *W 33*		Click Edit, click Redo	[Ctrl][Y], or [Alt][E], [R]

TASK	MOUSE	MENU	KEYBOARD
Rename a file, *W 60*		Click File, click Save As..., type filename, click OK	[Alt][F], [A], type filename, [Enter]
Repeat Go To, *W 347*			[Shift][F4]
Repeat last action, *W 125*			[F4]
Replace text or formatting, *W 116*		Click Edit, click Replace..., specify replace options, click Replace or Replace All	[Ctrl][H] or [Alt][E], [E], specify replace options, [Alt][R] or [Alt][A]
Revisions, accepting or rejecting all, *W 360*	Double-click MRK in status bar, click Accept All or Reject All	Click Tools, click Revisions..., click Accept All or Reject All, click OK	[Alt][T], [V], tab to choose Accept All or Reject All, [Enter]
Revisions, accepting or rejecting individually, *W 362*	Double-click MRK in status bar, click Review...	Click Tools, click Revisions..., click Review..., accept or reject revisions, click OK	[Alt][T], [V], tab to Review..., accept or reject revisions, [Enter]
Revisions, Marking, *W 350*	Double-click MRK in status bar, choose options	Click Tools, click Revisions..., choose options, click OK	[Alt][T], [V], choose options, [Enter]
Right-align text, *W 83*	(icon)	Click Format, click Paragraph..., click Indents and Spacing tab, click Alignment arrow, click Right, click OK	[Ctrl][R], or [Alt][O], [P], [Alt][I], [Alt][G], click Righ[t], [Enter]
Right-aligned tab, insert, *W 73*	(icon)	Click Format, click Tabs..., click Right, click OK	[Alt][O], [T], [Alt][R], [Enter]
Save a document for the first time, *W 25*	(icon), enter filename, click OK	Click File, click Save or Save As..., enter filename, click OK	[Ctrl][S] or [Alt][F], [S] or [A], enter filename, [Enter]
Save a document, *W 35*	(icon)	Click File, click Save	[Ctrl][S], or [Shift][F12], or [Alt][F], [S]
Single space text, *W 81*		Click Format, click Paragraph..., click Indents and Spacing tab, click Line Spacing arrow, click Single, click OK	[Ctrl][1], or [Alt][O], [P], [Alt][I], [Alt][N], click Single, [Enter]
Sort rows in a table, *W 122*		Click Table, click Sort..., specify sort options, click OK	[Alt][A], [T], specify sort options, [Enter]
Spacing before or after a selected paragraph, change, *W 137*		Click Format, click Paragraph..., click Indents and Spacing tab, change Spacing Before or After options, click OK	[Alt][O], [P], [Alt][I], chan[ge] Spacing Before or After options, [Enter]
Spelling, check, *W 36*	(icon)	Click Tools, click Spelling...	[Alt][T], [S], or [F7]
Splitting cells, *W 399*		Click Table, click Split Cells..., select options, click OK	[Alt][A], [P], choose options, [Enter]
Standard toolbar, activate/ deactivate, *W 14*		Click View, click Toolbars..., click Standard, click OK	[Alt][V], [T], click Standar[d], [Enter]